LeAnne Millian
19596 Glendale Ave.
South Bend, Indiana
46637

READING DISABILITIES

Selections on Identification and Treatment

READING

DISABILITIES

*Selections on Identification
and Treatment*

edited by

HAROLD NEWMAN

THE ODYSSEY PRESS
The Bobbs-Merrill Company, Inc., Publishers
Indianapolis · New York

The Odyssey Press
A Division of The Bobbs-Merrill Co., Inc.
Printed in the United States of America
Library of Congress Catalog Card Number 70-80026
ISBN 0-672-63098-2 (pbk)
Third Printing

TO *Lona* AND *Alan*

Preface

This book of readings was compiled to fulfil the request of undergraduate and graduate students as well as their professors for a collection of good articles dealing with the identification, needs, problems, concerns and remediation of the disabled reader. Who is he? Why did he become disabled in reading? What are his problems? What is the etiology of these problems? How can teachers diagnose his needs? What constitutes a good remedial program? What specific techniques can the classroom teacher use to help him to improve his word attack and comprehension skills? What are some of the techniques that teachers can use to diagnose their students' needs? How can teachers motivate reluctant readers? What materials seem to be most conducive to their growth? These are just a few of the many questions to which adequate responses are given in this collection.

The articles that found their way into this book were selected from over seven hundred possibilities. Specifically, the anthologized material had to meet the following criteria:

Authenticity. The authors write with a realistic sensitivity of their topic, reflecting an understanding based upon years of experience.

Readability. Informative, well-organized and interestingly written articles predominate. Scholarly articles were rejected when they were too technical, rambling, or turgidly written.

Applicability. Many of the ideas expressed in these selections can be adapted and implemented at virtually any level of instruction.

Length. No rigid requirement was followed. Some excerpts are two or three times longer than others because of the uniform high quality of presentation.

Timeliness. Although the bulk of the articles included were published within the last twenty years, a few articles written in the thirties and early forties were included because they are exceptionally informative and quite applicable to today's problems.

Representative selection. This final criterion was based on a survey of student opinion concerning the topics they thought most pertinent to the teaching of reading.

An appendix of lesson plans devised by the New York City Board of Education has been included to help meet the practical needs of teachers of retarded readers.

Introductions to each chapter have been omitted purposely because of the clarity and the self-explanatory nature of the articles in general and the lead-in articles in particular. The editor believes that it is best for the instructor to personally introduce each chapter with essential background material, clarifying any anticipated difficulties, highlighting salient issues and points of view, and providing the students with a few questions beforehand to stimulate critical reading and to guide any consequent classroom discussion.

I would like to express my appreciation to the authors and publishers who have permitted me to include their selections in this anthology. In particular, I would like to thank the New York City Board of Education, Dr. J. Wrightstone of their Bureau of Educational Reseach, Mr. Thomas P. Casserly of Columbia University's Teachers College Press, and Dr. M. Jerry Weiss of Jersey City State College, who enables me to "grow" on the job.

Contents

READING DISABILITIES

Selections on Identification and Treatment

CHAPTER I

THE RETARDED READER AND HIS PROBLEMS

1. THE NON-READING PUPIL IN PERSON

Harrison Bullock

If school people are to meet the needs of non-reading pupils, it is necessary first to learn to know and appreciate them as human beings. Opportunity to make the acquaintance of a number of them will be provided in this study, in the hope that increased understanding and insight into their development, their feelings, and their needs may emerge.

The present chapter will present five non-reading pupils. One of these boys, more communicative than some of the others, will reveal through tape-recorded interviews many of the feelings common to non-reading pupils.

THE CASE OF TED

Ted was fifteen years old. His manner and physical development seemed somewhat beyond his age and compact size. His fingernails, badly bitten, were constantly in his mouth unless a toothpick, wad of gum, or cigarette was there to take their place. On the Wechsler-

Reprinted with permission of the publisher from Harrison Bullock: *Helping the Non-Reading Pupil in Secondary Schools* (New York: Teachers College Press), pp. 14–35, Teachers College, Columbia University, copyright 1957.

Bellevue scale he scored a verbal IQ 81, performance IQ 110, with full scale IQ 95. Excerpts from an interview with him will provide information about his home and school environment and reveal attitudes and feelings about himself and others and about his world.

Worker: Tell me, why are you coming here to the reading center?
Ted: Can't read.
W: Can't read. . . . Was it your idea of coming here, the school's, or whose?
T: The school's. I always wanted to read. Tried, but I couldn't. So I wasn't going to argue with them.
W: Oh, it was their idea, but you're coming here of your own accord. You'd like to come—
T: I'd like to read very much. Right now.
W: Are there certain kinds of things you can read, if they're not books?
T: I can't read nothing. I know a couple of little words.
W: Like "No Smoking," and—
T: Yeah, I know that, "No Smoking."
W: "Stop," "Go"—
T: Yeah.
W: —and "Push," "Pull." . . . You never have been able to read?
T: I was tongue-tied when I started school.
W: Then it took you some time to get started talking.
T: Yeah, I'm still tongue-tied a little, but not as much as I was. I can't pronounce nothing at all. Some words I still can't pronounce. Like when I say "scissors," I used to say "stissors," you know. "Cigarette," "tigarette."
W: Yes. S's were hard for you.

Confused Response to Phonetic Instruction. Ted's discussion of his difficulties in speech led to another area of verbal difficulty for him: phonics. He clearly demonstrated his confusion in this area, at the same time telling us a few more of the facts of his life:

T: That's the only thing I don't know is my nouns, you know. Like D-duh. Like that, you know.
W: You mean, you don't know the letters?
T: Oh, I know all of my alphabet. But I can't pronounce them.
W: You can't say all the letters of the alphabet?
T: I can, but what I mean is D, as a sound. *(Gives examples of phonetic sounds of various consonants, all followed by the neutral vowel sound.)* I ran away from home. Then I went and stayed with my grandmother. Then every once in a while I went over to my aunt's. Then my other aunt bought a book for me. A-T. I started learning A-T, you know. Cat, bat, mat, all of that. Then she started me on a what do you call it? D-duh and all that, you know, and I started picking up a little. Then I never went over any more. I'd been going over there about three weeks straight. Once in awhile she didn't do nothing; she didn't have time.

Ted had apparently been exposed to a variety of phonic training. Without in any way discounting the need for phonics as an analytic method of learning to read unfamiliar words or to spell familiar words, we should recognize that the inconsistency of English spelling renders the method treacherous for the beginning reader and unsafe to use as the only method of attacking unfamiliar words. Furthermore, as Anderson and Dearborn point out, "Isolated letters do not say anything. Just as with the letter names, the sounds of the letters have no meaning in themselves" (1:028). They also caution that "phonics instruction, especially of the direct sounding variety, introduces the danger that the pupils will become too analytical in their word recognition" (1:276). Research cited by Dolch and Bloomster indicate that children are not likely to derive much profit from phonics instruction before they have a mental age of at least seven years (5). All of this seems to suggest that overemphasis or too early introduction of phonetic instruction can be confusing to a pupil.

Phonetic instruction in Ted's case had apparently been both confusing and inexpert. It confused him even to the extent that he used the word *nouns* when he meant *sounds*. It was inexpert in that it taught him to associate a neutral vowel sound inseparably with consonant sounds, a practice which makes blending of sounds much more difficult than learning consonant sounds either alone or in phonograms.

Emotional Response to Reading Disability. Ted continued to combine in his account the important events of his life and his learning experiences. This may make difficult any logical organization for summarizing the interviews, but it does illustrate the inseparability of learning from life. The emotional quality of his reactions to classroom experiences was very evident as Ted discussed his hopes of getting a job as a mechanic, and how his reading disability would hamper him in it.

W: Does trouble with reading spoil very many things you would like to do?
T: Yes. Most of all, it's the reading. I get very good marks in arithmetic. I can do that, but when it comes to, you know, like problems where you've got to read, then I guess at them.
W: Or if somebody reads you the problems, then it's all right?
T: Oh yeah. Then I get them.
W: Now, the trouble with reading bothers you in school; where else does it bother you?
T: (*After thinking for a long moment.*) I guess it bothers me when I go for a job or something. If I gotta fill out something.
W: Then you might have to ask what it says.
T: Yes.
W: Has this difficulty in reading ever embarrassed you?
T: Yeah, I'm with my friends in a car or something, you know, and somebody says, "Read that direction." I couldn't. "I can't make it out," I'd say (*in a casual quoting tone*).
W: Oh, you'd try to hide it a little.
T: My friends try to help me out. None of them knows I can't read, though, maybe one or two.

W: One or two . . . You don't talk about it.
T: I never talk about none of my marks or anything with my friends.
W: How do you get along in school, other than reading?
T: All right.
W: You say you do well in math. You like that. You get along well with your teachers? *(Ted nods.)*

Ted discussed his feelings about ways in which his teachers tried to teach him when the rest of the class was reading. This portion of the interview is quoted in Chapter VI on making a place for him in his regular classroom.

Ted has here demonstrated his extreme sensitivity to the emotional components of reading disability, in and out of the classroom. He has been very explicit about his embarrassment and its sources in the classroom situation. Some might say that such embarrassment is a natural result of his negligence in school work. Natural or not, the fact remains that such feelings seriously affect the pupil's learning process. They are part of a vicious circle: falling behind in one's work leads to embarrassment, which interferes with progress, which leads to further failure and embarrassment. Is it not the teacher's responsibility to provide a learning situation in which the pupil can succeed with reasonable effort?

Need for Success Somewhere. Ted, like anybody else, needed to bolster his self-esteem sometimes by reminding himself of the successes in his life. The worker, in an attempt to make an informal evaluation of Ted's reading level, gave him a copy of the *Skill Builder* (27) at third grade reading difficulty. Ted selected an article in the book and proved within half a dozen lines of trying to read it that the material was completely beyond his capability. Worker hastened to change the subject from what certainly must have been a painful experience for the boy.

W: By the way, what are you interested in, other than automobiles?
T: Swimming.
W: How far can you swim?
T: I never, you know, really figured it out. If I go swimming all day long, twenty-four hours, I'll be in the water at least eighteen hours of it. Be in for eight hours, ten hours. I'll be in the water for seven or eight hours. I learned how to dive before I could swim.
W: Oh, how old were you then?
T: I learned how to dive when I was about six years old, I learned how to dive. Then when I was about eight I learned how to swim. My uncle taught me.
W: Where was that? A pool or river somewhere?
T: I learned how to swim in a—I learned how to dive in a lake, you know, little lake, diving board. Then when I learned how to swim I went to the ocean. I learned how to swim there.
W: You learned how to swim when you were about eight, you say.

To counterbalance his dejection over his miserable performance in reading, and to prove both to himself and to the worker that he is not entirely inept in everything, Ted was glad to talk of his success in diving and swimming.

Relationships with His Family. In the illogical way that conversations seem to have, the interview veered from a discussion of how his voice sounded when played back on the tape recorder, through fingernail biting, to a long discussion of Ted's relationships with members of his family:

T: Doesn't sound like it.

W: No? What made the difference?

T: Oh, the voice.

W: Too low or too high?

T: I don't know. I can't make it out.

W: One reason is that you're talking past your hand all the time when you're chewing your fingernail.

T: When I have gum or a toothpick or something, I don't bite it. When I'm in the show I always eat them.

W: Do you enjoy biting them, or don't you even think of it?

T: Don't even think of it. When I'm watching television or something I chew them. My father's are worse than mine.

W: His are? Does anybody ever get after you for it?

T: Yeah. A lot of girls slap me around. *(Both laugh.)* Sister.

W: Your sister? What does she say?

T: She told me to stop it, her boy friend. She's getting married in March.

W: Oh? She is?

T: My brother's in the service. He's out in Austria now. He'll be coming home Christmas next year.

W: How long has he been over there?

T: Been over there about six months now. He was already through boot camp. He came home for about a week. Then he was shipped out, over to Austria. I didn't see him for about two years. Most I see him was for one day, in between those two years.

W: You haven't seen much of him. How old is he?

T: He's twenty.

W: Five years older than you. Quite a bit of difference.

T: Yeah. Sister's eighteen.

W: You living right with her?

T: No, my sister left. My brother left. And I left; I came back.

W: Had to have some place to live.

T: Yeah. I was staying at my grandmother's; I could've stayed over there, but I figured I'd cause trouble home, you know. School and everything.

W: You can't get along with your stepmother.

T: Yeah, I don't know. Slaps my father around a lot; they drink a lot.

W: Leaves you out in the cold. . . . The grandmother you stay with, that's where you live now?

T: No. I'm living home right now.

W: But your grandmother lives right near, though.

T: Yeah, my grandmother lives on ———— Street, right over the bridge.

W: That's your father's mother?

T: That's my mother's mother, my own mother's. All my mother's sisters, my aunts, uncles, they all live over there. They all live close together.

W: Well, when you left your father, you went to live with your grandmother. What took you back?

T: I don't know. My aunt started explaining, you know, my shoes were falling apart and everything. They came over and got me shoes and clothes. Then about two weeks later I went back home. Talked me into it.

W: Is it better than it was?

T: Still the same.

W: Do you get along with your father all right?

T: We get in an argument once in awhile, not too much.

W: Not too much. Do you get along better with your brother and your sister than anybody else?

T: Yeah, I have a younger brother, too. One twelve.

W: How about him?

T: We get along.

W: Does he get along with your father and stepmother?

T: She has two kids of her own, now. I have a stepbrother and a half brother. He's eleven and the half brother's about a month old.

W: How about the stepbrother? Do you get along with him?

T: Oh, we're always arguing. He likes to have his own way. My father sticks up for him too much. I don't mind about myself, but I feel sorry for my own brother.

W: Oh, he and the stepbrother don't get along too well?

T: No, they're always fighting. They both get jealous of each other. If he gets more money than my brother they start arguing. And if my brother gets more money than him they start arguing.

W: Well, at least you have no stepbrother your own age. . . . Where are you working now?

T: A paper. Truck. Throw the papers off. Sunday papers you have to count out on Saturdays, but I don't work on the truck then. I work in a stand putting them together for an old guy there.

W: Did you ever have a job delivering papers house to house?

T: No, I didn't. My brother wanted to get that job delivering from house to house, but he didn't. Too small. And then he was going to get that job I have on Saturday, putting papers together. But he was too small, you know, to carry papers up on his shoulder.

W: How big is he?

T: Last time he was measured he was up to here on me. Now he's down to here.

W: You've been growing faster than he is, haven't you. I guess you can take care of him if he tries to beat you up.

T: Oh yeah, I could beat him up all the time, but I don't know, when I was small I didn't like to hit him because I always used to get hit. So one day he hit me through a window, you know how he hit, and I tripped and fell through a glass window and went right out on the porch. So then he was always grabbing everybody and saying, "I beat him up! I beat him up! I knocked him through a glass window!" So one day I got sick and tired of it, just about five years ago, four years ago, so I told him, "If you don't shut up, I'll show you who's boss." So I beat him up real good. Then when I did, I felt sorry for him. Every time I beat him up, you know, or somebody else beats him up, I always feel sorry for him.

W: Then after you beat him up that time, did you get hit?

T: No, no more. I always told my father. My father sticks up for me a lot now. I don't like it, though.

W: Why's that?

T: I don't like being sticked up for.

W: You like to fight your own battles.

T: Yes. (*Long pause.*)

What satisfactions did Ted find in his family relationships? What frustrations? Could his ambivalent attitude toward his brother be a source of concern to Ted? Why did he so sternly reject his father's overtures toward him and efforts to "stick up" for him? It is apparent that there was little security for Ted in his home life. Perhaps the greatest satisfaction for him lay in his feeling of kinship for his younger brother, which emerged despite sibling rivalry.

Evidences of Tension in Ted. The boy's need of oral activity, such as the fingernail-biting, toothpick-chewing, gum-chewing, and cigarette-smoking, is but one of many indications of great tension in him. Aside from this, his behavior showed few other symptoms of tension except that, like many another adolescent, Ted was afflicted with extreme acne. Whether as a result or as a cause, the association of acne with other symptoms of tension has often been observed.

In various ways, Ted showed evidences of rigorous control over his emotions. His talking was casual, restrained; he spoke lightly of matters which could not but have strong emotional meaning for him, as for example, the death of his own mother, his relationship with his step-mother, the excessive drinking at home, the protracted separation from his older brother, and the impending separation from his sister. Such matters are of far more than casual concern to a boy like Ted; the fact that he spoke of them at all and in so carefully casual a manner suggests the magnitude of the distress he thus sought to conceal.

These current and recent situations were aggravated by an old factor in his life, his continued failure in reading. He mentioned being tongue-tied, whatever that may mean in his case, and illness and surgery during his early school years. Some of this was brought out in portions of the interview not quoted here. Other upsetting factors in his early life can only be surmised. At all events, life was difficult for him all along the way, so tensions in him are certainly to be expected.

Ted's Future Plans. Early in the interview Ted announced his plan to quit school in June, as soon as he was sixteen, and to go back to the small town where he had formerly lived.

W: Have you a job lined up?

T: Yeah, a mechanic's job. Going to try to get one or work in a factory or something. That's why I want to learn to read very much. Car mechanic. Then I'll know a lot about cars.

Toward the end of the interview he spoke of different plans:

T: I'm going to go in the service. I was thinking of making a pension out of it, about fifteen or sixteen years. Then I figure it was too long, so I just want to stick out my term.

W: Of course you can't tell till you're in whether you're going to like it that well or not. Generally it isn't too bad.

T: Well, Navy's good. That's what I want to go into. I know Army stinks. A lot of friends I know are making it, you know, career out of it.

W: Does your brother find the Army so bad?

T: Yeah, he don't like it. I wouldn't either. He's right up in the front of the line. He carries ammunition, shells, and everything. He's right up in front of the line. I hear it's real cold over there in Austria. They're having earthquakes and everything, snow.

In these excerpts it is quite evident that Ted was poorly informed about many matters. Elsewhere he explained to the worker that he was not sure whether his brother "carried ammunition right up in front of the line" in combat or not, but he rather thought there was fighting going on. This amid the "earthquakes and everything, snow" in Austria!

His plans for the future were obviously vague and nebulous, except for his intention to quit school when he reached the age of sixteen, and to leave home at that time. And he did want to be able to read by that time.

When it became evident that Ted had no more to say about his future plans or his prospective life in the service, the worker took advantage of the boy's expressed interest in the Navy to present the book prepared for literacy instruction in the Navy (37). This book begins at the primer level with repetitious use of words, associated with pictures. The subject matter, life of a naval recruit, appealed to Ted, and he worked through the first unit of the book with interest and some degree of success. The worker listed seven words which Ted found difficult in the book and showed him how to trace them with his finger (6). Ted found that the method helped him to remember words, asked the worker if he could learn a "hard" word that way. The worker said it would be possible, so Ted asked if he might add the word *experience* to the list. Ted took the list home with him to study before the next interview, hopeful that he might have discovered a method of learning to read.

Ted's Difficulties and Potentialities. Ted has presented himself in his own words. He carried out his part of the interview in a self-possessed, restrained way, showing himself as a boy cruelly treated by life in many ways—being tongue-tied, having a serious operation, losing his mother, not getting along with his stepmother. At fifteen he was still a virtual non-reader. He showed many evidences of tension and deep disturbance.

In spite of Ted's difficulties, there are yet a number of bases for hope that he might make a reasonably adequate adjustment to life, including development of at least minimal reading skills:

1. There was evidence of at least normal intelligence, in spite of faulty information on such matters as Austria, confused plans for the future, and difficulty in expressing himself. His conversation was alert; his school attested to his ability in mathematics. His intelligence scores, much higher in performance than in the verbal component, may have been penalized, in the verbal, by the lack of information and background associated with his reading disability. His performance score was above average. At the moment, of course, exercise of his intelligence was blocked at many points by his emotional problems. Still it did emerge in the interview in a way it would not from a duller boy.

2. He had the courage to leave an intolerable home situation; going no farther than his grandmother's home, he served notice on his father about the way he felt about conditions at home. Yet, rather than make himself a financial drain on his grandmother and aunt, he went back to the home he had left. His course of action in this whole affair seemed to demonstrate a toughness of character combined with a grasp on reality which seemed to bode well for his ultimate ability to handle his own affairs.

3. His nervous mannerisms—the nail-biting, speech handicaps, etc.—seem relatively harmless outlets for the otherwise restrained deep disturbances which seemed to exist, in his casual mention of matters which must have had high emotional content. These mannerisms may well have taken the place of more destructive outlets for the release of tension.

General Observations on the Case of Ted. This boy's case has been presented here to illustrate how a non-reading pupil perceives his situation and to some extent how he feels about himself and his life conditions most closely related to the reading problem. Ted cannot be considered a typical non-reading pupil; no one is typical. Any attempt to learn the facts about and feelings of an individual will reveal the unique qualities of each individual.

Ted's prospects seem more hopeful than those of some other cases that will be considered later in this study. He has reasonable capacity, verbal ability, and motivation. He seems to be in touch with the reality of his immediate environment.

This discussion of Ted, the interpretation of his problems and appraisal of his assets, is actually on the basis of but a single interview, transcribed verbatim. This may therefore serve as an example of the initial impression of a non-reading pupil. Such an impression is extremely important, as it tends to affect much of what the worker does subsequently with the pupil. To fill out the picture of the non-reading pupil, however, it is well to consider pupils on the basis of much longer acquaintance.

Brief Glimpses of Four Other Non-Reading Pupils

The four cases in the present section will be discussed without reference to verbatim interview material. These boys will be considered, however, on the basis of more protracted acquaintanceship than in the case of Ted. Frank and Tip were met for periods of three hours daily during a six-week summer reading center. Jack was known over a period of three years in one school. Bill was met periodically at a reading center for a period of a year and a half.

The Case of Frank. Frank came to the reading center a neat, round-faced, stocky, tough-seeming boy of twelve ready to enter junior high school. His self-assurance seemed far beyond his years. He was alertly watching and listening to what went on about him, but saying little. When he did choose to speak, he was definite, to the point, and soft-spoken. He was reading at about second grade level at this time and his parents were greatly concerned. He would admit to some concern about the matter himself, if asked, but did not care to talk freely.

Frank's home was in a temporary war-time housing project which had survived the war by several years. To maintain safety and self-respect in this particular environment, it was necessary that a boy be able to defend himself, to give beatings and, if necessary, to take them without a whimper, and to maintain an attitude of strength and self-confidence. Frank could do all this without arrogance.

His aloofness and hardness would melt, however, whenever he talked about his brother Joey, who was seven years old and a cerebral palsied cripple. During the past year he had spent eight months at a state training school for cerebral palsied children. There he had learned to do a great many things which he had not been able to do before; he could feed himself and dress himself; he could even communicate better. Best of all he could walk better; it was no longer necessary for Frank or the parents to carry him wherever he went. Frank would talk of Joey with a tenderness and affection which contrasted strangely with his customary manner.

Frank was a boy of about average ability, IQ 95, with no particular personal characteristics which would seem to block achievement in reading. Apparently embarrassed about his poor reading ability, he would habitually attempt to avoid or escape situations which would require him to read. There was no evidence of extreme emotional disturbance.

Frank's lack of reading ability may have been associated with his younger brother's affliction. Perhaps the cerebral palsy became apparent just during the years when Frank was beginning school and should have been learning to read. Most of the family's attention and resources were required for the care of the crippled child. Even Frank, at around six or seven years of age, had to help in the family's parental duties. As a result, little attention may have been paid to Frank's education. Perhaps, during the first years of working out family routines in Joey's care, Frank felt himself neglected. He might have developed a sharp jealousy, except that he was really needed to help in the care of the cripple.

But meantime, with Joey at the center of his and his parents' attention, Frank was not progressing in school. His parents could do little to encourage his efforts there. Educational success had minor prestige among his neighborhood peers. The familiar vicious circle set in: lack of reading ability leading to lack of success in school subjects, leading in turn to discouragement and frustration, which led to compensatory behavior and blocked learning, so there was no progress in reading.

Probably this surmise as to reasons for Frank's disability is accurate as far as it goes; other factors may have also contributed, such as visual defects or late readiness for reading which left him behind his classmates from the earliest years of school. At all events, Frank seemed now ready to read, having sufficient intelligence and an awareness of the need, and having no strong apparent motivation against it.

The Case of Tip. Tip came to the reading center at the same time as Frank and was only a few months older. He was taller, more slender, more boisterous, and less self-assured than Frank. In many ways he seemed the type of boy one might be inclined to term the all-American boy.

When he arrived at the reading center he promptly attached himself to one of the workers and decided this was the man with whom he would get acquainted. His first move in getting acquainted was to ask the worker's name; his second was to show the man how he could remove his glass eye. He had acquired the distinction of a glass eye as the result of a wood chip's entering his eye when he was chopping wood. The demise of the affected eye was a lengthy process, ending with its removal approximately a year after the accident, when Tip was nine years old. Demonstration of the glass eye seemed to be part of Tip's standard routine in making acquaintance with his peers. He consistently treated the worker as an equal, addressing him always by the surname alone and without prefix, as he did all his contemporaries.

The right eye was not Tip's only major loss; it had been preceded shortly by the death of his own mother. His father, a painting contractor, had remarried. There were no other children in the family.

Tip's attitude toward reading was a mixture of fascination and avoidance. He said he wanted to read very much, but whenever a reading situation would occur, he would disappear, if possible; when physical escape was infeasible, he would attempt to escape by silliness, playfulness, boisterousness, or irritability. This summer reading center emphasized handicrafts and puppetry during part of each day's session, and Tip would frequently contrive to have his materials in such a state by the beginning of the reading period that it would take the entire reading period to get them in order and put away. Or else, during the break between periods, he would disappear into a far corner of the building and have to be found by the worker. And yet, in non-reading situations, he was the worker's veritable shadow.

Perhaps his attitude toward reading was a part of his general perfectionist attitude toward anything he might do. In making puppets, for instance, he was never able to finish. He would work and work on making the preliminary clay head, then begin forming the papier-mâché over it. Then he would presently destroy it and would soon be found starting work on another preliminary clay head. Assistance of any sort from anyone was not acceptable to Tip. On the day the worker finished his own puppet, Tip enthusiastically took it over and carried it about with him. That day members of the reading center went on a sightseeing boat ride on the bay. Tip brought the worker's puppet with him, wearing it on his hand all afternoon, making it gesture and posture. He would never, however, use it to act out a role.

During the course of the summer at the reading center it was not possible to learn much of the dynamics of Tip's attitude toward reading. Undoubtedly the two big traumatic losses of his life were a part of the picture; so also may have been his adjustment to his stepmother, although on the surface all looked placid there. For some reason he was dreadfully afraid of any sort of failure or show of inadequacy on his part. He related well with people up to the point where an inadequacy on his part might be exposed. Then he would try to escape.

Tip's case was one where psychotherapy would seem to be advisable. Any instruction or tutoring of him would have to be a patient, gentle, low-pressure process lacking any suggestion of reading itself until Tip himself felt ready for it.

The Case of Jack. As Jack approached his sixth birthday, still unable to talk, his family reconciled themselves to the idea that he was mentally retarded. By the time he entered school, he was well accustomed to the role of the retarded child. The impression was confirmed by a Binet test, administered by a school psychologist. He achieved an intelligence quotient just below 70. The role of the retarded child provided satisfactions and shielded the boy from responsibilities. In this role he learned winning ways and how to please people by "cuteness." His round baby face and infantile speech appealed to people's sympathy, so that he was shielded from problems and discouragement.

But all did not go too well at home. His father's matriarchal mother took care of Jack and his sister after the father's divorce. A few years later, the father found himself an attractive second wife who took an interest in the children and made a home for them. The grandmother and her younger, unmarried son, however, were still very much in the picture. They talked with Jack's father often in the language of the old country, which the children and their new stepmother did not understand. This not only served to retard Jack's linguistic development, but it also effectively kept the stepmother out of the inner group of the family. Finally it was arranged that Jack would live with his grandmother.

His grandmother did not believe in confusing Jack by teaching him two languages, so he learned only English. He never really learned to speak it well; his vocabulary was limited, his pronunciation infantile. Naturally Jack did not learn to read in school. No one expected him to learn; he was retarded. He developed an interest in drawing, modeling, making things with his hands; by this talent he achieved some success and recognition at school. He also found puppetry to his liking. Strangely, he could express the puppets' thoughts in language far more adequately than he could express his own. His imagination proved fertile in extemporaneous puppet plays, which were much admired by his schoolmates.

Retardation in reading seemed part of a general immaturity. At fourteen, Jack presented a rather infantile appearance with a chubby round face, with which his infantile speech seemed appropriate. He was in a regularly organized public school class for the mentally retarded on recommendation of the school psychologist. Certainly his verbal intelligence was very limited; in non-verbal activities, however, his ability seemed normal. An unofficial Wechsler test, administered by a student in training, bore this out with a verbal IQ of 58, performance 102. It is, of course, questionable whether this represented native endowment, or whether it reflected the overprotecting, inharmonious, bilingual home environment.

Jack seemed to feel no real desire to learn to read. From his point of view, he got along well enough without it. Urged to attempt exercises leading to reading, he would fuss, whine, or cry. The nearest approach to reading to which he would consent was to copy from a book in his neat, round, childish handwriting. Jack's family did not expect him to learn to read. With no stimulation within himself or from his family, it was unlikely he ever would.

The Case of Bill. Bill was an appealing boy, good-looking, neat, quiet, courteous. He seemed of normal intelligence; this impression was confirmed by an IQ of 95 on the Wechsler Intelligence Scale. He was unable to read at all, however, and was singularly lacking in general information. Although the name of George Washington was familiar to him, for example, he had no idea who that person might be or have been. Bill was fourteen then.

Why should a boy of this intelligence, one who had attended city schools all his life, have learned so little during the course of his education? His mother felt that it was a result of the family turmoil which preceded her separation from Bill's father when the boy was eight years old. She remarked that he had "heard what he shouldn't." She was also concerned about his associates in the rather tough neighborhood where they had lived for several years. At the time she brought him to the reading center she thought prospects were better, because she had remarried and the new home was in a much more favorable neighborhood. Bill had two younger brothers, both better readers than he; his mother reported that he got along well with them.

Bill was interested in music, but his greatest current interest was in the Bluejackets, a semi-military boys' organization devoted to seamanship and military drill. It is not at all unlikely that the uniform of the organization was part of its appeal to the boy. Nevertheless, he worked diligently to learn the subject matter taught in Bluejacket meetings, preparing for examinations which could result in his acquiring more "stripes."

Bill was pathetically anxious to learn to read, applying himself to the exercises given him in the reading center. After ten months of individual and group sessions he improved from zero to grade 2.3 on the *Durrell Reading Paragraphs* (40). At the end of this period he felt confident that he would not fail in any of his subjects at school.

He was apparently disturbed by his lack of general information, for his favorite part of his lessons at the reading center always seemed to be filmstrips on various subjects of general interest, geographical, historical, or industrial. He took an interest, too, in various reading games which he played with other pupils in the reading center.

It is quite probable that Bill's mother's impression, that he had "heard what he shouldn't" of the domestic disharmonies at home during the years when he should have been learning to read, was a major factor in his reading disability. Undoubtedly the relationships between Bill and the other members of the family, including his own father, with whom he seemed to have maintained contact, were rather more complex than the mother's theory recognized, but certainly the fact that he found himself in a disintegrating home prevented his achieving the learnings he should have achieved during these important primary years in school. The experience could have led to many emotional conflicts which would make him uncommunicative. His lack of aggressiveness, exemplified by his over-politeness, kept him from making progress he might otherwise have made. The lack of aggressiveness itself may well have resulted from the lack of security resulting from the family trouble. It could well have seemed to him the only safe attitude to take.

Hopeful features in this case were Bill's intelligence, his expressed hope to learn to read, his strong desire to do so, the existence of definite and specific interests on which reading could be based, and the apparent stability the family seemed finally to have achieved. If this latter should prove real and permanent, there was basis for reasonable hope of Bill's continued progress in learning to read.

How Much Hope for Non-Reading Pupils?

The non-reading pupil has been here introduced in the person of five boys with serious reading retardation. Distinct as each one is, they by no means exhaust the possibilities of variations in background, personality, intelligence, physique, and type of reading problem. In subsequent chapters other cases will be presented which will serve to broaden the conception of a non-reading pupil as a person. Teachers will continue to meet still others from time to time in their own classes.

Favorable and Unfavorable Prospects. Of the five boys here presented, three seem to have had rather favorable prospects as far as learning to read is concerned, two had not. Ted, Frank, and Bill were all of about average intelligence. Each had had difficulties in his life which contributed to his reading disability. For Ted and Frank, while the difficulties were likely to continue, the boys seemed to have accepted them and made a reasonably adequate adjustment to the continuation of the difficulties. Bill's environment seemed to have changed for the better and there were signs that the indelible memories of the period when the difficulties most beset him need not handicap him indefinitely. Each of the boys had reached a stage where he felt the need of learning to read and where there no longer seemed any important reasons why he should not learn.

Tip and Jack, on the other hand, had not resolved their difficulties. Tip continued to nurse his fear of appearing inadequate, while Jack's greatest satisfactions seemed to come from being treated as a helpless, mentally retarded baby. These boys showed poor prospects of improving their reading, for the present at least, although each had intellectual potential for real improvement.

Systematic remedial instruction would probably prove immediately fruitful for Ted, Frank, and Bill. Little could be gained by requiring Tip or Jack to submit to such instruction unless they themselves should request it. The school can do much to help boys like these in other aspects of their lives. Each success they experience brings increasing confidence in such pupils. The time may come when growing awareness of the need for reading will overbalance the needs they have to maintain the attitudes which prevent their improvement at present. Psychiatric help, if available, would surely benefit such boys. Where psychiatric care is not available, the school can in its own way help such boys to feel of importance, to experience successes, and to grow in various ways, even without the invaluable help of reading ability.

The School's Attitude Toward the Non-Reading Pupil's Prospects. In the present chapter pupils with favorable prospects have purposely been presented along with pupils whose prospects of learning to read are questionable. This contrast has been made to impress on the teacher the idea that among non-reading pupils in the secondary school both types will be found. In any one teacher's experience the cases will almost certainly never be numerically balanced. A teacher may find the situation generally very hopeful, or quite discouraging. The main purpose of this study is to show how the school can help these pupils in various ways, whether the specific matter of reading can itself be remedied or not.

As long as there are individual differences, there will continue to be non-reading pupils at any particular age group in the schools. Whether they are found scattered throughout the grades and classes, are held back in the beginning grades regardless of age and maturity, or are concentrated in special classes of one sort or another will depend on the judgment of educators and the policies and facilities of the schools. Regardless of their educational needs, they will continue to be among the first to drop out of school at the end of the age of compulsory attendance, as long as they are frustrated by a curriculum which demands and expects of them what they cannot achieve. In Chapter V we shall attempt to see the school from their point of view.

Any pupil over borderline intelligence who is exposed to six normal years of school experiences should develop reasonable reading facility. Where this facility does not develop, conditions may be presumed to exist within the child's life or environment which serve to block the achievement. Not the least of these obstacles are those arising out of years of experience with reading disability: distaste for or anxiety toward reading, expectation of failure, defensiveness, compensatory behavior, and so on. Reading disability beyond the age of twelve is certainly a serious condition, demanding serious study of individual cases. Serious factors in the pupil's life obstructing achievement in reading will be found in every case.

Serious though these factors may be, however, there are other factors which favor progress in reading ability. The pupil's potential reading ability, limited though it may be to the degree of his intelligence, is nevertheless usually far in advance of his actual reading skill. In other words, even non-reading pupils of limited intelligence have room for improvement. A pupil who can achieve a score on a validly administered individual—or even group—intelligence test which corresponds to a mental age more than a year in advance of his reading age can reasonably be expected to have a potential for improved reading skill.

As a non-reading pupil reaches adolescence, he begins to see many reasons why he needs to learn to read, reasons which were not apparent to him during his years in elementary school. He can see how his lack of reading ability can be a real handicap for him in life out of school, how it will prevent him from accomplishing many things he really wishes to do. He becomes more and more aware of the way in which his reading disability tends to make him appear in an unfavorable light, to disgrace him, as it were. As the non-reading pupil approaches maturity he finds many motivations for putting forth the effort to learn to read.

The teacher's problem with the non-reading pupil is to seek to determine, so far as possible, the factors favorable to as well as those making difficult his learning to read. The teacher should be ready to utilize and reinforce the favorable factors; where the obstacles are too strong, the teacher should be prepared to help the pupil in other ways without insisting unduly on the reading.

Reading is only one aspect of a pupil's total adjustment. He is not likely to be able to improve it alone while other vital areas of his life remain unsettled; on the other hand, if he can be helped to find successes and satisfactions in various sectors of his life, he is very likely, given sufficient intelligence and motivation, to make real progress in his ability to read.

2. THE NATURE OF THE READING PROBLEM

Board of Education of the City of New York

IDENTIFICATION OF THE READING PROBLEM

Typical Manifestations of Reading Difficulty Appear in the Classroom.

What are the aspects of the "reading problem" that first command the teacher's attention? What are the typical manifestations of reading difficulty as they appear in the classroom? The teacher who is asked to identify the deficient reader frequently cites as most important the symptom or overt manifestation. She tends to measure and describe the child's deficiencies largely in terms of his immediate responses to the material and the instruction presented. The following manifestations of reading difficulty are most commonly reported by teachers of the lower grades.

Phonic Difficulties. "Insufficient phonetic training," "poor in phonics," "no phonics sense," etc. What the teacher is actually contending with here is not simply a matter of phonics, but the fact that mastery of mechanics, regardless of how reading is taught, must result in the power to read new material independently. The difference between the good readers and the poor readers in her class is not that the good readers have "sufficient phonetic knowledge, etc.," but that they have developed the power to work independently with unfamiliar words and materials. As a matter of fact, the teacher is probably quite unaware of the variety of methods used by her good readers to attack new words. She might be surprised to learn how unimportant is the application of phonics with many of these children and how naturally they learn to use meaning and configuration clues.

Reprinted from *A Diagnostic Approach to The Reading Program, Part I*, Educational Research Bulletin of the Bureau of Reference, Research, and Statistics, No. 3 (March 1942), pp. 5–10. By permission of J. Wayne Wrightstone, Bureau of Educational Research of the New York City Board of Education.

Difficulties in Visual Retention. "Poor visual memory," "poor visual discrimination," "weakness in visual memory," etc. These descriptions are characteristic of the school in which visual methods of teaching dominate. The teacher is sensitive to the fact that even after repeated exposure the child does not seem able to retain what he sees.

Behind these manifestations of visual or phonetic inadequacy, we find the typical pattern of the dependent reader who has not mastered any method of attacking new words.

Word Reading. This manifestation is also cited with great frequency as an identifying characteristic of the poor reader. Related to the reports on "word calling" are descriptions of defects in terms of "poor eye span," "poor span of recognition," "reading words instead of thoughts," etc.

Again the teacher's real problem goes beyond the mere observable habit of reading words. The "word-reader" is seldom strong in comprehension. Perhaps he has been forced constantly to read material that is too hard for him; the number of new words and ideas that he must grasp per page has increased beyond his power to deal with them. Perhaps over-routinized school reading experiences have prevented him from developing an awareness of reading as a purposeful activity. Whatever the original source of difficulty, the significant fact is that for the "word-reader" reading has become an experience unrelated to meaning.

Guessing. The child who is referred for "guessing wildly" and "bluffing" is quite likely to be a serious reading problem. "Guessing" through context and picture clues is a useful technique which adults employ regularly and which children often have to be taught to use intelligently. It is a serious situation, however, when the child enters the second or third year dependent mainly upon guessing for the meaning on a printed page. In the experience of the reading clinics, it was the child with this pattern of difficulty who offered the greatest resistance to instruction.

It is usually the poor reader with superior intelligence who develops, as if through some intellectual "osmosis," the ability to absorb meaning from a page which he cannot actually read. He has a strong need for meaning, so he "guesses" or "makes it up." It is most important therefore, that in the primary reading program there be some provision for check-up on word recognition skills, particularly in the case of the alert child who memorizes easily but seems slow in acquiring a sight vocabulary or a method of word attack. This type of check-up is especially necessary in a program of experiential learning. Here the bright child has opportunities for intelligent participation which may tend to obscure the fact that he is not acquiring certain essential reading skills. Where these early needs are not recognized and met, such a child, through compensations or habits of evasion, may make undesirable adjustments to his reading difficulties which may, in turn, influence his whole personality development.

Undesirable Attitudes. Teachers also refer regularly to "attitudes" as manifestations of reading difficulty. They report as typical of their poor readers "a sense of failure," "a lack of desire to learn anything," "carelessness," "fluctuating attention," "timidity," "lack of desire to read," "no enjoyment in reading," "lack of confidence," "lack of concentration," etc.

It is hardly surprising to learn that unsuccessful readers do not like to read, or that children with records of reading failure have hostile or negative attitudes toward reading. In the remedial reading project conducted in the Probationary School by the Bureau, where the boys taught were over-age, seriously retarded, and had histories of delinquency, their own consensus was that they had lost interest in reading "when it got too hard," a feeling they vaguely associated with the second and third grades.

It is unfortunate that the attitudes described by teachers as characteristic of poor readers are so often dismissed in terms of "laziness" and "unwillingness to work." They should rather be interpreted as indications that the reading program is in need of some vital re-motivation— motivation which for one child may mean only easier material to be read with enjoyment, and which for another may require a drastically changed instructional approach.

Some Reading Difficulties Have Deep-Seated Origins.

These manifestations of reading disability—most frequently reported by teachers—may in certain cases be symptoms of deep-rooted difficulties. The intensive study of poor readers referred to the reading clinics revealed again and again the extent to which a child's real problem may go undetected or unrecognized.

One child, for example, reported for "poor visual memory" actually had severe eye-muscle difficulties. A boy who seemed unable to "keep the place" and who made many reversals was found to have serious directional confusions. A photograph of his eye movements revealed the struggle that took place when he attempted to make proper return sweeps. A further study of his background disclosed the left-handed child who had been trained to use his right hand. In another very similar case, the directional confusions appeared to arise from lack of dominance of either right or left side. One little girl who refused to try unfamiliar words, who seemed to have "no method of word attack," was revealed as an over-protected, home-oriented youngster who was enjoying her dependency and clinging to it as a source of satisfaction even in her reading. It was, as a matter of fact, in the area of emotional and personality difficulties that clinical examination and study often proved most effective. Experience in the reading clinics demonstrated repeatedly the need for developing new and positive attitudes in children before their reading problems could be solved. Identification of the reading problem in the fullest sense involves, therefore, not only recognition of overt manifestations but also study of underlying difficulties.

The Reading Problem Appears at All School Levels.

There is no one age or grade level to which the problem of reading failure is unique. Typical patterns of reading difficulty are to be found at practically every school stage. At different grade levels, however, there is changed emphasis on what seems to be the primary factor in poor reading.

What does the first year teacher, for example, find to be typical of the failure in her grade? Here are a few descriptions of children not responding to instruction, cited from reports of teachers of the 1A grade:

"Shy, too dependent on mother, needs encouragement."
"Not able to work alone, too dependent on mother and teacher, needs urging. . . ."
"Inattentive, too babyish, slow in grasping thought, poorest in class. . . ."
"Slow, long absence due to illness, difficult to make up even with individual help."
"Unstable, would rather play than learn. . . ."

Included, of course, in the picture of failure in the first year is the child who is actually retarded mentally; that is, whose mental age is considerably below the level at which the average child is expected to read. Even for those, however, with average or superior intelligence ratings, again and again the words "shy," "timid," "dreamy," "dependent" appear in the teachers' reports.

The composite *first year* reading problem, then, is a child essentially immature—physically, intellectually, or emotionally. He has been forced into intellectual activity—learning to read—for which he is not prepared. He is inattentive and, eager as he may have been to go to school, by the end of the first term he dislikes reading very much. He has also begun to develop habits of evasion or "cover up," or else, trying desperately to read, has begun those erratic mechanical habits which are fully evident only later and by then are chronic.

In the *second and third years*, when it is assumed that the child has acquired the mechanics of reading, reading failure is usually interpreted in terms of the mechanical difficulties observed. Reversals, confusions of similar forms, omissions and substitutions of letters, words, or phrases are common at this level. In the *third year*, such deficiencies take on an acute character because so much more is demanded than the poor reader can perform. This is the point at which the "no phonic ability, word-reading, poor visual discrimination" complaints are most numerous. Here, too, lack of interest is evident.

In the *fourth year*, inability to comprehend reading materials becomes marked, and in the *fifth and sixth years*, increases in seriousness as the scope of reading expands. "Reads words instead of thoughts," "limited vocabulary," are typical reports. The difficulty is often attributed to attitude: "Can't concentrate," "lethargic," "nervous," "not interested." The inability to attack words independently and specific mechanical difficulties, such as reversals and confusions, are recognized as very serious if they persist at this level.

Beyond the sixth year, reading failure is most generally identified with weakness in one or another of the many types of comprehension demanded in these grades. The child who has not learned from the beginning to extract the fullest meaning from his reading is often penalized in these upper grades where he is called upon to interpret a wide range of materials. Perhaps in the lower grades his understanding of material has been measured only by his ability to reproduce what he has read; or perhaps his weaknesses in the subtler aspects of comprehension have gone undetected because he has always been a fluent reader and his teachers have therefore assumed he understood what he read. At any rate, in these upper grades it becomes most evident that, in the teaching of reading on *all school levels,* a more analytical attitude is needed toward the development of comprehension.

With a better understanding of reading disability and the many-sided nature of retardation, it is possible to interpret more intelligently the common manifestations of reading difficulty. Identifying the poor reader and achieving a perspective on his present reading status is thus a first step; inevitably, it leads to the question: *Why* can't he read? There have been many approaches to the study of the origin of reading failure. In the following pages, several of these approaches will be discussed.

3. EMOTIONAL DIFFICULTIES IN READING

Beulah Ephron

THE SURFACE THREADS

I Am a Poor Reader

Almost everyone who comes for reading help has the self-concept that he is a poor reader. The qualifying word "almost" is used because of those adolescents who reluctantly come to the reading clinic at the behest of parents and/or teachers, though they themselves see no need for it.

At Teachers College, the course called "The Improvement of Reading

From Beulah Ephron, *Emotional Difficulties in Reading* (New York: The Julian Press, Inc., 1953), pp. 3–27. Reprinted by permission of the publisher.

for College Students and Adults" is composed mostly of graduate students, people who have read well enough to attain the graduate-school level of academic achievement. There are also in the group some college students, a few high school students, and occasionally one or two foreign students having a language problem.

The range of reading ability as objectively measured by a standardized test runs from zero to the ninety-ninth percentile, yet all of the sixty or more students consider themselves poor readers, else they would not have enrolled in this course. Because of their eagerness for help, their low self-evaluation as students, and their anxiety about their work, this group has been described as being "highly motivated and full of despair." Despite great differences in actual skill, they show this universality in self-concept: "I am a poor reader."

I Want to Learn to Read Faster

In five years of work in remedial reading, this writer has never heard anyone ask for help in obtaining more pleasure from reading. The idea of enjoying oneself with a book does not appear among the requests for help. The most frequent, perhaps universal, request is for increased speed. These are familiar questions: "What is considered normal reading speed . . . ?" "How fast should I be able to read . . . ?" "Will I be able to read more words per minute, more pages per hour if I take the course . . . ?"

I Need Help with Retention

"I read and read and then can't remember what I've read . . ." "I realize as I get to the bottom of the page that I have not really *seen* a word that I've 'read.'" This surface thread is tied in with a lack of interest, for many possible reasons, in the reading material. The individual is not paying real attention, for many possible reasons, to the printed page. He cannot follow this surface thread to its interconnections in order to see why this is happening to him. Without help, he does not realize the existence of the interconnections. He keeps trying to force himself to pay attention, and he feels more and more defeated and hopeless as he fails to remember because he is not really seeing.

I Cannot Concentrate

When this thread is followed all the way, it usually leads to the sources of all the other reading troubles. One who cannot concentrate will soon add, "My mind wanders away from what I'm reading." Now, one of the most interesting bits of data in the whole collection of material is this fact: In over two hundred instances, the writer asked the question, "Where does your mind go when it wanders?" In every case, without exception, the individual seemed surprised by this question; he had never thought to follow the wanderings of his mind to see what was distracting him. His energies were expended in a strenuous effort to force his attention upon the task at hand, away from whatever preoccupations were clamoring for attention, away from problems calling for solution. Since forcing is unsuccessful, the result is a losing battle, accompanied by feelings of helplessness and bewilderment.[1]

I Have the Bad Habit of Reading Word-by-Word

The reader who reads "word-by-word" gives equal stress, time and value to every word. He cannot omit a single word without a nagging feeling that something important has been missed, and he retraces his steps to pick up the missing word. It is chiefly because of the word-by-word reading that the Harvard Films[2] are used in the Improvement-of-Reading course. There is no magic in a mechanical stimulus, but the films do lead the students to make an important observation about themselves. Phrases flash by, never to return. The students groan. They have not had time to look long and thoroughly at every word, to go back and make sure they have missed nothing, and they are certain they will not be able to recall much of the material. However, when they are tested on their retention of the article, they are pleasantly surprised to discover that most of it has been absorbed. They learn, therefore, that they are capable of observing a great deal without conscious awareness of the act of observation. They learn that a quick exposure to the material is sufficient, that lingering and re-reading is unnecessary. The next step is to transfer this learning from the films to the printed page. Unfortunately, making this transition is not easy. Too many unconscious forces get in the way.

There Must Be One Best Way to Read

The conception of being "a better reader" is usually expressed in terms of reading faster and remembering more. To achieve this goal, all other

---

[1] Reik states: "We often hear that a patient cannot concentrate his attention, without thinking that it is already concentrated upon a subject, unknown or unconscious to him." Reik, Theodor (50, p. 169).

[2] A tachistoscopic device by which phrases are flashed in sequence on a movie screen.

reading goals are abandoned, and the student applies to every reading challenge his chief objective: "Faster!"

Professor Strang tries to meet this demand by suggesting that good reading consists of developing a repertory of reading skills and applying these skills appropriately in terms of the kind of material being read and the purpose for which it is being read. One would not sensibly read Keats, Dickens and Dostoievsky the same way one would skim the headlines of the *New York Times,* study a chemistry experiment, think through an engineering problem or peruse a lease on an apartment. Each reading situation calls for an appropriate response.

Students do not reject this approach to reading, since its validity is self-evident. However, they tend to veer back irresistibly to the expression of a wish for *faster reading*—no matter what the material may be. "Look at our bibliographies for all our courses," they say. "We have to read fast or we can't get through the semester." Yet, "We have to read slowly and carefully, else we won't remember." It is as if, to meet this dilemma, there must be *one best way to read.*

I Have the Bad Habit of Procrastination

Recently, a young man who had come to the Reading Center to speed up his reading confessed that he had carried an "incomplete" at a graduate school for five years. All he had to do to fulfill his obligations to the course was to write a brief essay. He had the intelligence, the experience and the knowledge, but he could not get the paper written. It is unusual for an incomplete to stand for five years, but it is not unusual for students to procrastinate.

The "bad habit" of procrastination is so prevalent, in fact, that the colloquialism, "cramming," came into existence to name the feverish activity which is the inevitable sequel to procrastination. A graduate student said, "Cramming became so ingrained in me that now, even when I am thoroughly well prepared for an examination, it is hard for me to resist staying up all night to study, though I know it would do me more good to get eight hours' sleep."

Procrastination and cramming: twin socio-psychological phenomena that haunt every campus. What are the underlying causes?

Reading Makes Me Nervous

Restlessness, irritability, drowsiness, unaccountable fatigue, a desire to close the book and do almost anything except read—these complaints are frequent. "I haven't the patience to sit still. ... " "I keep getting up and going out for coffee or a cigarette—anything for an excuse. ... "

"Gosh, I keep thinking how I'd rather be outdoors. . . . " "I get so fed up, I feel as though I'll shriek if I have to sit there and read one more minute . . . !" "I get so nervous sitting in the library. I always think I'll do better at home. But at home it's worse, because I start wandering around. . . . . " "I've always loved reading novels, but as soon as I have to read something for school, I get jittery. . . . . " "It's hopeless. It's too much. What's the use. . . . "

THE UNDERLYING THREADS

All the underlying threads emerge as various expressions of fear. The list is long and intertwined. Enumeration of the most important threads will involve unavoidable repetition and overlapping. But fear is basic:[3] I am afraid to take chances; I am afraid to make a mistake; I am afraid of freedom; I am afraid of responsibility; I am afraid to succeed; I am afraid to fail; I am afraid of my own feelings; I am afraid of criticism; I am afraid I'll appear ridiculous; I am afraid people will find out; I am afraid of being imperfect; I am afraid to have fun. . . . Each unconscious attitude, or underlying thread, involves many of these and other fears, all interrelated. The individual does not sense them as specific fears; he is aware only of vague anxiety, emotional and sometimes physical malaise, feelings of helplessness, hopelessness, bewilderment, "lack of self-confidence," "nervousness" and other signals of deep distress.

I Do Not Know What to Feel

When the Spaniards conquered Peru, they found in this strange land a belief in one virginal goddess, which reminded the Spanish Jesuits of the Holy Virgin and provided a connecting link between an alien culture and their own. This bit of history comes to mind in connection with a story about a Philippine girl who was a student in an American college. Because the external circumstances of her case were so strikingly different from those of the other students, the connecting links made by similar unconscious attitudes were dramatically highlighted. Let us refer to her as "Jasmine." She was so much like a flower, delicate, fine-featured, with creamy skin and soft ways. She came into the Reading Center one day for an interview, which proceeded as follows:

"I say I have a reading problem. I take your course because I cannot read; I cannot get my work done. But this is silly, because I can read, but I cannot concentrate!"

---

[3] According to Theodor Reik, the goal of psychotherapy was formulated by Ernest Jones as "the achievement of relative fearlessness."

"You mean your mind wanders away from what you are reading?"

"Yes! It wanders and wanders."

"Do you ever follow it to see where it wants to go?"

"Well . . . no. I try to make it stay where it should!"

"Perhaps the problems it is trying to solve are more urgent than the reading."

"Oh. . . . " She gazed out the window.

"Tell me about it."

"Shall I start from the beginning?"

"Start wherever you like."

"Well. . . . I was living happily at home, in the Philippines. I was content. I was engaged to be married, and I was content. One day I got a letter from my uncle and aunt who live here in New York. They said, 'Jasmine, why are you content to go on that way? Don't you want to be an educated, cultured person? Come to New York. Go to a graduate school. Get a higher degree. Make something of yourself. You could live with us. Come!' " Jasmine began to weep.

"My boy-friend did not want me to go. It meant postponing our marriage for a year. He said he would break our engagement if I left. I did not believe he would. He has not, but I miss him.

"My aunt and uncle have four little children. The youngest is less than a year, the oldest is eight. The same week I got here, my aunt and uncle left for a trip to California. They are still gone. I sit in the library and I try to concentrate, but how can I concentrate if I am wondering what to buy for supper that all the children will be sure to eat. I cook for them and take care of them, and it is a very big responsibility. I do not know what to feel."

"You do not know what to feel?"

"Well, you see, I know I should be grateful to them for this big opportunity which they have given me, but I do not feel grateful! I feel I would like to move out. I would so much like to live in the International House. I think if I could live in the International House and no longer have to take care of the four little children, I could study and I could concentrate."

She paused, sighed, and looked at the interviewer apprehensively.

"Do you think I am very wicked and ungrateful?" she asked.

"No, I do not."

"Do you think I would be very bad if I moved out and lived in the International House?"

"It sounds sensible."

"Oh, thank you! That is what I have done, but I was afraid I was being very ungrateful. I did not know what I should feel."

Jasmine had already summoned her relatives home and had arranged for a room in International House, but she became frightened that she had done something wrong. During the rest of this interview she talked of other experiences in which she had been similarly afraid. As she left, she said, "Now I shall have no reading problem." And this proved to be correct.

Jasmine's story is not presented here to show how much can be achieved in one interview. It is rare that this much is accomplished so quickly. One wonders whether she has, since then, had any further trouble with trusting her own feelings and taking a chance on them. One would guess that she has had more of the same self-doubt, as such basic fears are not fully routed quite so easily.

What were Jasmine's fears in this particular instance? She was afraid of feeling what she did feel, anger. She was afraid no one could like her if she felt angry when she was expected to feel grateful. She was afraid she could not like herself if she did not live up to her own standards of feeling only what one *ought* to feel. Her fears carried her away from a belief in her own feelings and their validity; she became confused and ended up with, "I do not know what to feel."

This fear of feeling what one really does feel—especially if the feeling is rage—is so prevalent that one must watch for it in every case. Almost everyone feels it is dangerous to be angry. An angry person is not a lovable person. An angry person will be punished for his anger. Someone will get back at him. No one possibly can like him. No one will want to be with him. He will be all alone. These are the frightening exaggerations that cause the true emotion to be forced out of awareness. It requires energy to keep it out of the way, to hold it back. Sometimes this effort is so fatiguing that little energy remains for work (1). Also, holding back one strong feeling may involve holding back all strong feeling; if a little bit is let out, more may come bursting forth. Thus, when one tries to encourage a very slow reader to develop "a positive attack on the printed page," one may be urging him to do something he is not able to do, because he is afraid of letting out any aggression whatsoever; to actively "go after" the words and concepts on a page would mean a freeing of energies which he has all tightly dammed up, for safety's sake.

"I am afraid to feel what I feel" may refer to any number of emotions which, because of some conditioning in the person's life, it seems dangerous to sense. Love, affection, passion, ambition, hope, joy—any of these, all of these, and many more than these may be freighted with feelings which the individual is afraid to face, afraid to feel, afraid to know.

It is oversimplification merely to state that the fear of one's own feelings interferes with reading enjoyment and reading efficiency. Seeing this important fear as it manifests itself in actual case material is the best, perhaps the only, way to obtain a clear understanding of its many ramifications. The reader will recognize its powerful role in a human being's life when reading about a young man named Ralph later in this study (cf. 4). It is a thread that runs through and around all the other threads of unconscious attitudes about to be enumerated.

I Am Afraid to Take Responsibility for a Choice

A young man having trouble with his law books was asked, "Is this the study of your choice?" He replied, "What do you mean?" The question was rephrased, "Have you always wanted to study law?" He replied, "Of *course* I want to be a lawyer." He thought a moment, then, "I don't know what else I could be."

Trouble with concentration is often a clue to poor vocational choice, or, rather, no vocational *choice*. The individual has made no active selection of career; he simply finds himself preparing for one. He is sitting in the library, struggling to learn history, or psychology, or chemistry, or engineering, or business administration, or transportation, or textiles, or pharmacy—and he has never given time or real thought to what he most wants to do with his life.

Perhaps he is reading law books because it has never occurred to him to actively question his father's expectation that he join the firm. His attention, therefore, is not on the material in the books, since he has no vital interest in *learning law*, but only the goal of *becoming a lawyer*. To have a goal instead of a purpose and direction means that attention is not flowing into the learning process itself, where it belongs, but is caught in a vision of a final position in life.

Perhaps the channels of communication are so inadequate between him and his parents that he cannot express to them any doubts he may have about their choice for him. Self-assertion then may make its way through distorted channels. Instead of realizing and saying directly, "I am not so sure, Mother and Dad, that I am interested in law; I'd like time and opportunity to explore some other studies"—instead of speaking these words, he may express them indirectly and unconsciously through self-sabotage, failing the courses, not being able to concentrate on his books, not being able to remember the lectures. For further discussion of this thread, see the paragraphs about "Inner Resistance."

To change one's vocational plan seems to mean admitting a mistake. This puts an additional burden on the individual when he tries something new, for to change *again* would be unbearably humiliating. Changes of direction that often quite naturally result from growth are not regarded as evidence of expansion and learning, but as signs of weakness, vacillation, defeat, undependability.

Teachers and parents create and continually reinforce this fear of change. A high school lad of sixteen was chided by his guidance teacher for wanting to drop a certain subject and change to another closer to his heart's desire. The teacher said, "Don't be a quitter." This was outrageously inappropriate to the circumstances, since this particular boy had always had the problem of erring on the side of excessive diligence and rigid self-discipline. He was in the habit of arising at five each morning to study, and his dedication to his work excluded all play and social activities. It had taken him a long time, and considerable work with a counselor, to achieve the courage to make a change in his courses. This had necessitated some freeing of his initiative and acquiring more respect for his own feelings. The teacher's contemptuous, "Don't be a quitter!" dealt a blow to his newly won courage to go after what he really wanted.

Vocational guidance people are familiar with the picture of parents bringing adolescent children for aptitude testing with the request, in effect, "Test him and tell us what he should be." This attitude leaves the adolescent very little leeway to explore, to change his mind, to seek himself in his own changing and growing world. The parental illusion, well-meant but devastating in its effect, is that there is one right way for the child to go, one right path for him to follow, and, if the experts set his feet on that path, all he need do is work hard and he will reach that one right goal with no time lost.

It is generally accepted—as an abstract theory—that learning from experience is valuable. Taking action and making changes in vocation on the basis of new knowledge is another matter, usually regarded not as "learning from experience" but as "wasting time" and "not knowing what he wants." A young man of nineteen said, "I *can't* tell my father I don't want to be a doctor, because he'll ask me, 'Then what *do* you want to be?'—and I don't *know* what I want to be." This lad felt it would create great turmoil in his family if he registered indecision. He also felt he would be hurting his father by saying he did not want to study medicine, since his father was a doctor, and the boy sensed that his father's feeling of worthwhileness was completely in terms of being a physician. The father lived for his work; the boy feared that to say he did not want to do the same work would constitute a criticism of the father. (On the unconscious level, there was more to it than this.) The result of this impasse was that the boy registered his complaint by failing his premedical courses, and dropped out of school in a painful state of confusion, bewilderment and humiliation.

Boys and girls of adolescent age invariably apologize when they "admit" that they "still don't know what they are going to be." It is astounding to realize that these youngsters feel it incumbent on them to know the world before they have seen it, and to be aware of their own personalities and powers without experience and without ever having been encouraged or helped to study themselves, to know themselves as persons.

Perhaps the young law student, after he has had the opportunity to explore his real self, with all his hidden wishes and hidden fears, will find he really does want to study law after all. But what a difference there is now—to go ahead out of free choice, knowing and deciding that *he* wants to study law, no matter what anyone else expects of him. He has made a choice, for which he takes responsibility, and the self-affirmation exercised in making his choice gives him great pleasure. His work, unhampered by the effects of the former slavery-defiancy pattern, will now be an expression of himself. His assertive and creative energies are liberated to flow into his purposeful study activity.

It's an Inner Resistance

"Johnny is not responding to our tutoring. I have a feeling he is resisting. His parents always put too much pressure on him, and now he is resisting them. He wants to defeat them. He is being contrary, defiant, uncoöperative. But he's so foolish to cut off his nose to spite his face. Doesn't he realize it's his own life that's at stake? Defeating his parents won't help him any, nor do him any good."

The adolescent boy is being "negative." Why does he cling so stubbornly to his "negativism?" If our understanding of the boy stops here, we are indeed defeated, and so is the boy.

The words "resistance," "negativism," "defiancy," "stubbornness," "spite,"—all these words (like "lazy") are pawns being pushed back and forth across a chessboard. They are busy words, much in use, which explore no depths and explain nothing.

To understand Johnny, and to help him, it is necessary to find out what "resistance" really means in his life. Why is it apparently more vitally necessary to him to resist authority than to pass his subjects? He cannot see what it is he is doing unless he is helped to find the underlying causes of his behavior, and to overcome them with strength and new attitudes gained in a therapeutic relationship.

What is seen behaviorially as "negativism" often turns out to be a kind of "positivism" in a different context. Perhaps the adolescent boy who behaves with "resistance" cannot afford to succeed in his school work because he is playing for higher stakes. If his whole life has been one in which authority persons have made it difficult for him to establish a sense of self, his one desperate goal is to save his own life by rescuing whatever sense of self he has managed to maintain. The feeling of intactness is essential to emotional health. Academic work may represent just one tiny corner in which he fights for the feeling of intactness, and if failing academically gives him that sense of intactness, then this price must be paid. Guarding a sense of identity, of integrity, the knowledge of *who he is* is more vital to his emotional health and survival than is academic achievement. If defying the expectations of authority figures is the only way open to him for feeling like a person, then he is making the wiser choice, even though it may mean school failure.

The task in such a situation is to permit the "defiant" boy to have, as one lad so beautifully expressed it, " . . . the freedom of his failures." When he finds he is respected in his own awkward, fumbling, experimental approaches to life, free of the former prying, pushing, overzealous, overanxious, hypercritical supervision of parents and teachers, he will take courage to build on his own valid foundations—valid because they are his own. (The case of Donald in this study illustrates this struggle and presents it more clearly than can any descriptive formulation.)

Does "resistance" belong only to the adolescent? Or, rather, one may ask whether the end of adolescence is marked by chronological age or by the achievement of comparative maturity. Many "adults"—graduate students, teachers, mothers, fathers—have never finished the business of adolescence, the important chore of individuation, of seeing parents and teachers as persons and the self as a separate, grown-up human being. These old adolescents feel "like kids" all their lives. They have great trouble feeling equal to their peers, and they have an excessive respect, sometimes amounting to awe, of persons in positions of authority.

Thus it is not unusual to find a student in his thirties showing the same "resistance" to his studies as does the "defiant" sixteen-year-old boy. The older adolescent is, like the boy, trying blindly to maintain a sense of self, and his struggle may come to his awareness in a feeling that he is "up against a stone wall." He says, "I feel there is something within me that stops me, a kind of inner resistance which makes me my own worst enemy." He is confused. "It doesn't make sense. Why should I want to defeat myself?"

It's Never Good Enough

When the little child in school spells "cat" with a "k," he does not get two-thirds credit for the "a" and the "t." He is either *all* right or *all* wrong. When the mother says to the little child, "You were bad today," the little child feels he has been *all* bad, that goodness is entirely excluded. He is one or the other, right or wrong, good or bad. He feels he cannot be both good and bad, both right and wrong at the same time. Absolutism and perfectionism rule the day.

A college student said, "I feel I have to read every word of every page of every book on every bibliography. It's slavery! If I don't do it that way, I feel I'm doing something wrong, almost as if I am doing something *bad*." To counteract this slavery, he decided that he would not read a word again until he felt like it. He stopped reading altogether for quite a long time, because it had to be all or nothing, and to give up the nothing meant taking on the tremendous burden of the all, which created unbearable anxiety.

Another student with the same conditioning reported the same feelings. He quickly saw how his pattern of reading mirrored his pattern of meeting other life challenges. He reported that when he has to buy a pair of new shoes, he searches all the stores for the best possible pair of shoes, the one best pair for him. Buying a pair of shoes becomes a test situation, as does his every life experience, and all pleasure is missing.

The phenomenon of "cramming" mentioned in "The Surface Threads" is understandable as a time mechanism for relieving the pressures of perfectionism and absolutism. When one has all semester to read a textbook in history, or economics, or accountancy, or whatever the subject may be, he feels there is no excuse for not learning *perfectly*. With oceans of time ahead of one, what reason can one have for not living up to one's standards of absolute perfection? "If, however," the student says, "I have only these eight hours remaining in which to cover this big book, then I must be practical and realize I can hope to do only so much in those eight hours. I'll be satisfied just to pass the course. I'll give up the wish for an A-plus and settle for a B-plus, since it will be remarkable for me to pass at all in the short time left for study."

In other words, when there is no longer a time freedom-of-choice, one is somewhat freed from the crushing burden of having-to-do-the-work-perfectly. One pressure is traded for another, and that should convey an idea of how dreadful the pressure of perfectionism is. The anguish of last-minute study imposed by the clock is preferred to the anguish of the self-imposed pressure of perfectionism. It is such a familiar picture: Midnight, and a big book on the desk out of which one must get at least the main ideas. The fatal moment is eight hours away. "With so little time left, all I can be expected to do is pass this test. If I just pass it, okay." That is the bargain with destiny.

Having thus negotiated with the gods, the student sometimes experiences, to his surprise, a feeling of exhilaration during this last-minute studying, provided he is not too exhausted, and if his supply of benzedrine does not run out. (It used to be coffee and caffeine tablets; now it seems to be benzedrine for last-minute magic.) Why this unexpected upsurge of exhilaration at this harrowing time? This feeling frequently has been misunderstood and has been described as the beneficial effect of anxiety; that is, "some people do better under conditions of anxiety." The writer believes that it is not anxiety that helps the student to study well at the eleventh hour; on the contrary, anxiety itself interferes with integrated activity. What seems to happen is that there is a momentary freeing from the pressure of perfectionism, an excitement at being liberated from one's own harsh standards, and thus a more intensive application of one's energies to the challenge at hand.[4]

Regard our student: A whiff of freedom, like a breath of springtime, stirs his soul. The possibility of happier days ahead gently kindles his

---

[4] This picture is oversimplified for the purpose of making the one thread stand out clearly. Actually, the story of last-minute study is far more complicated, with many forces at play.

imagination. It is now that he makes resolutions for the next semester. He says to himself, "Why did I think this text was so much to do! There's nothing to it! Here I am, quickly covering the main ideas in only eight hours. With a *whole semester* to deal with it, what I *could* have done!" Here he begins to fall into grievous error, for instead of asking himself, "Then, why didn't I? What stopped me? What *really* got in my way?" he turns his eyes towards new resolutions without new understanding, thus doomed to repeat old mistakes. "Boy, *next* semester things are going to be different! I'll tackle the text the first night I get it, not the last night I need it. I'll be all ready for finals by the end of the first week, so far as the book goes. I'll know it cold."

Thus, in the midst of the joy of newly glimpsed freedom, in a moment of relief from perfectionistic standards, shackling resolutions are made that close the door to freedom. The student promises himself he will do much better next time—no, not much better: He will do perfectly next time. As ever, the overdisciplined person seeks salvation in more discipline. Then, bewildered and unhappy during the middle of the following semester, he finds himself not able to concentrate. Naturally, he is in reaction against the crushing standards he has set up for himself. When cramming time rolls around again, he curses himself for having all semester failed to live up to his resolutions. Then the clock, on the eve of the examination, gives him a brief respite from his self-imposed burden of perfectionism.

Many students are puzzled by their own pattern of starting a task with high enthusiasm and soon losing interest. This pattern is another manifestation of the perfectionistic, absolutist conditioning. The individual begins with a dream of what he would like to do and be; the first time he fails, or thinks he has failed, in any little step on the path to the dream, he feels the dream is totally spoiled. Excitement dies and boredom arises. He loses interest in the task, or in the vocation, because it no longer holds the magic promise of making him a perfectly wonderful, or wonderfully perfect, person.

Why does he need to be this wonderful? Why does he cling to grandiose dreams of perfection? He dreams the dream of perfection because he needs it to save him from his own cruel self-criticism.[5] He was conditioned to feel that one had to be perfectly good and perfectly perfect in order to be lovable, in order to be considered a worthwhile person, in order to "count." Since his conception of perfection is impossible in reality terms, he is repeatedly facing the selfconcept of being a failure.

Finally, his only escape from constant feelings of failure is to try nothing, risk nothing, want nothing. He feels bored with life, because he

[5] The reader is referred to Karen Horney for her discussion of "the idealized image and the despised image." *Our Inner Conflicts.* New York: W. W. Norton and Co. Inc., 1945, pp. 96–114.

has not the courage to be his real self. His real self does not seem to him to be good enough to make him acceptable. Perhaps he will just stay in his room and do nothing at all, to avoid the whole painful prospect of meeting nothing but his own self-criticism, cruel, constricting, unrelenting. One young woman said, "I stayed in bed almost the whole weekend. At least for two days I felt I would avoid any chance of making mistakes."

The perfectionist is defeated before he begins, because to succeed on his terms is hopeless. His teachers, parents and friends may call him "lazy," when the opposite is true: He is excessively ambitious, and his inertia is filled with desperation. His self-criticism and his compensatory strivings must be understood and their irrationality ameliorated before he can mobilize the courage to make mistakes and the resulting energy to be productive. If a student's eggs are all in one basket, that is, if his feeling of worthwhileness depends on his perfect success academically, then he must have a guarantee of success before making any efforts. He cannot afford to take chances, because too much is at stake. Writing a term paper may seem to hold the promise of magic, complete fulfillment (unreal because measured by perfectionistic standards) or the danger of complete nullification. The risk is too great, and he prefers to choose failure than to chance it. He holds onto his dream of perfection, and his activity in reality terms is paralyzed.

The word-by-word reader, making sure he is missing nothing, suffers from these fears of being nothing if he is not perfect. He shares the too prevalent misconception that it is noble to have irrationally high standards, even though they are so high that no one could possibly achieve them, and even though the constant measuring of what one really is against the vision of what one "ought" to be leaves one too heartsick and hopeless to do what one is able to do.

Despite the fact that this way of life is inefficient, the person caught in it makes a virtue of his irrational necessity in order to maintain it, since he has the illusion that in this way lies safety. Thus, a student coming for help to overcome his word-by-word reading may gradually become aware that he wants the practical advantages of giving up his crippling perfectionism and, at the same time, wants to cling to the unreal "safety" of his perfectionism.

On the surface, this pattern gives rise to what looks like paradoxical behavior. The word-by-word reader asks for help to overcome his habit; he claims he wants to read faster, with more fluency. However, when encouraged to be less "sticky" and more selective in his reading, to skip words that are not essential to the meaning, he becomes ruffled and a little resentful, petulant and defensive. The suggestion that he try to do just an adequate job, that he strive towards being average rather than remarkable, gives rise to considerable strong feeling.

Sometimes the instructor is accused of promoting carelessness, inefficiency, mediocrity, even dishonesty—as though skipping a word were immoral. The instructor is reaping the results of exposing a weakness which has been exalted into a virtue as part of a safety system. The student's lack of self-confidence makes it impossible for him to be selective, to decide what words to read and what words to skim over; he sees this fear-ridden performance rather as evidence of his being an extraordinarily good child, perfectly "clean," conscientious and thorough.[6]

The excessive carefulness, despite all the trouble it causes, has become a source of pride, and the possessor of the perfectionistic attitude would like to be praised for it. When no special rewards are forthcoming for being so good—in fact, when it is intimated that one is foolish and ineffectual when one is *that* good—there is, quite naturally, a rage reaction. One young woman, proceeding from a discussion of her word-by-word reading to a discussion of her similarly cautious mode of activity in other life areas, said, "When I think of all the years I've wasted, never expressing my real feeling, never really living, always waiting for someone to reward me someday for my goodness, I could explode, I'm so angry!"

Thus, when an instructor or remedial-reading specialist tries to change reading habits, he is trying to change a great deal more than that. All kinds of feelings are stirred up, and safety systems erected to forestall anxiety are threatened. "Help me to read fast," the students request. "But," they add, in effect, "don't take away my perfectionistic standards."

I Am Afraid to Succeed

A woman in her middle thirties had made many sacrifices for several years to save money enough for a year's leave of absence from her teaching position, so that she might come to Teachers College for a Master's Degree. As the first semester drew to a close, she found herself having crying spells, and she came to talk things over. She said she was worried that she was not of high enough calibre for graduate-school work. She was not able to concentrate on her studies or get her papers written. She said she was a poor reader, and she wanted to take an intelligence test to make sure she had the intellect necessary for advanced study.

She rated high in the superior group on the Bellevue-Wechsler Test. Though this was reassuring to her, it also was surprising. "I never believed," she said, "that I was smart, though my teachers always told me I was." It followed now that she must wonder what in the world was making it so difficult for her to do her work. "I've wanted this chance for years," she said, "and now that I'm here at last, I can't make the most of it." She began to wonder aloud, and the underlying threads came to the surface:

[6] The reader who would like a more thorough understanding of this concept is referred to discussions in the psychoanalytic literature of the genesis and characteristics of the obsessive-compulsive character structure.

Grace[7] had had an unhappy childhood. Her mother died when she was a little girl. Her mother's sister came to live with Grace, her father and her baby brother, to take care of them all and, as it turned out, to terrorize them. This aunt was like a witch out of a storybook. At first Grace described her cruelties with calm and forbearance, but later she began to reexperience the emotional torment she had endured as a child, and angry tears poured.

To come quickly to the point: While still a child, she learned that her aunt was jealous of women better educated than herself. Grace became very ambitious, wanting nothing in the world so much as a higher education. She had fleeting glimpses of awareness that she was really working towards her day of revenge: She would have a Master's Degree, and her aunt would have to look up to her—a humiliating prospect for that bitter, envious woman.

This story did not go far enough, however, to account for the weeping and the inability to concentrate. Did she feel so guilty about her wish to humiliate her aunt that she must punish herself by defeating her own constructive efforts? This did not seem strong enough a wish to produce such powerful effects; there had to be more to it than that. There was. One day the fantasy spun itself out all the way: Her aunt would *drop dead* with jealousy the day Grace came home with her higher degree. This was the hope and the wish. However, since she, like most people, felt keenly the magic power of words, she feared it might really happen that her own triumph would kill her aunt. This fear gave rise to a subsequent fear: Destiny would punish her for her wish to kill. Her punishment would be death. Thus, to do her work successfully meant she would be killed, she would die!

During the session in which this fantasy emerged, Grace realized it was natural for her to have violent death wishes against her aunt, who had been so cruel to her during her entire childhood. She said, "I didn't know how *much* I hated my aunt. I was afraid to know." This was a turning-point for her. The weeping spells ceased, and her concentration improved. With more and more understanding of her feelings about her family relationships and her relationships with fellow students, professors and the counselor, she made steady progress. She gained weight, used more make-up, bought her first red hat and began to enjoy her courses and her extracurricular activities. She was a superior student, and she was an exceptionally gentle and kind person, with fine sensitivity to the needs of children.

This is a greatly oversimplified account of a case for the purpose of highlighting one important thread: My triumph will be at another person's expense! The example may seem so striking as to be unusual. In some ways it is, since the role of an intruder aunt in a family, replacing the mother, is not usual. However, the fear that success comes at another person's expense is not unusual. If one sees it in the setting of

[7] Names and identifying data have been changed.

competition between brothers and sisters, between daughter and mother, father and son, it becomes quite clear that this thread weaves through many lives.

It occurs with particular intensity in those families where it is considered unforgivable to express anger, and where rivalry is regarded as evil instead of natural. There comes to mind a family in which the mother boasted to her friends, "In *our* family we do not quarrel." The mother did not know that her little son wanted to hit his sister on the head with his baseball bat, that her daughter had a compelling impulse to push her mother down the stairs, and that both children were dreadfully paralyzed because their constructive ambitions were so loaded with the forbidden wish that their success would cause the rival to drop dead with envy. The daughter remarked to the Counselor one day, "No wonder people say, 'That'll really slay 'em!' "[8]

I Am Keeping a Secret Bargain

A graduate student unable to concentrate on her work began to explore with the Counselor some of the feelings lurking under the surface, feelings holding her *real* attention, distracting her from her studies. She discovered that she felt herself bound by an unconscious bargain, and that she was in rebellion against this bargain.

Laura, the student, had very early in life made an unconscious bargain with her sister, two years her junior. The sister was small, dainty, girlish; Laura was big and heavy-boned, with features that were not quite as fine as her sister's. "I'll be the smart one, and you can be the pretty one," was the unspoken bargain Laura made, not realizing she was afraid to compete with her sister in the area of femininity.

Now, after a triumphant academic career, nearing her doctorate, Laura seemed almost deliberately to be trying to sabotage the successful completion of her work. Further insights revealed her unconscious protest against the unconscious bargain. Her sister was married and had two children. The doctoral diploma seemed a cold substitute for love and family life. A bargain that involved suppression of her own femininity was too harsh a bargain, indeed. In a last-minute rebellion against the defeat of her womanly self, she was trying to break the bargain. It was as if she were saying to herself: "If I fail to get my degree, perhaps it is not too late to win in the other arena, in the world of competition with women, as a woman."

[8] The reader may consider this example too pathological to be representative. This is not so, however. The difference between the fantasies of these persons and the average person is not in kind, but in degree of intensity. The reputation of the young woman here described is that she is "such a sweet girl" (which she is), who "could not be mean if she tried" (also true, as she turns her bad feelings against herself and suffers psychosomatically). Since her friends do not have access to her fantasies, they are not aware of what is really going on inside her.

It came to her as a shock that she *could have everything*, her academic success *and* her feminine success. She recognized that she had carried through life the feeling of being handicapped, as handicapped as though physically disfigured, perhaps even more so. With a surge of relief she understood that she need not carry this self-imposed limitation, that she could break "the bargain" without disaster or dishonor. Further psychotherapy supported Laura's efforts to grant herself both her intellectual competency and a flowering of her womanly charm.

There are many different kinds of unconscious bargains. Often a young man or woman feels that he or she is going to college *for* a parent or sibling. One nineteen-year-old college girl said despairingly, "Mother is always reminding me how much *she* wanted to go to college, and that she couldn't go. She says, 'It hurts me that you don't make the most of the opportunity.'"

This girl felt that she had made a bargain with her mother: She was accepting tuition and living expenses in return for going to college *for* her mother. The impossibility of this goal, of *being* her mother, as it were, filled her with a hopelessness that permeated all her efforts. One day she burst out with: "The only way I can give my mother a college education is for her to go to college herself. That must be why I am always urging her to please go take some courses. I guess I want her to get her own education so there will be less of a burden on me."

When she realized that she had made an impossible bargain, and recognized how it had paralyzed her, enraged her, and filled her with hopelessness, she began to be more courageous and was able to assert to herself that she had a right to go to college for her *own* education. With increasing freedom to be herself, her energy for study increased, and her concentration improved.

There is also the unconscious bargain made by the one physically healthy child in a family in which the other children have been damaged by illness or accident. This child is afraid to succeed because his success would seem so unfair to those who are not able to compete with him. It is as though he has made a bargain with them: "I won't press my advantage of being the healthy one. I'll give myself the handicap of not really trying. In exchange for my health, I'll pay the price of failing in school."[9]

I'd Rather Be Loved Than Successful

This is a variation of the thread discussed directly above. It is another "unconscious bargain," another formulation of the fear of achievement. This attitude, "I'd rather be loved than be successful," is found in persons so intolerant of their own competitiveness that they feel no one will love

[9] Also, he is afraid to risk making mistakes, because, being well and strong, he has "absolutely no excuse" for not being perfect in his school performance.

them if their competitiveness is discovered. "If I fail," said one student, "I am no threat to anyone. If I am not a threat, they will like me."

Many years ago, Stuart A. Courtis at the University of Michigan introduced exercises in cooperation for students in the field of education. The writer recalls a discussion with a fellow student with whom one of the exercises was being carried out. Both wondered whether cooperation necessitated the complete obliteration of competitiveness. It seemed a goal impossible of attainment. Now, picking up that discussion at the present time, the writer believes that intolerance for natural competitiveness tends to inhibit natural capacities for cooperation. Perhaps an example will serve to make the point:

Consider a woman whose turn it is to entertain her bridge club. She is preparing a luncheon for her company, and she has at least two feelings about it: On the one hand, she enjoys the prospect of giving enjoyment to her friends by serving them excellent food, beautifully prepared; on the other hand, she has a secret satisfaction in feeling that the other women will have to recognize her superiority as a cook, since she is certain no one else has served anything quite so original, so dainty, so exquisite. Should she despise herself for the latter feeling? Must she hate herself for being competitive, for wanting so much recognition? If her conscience is overscrupulous and punitive, she will hate herself for contaminating her pure feelings with competitive ones. If she hates herself a great deal, she may have to project the hatred (unconsciously) in order to endure it. That means she will feel she does not like the other women, or she will feel they do not really like her. She is afraid no one will like her if her competitiveness is exposed. She finds one reason or another for dropping out of the club. Is this constructive and cooperative? No, for now the other women have lost her altogether. Though they are spared her competitiveness, they lose her friendship, since her warmth and goodness were not excluded by her competitiveness. Everyone loses.

How much healthier it would have been for this woman to feel something like the following: Well, that's how I am. It's true I'm competing with the other girls, but I expect them to compete with me, too, and no harm done. It's probably a hangover from my competition with my mother and my sister. Anyhow, I'm not hurting anyone by my thoughts. The only effect on them is to provide them with the comfort of my hospitality. They will have the opportunity to do the same thing when I go to their houses. We all get our chance to show off. That's how we human beings are, and it isn't so bad.[10]

Let us take another example, this time in the area of education. If several students study together for an examination—as they often do when preparing for matriculation or comprehensive examinations—

---

[10] Individuals who are excessively self-critical tend to regard many human attributes as *sub*-human, and angelic qualities as properly human and entirely possible if only one tried hard enough.

mutual helpfulness is not untainted by competitiveness, yet everyone profits. Each person shares his material with the others. Should each feel guilty for his secret thought that in some special way he will particularly excel on the examination? He does not begrudge the others' doing well, but he wants to express his own identity in his very own way, to make his own mark, to carve his own initials. If he feels guilty for this wish to be himself, which he may sense as wanting to be better than the others, at the expense of the others, he may stay away from the study groups altogether, rationalizing that he gets more work done when he works alone. He misses out, both academically and socially, on what is offered by the other students. He misses the valuable experience of formulating his own ideas to communicate them to others. He misses the fun of doing things together.

Freedom Makes Me Anxious

A student studying for his oral examination in English literature expressed fear that he would never finish all the books in time. He was asked, "Why did you hurry to set a date for your oral examination, when you have hardly begun the reading?" He replied, "Unless I set a deadline, I'll go all to pieces and won't be able to read at all. I get nervous, depressed, anxious and terribly inefficient if I have too much freedom."

At first this sounds like a person who has been so accustomed to functioning under rigid disciplinary conditions that freedom frightens him (21). One might say he has had "too much discipline." A great deal has been written and spoken about the evil effects of too much discipline. Recently, statements are beginning to come into the literature of child psychology about the deleterious effects of too little discipline, of failure to "set limits." The use of the words "too much" and "too little" are not helpful, however. It is the quality of discipline and the personality of the disciplining person that is of importance (3). The word "discipline" itself is a fighting word; hackles rise at the sound of it, because of its traditional authoritarian connotations. The expression "setting limits" came into being to avoid these connotations.

A young man is preparing for his oral examination, unable to work without setting a deadline. Viewing the situation from the outside, an observer of the family would unhesitatingly say that his father "over-disciplined" him and his mother "spoiled" him. His father terrified him with authoritarian demands for conformity. His mother waited on him, babied him and protected him from the neighboring children.

During the process of psychotherapy, the real picture emerges: The father is a frightened man. He shouts and blusters, and his son is frightened because he can get no strength from his father. What name can one give to this father's "discipline?" The mother turns out to be shadowy, indefinite, easily bullied; however, she, in turn, bullies her son.

She wins her way by weeping and begging. Can this method of intimidation be called "discipline?" Can it be called "spoiling?" If the popular notion of "spoiling" is that the child is always allowed to have his own way, then he was not "spoiled," for he was thoroughly dominated, not only by his father's weak blustering, but by his mother's tearful bullying.

In an environment so inconsistent, with a parental show of spurious strength belied by internal weakness, the boy was almost constantly in a state of anxiety, in a fog of uncertainty. He hungered for a really strong father, someone kind and consistent, who could protect him and give him a model to follow. He yearned for a mother who would not melt into tears at his every show of independence.

This young man repeatedly set up situations for himself in which he provided a structure of limits within which he tried to function with an alleviation of his confusion and anxiety. One might almost say he was trying to be a strong mother and father to himself. He said, on one occasion, "When I was a kid, it suddenly dawned on me: 'If they are so frightened of the world, who will protect me in the world?'" It turned out that setting a deadline meant to him establishing strong parents who cared about him and would take care of him adequately. The deadline became "someone who really cared"—not like his infantile parents, who were so immature that they clutched at him for support instead of being able to give him support.

Scheduling his daily activities had the same meaning for him: The schedule was a strong parent. His difficulty was that he overdid his efforts to provide structure. The systems he set up were too rigid, too exacting, and he was bound to experience reactions against them, thus throwing himself into helpless and hopeless confusion; for freedom to him meant chaos rather than an opportunity for strong self-assertion. When reading, he was so determined to remember every word he read, and so frightened that he would not remember, that he could not concentrate. Therefore, he found himself looking at pages without seeing them. This ineffectual reading would catapult him into the most distressing depressions and feelings of hopelessness.

My Desperation Leaves Me No Time for Discriminating

There is a kind of reader whose way of reading is characteristically described as follows: "He goes too fast, misses words, stumbles, loses the meaning, has to go back, starts up again at breakneck speed, rushes headlong into the material, gets lost again, stops, goes back and so on." If I were to give a name to this kind of reading, I would call it "stuttering reading."

It has long been recognized that stuttering in speech has psychogenic origins. "Stuttering reading" is perhaps closely related to speech stuttering; it demands and deserves an equal attention to underlying causation.

There is a quality of desperation in the reader who rushes and halts, speeds and stops. An observation one can make immediately is that these readers seem to be standing in their own way, and that there is in their reading some element of self-sabotage.

Another observation is that they seem to be gulping, not savoring what they take in. Why is there this great hurry? Can one hypothesize that this kind of person is so desperate for affection and for safety that he reaches frantically and grabs indiscriminately? Can one also ask whether he so fears punitive reactions to his competitiveness that he can be aggressive only surreptitiously and speedily? Questions like these point the way to an understanding of the underlying causes of reading disability.

These are some of the most important threads that emerge from below the surface when reading problems are studied carefully. The reader will recognize them in their interacting, overlapping, dynamic relationships in the case material presented in this study.

One major point will become increasingly clear when seen in the case material: Reading cannot be regarded as separate from the other behavior of an individual.

4. CHILDREN AND READING DIFFICULTIES

Gertrude Hildreth and Josephine L. Wright

ANALYSIS OF UNFAVORABLE BACKGROUND CONDITIONS AND DIFFICULTIES WITH READING[1]

In analyzing the case study summaries for each child, we found thirty-five indications of home background or previous school background having been unsatisfactory in some respect. The parents were uniformly over-anxious about the child's failure in reading and this anxiety served only to aggravate the child's problem. They seldom seemed to understand what was best for the child. They only knew that they wanted the child to "pass" rather than to "fail" in school, and not be a disgrace to the family. It was apparent even to the parent with least insight that a child must read in order to "pass" at school, and for that reason the child

Reprinted with the permission of the publisher from Gertrude Hildreth and Josephine L. Wright, *Helping Children to Read* (New York: Teachers College Press), copyright 1940 by Teachers College, Columbia University.

[1] This analysis includes two children studied by us, but not included in the class because they fell outside the age range.

was being forced to attend the summer reading class. Parents were over-solicitous or frankly ashamed of the child and displayed these attitudes in the child's presence. They were often domineering, dictatorial, harsh, severe, or unsympathetic in their attitude toward the child and his problems. They expressed many "musts" to the teacher on registration. "He's got to learn." "He's got to go on to the next grade this fall." "He's got to mind." "He's got to read better." "His father's spending all this money on his books, clothing, food, etc., so he can learn." "You must make him do better." "He's a disgrace to the family." There was little evidence of a sympathetic attitude.

Little attempt was made by parents to understand the case; no request was made for help in understanding the problem. Parents commented that they had to force the child to do his homework, but they showed limited ability to help him with his lessons at home. Few had any materials at home worth using. Most of the parents were inclined to use a spelling-out method when they did attempt to teach the child, or to complain, "He doesn't know all his letters yet." Most who selected books for the child chose those on the child's chronological age level—*Robin Hood* for the eleven-year-old—rather than the primer material suited to the child's present reading level. Most of them thought of a remedial reading program as a drastic curative process applied like a plaster or strong medicine, or similar to a major operation. They did not understand the child's part in the learning process. Few would believe that the child was not genuinely lazy or that his trouble was not due solely to poor eyesight.

In several cases, the child's former teachers had been more interested than the parents in seeing that the child received better reading training. One father told the home visitor that he did not know how to read well, that he seldom read, and yet he was very successful with his work. Few parents inquired during the term about the child's progress, or asked in what ways they might help. The grandmother of one child reported that the father was too easy on the child, indulged him too much, never said "no" to him, and gave him too much money. Although the father was lenient in these matters, he was unduly severe when the boy's former school report was marked "failure."

There were eleven indications of protracted absence from school, or frequent changes of school, during the primary years.

BEHAVIOR AND EMOTIONAL PROBLEMS

Unfavorable signs were found to the largest extent in unfavorable attitudes, emotional maladjustments, and behavior symptoms. Emotional maladjustments, erratic behavior trends, extreme manifestations, such as hypertension, depression, over-activity, anxiety, egocentricity, rebelliousness, insecurity, shyness, and nervousness in any new situation, were mentioned twenty-one times in the reports. Behavior problems were quite general and negative attitudes toward school were very marked. Feelings of failure, lack of confidence, failure to exert effort, inability to face difficulties and to assume responsibility were mentioned twenty-two times. There were eighteen indications that attention was hard to control or that work habits were unsatisfactory. Ability to study or work independently was a skill almost entirely lacking in the group in the beginning. The children showed a "defeatist" attitude; they were sure they could not succeed even if they tried. Many were negativistic, tending to withdraw, or to refuse to try. The children were on the defensive; they were non-conforming, apathetic. Even brief and casual observation revealed that quite a few in the group showed signs of tics and other nervous tendencies. An unusual number of the cases had bitten their nails down to the quick because of the emotional strain under which they had been laboring for a long period of time. Several of the children were clinical cases, so serious were their problems from an adjustment standpoint. Several seemed to enjoy the stir caused by their reading failure and manifested great satisfaction over the worry and concern their problems were causing parents and teachers. They could succeed in being disability cases, if in nothing else!

Retardation due to reading failure had obviously precipitated the children into maladjustment. Personality and behavior problems naturally arose from or were aggravated by failure in reading. The evidence on this point was incontrovertible. Since these unfavorable symptoms tended to clear up during the retraining program, we concluded that they were more the result than the cause of reading disability.

DIFFICULTIES IN READING AND CONTRIBUTING FACTORS

The first problem confronting us was to analyze the reading difficulties of each child. Although this process was begun immediately, it was not concluded until the end of the six weeks' term because each day's work revealed more evidence concerning the child's limitations with respect to reading. Lack of past history and developmental data prevented us from going any further into causal factors that operated in the child's early learning history.

During the registration period and the first week in school the most obvious fact was the distaste these children showed for anything connected with reading. Their fear of failure in reading and embarrassment were the result of former failures. The case studies yielded thirty-seven references to strong emotional reaction against reading, with marked fear or resistance toward reading. The most marked difficulties were shown in adjustment to reading. The children made unconscious attempts to escape from reading, the mental effort it entailed, and the dissatisfaction associated with the activity.

Unfavorable Attitudes. Fluctuating attitudes characterized most of the cases. One day certain children showed that they genuinely wished to improve. The next day the interest shown so intently the day before had evaporated. They might stay away on some trivial excuse or come late. All the children enrolled in the summer class had had previous school training in reading and six had had "remedial" work. We were amazed to see how relatively ineffective this work had been, so far as we were able to evaluate it. Children had spent years learning to read under intensive pressure with only scant results to show for all the effort expended.

Even with intensive instruction, most cases had not caught on to the reading trick, the process of thinking through and interpreting the printed page, of anticipating and grasping meanings and gaining ideas from sentences or paragraphs. Several had worked with teachers individually after school, before school, or at recess. Many had been given assigned lessons to take home daily. Some had had intensive work in phonics. All had been given textbooks to study or workbooks to labor over. Yet the gains these children had made were negligible, and little that could be called reading had resulted.

The specific reading difficulties in each case were studied intensively through the use of diagnostic tests and observation during reading activities. Close attention was paid to methods the child used in attempting to identify words, fluency in word recognition, perceptual and eye-movement habits, the character of oral reading, the child's response to difficulties encountered, the use of picture and meaning clues, the extent to which the child could comprehend what he read, the extent of his meaning vocabulary, habits in silent reading, and attitudes toward reading assignments. These diagnostic studies, for the most part, were made by student-interns. We were more concerned with identifying the child's difficulties than with trying to infer from the diagnostic study the causes of the inefficient habits.

Every child except one presented a serious problem in reading. No two children presented the same problem, although several showed similar traits and proved to be at the same levels in achievement. We found, however, few "pure" reading problems, that is, deficiencies in reading unaccompanied by other handicaps, limitations, or complications. More than one specific difficulty was usually found in each case. Reading failure was often only a small part of general failure. Difficulty with reading was only one symptom that a more general learning or personality adjustment problem existed. Reading problems were often subordinate to others more serious.

Aside from specific failures in skills, such as identifying and sounding word parts, or recalling the meaning of a word, the children as a group had two major troubles. First, they were afraid to try. They showed no tendency to go into a problem, to experiment with a feature causing difficulty, to show flexibility or versatility in attack on a difficult word, to respond actively, or to exercise intelligence when the need to study words arose. These tendencies were especially marked in the children who had the smallest recognition vocabularies. The situation seemed to be due to two causes: first, the conventional, mechanical methods by which most of the children had been taught, which allowed little time and opportunity for repeated trials; and second, fear of punishment associated with trials that resulted in error. The latter cause constitutes a serious handicap in learning to read or in reading improvement because active trial and experiment is inherent in all successful reading practice.

The second major handicap under which these children suffered, one that appears to be indirectly related to the first, was a tendency to show fatigue at the slightest mental exertion. Attention could not be long sustained, concentration was impossible for any length of time because continuous mental effort exhausted them so quickly. Several children commented on what hard work reading was, how tired they became when they read. They were extremely tense when doing any seat work, such as reading or writing. They showed evident relief when they were permitted to turn to cutting, pasting, woodwork, or printing with the stamp outfit—activities which did not entail sustained mental effort, or which the child could adapt to his own energy limitations.

Deficiencies in Specific Skills. Deficiencies in specific reading skills and techniques were indicated in thirty-four instances. There were fifty-five indications of inefficient, inadequate, or unskillful reaction to new words, or evidence that the child was lacking in word analysis and phonetic skills.

"Spelling-out" was the most common method of attack on new or hard words, though all the children had received reading instruction in fairly modern schools. This method slowed down word attack. The child first whispered each letter, sometimes twice, looking at each letter painstakingly. Then he tried to sound the letters, often making unsuccessful attempts at blending. The letter names gave no helpful associations with appropriate letter sounds. Eventually the child might pronounce the word correctly.

The children showed limited phonetic translation skill. They could not use the conventional phonics they had been taught. Attempts at blending the elements they had learned in isolation were unsuccessful. Another difficulty characteristic of the group and observable at the same time was difficulty in pronouncing any new or unfamiliar word, even after it was pronounced for them. For example, "Fiske," the name of the teacher whose class had extended our class an invitation to visit them was difficult; the first attempts at pronouncing this name were "Fits," "Frisk," "Fritz," although the children labored to pronounce it correctly. Eye-movements were irregular and ineffective because word recognition in many cases was so limited. Finger pointing was common. Random guesses and careless errors were numerous, and the group as a whole seemed below average in memory for verbal material. They tended to ignore punctuation marks in oral reading, phrasing was poor, and the result was often expressionless, monotonous word-calling. A few children who had been taught by the "whole method" tended to memorize everything they read, and were handicapped when they met the familiar words in new arrangements or settings. These children read carelessly in content material, often skipping words.

Early in the session a note was received from another class inviting our group to tell them about a trip we had made to the zoo. Although this invitation in letter form had been drafted by a child who used very simple words, the group as a whole failed to understand the message until it was explained to them. This was additional evidence that even their verbal understanding, to say nothing of verbal reading skill, was extremely limited. The children could pronounce the separate words of the message when it was written on the board, but it conveyed no meaning to them until it was all carefully explained. Then the faces brightened and the general response was, "Of course, we'll be glad to visit their class and tell them about our trip."

Inability to spell was related to phonetic deficiencies. Early in the session there was occasion for the teacher to write on the board the word "Vote." No one seemed to know how to spell it. The pupils' attempts at blending phonetic elements were unsuccessful. Volunteers in the class suggested "voat," "voet," "vout," "voute," "volt," and other alternatives closer to sheer guesses. The teacher's suggestion that the word was analogous to "note" was of little help. Finally, after many trials, one of the more competent members of the class spelled the word aloud correctly.

Few children showed one handicap to the exclusion of others; many deficiencies were found correlated in an individual case. Handicaps that alone might have been insignificant, in conjunction with others impaired ability to learn to read.

INFERENCES AS TO CAUSES OF POOR READING

The indications from present difficulties, in conjunction with school history and home background data, forced us to conclude that these children had become reading failures chiefly because they had received inadequate attention and inappropriate instruction in the first school years. Their needs as individuals uninitiated in school procedures had not been appreciated, understood, or provided for intelligently. Their slight deviations from normal learning trends had either not been detected at all or not early enough. Instruction had not been differentiated from that for typically normal learners before the lag became so great as to cause failure and attendant antipathy. These children were unable to meet the learning demands teachers had made of them. They lacked sufficient mental energy for sustaining attention to the learning task imposed on them. The work had been energy depleting, and hence painful when long sustained. The strain wasted their mental and emotional reserve power. They were emotionally shocked by reading, not emotionally satisfied as they should have been to insure positive learning attitudes. Yet these children had been conscripted for imposed learning at an early age and had no means of escape except through non-complaint behavior.

The children had inadequate oral language facility for learning to read at a normal rate in a normal way, as well as too limited experience and background. They also had certain physical handicaps and were affected by circumstances which interrupted the normal course of learning to read. Furthermore, the homes represented had little or no reading material to supplement or assist the school in its instructional program. Learning for these cases had been extremely wasteful, psychologically unsound in every phase.

Retraining Needs Revealed by the Diagnostic Study

We concluded from the foregoing analysis of the children's difficulties that no one method, however expertly applied, would remove the handicaps under which these children labored, or which these cases presented. After studying their informal responses for a week and analyzing their difficulties, we reached the following conclusions with regard to their retraining.

1. Each child required a highly individualized program, at least at the beginning, in order to relieve embarrassment and to focus attention.

2. To insure success, the children needed work on an easier level than had been customarily assigned to them.

3. An entirely new beginning was necessary in some cases to stimulate interest and restore confidence.

4. They required reading work in small doses and short drill periods.

5. They needed to learn to associate words with their meanings so that they could read meaningfully. They needed activities that would make reading meaningful, so that they could read with a purpose.

6. They needed to learn to study, how to find out facts for themselves and how to work without constant supervision, how to take directions and to follow them alone.

7. They required practice in giving attention and in concentrating on work involving individual study. Attention needed to be gained and

attention span lengthened if these children were to develop satisfactory reading habits.

8. They needed help in language, in speech, in using larger vocabularies, in hearing sentences properly enunciated; they needed practice in conversation and word pronunciation.

9. They needed much vocabulary repetition on a simple level.

10. They needed writing and spelling practice as much as reading, that is, writing in the sense of composition.

11. They needed experience wider and more thought-provoking than they had previously had, so that their curiosity would be stirred, and their interest aroused in how things are made, the causes of natural phenomena, appearances of things, their structure and composition. This kind of experience had been largely lacking in these children's lives. It could be provided only through integrated experiences in the classroom and some school supervised contacts outside.

12. They needed more opportunity in school for satisfying social experiences. Most of their social lives heretofore had been lived on the street. School had afforded meager opportunities for these children to live together. They needed to work together and to respond to one another as persons, not solely as competitive school pupils who must "do all their work by themselves."

13. They needed to develop feelings of security with teachers and other pupils, to feel that they had nothing of which they need be ashamed, that the teacher had confidence in their ability, that they could succeed if they tried, that learning in general and learning to read in particular could be a happy adventure; that satisfaction and fun could be derived from reading.

14. They needed to see and handle some books other than classroom textbooks or readers they had already failed to understand after several attempts. They needed to know what books contain. They needed to hear someone else read, both to stimulate interest in book content and as an example of how reading is done expertly.

15. They needed plays and games to relieve tension and make school experiences happier.

16. Their parents needed guidance and instruction in all of these matters, better understanding of the child and more sympathy with him, as well as assistance in helping him to better reading habits when he asked for and wanted help at home.

17. They needed to learn to give and take, to "play the game," to share and work together on a group project.

18. They needed a sympathetic listener when they wished to talk over their problems.

19. They needed to have their errors and mistakes in reading talked over with them so that they could more fully understand the nature of their difficulties.

20. They needed to be challenged to achieve, but to be given a challenge they could actually meet successfully.

21. They needed to get far enough into the process to see that reading could furnish experiences and ideas.

22. They needed varied exercises and techniques in learning to read, to read in content, to use picture and meaning clues, to see and study words intently, to see words in words, to see how to study words, to anticipate meanings, to guess more effectively, to help themselves out of difficulty, to be more aggressive and versatile in attacking reading work.

23. They needed the social satisfaction of reading in groups.

24. They needed opportunities for oral reading practice before an audience for the purpose of giving pleasure or information to a group, and for experiencing the satisfaction of group applause.

25. They needed to read silently more rapidly and effectively. Their silent reading needed to be checked more carefully.

26. They had to unlearn bad habits, finger pointing, inner speech, saying, "wait a minute," "oh," "ah," hemming and hawing that caused slow reading.

27. They needed to improve in phrasing and other aspects of oral reading.

It was obvious that few of these children were able to help themselves very much. They needed carefully controlled programs under close personal supervision in order to learn how to work out assignments for themselves.

We could not assume that correcting the reading deficiency would immediately alleviate all other problems, for the retraining program must necessarily be broad in character. However, it was obvious that reading instruction would give these children a skill greatly needed for any further progress in school. If they received ample individual supervision they could unquestionably learn to read. We believed that their school adjustments might improve, their behavior become better controlled and their work habits better organized, if they could acquire and use reading skills more effectively.

5. CAUSATIVE FACTORS IN
READING DISABILITIES

Marion Monroe

SUMMARY

The following outline is an attempt to list the factors associated with reading disabilities. For convenience, the factors are outlined under various aspects of reading. When the same factor may be viewed from different angles, it is mentioned more than once. We have attempted to list all the observed factors, although only a few aspects of some of them were quantitatively measured. In the following outline we refer to specific reading defects which may occur at any intellectual level.

I. Difficulties related to the visual aspects of reading
    1. Lack of clear-cut retinal images, due to defects in the refractive mechanisms of the eye, may impede progress in reading.

> *Manifestations in reading*
> The child shows evidences of eyestrain and confuses similarly shaped letters such as o, e, c, or b, h, n, etc. Reading errors consist of confusion of words such as "oat " "cat," "eat"; or "hand," "band," "hard," etc.

    2. Lack of precision in discrimination of complex visual patterns may impede progress in reading. The difficulty in discrimination of patterns in some cases may be associated with hemianopsia, or with injury to optic tracts or cortex. The difficulty in other cases may be due to poor acuity of the peripheral retina so that the child must bring small parts of the pattern successively into foveal vision. The difficulty in still other cases may be due, not to sensory defects, but to difficulties in correlating the visual impressions with language through functional, rather than organic, deviations.

> *Manifestations in reading*
> The child seems unable to react to words as units. He reads slowly, by spelling out the letters. He sometimes tries to identify patterns by tracing over them with the finger. His reading errors consist of omissions of sounds and filling in words by guessing from one or two recognized letters, thus producing vowel and consonant errors.

    → 3. Lack of precision in discrimination of the spatial orientation of patterns

may impede progress in reading. Space perception is usually developed
through motor reactions to objects, by looking at, reaching for, or
manipulation of the objects in positions up, down, right, left, near, far,
etc. A confusion in the directional movements of the hands, or of the
hand and eye, may result in confusion of the right or left positions
of patterns.

Manifestations in reading

The child confuses the patterns which are alike in shape, but which
are placed in different positions, as b, d; p, q; u, n; m, w; f, t;
"was," "saw"; "on," "no," etc. He confuses the sequence of words
and is often a fluent mirror-reader or mirror-writer. He sometimes
traces the words or letters with his finger in order to determine
their position. He slides a finger along the text to give a cue to
direction. His reading errors consist of reversals, repetitions, and
sometimes, because of correlating the sequence of sounds with the
reversed sequence of letters, of consonant and vowel errors.

II. Difficulties related to the auditory aspects of reading
   1. Lack of auditory acuity due to partial deafness may impede progress
   in reading.

Manifestations in reading

The child omits endings and non-stressed syllables because he
does not hear them. He confuses some of the consonant and
vowel sounds.

   2. Lack of precision in the discrimination of speech sounds may impede
   progress in reading. The difficulty in discrimination may be due to a
   defect in the auditory mechanism for some ranges of pitches and sound
   qualities. The difficulty is often associated with articulatory speech defects. The articulatory speech defect may result from the lack of precision
   in auditory discrimination, or if no sensory defect is present, may cause
   the lack of discrimination. In cases of articulatory defects, the words as
   presented to a child by himself and by others are different in auditory
   pattern and yet arouse a common meaning. The two diverse auditory
   patterns may become so closely associated in the common response as
   to be inseparable in discrimination.

Manifestations in reading

The child confuses words composed of similar sounds, such as
"send," "sand"; "bit," "bet"; "cashing," "catching," etc. He has
difficulty in forming visual-auditory associations. Reading errors
consist of vowel and consonant errors, additions and omissions
of sounds.

   3. Lack of precision in the discrimination of the temporal sequence of
   sounds may impede progress in reading. The difficulty in discrimination
   of sequence of sounds may result from inability to discriminate the
   separate sounds of the pattern. The child who cannot tell the difference
   between the separate sounds of the word cannot very well distinguish

which sound comes first. The difficulty may be due to poor retention of auditory patterns so that the patterns cannot be held in mind long enough for temporal analysis.

Manifestations in reading

The child has difficulty in applying phonics as a method of word-recognition. He may be able to give the separate sounds for each of the letters composing a word but cannot blend the sounds to get the complete word. He often reverses the sequence of sounds, in attempts at blending, as "p-a-r-t-y," blended to make "pottery." Reading errors consist of vowels, consonants, reversals, additions and omissions of sounds.

III. Difficulties related to the motor aspects of reading

1. Lack of precision in the motor control of the eyes may impede progress in reading. Children who cannot direct the eyes accurately to the printed words and maintain the motor adjustment for a period of time usually have difficulty in attending to the visual symbols with sufficient persistence to form the necessary associations.

Manifestations in reading

The child frequently loses the place of reading. He skips lines and words. He often follows the text with the finger as a means of keeping the place. Reading errors consist of omissions of words, omissions of sounds, reversals, and repetitions.

2. Lack of precision in the motor control of speech may impede progress in reading. Articulatory speech defects due to cleft palate, partial paralysis, clumsy movements of the speech-motor mechanism, or failure to establish proper motor habits of speech offer an impediment to precise auditory discrimination of speech sounds, and to the formation of speech-reading associations. Stuttering also presents an impediment to reading either as a disruption of motor speech or in association with other motor functions affecting reading.

Manifestations in reading

The child confuses words in reading which contain the confused sounds of speech. Frequent errors found in cases of articulatory defects are vowels, consonants, additions and omissions of sounds, and, in cases of stuttering, reversals and repetition.

3. Lack of precision in directional motor responses may impede progress in reading. Left-handed or left-eyed children, whose most facile direction of movement is toward the left rather than toward the right, have to make a motor adjustment which is opposite in direction from that of right-handed or right-eyed children. In trying to imitate the motor patterns set by social custom, left-handed or left-eyed children may become confused in directional responses. Children whose hand-and-eye preferences are mixed may also develop confusion in direction. In those cases in which the directional motor responses are inconsistent, difficulties in discrimination of spatial orientation of patterns may result.

Manifestations in reading

The child shows the manifestations described under failure to discriminate the spatial orientation of patterns.

IV. Difficulties related to the conceptual aspects of reading

1. Lack of vocabulary may impede progress in reading. Children who have not acquired the verbal symbols which are to be associated with the visual symbols are often delayed in progress in reading.

Manifestations in reading

The child fails to comprehend the meaning of the text. He cannot utilize context in giving cues to words since his vocabulary is too meager to suggest possibilities for the unknown words.

2. Lack of facility in the organizations of language may impede progress in reading. Verbal responses are organized and manipulated in many ways. Sometimes the relationships are simple, such as subject-predicate, adjective-noun, etc. Sometimes the relationships are complex, such as sentences containing dependent clauses, metaphors, contrasts, etc. Some individuals may manipulate a small vocabulary in complex organizations of meanings. Other individuals may manipulate a larger vocabulary in very simple organizations of meanings. Children whose facility in the organizations of language is limited may become confused in reading even though they possess adequate vocabularies.

Manifestations in reading

The child skips periods, or inserts pauses at illogical positions in the sentence. He fails to comprehend the meaning of text. The substitutions of words guessed from context are irrelevant or absurd.

V. Difficulties related to methodological aspects of reading

1. Overstress of speed of reading may develop habits which impede progress in reading.

Manifestations in reading

The child becomes breathless, excited. Reading errors of all kinds are increased, particularly omissions of sounds and words. Mannerisms to gain time appear, such as clearing voice between words, inserting "ah," repeating portions of sentences before hard words while the words are studied under cover of repetition. Many substitutions and illogical words, guessed hurriedly from context, appear. The child fails to give an accurate account of the content after reading.

2. Overstress of some methods of word-recognition may develop habits which impede progress in reading.

Manifestations in reading

Overstress of contextual cues to new words produces improvised or picture reading, substitutions, additions of words, and omissions of words. Overstress of some systems of phonetic analysis, such as explosive sounding (*guh* for g, *puh* for p, etc.), prevents sound-blending. Phonetic systems of rhyming, such as "cat," "hat," "sat," "pat," etc., may stimulate reversals if the child looks first at the ending to identify the family and then makes a regressive movement to the beginning of the word. Unwise selections of word lists may develop confusions, for example, "can," "cat," "car," "cap," "call," in a list to represent the sound of short a. Mechanical emphasis without attention to content may lead the child to ignore meaning.

VI. Difficulties related to environmental aspects of reading

    1. Among the environmental factors which impede progress in reading may be mentioned the following: foreign language, illiterate parents, truancy and poor school attendance, frequent moves from school to school, number of siblings or ordinal position of child among the siblings, etc.

VII. Difficulties related to emotional aspects of reading

    1. Among the personality and emotional factors which may impede progress in reading may be mentioned the following: attentional instability; resistance to reading; fear, timidity, embarrassment; withdrawal, etc. In some cases the emotional factors may be due to constitutional instability or poor habit-training. In other cases the emotional factors may result directly from the failure to learn to read due to other reasons, and then in turn aggravate the disability.

In summarizing the results of the inquiry into the factors which may impede reading, we make the following observations:

1. No one factor is present for all cases.
2. A number of the factors which were measured quantitatively show statistically valid differences between the reading-defect cases and the controls.
3. Each differentiating factor shows an overlap between the groups of reading-defect cases and controls. Some children who possess the impeding factor had learned to read and some children who do not possess it had failed to learn to read.
4. Factors that are not statistically significant in differentiating the groups seem to be definitely impeding factors in individual cases. For example, foreign language and defects in visual acuity as measured in this study appear with approximately the same frequency in good and poor readers and yet in individual cases offer marked impediments to reading. Refinement of technique of measuring certain qualitative aspects of such factors would probably indicate the conditions under which the factor becomes an impeding one.
5. It is probable that the reading defect is caused by a constellation of factors rather than by one isolated factor. Two children may therefore possess much the same impeding constitutional factor and yet one, through good environmental, methodological, and emotional factors, may overcome the disability, while the other, through poor environmental, methodological, and emotional factors, may become seriously retarded. *The reading defect may result in those cases in which the number or strength of the impeding factors is greater than the number or strength of the facilitating factors.*

6. WHAT DOES RESEARCH TELL THE CLASSROOM TEACHER ABOUT THE BASIC CAUSES OF READING DISABILITY AND RETARDATION?

Margaret J. Early

What Do We Mean by Reading Disability and Reading Retardation?

Standardized reading test scores of pupils in grade eight in a typical junior high school may range from grade 4 to grade 12, with 17 percent of this particular group scoring a year or more below grade placement (2).[1] All the pupils reading below the level of their grade placement may be considered "retarded readers," but many of them may be reading as well as they are able to. They are "retarded" only in the sense that they do not read as well as the average pupil in grade eight. Some of the pupils in the group reading below grade placement are cases of reading disability in the sense that their level of general reading achievement is below their general mental ability or their achievement in other types of learning. In a broader sense, pupils whose scores are at or above grade placement may also have reading disabilities. These are pupils of superior mental endowment whose reading ability does not measure up to their potential. The teacher's problem is to distinguish between "retarded readers" and "disabled readers," to provide an adjusted program of developmental reading instruction for the former, and to investigate causes of reading disability preliminary to providing a corrective or remedial program for the latter.

What Are the Basic Causes of Reading Disability?

In spite of years of research in reading and an accumulation of more than 3,000 studies, no easy answers are available. Because facts are meager, emotional bias slants many of the conclusions derived from limited research findings. One widely accepted conclusion can be stated: Reading disabilities are the result of several contributing factors. A major finding of Helen Robinson's study (31) is that the most seriously retarded of her

Reprinted from *Improving Reading in the Junior High School*, Arno Jewett, Editor, Bulletin No. 10 (Washington, 1957), pp. 16–25. United States Government Printing Office.
    [1] Bibliographical references are listed on pages 62–65 at the end of this article.

thirty cases showed the greatest number of anomalies, whereas those least retarded presented fewest.

A review of the research indicates to the classroom teacher both the complex nature of causation and the limitations of the studies undertaken thus far. Research is of two kinds: group studies comparing good and poor readers and case studies describing reading disabilities. Because almost all studies investigate the effect of single factors, representative studies will be reviewed according to (a) mental, (b) physiological, (c) emotional, (d) environmental and social, and (e) educational factors.

MENTAL FACTORS

Correlations between group verbal intelligence test scores and reading test scores are high—usually between .50 and .80. Correlations between reading test scores and intelligence tests that include performance as well as verbal scores are much lower (40). Teachers should therefore question group I.Q. scores of poor readers, realizing that an intelligent child who is a poor reader may appear dull. Many poor readers are, of course, of low verbal intelligence, and their slow learning affects all academic subjects. But teachers should remember that among cases of specific reading disability may be found pupils with low, average, or superior intelligence (45). One out of four poor readers will have average or superior intelligence, according to Donald D. Durrell (9) and may be expected to do better in reading. The relationship between mental age and reading ability appears to be less positive with beginning readers (16) and to become increasingly important as the reading task becomes more complex (3, 25).

Research into the intellectual factors basic to reading ability tells the classroom teacher that success in the earlier stages of reading development is more dependent on specific background skills, such as visual memory, auditory perception, and phonics than on mental age (9), suggesting that even pupils in the lower range of intelligence tests scores can be taught fundamental skills (41).

PHYSIOLOGICAL CAUSES

Vision—Investigations of visual defects among good and poor readers yield conflicting results, suggesting that visual anomalies alone are not necessarily causative. For example, Robinson (31) identified visual anomalies in 73 percent of her cases but concluded that in 10 percent of these the visual difficulties were coincidental. According to many studies, hyperopia, hyperopic astigmatism, binocular incoordination, visual fields, and aniseikonia are the visual difficulties most commonly related to reading disability (31). Teachers need to be aware of the contributory effects of certain types of visual difficulties and to include adequate screening tests in their study of poor readers (32).

Hearing Loss and Speech Defects.—No clear-cut evidence is found in the research as to the correlation of auditory acuity and reading level (4, 20). From their review of the research, Paul Witty and David Kopel (45) concluded that auditory factors appear to be related to reading only in individual cases where the defect is great. In the same way, speech defects have sometimes been associated with reading disability but the evidence of causality is inconclusive (1, 4, 28). Nevertheless, teachers should be aware of the possible influences of both hearing and speech defects in individual cases. Reasons for a poor reader's deficient phonetic skills, for example, may be traced to speech defects or hearing loss experienced during the earliest years of reading instruction and now corrected. Thus, re-training in specific skills in beginning reading may be a reasonable recommendation.

Neurological Difficulties.—Cases of extreme difficulty in learning to read led early investigators to hypothesize damage to specific areas of the brain, either from injury or lack of development, as a major cause of reading disability among otherwise normal subjects. *Congenital word-blindness* or *dyslexia* are labels that are still frequently used. These labels neither explain nor describe causes of reading disabilities. They simply say, in effect, that other possible causes have been ruled out and that symptoms of brain damage have been noted by neurological and psychological examination.

Ralph C. Preston and J. Wesley Schneyer (30) proposed an investigation of the interaction of neurological and psychiatric factors, justifying the need for this type of study on their review of 83 published investigations, of which 31 showed positive relationships between reading disability and neurological factors.

Research is still needed to determine the extent to which brain damage may prevent progress in learning to read when appropriate instructional methods are used. Grace M. Fernald (13) and Alfred Strauss and Laura Lehtinen (42), for example, have shown that brain-damaged children can be taught to read using special methods.

While the exploration of the effects of brain damage is of great interest to reading specialists, the classroom teacher receives little positive help from research in this area. Where resources for neurological examination are available, the teacher's role is to determine when referral is appropriate. Even when evidence of brain damage is clear in individual cases, the teacher must still decide what, if anything, can be done in the school situation to improve instruction for such pupils.

Mixed dominance is another type of neurological disorder that has been proposed as a cause of reading disability. Several persons have presented evidence to support the theory that more poor readers than good readers exhibit mixed dominance (10, 7, 1, 36, 22, and 17). Other investigators (e.g. 15, 19, 28) believe no relationship exists between dominance and general ability or specific errors in reading. In view of conflicting research, reading specialists should probably include the study of dominance in analyzing all aspects of an individual's problems and should investigate recently proposed training devices (23). However, classroom teachers will find little value in studying dominance until research tells them what they can do to affect the condition, if it proves an important causal factor.

Other Physical Factors.—Malnutrition, infections, and endocrine disturbances are the three general physical factors mentioned most frequently as possible causes for failure to learn to read (31). Thomas H. Eames (11) found considerably higher incidence of general diseases and defects among reading failures than among non-failures. Since poor health and low vitality may induce poor attention to learning and cause absences from school, teachers should examine pupils' medical records. Evidence of poor health in earlier grades warns the teacher to consider the skills, concepts, and habits included in the program of these earlier grades and to measure the extent to which they may be deficient in the retarded reader.

PERSONALITY FACTORS

Emotional difficulties are found among retarded readers, but, as Dr. Traxler has indicated, research has failed to define the extent to which personality maladjustment may be the cause or result of reading retardation. Some writers believe that reading disability is a symptom of basic emotional disorder and that treatment of the reading problem must be preceded or accompanied by attention to the emotional difficulties. Personality traits that have been suggested as causes of reading failure are dependency on one's mother and lack of responsibility, excessive timidity, and predilection against reading or against all school activities (29). W. H. Missildine (27) noted emotional disturbances due to sibling rivalry and to mothers who were hostile, tense, perfectionistic, and over-indulgent. George D. Spache (39) found retarded readers more likely than non-retarded ones to be submissive towards adults and aggressive toward peers. Max Siegel (35) found no pattern typical of retarded readers as compared with other emotionally disturbed children but noted fear and anxiety, sometimes accompanied by aggressiveness and hostility, sometimes by withdrawal.

Lack of interest, inattentiveness, daydreaming, defeatism, truancy, and nervous mannerisms have been reported as concomitant with reading disabilities (31, 33, 37, 44). Since emotional disturbances may result from reading failure, continued failure aggravates these conditions. The older the retarded reader is, the more intense and deep-seated these emotional reactions may become.

What should the classroom teacher do when signs of emotional disturbances are apparent among retarded readers? The type and degree of personality maladjustment (together with other causative factors and the nature of the reading problem) must be considered in deciding weather individual or small-group instruction is advisable, or whether no immediate attention should be paid to reading. The teacher may refer extreme cases for psychological therapy (when it is available) and advise against immediate remedial instruction. A skilled counselor or remedial teacher may provide both therapy and help in reading (5, 12). In many cases, a teacher's best approach may be a well-planned instructional program based on sensitive understanding of the pupil's emotional problems, his needs in reading, and his interests. Special efforts to motivate interest in learning to read are almost always necessary.

ENVIRONMENTAL AND SOCIAL FACTORS

Among the environmental and social factors that have been studied are the attitudes and interests of parents, language spoken in the home, economic status and neighborhood conditions, adjustment to school, and experience background. One of the most significant findings of Robinson's study (31) was that maladjusted homes and poor intra-family relationships existed in 54.5% of her cases. Sheldon and Carrillo (34) noted that as the number of books in the home increases, the percent of good readers increases and that good readers come most often from homes where parents have reached higher levels of education. Marion Monroe and Bertie Backus (29) found that illiteracy and foreign language in the home and insufficient background were characteristic of reading failures. In a study of 100 ninth grade poor readers, Paul Witty (43) listed the following characteristics: meager background of experience, impoverished play life, repeated failure in school, and frequent change of school.

The teacher's role in relation to many of these suggested influences on learning is necessarily slight. Understanding pupils' environmental needs, however, teachers can enrich classroom libraries, take into account experience backgrounds that may be lacking, and select materials and methods geared to their pupils' environment.

EDUCATIONAL CAUSES

Expert opinion, rather than research findings, must be called upon in exploring another possible source of causes for reading failure: ineffective educational practices. In American schools employing a variety of educational methods, the majority of children learn to read. Nevertheless, other children of equal intelligence are seriously limited in reading skills. William Kottmeyer (21), for example, reports that 2,169 out of 7,380 eighth grade graduates in a large city system read at or below norms for the sixth grade.

While it may be argued that additional causative factors tend to nullify the effects of teaching methods that are successful with most children, research is still not clear as to *what* physical, emotional, and environmental factors impede some readers or *why* some pupils seem unaffected by similar characteristics. When corrective instruction improves the skills of retarded readers, it seems safe to infer that unsuitable teaching practices have been at least partially responsible for reading retardation. Many studies demonstrating the improvement of reading ability through specific educational methods have been reported (41) and will be described in another section.

Durrell's recent listing of educational causes of reading difficulties (8) furnishes the background for the following summary:

1. *Lack of adequate background to perform the reading task set.*—For example, junior high school pupils may have insufficient meaning vocabulary, inadequate word-analysis skills, or inadequate background for comprehension tasks. In Witty's study of 100 poor readers in the ninth grade, 32 percent were found lacking in the ability to attack new words, and 56 percent were deficient in vocabulary (43). Spache (38) says "poor readers of all ages seem to be unfamiliar with phonic or structural analysis, use of context, or any of the other means of discovering the pronunciation and meaning of unknown words."

2. *Failure to master the early elements on which later abilities are based.*—Teachers who present "grade level skills" to all pupils ignore the possibility that the learning of lower level skills may have been fragmentary —for a variety of reasons.

3. *Confusions resulting from instruction not correctly adjusted to the level and learning rate of the child.*—Learners whose developmental rate is slower than average become increasingly confused if teachers set a pace of instruction that is too fast (14).

4. *The acquisition of faulty habits which impede progress.*—Durrell says ". . . learning to read is a highly complex process providing countless opportunities for confusion in learning." When teachers fail to recognize the pupil's faulty technique, it remains to impede progress and create more confusions. Teachers' failure to analyze the nature of the individual's reading skills and to plan systematic instruction on the basis of thorough knowledge of the pupil is probably a major cause of continued retardation.

Concluding Statement

Causes of reading disability are multiple. All research points to this conclusion, either directly as in Robinson's study, or indirectly by the very inconclusiveness of studies related to single factors. Future research should be concerned with broad studies, centered in schools rather than clinics, involving both retarded and able readers, to determine the interactions among causative factors. Of the physical, emotional, mental, environmental, social, and educational factors that may affect reading ability, what combinations produce what results?

Three implications for the classroom teacher, in addition to those already mentioned, are:

1. Insight into the causes of reading failure requires study of all phases of the learner: his health, home and family, personality, experience background and learning abilities, including detailed evaluation of the complex of skills that constitute reading. Adequate study of many of these facets is beyond the teacher, or reading clinician, or psychologist. Each of these persons needs to know when to make referrals when his diagnostic tools prove inadequate.

2. Since causation is multiple, remediation must also use many approaches. A single method of attack may be detrimental as well as useless.

3. As research in causation is tentative, so is diagnosis of individual cases. As hunches are confirmed or rejected by new insights, plans for treatment must also be changed. Diagnosis of the complex process of reading is continuous.

REFERENCES

(1) BENNETT, CHESTER C.   An inquiry into the Genesis of Poor Reading, Bureau of Publications, Teachers College, Columbia University, 1938.

(2) BLAIR, GLENN M.   Diagnostic and Remedial Teaching, New York, The Macmillan Co., 1956. (Rev. Ed.)

(3) BLIESMER, EMERY P.   Reading Abilities of Bright and Dull Children of Comparable Mental Ages. *Journal of Educational Psychology,* 45:321–31 October 1954.

(4) BOND, GUY L.   The Auditory and Speech Characteristics of Poor Readers, Contributions to Education. No. 657, Bureau of Publications, Teachers College, Columbia University, New York, 1935.

(5) BULLOCK, HARRISON.   Helping the Non-reading Pupil in the Secondary School. Bureau of Publications, Teachers College, Columbia University, New York, 1955.

(6) CLELAND, DONALD L.   Causes of Retardation, Ninth Annual Conference on Reading p. 50–60. Pittsburgh, University of Pittsburgh Press, 1953.

(7) DEARBORN, WALTER F.   The Nature and Causation of Disabilities in Reading, *in* Recent Trends in Reading, Supplementary Educational Monographs, No. 49. Chicago, University of Chicago, 1939.

(8) DURRELL, DONALD D.   Improving Reading Instruction. Yonkers-on-Hudson, N.Y., World Book Company, 1956.   p. 350–51.

(9) ——— Learning Difficulties Among Children of Normal Intelligence. *Elementary School Journal,* 55:201–208, December 1954.

(10) EAMES, THOMAS H. The Anatomical Basis of Lateral Dominance Anomalies, *American Journal of Orthopsychiatry*, 4:524–28, October 1934.

(11) —— Incident of Diseases Among Reading Failures, *Journal of Pediatrics*, 33:614–17, November 1948.

(12) EPHRON, BEULAH K. Emotional Difficulties in Reading, New York, Julian Press, 1953.

(13) FERNALD, GRACE M. Remedial Techniques in Basic School Subjects, New York, McGraw-Hill, 1943.

(14) GATES, ARTHUR I. Teaching Reading, What Research Says to the Teacher, No. 1, Department of Classroom Teachers and American Educational Research Association of the National Education Association, 1953.

(15) ——, *and* BOND, GUY L. Relation of Handedness, Eye-sighting, and Acuity Dominance to Reading, *Journal of Educational Psychology*, 27:455–56, September 1936.

(16) HARRINGTON, *Sister* MARY JAMES. The Relationship of Certain Word Analysis Abilities to the Reading Achievement of Second Grade Children. Unpublished doctoral dissertation, Boston University, 1953.

(17) HARRIS, ALBERT J. How To Increase Reading Ability, New York, Longmans, Green and Co., 1956. p. 249–60.

(18) HARRIS, THEODORE L. Implications for the Teacher of Recent Research in High School Reading, *The High School Journal*, 39:194–206, January 1956.

(19) HILDRETH, GERTRUDE. Bilateral Manual Performance, Eye-Dominance and Reading Achievement, *Child Development*, 11:311–17, Dec. 1940.

(20) KENNEDY, HELEN A. A Study of Children's Hearing as It Relates to Reading, *Journal of Experimental Education*, 10:238–51, June 1942.

(21) KOTTMEYER, WILLIAM. Improving Reading Instruction in the St. Louis Schools, *Elementary School Journal*, 45:33–38, September 1944.

(22) LEAVELL, ULLIN W. The Problem of Symbol Reversals and Confusions, Their Frequency and Remediation, *Peabody Journal of Education*, November 1954.

(23) ——. Manual of Instructions for the Leavell Language-Development Service, Keystone View Company, Meadville, Pa., 1955.

(24) LOUTTIT, C. M. Emotional Factors in Reading Disabilities: Diagnostic Problems, *Elementary School Journal*, 56:68–72, October 1955.

(25) MACK, ESTHER M. An Investigation of the Importance of Various Word Analysis Abilities in Reading and Spelling Achievement, Unpublished doctoral dissertation, Boston University, 1953.

(26) MCCALLISTER, JAMES M. Character and Causes of Retardation in Reading Among Pupils of the Seventh and Eighth Grades, *Elementary School Journal*, 31:25–43, September 1930.

(27) MISSILDINE, W. H. Emotional Background of Thirty Children with Reading Disabilities with Emphasis on Its Coercive Elements, *Nervous Child,* 5:263–272, July 1946.

(28) MONROE, MARION. Children Who Cannot Read, University of Chicago Press, Chicago, 1932.

(29) —— and BACKUS, BERTIE. Remedial Reading: A Monograph in Character Education, Houghton Mifflin, Boston, 1937.

(30) PRESTON, RALPH C., *and* SCHNEYER, J. WESLEY. The Neurological Background of Nine Severely Retarded Readers, *Journal of Educational Research,* 49:455–459, February 1956.

(31) ROBINSON , HELEN M. Why Pupils Fail in Reading, University of Chicago Press, Chicago, 1946.

(32) ——. Factors Which Affect Success in Reading, *Elementary School Journal,* 55:263–269, January 1955.

(33) RUSSELL, DAVID H. Reading Disability and Mental Health: A Review of Research. *Understanding the Child,* 16:24–32, January 1947.

(34) SHELDON, WILLIAM D., *and* CARRILLO, LAWRENCE. Relation of Parents, Home, and Certain Developmental Characteristics to Children's Reading Ability. *Elementary School Journal,* 52:262–70, January 1952.

(35) SIEGEL, MAX. The Personality Structure of Children with Reading Disabilities as Compared with Children Presenting Other Clinical Problems. *Nervous Child,* 10:409–414, 1954.

(36) SMITH, LINDA. A Study of Laterality, Characteristics of Retarded Readers and Reading Achievers. *Journal of Experimental Education,* 18:321–330, June 1950.

(37) SMITH, NILA BANTON. Research on Reading and the Emotions. *School and Society,* 81:8–10, Jan. 8, 1955.

(38) SPACHE, GEORGE D. Factors Which Produce Defective Reading, Corrective Reading in Classroom and Clinic, Supplementary Educational Monograph, No. 79, Chicago, University of Chicago Press, December 1953.

(39) SPACHE, GEORGE W. Personality Characteristics of Retarded Readers as Measured by the Picture—Frustration Study. *Educational and Psychological Measurement,* 14:186–92, Spring, 1954.

(40) STRANG, RUTH. Relationship Between Certain Aspects of Intelligence and Certain Aspects of Reading. *Educational and Psychological Measurement,* 3:355–59, Winter, 1943.

(41) ——, McCULLOUGH, CONSTANCE M. *and* TRAXLER, ARTHUR E. Problems in the Improvement of Reading, New York, McGraw-Hill, 1955.

(42) STRAUSS, ALFRED, *and* LEHTINEN, LAURA. Psychopathology and Education of the Brain-Injured Child. New York, Grune and Stratton, 1947.

(43) WITTY, PAUL. Reading Retardation in the Secondary School. *Journal of Experimental Education*, 15:314–317, June 1947.

(44) ———. Reading Success and Personal Adjustment, *Elementary English*, 27:281–96, May 1950.

(45) ——— and KOPEL, DAVID. Reading and the Educative Process, Boston, Ginn and Co., 1939.

7. PSYCHOGENIC FACTORS IN SOME CASES OF READING DISABILITY[*]

Phyllis Blanchard

Our first reports on reading disabilities, five years ago, stressed the significance of conditioned emotional responses or unfavorable attitudes to reading, in addition to the etiological factors suggested by other investigators, as contributing causes to failure in this school subject.[1] These early cases for the most part responded fairly well to remedial teaching methods, combined with simple measures for modifying the emotional reactions and attitudes. But further experience revealed that remedial teaching did not always produce such good results; some children failed to respond when it was undertaken at the clinic, others came to the clinic after months of special teaching elsewhere had failed to bring about any improvement in reading.

When remedial teaching had proven ineffective in certain instances, we turned experimentally to other kinds of treatment. We then found that children who could not benefit from the teaching approach were involved in emotional conflicts and difficulties of emotional development similar to those of children with neurotic symptoms. Frequently, when the conflicts were at least partially resolved through treatment, they learned to read without the aid of remedial teaching. While we do not claim that reading disabilities are invariably of complex psychogenic ori-

Reprinted from *American Journal of Orthopsychiatry*, Vol. V, No. 4 (October 1935), pp. 361–374. Copyright, the American Orthopsychiatric Association, Inc. Reproduced by permission of author, Phyllis Blanchard, and publisher.

[*] Presented at the 1935 meeting.

[1] Blanchard, P. Reading Disabilities in Relation to Maladjustment, Mental Hygiene, 1928, XII, pp. 772–78; Attitudes and Educational Disabilities, Mental Hygiene, 1929, XIII, pp. 550–563.

gin, our experience does indicate that in many cases the failure in learning to read may be a part of the child's more general difficulty in achieving normal emotional growth.

For this paper, we have selected certain treatment cases in which the child's own associations to the trouble with reading supplement the history from parent and school. One case is given in more detail, with brief summaries of three others.

CASE MATERIAL

An eight year old boy had remained for two years in the first grade without learning to read; he also continually wrote words and letters with reversals. The case is particularly enlightening because of the many phantasies and emotions related to reading and writing.[2] The associations to his difficulties with these school subjects have been spontaneous in the sense that it was not suggested that he talk about them nor was any special kind of play situation set up in an effort to get him to do so. But as he showed anxiety over his failure in school, this was recognized and interpreted to him. Otherwise, interpretations were used chiefly in connection with his changing transference feelings toward the therapist and to help him through his need to protect himself from anxiety and through the frequent periods of fear of punishment or guilt over his phantasies and the emotions accompanying them.

Before the boy came to clinic, we had information indicating that this should be a treatment rather than a remedial teaching case. He was an illegitimate child but his mother had supported him in a boarding house until he was about three years old; she then deserted him after the birth of her second baby, a girl. He came to the care of an agency and for a year was in two or three different foster homes, though the most of the year was spent with one foster mother, whom he loved. Toilet training was a problem when he was first placed with this foster mother but improved under her care. At the age of four, the ill health of this foster mother necessitated his removal to another foster home, where he has remained. Here he has had a rather strict foster mother and a gentle, kindly foster father. He reacted to the separation from the previous foster mother by an extreme infantile regression, with complete loss of bowel and bladder control, helplessness in dressing himself, etc. After this regression, toilet training was reestablished only in the year prior to his coming to clinic, with occasional diurnal enuresis still persisting even after the soiling had almost entirely ceased. At home he was fearful and submissive; in school, overactive and inattentive; both at home and at

[2] We express our appreciation to the Juvenile Aid Society for undertaking the responsibility for the child's coming to clinic during the long period of treatment which he needs.

school, he played by himself, being unable to compete with other children in games.

On four Stanford Binet tests he made the following ratings: I.Q. 95 at the age of three, I.Q. 76 at five years, I.Q. 74 at seven years, I.Q. 84 at eight and a half years of age. The last test was given by the same psychologist who had done the first three, between the forty-third and forty-fourth treatment interviews. She was of the opinion that an extreme fear of failure interfered with his effort and cooperation, and described more qualitative than quantitative improvement. In his twenty-sixth treatment interview at clinic, he drew a picture of a man which, scored by the Goodenough Scale, gave him I.Q. 104.

At the date of writing, there have been 46 treatment interviews. The first 16 hours were once a week, then there was a month's break when the psychologist was away on her vacation; when she returned a change to two hours weekly was made. The first interviews were concerned with developing a treatment relationship, with the boy's reactions to the necessity for leaving at the end of the hour and his feeling about the therapist's seeing other children. The 6 interviews preceding her vacation were devoted mostly to his feelings about it, since it evoked all the resentment for the therapist's desertion of him and fear lest she might not return to him that might be expected in view of his having lost both his own mother and one foster mother.

During the first 16 interviews, the only material related to his reading disability was in phantasies about his father and projection of his own anxiety about being unable to read onto the therapist. In the father phantasies, the father was described as a big, strong man, who could *read,* work and earn money. In one interview, he elaborated that his father had been a soldier and was given "fighting coffee" to drink. He, himself, never was given any of this fighting coffee; if children should try to fight, they would be killed. In the same interview, he said that his father and mother had left him all alone; he had tried to learn to do hard things all by himself but couldn't, because they were too hard. To the interpretation that he must be unhappy and worried, if he couldn't fight when he felt like it or learn to do as hard things as he wished, he replied: "I'm not worried, you're worried." But he immediately produced another phantasy to the effect that in the army you were given poison with which you could kill people, adding that he would not want to kill people, he was not permitted to do bad things.

In a somewhat later interview, he mentioned a desire to get stars for good work in school, but immediately projected his anxiety and the criticism he had accepted of himself onto the therapist, asking her, accusingly: "What's the matter with you, can't you learn to read? Why don't you work harder? Do you want to be a baby? Do you want to grow up and not know anything? Do you want to be a dumb-bell all your life?" When the therapist remarked that these sounded like things which might have been said to him and which must have made him feel both worried and angry, he countered: "I'm not worried. I'm not angry. Are you angry?"

In his very first interview, the boy's initial speech had been: "Do you have anything for me to eat?" and there had been repeated requests for food thereafter. From the seventeenth to twenty-third interviews, resentment toward the mother who had deserted her child and not provided him with food was projected very intensely into the transference relationship. The therapist was reproached with being a bad mother, who never fed her children; there was a new version of the rhyme about the old woman who lived in a shoe, revised to the conclusion that she gave away her children; there were many instructions as to what the therapist should do for him in order to be the right kind of mother. When his demands could not be gratified, there were violent hostility and anger, expressed in wishes to give the therapist poison, cut her into pieces, and do other things of this sort to her, accompanied by threats of never coming to see her again. After each outburst of hostility, came anxiety and guilt reactions, once to the extent of talking of how he could kill himself by falling out of the window. Connected with his anger and resentment was the complaint that the baby could never grow up if so badly treated by the mother.

After repeated interpretations that he was asking the therapist to do all the things he had wanted his mother to do for him and hating her because he believed that she was like his mother, not loving him enough or caring what happened to him, he reverted to a more positive feeling. By the twenty-fourth interview, he began to speak of the therapist as the only person who had ever wanted to help him, telling her that he was coming to see her until he had learned to do everything she could do. In this same twenty-fourth interview, he began the sequence of associations more directly related to his reading disability and the reversals in writing. He wrote on the blackboard, reversing letters and words, or making peculiar marks, and said he was "writing Chinese." Thereafter, references to writing Chinese, in connection with reversals in writing or making peculiar marks came into several interviews. But not until the thirty-third interview did other associations to Chinese appear. Then he made a knife from wood, which he said was a Chinese knife, elaborating that the Chinese tortured people with such knives or stabbed and killed people. When the therapist interpreted that he might sometimes feel like doing such things, he became fearful and anxious at first but finally said that if the knife were only sharp enough, he could stab her with it or skin her alive and cut her into little pieces. Toward the end of this interview, the therapist remarked that he seemed to know a good deal about the Chinese; that they wrote backwards and that they killed and tortured people with knives. She also suggested that when he wrote Chinese, he might be feeling like killing or torturing someone.

In the thirty-fifth interview, he returned to the subject of writing Chinese. He was asked what he thought about when he wrote that way. His reply was in a low tone, so that only the words *knife* and *kill* could be understood. The therapist asked if he had said he wanted to kill someone with a knife and he replied affirmatively. He was in a very affectionate mood toward the therapist at the time and immediately proceeded to write her name correctly. The therapist said that she believed he could write her name correctly instead of in Chinese, when he loved her and did not want to kill her. Still writing correctly, he wrote the therapist's first name with the last name of the first foster mother whom he had loved.

Further material related to the reversals in writing appeared toward the end of the forty-first interview, a short time after the patient had chanced to see the boy who came the following hour. He asked if he had to leave so "that other boy" could come and said he would like to kill him, he would write his name in Chinese. The therapist interpreted his fear that she might like the other boy better than him and his wish to get rid of the supposed rival; she also commented that writing his name in Chinese must be a magic spell to kill the other boy. This interpretation was willingly accepted.[3]

In the same series of interviews in which he produced the sequence of associations to the "Chinese writing," the patient continued the phantasies about the father, in relation to both the reading disability and an inability to use a saw when making things from wood. In earlier interviews, he had complained that sawing was too hard for him and asked the therapist to do it, saying sadly, "I can't saw, I can only sew." But he added that he was watching her in order to learn how to saw and in the twenty-fourth interview decided he was ready to try it. He used a small saw and accidently hit it against a large one so that the latter fell off the work table onto the floor. "Look, the baby saw made the father saw fall right down!" he exclaimed but then became frightened of continuing the sawing. Interpretations of his fear and guilt over his aggression were ineffective during the remainder of this interview and the two succeeding ones; not until the twenty-sixth interview did he dare to use the saw again. Then he had to sit in the therapist's chair before he felt safe in using it and has continued to need to sit there when sawing.

[3] There is no evidence that the theory of change in handedness in relation to reversals in reading and writing applies to this case. Nor has it been very strongly confirmed in 24 other cases, in which the Orton-Monroe as well as the Gates diagnostic reading tests were given. In 6 of these cases there had been a change from left to right hand; 2 were still left-handed, 16 had always been right-handed; 4 of the right-handed children reversed letters and 5 reversed letter sequences in words to some extent, while none of those changed from left to right reversed letters and only one reversed sequences; 5 of the right-handed were good at mirror writing but only 1 changed from left to right was good at it; similar figures appeared for the other tests of the Orton-Monroe series, when the right-handed cases and those changed from left to right were compared.

In the twenty-ninth interview, he produced a phantasy of cooking and eating up the therapist. He also started to cook a toy soldier in a small fire which he built in the sand box but was afraid to complete this activity. In the following hour (thirtieth), he was able to go on with play and phantasies of cooking and eating the soldier, wondered who the soldier was and asked the therapist if she could tell him. She reminded him that he had talked of his father being a soldier. This interpretation aroused fear and anxiety, so that he suggested putting out the fire. After interpretation of his fear, he continued to cook the soldier until it melted and said it had disappeared. He then asked to sit in the therapist's chair, at her desk, to read and write. He said he knew the words *father* and *baby* and asked, "Where is the baby?" He elaborated that fathers could have babies, could *read* and *write* and do other hard things. They were strong, like Tarzan, and could kill lions and tigers. He, himself, used to be afraid of mice but now he could pick them up and throw them out of the window. He proceeded to draw a picture of a mouse and wrote the word *mice* correctly. Next he drew a picture of himself, found the words *the big boy* in a book and copied them below this picture.

In the thirty-second interview, he again started to read and write but changed to making a soldier's hat and arm bands from colored paper. He put them on after they were finished and said he would be the soldier now. In the next interview (thirty-third), he made a wooden gun and dagger for his soldier's equipment. He also made "soldier soup" by boiling a toy soldier in some water along with some paints and cigarette stubs. He said it was like chicken soup, it would give you strength. He was pleased with the interpretation that he felt as if he had eaten the soldier and gotten his strength. He replied that he wanted to be stronger still, asked if he might make a bow and arrow like Tarzan's next time he came, and asked if the therapist would give him a "baby rabbit." The therapist agreed that they could make bow and arrows but did not try to interpret his request for a baby rabbit, beyond telling him she wouldn't be able to get him the baby rabbit, though she knew he wanted something like that from her.

When he came for the thirty-fourth interview, he immediately asked the therapist if she had gotten him what he asked for. When she showed him materials for making a bow and arrows, he flew into a violent rage, accusing her of being a bad mother, who never gave him what he wanted. After a half hour of intense anger, he finally revealed his disappointment over the non-fulfillment of the phantasies underlying the "baby rabbit" request. He reproached the therapist: "Why don't you get fat? Look at you, you're no fatter than you were last week. You're no fatter than I am." When the therapist recognized his wish to be the father and have a baby and his disappointment that she was not getting fat as she would if she were going to have a baby for him, he asked very sadly, "What grade were you in when you first started school?" As soon as he had asked this, he began to mix sand and paint together to form a black mixture, smeared some of the playthings with it, and toward the end of the hour was able to say he was making "good, black" faeces, he hoped the therapist would get it all over her when she cleaned up after him and that the smell would poison her and kill her. This was interpreted as his anger over his disappointment.

He started the thirty-fifth interview with intense fear and guilt over the soiling play which had terminated the preceding hour. He was afraid the therapist would consider him a bad boy, would not want to continue seeing him but would give his hour to a girl patient. This marked the beginning of phantasies and feelings related to his mother's having deserted him after the birth of a baby girl. In the fortieth interview, he set up dolls to represent the mother, little boy and baby girl, said he hated the mother and the baby and knocked them down. In the forty-fifth interview, he stated his suspicion that the therapist had a little girl of her own, for whom she did more than for him, anxiously demanding information about the matter. Instead of giving the information he asked for, the therapist interpreted his fear that she might love a little girl better than himself. He immediately reverted to more faeces play but in a fashion suggestive of a desire to be cared for like a baby rather than the hostility which had accompanied the phantasies previously associated with soiling.

In the forty-sixth interview, he mentioned the existence of the baby sister for the first time. The therapist said he must worry about his mother having a little girl. His reaction to this interpretation was playing with water and sand and talking about wetting and soiling himself so that he could be washed and bathed. The therapist interpreted that he might wish to be a baby, as small as the sister whom he remembered, because he felt it would be pleasant to be washed and bathed like a baby. As if he thought this a desire no one could help feeling, he asked wistfully, "Wouldn't you like to be a baby? Wouldn't you like to be washed and bathed?" The therapist mentioned that if this were done for him, he could feel sure he was loved. He then said that he knew a little boy who wet and soiled himself. "But when he does that, I whip him, I get so angry at him." The therapist interpreted that he might have been scolded and punished for wetting and soiling so that he felt he ought to be angry at himself; also, it was hard for him to have these wishes to be like a baby because at the same time he so wanted to grow up and learn to do hard things. He said he had learned to do many things since he started coming to see the therapist. "You know, when I first came I didn't know anything, I couldn't do one thing." Then he ran to the blackboard and wrote the words *love* and *good* quite correctly, asking the therapist if she knew what he meant. She replied that he might mean he wanted to be good, when he loved her or other people, in order to please them and be loved in return. While writing, he had been dancing up and down with obvious need to urinate and now he announced: "I have to go to the toilet," and ran to the bathroom. He returned with evident satisfaction at having accomplished this control instead of wetting himself.

From this last material, it seems clear that he has felt his mother deserted him because she loved the baby girl better than himself. Hence another factor in his inability to do masculine things—which from his viewpoint include reading and sawing—is anxiety over the loss of love as a result of masculinity.

It is not the purpose of this paper to discuss techniques of treatment, nor would there be time to do so. But it should be emphasized that this partial case report, consisting merely of excerpts from certain interviews, in no way presents a picture of treatment so far as the actual procedure is concerned. In limiting the material by selecting only that related to the reading disability and the reversals in writing, many things which were far more important for therapy have necessarily been omitted. If the form of the report should give an impression that the treatment consisted simply of watching the child play, listening to his remarks and giving interpretations, it would be a very erroneous one.

The treatment of a child with as many and complex conflicts is not such a simple matter. For example, with this patient, there were many initial problems in treatment arising from his need to protect himself from experiencing painful emotions, so that for some time there were defenses in the form of projecting his own feelings onto the therapist or retreating into wish-fulfillment phantasies to escape unpleasant emotions or uncomfortable reality situations. Also at first he could express his feelings only through behavior, often directed toward the person of the therapist, and only gradually became more capable of verbalizing his phantasies and the emotions accompanying them. The task of helping such a child give up his defenses and gain capacity to bear his conflicting emotions and talk about them, instead of having to evade conscious recognition of them, calls for clinical experience and knowledge of psychoanalytic approach, together with considerable flexibility in adapting techniques to the particular child.

While the treatment has not yet been completed in this case, thus far it seems fairly evident that the reversed writing of words and letters is a substitute for sadistic phantasies of torturing and killing or a magic spell to produce death. Most of these phantasies appear to have been originally toward the mother, since with one exception they were projected into the transference relationship when he was strongly identifying the therapist with the mother who deserted him and did not take care of him. His reading disability, his inability to use the saw, his complaints of being unable to do hard things, are more largely a part of the problem of establishing identifications with the father, which he can only attempt on a hostile and sadistic basis, to judge from his phantasies of cooking and eating the father to get his strength, destroying and replacing him. His guilt over these sadistic impulses and his fear of punishment have prevented him from carrying through the identifications, in all probability. As we have also seen, in his reactions to the mother's desertion after the birth of the baby sister, anxiety over the loss of love further interferes with masculine identifications.[4]

Sadistic and hostile phantasies clearly enter into the persistence of habits of wetting and soiling. But also in the wetting and soiling and in being unable to read, is the desire to obtain infantile satisfaction in being cared for and being read to, like a small child. At the same time, he can atone for his sadistic wishes and relieve his guilt by making himself very uncomfortable through the refusal of toilet training and failure in school, since he has been subjected to both punishment and severe criticism for these things. That he should have had all the hostility and resentment expressed in his sadistic phantasies is natural in view of his life experiences, but he has had too much guilt over his hostility and too much anxiety over loss of love, for normal emotional development. Since he was unable to resolve his Oedipus conflicts and make identifications with the parents, his only recourse was to regress to anal and oral levels.

An interesting part of the boy's response to treatment has been his real capacity for love and affection and his effort to make some identification with the therapist on a positive basis. Another aspect of treatment has been his need to use the therapist in the role of "protector against anxiety," as he brings out the phantasies and emotions in his ambivalent guilt conflicts. This has been shown in the continual necessity for interpreting his fear of punishment, fear that the therapist will be angry at him, and the like, and also in his having to sit in the therapist's chair very often before he has courage for reading, writing or sawing, as if in a magical manner this offers close identification with her and affords protection from guilt and anxiety.[5]

Reports from the foster home and school indicate steady improvement in the boy's outside adjustments. At present his teacher considers him a fairly satisfactory pupil. He now plays actively with other children, quite able to compete adequately in games; his foster mother says he has at last begun to act like other boys of his age.

---

[4] In a general theoretical discussion, Strachey suggests, among other things, that reading symbolizes eating the father in an attempt to gain control of his powers; also it represents an attack on the mother, as well as the father; therefore guilt over these sadistic wishes or the presence of unconscious unsublimated oral tendencies interfere with reading proficiency. See: Strachey, James. Some Unconscious Factors in Reading, Internat. Jour. Psychoanal., 1930, XI., pp. 322–331.

[5] For a theoretical discussion of ambivalence in relation to the feeling of guilt, see: Numberg, H. The Feeling of Guilt, Psychoanalyt. Quar., 1933, III, pp. 589–604. The patient's need of the analyst as protector against anxiety, in analytic treatment, has been described in Chapter X of Numberg's Allgemeine Neurosenlehre auf psychoanalytischer Grundlage, Hans Huber, Bern, 1932.

CASE SUMMARIES

An eleven year old boy had not learned to read although he was in the fifth grade. According to our tests, he was of average intelligence but had only low second grade reading proficiency. Remedial teaching was attempted but it soon became obvious that he was too much disturbed emotionally to sustain attention and effort for reading, hence a change to treatment was made. He showed considerable improvement in reading during a treatment period of 35 interviews, one hour weekly, without further remedial teaching.

This boy dated his trouble with reading from an occurrence when he was in the second grade. A teacher whom he liked and with whom he had done well in reading, went to the hospital for an operation; she never returned and he imagined that she had died. Actually, she recovered, but the pupils were never informed of this fact. There was a history, in the case, of early and difficult weaning; the mother had worked away from home for a time when the boy was between three and four years of age; when he was five, she had gone to a hospital for an operation; she went to work again when he started school. His emotional reactions to the nursing deprivation were suggested by phantasies about baby animals who could not live if the mother did not nurse them; his resentment toward the mother for leaving him to work was expressed in phantasies of preparing electrical shocks and chemical explosions to greet her when she came home.

He did not remember the mother's illness and operation at any time during our incomplete treatment period. Since her illness followed the nursing deprivation and her first leaving him to work, we may suspect that hostility toward her caused him to react to her illness and operation with phantasies of her death, for which the phantasy of the teacher's death was but a cover. The situation with the teacher apparently was for him a repetition of the earlier situation with the mother, so that it threatened to reactivate memories and feelings which he had repressed. Because he loved his mother, the partial revival of the early conflict about her produced anxiety and guilt reactions, as was clearly shown in his interviews. Hence, effort which might otherwise have been expended in learning to read had to be devoted to maintaining repression of the memories and feelings associated with his mother's illness and operation.

A nine year old boy came for treatment after an extended but unsuccessful attempt at remedial teaching in reading. His mother withdrew him from treatment soon after it was started but in the interviews he did have, there were constant protestations of wishing to be good, to love people and never want them to be hurt or killed, accompanied always by play activities of shooting and killing. Thus his ambivalence and feeling of guilt were at once evident. He told of an experience when he first tried to read: "When I was little, I tried to read a book, but I didn't like it because it was full of people getting killed or dying. I cried and cried whenever I tried to read it. I tore it up and threw it away so I would never have to see it again."

At the time this boy started school, an older brother, who had been the mother's favorite, died. Thereafter, the mother wished this boy to take the dead brother's place by doing good work in school. Probably the boy had been jealous of the favored brother and wished him dead, so that his actual death may have seemed to him the result of his unconscious death wishes. In reading the book which he described, his death wishes toward the brother may have threatened to emerge into consciousness, so that his weeping was a guilt expression. Thus reading became dangerous, from his viewpoint, as something which might destroy peace of mind; moreover, if he learned to read and was successful in school, he would be taking the dead brother's place with the mother, which he could not bear to do because of his feeling of guilt.

A seven year old boy, with I.Q. 112, failed in first grade because he could not learn to read. He also failed to respond to individual tutoring and was brought to the clinic for treatment, which was completed in 18 interviews, on the basis of one hour a week. The boy had three younger brothers who remained at home with the mother while he was at school. In the treatment interviews, it soon became evident that he spent the time in the classroom worrying about what the mother and brothers were doing at home and fearing that his mother cared more for them than for him. His first interviews were full of anxiety over the therapist's relationship to other patients, his belief that the brothers were treated better than himself, and his hatred of having to go to school "to learn to read."

During the first part of the treatment, he could not bear his jealousy and hostility toward other patients and toward the little brothers; whenever these feelings came close to consciousness, he turned his aggressive and hostile impulses back on himself, hurting himself or pretending to kill himself in his play. By the middle of the treatment period, he could say his brothers were a "pain in the neck," he wished they had never been born, etc. and express hostility to other patients, without the early guilt reactions. Toward the end of treatment, he could accept the necessity of sharing the therapist and his mother with other children without feeling this meant rejection for himself. He was also reading satisfactorily in school by the end of the treatment. Probably his favorable response to a short time of treatment was partly due to the fact that he was not, in reality, a rejected child but was sincerely loved by the mother, and partly to his not having the intense and complicated emotional conflicts such as were present in the first case we have reported, or even in the second case.

GENERAL DISCUSSION

Certain common psychogenic factors, evident in more or less degree in all these cases of reading disability, present at least superficial similarities to those which also enter into the formation of neurotic symptoms. In each case, there were anxiety and guilt over hostility and the sadistic phantasies in which this feeling found expression, together with expenditure of considerable effort to maintain repression of the phantasies and emotions; the neurotic also expends effort in repression. The first case shows marked regression to early infantile stages of emotional development, as do many neurotic patients. If the neurotic often represses aggression and turns it back on himself in his symptoms, likewise aggression is repressed and turned back on the self in these reading disability cases. And if the neurotic expiates his guilt and to some extent punishes himself in his suffering through his illnesses, it seems that there is also an element of atonement and self-punishment in reading disability cases, since by the failure in school the child produces a situation in which he is exposed to constant criticism and reproof from parents and teachers.

From the practical viewpoint of the approach to clinical work with reading disabilities, it is certainly important to recognize that in many instances this kind of difficulty may have a complex psychogenic background. If there are obvious neurotic characteristics, in addition to the reading disability, as in the first case reported, we may be sure that treatment rather than remedial teaching is required. Failure to respond to a trial period of remedial teaching usually is another indication of necessity for treatment.[6] Needless to say, we are referring to cases of reading disability where intellectual deficiencies are not involved but where the children are of normal or superior intelligence.

Probably the kind of treatment and the length of time required for it should vary with individual patients. Capacity to respond to treatment, the intensity and complexity of the emotional conflicts, the kind of relationships afforded the child in his actual living situation, all should be taken into consideration. So evaluated, the first case which we reported obviously needs a long time for the completion of treatment of a fairly intensive nature; the last case needs only a short time and a much less intensive sort of treatment.

DISCUSSION

MR. TULCHIN: Early studies of reading disability cases were made chiefly by physicians who were primarily interested in the physical aspects of their cases.

[6] A diagnostic testing program alone cannot clear up the question of remedial teaching versus treatment, since the same deficiences in the mechanics of reading-reversals, word confusions, etc.—appear on tests in cases of psychogenic origin as in any other type of case.

Later, attention began to be paid to the psychological and emotional factors.

Various personality and behavior difficulties may result from school maladjustment in children whose specific reading disability is non-emotional in character. We began to recognize that regardless of the etiology of the disability certain emotional factors entered in to complicate the clinical picture and in many cases it seemed that the emotional factors were primary. The lapse of time between the first manifestation of the reading difficulty and the time the child is brought to the psychologist may make it extremely difficult to determine the various elements responsible for the difficulty, and to evaluate their relative importance.

Feeling of inadequacy, attention, oversensitiveness to criticism, infantile behavior, resistance to authority, sibling rivalry, general instability, and other emotional factors, singly or in combination, may interfere with learning to read. On the other hand, these emotional reactions may in turn trace their origin to a reading disability based on other than emotional factors.

The importance of early experiences and emotional attitudes developed long before the child faces the task of learning to read, are shown in a case recently brought to our attention. This case is closely tied up with a sibling rivalry situation. A 9 year old boy of superior intelligence with exceptional interest and ability along mechanical lines showed a retardation of two years in reading. His reading difficulty was discovered as soon as he entered school and at irregular intervals special help was given with little success.

When asked, during the examination, whether he uses his left hand for throwing a ball he replied: "I use my left hand for only one thing—to punch my brother." When asked by the psychiatrist to mention one thing about his brother that is good he can only think of: "He can read and write better than I can." Challenged to say one other thing brings forth: "That's too hard—I'm stuck in the mud." The boy's older brother was able to read long before John entered school. In remembering an early scene of his brother reading to his mother, the two sitting together, himself a distance away, he describes his desire to "do something" to gain her attention. In a phantasy he fights with his brother and actually gets him away from the mother.

His interest in mechanical things seems directly associated with his strong urge to excel in a field of his own. A short period of tutoring, simultaneous with psychiatric treatment of the sibling rivalry situation, cleared up the reading difficulty and improved the rivalry problem. A later follow up report from the mother informs us that the improvement continued and John now shows an interest in reading and his work is up to grade.

In stressing the importance of psychogenic factors in reading disability cases, and in presenting her very interesting illustrative case material, Dr. Blanchard rightly warns us that not all cases of reading disability are of complex psychogenic origin. Dr. Blanchard feels that in cases in which psychogenic factors predominate, psychotherapy alone, without any remedial teaching brings about improvement in reading. Our own experience points to the desirability for remedial tutoring to be carried on simultaneously with psychotherapy.

The remedial program, of course, must be worked out in relation to the findings in each individual case. A rigid adherence to a single program is precluded by the very nature of the problem. The child himself frequently gives clues which can be utilized to advantage.

One needs to differentiate between the type of tutoring which merely repeats the classroom situation with perhaps minor changes and remedial training which recognizes the emotional attitudes and conflicts of the child and utilizes the clinical and psychological approach to the problem. The child is not aware of the psychogenic factors in the situation and may not relate his emotional disturbance to the reading difficulty but he does know that he is unable to read and may be willing to accept help. The need exists to overcome his resistance to reading, to restore his confidence in himself, and actually to help him with reading. Psychotherapy will undoubtedly tend to free him emotionally so that his progress may be more rapid but a child who is several years behind in his reading achievement is in need of specific help.

In some of the cases presented by Dr. Blanchard the emotional experiences and conflicts of the patient, although in themselves not specifically related to the reading disability, created the disturbance which interfered with the child's ability to learn to read. Dr. Blanchard finds that the energy and effort which might have been spent in learning to read was utilized by the child in repressing certain emotional experiences. One should like to inquire about the general school adjustment of these children and about their performance in subjects other than reading. In repressing certain of their emotional experiences, why did they utilize the energy and effort essential for learning to read, and not the energy needed for arithmetic or other subjects?

Dr. Blanchard, in her paper, makes clear very forcibly the need for adequate study and analysis of each case of reading disability. No single cause can adequately explain the nature and origin of reading disability, and the therapeutic technique must be sufficiently flexible to meet the problems presented by the individual child.

DR. OLSON: I believe that Dr. Blanchard has given us an excellent illustration of the multiple nature of causation in the field of reading. Her work, in a sense, confirms and elaborates that of Dr. Castner. There is a clear need for a pluralistic approach to the problem of reading disability. It may be necessary in each such case to set a series of hypotheses which should be checked for or systematically ruled out, as elements in the diagnosis.

Dr. Blanchard has performed a distinct service in calling our attention to the highly individual nature of some of the factors involved in the child who is failing to make progress commensurate with his capacity.

In our work we have tried to rule out of consideration as special disability cases, those in whom the failure to progress is adequately accounted for by a lack of readiness in the mental or chronological maturity of the child. There is considerable evidence, for example, that many of the reversal symptoms are not specifically diagnostic but are simply a part of a normal immaturity.

Another approach has been to determine whether a specific sensory disability related to reading was involved. We have been using the Betts telebinocular apparatus, and the audiometer in this connection. The third approach has been an examination of the instructional situation with particular reference to motivation and to learning.

The fourth approach comes squarely into the field of personality and at once raises a multitude of questions. We have some evidence in the light of this approach that reading is but one of many peripheral expressions of the personality. We have a number of cases in which the conduct and personality reaction of the child to social settings as a whole antedated the specific appearance of a reading disability, and in which the problem of desirable personality integration became much more basic than the peripheral expression in reading.

Cases of discrepancy between capacity and achievement come in disproportionately large numbers, from the highest 25 percent in problem tendencies on a generalized scale we have employed. The picture may be one of destructive aggression or withdrawal.

Dr. Blanchard has suggested a treatment approach for such cases in which the facilitation involved in the individual process may restructure the personality picture, so as to remove inhibiting factors and involve a general energy release favorable to expressive movement. She has suggested the existence of quite specific inhibiting factors—in the discussion of Chinese writing, in her case, and in the associations uncovered in connection with the knife. The length of the treatment program that Dr. Blanchard has undertaken indicates that the central tendency of personality is not rapidly affected.

I do not believe we can expect changes when involved personality problems are present. In a few instances, of course, pressure applied on an external basis for the acquisition of a specific skill of a complicated type, such as in reading, may be the occasion for the development of faulty attitudes. I cannot help but wonder whether some of Dr. Blanchard's material, as elicited in the interview, is evidence of peripheral social and emotional responses not directly related to reading, except as both are evidence of a problem of internal organization. The question is really one, theoretically, of the generality and specificity of behavior or of the existence of a third factor hypothesis. In reading disability cases, is one more likely to find a general personality involvement reflected in speech, movement, ideation, adjustment, and reading, or a specific connection between the reading and emotional content?

If all are related to a central pattern, then help at any point should assist at others. In such a case, help with reading may be a fundamental approach to personality adjustment. Similarly, an individual treatment approach directed at the personal problem, should facilitate expression in reading.

Dr. Blanchard has called our attention to a type of case which is fairly frequent, and to a treatment approach worthy of extensive exploration.

CORRECTION OF DISCUSSION

DR. BLANCHARD: I might say one or two things briefly. I cannot take time to reply in detail to Dr. Tulchin's question about other school work in cases of reading disability. In certain cases, the other school work is affected. This is more likely to be so as the child goes on into higher grades where reading is important for mastery of many subjects. But in many cases, there seems to be a specific reading disability, with very good achievement in such subjects as mathematics, excellent mechanical ability, etc. I hope to discuss this in another paper.

Time does not permit me to comment on the points made by Dr. Olson. I should like to mention, in connection with the previous paper presented by Dr. Castner, that when the boy whom I have described in some detail in my own paper first came to clinic he could not draw even the simplest forms, so poor was his motor coordination at that time. By the twenty-sixth interview, as I reported, he was able to draw a very good picture of a man, which gave him an I.Q. 104 on the Goodenough Scale.

I should like to mention one more thing, which may be related to Dr. Olson's remark as to the time element necessary for changes in cases with involved personality problems. Since this paper was written, and since the last interview which was included in it, the beginnings of a change in the boy's personality are strikingly evident. In the interviews reported, he was talking about wishing to learn everything from me and had to sit in my chair in order to attempt any reading or writing. In that part of the treatment, he was dependent upon borrowing strength from me and needed support from me quite extensively. He has suddenly blossomed out into saying that he used not to have brains, but now he does have brains, that he gets ideas out of his own head, and is able to do some reading and writing sitting in his own chair instead of mine. These and other similar changes indicate the beginning of changes in his personality, I believe.

8. LEARNING DISABILITY IN READING[1]

N. Dale Bryant

Reading difficulties may result from a learning disability or from non-disability factors such as low general intelligence, missed instruction, poor teaching, etc. Disability refers to an impairment—a lack of normal function—which is severe enough to be a handicap. The term disability does not imply a particular cause or even a particular kind of impairment; it merely indicates a relative inability to learn and retain. Inability to learn assumes ample opportunity, including some individual instruction by a competent teacher. If a child with reading retardation and normal intelligence has ample opportunity, tries, but is relatively unable to learn and retain simple materials at his level of functioning, the term reading disability is appropriately applied to him. This is exactly the condition of many children receiving remedial instruction.

If the teacher is aware of the complexities of reading disability and has a conceptual framework to view the child's impairment, the child's performance in a learning situation provides crucial information for diagnosis and offers an excellent guide for developing a remedial program. Without understanding and without a conceptual framework, the

Reprinted from *Reading as an Intellectual Activity*, J. Allen Figurel, Editor, International Reading Association Conference Proceedings, *Scholastic Magazines* Vol. 8 (New York, 1963), pp. 142–146. By permission of N. Dale Bryant and The International Reading Association.

[1] Work contributing to this paper was supported in part by a PHS project grant OM 225 from the National Institute of Mental Health, Public Health Service and also a research grant from the Association for the Aid of Crippled Children.

teacher often overlooks important data and fails to interpret the child's behavior so that it is useful as a guide to remediation.

In considering the nature of reading disability, every teacher should be aware of the following basic concepts:

1. "Disability" is meaningful only with reference to the material and methods used in instruction. A child may be unable to learn by one method but not be "disabled" if a different method is used. However, in learning to read, the normal child shows great ability to learn by almost any method and sometimes without formal instruction. The child who is unable to learn by one method, is likely to have difficulties with other methods.
2. Reading disability is not an entity. It is an extremely variable symptom. Children with reading disability do not all have the same basis, degree, or type of impairment, though there are some characteristics that are common to most cases.

Practically every case of reading disability is a complex interaction of such factors as the following:

a. A *basic cause* (or causes) of the disability (e.g., neurological dysfunction, emotional interference, or confusion from missed or erroneous learning).
b. A *secondary effect* of the disability (e.g., feelings of inadequacy arising from reading failure).
c. A *contributing difficulty* which is not sufficient to cause the disability itself, but is enough to complicate the reading problem and make it more severe (e.g., the secondary effect of feelings of inadequacy may make the child avoid involvement in reading situations and thereby be less responsive to remedial help).
d. A *correlated resultant* which results from the same factors which cause the disability even though it has no effect on the disability nor is it effected by the disability (e.g., neurological dysfunctioning that causes a reading disability can also impair the development of balance and motor coordination).
e. *Incidental* factors which occur in a reading disability sample just as they would in any sample (e.g., it is meaningless to identify that children with reading disability come from homes in which there are frequent family arguments unless a comparable sample without reading disability is found to have fewer family arguments).

f. *Expectations of performance* arising from the child's self-concept, family orientation, subcultural attitudes, perception of boy *vs.* girl role in school, and other socio-cultural influences. (A boy from a lower class home may be under less personal and external pressure to try and overcome reading difficulties than a girl from a middle class, education-oriented family.)

Within the context of expectations of performance, the basic causes and contributing difficulties bring about an impairment in a child's ability to learn. Let us consider the nature of factors causing or contributing to reading disability. The following causes are arranged in order of increasing involvement of the organism so that disability from a more involved cause is almost sure to have elements of all preceding causes.

1. *Confusion from Missed or Erroneous Learning.* The simplest cause for reading disability (and one which is almost always involved even where there are other causes) is confusion and erroneous learning. Missed instruction, poor teaching, or lack of learning due to other causes (including learning disability) can result in gaps of basic skills and in incorrect concepts that "disable" the child in accomplishing new learning. It might be argued that this is pseudo-disability, but remember the previous point 1: that every disability is meaningful only in terms of the method and materials of teaching. When confusion interferes with the usual methods of instruction, some degree of disability exists. However, unless confusion is maintained by other causes, it is likely to be quickly overcome if instruction is made simple and deals with the problem area. When teaching methods are not adapted to the child's level of understanding and when instruction is not focused on his confusion and errors, this represents *teacher perpetuated reading disability.*

2. *Emotional Interference.* The second cause of reading disability (either basic or contributing) is emotional interference with attention and concentration. Most reading disability cases have emotional problems, particularly feelings of inadequacy, but in order for emotions to be considered as a cause of reading disability, a way in which learning is interfered with needs to be stipulated. Many emotionally disturbed children learn to read easily. Furthermore, emotional difficulties may be present and represent only a contributing difficulty rather than a primary cause.

When the child is obviously *involved and trying to learn,* it is unlikely that emotional factors are a primary cause of the reading disability. The reverse is not necessarily true; the presence of anxiety, fantasy, blocking, or depression do not enure that these are the primary cause of the reading disability. Emotional factors are almost always involved in any case of disability, if for no other reason, as secondary reactions to repeated failure and conflicts arising from the disability. Secondary emotional factors can be a more serious problem than the reading retardation and, in most cases, do contribute to the child's reading difficulties. Reading disability basically caused by emotional factors is likely to be associated with learning difficulties other than just reading and spelling. There are techniques for reducing each of the emotional factors that cause or contribute to reading disability though their elaboration is beyond the scope of this paper. A knowledge of behavioral principles, a warm relationship, and a flexible approach to adjusting the situation so as to modify the child's emotional reactions can provide reduction of emotional interference with learning to read, whether it be primary or secondary.

3. *Neurological Dysfunctioning.* A third cause of reading disability, which Rabinovitch[2] has called *primary reading disability,* is neurological dysfunctioning. This can readily be conceptualized by teachers as massive unreadiness. The author has discussed elsewhere[3] a neuropsychological model which provides a basis for understanding the way in which neurological dysfunctioning can produce the defects seen in cases of reading disability. Probably a number of factors can produce a similar kind of neurological inefficiency in the association areas and connections within the brain that serve reading:

a. *Damage* can obviously produce loss of ability to read (alexia) in an adult and prevent learning (dyslexia) in a child. Damage does not have to be gross to reduce the efficiency of one of the brain's most vulnerable areas of neurological functioning. Pasamanick[4] postulates a continuum of pre- and neonatal damage ranging from spontaneous abortion and infant death through gross brain damage to a much more frequent minimal damage with no gross signs (particularly in the more vulnerable males). Damage results from complications of pregnancy, prematurity, anoxia at birth, concussions, and very high fevers. Interrelationship of factors is seen in the fact that prematurity and conditions indicative of possible minimal damage occurs many times more frequently among groups with poor prenatal diet and care—the same group whose children will likely be "culturally deprived."

b. *Genetic factors* are sometimes a cause, but are difficult to differentiate from effects of family environment. Sometimes, reading disability does tend to "run" in families, particularly among male members. Hermann[5] reports that in 45 sets of twins, where one had a reading disability, all 12 of the one-egg twins showed an identical disability, but in only 11 of the 33 two-egg twins, did both have reading disability.

c. In many cases of reading disability, the child appears to be matur-

[2] Ralph Rabinovitch, "Reading and Learning Disabilities." In *American Handbook of Psychiatry* (S. Arietti, ed.). New York: Basic Books, 1959.

[3] N. D. Bryant, "Reading Disability: Part of a Syndrome of Neurological Dysfunctioning." In *Challenge and Experiment* (J. Allen Figurel, ed.). New York: Scholastic Magazine Press, 1962.

[4] B. Pasamanick and H. Knobloch, "Epidemiologic Studies on the Complications of Pregnancy and the Birth Process." In *Prevention of Mental Disorders in Children,* G. Kaplan, ed. New York: Basic Books, 1961.

[5] Knud Hermann, *Reading Disability.* Springfield, Ill.: Charles C. Thomas, 1959.

ing slowly. A *maturational lag* in certain abilities is a common conception applied to reading disability cases and in the late teens improvement is often seen that appears to be maturational.

d. It is possible that *extreme deprivation of perceptual and associational experiences at crucial* times in the development of the child may prevent the development of an efficient neurological functioning.

Whatever the source of impairment, many cases of reading disability seem to show symptoms of neurological dysfunctioning, including:

1. Motor impairment (below the norms for his age on the Lincoln-Oseretsky Test of Motor Development—usually not identified in a pediatric or neurological examination).
2. Left-right confusion or history of confusion past age of seven or eight.
3. Abnormal or borderline EEG.
4. Aphasoid confusion with respect to time, size and distance estimation, months and seasons.
5. Inability to consistently perceive spiral after-image effects. This may represent distractability since subjects must fixate for 30".
6. Lack of certain perceptual skills (ignore details within known words when the words are flashed at 1/10" and even when encountered in sentences).
7. Sound-symbol association difficulties as reflected in reading errors and defects in learning new words.

In addition, a higher percentage than normally expected have speech difficulties or a history of such difficulties, have other members of their family who had similar reading disability, have minor visual or auditory discrimination difficulties. Some of the children also show the hyperactive-distractable syndrome common to children with known brain damage.

The reading specialist, particularly the remedial teacher, can appropriately ask at this point, "Why this great concern with basic and secondary causes of a child's disability?" The answer is that diagnosis provides a structure which suggests a designed and purposeful approach to remediation. This is in contrast to the reliance on the folklore of reading and "magic" procedures and materials that are too common today. Cases with reading disability frequently get years of remedial help without any real improvement in usable skills. The reason is not just the child's disability since brain damage, maturational lag, and emotional interference cases can all make steady (albeit slow) improvement toward usable achievement. The reason for lack of success is often that the teacher is oriented to materials and techniques irrespective of the needs reflected in the child's performance.

Strangely enough, as we more fully understand disabilities, we find that certain common remedial approaches, if used flexibly, appear applicable to reading disability cases almost irrespective of cause.

When disability results from neurological dysfunctioning, we must program remedial instruction in such small units that the child's learning impairment will not prevent him from dealing with the units we are using. We must only use a small number of units at any one time so that the child can handle the required number of discriminations and associations. We must have him overlearn each simple skill until he can consistently and automatically use it. The author has discussed elsewhere principles of remedial instruction for dyslexia .

The principles and methods appropriate for *primary* reading disability (caused by neurological dysfunctioning) are not inappropriate for disability cases resulting directly from the second cause discussed above: emotional difficulties. The methods need only be supplemented by procedures designed to cope with emotional difficulties. In every case of neurologically based disability, the emotional factors must be considered and handled by the teacher. Furthermore, one of the most therapeutic experiences for reading disability cases is *success*—repeated and consistent success.

All of these points suggest that in approaching remediation of reading disability, we should (1) adhere closely to basic learning principles; (2) design our instruction so that it is not blocked by either the impairments that make up the disability or confusion that blocks new learning; and (3) establish an instructional relationship which reduces the emotional contribution to the continuing reading difficulty. The keys to successful treatment of reading disability are *understanding* the nature of the child's impairment and *flexibility* in modifying the general approaches to fit the child's needs as reflected by his errors and behavior.

CHAPTER II

DIAGNOSIS OF

READING PROBLEMS

9. INTEGRATING DIAGNOSIS WITH REMEDIATION IN READING[1]

George D. Spache

Despite refinements in diagnosis and remediation in reading in the last twenty or so years, there is still widespread lack of integration between these two processes. Numerous reports of remedial work give evidence that the procedures used are not directly related to the detailed diagnostic findings. In many instances it would appear that these two processes are carried on by different persons between whom there is a distinct lack of communication.

One cause of lack of relevancy between diagnosis and remediation is the presence of biased or prejudiced thinking, resulting in limited diagnostic efforts or in stereotyped remedial programs. A second cause may lie in the differing emphases in the training of clinicians, who are likely to do the diagnosis, and of remedial or classroom teachers, who are so prominent in remedial work. But whatever the reasons, the inco-ordination between diagnosis and remediation is a relatively common phenomenon, as we shall attempt to show.

Reprinted from *The Elementary School Journal,* Vol. 56 (September 1955), pp. 18–26. By permission of the University of Chicago Press, copyright 1955 by the University of Chicago Press.

[1] Address presented on November 26, 1954, at the annual meeting of the National Association for Remedial Teaching held at Detroit.

EVIDENCE OF THE NEED FOR BETTER INTEGRATION

There is evidence of bias or a priori thinking in the diagnostic statistics reported by many clinics and teachers. In an investigation of the incidence of personality disturbances among retarded readers, a clinic in Boston reports that 39 per cent of the cases had significant emotional problems. A clinic just outside of Chicago reports 50 per cent; the St. Louis clinics find 4–6 per cent; while we at the University of Florida feel that at least 70 per cent of our reading cases (23) show emotional maladjustment. Certainly these differences reflect the breadth and depth of the diagnostic procedures used by these various clinics rather than any real differences in the extent of personality problems in various geographic areas.

In the case of other diagnostic steps, such as the measurement of vision or reading skills, there are similar contradictory reports. One clinic in New York claims that 95 per cent of all retarded reading cases are due to difficulties in the convergence-divergence ratio in vision, while another finds that most retarded readers are in dire need of visual training. Two other clinics spend three or four days in extensive medical examinations, despite their admission that only a very small proportion of their cases show related organic defects. The report form a group of public school clinics in a large midwestern city finds that 96 per cent of the patients lack skill in word analysis and concludes, logically enough, that poor training in word analysis is the primary cause of reading retardation.

These four clinic reports are typical examples of the circular reasoning present among many diagnosticians. They reason backwards from effect to cause, assuming that, if a certain characteristic is found to be common among retarded readers, it must be a cause of the reading failure. As in the case of those who stress lack of word analysis as a cause, these diagnosticians assume that, since these children are weak in an educational tool, the cause of the reading failure must be found in the reading methods or training. This is about as sensible as concluding that, since all retarded readers are deficient in the school-trained skill of reading, the cause of the failure must lie somewhere in the school. These diagnosticians fail to try to discover the reasons *why* this methodology or training, which is so beneficial to so many children, has failed with the retarded readers. In our opinion, these exaggerated reports reflect a diagnostic prejudice which practically dictates the remedial approach and makes diversified remedial programs, keyed to the true causes, almost impossible.

Lack of direct thinking which would promote better integration between diagnosis and remediation is also shown in the tendency toward stereotyped remedial programs. For example, all the cases in a clinic in the Far West seem to be given the kinesthetic approach to reading without reference to their capacities to learn by other methods. Certain proponents of psychotherapy (2, 6, 17) act as though remedial work in reading was synonymous with nondirective therapy. Apparently some of these authors would use play therapy for all types of emotionally disturbed retarded readers, despite the fact that the cases exhibit a variety of personality adjustments (23), for some of which the nondirective approach would probably be quite inappropriate.

In programs using mechanical devices extensively, there is a tendency to employ such devices with little attention to the exact characteristics of each case. These atomistic training courses leave unanswered such questions as the kinds of remedial cases for which such a program is most or least effective. Apparently no training distinctions are made between slow readers with good comprehension and vocabulary, who might conceivably profit from mechanical acceleration, and cases with multiple difficulties in reading background, comprehension, vocabulary, and word-analysis skills. In the widespread mechanistic programs for adults, there is similar lack of discrimination between adults who are merely slow readers and those who are deficient in a number of reading skills.

Other facts which must be known before the success of mechanical programs can be considered real are the optimum length, intervals, and intensity of such training. Should this training be continued for a few hours, a few weeks, or indefinite periods? It appears from some research that the values of this approach tend to disappear after a very short period of exposure (9).

One other serious objection to the stereotyped use of mechanical devices has been explored by Traxler (34), who pointed out the extent of individual differences in fluency, in speed of associative thinking, and hence in potential for growth in rate. For the past two years we have been following this type of research with modest success in attempting to find a means of identifying those cases likely to profit from rate training. Frankly, practically nothing is known about techniques for careful selection of cases for training in speed. As long as such training continues to be successful with only a moderate proportion of cases, as is generally true, there will be a crying need for better diagnostic criteria rather than for wider use of this method. In our opinion, the use of mechanical training with large numbers of retarded readers is another example of the lack of clear-cut relationships between diagnosis and remediation in many places.

Finally, one other body of evidence showing poor communication between clinicians and remedial teachers is found in a great number of reports on purely formal remedial-reading programs. In many places, reading cases differing widely in etiologic and prognostic details are offered formal reading instruction exclusively. In reports from some clinics, groups of teachers taking university courses in remedial reading are merely matched with an equal number of retarded readers. All that seems important is that the case load per teacher is equalized. All that the teacher has to have, apparently, is a modicum of training in reading methods in order to be ready to do successful remedial work with almost any retarded reader. Actually we still do not clearly know what kinds of cases should or should *not* be given direct reading training. Nor is it entirely clear what types of emotionally disturbed poor readers profit from the usual remedial work (23).

Futhermore, apparently in an effort to widen the disparity between diagnostic implications and the remedial therapy, many training programs are carried out largely by visual methods practically identical with those used in the early training of the retarded reader—the same methods by which the student failed to learn to read successfully. Emphasis upon visual methods in reading is often used with visually handicapped students, despite the evidence of Fendrick (7) and others of the doubtful values of this approach in such cases. No real attempt is made to explore and relate the organic or learning capacities of the student to various basic methods of teaching reading, despite the available diagnostic techniques (15).

IMPLEMENTING DIAGNOSTIC FINDINGS

To attack this problem constructively, it is possible to point out a significant number of ways in which the facts found in common diagnostic procedures may be better implemented by closely relevant remedial or therapeutic steps. We shall first name the characteristics of the retarded reader which are commonly evaluated because the research evidence indicates that they may play a part in the causation of reading failure. Following each diagnostic step, we shall point out the most widely used related remedial procedures and their probable inadequacies. Finally, we shall suggest alternative remedial efforts which may not be widely known. It is our hope that the use of these additional remedial procedures will strengthen a more direct relationship between the causes found by diagnosis and the corrective steps used to relieve reading disability.

Vision

Testing the vision is probably the most common diagnostic step used in this country. Among the visual characteristics which are found to contribute to reading difficulties are deficiencies in visual acuity, hyperopia (farsightedness), astigmatism, and binocular inco-ordination resulting in abnormalities in fusion of the phorias, or in marked monocular preference. One other defect, aniseikonia, seems to be important, but its measurement is probably too difficult for most teachers or clinicians. Myopia (nearsightedness) is also commonly tested, but there is great doubt that it contributes to reading difficulty except in rare cases. With the instruments now available, such as the Ortho-Rater, the sight-screener, the Binocular Reading Test (24), and a few others, relatively complete and reasonably accurate diagnosis is quite possible.

The initial remedial step when visual irregularities are diagnosed is usually to refer the case to a local "eye specialist," who, presumably, will make any corrections that are necessary. At the risk of offending many competent vision specialists, it must be pointed out that simple referral does not relieve the reading teacher of further responsibility in this diagnostic detail. As in every area which involves dealing with humans, there are conflicting philosophies of remediation. For example, many medically trained specialists have, in our opinion, little training or time to engage in orthoptic or visual-training corrective methods. It would seem that, in many parts of our country, visual training is better understood and more widely used by optometrists than by ophthalmologists. This type of training is certainly not the panacea that some reading clinics and some optometrists seem to think it is, but there is a great deal of evidence which indicates that many of these visual handicaps can be relieved, if not entirely eradicated, by this calisthenic approach alone or in combination with other corrective efforts (4, 12, 21, 32).

It may be only a reflection of personal experience, but it also seems that many vision specialists are not aware of the peculiarly intensive demands in near-point work imposed on the high-school or college student. Perhaps that is the reason for the failure of some visual practitioners to make corrections which relieve the symptoms of distress or even actually aid the student in his near-point task of reading or studying.

In our opinion, it is the responsibility of the reading diagnostician to recheck the visual functioning of the retarded reader to determine whether the distress or handicap imposed by visual abnormality has been relieved as much as it is humanly possible to do so. This does not imply that the reading teacher is to attempt to judge the accuracy of the optical prescription or the competence of the visual specialist. Rather, the reading diagnostician should continue to explore the possibilities of further aid to the visually handicapped student by consultation with several eye specialists who may represent different schools of philosophy of remediation.

Other possible remedial steps to aid this type of case are the use of reading materials especially prepared for those of limited vision, as listed by Matson and Larson (13) and Galisdorfer (10); instructing the student in manuscript writing because of its greater visibility (11); and teaching the student better visual discrimination of forms by the use of such training materials as those of Durrell and Sullivan (5) or Thurstone (33). Four possible sources of further aid for the visually handicapped student are state commissions for the blind, the two national vision societies,[2] and local service clubs such as the Lions, which, we understand, are participating in a nation-wide interest in visual problems. Help in financing such steps as visual treatments, mechanical aids, and the hiring of readers is often found through these sources. One further effort that we have found desirable is for the reading teacher to give training in efficient reading

[2]National Society for the Prevention of Blindness (1790 Broadway, New York 19, New York) and American Foundation for the Blind (15 West Sixteenth Street, New York 11, New York).

or study methods to persons who read to the blind or the extremely visually handicapped.

Hearing

Ordinarily, auditory acuity and discrimination are explored in the diagnostic procedures. The ability of the poor reader to hear sounds of normal intensity, or sounds at various pitches, or to recognize similarities and differences in speech sounds are usually evaluated in this auditory testing. The common remedial steps are to refer the auditorily handicapped cases to an otologist and to avoid auditory or phonic methods of teaching. Because of the assumption that such cases cannot employ phonic approaches to reading, we seldom see any attempt to improve the situation by auditory training even though teaching materials are available (5). Actually we know that discrimination often can be improved, particularly if hearing is reinforced by such devices as hearing amplifiers. In the absence of actual hearing loss, poor auditory discrimination may be treated like any other undeveloped skill and repaired by appropriate teaching.

Intelligence

Measurement of intelligence today usually includes evaluation of verbal and nonverbal capacities. Remedial procedures are usually predicated on the results of the intelligence testing, and the mentally retarded are often given the kinesthetic approach to reading, particularly if nonverbal intelligence appears to be significantly greater than verbal. The assumption behind this procedure is as yet unfounded, first, because several studies show that most retarded readers (and, in fact, most children) score higher in nonverbal than in verbal capacities (16, 26) and, second, because there is very little evidence that the kinesthetic approach is peculiarly suited to poor readers who are mentally retarded.

There are several additional steps which, if employed, would further a more direct relationship between diagnostic estimates of intelligence and subsequent remediation. The use of the Learning Methods Test (15) will usually reveal which of four approaches to reading are desirable in each case. Briefly, the procedure in this test includes four teaching lessons, each based on a different reading method, with testing of immediate and delayed recall. Thus far the research data being compiled in use of this test give no indication that level of intelligence or differences in verbal or nonverbal abilities bear any direct relationship to the reading method best for each individual. When verbal ability is significantly lower than nonverbal, the difference may be interpreted as indicative of poor cultural, linguistic, or reading background. If this interpretation is made, then remedial efforts will take the form of providing numerous firsthand and vicarious experiences as well as extensive reading of simple, realistic materials.

Furthermore, we would disregard mental age as a guide to maximum level of potential growth. Many children exceed their own mental ages in reading achievement, while many others fail to progress to this point even under excellent instruction. We prefer to measure potential for growth in comprehension level by estimating the highest level at which the individual can show adequate comprehension when standardized paragarphs are read to him. We have found this method of estimating potential for growth quite feasible with children of the first six or seven grades. For testing from the seventh-grade to college Freshman level, there is available an Auditory Comprehension Test (25), which, when used in conjunction with a parallel measure of silent-reading comprehension, yields similar estimates of potential. Faulty integration of diagnosis and remediation is fostered, in our opinion, by overdependence upon mental age or mental-test performances as the criteria of potential or of the reading method to be employed.

Reading Rate

Present status and the prognosis for growth are commonly measured in the skills of rate, comprehension, vocabulary, and word analysis. Remedial procedures to improve rate are usually of two major types: timed reading with comprehension checks or mechanized programs.

We have already indicated some objection to indiscriminate mechanized procedures and here shall point out several other doubtful assumptions that underlie such methods. Use of this type of training for speed ignores the fact that the reader's eye-movements, phrasing, and the like are often merely a reflection of the difficulty of the reading materials. Even good readers show the same irregularities when reading complex matter, as Anderson has shown (1). It would seem more logical to implement the diagnosis of slow reading by providing simpler materials in which these irregularities do not appear, or to attack the problem more directly by trying to improve the poor vocabulary, word-recognition, or word-analysis skills which may be directly causal.

We also consider that the other type of approach, timed reading or reading under pressure, is inadequate for many slow readers. Extended practice with selections from the various content fields, which we commonly see, leaves the student ignorant of the basically different reading demands of each field. Such practice leads the student to expect naïvely a significant rate increase in all kinds of reading. We doubt that there is a general rate improvement which, as both timed reading and mechanized programs seem to assume, transfers automatically from reading in one content field to another.

More real and permanent growth in rate can be accomplished by teaching the student *how* and *when* to use rapid reading and by direct instruction in reading for ideas, scanning for single facts without actual reading, and skimming by reading only headings and topic and summary sentences. The student achieves flexibility in rate (which, after all, is the real aim of rate training) only by learning to vary his speed and reading techniques according to his purpose, the difficulty and style of the reading material, and his familiarity with the content of the reading matter. This type of rate improvement is best accomplished by instruction in intelligent use of the rapid-reading techniques suggested above in the types of content and reading situations in which they are appropriate.

Vocabulary

Common remedial steps to overcome poor vocabulary include training in word recognition, word meanings, and word relationships, as synonyms and antonyms. Other remedial approaches include emphasis on use of the dictionary and giving the student word lists or lists of affixes and roots to learn. Except at primary levels, there is serious doubt of the values of programs stressing words as contrasted to those stressing tools for vocabulary growth (3). In view of our lack of knowledge of the words actually essential for reading success at upper-elementary or higher levels, it is presumptuous for remedial teachers to offer any particular word list or "all-inclusive" list of affixes or roots for student learning. We do not know accurately how great the whole mass of our language is, or how rapidly it is increasing, or how to make a cross-sectioning sample which would meet the needs of a particular student. We do not know how to anticipate the vocabulary needs of each individual. Perhaps the most we can do is to offer small lists of technical terms which seem to be important in circumscribed areas of study. The general vocabulary needs of each individual are still beyond our measurement or prediction skills.

If we accept this premise, then remediation will stress training in use of tools for vocabulary growth rather than in words or word relationships. Remedial work will include (1) practice with dictionary use for meanings, pronunciation, usage, derivation, and spelling; (2) practice with concentrated, small groups of affixes and roots in analytic attack upon words in context rather than synthetic juggling of lists of words; (3) training in the use of the context to derive meanings by such approaches as inference, direct explanation, structural cues, figures of speech, and tone or mood; and (4) instruction in personalized use of a card file to study the new words that each individual meets in his work-type reading.

Comprehension

In remedial training to improve comprehension, we usually see two types of programs: (1) a drill program in simple varied materials stressing main ideas, details, conclusions, and the like, (2) the use of basal reading materials supplemented by recreational reading. In both programs there is an assumption that repeated practice in answering certain types of questions results in more intelligent reading and in growth in the level of material that can be read. Above primary levels, we believe that there is much more to the act of reading than this semi-mechanical process of reading

and answering questions. There is considerable evidence that general training does not transfer to each content field and that specific, insightful
training is necessary for each basic reading situation (19).

Rather than general drill in comprehension, the student should be
taught how to read for differing degrees of comprehension. This type of
instruction is already available in a few materials (30, 31) and will be
stressed in others as yet unpublished (27). The training to produce intelligent reading includes at least five major points:

1. Planning each reading and its purpose in relation to the whole area of
study, the demands and general purposes of the instructor, and the specific
purposes of the reader.

2. Teaching the student different ways or rates of reading and their effect
upon comprehension.

3. Instructing him in a systematic approach to difficult materials, such as
Robinson's Survey QRRR (18) or some similar study procedure which will
promote thorough retention.

4. Training in critical reading, as in social-science and propaganda materials.
This involves practice in identifying the facts given, evaluating the ideas offered,
and detecting bias, omission, distortion, and the like.

5. Giving the student practice in applying his reading skills in the various
content fields.

The student must understand the demands of reading in literature of
various types, in social science, mathematics, and science—the nature of
the material, the types of thinking needed, the kinds of interrelationships
present, and appropriate rates for accomplishing his various purposes. Fortunately for those attempting this type of approach, there are available
several recent manuals which offer numerous suggestions as to procedures
and materials (20, 28, 35).

Word-Analysis Skills

Diagnostic steps in this area usually include an evaluation of the pupil's
ability to make a systematic but varied attack upon unknown words met in
context. Despite the recognition that word-analysis skills must eventually
function during the act of reading, there is a tendency to retrain these skills
atomistically and in learning situations which do not involve contextual
reading. Many remedial programs stress letter phonics, or letter combinations, or formal syllabication, and the like, which deal only with
isolated words.

It is true, as some of the clinic reports cited earlier show, that one of the
most prominent disabilities of retarded readers at all levels is ineffective
word attack or word analysis. Students may know and understand phonic
principles or syllabication rules, but they seem to make no transfer or use
of this theoretical knowledge when actually reading. A simple experiment
that we carried on at the college level confirms this inability to apply

principles of word analysis. We found practically no statistical relation between the ability to quote the essential parts of syllabication rules and the ability to syllabify.

This lack of relation between formal knowledge of word-attack principles and success in word analysis in contextual reading is widely recognized by diagnosticians. Yet most of the teacher-made or commercial materials that we see persist in using a synthetic approach, involving drills on sounds or word construction rather than word analysis in context. If we agree that most retarded readers need training in word analysis and that formal training does not transfer readily, then there is a need for remedial training in varied methods of word attack *while reading*, rather than programs stressing sounds, isolated words, and the like.

Personality

Many diagnosticians are making some effort to detect the extent and severity, and perhaps the nature, of emotional problems affecting reading performances. There is undoubtedly a growing recognition of the absolute necessity of evaluating by some objective means the influence of personality upon reading. Yet despite this increasing exploration of emotional concomitants, most retarded readers are being referred to the remedial teacher for formal reading instruction. A few diagnosticians may refer children with severe emotional problems for play therapy, if such facilities are available. Other diagnosticians, as we have mentioned earlier, would apparently refer all retarded readers for psychotherapy. There are a number of questions to be answered before we know which of these three courses of action should be taken.

We still do not know what personality patterns are peculiarly characteristic of retarded readers. We are not certain what kinds of maladjustment problems we are attempting to treat. Most studies of the personalities of retarded readers are based on personal experience or opinion. The few studies available employing objective measures of personality have dealt with small groups or economically restricted samples (22, 29, 36). One recent exploratory study (23) points out at least five major personality types in an unrestricted sample of 125 retarded readers. Based on the Rosenzweig Picture-Frustration study, the patterns found in relatively large subgroups are the aggressive, defensive, adjustive, solution-seeking, and autistic or withdrawn. Specific suggestions for therapeutic approach to each type are offered in this study, but these suggestions are based largely on opinion rather than controlled research. We still do not know exactly what kinds of therapy to use or how to relate these to the particular personality problems which we may eventually identify as common to poor readers. Lack of integration between diagnosis and remediation is evidenced in this area also.

There are numerous remedial or therapeutic approaches that we must explore by controlled research in the near future. We should investigate the emotional relationships of the family of the retarded reader and the possibilities of therapy for the parent as well as the child. If, as seems true in certain types of emotionally disturbed readers (6, 23), parental perfectionism or inconsistency is a predisposing factor, we must find means of extending guidance to the parent also. We should make wider use and careful evaluation of a number of approaches which have shown some merit in isolated studies. The values of bibliotherapy, play therapy, and ordinary remedial instruction used alone, or together, or successively in varying arrangements (14), still need extended research. Using the child's original stories of his verbal or artistic interpretation of other stories to gain insights into his feelings and attitudes will be another profitable approach.

Various types of group therapy, used alone or in conjunction with the usual remedial instruction, need further investigation (8). These groups may range from bull sessions providing an opportunity for verbalizing feelings about reading through varying degrees of permissiveness to semi-directive discussions of reading techniques. We also need to discover the types of individuals among high-school and college students for whom directive, semi-directive, or permissive psychotherapy may provide a better answer than formal skill instruction.

We must explore all the possibilities of counseling and guidance procedures in the remedial-reading program. In our reading clinic at the University of Florida, we have found an individualized approach in testing and remedial instruction, with approximately a fourth of the time spent in personalized, semi-directive counseling, the most effective procedure despite a case load of almost one thousand each year (28). We feel strongly that the tendency to formal, group instruction at high-school and college levels must be modified to something approximating the counseling approach used with younger pupils.

In concluding, may we repeat the suggestion that, despite our advances in diagnostic and remedial techniques, there is evidence of a lag in the co-ordination of these processes. We have tried to point out a number of ways in which diagnosis may be made more truly effective in finding the real causes of reading failure and remedial work can be made directly relevant to our diagnosis.

BIBLIOGRAPHY

1. ANDERSON, I. H. "Research in the Psychology of Reading," *Journal of Exceptional Children,* IV (January, 1938), 57–60.
2. AXLINE, VIRGINIA MAE. "Play Therapy—A Way of Understanding and Helping 'Reading Problems,'" *Childhood Education,* XXVI (December, 1949), 151–61.
3. COLVIN, CYNTHIA. "A Re-examination of the Vocabulary Question," *Elementary English,* XXVIII (October, 1951), 350–56.

4. DAVIS, LOUISE FARWELL. "Visual Difficulties and Reading Disabilities," *Recent Trends in Reading*, pp. 135–42. Supplementary Educational Monographs, No. 49. Chicago: University of Chicago Press, 1939.

5. DURRELL, DONALD D., and SULLIVAN, HELEN BLAIR. *Ready To Read.* Yonkers-on-Hudson, New York: World Book Co., 1941.

6. EPHRON, BEULAH KANTOR. *Emotional Difficulties in Reading.* New York: Julian Press, 1953.

7. FENDRICK, PAUL. *Visual Characteristics of Poor Readers.* Teachers College Contributions to Education, No. 656. New York: Bureau of Publications, Teachers College, Columbia University, 1934.

8. FISHER, BERNARD. "Group Therapy with Retarded Readers," *Journal of Educational Psychology*, XLIV (October, 1953), 354–60.

9. FREEBURNE, CECIL M. "Influence of Training in Perceptual Span and Perceptual Speed upon Reading Ability," *Journal of Educational Psychology*, XL (October, 1949), 321–52.

10. GALISDORFER, LORRAINE. *A New Annotated Reading Guide for Children with Partial Vision.* Buffalo: Foster & Stuart, 1950.

11. GRILL, E. "Manuscript Writing and Its Value to a Sight-saving Child," *Educational Method*, IX (April, 1930), 407–12.

12. LANCASTER, JULIA E. *A Manual of Orthoptics.* Springfield, Illinois: Charles C. Thomas, 1951.

13. MATSON, CHARLOTTE, and LARSON, LOLA. *Books for Tired Eyes.* Chicago: American Library Association, 1951.

14. MEHUS, HILDA. "Learning and Therapy," *American Journal of Orthopsychiatry*, XXIII (April, 1953), 416–21.

15. MILLS, ROBERT E. The Learning Methods Test. Dade City, Florida: The Author (903 South Tenth Street).

16. MONROE, MARION, and BACKUS, BERTIE. *Remedial Reading: A Monograph in Character Education.* Boston: Houghton Mifflin Co., 1937.

17. POTTER, MURIEL. "The Use of Limits in Reading Therapy." *Journal of Consulting Psychology*, XIV (August, 1950), 250–55.

18. ROBINSON, FRANCIS P. *Effective Study.* New York: Harper & Bros., 1946.

19. SHORES, J. H., "Skills Related to Ability To Read History and Science," *Journal of Educational Research*, XXXVI (April, 1943), 584–93.

20. SIMPSON, ELIZABETH A. *Helping High-School Students Read Better.* Chicago: Science Research Associates, 1954.

21. SMITH, WILLIAM. *Clinical Orthopic Procedures.* St. Louis: C. V. Mosby, 1950.

22. SOLOMON, RUTH H. "Personality Adjustment to Reading Success and Failure," *Clinical Studies in Reading. II*, pp. 64–82. Supplementary Educational Monographs, No. 77. Chicago: University of Chicago Press, 1953.

23. SPACHE, GEORGE. "Appraising the Personality of Remedial Pupils," *Education in a Free World*, pp. 122–32. Washington: American Council on Education, 1955.

24. SPACHE, GEORGE. The Binocular Reading Test. Gainesville, Florida: The Author (University of Florida).

25. SPACHE, GEORGE. "The Construction and Validation of a Silent and an Auditory Work-Type Comprehension Reading Test," *Educational and Psychological Measurement*, X (Summer, 1950), 249–53.

26. SPACHE, GEORGE. "Intellectual Characteristics of Retarded Readers as Measured by the WISC" [to be published].

27. SPACHE, GEORGE, and BERG, PAUL C. *Better Reading for College Students.* New York: Macmillan Co., 1955.

28. SPACHE, GEORGE, and BERG, PAUL C. *Instructor's Guide for "Better Reading for College Students."* New York: Macmillan Co., 1955.

29. STEWART, ROBERT S. "Personality Maladjustment and Reading Achievement," *American Journal of Orthopsychiatry,* XX (April, 1950), 410–17.

30. STRANG, RUTH. *Study Type of Reading Exercises.* New York: Bureau of Publications, Teachers College, Columbia University, 1935.

31. STRANG, RUTH. *Study Type of Reading Exercises—College Level.* New York: Bureau of Publications, Teachers College, Columbia University, 1951.

32. TAYLOR, EARL A. *Controlled Reading.* Chicago: University of Chicago Press, 1937.

33. THURSTONE, THELMA GWINN. *Learning To Think Series.* Chicago: Science Research Associates, 1949.

34. TRAXLER, ARTHUR E. "The Relation between Rate of Reading and Speed of Association," *Journal of Educational Psychology,* XXV (May, 1934), 357–65.

35. TRIGGS, FRANCES O. *We All Teach Reading.* New York: The Author (419 West 119th Street), 1954.

36. VORHAUS, PAULINE G. "Rorschach Configurations Associated with Reading Disability," *Journal of Projective Techniques,* XIV (March, 1952), 3–19.

10. INFORMAL TECHNIQUES FOR APPRAISING READING ABILITIES

Board of Education of the City of New York

The objectives of the reading program that were suggested in the previous chapter were:

1. The child develops interest in reading.

2. The child gets meaning from the material he reads.

3. The child becomes independent in basic reading skills.

4. The child learns how to find and use printed matter.

In this chapter, the informal techniques best adapted for appraising the

Reprinted from the *Informal Appraisal of Reading Abilities,* Educational Research Bulletin, Bureau of Educational Research Evaluation Series No. 2 (June 1955), pp. 7–29. By permission of J. Wayne Wrightstone, Bureau of Educational Research of the New York City Board of Education.

abilities which are related to these objectives will be indicated. The abilities to be discussed may appear to be treated as separate entities. This is not the case, however, for these abilities are interrelated and interdependent. They are all essential components of general reading ability. In making a comperhensive appraisal, however, it is expedient to examine them one at a time. This procedure is also highly desirable, for such an analysis helps to reveal areas of strength and weakness in the child's reading.

OBJECTIVE 1

The Child Develops Interest in Reading

In achieving this objective, the child displays many desirable attitudes toward reading. He has a desire to read. At a young age he likes to look at pictures and he tries to read labels, signs, posters. At a later age, he likes to read books, magazines and newspapers for entertainment and information. He appreciates and enjoys materials of varying forms and content— fairy tales, adventure, biography, science, poems, comics, etc. He takes care of the physical condition of books and he wants to have books of his own. In order to estimate the child's interest in reading, the chief techniques for gathering the evidence are observation and records.

Observation

The teacher gets a general impression of the child's interest in reading from direct observation of the enjoyment he displays during reading activities.* She notes the eagerness with which he seeks materials from the class, school or public library and the number and variety of pamphlets, magazines and other printed matter he brings to school. She recalls the contributions he makes to group discussion from books he has read and his oral and written expression of literary appreciation and reading preferences. The teacher may occasionally make written note of these observations. She may report them in anecdotal records for a few children. She may also keep a list of the readings completed by the members of a group.

Pupil self-records

Records which pupils keep help the teacher to judge their interest in reading. These are some devices for record-keeping by the child:

* See *Guiding the Growth of Reading Interests,* Educational Research Bulletin Number 8 of this series.

1. Have the child keep a cumulative list of stories, poems and books read in school, at home or in the library in connection with a particular topic or unit.

2. Ask the child to submit at the end of a unit study period a list of the references he has read.

3. Suggest that the child write in his notebook useful bits of information he has found in research materials and direct him to indicate the source of such information.

4. Have the child keep a cumulative list of readings throughout the term with or without his reactions to and evaluation of them.

5. Have the child collect in a folder book reviews, illustrated book covers, drawings, paintings and posters which he has made in connection with the various study areas.

6. Have the class librarian keep a record on cards of materials withdrawn from the class library. These cards become a permanent inventory of the reading interests of the various children.

7. Have the child maintain a log or diary which may be examined by the teacher for references to materials read and commented on.

If the records which children keep are to be useful in appraisal, however, they should grow out of some classroom activity, for the accuracy of the information which the child provides depends in part on what he is being asked to report and what he thinks the teacher is going to do with it. If he knows, for example, that he will be judged by the number of titles he lists in his records, reading, to him, may become a compulsory task. Indeed, such a procedure may even tend to discourage his taste for reading. This precaution regarding the integration of children's record-keeping with the normal procedures of the classroom is necessary also in the use of questionnaires, checklists or inventories.

Questionnaires

The pupil may provide the teacher with a record of his reading preferences and of his general attitude toward reading by answering a special questionnaire designed for this purpose. Such information may be obtained, for example, as part of a general questionnaire, called perhaps a *Hobby Record.* The pupil might be asked to fill in what he thinks he would like to be some day, what he likes to do in after-school hours, whether he does any outside work for which he is paid, what his favorite games or sports are, whether he does any reading, manual work, or drawing and whether he plays a musical instrument. He might be asked how often he goes to the movies, what his favorite radio and television programs are, the name of his favorite motion picture hero, titles of his favorite books, stories, poems, etc. In using a questionnaire of this type, it would be advisable for the teacher to give an appropriate introduction, explaining that the results would be used in providing for activities in which the children are interested and in helping them plan for their future studies.

The questionnaire may be more specifically related to reading. It may take the form of a poll of reading done during a week's vacation, for example. The teacher might explain that she is conducting this poll on how much and what children have read outside of school and that she knows that some children like to read and that some don't. She should encourage the children to report their actual reading and to include all types of material including books, magazines, comics, recipes, directions for making airplanes, etc.

Checklists and inventories

Instead of requiring the child to write out answers on a questionnaire the teacher might present him with a list of possible responses and direct him to check those he prefers. Checklists in this form may be drawn up to relate to a variety of interests, activities or fields or to reading alone. An adaptation of such a checklist of reading interests might require the child to indicate with an *L* the kinds of stories he likes to read, a *D* those he does not like, and an *I* those about which he is indifferent or is not sure. An interest inventory might instead include items like the following to be answered with *Yes, No* or *Don't Know.*

Do you like to read stories about:

animals?	Yes	No	Don't know
fairies?	Yes	No	Don't know
children in other lands?	Yes	No	Don't know
airplanes?	Yes	No	Don't know
adventure?	Yes	No	Don't know
science?	Yes	No	Don't know
mysteries?	Yes	No	Don't know

Questionnaires, checklists and inventories, when properly constructed and administered, become valuable guidance instruments especially when followed by an interview with the child regarding specific items. It should be noted that children may need help in filling out these records. With some children, it may be necessary for the teacher to read the text aloud as they read it silently. In some cases, she may even have to write the child's oral responses to the items. The questionnaire may become the basis for a pupil-teacher interview.

Rating scales

Having observed the child carefully and having obtained supplementary information from questionnaires, inventories and checklists and by direct oral questioning, the teacher is now in a position to rate his interest in reading. She may simply assign a rating of 1, 2 or 3 according to the degree of interest exhibited. If she uses this method, it is helpful first to select one or two children to represent the three points on the scale: (1) low, (2) average and (3) high. Using these children as criteria, the teacher may then rate the others relatively. If a finer differentiation is desired, 1, 3 and 5 may be assigned to the children selected as the standards of low, average and high, and intermediate scores of 2 and 4 may be given to those who fall between. Qualitative judgments such as *poor-fair-good* may be used instead. Whether the ratings are given in numbers or in descriptive terms, no more than five levels of judgment are advisable.

A more objective method, however, is to construct a scale and set up criteria for rating in advance. When more than one teacher uses the scale or where the results are passed on from one teacher to another, it is important that there be agreement as to the meaning of the ratings assigned. In constructing such a scale, therefore, definitions in terms of concrete evidence should be worked out for each rating. These definitions might include details as to frequency of visits to the class and public library, contributions to discussion from materials read, and perhaps, too, the number of books or stories or pages read. An alternate or additional technique would be to select children known to all the teachers involved to represent the various ratings, or to write a brief description of the reading interests of these children. Such implementation of the following four-point scale for interest in reading, for example, would tend to make each step clearly distinct from the others and would increase the possibility of teachers arriving independently at the same rating for a particular child:

1. Avoids reading.

2. Reads what he is asked to read but engages in little or no voluntary reading.

3. Does some reading on his own.

4. Does considerable reading on his own.

The results from the use of a rating scale become more reliable, also, if the scale is itself more specific. A scale like the following, for example, may be found useful with very young children.

1. Disregards labels, signs or books.

2. Occasionally attempts to read labels, signs or books.
3. Shows persistent interest in reading labels, signs or books.

The objectivity of this type of scale could be increased by selecting children as standards for the various levels of interest indicated. For example, a teacher may use Jane as an illustration for a rating of 1. Jane pays no attention to any labels or signs. She does not mention them, ask any questions about them or attempt to read them. Tom, on the other hand, displays a persistent interest in labels and signs. He asks such questions as: "Does that label say Post Office or Post Toasties?" His manifest interest in labels, signs and books marks him as a standard for a rating of 3. Thus, by selecting certain children as examples of rating levels, it is easier to assign ratings to other children on a comparative basis.

A single form may be drawn up to record the general evaluation of the child's attitude toward reading. Such a summary would include the various items which are considered as components in general attitude toward the reading. The record may also be presented graphically as on the following qualitative rating scale.

Interest in reading books	Shows no interest	Is interested	Shows exceptional interest
Interest in reading magazines and newspapers	Shows no interest	Is interested	Shows exceptional interest
Variety of subjects read	Range of subjects is very limited	Range is fair	Range is very broad
Literary quality of material read	Voluntarily selects material of low literary quality only	Reads material of acceptable literary quality	Choice of materials shows exceptional appreciation of good literature
Physical care of books	Does not take care of books; defaces books	Keeps books in fair condition	Takes very good care of books

The hints given for constructing and using rating scales in appraising attitudes toward reading may be applied also in constructing scales for other purposes. Scales may be found helpful in recording general evaluations of basic skills, comprehension and study skills. They are especially useful in appraising attitudes gained from reading. In constructing scales for these purposes as well, attention should be given to the specificity of the items to be rated, the concrete definition of the various ratings to be assigned and the methods for accumulating objective evidence on which the ratings are to be based.

OBJECTIVE 2

The Child Gets Meaning from the Material He Reads

Reading comprehension is a major objective of instruction and much of the total elementary school program is devoted to the development of concepts and meanings. Comprehension involves a number of specific abilities which have been given various names and assigned different classifications by various authors. For this discussion the specific abilities involved in reading comprehension may be grouped into three general categories which are somewhat overlapping, as is inevitable, but which represent three somewhat different types of reasoning required of the child in comprehending what he reads. These categories are:

A. Getting the literal meaning of the words, phrases and sentences
B. Seeing relationships among the ideas expressed
C. Getting the main thought and the general tone of the material

Appraising the abilities included in each of these categories requires different techniques. Direct observation and testing are, however, the chief methods. Objective-type pencil-and-paper tests of silent reading are particularly economical and efficient in yielding evidence for the appraisal of reading comprehension.

Observation

The teacher gets a general impression of the child's comprehension of what he reads from the use he makes of what he has read. She notes his comments and his questions, and the references he makes to the content in later discussion or written report. She estimates his understanding from his responses to printed directions and questions, from the illustrations he draws or paints or finds for selections and from his participation in dramatizations. She observes also how he applies ideas gained from reading.

The teacher occasionally uses oral questions and answers in her day-to-day testing of reading comprehension. She may ask for specific details in a selection or for its general content. She may call for the meaning of an unusual word. She may ask the child to predict the next event in a story. She may direct him to find the part that tells why a certain thing happened or a certain relationship exists. She can tell also from the way the child reads a passage aloud whether or not he is comprehending what he is reading.

Informal pencil-and-paper tests

The teacher appraises the child's reading comprehension also from his performance on written tests. Informal tests are found in workbooks, exercise booklets, children's graded newspapers and publishers' manuals for teacher's use with readers. Similar exercises frequently appear at the end of stories in readers and in social studies, elementary science and other textbooks. The tests in these sources should be examined carefully and selected with the following considerations in mind:

Does the test deal with a subject or unit in which the group is interested?
Is it drawn up in vocabulary familiar to the children?
Does the child or group need to be tested in the particular aspects of reading comprehension that are measured by the questions?
Does the test measure the aspect or aspects of comprehension which the teacher has been emphasizing?
Is it appropriate for the level of ability of the child?
Do the tests as a whole relate to all fields in which the child reads?
Do they adequately measure all important aspects of reading comprehension?

Unfortunately, some published informal tests, and standardized tests as well, are mainly tests of the child's ability to get the literal meanings of the words, phrases and sentences. They place little emphasis on getting the general thought, seeing relationships and making inferences. In addition, few standardized tests are available which are framed in the vocabulary of the various subject matter fields.

The teacher, therefore, finds it necessary to revise and supplement published tests. She may construct original test items using the vocabulary taught informally in the course of classroom activities. She may test the child's comprehension of: an original or an adapted passage, a story that is new to the children, a poem, an excerpt from literature, a selection from a social studies or science book, a problem from an arithmetic text, a health leaflet, or an article in a newspaper or magazine related to the subject of study. In the lower grades, material from experience charts, children's logs and notes may also serve as the basis for test items.

Reading tests should be related to all the subject matter fields; and test items should measure all the specific abilities involved in getting meaning from printed matter. Suggestions will be given for the kinds of items which can be used to measure these specific comprehension abilities.

A. *Getting the literal meanings of words, phrases and sentences.* This aspect of reading comprehension involves knowing the meaning of the words used, selecting the particular connotation of the words as intended by the author, getting meaning from groups of words and noting details contained in the material.

In the beginning stages of learning to read, pictures may be used to help appraise this aspect of comprehension. A series of words may be presented with an easily recognizable picture which illustrates one of the words. The child should be directed to circle the word or draw a line under the word which gives the same meaning as the picture or to draw a line from the picture to the word. This form of picture item may be used also with a series of phrases or short sentences.

For children whose reading comprehension can be tested with reading matter, items like the following may be found useful:

1. Present a word followed by a series of suggested meanings. Have the child underline the meaning which is best for the key word; e.g.,

    To *possess* means to _____claim   borrow   own   reach

    This type of item may be used also with phrases and short sentences.

2. For a word with several connotations depending upon the context in which it appears, present the several meanings and have the child select the connotation intended from the context; e.g.,

    He found the information he wanted in the *body* of the letter. In this sentence, *body* means

        an individual
        the physical person
        the chief part of something
        a group of things or facts

3. Direct the child to classify words into several categories. For example, list the following words under the headings *Industry, Government* and *Entertainment:*

    ambassador, theatre, mining, legislation, baseball,
    suffrage, manufacture, excursion, transportation

    Or, find the word which does not belong:
    mining, manufacture, theatre, transportation

4. Prepare a list of paired words, some pairs having the same meaning and some having different meanings. Provide a space between the words of each pair. Direct the child to write in the space S for *same* or D for *different*; e.g.,

        sad_____gloomy
        praise_____disapprove

    This type of item may be used also with phrases and short sentences.

5. List a number of words which are to be matched with words or phrases in a parallel column. Have the child draw a line between those which mean the same or direct him to write the appropriate letter in front of the number, e.g.,

	a. troubled
_____1. roam	b. scatter
_____2. anxious	c. drown
_____3. vicinity	d. neighborhood
	e. wander

This type of item may be used also with phrases and short sentences.

6. On a sheet of paper or a card, print a direction and observe the child's performance of the task assigned; e.g.,

Color the ball red.

Turn to page 42 in your reading workbook and do the best exercise you find there.

7. Prepare objective-type items calling for specific details to be found in a selection; e.g.,

Completion: The birthday party was for _____

Multiple-choice: The birthday party was for
           Betty   Jean   Susan   Jane

True-False: The birthday party was for Jean____ True   False

B. Seeing relationships among the ideas expressed. Reading comprehension involves weaving together the ideas expressed, bringing together associated details, explaining some details in terms of others, noting direct and indirect relationships, making inferences from the facts given. Items of the objective type are especially useful in testing for understanding in reading. The particular items to be used depend, of course, on the passage to which they apply. Some passages lend themselves more to testing for specific details or getting the general thought than for seeing relationships. The general test of reading comprehension, however, should include some items calling for seeing relationships and making inferences.

Completion items like the following, the answers to which may or may not be given in the passage, are useful in appraising the ability to see or infer relationships:

Johnnie lost his way because_____
Johnnie lost his way probably because_____
Plants need sunlight because_____
Many railroads were built after 1849 because_____
If Mr. Jones had not gone to the store, he probably would not have_____
What do you think Robbie did then?_____

Multiple-choice items may be used, for example:

Johnnie lost his way because
———— it was dark
————he had been chasing butterflies
————he wanted to run away
————he was far from home

This item may also be presented in the true-false form, thus:

Johnnie lost his way because it was dark_____True   False

The advantages and disadvantages of these various types of objective items are discussed in Chapter III.

In certain types of printed matter, seeing relationships depends especially upon the ability to note the order in which the ideas are presented. This ability is needed, for example, in order to appreciate action in narratives, note cause and effect in expository passages and in order to follow sets of directions, as for cooking or constructing something. The devices listed below are useful in helping to determine whether or not the child is able to follow the organization of this type of material.

Direct the child to list the events or steps in order in which they occur.

Present the events or steps in scrambled order and have the child arrange or number them in correct order.

Present key words, phrases or sentences in scrambled order and have the child arrange or number them correctly.

Have the child outline a given selection.

Present several main headings for a selection of two or more paragraphs; direct the child to outline the ideas under these headings.

Present the main headings and the subheadings for a selection in scrambled order; direct the child to arrange them in correct order.

Have the child follow a set of printed instructions and judge from the finished product whether he has been able to follow the directions in sequence.

C. *Getting the main thought and general tone of the material.* Comprehension involves also selecting the main idea, getting the general thought and reacting to the material as a whole. The child may be asked to reproduce the gist of a passage in a one- or two-sentence summary. He may be directed to find the summary sentence, if there is one. He may be tested with objective items which start with:

The main idea in this article is
This paragraph is mostly about
The best title for this story is

With descriptive matter, an item like the following may serve to summarize the general thought or tone:

The boy in this story is very
    happy
    lonesome
    brave
    selfish

The child judges the quality of literary materials. He catches their mood. He notes their style. He detects the author's personality. The depth of the child's appreciation of literature and his sensitivity to its emotional overtones may be revealed by means of essay questions which direct him to evaluate selections with respect to specific points. Testing by means of essay questions is discussed in Chapter III. Objective items like the following may be found useful and less time-consuming:

This poem makes you feel
    sad
    joyful
    angry
    disappointed

The style of the author is
_____light   or   _____heavy
_____complicated   or   _____simple
_____interesting   or   _____dull
_____ matter-of-fact   or   _____imaginative

The writer is probably
_____mean   or   _____kind
_____happy   or   _____unhappy
_____rich   or   _____poor
_____young   or   _____old

With materials of a persuasive nature, the child needs to recognize the author's general purpose or his point of view. Items like these may be found useful in testing for this ability:

The author wrote this mainly to
    entertain you
    give you some facts
    tell you how to do something
    make you want to do something

This author would be considered
    very old-fashioned
    conservative
    very modern

Similar generalizations based on an evaluation of the material as a whole may be presented as statements with which the child is asked to express his agreement or disagreement; e.g.,

The main point is that foods should be chosen carefully   Agree   Disagree

The chief purpose of this article is to make you buy Cracklies	Agree	Disagree
The story shows that the author does not like children	Agree	Disagree
The writer of this selection is probably foreign	Agree	Disagree
This story is full of mystery	Agree	Disagree
This poem is written in a dignified style	Agree	Disagree
This writer likes to give many colorful details	Agree	Disagree
The clock in this story is treated as if it were an old man	Agree	Disagree

Planning the Informal Test of Reading Comprehension

In constructing an informal test of reading comprehension, the teacher will need to select the aspect or aspects of comprehension she wishes to measure—getting the literal meaning of the words, phrases and sentences, seeing relationships among the ideas expressed, getting the main thought and the general tone of the material, or some combination of these. If she plans to test only one aspect of comprehension, she will direct her questions accordingly. For example, if she has been emphasizing the ability to get the general thought of a passage, she may draw up a series of items which reveal this ability specifically. In this case, she might direct the child to skim a number of selected paragraphs and answer an appropriate question for each; e.g., a multiple choice item, a completion item or a summary sentence.

She may, however, plan to measure a number of aspects of reading comprehension. For this purpose, she may use a single selection, and prepare a number of different items appropriate for testing these various aspects. The items should be of appropriate difficulty. They should permit the child to display his full ability in the aspects of reading being appraised, but they should not be so difficult that his reading ability is not measured at all. A survey type of examination is economical and efficient. It is comprehensive and at the same time useful in diagnosis. It gives both teacher and pupil an appreciation of the various abilities which are components of reading comprehension.

A survey test like the following, for example, may be found useful in appraising the reading comprehension of a particular group. The paragraph was adapted from an elementary science textbook. The aspects of comprehension which the items were designed to measure are indicated for the teacher in the right-hand column.

Directions: Read this paragraph carefully and answer the questions about it. For each question, you are given four answers. Check the one which best completes the statement.

In very high mountain regions there are places where the snow falls frequently, and most of the time it is so cold that the snow does not melt. When the snow gets to be hundreds of feet deep, it packs down hard and the bottom turns into a solid layer of ice. As the snow continues to fall on the top, more and more ice is formed and the frozen mass becomes heavier and heavier. Finally, after many years, this enormous mass begins to break away and slip down the mountainside. It acts like a river, moving slowly, very slowly. In a day, it advances perhaps only a few inches. This great river of ice is called a glacier.

1. This paragraph tells chiefly about the way
    a river moves
    snow changes to water
    a glacier is formed
    ice is formed

Item 1 is intended to measure the ability to recognize the main idea in a paragraph.

2. The author is trying to
    tell you how to travel in high mountains
    tell you to be careful when ice breaks
    give you information about glaciers
    make you afraid of glaciers

Item 2 is intended to measure the ability to recognize the author's purpose.

3. In size, a glacier is most like
    an icicle on your roof
    an ice pond in your backyard
    a rock as large as this room
    a tall apartment house

Item 3 is intended to measure the ability to make a general inference from the facts given.

4. In a glacier, ice is found mostly
    at the top
    at the bottom
    in the front
    at the sides

Item 4 is intended to measure the ability to note a detail.

5. The snow piles up high because
    the mountains are high
    glaciers are formed
    snow turns into ice
    the snow does not melt

Item 5 is intended to measure the ability to see a relationship.

6. A glacier begins to move because it is
    heavy
    frozen
    melting
    in layers

Item 6 is intended to measure the ability to infer a relationship.

7. The snow falls and gets very deep. Then it

    moves slowly, packs down hard, turns to ice

    packs down hard, moves slowly, turns to ice

    slips, turns to ice, packs down hard

    packs down hard, turns to ice, moves slowly

Item 7 is intended to measure the ability to follow the organization or sequence of ideas as presented in the paragraph.

8. To *advance* means the same as to

    increase

    go ahead

    pile up

    turn

Item 8 is intended to measure the ability to get the literal meaning of a word.

9. *Mass,* as used in the paragraph, means

    something crowded and jumbled

    something big and weighty

    a collection of things

    a great body of people

Item 9 is intended to measure the ability to select the appropriate connotation of a word from its context.

10. According to the paragraph, a glacier *acts like a river.* This is true because a river

    is water

    sometimes has ice in it

    is in motion

    is very deep

Item 10 is intended to measure the ability to interpret figurative language.

OBJECTIVE 3

The Child Gains Independence in Basic Reading Skills

One of the most important objectives of the reading program is the child's development of independence in basic reading skills. At the start of the school program, the child is just beginning to recognize slight differences in pictures, geometric forms, numbers and general word configurations. He is still somewhat far-sighted. He may tend to examine the printed page from bottom to top or from right to left, as if it were a new toy. He has difficulty in handling a book and in turning pages. With increasing muscular development, his eyes become accommodated to printed matter close to him. He becomes able to make fine ocular adjustments and to discriminate among word patterns, among words and among letters.

He will need to establish the essential reading habits—for example, to move his eyes from left to right, to keep them on a line, to sweep them back to the next line, to proceed from the top to the bottom of the page. He must acquire the meaning of and learn to recognize at sight a large number of printed words. He must develop power in using a variety of techniques to work out the recognition and meaning of unfamiliar words. Gradually, with continued reading experience, he will increase the number of words he can perceive with comprehension in one eye-fixation. He will speed up his reading and he will be able to vary that speed to meet the nature and difficulty of the material and his purpose in reading. These are among the basic reading skills which the teacher observes as she helps the child from day to day in learning to read.

Observation

The teacher is especially watchful for any disabilities or difficulties which the child may develop. She is sensitive to limited sight vocabulary, unfamiliarity with common phonograms and to poor techniques of word analysis. She notices finger-pointing, mouth-moving, squinting. She is conscious of such deep-seated causes of difficulty as poor vision, limited hearing, foreign-language background, emotional disturbance, or low intelligence.*

Records and checklists

At times the teacher may merely make a mental note of these deficiencies. Sometimes, she may jot them down. For a few selected children, she may keep anecdotal records. Periodically, she may write a brief report of the reading progress of each of the children in her class.

A convenient device for recording difficulties in basic reading skills is a checklist like the one which appears on page 115. In preparing such a checklist, a list of possible items is made up in advance, and the form is mimeographed. After observation and testing, the teacher checks those items which apply to the child and enters additional comments on either the face or the reverse side. The same copy of the checklist with double entries may be used for a child at the beginning and end of the year. The sheet may then be passed on to the child's next teacher who may enter her appraisal by drawing two vertical lines and checking in these new columns the items which apply at the time of her report. In making such reports it is important to indicate the date to which they apply and the grade level of the reading matter on which they are based.

* For suggestions for the study of reading failure, see A *Diagnostic Approach to the Reading Program, Part I*, Educational Research Bulletin Number 3 of this series.

Tests

Silent and oral reading tests help the teacher to direct her observation. Some of these tests are especially useful where diagnosis is required as in cases of retardation in reading.

The oral reading test. Occasionally the teacher asks the child to read a passage orally so that she may examine his basic reading skills more closely.* Sometimes, she may select a passage particularly suited to the reading level of a group and have the various members of the group read it individually. She may, however, construct a special oral test by means of which she can estimate the child's reading grade placement either for instruction, for easy independent reading, or for supplementary materials. This test may be prepared by selecting a paragraph or two from each of a series of graded basic readers or textbooks. The child starts with the passage which he can read with ease and proceeds through the more and more difficult passages. When he reaches a word which is difficult for him, he is allowed a little time to work it out; if he still fails, the teacher reads the word for him and records his attempt on her copy of the passage or on a separate piece of paper. The test may be followed by a short oral quiz on general content. The teacher jots down other observations and may later analyze her notes for common errors, weaknesses in word analysis and other basic difficulties, or she may use a checklist to record her observations as the child reads.

Checklist of Difficulties in Basic Reading Skills

Word Recognition

Has limited stock of sight-recognition words
Does not recognize common phonograms
Reverses letters
Reverses simple common words
Reads many words incorrectly
Omits words
Adds words

Word Analysis

Hesitates to try unfamiliar words
Recognizes word beginning and guesses rest incorrectly
Does not use context clues
Depends too heavily on context clues
Does not look for recognizable parts

* For this and other diagnostic classroom methods, see also *A Diagnostic Approach to the Reading Program, Part II,* Educational Research Bulletin Number 4 of this series.

Depends too heavily on phonetic analysis
Substitutes words
Does not recognize word errors

Phrasing, Fluency

Ignores punctuation
Reads word by word
Habitually repeats words or expressions
Reads too slowly, ploddingly
Reads too fast, carelessly

Ocular Motor Skills

Holds book too close
Loses place
Does not have left-to-right directional habit
Return sweep to next line is too slow
Points finger
Moves head
Eye-voice span too narrow
Eye movements poor

Speech

Mispronounces certain words frequently
Enunciates poorly
Stutters or stammers
Voice weak
Voice loud

General Observations

Does not understand what he is reading
Does not show interest in reading

Other Characteristics

Unfavorable attitude toward school
Poor work habits
Emotionally disturbed
Socially immature
Low intelligence
Limited speaking vocabulary
Foreign language background
Poor home environment
Poor hearing

Poor vision
Poor motor control
Other physical handicap

Testing visual discrimination. The child's general ability to make visual discriminations may be tested by asking him to detect likenesses and differences. The material to be used and the fineness of the discrimination to be required depends on the maturity of the child. Generally, pictures and geometric forms are suitable material for the reading readiness stage. Groups of words, single words and later, letters may be used in the beginning reading stage. The following types of exercises lend themselves especially to group testing:

Present several pictures, all the same except one. Ask the child to find the one that is different. This item may be made difficult by using for the unlike picture one which is very similar to the others. The pictures may be kept in an envelope and used repeatedly with individual children. A test would include a number of items arranged in horizontal rows across the page. This type of exercise may be used also with designs, patterns, geometrical forms, numbers, groups of words, words or letters.

Present several pictures, some the same and some different. Ask the child to find those that are the same. This type of item may be treated as above.

Present pairs of pictures, geometric forms, patterns, numbers, words or groups of words, some of the pairs being the same and some different. Ask the child to mark those that are the same with an *S* and those that are different with a *D*. If this exercise is used with words, a test may include pairs like home—dome, house—horse, was—saw, no—on, bone—done.

Prepare a passage using repeatedly a number of words which look very much alike. Present in print one of these words. Ask the child to underline or circle it wherever he finds it on the page.

Compile a list of the words which appear in the classroom on signs, labels, posters, directions. Include also words from experience charts, and those placed on the blackboard in planning the daily program. Arrange these words in four or five columns on a mimeographed page. For each row across, pronounce one of the words and ask the child to find it and mark it. The list may be used four or five times, each time for recognition of a different set of words, one word in each row. The child is supplied with a fresh copy for each set. This exercise may be made more difficult by placing in a single row words which look somewhat alike.

Testing directional orientation. It is sometimes desirable to test for directional orientation because it has been found that children who are left-handed and right-eyed or right-handed and left-eyed may have difficulty in acquiring the left-to-right reading habit. Eye dominance may be discovered by requiring the child to sight an object through a one-inch square hole made in a sheet of paper. Ask the child to pick up the paper, and as he does this, note the hand he prefers to use. Tell him to hold the paper at arm's length and look through the hole at a specific object some distance away. The teacher stands near the child, facing him, and observes to which eye he spontaneously places the hole. This method yields only a rough index of eye preference and the child should be given a number of trials.

The tendency to make an excessive number of reversals may be discovered by having the child copy numbers like 3, 6 and 9, and letters like Z, N, E, b, d. Mimeographed copies of this test may be prepared for all the members of a group. The letters and numbers should be large so that the child will have no difficulty in seeing them before he is asked to copy them.

Testing eye movements. The teacher may study the child's eye movements by watching his reflection in a mirror as he reads. Sitting at his right with the mirror in her hand, which she can focus on the child's eyes as he reads, she notes how smoothly the child's eyes move along the line, how many regressive movements his eyes make, and how many stops (eye fixations) he has for each line. She would be in a better position to observe, however, if she were to face the child directly. The following device is useful for this purpose.

Cut a hole about 3/16 of an inch square in the center of a piece of cardboard about 9 x 12 inches. Paste 3 or 4 paragraphs cut from a reading text, on the cardboard. The child sits facing the teacher. The teacher holds the cardboard so that the child can read the paragraphs naturally and so that she can see through the peephole. As the child reads silently, the teacher may observe the number of eye fixations and regressions per line as well as possible confusion of eye movements.

Testing eye span. The following methods are useful for studying the child's eye span, that is, the number of words he can take in with comprehension at one glance. By counting the number of words which the child can read during a brief exposure, a rough index of eye span may be obtained.

Direct the child to read a passage orally. As he approaches the end of the line, cover the last few words with a card. Note how many of the covered words the child can reproduce.

Prepare a series of flash cards on which are printed words, phrases and sentences of varying lengths. Direct the child to read them aloud as they are exposed for a few seconds.

Print a series of words, phrases or short sentences in a column on a large sheet of paper or cardboard. Direct the child to read each item aloud as it is exposed for a few seconds. To form a shutter for exposing one item at a time, hold a small card directly above the item and another card directly below it. To close the shutter, bring down the upper card to meet the lower one. After the child has given his response, move the lower card down to expose the next item.

Testing speed of reading. Speed of reading depends, of course, on the material being read—the difficulty of the vocabulary, the type of sentence structure, the number of details presented, and the technical nature of the content. The teacher notes the child's varying rates of reading as he handles materials for recreational and study purposes. For the different types of materials, she gets a measure of the relative speed of the child in comparison with the rest of his group or the rest of his class.

Rate of reading a particular passage may be roughly measured by means of group techniques. A passage should be selected which most of the group can be expected to finish in a short time, perhaps in three to five minutes. Before starting, inform the children that when they have finished, they will be asked a few general questions on what they have read. A short objective test of four or five items relating to the main idea or general content should be ready. After the signal to start has been given and the time noted, any of the following procedures may be followed:

At the end of the time alloted, direct the children to stop and note the last word read (the number of the line and the number of the word). Have them count the number of words read and divide by the number of minutes. The quotient gives the average number of words read per minute.

Direct the children to raise their hands when they have finished. When a child raises his hand, note the time and the child's name on a time record. It would be convenient to prepare this time record in fifteen second intervals; the children's names may be recorded next to the appropriate time. The average speed is computed by dividing the number of words in the passage by the number of minutes and quarters of a minute consumed.

A variation of the above is to have the children record the time elapsed. Direct them to look at the blackboard when they have finished, and jot down the number they find there. Fifteen seconds after the signal to start, write 1 on the blackboard. Fifteen seconds later, erase 1 and write 2. Fifteen seconds later, erase 2 and write 3, and so on until all children have finished. The children or the teacher can compute the average speed of reading by first dividing the number they have recorded by 4, thus converting it into minutes, and then by dividing the number of words in the passage by the result.

Such procedures require careful explanation and a sample demonstration. Otherwise, the children may be influenced by the novelty of the timing and not give an adequate or representative performance in reading.

OBJECTIVE 4

The Child Learns How to Find and Use Printed Matter

Another objective of the reading program is to develop in the child the ability to find and use the printed materials he needs for both recreation and study. The abilities which are involved in finding and using material specifically for the purpose of information or study are generally called *study skills* and the chief techniques for appraising them are observation and testing.

Observation

The teacher may informally observe the facility with which the child finds desired information in sources like the dictionary, textbook, encyclopedia, reference book or newspaper. She may note the frequency of his visits to the class, school or public library and his ability to find books, magazines, newspaper articles, graphs or pictures on various subjects. She may judge whether the child is learning when to refer to printed matter, whether he is becoming familiar with the best sources for particular kinds of information and whether he is growing in ability to evaluate independently the appropriateness of material for his purpose. She may note whether he is developing a critical attitude toward printed matter and is judging the reliability of the information it contains as well as the conclusions that can be drawn from it.

Tests

Tests aid in the appraisal of study skills. Appropriate test exercises and items are suggested here.

Testing the ability to locate material in given sources. In order to appraise the child's ability to obtain information from various reference materials, he may be given exercises of the following types:

Using a dictionary or an encyclopedia indicate: (a) the pages on which the specified words will be found; or (b) the definition, pronunciation or spelling of given words; or (c) arrange a series of words in alphabetical order, and then look up their meanings.

Consult the table of contents in a given book and indicate the page or pages on which specified stories, topics or chapters may be found.

Using the index in a textbook, indicate the page or pages on which information about given topics can be found.

Using an encyclopedia, indicate the page or pages for articles on specified topics.

Using a railroad time schedule, find out what time the next train leaves for Albany.

From a bar, line or circle graph, or a pictograph, find out what country needs the most food.

Using a map or globe, find out in what direction Hollywood lies from New York; or approximate the distance between New York and Chicago.

From an automobile map determine what route numbers you must follow to get from New York to Buffalo.

Find from the World Almanac what important event occurred on August 14, 1945.

Find the telephone numbers for given individuals from the telephone directory.

Order a dinner from a menu.

Order items from a store catalog, giving item number and price.

Testing the ability to locate sources of information. To help discover whether the child knows where to look for particular materials, the teacher may ask him to indicate the best sources for specific topics. These topics may relate to the social studies, science, biography, literature or to any of the other subject matter areas. He might be given exercises of the following types:

In which of the following books might you find an interesting short story about a famous individual? (Teacher gives the name of the individual and suggests several source books.)

11. DIAGNOSTIC METHODS IN THE CLASSROOM

Board of Education of the City of New York

In the preceding bulletin the underlying approaches to the reading problem were discussed. Against this general background, the present bulletin will describe the application of specific diagnostic procedures, both in the appraisal of reading achievement and in the analysis of reading difficulties. Because the field is so extensive, the emphasis has been placed

Reprinted from *A Diagnostic Approach to the Reading Program, Part II,* Educational Research Bulletin of the Bureau of Reference, Research, and Statistics, No. 4 (April 1942), pp. 1–21. By permission of J. Wayne Wrightstone, Bureau of Educational Research of the New York City Board of Education.

upon techniques related to classroom needs. These methods and techniques must, of course, be interpreted in terms of the grade being studied. It is obvious that the diagnostic methods employed in the study of first year children will differ considerably from those used in the study of fifth year children. Although many of the phases of diagnosis presented here will have applicability to all grades, the emphasis is largely upon those procedures suitable in the middle grades. For discussion purposes these procedures are treated separately. In a balanced program of diagnosis, however, they are recognized as interdependent.

1. The Measurement of Achievement in Reading

Standardized tests are widely used in diagnosis.

It is hardly necessary to discuss here the place or the value of standardized tests. Tests are perhaps the most widely used instruments of diagnosis in the school reading program. The schools have accepted their use on such sound bases as: (1) the standards which they offer for the measurement of pupil achievement; (2) the scientifically devised content; (3) the objectivity of administration and scoring; (4) the availability of parallel forms for comparison. In the second bulletin of this series,[1] tests and measures were discussed in terms of reading objectives and appropriate tests were suggested for each objective. The standardized test will, therefore, be considered here primarily in terms of its place in the diagnostic program.

The selection of tests involves certain problems.

There are a number of considerations which should influence the selection of tests:

(1) *The purposes of the testing program need to be clearly defined.* Tests should be selected with specific purposes in mind. If, for example, the teacher wishes to ascertain the general reading ability of her class, she should plan to use the type of test best designed to give such an overview of her group's achievement. It was pointed out in Bulletin No. 2 that an appraisal program includes the evaluation of many aspects of reading.

(2) *It is important to determine how suitable a test may be for a specific grade.* Publishers sometimes claim too wide a range for their tests; for instance, a "primary" test recommended for grades one to three

---

[1] *Appraisal of Growth in Reading.* Educational Research Bulletin, No. 2.

may actually be of value only in the second year. Nor is a test in which an appreciable number of children make maximum scores a good instrument for the class concerned. It is well worth setting up a grade committee to study a number of tests from these viewpoints before a final selection is made.

(3) *An intensive diagnostic study would involve several steps in testing.* In such a study the results of a general survey test would be found adequate only as a first step. The test results would then be analyzed and the poorest readers selected for more complete diagnosis. A diagnostic test would then be given for the purpose of acquiring greater insight into their difficulties.

(4) *It is always necessary to keep in mind the limitations of any one test.* No single test can be all-inclusive since it is practically impossible to represent within one test all aspects of reading. Even the best of tests is, therefore, only a guide—a diagnostic check or inventory of certain specific skills or abilities which the author has aimed to measure. If the test is used as the sole criterion of achievement, serious distortions in the instructional program may occur. Not only may the temptation arise to teach pupils to meet test requirements but the need for developing a variety of reading skills and a well-balanced reading program may become obscured.

Tests should be administered with care.

To maintain objectivity. Certain precautions in the use of tests cannot be over-emphasized. The whole complex and scientific process of standardization aims to produce a test as objective as it is humanly possible to obtain. To that end, the instructions for giving, the timing, and the scoring guides have all been carefully worked out in order that the teacher who uses the results may, with confidence in their reliability, compare her pupils with similar groups of the school population. Where this objectivity has been destroyed by any departure in the administration or scoring of the tests, the results are not merely invalid; they are likely, if utilized, to do more harm than good. Where, on the other hand, the instructions have been carefully observed, the teacher has in her hands a scientific check-up on her own subjective judgment.

To secure maximum response. It is also important that the tests be given in an atmosphere which will stimulate the fullest cooperation of the children. The most dependable measure of achievement is secured when the child puts forth his best effort. If he does not respond with maximum attention, the score which he achieves will not give a true picture of his ability. A child's performance may be influenced by many different factors; emotional difficulties may produce lack of cooperation;

poor physical conditions at the time of the testing may interfere with ability to work well; and so on. The presence of such difficulties should be noted on the cover of the test, the ratings on such papers discounted, and, if possible, another test administered under more favorable conditions. Where more permanent factors operate to the child's disadvantage, such as defective vision or hearing, they should be made an integral part of the record, in order that the ratings may at all times be properly interpreted.

Test results yield valuable data.

The exacting process of testing with a standardized instrument of measurement would hardly be said to justify itself if all that resulted were age and grade scores. Experience has shown that the results secured through these tests can yield a wealth of information. The quality and quantity of this information, it should be added, will depend to a great extent on the degree of "digging out" that takes place. Suggestions for the study of test results will be presented in the following pages.

The study of test scores involves several procedures.

Finding the average achievement. What is the general picture of the achievement of the class? How does it compare on the whole with other similar groups? The answers to these questions may be determined by comparing class results with the norms furnished by the author of the test. The first step in such a study of class achievement is to make a distribution of the children's scores. Then, by securing the median or the arithmetic mean, the teacher is able to compare the average achievement of her class with the average attainment of the groups upon which the tests were standardized. If, at the beginning of the term, a teacher of a 5A class finds that the highest grade score obtained on a reading test is 4.5, the obvious and practical conclusion she may draw is that her instruction for the time being cannot be geared to a 5A level. Should she find, on the other hand, that her 5A class has an average grade score of 5.2, she may assume that this test indicates—for the type of reading measured—satisfactory achievement for her class as a group.

Finding the range of achievement. It will soon become apparent to this teacher, however, that the average of 5.2 tells only part of the story. Upon further examining the distribution of scores she notes wide variability. Three children have scored below 3.0 and seven have scores of 6.0 or over. Perhaps this range of differences comes as a surprise; perhaps it merely confirms a subjective judgment already formed. In either case, such a study of the range of achievement reveals the complexity of the instructional problem and can be used to lay the groundwork for the later organization of group instruction within the classroom.

Recording the results. The scores obtained are an important part of the child's record of achievement and should, therefore, be entered on some form of summary sheet or on pupil record cards. It would scarcely seem necessary to emphasize the importance of insuring accurate scoring, yet experience has shown that this need is frequently underestimated. Computations based on the scores must also be made with the greatest care. If the instructional program is to be influenced by achievement and intelligence ratings on standardized tests, it is imperative that these records be accurate. In computing an IQ, for example, the simple reversal of the MA and the CA will cause a child with an IQ of 125 to be reported as having an IQ of .80. It is obvious how such an error once recorded officially can become a continuous source of confusion and misinformation.

The analysis of test items is an essential step.

Even the group test which has not been labeled "diagnostic" can be made into an instrument of diagnosis. The teacher is, of course, interested in discovering the types of errors made and the nature of the material which presented special difficulty. It is through a study of test responses that she secures this information. The more intensively she examines test items and analyzes test responses, the greater is the diagnostic value of any test she administers.

Finding types of errors. In making this kind of inventory of achievement, a summary of the frequency of failure of the test items is extremely helpful. Common weaknesses will then stand out in bold relief. Naturally, many children will not be equal to the difficult parts of a standardized test and a fourth year teacher, analyzing the responses of her class, need not be much concerned with the items failed on sixth and seventh year levels. It is quite likely, however, that as she makes the analysis she will find herself becoming greatly interested in the way her good readers have functioned in these upper levels. The extent to which they have handled successfully the more difficult material will sometimes furnish clues to the type of enriched instruction which should be planned for this group of superior readers.

Such an analysis of the strengths and weaknesses of class reading achievement can be an invaluable guide to instruction. For example, in one study of the responses on the test papers of second, third, and fourth year children, it was found that—

1. Many children were unable to identify or interpret words that ask questions, such as *what, why, when, who,* etc.

2. Many children had concepts of distance and size which (as indicated in their reactions to such words as *far, large,* etc.), were greatly confused and in need of clarification in terms of their own experience.

3. There was marked inability to follow exact directions. After reading a paragraph the children would be given such instruction as: "Write *one word* which tells about. . . .," or "Name the *three things* mentioned. . . .," etc. Their responses frequently showed good general comprehension but failure to interpret correctly specific directions of this kind. To such a question, for example, as "*Which word* tells how Helen's sister felt?" a typically incorrect response would be a full sentence, "She felt very sad."

4. When asked to indicate the meaning of a word, many children responded with other associations rather than with synonyms. In each of the following multiple choices, for example, the child was asked to draw a circle around the word "that *most nearly means the same* as the first word in the row." The words italicized indicate the choices frequently made by the children.

cap	—	house	hat	*head*	face	hair
small	—	*big*	funny	wide	little	child
canoe	—	team	boat	sleigh	trunk	*Indian*
shut	—	*door*	street	open	leave	close
lamb	—	goat	ham	sheep	*fleece*	calf

Even a superficial examination of these responses shows the nature of the association underlying each incorrect answer. This tendency of young children to interpret meanings through associations rather than synonyms appears to be a developmental phase suggestive of broader teaching approaches to vocabulary building. Perhaps there should be fuller use of the specific associations children bring to words before the generalization is even attempted.

Using test results in teaching. Many implications for the instructional program emerge from such analyses of test responses. In the process of translating test data into teaching, however, certain dangers should be avoided. Few teachers need to be told that to teach material *in the test* is not only unethical but a step that renders the test useless as a measure of growth or as a diagnostic instrument for future use. If a test reveals that many children failed to answer questions correctly because they did not recognize or understand the use of *what, how* and *who,* the teacher would, of course, make sure that these words were learned and understood. She would do so, however, in a variety of situations apart from the context of the test itself.

Another danger which has been mentioned before is that of interpreting test results in such a way that teaching tends to become restricted to the type of reading which is being measured. An analysis may show, for example, that on a certain test most of the children responded correctly when the information was stated in the text but were unable to answer several questions in which they were called upon to predict a future happening which had been merely implied. The teacher who thereupon concludes that she must "teach how to predict outcomes" is interpreting her findings with unfortunate narrowness. A far more tenable conclusion would be that the simplest types of comprehension in reading have probably been over-emphasized and that what her pupils now need is every possible opportunity to use their critical powers—to infer, to generalize, and to form judgments on the basis of what they have read. It is safe to predict that one of the outcomes of such a reading program would be an increased power to predict outcomes!

Studying the factors that influence scores. A test score is never an absolute value and should never be used as though it were. Sometimes the child's performance on a standardized test is affected by unexpected or unpredictable factors. In the course of analyzing test items, it is often possible to estimate the effect such factors may have had upon the test score. It has already been pointed out how lack of rapport or physical inadequacy may influence responses to the test situation. Factors inherent in the structure of the test may also be significant. In the experience of the reading clinics and the experimental classes, some of these factors operated frequently to affect test responses.

1. *Test format.* The organization of content, the placement of items, and the format of the test itself may operate to produce unnecessary errors. Children frequently omit lines and even paragraphs where material runs over to a second page. Some children, particularly those with poor coordination, have real difficulty fitting a written response into the space allotted. Still others will often misinterpret the pictorial materials included in many tests.

2. *Time limits.* Short-timed tests, such as those with six- or eight-minute limits, will for many children give only an incomplete picture of reading power. It was found in the clinics that after remedial instruction many fifth and sixth year children were able to reach their grade levels on the New Stanford Reading Tests, whereas they frequently were unable to achieve more than third and fourth grade scores in such short-timed tests as the Gates Silent Reading Tests. For some of these children it was not only speed of reading that was being tested but also speed of reaction. It was not unusual for a slow-moving child to take so long to organize himself for a rapid reading situation that he would hardly have begun before the time was up.

3. *Guessing.* Another factor which may affect a test score is the element of guessing. Two children of definitely unequal ability to read may both obtain the same score. It is most important for the teacher to know that one child worked carefully and accurately, omitting responses to items beyond his reading ability while the other, guessing wildly and often successfully, appeared to

cover more ground. In the course of a testing program administered to some fourth year classes it was found necessary to study carefully the results of the subtest on word meaning. This particular test contains 80 words, progressing in difficulty. The child is asked to indicate the meaning of the word by underlining one of five choices. It was obvious from an analysis of the test papers that a number of children by mere chance had underlined correctly an appreciable number of words they did not know. Some of them had succeeded with words in the upper levels of the test such as *choleric,* *elucidate,* and *fundamental,* when they were unable to read even the simplest words at the beginning of the test such as *grape, tall,* and *breeze.* These papers were noted "unreliable because of guessing." When these children were later retested, after remedial instruction which developed word-building skills and habits of greater accuracy, some of them made scores lower than previously. On the surface, to judge only the scores, they seemed to have retrogressed. A follow-up study of these test results showed, however, that guessing was no longer rampant and that the scores were beginning to register achievement more reliably. Only the fact that the test papers had been studied made it possible to interpret these lower ratings in their relation to the improvement which had actually taken place.

Informal or instructional tests are useful.

For testing and teaching. The more information one can gain about a child's responses to a test, the greater is the diagnostic value of such material. Why, for example, does he underline one word rather than another? What makes him draw a line to the picture which is so obviously incorrect? Is he guessing or is there behind the wrong response a reason important to the child? What confusions and misunderstandings are in his mind when he responds as he does?

For acquiring knowledge of this nature the informal instructional test is invaluable. The limitations which have been indicated in the use of the standardized test—where content must not be used as teaching material—do not affect these informal materials. They may be used *both* to diagnose weaknesses and to correct them. In the reading clinics and experimental classes extensive use was made of exercises of this kind. When difficulties were revealed in a standardized test, informal tests were devised to teach and give practice in the necessary skills.

For interpreting responses. Many workbooks contain this informal type of testing-teaching material. The full diagnostic value of these exercises cannot be obtained, however, unless through question and discussion with the children their reactions are studied. Through such an approach it is often possible to gain insight into the origin of certain errors. One child, for example, had answered incorrectly in his exercise a question on telling time. The right answer was "twenty-five minutes to three." He had written "a quarter to three." When the teacher asked him to explain his answer he did so with unexpected logic. "Twenty-five cents is a quarter so why can't twenty-five to three be a quarter to three?" In another exercise, the children were instructed to "cross out the word which does not seem to belong: Dolly   Sally   Tom   Polly." One of the boys crossed out "Polly." Upon being questioned, he replied, "Dolly, Sally, and Tom are children's names and Polly is a *bird*." He had never heard of "Polly" as a girl's name.

2. Systematic Observation of Children

Direct observation provides essential information about the child.

Emphasis has been placed increasingly on the study of children through direct observation, and much research is at present being devoted to the development of scientific techniques in this field. The type of information which can be gathered through procedures such as testing needs to be supplemented by a picture of the child in action. Test analysis will reveal the respone in a relatively static situation; direct observation makes possible the study of reactions in living, changing situations.

Although the teacher may not be equipped to carry on an elaborate program of observation, she has many opportunities in the classroom to "diagnose" in an informal manner through direct observation. She looks at the children in her class for most of the school day. When she not only "looks" but "sees" and is able to interpret what she sees, in a diagnostic sense she begins to observe.

There are several characteristics of good classroom observation.

It is organized. Many phases of classroom activity lend themselves to fruitful observation. The teacher needs, therefore, to systematize her program; to arrange in some order suitable to herself the method by which she will study such aspects as vision, language development, etc. Sometimes a check list of factors to be watched for under these headings is a useful guide which helps the teacher to keep before her the particular problem which she has set for herself.

In some of these areas of observation it is possible to take reading achievement as a point of departure. At other times the study of some apparently unrelated factor may, in turn, shed much light on reading achievement. Some of the interesting areas which may be observed in the classroom include:

Work Habits: With what degree of independence do the children in the class work? What is the nature of the help they demand? How do they attack a problem? How sustained is their effort? Their attention? What errors persist? Are there constant confusions, for example, of such words as *through* and *though*, *mouth* and *month*, *head* and *hand*?

Attitude toward Reading: Which children seem interested in hearing stories but not in reading for themselves? Which children seem discouraged about their reading? Apparently indifferent? Eager to avoid reading situations? Is there expression of an active dislike for reading? Is there evidence of over-compensation in other activities? Of failure to face difficulties?

Language Development: How do the children in the class express themselves? In how many cases does language indicate either poverty or adequacy of experiences? Does the young child, particularly, talk in sentences or words? How much communication by language does he seem to need? With teacher? With classmates?

Speech: What speech defects need immediate attention? Do they appear to be related to some physical defects such as adenoids? How many children are in need of speech improvement? What are the most frequent mispronunciations? Poor enunciations? Foreignisms?

Motor Behavior: What children seem over-active? Sluggish? Do they have special difficulty in writing? Is there excessive pointing, vocalization, or body movement during reading? Are there evidences of directional confusions, such as persistent reversals in writing and word recognition, or of the absence of clearly dominant handedness?

Vision: What evidence is there of visual difficulty other than that indicated on the Snellen Charts? Do any of the children show tendencies to squint, strain, or assume distorted positions of the eyes or head when materials are being read on the board or at the desk?

The teacher will also find it valuable to study occasionally a somewhat formal problem—to note for a whole morning, for example, the extent to which the assertive child succeeds in dominating the class situation, or the number of times the bright child participates as compared with the slower, less developed pupil. Another method of systematizing an observational program is to set aside some definite time for focusing attention on the reactions of certain individual children.

It is objective. One aspect of good observation is objectivity of reporting. The teacher's point of view needs to be as impersonal as possible. One of the most worth-while outcomes of the technique of observation is the fact that the teacher who makes frequent use of it learns to control or to evaluate any prejudice which may be influencing her judgments of children. She becomes more analytical as well, and instead of a notation: "John is lazy and won't study his words," there will appear a comment such as "Today John missed these words again. He appears to have some special difficulty in retaining them. Visual? Auditory?" Instead of such a judgment as "Helen is a slow child," there will be an effort to interpret this slowness as a physical, emotional, or intellectual phenomenon.

It is applied against certain standards. If direct observation is to yield greater insight, the teacher must be able to decide which of the reactions she observes are most significant. She will need to be aware of the range of differences in her class and to discover "norms" among them so that she can identify and describe the deviates among her pupils. She needs also to understand the appropriateness of any manifestations of difficulty she may find. In the course of her observation she may note, for example, the presence of some infantilisms in speech. Obviously, she would not consider this as serious in a six-year-old as she would in the case of a ten-year-old. Then, too, she must be able to interpret a generalization in terms of the individual. First year children, still learning the directional movements of reading, frequently will make reversals. Even in the first year, however, this tendency may be indicative of a more serious problem. Observation must help the teacher to decide from the very beginning whether such reversals are only simple learning errors or evidences that lateral dominance is not clearly established. The technique of classroom observation has, on the whole, special application in the first year where the immaturity of the child makes such study a primary and essential source of information.

The results of observation should be recorded.

The success of a program of observation will often depend on the recording of the data observed. Later in this chapter the function of records in a diagnostic study is discussed. It should be emphasized here, however, that in the case of direct observations the important thing is not how the observation is recorded but that some record be made. Two notations in juxtaposition may sometimes suggest more than many casual mental observations. The teacher may have recorded the fact that on Thursday James, despite his glasses, was peering at his book. On Monday she may note that his written work is becoming increasingly careless and seems to show no regard for the lines on the paper. The two observations made under this boy's name may for the first time call sharply to her attention the possibility that his glasses need correction.

The methods of note-taking can be varied and informal. Some teachers keep a small notebook with pages conveniently indexed for each child. Others use small index cards; still others prefer folders for accumulating significant memoranda. Each teacher should determine which, for her, is the simplest, most direct, and efficient procedure; once she determines the method she should train herself to use it systematically. The technique of classroom observation has the interesting aspect of a "self-training" procedure, sharpening the teacher's power to see what goes on in her classroom and, through accumulated experience in seeing, enabling her to interpret. More and more as the program of elementary education creates a freer classroom situation, there will be dependence on the teacher's trained observations for significant diagnostic data.

3. The Study of Achievement in Related Instructional Areas

Reading ability is related to achievement in other "subjects."

The modern view of reading as one phase of a program of language arts emphasizes the relationship that exists between many of the school's instructional activities. Reading, spelling, language usage, oral and written expression are all seen in truer perspective as different aspects of a basic ability to use and to understand language, to receive and to communicate ideas. The whole trend in teaching is toward the integration of these instructional activities. The study of reading difficulty needs the same integrated approach. The teacher who obtains a complete picture of the child's spelling, writing, and language achievement will understand better his poor attainment in reading and will in turn see more clearly the negative effects of poor reading on these other aspects of his school work.

It was found very early in the clinics that most of the children referred for reading difficulty were also extremely poor in spelling and greatly inhibited in written expression. To encourage fuller expression, to free it from the confines of the few words that they could spell, the children were invited to dictate their stories to the teacher. At the same time an analysis was made of the spelling errors most frequent in the children's compositions. A basic list of 228 words was compiled, and it was considered necessary to teach these spelling words in conjunction with the reading and writing aspects of the whole remedial program. Any teacher can cull the written work of her class for such a basic spelling list. Teachers have only too often looked at the "spellers" they have been obliged to use and wondered why the next spelling lesson had to be concerned with *mosquito* and *peculiar* when *does* and *who* were still so vaguely apprehended by the children and so individually spelled. The same situation has existed with much of the drill in language usage which in the past has been "required."

Instructional approaches should be integrated.

Because of the relationship that exists between the various phases of the instructional program, the reading problem cannot be approached purely through "reading" techniques. It was found in the clinic, for example, that several of the children depended heavily upon the spelling out of words for recognition. Frequently, in the course of his reading, a child would look at a word, remark, "Oh, that's one of my spelling words!" spell it out, *and only then, recognize it.* Children who have acquired no basic power of word recognition by the time spelling instruction begins will often seize upon this "deciphering" technique. At first such children spell out merely their "spelling" words. Later, particularly if they continue to have difficulty in word recognition, spelling out becomes their method of word attack in reading. Moreover, a spelling method which does not demand of children that they be able *to read* the words they are learning to spell will help to create such habits.

Corrective procedures in reading will, therefore, frequently depend for their effectiveness on the extent to which they involve related areas or "subjects." The integrated program which is today being introduced into elementary education should do much to facilitate the use of such procedures and to encourage the teaching of reading as one of many related language arts.

4. STUDY OF INTELLECTUAL CAPACITY IN RELATION TO READING ACHIEVEMENT

Appraisal of intelligence is an important phase of diagnosis.

With the primary emphasis in diagnosis shifting from the analysis of achievement to the study of the child, the appraisal of intelligence becomes an integral part of the diagnostic program. Without some knowledge of her pupils' capacities to achieve, the teacher is unable to evaluate the task before her. Through careful study of their abilities she can help them better to attain their maximum achievement.

Using intelligence tests. It is desirable to include in the diagnostic program a good intelligence test. The data secured through intelligence tests enable the teacher to establish the relationship between the child's reading level or reading age and his mental level or mental age or—in other words—between his *achievement* and his *capacity to achieve*.

In general, however, it is difficult to secure a dependable measure of intelligence for the extremely poor reader. Group verbal intelligence tests penalize the poor reader because they so frequently involve reading items. Often, the child's "intelligence" has to pass through many reading skills before it even becomes measurable by means of such an instrument. Experience in the reading clinics has shown that an appreciable number of children referred as dull—with IQ's of between 80 and 90 on group intelligence tests—have scored as much as 20 to 30 points higher when given individual tests. The individual intelligence test, of course, gives the opportunity to observe responses directly and is, therefore, not only more diagnostic but also more reliable. However, when dealing with the poor reader it is wise to view with reservation and to regard as highly tentative the IQ derived from any test involving the use of language. If the results of intelligence tests are to be utilized properly in the instructional program the important consideration should not be an IQ which may be unreliable but the needs which have been revealed. Whether or not the rating is a true index of his ability, the child who scores lower than others in his class on verbal intelligence tests has some special instructional needs.

Supplementing test ratings. Even where the test data are quite valid, the picture of the child's intelligence which is obtained by testing is necessarily an incomplete one. In the study of intellectual capacity, particularly, the approach must be dynamic. No matter how many tests have been given, the teacher in the role of alert observer needs constantly to be searching out abilities and skills as well as problems and difficulties. Test ratings should be supplemented by the observation of intelligence as it operates from day to day in various classroom situations. The teacher has the opportunity to note the child's general alertness, his ability to follow directions, to ask good questions, and to reason in arithmetical situations; she can appraise such aspects of intelligence as retentive ability, reasoning, and judgment in practical situations. These observations are of particular value in the case of children who are not adequately measured by the tests and who seem to possess greater ability than school progress and test ratings indicate.

Today the concept of "achievement expectancy" is interpreted broadly. It stresses the relationship not only between achievement and capacity but between many important factors in the child's development. There is the feeling that all factors—of growth as well as of intelligence—must be considered in estimating such development. Certainly, experience in the reading clinics tends to support the point of view that the child's progress in reading should be viewed "against the broad background of total growth" and "that much more is involved than the immediate learning experience."[2]

[2] Olson, Willard C. "Reading as a Function of the Total Growth of the Child." *Reading and Pupil Development.* Chicago Supplementary Monographs, No. 51. Chicago: The University of Chicago, 1940. p. 233.

5. Survey of Reading Interests

Children's interests often disclose vital information.

In the process of "finding out about the child," some areas of information are more accessible than others. It is relatively easy to analyze school achievement or to observe the way a child functions in a classroom. It is more difficult—and sometimes more significant—to learn the nature of those reactions which are not entirely confined to the schoolroom. The study of children's interests has been shown through wide experience to be a most rewarding field of inquiry. It is possible through such a study to gain some knowledge of the child's background and "way of life," to learn what part reading plays in the meaningful hours he spends outside the school, and to secure an insight into the kind of motivation which in the classroom will draw from the child the most active and whole-hearted response.

There are many methods of ascertaining children's interests.

What are the general interests of the children in the class? What do they like to do? What are their hobbies, their enthusiasms, their ambitions? What are their reading interests? Do they read in connection with their favorite activities? What kinds of books do they like? Do they read exclusively one type of material, or are their reading interests well balanced? There are a number of techniques through which such information may be acquired over a period of time.

The interest inventory. Many of the extensive investigations undertaken by research workers into children's interests have depended largely upon the interest inventory and questionnaire. The range of these questionnaires is usually quite wide. On the Diagnostic Child Study Record prepared by Witty and Kopel[3] there are, for example, such questions as: "When you have an hour or two that you can spend just as you please what do you like best to do?" "What are the names and ages of your close friends?" "Where did you go during your last summer vacation?" "What things do you wonder about?"

The study of special reading interests made by Lazar[4] included such items as: "What magazines have you at home?" "Which newspapers do you read?" "Do you have a library card?" "Check the kinds of books you like...."

[3] Witty, Paul and Kopel, David. *Reading and the Educative Process.* Boston: Ginn and Co., 1939. pp. 311–34.

[4] Lazar, May. *Reading Interests, Activities, and Opportunities of Bright, Average, and Dull Children.* Contributions to Education No. 707. New York: Bureau of Publications, Teachers College, Columbia University, 1937. p. 121.

Although a number of such published interest inventories are available, the teacher can in many informal ways adapt the questionnaire technique to her own classroom needs. She may be interested in a special aspect of the children's reading interests and devise a brief inventory dealing only with this phase; or she may wish to compare two groups on the basis of their extensive reading in order to plan an improved library program. Perhaps she is curious to see if there has been some growth in interests and tastes, and she will plan to use the same type of inventory at different periods during the school year. The questionnaire technique is extremely flexible, and the information obtained through its use will often serve as a source of new motivation to the reading program.

The library record. Whenever the children have an opportunity to choose a book there is opportunity to observe some aspect of their needs, interests, or attitudes. It was noted in the clinics that one child would select a "little book" which he could finish within a half hour. Another would read only books on "tools" or "boats." Still another, with an IQ of 123—talented and with many interests—would alone in his group show no desire for any library book. Direct observation is an excellent method of learning about children's reading habits and tastes.

It is wise to provide for the recording of choices made in the class or school library, and to note as well the books obtained from the public libraries. These records may be placed on index cards, class charts, or individual lists kept by the children in special notebooks. Book reports are obviously useful in determining the direction of children's reading, but a word of caution must be said concerning their use. The book report can be made one of the liveliest and most socialized means of communicating reading experiences. Unfortunately, too often "having to write a book report" has been one of the reasons why more books are not read by children. It would be better to have no book report at all than to make it a routine "lesson" which creates antagonism toward reading. The book report should be thought of in terms of a lively, enjoyable, and purposeful sharing of opinion. Every means should be utilized for stimulating such a "book-reporting" atmosphere.

Language activities. Almost any activity in language development lends itself at some time to the gathering of data on children's interests. The *oral discussion* provides frequent opportunity for reports on personal activities and experiences, on follow-up assignments undertaken by children with special enthusiasms, on books disliked or enjoyed. *Written expression,* whether creative or reportorial, is often highly personal and reveals such aspects of a child's life as his drives, his leisure-time pursuits, and the kind of reading that really matters to him.

The study of children's interests has been discussed here as a technique of diagnosis. Actually it is hardly possible to separate the factor of "reading interests" from its place in the whole instructional program, and it is planned in a subsequent bulletin on instructional procedures to discuss the role of interests in the reading program from this point of view. Finding out where the child stands and the level at which his interests lie can be only a first step. From then on this knowledge of his vital interests should serve to motivate his learning and his growth.

6. Recording Diagnostic Data

Records are indispensable in a diagnostic study.

Reference has been made throughout this chapter to the recording of diagnostic data. In summarizing here the matter of records, it is important to emphasize the function of recorded information in any diagnostic study. It has already been pointed out that greater objectivity of judgment is achieved when an observation is set down in words. "You don't see a child," says Baruch,[5] "till you write down what you observe about him." When records are kept, objective evidence tends to become a substitute for the vague impression and the fleeting recollection.

It is the record which makes possible continuity in the study of a child. The value of much careful observation and analysis may be entirely lost when no report remains of what has been found. The teacher who, studying John's test record, can say, "John's test score shows little improvement in reading, but here is a series of observations made on many different occasions which show real improvement," speaks with greater authority than the teacher who can only sigh and say, "Despite this poor test rating, I just *know* that John has improved!"

Often the most vivid picture of emotional and personality growth is secured from the informal cumulative record. When each person who comes in contact with the child must rediscover for himself essential background or personality data, there is little opportunity to trace development. Good records make it possible to study and to direct growth.

There are many approaches to record-keeping.

Class summary chart. Different types of records serve different purposes. There is, of course, the standard procedure of recording quantitative data on cumulative pupil record cards. Another of the most generally useful types of records is a summary of test data which affords a quick overview of class achievement. Such a summary chart can include any aspect of achievement in which the teacher is interested and may be organized somewhat as shown in the illustration.

[5] Baruch, D. "Whither the Kindergarten?" *California Journal of Elementary Education,* 9:106-13, November, 1940.

CLASS 5A2—GRADE SCORES—SEPTEMBER 1941

Name of Pupil	Chron-ological Age	NEW STANFORD READING			GATES SILENT READING				Spell-ing	IQ
		Test 1	Test 2	Total Read-ing	Type A	Type B	Type C	Type D		
Frank L.	10-6	4.8	5.5	5.2	4.8	5.3	5.9	6.0	4.0	107
Charles B.	10-3	4.9	4.9	4.9	3.8	4.2	5.0	5.0	4.1	116
John S.	11-4	4.1	4.8	4.5	3.6	4.6	5.2	5.0	3.8	93
Louise G.	10-1	5.2	4.4	4.8	4.8	4.9	5.3	5.7	3.5	113
Rose M., etc.	10-8	3.9	4.4	4.2	4.3	4.7	4.7	4.9	4.2	98

In studying a chart of this kind the teacher would be able to note for further follow-up such problems as these:

1. The spelling appears to be generally poorer than the reading.

2. Some children, Charles and Louise, for example, do not seem to be working to their mental capacities.

3. The best scores on the Gates Tests were in Type D, which tests ability to note details. The poorest scores were obtained in Type A, which measures ability to derive general significance. Since Type A is a short-timed test (6 minutes) it would be useful to examine the low scores to determine whether they were primarily the product of inadequate speed of reading or definite weakness in comprehending general significance.

4. In general, the scores seem lower on the tests of interpretation and inference. The trend of the scores in paragraph meaning (New Stanford, Test I), in general significance (Gates, Type A), and in the prediction of outcomes (Gates, Type B) would seem to indicate the need for fuller comprehension activities.

Such a summary chart is particularly compact and useful when, after a period of time, retests are given and a comparative study of the results is being made.

Check lists. The check list has been frequently recommended as a type of record that goes beyond test score data and by the enumeration of certain items directs attention to important aspects of behavior or achievement.

The process of checking off traits or reactions, however, has a tendency to give to the study of children a routine quality. It becomes easy to carry out perfunctory observation. It is also possible, in using a check list, to err in the other extreme. Looking too carefully for items that have to be checked sometimes results in "observing" a manifestation which does not exist. In this process of "looking for" the items on a check list, much significant behavior may be overlooked. Were it practical to use in a classroom a thoroughly comprehensive enumeration of factors, this technique might on the whole have greater usefulness.

Unquestionably there is great value in focusing attention on specific reactions to be observed. Rather than using someone else's interpretations of important items, however, the teacher would profit more from a check list of her own making. Keeping in mind primarily what it is she wants and needs to know about the children in order to help them in the classroom, she can construct a simple list of factors—posed either as questions, statements, or one-word items—which can serve as a spur to her observations. She will probably have to make a conscious effort to include on such a list positive and desirable aspects, lest the tendency develop to seek out only difficulties and to work only with problem children.

Perhaps the wisest use the teacher can make of such a personal check list is to use it not as a check list at all but as a general guide to observation and as a basis for making her informal anecdotal records more complete and objective.

Anecdotal records. The anecdotal record kept over a period of time is the type of record which modern educators regard as of greatest value. The teacher's notes serve to clothe the framework of test score data or check list items. They fill in the picture of day to day reactions and provide source material for the study of children's growth. The following entries indicate the type of observations recorded in the case of a third year child with special reading difficulty:

Record of Anna M., Class 3A2

4/3/40   Can't pronounce *sh,* says "fis" for "fish." Some difficulty with *ch* as well. Seems quite immature and dependent. Waits for words to be told to her.

4/18/40   Difficulty distinguishing between sounds; doesn't know initial consonants. Can't concentrate on a job. Sat with work before her, dreamily absorbed. Moves slowly, with same dreamy air.

10/26/40   A. was very happy to discover that she could read the directions in her book by herself. Felt a sense of achievement. Asked, "Can't I have an extra reading period because I did good work?"

12/15/40   Has great difficulty noting similarities and differences in words. A. needs ear training. May be some relation between her poor auditory acuity and speech infantilisms.

2/18/41   Is beginning to use a familiar element in word recognition.

3/1/41   Marked improvement in blending, although still hesitant. Grouping A. with Mary has had a very enlivening effect. Affected by Mary's sprightliness, A. is very wide awake.

4/17/41   A.'s development has been most gratifying. Great advance in social maturity. Speech infantilism has completely disappeared. There is an integration of her whole personality. She talks well, is animated and energetic. Reading has improved in all aspects although not yet up to grade.

Naturally, such records cannot be kept for a whole class at one time. If these running commentaries are made, however, for a few children at a time, if they aim to record all evidence of growth, and if they are jotted down when the teacher's reaction is fresh, a significant record of development will emerge.

Other informal records. Many of the classroom activities and much of the children's own work can serve as a check on learning responses and a record of personal development. These records may take many forms such as:

(1). *Class Charts.* Records of new words learned or new books read appear on such vocabulary or library charts as "New Words for Old," "Books I Have Read," etc.

(2). *Class and Individual Graphs.* The results of tests and practice materials recorded this way enable the child as well as the teacher to trace improvement.

(3). *Children's Logs and Class Diaries.* Such records offer insight into the effectiveness of certain classroom experience and growth in power of expression.

Various records should be studied together.

Each type of record that has been discussed emphasizes only certain aspects of the child's reading status. The class summary chart surveys his achievement in terms of standardized measures, the check list highlights other phases of his attainment or behavior, the teacher's notes and the class records add still other dimensions to the picture of his development. If the object of record-keeping is to bring together and to set down all one can learn about a child, then these varied types of records will need to be used constantly in combination with one another.

Throughout this chapter the point of view has been that diagnosis is not a series of narrow techniques but a pattern of study. In this conception every aspect of the school program that opens up another path toward understanding the child is properly a "technique" of diagnosis.

12. DIAGNOSIS AND REMEDIATION OF DISABILITY IN ORAL READING

E. W. Dolch

In discussing the subject, "Diagnosis and Remediation of Disability in Oral Reading," we must first define our terms so that we know exactly what we are talking about.

DEFINITIONS

First, the reading we are talking about is to be thought of as a process of "taking in," or of "getting the meaning." This is the ordinary meaning of reading, as distinguished from many special meanings with which the school may be concerned. By "ordinary reading" we mean the kind you usually do when you pick up a newspaper or a magazine or a book. In this case you are not looking for anything special, such as *finding an answer*. You are not trying to cover a great deal of material in a short time. That is *skimming* or *skipping*. And you are not *studying* so that you may tell others. You are just reading. This means following the thought of the author, wherever it takes you.

Please note that this ordinary reading may mean reading to yourself or to someone else. If you are reading a magazine, and I should say, "Read it to me, I want to know what you are reading," you usually go on doing exactly the same kind of reading—that is, following the author wherever he takes you—but you simply add the saying-aloud of the words you are going over.

Second, by "ordinary reading," we mean first reading. That is the kind of reading you are doing all the time and that you will always do. Look at a hundred men or women in a waiting-room who are reading until train time. How many of them, do you think, are puzzling something out and then rereading? I am sure none of them are. They are just reading, which means getting what they can get, or do get, the first time over. If you cannot read an article the first time over, you cannot read it. You will have to puzzle it out and then reread.

Reprinted from *Oral Aspects of Reading*, Helen M. Robinson, Compiler and Editor, Supplementary Educational Monographs No. 82, pp. 91–95. By permission of the University of Chicago Press, copyright 1955 by the University of Chicago Press.

Third, we are speaking then of ordinary reading, the first time over, and, now let us add, with full *comprehension*. We know all about this in our everyday life. If I gave you something hard and abstract to read and then asked you if you had read it, you would say, "Well, I got most of it." You would mean that you did not completely read it. You could not. You therefore did less than real reading, for real reading means full comprehension.

Fourth, this ordinary reading with which we are concerned implies getting the meaning, but it is not concerned with how fast we get that meaning. It is just like walking: everyone could walk faster if he wanted to, but he does not want to. Everyone could read faster if he wanted to, but most persons are not concerned with speed. They are concerned, first, with interest and, second, with understanding.

Since speed of reading has come up, we must point out that the difference between oral and silent reading is basically just a difference in speed of the reading operation. The words "oral" and "silent" really falsify the situation. These words say that you either make a noise or do not make a noise as you read. But making a noise or not making a noise is not the question. Instead, in speed of reading there is a natural progression from one extreme to the other. In short, this ordinary reading, first time over, with full comprehension, can be done at varying speeds. Therefore, it can be studied or judged at varying speeds.

This fourth requirement is emphasized because we are here concerned with diagnosis and remediation of *oral* reading. The reading is to be done aloud. It has to be done aloud so that we can hear it and diagnose it. It has to continue aloud so that we can tell what the reader is doing.

DIAGNOSIS

We now come to the actual method of diagnosis of oral reading. Here let us emphasize that we are not speaking for the handful of clinical workers in this country but for the million teachers who deal every day with children. In addition, let us emphasize above all else that we are chiefly concerned not with the child's reading "product" but with his "reading process." What does he do when he is in the process we call reading?

The problem of diagnosis of reading is based on the answers to four distinct questions. The *first question* in diagnosis is, "How does the child feel about reading and about the persons and things connected with it?" What we do or say at any step is directly determined by how the particular child feels about it. The more deficient the child may be, the stronger those feelings are likely to be, and the more we must regard them. It is the ignoring of the particular child's feelings that has resulted in most of the lost effort and labor in teaching reading.

Let us consider a typical situation of diagnosis. Let me speak of my own experience because, of course, I know that best.

First of all, I try to learn beforehand the child's first name and as much as I can about him, his family, and his teacher. All these things are involved in understanding the child and his situation.

When the child comes into the room, I call him by his first name and greet him at once. On the table I have a number of attractive books, carelessly scattered about. They will have been chosen according to what I have learned beforehand. They will range both above and below the level at which I guess the child will be able to read. If possible, they will not be schoolbooks or look like schoolbooks.

After the child is seated, I will say as casually as possible, "Have you seen any of these books before?" The child may point to one or other of the books, and I will just push them to one side. All this time I have been watching the child's reaction to the books and to the surroundings. I am looking for evidences of the two usual states of feeling of all school failures, either fear and timidity, or aggressiveness to make up for failure.

Here I must add that further answers to the question, "How does he feel?" are gained through all the rest of the examination. Tone of voice and expression of face continue to tell about the child's fears or his aggressiveness.

Especially important is the later discovery of how the child feels toward the teacher or the parent or toward anyone who might help him. How the child feels toward tests of any kind is most important in determining what kinds of tests to give, if any, and how to give them.

We come now to the *second question*: "How well does the child read?" Here the word "read" means to read, not to puzzle out or guess. To return to the table of books, we will say, "Look at these books and see if any look interesting." The child will pick up one that appeals to him and look into it. If he lays it down at once, we know it looks too hard. Sooner or later he will pause and keep looking into some book. Then we will say, "Read me a little from that one." If the child reads haltingly, with obvious puzzling out, just thank him kindly and take the book away and hand him another that you know is easier. Finally you will come to a book that he can read, that is, one in which he keeps going ahead, no matter how slowly, but without puzzling out.

Here a caution must be given. Usually we can tell from the way a child reads whether he is understanding, but not always. As a check, after the child has read rather smoothly, we should take the book from him and say casually, "Tell me what you have just read."

Regarding our question, "How well does he read?" we may have located a *level* of reading, but how fluent is the child at that level? One way of finding out is to say to the child, "That is fine, but you can read that page much more easily. Try it. Just start at the top and go on down as fast as you can." If the trouble has been a general uncertainty, there will be much better speed. But if there is uncertain word recognition, there will be little improvement.

Our first question was, "How does he feel about reading?" Our second question was, "Where can he actually read?" The *third question* must be, "How well can he puzzle things out?"

1. To diagnose puzzling, we watch until the child hits a word he cannot recognize. Then we may say, "Just jump over the word and read to me the rest of the sentence." If he can do that, then say, "Now what do you think that word might be?" Since sentences and suggestions from *context* vary, we cannot say how often you should do this, but you should try out the situation to get an idea as to whether the child is using, or can use, guessing from context to get a word.

2. Quite apart from context, one should try out the child's use of *word parts.* If the child stops at a word, you can ask, "What word do you think it looks like?" Or, "Do you see any parts of it you know?"

3. The use of *sounding* is diagnosed in a similar situation. If the child does not meet strange words in his easy book, give him a little harder book. When he stops at a word, you can ask, "How does the word start?" He will probably give you the letter name, since most poor readers have been taught to spell rather than to sound. Then ask, "What is the sound of that letter?" In this way you may find out if the sounds of few or many letters are known. If the letter sounds are known, have the child sound the letters through a word or syllable and then ask what the word or syllable says. You are trying to find out whether the child can or cannot blend letter sounds into syllable sounds.

Our three questions lead to the *fourth question*, which is often overlooked: "How much does he think about what he reads?" In the first place, interest means thinking, and thinking means interest. If we are interested, we cannot help thinking about material or ideas. If we are not interested, it is practically impossible to do thinking. So for reading, we can use thinking as a yardstick of interest. And interest means drive or lack of it.

The implications for this question are very important. For instance, if the child naturally thinks about his reading, he will wonder about words and will guess at what they mean. If not, he will just skip them without any idea of meaning. If he is a thinker, he will wonder when, because of misreading, a sentence does not make sense. Second, the thinking child will want to read. He will want to get at books. He may know that being a poor reader is blocking him, and want to overcome that block. The nonthinking child will consider reading just a nuisance and try to get away from it.

Remediation

The chief problem behind remediation is correct diagnosis. This is very true, as you know, in medicine. Correct diagnosis is the key to medical treatment—and is the hardest part of it. This is also true of remedial work in reading.

Suggestions for remediation have necessarily been mentioned in the discussion of diagnosis which we have given.

How does the child feel? The remediation here is merely that, if he feels wrongly, he must learn to feel rightly. If he is afraid of teachers, he must learn to like teachers. Teacher friendship will solve that, and nothing else will. If the child is afraid of reading, he must discover that there are books he *can* read and books he *wants* to read.

Where can the child actually read, and how well can he read there? The remediation for maladjustment of child and reading is to give the child something that he can read and that he will find *fun* in reading. The independent-reading period, where "every child every day reads something on his interest at his level" is the answer. This period is indispensable to any attempt to improve poor reading.

Incidentally, we have the problem of the child who has so small a stock of sight words that we can find nothing that he can read. Then these necessary sight words can be learned by such a child through the playing of games with other children or at home.

To conclude, a child must read where he actually *is* to get ease and confidence and desire to read more. Soon he gets fluency, and he will be ready to attack a higher level with confidence and pleasure.

The school has shown most concern about teaching the third step, *word attack*. Here the great mistake has been in making this a hard step and in losing patience when the child did not succeed.

We have already emphasized that every child must actually be reading on his interest at his level. At the same time, however, there will be harder reading so that word attack can be learned and practiced. This reading will naturally be oral, since no one can help a child unless he knows what the child is doing. Here the three points we have made will be watched.

First, if the child needs to learn the habit of using context, the teacher will ask that the rest of the sentence be read and that a guess be made as to what the unknown word may be. Here the important thing is the *habit* of guessing, not an actual correct guess.

Second, if recognition of word parts or syllables is to be emphasized, the question will be, "Do you see any part you know?" This again is to instil a habit rather than to teach certain word parts.

Third, the practice at sounding attack is the one that will really count in improving reading. For this purpose the teacher has in mind the series of principles in sounding. He has found out just about how far the individual child is in the process of learning sounding. Thus the teaching will go on from the point at which the individual child's knowledge stops. Time will not be wasted in asking questions that are either too easy or too hard.

Fourth, the question of how much a child thinks must be given more attention than it seems to be given at present. We have the strange idea throughout the school that we do not have time for children to think. Since many children have never been asked what they think about what they read, most of them are completely dumbfounded when you say, "Well, what do you think about it?" They are not supposed to think; they are just supposed to read.

CONCLUDING STATEMENT

The reading examination has been discussed as a means of diagnosis. In this examination we have sought answers to four questions: (1) "How does the child feel?" (2) "Where does he read and how well?" (3) "How does he use word attack?" (4) "How much does he think about his reading?" Our suggestions for remediation depend on our answers to these four questions.

Diagnosis and remediation in reading mean simply finding out just where the child is in this complex reading process and helping him to grow from that point on, according to the laws of growth and learning.

13. NATURE OF AN INFORMAL READING INVENTORY

Marjorie Seddon Johnson and Roy A. Kress

BASIC CONCEPTS

The term *informal reading inventory* is one in our language which expresses three fundamental concepts with three words. Consider first the basic noun in the title. This technique of evaluating a child's performance is an inventory in the sense that it is a detailed study of his whole performance in the reading area and those language and thinking functions related to reading. The second major concept is that of reading itself. In the label informal reading inventory, the function reading is widely conceived. The interest is not in mere pronunciation of words, but also in the manipulation of ideas which are represented by these words. Finally, the technique is an informal one in that specific methods are not standardized, and no norms have been established for performance to be compared with what other students can do. Instead, evaluations are made in terms of absolute standards. A child's performance is judged against virtual perfection rather than compared with what the majority of children might do if given the same job.

An informal reading inventory, therefore, offers the opportunity to evaluate a child's actual reading performance as he deals with materials varying in difficulty. While an appraisal of these specific reading abilities is being made, opportunities also arise for making informal evaluations of his expressive and receptive abilities in the oral language area, for reading is only one facet of verbal communication. As such, it is inextricably bound in with listening, speaking and writing—the other facets. An effective evaluation of a child's ability to read must take into consideration this interrelatedness of the receptive and expressive functions of total language performance.

Reprinted from *Informal Reading Inventories,* Ira E. Aaron, Editor, Reading Aids Series, International Reading Association (Newark, Delaware, 1965), pp. 3–14. By permission of Marjorie Seddon Johnson and The International Reading Association.

SPECIFIC PURPOSES

A number of very specific kinds of information can be obtained from careful administration of an informal reading inventory. Accomplishing these purposes is inherent in the administration of the informal reading inventory provided a competent examiner makes the evaluation. Because the usefulness of the inventory depends on accurate observation of the individual's performance in the testing situation, and interpretation based on these observations, only a competent examiner can accomplish the purposes.

Careful administration of an informal reading inventory can determine the level at which the child is ready to function independently, the point at which he can profit from instruction, the level where he reaches complete frustration with the material, and his level of hearing comprehension. Three of these four levels have special significance for the teacher. It is necessary to know the level of material the child can handle adequately when working on his own. Much of the child's school work, and certainly that reading which will make him a mature and avid reader, is done on an independent basis. Unless materials at the proper level are provided, the child can hardly be expected to do an adequate job in independent work and thereby establish for himself high standards of performance. All instructional work must be provided at a level where the child meets sufficient challenge to learn and yet has adequate readiness for learning. This means that he must achieve well enough to be able to absorb the instruction which is being given. However, to give instruction in materials which the child can handle virtually independently would be foolhardy. Finally, for oral activities it is important to know the child's hearing comprehension level. Too often the false assumption is made that if material is read to the child, he will be able to understand it regardless of the level of complexity it represents. For profitable listening activities one must know the hearing comprehension level.

A second purpose to be served by the informal reading inventory is the determination of the child's specific strengths and weaknesses. Only in terms of such analysis of specific skills and the pupil's adequacy of achievement in these skills can a suitable instructional program be planned. Teaching at the right level is not enough. It must be directed toward overcoming any specific weaknesses that exist. It must also be given in areas where the child has adequate readiness for learning.

For instance, a child may be weak in auditory discrimination of long vowel sounds and show no appreciation of vowel digraphs which represent such sounds. Readiness for the second area involves the first. It might well be possible to teach, at this time, to overcome the lack of auditory perception. However, it would be foolish to launch a program of instruction on the vowel digraphs before readiness is established.

A third purpose of the inventory is to help the learner himself become aware of his levels of achievement and his specific strengths and weaknesses. As he works with materials of increasing difficulty, he should be able, with the aid of the teacher, to determine where he functions well and where he needs assistance. In the same fashion, he should develop an awareness of the kinds of thinking and word recognition which he is capable of handling, and those in which he needs to improve. Without adequate learner awareness, instruction becomes exceedingly difficult if not impossible.

A final purpose to be accomplished by an inventory is that of evaluation of progress. Repeated inventories at periodic intervals should make it possible to determine changes in levels and in the handling of individual skills and abilities. In this way a true measure of the child's growth can be obtained.

CRITERIA FOR LEVELS

One of the problems in determining independent, instructional, and hearing comprehension levels is the variability which exists in the criteria used for judgment. All too often, the criteria are quite low. Consequently, the level at which a child's performance is judged adequate for independent work often turns out to be one at which he has many problems. Instead of doing a high quality job with the material, he is perhaps operating at something close to the old seventy-percent-passing level. In the same fashion, children are often considered ready for instruction when they have a great many deficiencies in their operating patterns at a particular level. Experience has shown that when there is too much to be accomplished through instruction, the child does not adequately profit from instruction and retain those things which are taught. In order to overcome these weaknesses, high standards must be used for judging the achievement levels. In the following pages, each of the four levels previously noted is discussed in terms of the specific criteria to be applied.

Independent level. This is the level at which a child can function on his own and do a virtually perfect job in handling of the material. His reading should be free from observable symptoms of difficulty such as finger pointing, vocalization, lip movement, and other evidences of general tension in the reading situation. Oral reading should be done in a rhythmical fashion and in a conversational tone. Materials, in order to be considered to be at an independent level, should be read with ninety-nine percent accuracy in terms of word recognition. This does not mean merely final recognition of the words in the selection. Rather, this means that even in a situation of oral reading at sight, the child should be able to handle the material accurately, making not more than one error of even a minor nature in one hundred running words. In terms of comprehension, the score should be no lower than ninety percent. Whether the reading has been done silently or orally at sight, the child should be able to respond with the same degree of accuracy to questions testing factual recall, ability to interpret and infer, and should have the comprehension ability required for full understanding of the material. He should be able to respond adequately to humor, for instance, or to follow any sequence of events involved in the material. In addition, the child should be able to make adequate applications of information and ideas to other situations.

Attention to the independent level can be a key point in the determination of progress in reading. The child, his teacher, his parents, and the librarian should all be concerned with this level. All are involved in the process of selection of materials for his independent reading. Books bought for his own reading, his personal library, should be ones he can read well. References suggested to him by the librarian, as she helps him get resources for carrying out a project, must be ones he can use successfully. Homework assignments should be ones he can read without assistance. It is through wide reading at the independent level that the child has opportunities to apply the abilities he has acquired, to learn through his own efforts, to increase the rate and flexibility of his reading—in short, to bring his reading ability to the point that it provides him with real satisfaction. Only through his independent reading will an individual become a "spontaneous reader," one to whom reading is a natural part of living.

INDEPENDENT LEVEL

Word recognition: 99%   Comprehension: 90%

Related Behavioral Characteristics

Rhythmical, expressive oral reading
Accurate observation of punctuation
Acceptable reading posture
Silent reading more rapid than oral
Response to questions in language equivalent to author's
No evidence of:

lip movement	vocalization
finger pointing	sub-vocalization
head movement	anxiety about performance

*Must be met without aid from the examiner.

Instructional Level. This is the level at which the child should be and can profitably be instructed. Here again the child should be free from externally observable symptoms of difficulty. Again, as at the independent level, he should be able to read rhythmically and in a conversational tone. One would expect that certain difficulties might arise in the course of oral reading at sight; however, when the child has a chance to read the material silently, most of these difficulties should be overcome. Consequently, oral rereading should be definitely improved over oral reading at sight. The child, in order to profit from instruction, should encounter no more difficulty than can reasonably be expected to be overcome through good instruction. In terms of specific criteria in word recognition, this means that he should perceive accurately at least ninety-five percent of the words in the selection. In terms of comprehension, he should attain a seventy-five percent level of understanding of the material without instructional aid. When these criteria are met, the child in all probability will be able to reach, with teacher help, the same high levels of performance as were indicated as criteria for the independent level. In general, one should strive in instruction to have the child handling the material independently by the time the lesson is completed. If he begins the lesson with less adequacy than ability to get ninety-five percent word recognition and seventy-five percent comprehension, there is very little likelihood that he will overcome all of his problems.

Certain other evidences of ability to profit from instruction can be observed at this level. The child should know, for instance, when he is running into difficulty. He should be able to profit from minimal clues offered by the teacher to help him overcome any difficulties he may encounter. He should also know when he needs to ask for direct help because he lacks the skills necessary to solve problems he meets in reading. Here, as at the independent level, the child should be able to set continuing purposes for reading once he has been helped to develop an initial readiness.

It is in guided work at the instructional level that the child will have the opportunity to build new reading and thinking abilities. Building on the foundation of his previously acquired skill, he can profit from teaching and thus extend his concepts, his word analysis skills, and his specific comprehension abilities. Extension of these skills through both increased range of abilities and greater depth of applicability is the purpose of instruction. If this is to be accomplished, knowledge of the child's instructional level is essential to the teacher.

INSTRUCTIONAL LEVEL

CRITERIA*

Word Recognition: 95%   Comprehension: 75%

Related Behavioral Characteristics

Rhythmical, expressive oral reading
Accurate observation of punctuation
Conversational tone
Acceptable reading posture
Silent reading more rapid than oral
Response to questions in language equivalent to author's
No evidence of:

lip movement	vocalization
finger pointing	sub-vocalization
head movement	anxiety about performance

*Must be met without aid from the examiner.

Frustration Level. The point at which the child becomes completely unable to handle reading materials is of more clinical than classroom importance. For the classroom teacher, however, knowing this level may serve two purposes. Information on the frustration level may give the teacher some guidance about the kinds of material to avoid for this child's work. It may also give him some indication of the rate at which the child might be able to progress when he is taught at his proper instructional level. If a child is ready for instruction at one level and completely frustrated at the next, there is clearcut evidence that he has many problems to be overcome at the appropriate instructional level. It is not likely that this instruction will progress rapidly because of the complexity of problems. On the other hand, if there is a considerable spread between the instructional and the frustration levels, a better chance for fairly rapid progress exists. There is evidence that a child can continue to use his reading abilities with fair effectiveness when he meets more difficult material than that truly appropriate for instruction. This fact would seem to indicate that the needs to be met at the instructional level and somewhat above are not terribly serious or complex ones. Consequently, he might be expected to solve any problems encountered relatively rapidly with good teaching to help him.

Specific criteria for the frustration level are these: comprehension of fifty percent or less and word recognition of ninety percent or less. Failure to meet the other criteria already described for independent or instructional level would also be indicative of frustration.

FRUSTRATION LEVEL

CRITERIA

Word recognition: 90% or less   Comprehension: 50% or less

Related Behavioral Characteristics

May show one or more of the following:
  abnormally loud or soft voice
  arhythmical or word-by-word oral reading
  lack of expression in oral reading
  inaccurate observation of punctuation
  finger pointing (at margin or every word)
  lip movement—head movement—sub-vocalization
  frequent requests for examiner help
  non-interest in the selection
  yawning or obvious fatigue
  refusal to continue

Hearing Comprehension Level. This is the highest level at which the child can satisfactorily understand materials when they are read to him. The hearing comprehension level can serve as an index to the child's current capacity for reading achievement. It indicates, in other words, the kinds of materials that he would be able to understand if his reading levels were at this moment brought to a maximum point. Criteria for judgment of adequacy of hearing comprehension are similar to those for the establishment of the instructional level. The child should be able to understand at least seventy-five percent of the material when it is read to him. A second measure, and a very important one, is the index given by his own speaking vocabulary and language structure. He should, in responding to the material, show an oral language level which is comparable to the language level of the material which has been read to him. The necessity for the examiner to translate questions down in language level or for the child to answer in a lower level of language would indicate that he is not comprehending fully at this point.

All instructional activities involving listening should take into account each child's hearing comprehension level. Whether materials are being read to the class or spoken, there can be no real profit to an individual if they are beyond his hearing comprehension level. He may simply tune out when he finds himself failing to understand. Knowing the appropriate levels of oral language activities can lead, then, to better classroom attention and thus to greater learning.

The hearing comprehension level has one other kind of significance for the teacher. It gives him an indication of the level at which the child *should be reading*. The criteria in terms of comprehension are the same for the instructional reading level and the listening level. One should not feel completely satisfied until the child can do as well with the material when he reads it himself as when it is read to him. Therefore, a goal to aim for is equivalence of the reading instructional and the hearing comprehension levels.

MATERIALS

The types of materials to be used in an informal reading inventory are dictated by the purposes of the inventory itself. Because the establishment of levels is one of the expected outcomes of the administration, it is obviously necessary that the materials represent a variety of levels. In a clinical instrument, for instance, it is usual to have the difficulty level of the material progress from preprimer level to the highest point that one is likely to need. These materials may represent a variety of subject areas and types of writing. However, if one were interested primarily in the achievement levels of the child in the science area, then materials relevant to this content field should be used for the inventory. Because

HEARING COMPREHENSION LEVEL

CRITERIA*

Comprehension: 75%

Response to questions in language equivalent to author's

*Must be met without aid from the examiner.

an evaluation of competency in handling specific skills and abilities is the desired outcome, the materials of the inventory must present the opportunity for evaluating this competence. Obviously, not every ability which is a part of reading comprehension could be tapped in the course of each inventory; however, an adequate sampling should certainly be made.

The length of materials must be controlled sufficiently to allow the inventory to be administered without undue fatigue on the part of the child. In general, selections of increasing length can be handled as the difficulty level of the material increases. As few as thirty words might be used at preprimer level and yet two hundred fifty to three hundred at ninth reader level. Specific materials and arrangement of them for the inventory depend, to some degree, on whether the evaluation is to be in an individual or group situation. For an individual inventory, most frequently used on a clinical basis, two selections, preferably connected, should be chosen for each level, from preprimer to the highest level to be tested. One of these is used for oral reading at sight and the other for silent reading. Oral rereading ability is evaluated by having the child reread aloud a portion of the material designed for silent reading. For a group inventory, one level at a time might be handled in a directed reading situation slanted toward evaluation or, at most, possibly two or three levels of material incorporated into one directed reading activity. It is very unlikely that a full range of materials from preprimer level on would be used in one group inventory. Instead, the total inventory process might continue over a number of related sessions. In the group inventory, definite portions of the materials would possibly not be set aside for silent or oral reading. When the children are operating in a group situation, there appears to be no justification for asking them to do oral reading at sight. Rather, materials should first be read silently as in any good instructional situation. Portions to be used to evaluate oral rereading should be selected so that the rereading is a natural part of the evolving group activity.

Ideally, the materials chosen for the inventory should parallel as closely as possible those materials which will be used for instruction. However, they should not be materials which the child has actually encountered in his instructional program. The inadequacies of the material which has been used for instruction seem obvious. There would certainly be the real possibility that the child would respond in terms of what had gone on in the classroom rather than in terms of what he was reading at the moment.

14. GIVING AN INFORMAL TEXTBOOK TEST

Board of Education of the City of New York

The informal textbook test is an important measurement instrument in teaching reading.

At the beginning of the school year, the test is used:
1. To determine a child's instructional reading level.
2. To aid in requesting appropriate reading material.
3. To diagnose abilities and deficiencies in skills.
4. To aid the teacher in grouping children for reading.

During the school year, the test is used:
1. To move a child from one instructional level to another when his reading material is too easy or difficult.
2. To evaluate his mastery of skills taught.
3. To determine the instructional level of a newcomer.
4. To complete the record of a child being transferred.

At the end of the school year, the test is used:
1. To evaluate a child's reading progress.
2. To complete his reading record before sending it on.
3. To provide supervisors with information that will help them in planning their next school organization.

TESTING AT OR ABOVE PRIMER (1^1) LEVEL

1. *Conditions.* Each test is to be administered individually. Other children should not hear the responses.
2. *Materials.* Obtain basal readers in a specific series, ranging from one year below to one year above the child's reading level, as noted on his Reading Record. Use, if available, the free Informal Textbook Test pamphlet prepared by the publisher of the series being used (this pamphlet indicates by page numbers the selections best suited for use in tests and provides suitable comprehension questions for each indicated selection).

Or, prepare an original test: *(a)* Select a passage of about 100 running words in a story without too many unfamiliar concepts. *(b)* Prepare four

Reprinted from *Sequential Levels of Reading Growth in the Elementary School,* Division of Elementary Schools, 1963, p. 44. By permission of the New York City Board of Education.

comprehension questions based on the selection, including literal meaning and finding details; getting main idea; drawing inferences; and reacting to the story.

3. *Procedure.* Choose a basal reader corresponding to the child's instructional level as noted on his Reading Record. Introduce the selection, establish rapport, tell a little about the story, tell the proper names, and ask the child to read *orally without previous silent reading.*

4. *Scoring.* Note and count errors as follows:

Nonrecognition Errors. Each *different* word a child does not know (tell him the word after five seconds) or mispronounces counts as one error. Words mispronounced because of foreign accent are *not* counted as errors.

Addition Errors. Count as one error all words the child adds, regardless of the total number of additions.

Omission Errors. Count as one error all words the child omits, regardless of the number of omissions.

Endings Errors. Count as one error all endings the child omits, no matter how many endings are omitted.

INTERPRETING THE INFORMAL TEXTBOOK TEST

1. *If a child makes fewer than 5 errors,* repeat the test on a reader at the next higher level. Continue until the level at which he makes about five errors is reached.

2. *If a child makes more than 5 errors,* repeat the test on a reader at the next lower level. Continue until the level at which he makes about five errors is reached.

3. *If the child makes about 5 errors,* then ask the four comprehension questions. A score of 75 percent or higher indicates that this is the child's instructional level. If he scores lower than 75 percent, then:

If the child is at or below third-year reading level:

a. Prepare another test of 100 running words from a story at the level on which he scored about five errors.

b. Have the child read the new selection *silently.*

c. Ask him four comprehension questions.

d. A score of 75 percent or higher indicates that this is the child's instructional level; but if the comprehension score is lower than 75 percent, then assign him the reader *one level below* the one used in this test, for this is the child's instructional level. Work closely with him on his comprehension skills.

If the child is above third-year reading level, follow the procedure just outlined but use three pages in a story instead of just 100 running words.

TESTING BELOW THE PRIMER (1¹) LEVEL

When testing below the primer (1^1) level, select 15 different words (no proper names) from the back of all pre-primers in the basal series being used for the test—perhaps every fifth word from a list of about 75 words.

Type (primer typewriter) or print (manuscript) the 15 words in a column or on separate cards. Ask the child to read the words aloud. Note his errors and evaluate:

1. *If he does not know any of the words,* provide him with a reading-readiness program.

2. *If he recognizes between 1 and 12 words,* then provide him with more pre-primer work, for this is his instructional level.

3. *If he recognizes 13, 14 or 15 words* (does not miss more than 2 words), then start him on the primer (1^1), for this is his instructional level.

CHAPTER III

PRINCIPLES AND PRACTICES OF REMEDIATION

A. Philosophy and Perspective

15. WHAT WE KNOW AND CAN DO ABOUT THE POOR READER

Arthur I. Gates

Like susceptibility to colds and other common bodily ailments, reading disabilities and failure have always been with us. The statements of certain journalists to the contrary notwithstanding, retardation in reading is not a development of the last two or three decades. What has developed during this period is a vigorous program of study designed to correct and prevent reading difficulties. This intensive research enterprise was the result of the recognition of the extent and seriousness of difficulty and failure in reading which prevailed in 1920 and earlier. At that time, during the heyday of phonics and "meaty," primary material, one child in every five or six, as shown by Percival's study,[2] was required to repeat

Reprinted from the May, 1957, issue of *Education*. By permission of the publishers, The Bobbs-Merrill Company, Inc., Indianapolis, Indiana.

one or both of the first two grades primarily because of retardation or failure in reading. Difficulty in learning to read plagues the teachers and children of all nations, even those in which the relationship of letters and sounds is not so distressingly inconsistent and bewildering as it is in English.[1]

Learning to Read Is Hazardous

It is important that parents and inexperienced teachers realize that learning to read is one of the most critical and difficult tests of a person's lifetime. For many it represents as serious a problem in adjustment as leaving home for the first time, going into the armed services or getting married. The seriousness of the task results from the fact that learning to read is for many a very difficult and subtle task. It comes at a time when the child is so young and inexperienced in learning in a new and often confusing group situation and one which demands so many other new adjustments. Difficulty springs, too, from the fact that his success or failure in learning to read is fraught with serious social consequences. If he learns to read well, all is well; if he does poorly or fails, the respect of his parents and acquaintances and his own self-esteem are threatened. When the test of learning to read becomes a test of a child status as a total person, it becomes an ominous source of anxiety which increases the difficulty of learning and subtly induces many children to seek some sort of "escape" from the test. Unfortunately for the youngster, there is no satisfactory escape from learning to read, as there are from most of his other activities. If a child doesn't get on well in hopscotch or baseball or singing, he could turn to something else and save face. But, there is in school and elsewhere today, no satisfactory substitute for reading. The difficulty and cruciality of the learning-to-read period combine to make it a cauldron of anxiety and trouble, perplexing to child, parent and teacher. And herein lie the major "causes" of retardation and failure in reading.

After little more than three decades of study of the processes involved in learning to read in school, studies carried on by many specialists-teachers, educational diagnosticians, psychologists, neurologists, psychiatrists, oculists, anatomists, and others—it is recognized that to learn to read successfully a child must be pretty well equipped with aptitude for this type of symbolic learning; he must enjoy quite good health and vigor; he must be well taught; he must be well adjusted to the teaching mentally and emotionally, and he needs to be pretty lucky. Conversely, it is recognized that a deficiency in any of these areas may cause trouble in learning. There is nothing startling in this view. Every good physician knows that a similar situation exists in relation to keeping a person "in the pink" of physical condition, especially during a period of new and crucial adjustment. Whether a child's health and vigor are excellent, average or poor depends upon his general physical equipment, how he is nurtured and taught, the nature of his mental and emotional adjustment, the kind of habits he forms and, to some extent, on his luck.

Prevention and Correction

Efforts to improve the program for securing better development of reading interests and ability, of preventing difficulties and diagnosing and correcting those which appear are substantially the same in character as the corresponding approaches of medicine. All phases of the work depend upon achieving an understanding of all the factors which help and hinder improvement and of discovering and controlling their role in the case of each individual.

To prevent or cure reading difficulty, a teacher or reading specialist must determine the role of many factors quite as a physician must consider the effects of many influences if he is to prevent or cure indigestion, headaches or insomnia. Among the former are intelligence, or general aptitude for scholastic, especially symbolic learning, which may be gauged by using a "general intelligence" test. The reading specialist may use several tests of special abilities such as ability to perceive and recall word-like symbols; and ability to perceive similarity and difference in word-like sounds. Such tests are similar in character to the physician's tests of blood pressure, pulse rate and temperature. A physician's or specialist's diagnosis of vision, hearing, and general physical condition are also often needed. The reading specialists, like the physician, will take a careful case history, giving the same attention to the psychological and educational factors that the physician gives to the physical, and both would take account of the character of the child's activities and relationships in the home, the neighborhood and the school.

Emotionality

Reading difficulties, like indigestion, may be produced or aggravated by emotional factors existing in the home or playmate groups or the school. Indeed, both may arise from the same conditions—from such influences as overprotection, or overly severe discipline, or indifference of the parents or other older members of the family. The child who is "babied" too much may resent the inability of the teacher to lift him individually over every hurdle in learning to read and lack the initiative to learn by himself. Indeed, many children are dismayed to find that one cannot learn to read without effort. They may expect the story to come to them from the printed page as easily as it does from the movie or the television screen, and when it does not, they may become so discouraged or resentful as to seek to escape responsibility by refusing to try to learn or so jittery or apprehensive as to be unable to learn. Overanxiety of the parents or siblings or teacher may have the distracting effect that severe stage fright has for an adult. In such cases, urging the child to try harder or even trying inexpertly to help him learn may tighten rather than loosen the child's strait-jacket of doubt and tension. In all such cases— and they take many other forms—some sort of psychotherapy is essential.

By "psychotherapy" is not here meant special treatment by a psychologist or psychiatrist, although on rare occasions the help of such a specialist is indicated, nor is a separate period or provision of therapy necessarily required. What is suggested is that once the existence and nature of unfavorable emotional conditions and misleading personal relations are discovered, steps should be taken to relieve them. This may often be accomplished best by a shrewd teacher or reading specialist— who is or should be an exceptionally insightful teacher—in the course of normal classroom activities and often combined with suggested modifications of the pattern of family life. Usually, however, the demand for this type of therapeutic re-education of the child and his family or both calls for a considerable amount of extra time for diagnosis and individual counseling by the teacher. One of the tragedies is that a teacher who possesses the ability and desire to grapple successfully with such subtle problems simply does not have the time. She has many other problems, many other subjects and many other phases of instruction in reading to attend to.

Reading Skills

Reading is probably the most difficult and subtle of all the scholastic abilities and skills to teach and the critical period comes at the very beginning of school life when the children are least experienced and most readily bewildered. It is very difficult to show a child, for example, all the tricks of working out the recognition and pronunciation of the weirdly artificial little hierglyphic which printed words are. To be successful a child must catch on to good techniques. What is good for one word is often poor for another. To learn to recognize, sound and blend the sounds of the letters may suffice for *hat* or *bag* but be utterly confounding for *haughty* or *hippopotamus,* the former because of phonetic inconsistence and the latter because the number of letters exceeds the child's immediate memory span. (The adult reader might try to blend the letter sounds of *zhljrpaufiom* from memory—it should be less puzzling because of his many years of experience with letters and their sounds).

The child must learn much by trial and error, and inappropriate techniques await at every hand to lead him astray quite as they do the adult who tries to learn to play golf or bridge or the violin without continual, expert, and individual instruction. Here is where "luck" enters. In learning to read, many children have the bad luck to hit off on faulty techniques which handicap them seriously. If a child, for example, begins to look first at the *end* or the *middle* of the word, rather than the beginning—a technique that works perfectly well in recognizing coins, insects, earrings, faces, and almost every object on earth except printed words— he is in for trouble. The woods of beginning reading are full of such treacherous pitfalls. Hence the need of a careful diagnostic inventory of the skills, insights, techniques and devices used by each learner.

Skill in using some one or a combination of several such diagnostic inventories now available is part of the equipment of every good reading specialist and an increasing number of teachers. They help the diagnostician discern the good and poor techniques used by a youngster. Using them gives no automatic insight; much depends upon the shrewdness of the teacher as, of course, it does in the case of the physician or music or golf instructor. The insightful diagnostician in all these fields uses the data from the diagnosis as a basis for planning a program of therapy or instruction tailored to fit the needs of the individual. This is called "corrective reading" or "remedial reading" but it differs in no important respect from the best types of everyday instruction. Indeed, the work of the reading specialist at its best differs from that of the regular classroom teacher only in being more expertly conceived, more skillfully conducted and precisely adjusted to the needs of each child.

To teach such a subtle skill as reading to thirty to forty children is a formidable task for the best teacher and, of course, not all teachers are perfect. Some children are unlucky enough to get a relatively poor one —one who is so easy going or unsympathetic that children become passive or aimlessly active, or one who is so autocratic as to make them jittery or fearful or angry, or one who is so uninspiring or inept, or one who is so blind to individual difficulties and needs as to leave children groping in uncertainty and confusion. Some children, moreover, are so unlucky as to miss school or change schools or teachers or encounter shifts in teaching methods or stumble into a change of interpersonal relationship in school or home at critical periods, and any gap not skillfully and individually bridged or any change not adequately guided may plunge the youngster into trouble. Emotionally unsettling events such as illness or misfortune or anger occurring to a member of the family or to the teacher or a playmate may be sufficient to reduce greatly the child's learning. The reaction of the teacher or pupils to a youngster on an "off day" may have a persistingly destructive effect. The writer recalls the occasion when one of the world's outstanding actors, who specializes in oral reading, made four or five "slips of speech" in each of a half dozen brief introductions of the artists participating in a program. If the most experienced and expert performers have such conspicuously bad spells, it is to be expected that a rank beginner will often have pathetically bad days. To offer crude, unsympathetic treatment at such a time is to sow the seeds of rebellion or failure.

Panaceas

The considerations just presented should convince the parent that there can be no panacea for the troubled reader. There are unfortunately many panacea peddlers for poor reading, as there are for all sorts of physical ailments. Popular among them are various systems of formal phonics, most of which have appeared and reappeared for more than a century. Certain forms of psychiatric or psychoanalytic procedures have been advocated as sufficient for all cases. Recently popular are various mechanical gadgets such as rapid exposure apparatus, motion picture materials and various pacing machines. There are also a number of highly artificial and therefore novel forms of practice methods such as the kinesthetic method (tracing the outline of letters, etc.) flash card methods, experience story methods, reverse image exercises, visualization and other methods. None of these is good for all cases; to use any one in certain cases would be to add oil to the fire. Some of them are valuable for limited uses with certain cases. One should be suspicious of all panaceas, especially any rigid scheme of formal or freakish drills or mechanical gadgets.

Parents and Reading

Parents often ask whether there is anything they can do to help a child learn to read or to improve his reading ability and interests. There are, indeed, many things parents can do. There is evidence that much of the basal equipment for reading is learned at mother's knee. Mother and father may contribute richly during all the pre-school years by helping the child engage abundantly and enjoyably in language activities. Answer the child's questions as fully and meaningfully as possible. Talk to him, tell him stories, report your daily experiences and encourage him to talk to you—the more the better. Take him on tours to the local stores, museums, factories, plants and other places and while doing so engage him in conversation, read the signs, placards, advertisements and talk about them. Provide him at home with reading matter, signs, ads, picture cards, magazines and books—alphabet books, picture books, story and other books. Read them to him, observe the pictures and diagrams together.

Television programs, wisely selected, provide excellent opportunities for family enjoyment of great value. In using all these materials, read the words and text to the youngster, look at the pictures and talk about them together and *answer the child's questions,* listen to his comments, and respond as helpfully to them as you can. If he asks the name of a letter or a printed word, tell him. Run your finger along under the line of words you are reading as he observes. Put words and phrases on objects and pictures in his room and answer the questions he asks about them. Play word sound games. "What words begin with the same sound as *cat*; or ends with the same sound as *sing*?" Should you teach him? No, not in a formal sense. Try, rather, to help him enjoy and engage at length in all kinds of verbal activity. If you can do that, you will have introduced a superior type of teaching. You will have helped your child enormously to make learning to read in school more certain and easy. If he learns to read before entering school, as many children with special aptitude will, so much the better. But don't undertake to teach him a heavy, formal system of phonics. This is a job for an experienced teacher.

The child will be helped enormously by the same pattern of family activity all through school, even into college. Let there be, at the appropriate level and in the proper areas, lots of conversation, reading aloud, reporting experiences and problems in which every person's contributions are welcomed and respected. Let there be a daily reading period, observed with the same regularity and conducted with the same spirit of enjoyment as the evening meal. Let each person read what he likes and feel free to talk about it to others.

Before a parent implies that his children's questions and comments are too silly and childish to merit respectful consideration, he might remind himself that in a few years his comments will seem equally naive and ignorant to the son or daughter who comes in fresh from study of up-to-the-minute knowledge in high school and college. The parent may expect to get, and deserves, the same treatment from his grown-up son or daughter as he gave them when they were children. Good readers, good students and good citizens tend to develop in homes in which good reading and good talk is a regular and enjoyable part of family life. A good reading specialist can spot in a few minutes a child who has suffered linguistic malnutrition in the home. And let no teacher or parent believe that a heavy dose of formal phonetics, or any other similar panacea, whether administered in the home or school, is a substitute for a wholesome diet of verbal food.

BIBLIOGRAPHY

1. KARLSON, BJORN, "We Have Remedial Reading in Europe, Too," *California Teachers Journal,* May 1955.

2. PERCIVAL, WALTER E., *A Study of the Causes and Subjects of School Failure,* Unpublished Doctor's Dissertation, Teachers College, Columbia University, New York, 1926.

16. GENERAL CHARACTERISTICS OF CLASSROOM INSTRUCTION AND REMEDIAL INSTRUCTION

Arthur I. Gates

In the minds of many persons there is a sharp distinction between typical classroom instruction and remedial instruction. It is the purpose of this chapter to discuss the relationships of the usual types of classroom teaching and remedial teaching. No effort will be made to discuss particular teaching or remedial activities or exercises or devices but rather to consider the features which characterize all types of good teaching and good remedial work.

CLASSROOM INSTRUCTION WITH REMEDIAL INSTRUCTION

The phrase "remedial instruction" implies that it is a process of teaching for the purpose of remedying some difficulty or deficiency. In current usage remedial instruction is the form of teaching undertaken to improve abilities in which diagnosis has revealed deficiency. Remedial teaching is thus intended to correct demonstrated weaknesses, to remove inappropriate habits, or to substitute a good technique for a poor one. Remedial instruction emphasizes administering to individual needs. For example, certain skills, such as those involved in working out the pronunciation of a word by giving the sounds of the individual letters and blending them, may be inadequately developed by one child, properly mastered by another, and so strongly emphasized by a third as to interfere with quick recognition. The first pupil may need further intensive training in using the letter-by-letter phonetic analysis, whereas the second may need no special instruction apart from that provided for the class as a whole, and the third may need guidance in the development of other techniques and in restricting the use of the more detailed analysis. Remedial instruction, then, is first and primarily individual prescription for individual needs.

Every specialist in reading, however, advocates the greatest possible adjustment of instruction to individual needs for all children. Teachers are accustomed to using a variety of devices for gaining insight into the abilities and difficulties of individual children and of organizing ordinary classroom activities to permit guidance in accordance with individual needs. As a general theory of teaching, therefore, there is no distinction between regular developmental classroom teaching and remedial instruction. The difference in practice is one of degree. In remedial instruction, individual differences in abilities and difficulties are sought more extensively and thoroughly and remedial instruction consists in setting up a program to permit the maximum intensity of specialization to meet individual needs.

Some persons are inclined to think of remedial instruction as individual work in which the teacher and one pupil work face to face. In such a situation very searching diagnosis of the individual's strengths and weaknesses and very precise teaching to adjust to his special needs are, of course, possible. However, the classroom teacher is urged to employ methods of subgrouping and other devices to enable her to do some individual intensive work with one pupil at a time as part of the daily program. Here again the distinction between remedial instruction and first-rate classroom teaching is not a distinction of kind; it is one of degree.

Many teachers have the impression that in remedial instruction the materials are different from those used in the best classroom instruction. Their impression is that the content and organization of the materials are of a peculiar type called "remedial" materials. It is true that many organizations of materials advocated by reading specialists are very different from those used in the best classrooms. Some of them are very artificial in form, meager and restricted in content, and organized in highly artificial ways. In the opinion of the present writer these materials are distinctly inferior for all except exceedingly rare cases to the richer, more meaningful, more challenging, more normal content used by good teachers. It is the author's opinion that remedial instruction, with rare exceptions, would be more fruitful if the remedial materials were more like, indeed even better than, those used in the best classroom practice in such respects as interest-provoking qualities, educative values, and general utility in content. Indeed, in the author's opinion, where a need for intensive individual remedial work exists, it is of unusual importance to secure the highest possible levels of quality in form and content of the materials.

It is sometimes assumed that remedial instruction is based upon unusual, novel devices, practice exercises, and stunts of the type often disapproved for classroom usage. Many of the artificial and unusual devices used in remedial reading are the results of work of specialists such as psychologists, ophthalmologists, and psychiatrists who do not have a full understanding of modern educational methods and objectives. Some of the teaching devices found in remedial programs may be properly recognized as thoroughly unsatisfactory devices and quite inadequate teaching methods. The remarkable thing about many types of

remedial work is that they succeed despite exceedingly poor materials
and techniques. With rare exceptions the best methods and devices used
in classroom teaching are the best possible ones to employ in remedial
work. Indeed precisely because remedial instruction is typically given to
the pupils who have the greatest difficulties, the need for the richest, best,
and most effective materials and devices is particularly acute. Due to the
fact that remedial instruction often represents an emergency measure
there has been a disposition to feel that a form of teaching radically
different in type and intent from that employed in the schoolroom is
desirable. The objectives sought in remedial teaching are substantially
those which every good teacher seeks to achieve in her individual and
group work in the classroom. She wishes to build up a high level of skill
and interest in reading. She desires to give her pupils a well-rounded
assortment of techniques and versatility in using them to meet particular
needs. She aims to develop proficiency in such techniques and abilities
as those outlined in Chap. 2.

Remedial teaching should follow the same general principles that are
or should be observed in any other type of instruction. There are
instances in which it may be advisable to use apparently different
methods or devices in remedial work. When, for example, a pupil has
failed after a prolonged period of work with one kind of practice
material or one type of oral device an apparent change may be advisable
lest the pupil conclude, "Well, this is the same old thing and I will fail
again as before." The variations, however, should represent equally good,
if possible better, embodiments of the same general principles. It would
be a serious mistake to shift from a moderately good teaching procedure
to a much poorer one just to be different, when there is plenty of opportunity to choose sufficiently different procedures which are as good as
or better than the one originally used. These variations represent not
contradictions of the main principles of teaching but special applications
of them which require unusual skill and understanding. In many instances they can and should represent a modification designed to provide
more exact adjustment to individual needs. The general characteristics
of good remedial treatment are precisely the same as the general
features of good classroom procedure.

It may be said that, in general, a person should be suspicious of any
form of remedial teaching which is highly artificial, unnatural, and
which utilizes narrow, barren content, or artificial gadgets, mechanisms,
stunts, and devices. There may be instances in which good teaching
materials and methods may be embodied in an unusual form. There is
no objection to novelty per se. Indeed, in many instances, an apparently
new organization may have special merit. Novelty, in organization or in
apparatus or in procedure, however, is not alone sufficient. It is imperative that in appraising remedial procedures the teacher examine below
the surface to determine precisely what type of activity the pupil is

learning and the merits of the content itself. The remedial program should contribute to enrichment of ideas, the enjoyment of stories, and other forms of content, the development of information of educational value, the cultivation of artistic, constructive, and other abilities, and should in other ways meet the broad objectives of the normal teaching program.

CHOICE AND ORGANIZATION OF MATERIALS FOR REMEDIAL WORK

In choosing and organizing materials for remedial work in reading six points should be borne in mind:

1. *The material should be highly interesting to the pupil.* A first requirement of remedial work is that the pupil's interest be captured. Of the several factors which contribute to the pupil's interest in the program as a whole, an important one is interest in the reading content. The remedial teacher should, therefore, by talking to the pupil and his teacher and by trying out samples of material through oral reading, attempt to discover the types of material which make the greatest appeal.

   In this respect, the writer's opinion differs from the opinions embodied in certain programs of formal training in which the desired skills are sought by what are considered the most direct means, irrespective of content, on the assumption that if the pupil can be drilled into ability to read, interest will take care of itself. While it is quite true that developing ability is often sufficient to arouse interest, there are times when a spark of interest must be activated before the pupil can be aroused sufficiently to make continuous effort to learn to read.

2. *Materials of outstanding popularity among children should be chosen.* Although, as indicated in the preceding section, interest in learning to read can be increased by capitalizing upon a unique or special interest of the individual child, it is not necessary, as has occasionally been contended, to limit all remedial instruction to one topic or area. It is no more necessary or no more desirable to do this in remedial work than in classroom teaching. It is desirable in both cases to make available to the child a generous amount of reading matter which has proved to be of outstanding interest. Dull, monotonous, uninspiring material should be replaced by selections embodying high comedy, adventure, and other challenging content. Indeed, the fact that the pupil has had special difficulty and is likely to be somewhat resistant to learning makes it even more important in the remedial instruction to have the highest possible proportion of the most thrilling, humorous, and otherwise satisfying content. The notion sometimes encountered that remedial materials may be confined to poorly written, uninviting content so long as it is within the pupil's field of major interest and

embodies the proper repetition of words and other mechanical features, is entirely unjustified. It may take ingenuity to adapt the most outstanding examples of children's literature to the technical needs of the remedial work but it can and should be done. The good remedial teacher has at hand a large stock of the most entrancing materials and has ability to work many of them into the remedial program.

3. *The materials should be of proper difficulty.* Pupils suffering from difficulties in reading have nearly always spent much time struggling with materials too difficult for them to read. It is of utmost importance that remedial work be conducted with material within the pupil's range of mastery. In the case of nonreaders or seriously retarded pupils, it may be difficult to secure material which is both of intrinsic interest and sufficiently easy. Within recent years, great progress has been made, however, in the writing of substantial and interest-provoking selections within the limits of a small vocabulary. Some of the organized systems in which readers are combined with preparatory or workbooks, both based upon the same vocabulary, are highly satisfactory for remedial instruction. In many instances, pupils may become highly interested in such books several grades below those corresponding to their chronological or mental-grade level. In other cases, additional activities or additional workbooks may be developed to prepare for and supplement books in which pupils are likely to show strong interest. By means of selection and supplementation, the materials as a whole must be made easier until a vocabulary burden is achieved which the pupil can carry. To enable the pupil to succeed as soon as possible in really doing full-fledged reading is one of the requirements of remedial instruction. To achieve this result, the materials must be easy to understand and must comprise a vocabulary relatively light for the particular pupil.

4. *The materials should be of various types.* In remedial instruction one usually has to deal with the type of pupil who has found his classroom selections difficult, long, and boring. In the first lessons in remedial work, even if they are highly successful, the time required to cover a given selection will be greater than that required by the able pupil, and the work is likely to be fatiguing. Many remedial cases are conspicuously prone to boredom in reading in any circumstances. Hence, the selections should be relatively short as well as easy, and should be varied in character. The ideal is to have a series of selections of different types, each written largely within the limits of the same vocabulary. Thus, the pupil is enabled to read stories of different types —humorous material, informative selections, directions to be executed in different ways, verse, problems of different sorts, instructions to be carried out in various types of projects, comprehension exercises of several forms, various questions to be considered, and so on. As different topics, types of materials, and forms of correlated activities

are tried out, the teacher can discover which ones are most, and which ones least enjoyed, and the proportions can be varied accordingly in later work. Over a period of time, all types should be sampled.

5. *An abundance of easy reading should be provided as a substitute for review.* The pupils who have had difficulty with some aspect of reading will usually need more review than the others. It is dangerous, however, to require a large amount of formal review, since mere *re-view*, without motivating incentives or purposes, will increase their distaste for reading. These pupils are usually already surfeited with review that has been conducted during and after school hours. Instead of such work, they should be given additional experiences on the same level, but with varied types, content, and purposes, as have been suggested above. In many instances, the teacher may need to make up much supplementary material herself. Another device is to develop incentives which make rereading purposeful and zestful. Thus, a series of thought-provoking comprehension questions may arouse a pupil's interest in rereading the material to find the substance bearing on a particular problem. Disagreement with another pupil or the teacher concerning the correct solution of a comprehension exercise may motivate rereading "to find out." Again, various new projects—such as making up a series of comprehension exercises for another pupil, selecting characters and episodes for a play, or a series of illustrations to be drawn and colored or sentences to combine into a summary—may be developed, which make rereading seem interesting and purposeful. Finally, the teacher should be able to supply additional selections which will carry the pupil on by as easily graded stages as may be desired. Familiarity with a wide variety of the best available materials for children's reading and skill in writing suitable materials when other resources fail, are assets in a remedial teacher.

6. *The teacher should help the pupil develop the need for reading.* Many children are poor readers chiefly for the reason that they have actually done very little reading except what they have been required to do in school. This is true of many children who have met the challenge of the initial stages of reading and acquired reasonably good reading ability in the first and second grades. Some children develop emotional resistance to reading when the task in school has been largely a rather arduous study-type of reading. In out-of-school hours they have spent their time in playing, working, talking, attending the movies, and listening to the radio. They have found it possible to get along comfortably and enjoyably without reading. In many cases the home provides few, if any, incentives. Other members of the family may read very little and spend their time talking and listening to the radio. The home may contain little reading matter attractive to children. These pupils gradually fall behind the normal reading development from lack of practice. The lack of practice comes from lack of

incentive or need. They really have found little or no insistent need for reading.

In such cases as these a major task in remedial reading (and in ordinary reading teaching as well) is that of trying to modify the pupil's life pattern in such a way that reading will serve a need in a highly satisfying way. The exact steps to take to achieve this end will differ with different children. In most cases finding highly interesting material which makes a contribution over and beyond that easily secured from the radio or other sources is another. Providing an opportunity for enjoyable free reading in the school may be a valuable step. Fuller returns will be secured if equally attractive provisions are made in the home. This may mean enlisting the services of parents to subscribe to attractive children's magazines, purchase interesting books, or secure them from public or private libraries. In some instances it may mean budgeting a particular time for reading. For example, the whole family may agree that at a certain time each evening everyone will read. The pupil is likely to join in with the family plan, especially if the parents make available challenging and interesting reading matter. In later pages suggestions will be given for making reading fill a greater need by providing opportunities for tangible use of the results of reading in the school and in the home.

MANAGEMENT OF THE REMEDIAL INSTRUCTION

Remedial instruction should be properly scheduled. One of the most serious defects of much remedial work is to be found in the lack of a proper program. When the remedial instruction is offered a bit now and a bit then at odd moments, it can hardly be highly effective. Deficiency in reading is serious enough to justify giving the remedial treatment a definite and preferred place in the daily program. The time usually spent in regular reading instruction should be utilized if possible. Additional periods should also be provided. A careful study of the pupil's attainments in other activities should be made to ascertain the most suitable periods for additional work. Some of the time customarily spent in activities in which the pupil is well advanced or which are of relatively little importance may be devoted to instruction in reading. In formulating such a program the following cautions should be observed:

1. *Remedial instruction should not be substituted for enjoyable activities.* It is of first importance to be certain that the remedial instruction does not result in depriving the pupil of highly cherished activities. For example, the pupil should not be deprived of recess time or of school activities which he especially enjoys. To do so is likely to arouse his resentment at once. A resentful pupil is not a good subject for instruction. Everything possible should be done to make the new program more enjoyable than the one it replaces.

2. *Remedial instruction should be managed so as not to classify the pupil*

in an embarrassing way. It is highly important to arrange the program and designate the periods and methods of remedial reading instruction in such a way as not to imply, or let other pupils feel, that a penalty is being applied. Pupils undertaking remedial work should not be classed as failures, "dumbbells," or commented upon as having to stay after school for punishment. One clever remedial teacher usually seizes upon some meritorious achievement of several pupils, among whom are those who are scheduled for remedial work, and offers as a reward a revised program for each. Thus, the programs for some very able readers as well as the poor ones are rearranged at the same time. In some cases, the very able readers follow a program essentially the same as that of the remedial cases, except that the former do advanced work on more difficult material. In some cases, the teacher arranges for all the children a program including several periods for individual or small-group enterprises of which the remedial work in reading is one. Thus the exercise of a little ingenuity may result in making the remedial program socially acceptable.

3. *The time allowance for remedial work should be generous.* If a pupil is seriously deficient in reading, abundant time should be provided for remedial instruction and for reading experience. To assume that a few minutes of drill now and then will suffice is quite unsafe. Cases that bring to the work inappropriate techniques, well habituated, and a history of boredom and distaste for reading are not corrected by a limited amount of effort. For the really serious cases, provision should be made for systematic instruction and for experience with the remedial materials *several times every day.* More than that, the pupils should be provided with opportunities to have carefully arranged reading experiences during as much of the remainder of the day as possible. Indeed, the best remedial work provides not only the definite instructional periods, but a whole program including activities in other subjects worked out around reading as a center. This, in its ideal form, includes the use of many exercises and directions in self-manageable form, supplementary materials of suitable difficulty for use in connection with other subjects, free reading of library materials, and opportunities to do enjoyable reading at home or elsewhere in out-of-school hours.

It should be recalled that we are now considering the pupil whose deficiency is serious and who has much ground to cover before he can read as well as he should. At the other extreme are pupils for whom one brisk remedial exercise a day in addition to the regular work is sufficient. But these pupils also should be provided with opportunities for much additional experience in reading. The remedial instruction and the teacher-directed practice should give birth to the essential techniques which must be developed into flourishing health and vigor through extensive, varied, and zestful reading experience.

4. *The teacher should have sufficient time to arrange and supervise the*

remedial work. Progressive schools are rapidly coming to realize that the costs and deprivations to both the pupil and the teacher of backwardness in reading are so great as to make adequate provision for prompt and effective remedial work an obvious economy. In such schools the teacher who discovers the need of instruction is either provided with a specialist in this work or with some assistance in her other work to enable her to formulate and carry out a thorough program. When such assistance is not available, the teacher should try to schedule her program, to utilize self-directive materials, to provide special educative projects which permit abler pupils to be of assistance in conducting class activities, and in other ways to conserve some time for the needs of the poor readers. Such activities as looking up material for and assisting the remedial cases in their projects, reading with them, giving them special suggestions or techniques, are often more educative to the abler pupils than strictly private enterprises would be. The poor reader requires for a time very careful and intelligent supervision, and he should have it!

5. *Remedial work may be either individual or cooperative.* Remedial work demands that much attention be given to the individual case. This does not mean, however, that the pupil who is deficient in reading must do all his work apart from other pupils. Indeed, there are certain advantages in having several pupils work together at times. As suggested above, the program should include periods devoted to individual instruction and check-up, alternating with periods of work of a self-manageable character done on materials which the pupil, because of familiarity with the vocabulary and subject matter, is prepared to handle with little or no help. While the teacher is devoting herself to one pupil, the others may be doing independent or cooperative work. Cooperative enterprises may be developed by having a small group work upon the same general topic. The pupils may be reading different selections, some much easier than others, but the common interest provides an incentive for reading choice bits aloud to each other, giving oral reports, and engaging in various related enterprises, such as searching the files of the library, visiting a museum, making posters, developing bulletin-board announcements, making a picture book, constructing objects, decorating the room, and so on. All these cooperative enterprises are made more workable by utilizing generous amounts of self-manageable materials related to a topic which lends itself readily to correlated activities and projects. Examples of such materials will be given in later chapters.

It is impossible to state definitely how many remedial cases a teacher should attempt to handle at once. The number will vary with the teacher's ability in the remedial field, the nature of the pupils' difficulties, their general competence and self-educative ability, the nature and amount of available instructional material, and many other factors. It is necessary, however, that the teacher have plenty of time to devote to the special needs of the individual case. Remedial instruction should not be primarily mass teaching. The serious reading case absolutely must have a generous amount of individual instruction.

6. *Remedial work should be begun at a favorable time.* The first meetings for individual remedial instruction are very important ones. The work should be started under favorable conditions. The pupil should not be tired. His mental attitude should be favorable; he should be caught in a cheerful and cooperative mood. He should not be in a state of readiness for some other attractive activity. The teacher should exercise ingenuity to establish a happy relation with him and to arouse his confidence and optimism. It is imperative that the first meetings develop in the pupil a feeling that the teacher is a good sort and that she will surely succeed in helping him out of his difficulty. Many remedial teachers make a practice of observing each case several times in the classroom before seeing him alone, and then of having several pleasant informal meetings with him before the reading problem is touched upon. In this way the remedial teacher finds out how best to get the child's interest and cooperation.

7. *Successes should be emphasized in remedial work.* For the pupil who appears for remedial work, reading has probably meant a long succession of difficulties and failures. He will probably be discouraged if not downright hopeless. Part of the strategy of remedial work is to shift the emphasis from failure to success. It is important to select and manage the first lesson so that something positive will be accomplished. The successful accomplishments should be featured and the difficulties disregarded. This policy, indeed, should be pursued throughout the work. Difficulties can be recognized and dealt with without implying failure or incompetence. Achievements worthy of recognition as successes can always be found even when the pupil has fallen far short of a perfect performance as a whole. To develop a taste of success after prolonged failure is one of the devices which ensures continued success.

8. *Improvement should be measured and the record shown.* In remedial instruction it is highly important not only to make the pupil's progress possible, but also to make clear to the learner the improvement he has achieved. He needs both the teacher's assurance that he is getting on and objective evidence of improvement. Better than vague assurance is a definite, intelligible expression of the amount of advancement. For these reasons one may often use in remedial work devices for demonstrating a pupil's achievement each day and thereby make possible a convincing expression of progress. The daily achievements may be recorded in graphic or other form so as to indicate the curve of improvement. The statement "Nothing succeeds like success" should, perhaps, be changed to "Nothing succeeds like observed success."

9. *The pupil's particular errors and successes should be detected.* The devices for appraising achievement and progress should be sufficiently definite, furthermore, to reveal the particular successes and errors made in daily work. The teacher may utilize such records as means of further diagnosis, of discovering in what particulars the pupil errs and requires further experience. The pupils themselves may be taught to check their own errors and to seek for their causes. A child can recognize his errors without feeling that he is failing in general. The obscurity which, from their point of view, surrounds the efforts of young learners is not infrequently one cause of loss of interest in improving. To have their successes and errors become apparent is often a means of arousing interest and of inspiring effort to understand and correct defects.

In many cases, the teacher can help the pupil effectively by discussing with him the nature of his difficulties. Children who have had trouble in reading have sometimes overheard discouraging, if not terrifying, explanations or terms—have caught such expressions as "word-blindness," "moron," "laziness," "brain injury," "something wrong with his mind," and so on. As a result a pupil may harbor insidious impressions of which his teacher is unaware. To explain the facts, pointing out that the difficulties are merely matters of incorrect knack that the pupil has acquired just as one might develop wrong methods of handling a baseball bat or of diving, may result not only in helpful insight, but also in a vastly improved emotional adjustment. Indeed, most of the tricks of the business of reading can be explained to the normal child to his advantage. To be a skillful remedial teacher, one must learn the possibilities and difficulties of explaining things to the pupil.

10. *The teacher's attitude should be optimistic and encouraging.* Encouragement and cheerful assistance may frequently be needed. Children of the type most likely to be in need of remedial treatment are notably susceptible to "off days" and to periods of apparent or real stagnation in interest. At such times they should realize that the most skilled baseball players, golfers, composers, artists, and others are subject to the very same difficulties—that even to the seasoned expert such periods come at times. Indeed, it is not at all improbable that disabilities in and distaste for many activities among children originate in the throes of such "plateaus" in the curve of learning. It is, therefore, important that the teacher detect such crises and that she deal with the child at these times with greatest skill and tact.

11. *The teacher should help the pupil avoid overanxiety and unduly extreme effort.* A common mistake in dealing with pupils who have had great difficulty in reading, especially the reading failure, is to assume that they have failed because they have not tried hard enough. Except for certain cases of misleading motivation discussed in the preceding chapter this is a very rare characteristic. Children are much

more frequently trying too hard than not trying hard enough. They are more typically overly anxious and prone to exert themselves to a point of tension and distraction. In many cases the pupil shows a tendency to shift from extreme effort to refusal to work. For example, if a child applies himself with intense effort but fails to master the assignment he may react by falling into a period of discouragement in which he really refuses to try. After a long period of frustration a pupil's emotional adjustment in the reading situation is likely to be tense, or flighty, or both, at times. Much of the success of the instruction depends upon the teacher's ability to get the pupil into a favorable emotional attitude.

An ideal attitude is one of almost carefree, zestful action characteristic of a pupil in some enjoyable game. Attempts of the child deliberately to arouse himself to an intense pitch of determination, the much applauded do-or-die attitude, are likely to do more harm than good. Trying too hard is often one of the main obstacles to learning. Dr. Fernald, who has spent a lifetime teaching nonreaders to read, states, "In all these cases conscious effort to do well resulted in a decrease in efficiency." Efforts to increase the intensity of the work are likely only to produce tension. A free, confident, "Isn't this fun?" attitude is the one in which individuals learn most effectively. Unfortunately, this is a fact which many parents and teachers do not believe.

To get the pupil into a favorable learning attitude and to keep him there the teacher must exercise continued caution. She must avoid becoming tense and discouraged herself. She must avoid letting the child sense any anxiety even if she feels it. She must beware of urging him to extreme effort. She must avoid giving the appearance of checking up on the pupil too rigorously. At least she must avoid giving any expression of disapproval or concern over his errors. Even adults can be disturbed when others follow their every move in adding up a bridge score or in reading a bit of verse. Poor readers usually develop undue sensitivity because of many unfortunate experiences resulting from their blunders in the past. It would be undesirable to introduce undue tension into the reading activity even if it should foster learning—which it does not. The reason for this is that the tension might persist as part of the reading process after the pupil has become a proficient reader, with the result that every time he engaged in reading he would be wasting his energy through emotional tensions, as many of us do when we talk before an audience.

12. *Practice should be so distributed as to avoid fatigue and boredom.* Care should be exercised not to permit the remedial lessons to continue at any one time to the point of fatigue or boredom. Several short periods of lively work are superior to an equal total time devoted to continuous study. Although the optimum length of the remedial lesson varies so greatly with the age, interest, strength, freshness, and stability

of the pupil and with the character of the practice that no single
guiding rule can be offered, the teacher may, by carefully observing
signs of waning zeal, acquire good judgement in deciding when a
lesson has run its fruitful course.

13. *A variety of exercises and activities should be provided.* Fatigue and
loss of zeal in remedial work may result from prolonged use of the
same type of material and device and, contrariwise, interest and
application may be preserved by variety. Since in remedial instruction
the pupils are engaged in mastering skills that have proved troublesome, they are more likely to tire quickly than in other types of work.
The need for variety in content, activities, exercises, and checks is therefore especially great. Projects which require much accurate reading,
such as reading coupled with comprehension checks which take the
form of selecting, drawing, or coloring illustrations, the use of puzzle
paragraphs to be solved, or of individual and group competitive games
in which the reading is realistic and abundant are types of activities
that may often be enlisted to increase interest. Indeed, it would be
desirable to have for each specific purpose a sufficient variety of
remedial devices to make it possible to provide the pupil with a
choice.

14. *A plan should be dropped when it fails to produce results after a fair
trial.* The preceding statement is obviously trite. It is nevertheless true
that while remedial instruction of a given type is sometimes dropped
too soon, it may be continued too long. The teacher must always be
critical, as skillful physicians are, both of her diagnosis and of her
remedial treatment. One type of treatment will be highly successful
with one pupil but will fail to help another who seems to have substantially the same difficulty. The teacher must constantly, while teaching,
diagnose the pupil's difficulty and his reaction to the instruction. She
should experiment skillfully with different explanations, demonstrations, instructions, and related devices. While it is hazardous to attempt
to state any general rule about changing instruction, it is a rare case
which should not, in three or four weeks, show pronounced improvement from daily instruction. One should be very suspicious of the
diagnosis or the remedial program or both if the pupil does not show
a marked gain in this time.

15. *Individual supervision should be continued until the pupil has his
improved techniques well habituated.* Individual remedial instruction
frequently produces remarkably rapid growth of reading skill. The
teacher should remember, however, that it takes time to habituate
quite new techniques. The teacher can probably recall experiences of
her own in adapting a new method of writing, typewriting, pronouncing words, swimming, or what not, in which the old habits were
likely to pop up in moments of fatigue or tension or relaxed attention.
Pupils are prone to relapses to the older bad habits or to a state of

discouragement. It is therefore advisable for the teacher to continue to keep the pupil's reading under supervision until she is quite certain that he is safely established in the better methods. A relapse in reading, as in disease, is very discouraging to the patient.

16. *The pupil must be induced to read widely in order to ensure further growth in reading.* A mistake sometimes made is to assume that reading, as in disease, is very discouraging to the patient.

intensive remedial work will take care of itself in all future reading situations. Superior readers are typically persons who read more than the average. Skill in reading is like skill in singing, playing the piano, painting pictures, and doing other subtle artistic acts. To achieve high levels requires continuously spending much time in the activity. Two children of equal reading and other abilities at the beginning of the third grade are likely to differ widely in reading ability a few years later if one does a great deal more reading than the other. No child is likely to continue to grow in reading ability or to maintain a high level of proficiency if his reading is confined to the necessary assignments in school. Reading ability can be carried forward only on the basis of the full school program supplemented by considerable free reading for the fun of it and for other purposes in out-of-school hours. The remedial case brought to a relatively high point by an intensive program will fail to keep pace with his companions, indeed is likely to retrogress, if his total volume of zestful reading in the future falls short of that of his classmates.

REFERENCES

The topics introduced in this chapter are especially well treated in the following books:

Betts, Emmett A., *Foundations of Reading Instruction,* American Book Company, New York, 1946, especially pp. 1–114, 438–488.

Durrell, Donald D., *Improvement of Basic Reading Abilities,* World Book Company, Yonkers-on-Hudson, New York, 1940, Chap. I.

Gans, Roma, *Guiding Children's Reading Through Experiences,* Teachers College, Columbia University, New York, 1941.

Newer Practices in Reading in the Elementary School, Seventeenth Yearbook of the Department of Elementary School Principals, National Education Association, Washington, D. C., 1938.

Witty, Paul A., and David Kopel, *Reading and the Educative Process,* Ginn & Company, Boston, 1939.

17. THE TEACHING OF REMEDIAL READING

Board of Education of the City of New York

A. Preparing to Teach Your Students

1. *Discipline*

Class control is not a matter of babysitting or policing your students. It is an art the teacher practices by:

a. disciplining his own emotional attitudes towards the students.

b. developing desirable emotional attitudes in the students.

2. *The Teachers Attitudes*

a. *The use of fear* as a weapon and the display of negative emotions (impatience, irritation, sarcasm, etc.) have no place in a remedial reading class. These students are already bogged down by reading blocks acquired through the years (sometimes because they were subjected to embarrassment and unsympathetic treatment in the classroom); you do not want to add to these reading blocks.

b. A "soft" and excessively tolerant attitude, however, can be more detrimental than the fear-inspiring attitude. (Note to new teachers: Do not try to make your class like you; it will like you in time when it sees that you understand and respect your job).

c. *In handling the recalcitrant student,* you will find that firmness with quiet humor is more effective than firmness with intimidation.

d. *Show your students* that you have faith in their ability to raise their reading levels and that you understand their problems.

For example:

(1) In motivating them to read the thumbnail character sketches of under par readers in *Reading Skills*, you must first weed out their sense of shame. You will see your students come to life at once if you say, "You haven't failed to learn to read. Do you know who failed? Some individuals in your past—in school, perhaps at home. They didn't stop to give you help when you needed it. . . . "

(2) They will then not only read with interest; they will surprise you with their ability to spot the emotional difficulties which underlie the reading problems of the fictitious characters.

3. *Developing Desirable Attitudes in the Students—Routines*

Reprinted from *Teaching English for Higher Horizons,* 1965, pp. 336–343. By permission of the New York City Board of Education.

a. *The very first day,* establish class routines. Train students to get down to work as soon as they enter the room.

    (1) They copy the homework assignment.

    (2) Following instructions on the blackboard, they work on a daily drill in their notebooks. The daily drill, review or a preparation for a new lesson, makes your class "self-starting."

    (3) Always follow up by calling on a student to read aloud the homework assignment to make sure it has been properly understood. While students are working with their notebooks, it is important to walk around and check on individual performances. Encourage the dreamers and doodlers to get down to work. (Remember: these individuals are expert escapists!)

b. *Acquaint* the students with your standards of performance. They have to know what you expect from them. Show them your Delaney book, your marking book; explain exactly how you will keep track of their progress. Explain your class laws—they respect laws, they want them. They also want to see you respecting your own laws. To carry them out check homework, grade written work, appreciate their efforts. Reward those who conform; punish those who do not go along with the class with a minus or zero—quietly, firmly, unemotionally.

4. *Classifying Your Students*

a. *Diagnose* the reading problems of each student. Procedure: Keep the class busy reading a simple story and writing answers. One by one, invite individuals to the privacy of the rear of the room. Reassure them; engage the nervous ones in a friendly conversation. Explain, "You and I are trying to find out where you need help. Don't read too fast. If you come to a word you don't know, I'll help you." After each reads, point out his difficulties. "This is what you and I are going to work on." (This individual approach will also strengthen your class control and eliminate discipline problems).

b. *Record* for each student:

    (1) In oral reading—his problems with phonetics, faulty eye movements, habits of repeating phrases, finger pointing.

    (2) In silent reading—comprehension, speed, lip reading.

    (3) Clues, if any, to personality difficulties.

c. Classify them:

    (1) Group I—the non-readers (they are confused by consonant combinations—st, str, ch, cr, cl, etc. They cannot sound out vowels and confuse bit, bet, bat, but).

    (2) Group II—students with crippled reading habits: faulty eye movements, lip reading, stalling and repeating words, inability to sound out words, guessing "river" for "lake," "people" for "passengers."

(3) Group III—students who need training in comprehension, reading speed, skimming.

B. Teaching Your Class

1. *Speaking and Listening*

Before you start to teach reading, it will be ultimately rewarding to you and the students if you concentrate for a few days on teaching them to listen and speak.

These are frightened, defeated children. Too often humbled, they have learned to escape from demanding situations. Withdrawn, they have learned how not to hear. Too often wrong, they have learned to mumble through their recitations, faking words they cannot read. They have become like clams which you must learn to open up.

One method which has been found effective is the following:

a. *Homework assignment*
    (1) Find a newspaper story (not a picture with caption) which is a happy story. (Teach students to look for examples of heroism, humanitarianism, honesty, etc.).
    (2) Write an outline, stating:
       i.   *Whom* is the story about?
       ii. *Where* does it take place?
       iii. *What* happens?
       iv. *Why* do you think it is a "happy" story?
       (Note: These questions begin to form the foundation for ultimate reading for *main* ideas).

b. The *next* day, hammer away to fix the four W's in the students' minds. Ask them, "What are the four W's?" Write the W's on the board—large. Have the students go over their outlines to make sure they have followed instructions.

c. *Now they* are ready to make their oral reports—without referring to their outlines.

d. *The audience has* to listen because its job is to report whether the speaker has covered the four W's. Each student records on a sheet of paper the speaker's name and a brief account of the speech.

e. *The speaker has* to speak clearly to make himself understood. (Be a humanitarian: unobtrusively, help out the speaker who is numb with shyness by questioning him with interest).

f. *The teacher must* check the papers (for performance, not accuracy) —or he will lose his class in subsequent recitations of this sort.

2. *How Do You Teach Three Groups in One Class?*

Not all remedial classes fall into three groups; some may even be homogeneous. If, however, your class requires group treatment, you become a conductor leading an orchestra. Give your most advanced group its lesson for the day (while the rest work on a special daily drill); then leave it on its own with reading and writing papers which will be checked. Proceed to the middle group. Finally, work with the non-readers in the back of the room.

3. *Handling Group I (non-readers)*

a. *It is* too late in their lives and there is too little time in class to concentrate on teaching these students sight reading. You must find short cuts to reach them; melt away their reading blocks and give them what they have never had before: a sense of achievement. What materials do you use?

b. *The materials* lie in the students themselves. Let's start there. They cannot distinguish, for example, between "bat" and "bet." You decide the lesson for the day is the short "e."

   (1) *Write* "Senator Kennedy" on the board. When the student learns to associate "e" with some common experience, he will learn to read that "e." Is there an **Ed, Fred, Emma, Eleanor** in the class? The students write these names in their notebooks; they underline the "e's." These are key words which will keep reminding them how to sound out the short "e."

   (2) *You dictate simple* words with "e"—met, let, get, set, jet, etc. When necessary, you stop to teach consonants.

   (3) *All* these words, together with more difficult ones, are available for reference on the blackboard. Now drill with them orally, progressing from the simple to the most difficult.

   (4) The *next day* you hand the students a simple typewritten story. (You've composed it yourself.) It concentrates on the "e." (It may be an absurd little story, but it has a beginning, middle and end.) It might read like this: Then the ten men went to Ella's wedding. When they entered, everybody went home. What happened? The wedding depended on Eddie, the groom, but he had chickened out.

   (5) *The students* find they cannot read the story. You promise them, "You're going to read it, each one of you, before the end of the period."

   (6) *On the blackboard*, you have listed the underscored words what happened? The wedding depended on Eddie, the groom, together with many others. You drill the students. Ask for volunteers. Encourage the backward. Make it a game. Make them feel they have all the time in the world. Give hints.

   (7) *You return* to the story. The quicker students read first; the slower follow. In the end, all are able to read the story. Your non-readers walk out of your class—with an experience.

   (8) To *guide you*, the English Department will provide you with

Dolch's list of basic words. Ready-made materials, however, can be like dehydrated soups—dull and uninspiring both to student and teacher. There are live materials all around you. For example, ask the students if they are interested in driving a car. "But can you *read* all those traffic signs?" With this motivation, will they resist when you begin to teach the short and long "o's" with "Stop" and "Go."

4. *Handling Group II (faulty eye movements, lip reading, phonetics)*
   a. We have worthwhile books which take the student and teacher step by step through the reading skills to be mastered. Students love to keep charts of their own progress through drills and timed reading. They relish small experiments suggested by the textbook. They like all this, however, only if the teacher makes them aware of what skills they are trying to acquire.
   b. *It is enjoyable* to supplement the material in the textbook with live materials or devices that crop up each day:
      (1) Newspaper headlines and stories—reports, hurricanes, domestic incidents, etc.
      (2) *Accounts* of a big fire or a nuclear conference will make the students interested in reading those dull air raid and fire drill charts on the bulletin board.
      (3) *"I've* received a letter which I've been too busy to open and read," says the teacher. "Do you want to help me read it?" He promises that tomorrow he will mimeograph the material and the class will read it together.
      (4) *The students,* entering the classroom, become fascinated by some object planted on the teacher's desk—a horseshoe crab, milkweed pod, gadget—some visual expression of what the teacher experienced over the week-end. They ask questions, their curiosity rising when they see the teacher deliberately pretending lack of interest. Finally—"Do you really want to know?" On the board, or on mimeographed sheets, there is the story which they are clamoring for.
      (5) *Have you* noticed how eagerly they work when you tell them to fold their papers into four columns or show them how to prepare a chart? They like to make things. They are good at reading instructions and following them through. You can, by guiding them to sources, inspire them to bring in instructions on how to make something. From this material you can evolve live lessons for a week or two.
      (6) *To teach* them new words or phonetics, you might ask them to bring some particular advertisement in color from the Sunday newspaper. It will show many different items. On the board, list the names of these objects. The class reads these

words aloud; writes them in their notebooks; drills orally. Finally each student writes the proper word beside each object in the advertisement.

(7) *These* are only a few suggestions. You will find the world around you providing many more ideas.

5. *Handling Group III (comprehension, grasping of main ideas, details, increasing speed, learning to skim)*

a. *We have* textbooks which take us expertly through these phases but they can be enervating if the teacher does not stay alert.

b. *Students* must be made aware of the *purpose* of each lesson; they must recognize the *immediacy* of its importance to them; and, above all, they must be guided through experiences which prove that they are making progress.

c. *Example*: A lesson in learning how to skim.

(1) Students receive a list of questions in social studies.

(2) They have before them the textbook opened to the right chapter.

(3) You tell them, "I am going to give you exactly one minute to write the answers to the first three questions. Do not read the chapter word by word. Find the answers and write them down. When you are finished, raise your hand."

(4) At first the students may be dismayed and protest. You remind them of previous experiences through which you led them to successful performances.

(5) They settle down to their task. They are not wholly aware you have been working with them for this particular experience. For weeks, you have drilled them to find main ideas in paragraphs and entire essays: you have trained them to spot clues—key words, italics, capitalized words, dates, figures.

(6) Before the minute is over, hands are raised, faces beam. You encourage the slower students with a hint or two.

(7) You listen to their answers. "How did you do it?" you ask with disbelief. They respond, "Well, you find the main idea— italics—dates—etc."

(8) "What is this called?" you ask. You get your answer from them because they really know: "Skimming."

6. *Teaching Them Vocabulary*

The vocabulary of these students is often so limited that some of them believe "comets" and "comments" mean "comics." How do you attack the problem of vocabulary with students so poor in background experience? You will devise methods of your own to fit your particular students. Here is one procedure, however, which can be rewarding:

a. *Using* words which they will encounter in a future reading assignment, compose a story and have it rexographed.

b. *The story* is designed to stir them up; it invades *their own areas of living*. They read the title: "Mike, Our Delinquent Hero in the Cafeteria" and, with some prodding from you, they identify themselves with Mike, the hero.

   (1) *They attempt* to read the story—only to become frustrated. "What do these big words mean?" (What are they saying about Mike—me—my secret Walter Mitty self?)

      "Mike *consistently* strutted into the cafeteria and *ogled* the girls. *Belligerently*, he defied the teachers. *Reprimanded* for his obnoxious behavior, he . . ."

   (2) *For homework*, the students write the dictionary definitions of the underscored words. (You've taught them how, of course.) In addition, they translate the story into their own words.

c. *Learning* new words is not easy even for brighter students. The teacher MUST STAY with the vocabulary list until the students enjoy the success of having learned most of it and can pass a test. How is this done?

d. *Varied Drills*

   (1) One day they copy the list from the board (practicing the sounding out of the words); then they select the correct meaning for each word from three suggested definitions.

   (2) The next day they again copy the list and find the definitions suggested in a matching list.

   (3) The third day they are given a homework assignment to write sentences, using the new words. (Caution: they must first be trained to write sentences that are meaningful and conducive to learning the words: *not* "Jim was an obnoxious boy," but "Mary thought Jim was obnoxious because he was rude to his grandfather.")

   (4) The next day (while the class is working on the daily drill), you walk around and check the homework, and have the best sentences written on the board—with a blank left where the new word is used.

   (5) The students copy each sentence in their notebooks and supply the missing word.

   (6) The author of each sentence reads it aloud, asks the class to supply the missing word and spell it out while he writes it in the blank space.

   (7) Has the class learned the vocabulary? Not yet. You teach the students how to study and memorize. One day you allot 10 or 15 minutes for actual memorizing. Then administer a pretest and self-grading.

   (8) Finally, you give the real test—and reap the tens.

7. *All This Is Not READING*

You have merely been preparing your students to read. Now you must provide them with a real reading experience—reading for pleasure.

a. *You make a date* in the library. Inform the librarian of the approximate reading levels of your class. You stir up your students with the fact that very special books have been selected—just for them. Instruct them to listen to the librarian carefully. Tell them you expect to be proud of their intelligent conduct in the library.

b. *After the librarian* talks to them about the books she has selected, if you have stirred them up sufficiently, some will try to take out three, four books at once. (Limit them to two.)

c. *Escort the class* back to your room as soon as possible. Start the students reading their books immediately. Homework assignment: "Read the first two chapters. Write an outline: *Who? Where? What* happened? *What* do you think will happen next?"

d. *The following day,* have them give oral reports and share their experiences with the class.

e. *You must stay* with the students until they finish their books. For a few days let them read in class, writing a précis for each chapter. (You can then work with your non-readers.) Every day assign two chapters and a written report for homework. Eventually, they will write a final book report.

f. *Some will* finish their books in two or three days. (Do not insist on a chapter-by-chapter report from these students.) Others will take a week or two. Those who finish will start on another book—usually on their own. Praise and encourage both the quick and the slow. Never make the slow feel inferior but be firm and insist they finish their reports by a given deadline.

g. *How do you grade* the reports? Give them A, B, C, or D, according to neatness and fullness. (Do not attempt the impossible task of reading each report carefully. You do not have this kind of time. After all, this is a *reading* class and teaching it to write is incidental.)

h. *Arrange for another visit to the library.*
This time introduce the students to the pleasures of reading magazines. Inform the librarian that you are supplying the class with topics: automobiles, planes, carpentry, boats, beauty, homemaking, love, mental illness, art, etc.

B. Diagnostic Teaching

18. DIAGNOSTIC TEACHING IN UPPER ELEMENTARY GRADES

Margaret J. Early

How will teaching reading in the upper elementary grades be affected by the overwhelming attention currently being paid to beginning reading instruction? How will it be affected by changes in curriculum and organization such as the middle school, non-graded programs and varying degrees of departmentalization?

There is the possibility that upper elementary teachers will once again listen to the siren song of "learning to read in primary grades and reading to learn thereafter." The grain of truth in this cliché seems to be supported by claims of newer basal programs and linguistic-phonics approaches that all the word-analysis skills, from letter-sound relationships through use of the dictionary, can be learned by the end of third grade. Suppose that excellent teaching in the primary grades did indeed insure mastery of this stepped-up program, so that by fourth grade most children could decode any printed word and use context and other comprehension skills to discover meanings. Would teachers in grade four and beyond then be justified in adopting "reading to learn" as their watchword? No, not if that slogan is interpreted as assigning students to read without teaching them how. But if "reading to learn" is interpreted as teaching youngsters *how* to learn through reading, there is reason to believe that reading programs in upper elementary grades may be greatly strengthened. Real improvements in materials and methods of teaching beginning reading have appeared in this decade. Teachers in grades four to six now have the chance to build stronger programs on the improved foundations of primary reading instruction if they refuse to believe that a good start means that "reading to learn" just happens.

Upper elementary teachers who have learned to analyze the reading process and to observe its development in individual children are prepared to teach reading-to-learn skills or to re-teach learning-to-read skills. They know that some children who have "been through" the 3-2 reader

Reprinted from *Vistas in Reading*, J. Allen Figurel, Editor, Proceedings of the Eleventh Annual Convention, International Reading Association (Newark, Delaware, 1966), pp. 245–248. By permission of Margaret Early and The International Reading Association.

have not necessarily mastered skills of beginning reading. On the other hand, they know that some children at the beginning of fourth grade have not only mastered beginning skills but are able to apply these skills in increasingly complex materials. Diagnostic teaching is as vital a service to advanced students as it is to the retarded.

A second influence on teaching reading in upper elementary grades— the burgeoning curriculum and new organizational patterns—may be positive or negative. Teachers' skills in diagnosis can determine which. Surely the reading program stands to suffer from increasing specialization in the upper elementary grades if the experience of the junior high school is duplicated. Here we have seen departmentalization make every teacher a subject specialist (in intent, if not in fact) and none a teacher of reading. We have tried to patch up the situation by creating "extra" reading classes that isolate skills instruction from the learning of subject matter, or we have tried without notable success to train subject specialists in methods of teaching reading.

The way to avoid similar problems in the elementary school is to keep the self-contained classroom, bringing subject-matter specialists to the children instead of dispersing them on a fixed schedule to teachers who lose track of individuals when they have pupil loads of one hundred or more. In a design that allows for specialization without departmentalizing, language learning (including reading) is central to the whole curriculum and the core of the classroom teacher's education. The help he needs in teaching math and science, social studies, art, and music comes into the classroom in the person of the teacher-consultant who adds depth, richness, and accuracy to the curriculum. But the children continue to be observed and guided by the one who knows most about their learning processes. I am suggesting that reading specialists in the intermediate grades should be the classroom teachers. The subject specialists should be the "floaters," working with teachers and pupils but without permanent relationships with or responsibilities for grading any groups.

What turns a classroom teacher into a reading specialist? More than anything else, it is the ability to diagnose and to develop strengths and correct weaknesses. Any teacher can distinguish good readers from poor and fair-to-middlin' ones. During the first week of school, without consulting the cumulative folders or the standardized reading-test scores, Miss Jones can tell which of her students can read the fourth grade texts with ease and which cannot. But so could any layman. What makes Miss Jones a professional is her skill in analyzing *why* pupils can read some books fluently and with understanding and others haltingly and without comprehension. We mean "why" in the sense of what specific reading skills are present or lacking. The deeper "why" of causation is one that Miss Jones should also explore, with help from the school psychologist, physician, the child's family, and others; but when she finds pupils who are severely and inexplicably retarded, she will have to refer them for clinical diagnosis and treatment.

Determining the readability level at which a child can learn through reading is a necessary first step. It is accomplished through the informal inventory based on graded selections from basal readers, which serve also as a limited vehicle for analyzing the reading performance. This crude instrument allows a sensitive teacher to guess at how a child normally attacks silent reading by sampling how he reads at sight and by comparing comprehension after silent and oral reading. Analysis of oral-reading errors can reveal specific weaknesses in word attack—errors on medial sounds are most common among poor readers in intermediate grades—and in use of context. But the significance of specific errors varies widely. A meaningful substitution is a far different order of error from a mispronunciation or wild guess. Refusal to try a word indicates the most serious weakness. Similarly, comprehension errors vary in significance. Accurate comprehension after silent reading alters our evaluation of the oral-reading performance.

So, merely quantifying errors on an informal inventory is no more revealing than on a standardized-test score. Each error must be weighed sensitively if appraisal is to be accurate. Even so, an informal inventory, like any other test, only starts a series of hypotheses. Diagnostic teaching is the process of continuously checking hunches.

The classroom teacher uses the informal inventory only on those pupils he suspects of reading below grade level. He identifies these through testing oral reading in small groups and notes on index cards the nature of each child's performance. Children who read a sample passage from a grade-level reader with at least 70 per cent comprehension and few gross oral-reading errors may be grouped for instruction at this level. Excellent readers form another group, perhaps to be instructed from a higher-level basal. After individually testing the poorest readers, the teacher knows the level where developmental-reading instruction can safely begin for them, and he knows the types of weaknesses that require supplemental skills instruction. Moreover, through individual and group testing of this kind he acquires a first rough estimate of the independent-reading levels of average and poor readers.

Since the basal program is but one phase of teaching reading, diagnosis extends to the subject texts and to analysis of study skills. (Children reading on primary levels are excused from this phase of the diagnosis. They are not yet ready to learn very much through reading; their study of math, science, social studies, and literature must be largely accomplished through listening and oral participation, with tape recordings and visuals supplementing class discussions.) We cannot assume that children capable of reading grade-level basal readers will learn through reading subject texts at corresponding levels.

Diagnosis should begin with the teacher's careful analysis of these textbooks, which will reveal the need for types of reading not ordinarily encountered in basal readers, workbooks, or skills exercises. For example, successful reading of science texts requires initial understanding of the organizational pattern of the whole book and of individual chapters, the ability to integrate the reading of experiments (following directions, using diagrams and pictures) with the basic text, skill in noting details, ability to construct concepts and to hypothesize ability to evaluate and revise generalizations, and habits of flexible reading. Skill in identifying major and minor ideas, which is developed on well-structured expository prose in reading workbooks, must often be abandoned or greatly modified for reading science, math, and even social studies books, which employ single-sentence paragraphs, omnibus paragraphs containing more than one main idea, and transitional paragraphs that express no main idea. Outlining based on following the author's organization does not work in many textbooks which instead require the student to reorganize the author's ideas into a logical, easily retained structure.

Analysis of subject texts will convince the teacher that the spectrum of reading skills to be developed in upper elementary grades extends far beyond the basal. Thoroughly acquainted with the styles of textbook writing and publishing, the teacher will observe carefully how students respond to problems such as those noted above, will estimate how much assistance they need, and will decide when and how to offer it.

The diagnosis which precedes teaching will have to be limited. One clue to the readability of a specific text may be obtained by duplicating a passage omitting every fifth or seventh word. Children who can restore about 70 per cent of the deleted words (or their equivalents) can probably learn from this text.

Teaching the over-all structure of the whole book should be a first step, followed by frequent checks of ability to use the table of contents, index, glossary, and special features. Diagnosis continues as the teacher evaluates children's readiness for each assignment in a subject textbook, observes their attack, and listens to their discussions of what they have read.

Since there will be differences in the abilities of a group of children for whom a single textbook is a' reasonably good choice, differentiated study guides will provide more direction for some, less for others. A study guide for one group may re-word complex passages or supply help with concept formation or call attention to context clues. For another group using the same text, the study guide may call for more subtle inferences or may challenge pupils to question facts and generalizations.

In the upper elementary grades, children of comparable abilities in word skills and basic comprehension develop divergent rates of reading. Diagnostic teaching uncovers such differences and makes provisions for them.

Diagnosis of reading and study skills means probing children's responses to reading and their uses of ideas obtained from reading. Comparisons must be made between the ability to recognize ideas on objective-type tests and to reproduce them in free responses and the ability to interpret and extend ideas. Since facility in expression is crucial in measuring comprehension, written and oral responses should be compared.

Yet diagnostic teaching is not simply a matter of varied testing procedures. It is more a matter of observing how children respond to various approaches, how they answer questions phrased in different ways, and how they react to different degrees of teacher direction. Diagnostic teaching means observing how a child attacks an assignment in a textbook, how he uses references, how he chooses books, how he behaves while reading, and what his attitudes are.

The object is to find out what lies behind a test score and how a pupil learns best in order to facilitate learning to read and to make learning through reading not merely possible but desirable in his eyes.

19. DIAGNOSTIC TEACHING OF READING IN HIGH SCHOOL

Ruth Strang

What is the diagnostic teaching of reading? It is teaching that is based on an understanding of individual students and of the class as a whole. It is a process of identifying, appraising, diagnosing, and evaluating. It goes on continuously during the school years. In this process the teacher learns how each student reads—what his strengths and weaknesses are; what the student reads; why he reads—what his purposes in reading are; and what conditions facilitate or hinder his reading development.

The teacher makes immediate use of much of the understanding thus obtained. He interweaves diagnosis with instruction, and, in fact, with the total educational process. The entire school staff uses this information about students in building the curriculum and in selecting the texts, other instructional materials, and even the specific stories, poems, novels, or articles to be read by a given class. In every reading lesson, the teacher uses his knowledge of the students in setting up the objectives, orienting the students, giving instruction, guiding their thinking, and

Reprinted from *The Journal of Reading*, Vol. 8 (January 1965), pp. 147–154. By permission of Ruth Strang and The International Reading Association.

testing and evaluating the knowledge and the reading skills that they have gained from their learning experiences.

COMPLEXITIES OF DIAGNOSTIC TEACHING

The diagnostic teaching of reading in high school is as complex as it is necessary. Students may range in ability from nonreaders to college preparatory students who want to increase their reading efficiency. In high schools today there are many students who lack word recognition skills and a working knowledge of the basic elements of a sentence. There are others who understand the relation between subject, verb, and object in a sentence, but are unable to see relationships among the ideas in a paragraph. There are others who lack the necessary experience with life and literature to interpret the words and literary passages they are expected to comprehend.

Moreover, departmental organization offers the teacher less opportunity for observation and personal contact than does the self-contained classroom. And the larger majority of high school teachers have had little or no preparation for the teaching of higher-level reading skills—recognizing the author's intent, mood, and purpose; interpreting character and motivation; tracing sequences in thought; and reading critically and creatively.

Diagnosis of the reading proficiency of high school students is further complicated by social and emotional factors. Some students seem to feel no need to improve their reading; their daily activities require a minimum of reading. Only when they are confronted with the need to get a driver's license, fill out an application blank, pass the army classification test, or get training for skilled work do they become aware that they need more reading ability.

It is even more difficult to understand and help the student who feels no responsibility for developing his potentialities or for contributing to the work of the world. Others have become apathetic, have cultivated an aloofness from the realities of life, or have developed feelings of worthlessness and hopelessness. Some have never had successful reading experiences or been in an environment in which people enjoy and profit by reading. Still others have not been helped to take advantage of crucial periods of learning readiness in early childhood, and have consequently not developed a love of learning. At first glance it seems impossible for high school teachers to diagnose the multiple factors that are involved in reading development and reading difficulties.

However, if we view the diagnostic-teaching process as a continuum, we see that one end comprises many tasks that every teacher can do; at the other end there may be a need for expert clinical, psychological, or psychiatric service.

SCHOOL AND CLASS RECORDS

It takes time to study every student's cumulative record. If a teacher were to spend only ten minutes on each record, it would take twenty-five hours to examine the records of 150 students—the average high school teacher's load. It is unrealistic to expect every teacher to spend as much time as this.

However, the teacher may ask each student to prepare a personal data card. If this card is introduced as an opportunity for self-appraisal, students are likely to fill it out fairly accurately and frankly.

This record includes blanks for the student's name, age, and address; the subjects he likes best and least; his educational and vocational plans; his special interests and hobbies; the titles of the books and articles he has read during the past month and the past year; and other information that the teacher thinks is particularly pertinent. Having these cards filled out not only lightens the teacher's clerical work, but also gives each student a certain perspective on his educational plans and progress. The "Reading Autobiography"[1] accomplishes this purpose still more effectively.

To the information supplied by the pupil the teacher may add, in all or only in certain cases, test results and other significant information from cumulative records. By spending a short time reading these cards, the teacher will get an idea of the make-up of the class as a whole, and some understanding of the individual pupils. This information he can use immediately in selecting books and in planning instruction.

UNDERSTANDING GAINED THROUGH ORAL RESPONSES

In an oral English period, at the beginning of the school year, each student may be asked to tell about his vacation. The film "Helping Teachers Understand Pupils" (McGraw-Hill) shows how this practice gives the teacher some understanding of each student and of the class as a whole. The teacher notes indications of the individual's interests and of his social attitudes and relationships. He appraises pronunciation, speaking vocabulary, sentence patterns, and organization of ideas. He can quickly identify adolescents from culturally deprived homes or homes where no English is spoken; these youngsters need special practice and instruction in speech and functional English grammar. The glimpses he gets of the student's personal relationships aid him in forming congenial groups whose members will be mutually helpful.

In other subjects, a period of oral reporting enables the teacher to learn something about each student's background and special interests in the subject. The teacher is often amazed by the quantity of knowledge some individuals have gained from radio, television, and other out-of-school sources. Such information enables the teacher to gear his class-room instruction to outside interests and experience, and to supply the experience background which some of them lack.

UNDERSTANDING GAINED WHILE TEACHING

Diagnostic teaching should be an intrinsic part of the teacher's day-by-day instruction. The skillful teacher is always gaining insights that he uses in meeting individual needs; he guides as he teaches. The following excerpts are examples of diagnostic teaching that occurred in an English lesson on a short story:

Teacher: "The first question I want to ask you is, 'How did you like my choice of story?' "
Helen: "I liked it."
Teacher: "Why?"
Helen: "Well, I liked the style—the way she wrote it."
Teacher: "Any other reasons?"
Patty: "I don't know. You usually give us something where we have to dig for the meaning, but in this story the meaning was right on the surface.
Donald: "I didn't like it."
Teacher: "Why?"
Donald: "I thought the story and the plot and everything was too simple to have all those big words and mythological references."
Teacher: "That's an interesting statement."

Here the teacher elicited differing appraisals of a piece of writing. Donald was skillful in recognizing a *phony* story and in pointing out its wordy, inappropriate images. Others were not so discriminating. They either did not recognize the poor quality of the story, or were not morally courageous enough to mention it because this author's books had been highly recommended.

The teacher also noted wide differences in the students' ability to express themselves clearly, as in the following excerpt:

Teacher: "Does 'Boy Meets Girl' accurately describe the plot?"
Charles: "No."
Teacher: "Why not?"
Charles: "Because the girls, except one, have already met him and they are chasing *him*."
Teacher: "You don't see this as a simple boy-meets-girl plot?"
Charles: "No. . ."
Teacher: "What are the boy's characteristics?"
Claire: "Well, first of all, why, he has a mechanic's job; he is always greasy."
Teacher: "Is that unrealistic?"
Claire: "Well, I mean for a mechanic, it isn't, no, but I mean, it's the greasy character that, you know, most girls—if he has grease on his hands you know or all slouched up, that puts a bad impression into the girl's mind."

Charles tends to speak thoughtfully and to the point. Claire is fuzzy in her thinking and incoherent in her oral expression.

This technique may also bring out a student's creativity. In the same story the author thus described the main character: "At the stroke of twelve his work-a-day garments dropped from him magically as though he were a male and reverse Cinderella." One student interpreted this figure of speech as follows: "Cinderella at twelve o'clock became grubby again, but at twelve o'clock *he* became ungrubbier."

The teacher can usually tell whether a class has the readiness for reading a given assignment by asking them a few preliminary questions. In teaching the story of Casey Jones, one teacher assumed much more knowledge about railroads than the modern boy or girl possesses. He found that the students were unable to make inferences about who was to blame or how the accident could have been prevented because they understood so little about trains. They consulted the dictionary for words such as "switch" and "Pullman," but came up with inappropriate meanings. This experience taught the teacher to check the students' backgrounds before reading other stories.

In dictionary study, a teacher discovered that though the students knew the alphabet and knew how to use the guide words, they would accept the first meaning given after the entry word. They needed to recognize that a word may have multiple meanings; they needed practice in selecting the meaning that is appropriate to the context. The teacher encouraged them first to apply their knowledge of structural analysis and guess the meaning of the word in its context, and then use the dictionary to see whether they were right. They began with simple words in a context where the meaning was clear. Later they went on to more difficult exercises.

During a silent reading period the teacher observed the way each student approached the material: Does he appear to enjoy it? Is he absorbed in his reading? Does he consult other sources? Is he enthusiastic in his discussion of what he has read? If the answers to any of these questions are negative, the teacher reevaluates his teaching: Did he provide sufficient motivation, instructions, and background? Was the material too hard or too easy? Did the student clearly perceive the purpose of reading the selection? Would it be helpful to have a personal interview with the student, or could the problem be handled better in a group situation?

The diagnostic information that the teacher may gain while teaching is not limited to the reading process. In compositions in which they are free to express their own thoughts and feelings, students often reveal previous experiences that are having an important bearing on their present attitudes and behavior. For example, a sophomore revealed that she had an illegitimate child and that her cousin was making it possible for her to attend school in another town. By means of several conferences, the teacher helped this girl overcome her indifference toward school, and to accept it as an opportunity to make the most of herself.

The student who is making progress in reading gains a sense of acceptance and personal worth if his progress is noticed and praised by the teacher or by his classmates. Opportunity to express one's opinion, especially if it is a divergent point of view, encourages students to take initiative and to become independent in their thinking about what they read. If the class reading periods are enjoyable and rewarding, adolescents are likely to continue reading when they leave school.

DIAGNOSTIC VALUE OF INFORMAL TESTS

The quickest and best way of assessing each student's ability to comprehend and communicate what he reads is to give him an informal test on a selection from a book he will soon be expected to read. The selection should be long enough—500 to 1,000 words—to test his ability to grasp the structure of the passage. He reads the selection in his usual way and, without looking back, answers two types of questions. The first is unstructured—"What did the author say?" or "What did you get out of the selection you just read?" The second comprises a series of short-answer, multiple-choice, or other objective questions that are designed to ascertain his ability to recognize and remember the main ideas and important details, to interpret and generalize, to draw inferences and conclusions, and to determine the meanings of key words in a given context.

As the students finish the selection, they record how long it took them, and begin to answer the questions. Later the teacher then shows them how to rate the free response and how to score the objective-type questions and answers. A student may want to know *why* his answer is not the best answer. This discussion will motivate him to learn to read more accurately the next time. Instruction follows immediately. In two or three weeks the teacher will give a similar informal test. The students will again go through the process of reading the selection and scoring, recording, and discussing their responses. This informal diagnostic-testing-teaching process continues throughout the school year. After the second try, many begin to see that they are making progress.[2] In some classes, the first informal test may show clearly that the grade text in a given subject is far too difficult for some of the students. Further diagnosis of their reading is indicated.

If the teacher has time for conferences with individuals during a free period or while the class as a whole is reading or studying independently, he can learn more about the problems of retarded readers. If he finds that they cannot quickly recognize the basic sight vocabulary of 220 frequently recurring words, he will give them practice with the Dolch games (Garrard Press) or other practice material. If an individual tachistoscope such as the Flash-X (EDL) is available, he will let them use it to develop instantaneous recognition of these 220 words. If the problem seems to be difficulty in pronouncing unfamiliar words, the teacher may use the Phono-Visual charts for diagnosis and practice. If the student does not know the meanings of words even when he can pronounce them, he may be encouraged to read more widely and to build up a vocabulary file of key words.

If the student knows the separate words but has not acquired the ability to comprehend the meaning of sentences, he needs instruction and practice in the comprehension of sentences, paragraphs, and longer passages. The customary practice of testing students exclusively or principally on the literal meaning of reading material has left many of them weak in interpreting meaning, making inferences and generalizations, and drawing conclusions. These students may need extra instruction, individually or in small groups, in addition to the practice that is regularly given in class.

Although most standardized reading tests are of the survey type, some diagnostic value can be extracted from them. Teacher and student can go over the completed tests together, noting the total score and the subtest scores, noting errors, trying to determine the causes of these errors, and discussing ways of correcting them. This use of standardized tests for instructional purposes is now sanctioned by experts in the field of testing. Of course this procedure would not be used with tests that have been given for research purposes or to measure pupil progress.

THE INCOMPLETE SENTENCE TECHNIQUE

If there is a mutual relationship of trust and respect between students and teacher, the incomplete-sentence technique will reveal students' attitudes toward themselves and toward reading.[3] For this purpose items such as the following are pertinent:

I like to read about
Comic books
When I have reading to do, I
When I read math
I like to read when
For me, studying
Reading science
I'd read more if
I'd rather read than
When I read out loud
To me books
I wish my parents knew
I wish teachers
I can't understand why
I wish
Today I feel

The teacher interprets the replies, which are always to be given voluntarily, as he would interpret any other observed behavior, and checks his interpretation against his daily observation.

REFERRAL OF COMPLICATED CASES

There will be individuals who do not respond to any "reading first aid" that the teacher can give. These adolescents have difficulties that need deeper diagnosis. The reading specialist explores deficiencies in visual and auditory acuity and discrimination, and in conceptualization. He measures different kinds of mental ability such as those assessed by the Wechsler Intelligence Tests.

It may be that the student has emotional difficulties or a negative self-concept that limits his functioning in reading. If so, the teacher may refer him to the school counselor who, in turn, may refer him to a psychologist, psychiatrist, or neurologist for deeper diagnosis.

Without departing from the area of his competence, any high school teacher, whatever his subject, may help his students to improve their reading. As they see progress and experience success, they become more self-confident and put forth more effort. "Nothing succeeds like observed success." The distance between a low self-concept and a high level of aspiration can thus be reduced. Students who know they are making progress in reading have less need to cover up their failures by resorting to attention-getting devices. They no longer feel hostility toward the teacher or the school. As they become more competent in reading, they are likely to elicit a more favorable response from their parents, teachers, and classmates. If this process of diagnostic teaching were to be adopted in every subject, it might well have an enormous effect on the personal growth and reading development of every student.

REFERENCES

[1] Thomas Boning and Richard Boning, "I'd Rather Read than . . . ," *The Reading Teacher*, X (April, 1957), 196–200.

[2] For more detail on this procedure, see Amelia Melnik, "The Improvement of Reading Through Self-Appraisal," *A Procedure for Teaching Reading in Junior High School Social Studies* (Unpublished Doctoral Project, Teachers College, Columbia University, New York, 1960).

[3] Ruth Strang, *Diagnostic Teaching of Reading* (New York: McGraw-Hill, 1964), pp. 76–85.

C. Improving Word Recognition Skills

20. TEACHING WORD RECOGNITION SKILLS
Board of Education of the City of New York

It cannot be assumed that all boys and girls entering junior high school are able to read the printed materials used in their English, social studies, and other classes. Junior high school teachers know that many of their pupils have not acquired the fundamental skills essential to independent reading, and they realize that training must be given in elementary reading techniques. Little can be expected as far as comprehension is concerned unless a pupil can recognize the most common words and can work out the identities of unfamiliar ones; the area of word recognition, therefore, is of primary concern to the reading teacher. It is important that junior high school teachers and supervisors understand how independence in word recognition is acquired and that they accept the fact that instruction in the junior high school has to extend far back to elementary grade levels in order to reach some of their retarded readers.

The term word recognition as used in this Guide means more than ability to pronounce words that are met in reading. Mere fluency may be confused with real recognition which implies a degree of familiarity that enables the pupil to understand the meaning of a word when it is seen or heard and to use it in speaking and in writing. Familiarity comes from direct life experiences or from carefully interpreted vicarious experiences which provide the background of meaning needed in interpreting words. In addition to a variety of concepts, a pupil must bring to reading material certain word recognition techniques. The acquisition of recognition skills cannot be left to chance; a systematic program of diagnosis and training has to be followed. In order to guide teachers in developing such a program, the diagnosis and teaching of the various phases of word recognition will be presented here under the following headings: Using Oral Reading for Diagnostic and Teaching Purposes, Building a Sight Vocabulary, Utilizing the Context, Employing a Phonetic Approach, Employing a Visual Approach. Most retarded readers require training in more than one of these areas. Furthermore, they need help in shifting

Reprinted from *The Retarded Reader in the Junior High School: A Guide for Supervisors and Teachers*, prepared by the staff of the Reading Guidance Center, Division of Instructional Research, Publication No. 31 (September 1952), pp. 62–79. By permission of J. Wayne Wrightstone, Bureau of Educational Research of the New York City Board of Education.

readily from one approach to another that is more appropriate and in combining different techniques in attacking words.

1. Using Oral Reading for Diagnostic Purposes

The diagnostic aspect of oral reading is basic

Diagnosis is important not only at the beginning of the work with retarded readers but also throughout the entire training period. In the reading project in the junior high schools, both standardized oral reading tests and ordinary reading material were used as diagnostic instruments.

Using Standardized Oral Reading Tests

Oral reading tests generally include a series of paragraphs or stories arranged in order of difficulty; as the pupil reads, the teacher records on another copy of the test the time taken in reading each section of the test and the errors made. Later the teacher compares this record with the test norms. In recording errors, the teacher may adopt a code suggested in a test manual or improvise until he arrives at the system that is most rapid for him. For example, the following entries might appear on the teacher's copy of the paragraphs the pupil is reading:

> (r)
> house   (*house* was read as *horse*)
> paint(ing)   (*painting* was read as *paint*)
> (a)round   (*round* was read as *around*)

Accompanying some tests are detailed record sheets that list types of errors to be noted; directions for using the record sheet as well as for administering and scoring the test appear in the test manual. A teacher who has had little experience in diagnostic procedure, however, may find it confusing to consider many different errors. At first, he may look for only one weakness, such as phrasing, and as he acquires facility in noting and recording information, he may add other items. Later he may devise a check list similar to the one on the following page.

Diagnostic reading tests by Gates, Gray, and Durrell are described in the Supplement to Part I.

Using Books

Some books found in the reading rooms and in junior high school classrooms were used for diagnosing reading difficulties. In utilizing such materials for this purpose, it is possible to maintain the informal relation-

TECHNIQUE	SYMPTOMS NOTED	DATES				
Phrasing	Word-by-word reading.	✓				
	Wrong groupings of words.					
	Punctuation ignored.	✓				
Word Attack	Weakness in phonetic approach.					
	letter sounds.					
	common phonograms.	✓				
	Misuse of context.					
	over-dependence.					
	little utilization.					
	Limited sight vocabulary	✓				
	Weakness in visual analysis					
	Dependent upon:					
	general configuration.	✓				
	initial parts.					
	striking features.					

ship between pupil and reading teacher that is so desirable in a testing situation and that is difficult to achieve when a standardized test is administered. To find an individual's oral reading grade, the teacher selects a book at the retarded reader's silent reading level or slightly below it. A section at the middle of the book is assigned and if it is too difficult or too easy, the pupil is directed to the beginning or to the end of the book or to a book at a higher or lower level. The pupil may glance at the selection before starting to read it aloud. He reads orally to the teacher, and when he encounters two or three word recognition difficulties per page and shows by his answers to a few pertinent questions that he comprehends what he reads, his approximate oral reading level has been reached, e.g., first half of third year, end of second year. It is a point just beyond which he begins to show signs of tension—body movements, finger-pointing, repetition of words, and mispronunciation. Betts gives a full discussion of the problem of reading levels in *Foundations of Reading Instruction*, Chapter XXI. (See Appendix A, Section 1, 2.)

The oral reading grade is compared with the silent reading grade to determine the amount of emphasis that should be given to oral reading. In noting the discrepancy between the silent and the oral reading levels, teachers should be aware that for extremely retarded readers the difference may not be so great as it appears. Because of the inadequacy of the grade norms at the lower levels of some silent reading tests, pupils may be assigned grade scores higher than the ones they would achieve on a more appropriate test. A grade score—silent or oral—has a limited value only, for it does not give the teacher all the information he must have. It is a composite of various elements and indicates the approximate reading level at which a pupil functions at the time, but it does not indicate the specific techniques that he lacks.

In order that a pupil's word recognition needs may be revealed, he is required to read aloud material that is somewhat difficult for him and which he is not permitted to see before reading orally. At one sitting, the teacher supplies the words on which the pupil hesitates and makes a list of these words for future analysis. A study of the list discloses the kinds of words not recognized: common sight words, words not phonetic in character, unusual words, words that should be recognized from the context. At another sitting, the pupil is not given help with unfamiliar words but is encouraged to ascertain them for himself. The teacher notices to what extent phonetic and visual approaches function and how versatile a pupil is in shifting from one to the other as he tries to identify a word in its context.

Inadequate word recognition techniques result in impaired comprehension which may be detected through oral reading. The pupil who does not understand what he reads cannot convey meaning to the listener. One or more of the following symptoms may characterize his reading: failure to group words into thought units; lack of stress on the most important word in a phrase; excessive speed or slowness; regular repetition of one or more words; disregard for punctuation marks.

Books serve another purpose in the study of the retarded reader. After selecting a book at a level more advanced than the books used in the diagnosis, the teacher reads a passage to the pupil and questions him on the content. If the material is readily grasped, a selection at a higher level is tried. The highest level at which the retarded reader understands selections read to him represents the approximate level at which he is capable of comprehending such material. The spread between his reading capacity and his actual reading achievement indicates the degree of retardation. This information about a pupil's reading expectancy is valuable to the teacher in choosing materials for him and in planning his program.

The same procedure may be employed in determining the extent of the pupil's meaning vocabulary. A sampling may be taken from the new word lists in several readers of a graded series. As the word is pronounced by the teacher, the pupil defines it, or gives synonyms for it, or uses it in context. Thus his capacity for understanding the vocabulary of the readers used is revealed. For further discussion of the use of books in diagnosing reading difficulties see "Testing Reading With a Book" by E. W. Dolch, *Elementary English*, March 1951.

Diagnosis is continuous after the initial study of difficulties. In the teacher's daily work with the child, he frequently listens to the child read, questions him about meanings, and observes his responses to suggestions. Thus the reading teacher's understanding of pupils' reading problems grows continuously; he is, therefore, better able to direct his teaching toward the specific reading needs of the retarded boy or girl.

Just as the individual's problem is analyzed factor by factor, so the pupil is made aware of one fault at a time and guided in eliminating it. For instance, a pupil and teacher have worked together to correct word-by-word reading; the pupil has improved in certain word recognition techniques necessary for fluent reading and is now phrase conscious and can read in thought units except when a phrase is broken at the end of a line. The teacher explains and demonstrates the technique of pausing after the preceding phrase while the eyes travel on to the next line and the voice is withheld until the complete phrase can be said. After the pupil has grasped the idea, he is given assistance in his first attempts, and then he is left to practice by himself. He knows that during the following reading period the teacher, his sole audience at the beginning stages of his development, will listen for this aspect of phrasing. In the meantime, the teacher has recorded the pupil's progress and has indicated the technique to be checked; the next time he sees the pupil, he follows through with encouragement and with whatever additional instruction is needed. Such a brief daily check-up of oral reading for a specific purpose stimulates interest in self-improvement while the personal concern of the reading teacher gives the pupil satisfaction and contributes towards the development of self-esteem.

2. BUILDING A SIGHT VOCABULARY

Retarded readers generally lack competence in the recognition of words

The problem presented by the junior high school pupil who has a limited sight vocabulary can be understood better if the teacher appreciates the way in which a young child's sight vocabulary is developed. The first few times a child meets a word, he may have to be told what it is or he may be able to work it out for himself. After a few visual presentations of the word on experience charts, in incidental reading, or in books, he recognizes the word; that is, he associates its printed form with its sound and with its meaning. He can do this because in some way he has experienced the activity or object which the printed symbol represents. The more comprehensive and intense such experiencing has been, the more readily will the pupil recognize the word.

For certain children many additional experiences with a word, and often direct teaching or drill, are necessary before it is incorporated into their sight vocabularies. In large classes, it is very difficult to provide each child with the number of contacts with a word which he may need to ensure its immediate recognition. Continuity of vocabulary experiences from grade to grade is often lacking. As a result, some pupils reach junior high school with very inadequate sight vocabularies. Others have limited sight vocabularies because they have not acquired a good method of perceiving words clearly; they read "then" for "than" and "house" for "horse" and make similar errors. If a word is not perceived clearly at first, it cannot be recognized on sight, and the pupil relies on guessing. Sharpness of perception is a definite asset in word attack. Retarded readers who have inadequate sight vocabularies have been aided by training in visual perception and by an increase in the number of contacts with each new word.

In addition to poor visual perception, there is another cause of inadequate sight vocabulary which occurs infrequently but which should be recognized if both teacher and child are not to become discouraged. Some pupils, even with normal vision, have poor "visual memories." Despite good teaching the child does not recognize many words which he seemed to have learned in previous lessons. Even if we assume that the condition itself cannot be corrected by the teacher, instruction has to be modified to cope with the child's limitation. All avenues by which the child can learn must be utilized to greatest advantage; auditory training is given more emphasis than visual; kinesthetic exercises which include copying and tracing are helpful in some cases in giving the pupil the "feel" of the word. Some teachers of reading may find Hildreth's discussion of the kinesthetic approach helpful. (See Appendix A, Section I, 17.) Since children who are thus limited need many repetitions of a word before they can recognize it on sight, it is desirable to provide them with frequent, brief, and varied exercises. Copying and tracing as well as writing a word from memory and then checking on its accuracy were found to be effective procedures for slow-learning pupils, but they were very time-consuming. For this reason and because there was danger that it would become monotonous and that some pupils would associate it with punitive assignments, the kinesthetic approach was used only as a last resort.

The suggestions given here for helping junior high school pupils increase their sight vocabularies are by no means the only procedures and may not be suited to all cases:

Extensive reading of easy interesting material at a level below the pupil's reading grade level is probably the most pleasant way of reinforcing sight vocabulary. Unfortunately, the amount of literature that *seriously* retarded junior high school pupils can read with *interest and enjoyment* is extremely limited. There is much material available, however, at the fourth grade reading level and higher.

Pupils kept individual notebooks in which they wrote the words not recognized instantly in context, illustrated them pictorially when possible, and used them in sentences that clearly showed their meanings. Teachers in the various curriculum areas encouraged retarded readers to make special vocabulary books with such titles as "Science Words," "Transportation Dictionary," "Expressions Used in Art." When a pupil finds that he has insufficient skill to read fluently he will see the need to study individual words or groups of words.

Teachers introduced abstract words such as "often," "freedom," and "quiet" in meaningful phrases or sentences and presented them on illustrated charts whenever this served a purpose. Action words like *sift* and *pour* used in homemaking classes were taught in the same way.

The writing of a few sentences about something that is of personal interest to a pupil calls for the functional use of the most common sight words such as, *and, were, does,* and it involves kinesthetic learning as well. For nonreaders and for those just above that level, this procedure was found to be one of the best. When a pupil was unable to write his own story, he told it to the teacher who recorded a sentence or two for him to copy and then read aloud. Usually the pupil made an illustration which later served as a clue in rereading the story after it had been incorporated into his own storybook or had become part of a group collection. If a retarded reader was able to write reasonably well, he prepared his own brief story, and the teacher showed him how to correct any errors he had made. He was then allowed to typewrite his story; this aided in the development of left-to-right progression and afforded further pleasurable experience with basic sight words. In the beginning the pupil's original writing was confined to one or two sentences lest he become involved in the mechanics of writing and the main purpose of the activity be forgotten.

The word-picture type of approach to building a sight vocabulary was employed for pupils who read at a primary grade level. It took several forms:

Printed labels on pictures or objects in the room.

Illustrated charts which showed the meaning of words or phrases that the pupil was going to meet in his reading.

Illustrated word cards such as the Dolch Picture-Word Cards, a sample of which is given here.

Front   Back

Picture of tree	the word
and	
the word "tree"	"tree"

Since the meaning and the visual appearance of a word are presented simultaneously, these cards were used for initial teaching. In addition, they were studied independently by a pupil as he tested himself and checked his own responses; or partners tested and checked each other. The word-side of the cards was exposed rapidly by a teacher who wished to discover the extent of a pupil's knowledge of common words; later a diagnosis of errors was made and thus further insight into the pupil's basic word recognition difficulties was gained.

Original picture-word cards using the vocabulary of the pupils' daily experiences.

Individual word lists, such as the Dolch vocabulary which follows, were invaluable for discovering the extent of a seriously retarded pupil's sight vocabulary, for diagnosing his errors, and for encouraging self-improvement. By a rapid exposure of each word the teacher determined the extent of the individual's sight vocabulary. The number of words tested at one time depended upon the pupil's response. He might have been tested on the first five words only or on the first column. Pupils who functioned on a fourth grade reading level or higher generally were ready for the entire list.

Each pupil had his own list which enabled him to study by himself the words he did not know, to work with a partner, and to see evidences of his own progress as the number of known words increased. The method of studying the unfamiliar words varied, e.g., the sounding approach was used for words that are phonetic in character; a visual study of other words was made. Since this method of study and the word-picture approach do not ensure transference to reading situations, ability to recognize the new words in context was checked and practice subsequently given. Because these two hundred and twenty sight words occur again and again in all reading material, instantaneous recognition was required before a word was regarded as known.

The Dolch list was derived from a comparison of three basic word lists and consists of two hundred and twenty words found very frequently in elementary school readers and textbooks. The three lists are:

CHILD STUDY COMMITTEE OF THE INTERNATIONAL KINDERGARTEN UNION, *A Study of the Vocabulary of Children Before Entering the First Grade*, Washington, D.C., 1928.
ARTHUR I. GATES, *A Reading Vocabulary for the Primary Grades*, New York, Teachers College, Columbia University, 1926. A revision of this list has appeared since this study was made but does not change the results.
H. E. WHEELER AND EMMA A. HOWELL, "A First-Grade Vocabulary Study," *Elementary School Journal*, 31:52-60 September, 1930.

3. UTILIZING THE CONTEXT

The setting in which a word occurs often indicates clearly the meaning of that word

With meaning thus implied by the context, the reader who has acquired some visual and phonetic techniques can recognize a word that is already in his listening and speaking vocabularies. Many retarded junior high school pupils are unable to utilize the context as an aid to word recognition; that is, they cannot discover the identity of an unfamiliar word through a consideration of the meaning of the material that surrounds it. Some of these retarded readers are unable to concentrate on the thought of the selection because they have acquired neither a basic sight vocabulary nor elementary techniques of word recognition. For such pupils, who are functioning at a primary reading level, utilizing the context is not given special emphasis. Instead, skill is developed gradually along with other word recognition techniques through the use of easy material that is meaningful. There are other retarded readers, however, who have acquired various basic skills but have never had sufficient training in using the context. Although they may be reading on a fifth or sixth grade level, their reading is not so efficient as it might be. It is these pupils who profit from immediate guidance in utilizing the context to identify unfamiliar words.

For the retarded reader as well as for other readers, the context approach is valuable only when it is employed along with one or more visual or phonetic clues. If it is used exclusively, indiscriminate guessing and distortion of meaning may result. In identifying an unfamiliar word, the skillful reader uses several techniques simultaneously; he is able to make use of the hints that he gets from the context at the same time that he is looking at the word for visual and phonetic characteristics. The context approach to word recognition is more easily acquired by the junior high school retarded reader than by the younger child. This is true because the older pupil has a comparative wealth of experience to bring to reading material at the lower elementary school reading level.

In order to teach retarded readers how to make effective use of the context, it is desirable for the junior high school teacher to know something of the early stages in the development of this technique. In the prereading period, the child completes sentences which the teacher starts; for example, "The boy was bouncing the——." The meaning of such a statement is so clear that the child readily finishes it. He is then led on to completion exercises where the meaning of a whole story or a part of it must be considered. For instance, in a story about a boy losing his dog, the sentence to be completed is "John lost his——." If the child does not think of the meaning of the whole story, he may name any one of many articles which he knows from experience that boys sometimes lose. However, in the setting of the particular story, the response is limited. Later, when the child is able to read, he applies the techniques of utilizing context clues in exercises similar to those which he had in his prereading program. When he has acquired some skill in other word recognition techniques, he may try simple exercises like the following which involve visual discrimination as well as context clues.

Tom caught a fish on his book.
hook.

In such an exercise, an oral response is not sufficient. Precautions must be taken lest the pupil say "hook" while indicating the word "book." (For additional exercises in developing the technique of using the context along with other word recognition clues see *Eye and Ear Fun*, Appendix B, Section I.)

In addition to clues found in the story, the reader uses any others that may be present in illustrations and in titles. How the various clues function in a reading situation may be seen in the following illustration in which a difficult word, *capsized*, is used to point up effective use of the context.

Let us suppose that in reading about the adventures of two boys at a camp, a pupil meets the following sentence:

"Suddenly the canoe capsized and the boys found themselves in the water."

The word *capsized* is not recognized at sight. However, a hint as to what happened to the canoe may be found in an illustration, in the title of the story, or in the introductory sentence; or if the pupil has not found any clues to the meaning of the word previously, at least after he has read the remainder of the sentence he will know that the canoe must have overturned. He then goes back and looks at the word. He may recognize the syllable "cap." This clue, or any other, in addition to the knowledge

A Basic Sight Vocabulary of 220 Words—E. W. Dolch
(Reproduced with permission of the author)

These words make up 50 to 75 per cent of all school reading matter. They are arranged in order of difficulty.[1] For instructional purposes it is important that they be known in any order and not just as they occur in the columns.[2] The list may be divided into small units for use with very poor readers.

a	one	get	ran	where	does
I	black	if	work	many	show
too	my	soon	with	warm	any
to	at	its	there	laugh	try
the	all	some	about	live	kind
two	so	from	after	now	wish
in	by	fly	what	came	carry
see	do	then	ask	buy	know
into	are	but	sing	very	only
and	him	as	must	hold	pick
up	her	under	five	would	don't
blue	on	before	myself	hot	gave
she	green	walk	over	open	every
yellow	eat	stop	cut	light	which
he	four	out	let	their	our
go	said	his	again	pull	want
you	away	make	new	may	thank
we	run	your	well	goes	better
big	they	ride	have	small	clean
red	that	help	how	find	been
jump	going	call	keep	could	never
it	did	here	drink	fall	those
play	who	sleep	sit	think	write
down	like	cold	made	far	first
for	come	will	went	found	these
old	had	pretty	has	read	both
is	saw	them	seven	were	shall
me	no	when	right	best	own
look	long	round	why	because	hurt
can	yes	am	please	grow	eight
good	an	white	upon	fast	wash
brown	three	funny	give	off	full
six	this	put	once	draw	use
be	around	take	together	bring	done
today	was	of	us	got	start
not	just	say	tell	always	
little	ten	or	ate	much	

[1] NEMEC, LOIS G. AND LOSINSKI, BLANCHE. "A Study of the Difficulty of Dolch Basic Sight Vocabulary in the Second and Third Grades of the Rural Schools in Twenty-two Counties of the State of Wisconsin." *Journal of Educational Research,* 35:211–14, November, 1941.

[2] The list is arranged according to parts of speech and in alphabetical order in *Better Reading,* E. W. Dolch, Garrard Press, Champaign, Illinois, 1951.

that the canoe upset, helps him recall the word "capsized" which he has met previously either in some outside experience or during the *preparatory* activities for the reading lesson.

In guiding retarded pupils toward the discovery and use of contextual clues, the reading teacher at first demonstrates the procedure for the group and works with individuals in their early attempts. As soon as a pupil understands the technique, he is given many opportunities to apply it independently. For example, in preparing a group for some stories, the reading teacher did not present a new word on the blackboard or on charts. Instead, he used the word several times in meaningful spoken context, and the pupils were encouraged to include it in their oral contributions to the discussion. Then they had an opportunity while reading to apply the technique of utilizing the context to a word previously heard and spoken.

The context approach was found valuable in developing comprehension as well as in promoting skill in determining the identity of a word. It was a particularly worth-while aid to word recognition for *mature* pupils who derived little satisfaction from the more or less mechanical analysis of words. Other suggestions for utilizing the context will be found in the section of this book that deals with vocabulary development.

4. Employing a Phonetic Approach

Some pupils have little skill in attacking words

It was found that an appreciable number of junior high school pupils required instruction in the phonetic approach at the most elementary level. Visual techniques were used to some extent by these pupils, but in many cases facility in the phonetic approach was entirely lacking. Where the visual approach has failed as a major technique for some children, the phonetic approach often "works" to a considerable extent. It must be remembered, however, that the use of phonics is not a complete method of teaching reading but is only one approach to word recognition. When pupils have been through six grades of the elementary school and do not yet possess a sight vocabulary necessary to good reading achievement, every technique possible must be employed until some favorable result is obtained. It is agreed that reading is really a process of getting thought and the main goals are to strive to place word recognition skills in meaningful context and ultimately to have the child comprehend and enjoy the content. Although major emphasis should be placed on these goals some attention must be given to the place of phonics in the program of retarded readers.

Phonetics, the science of speech sounds, and phonics, the application of phonetics to reading, are both included in this approach. Skill is acquired through training in auditory perception to ensure the correct hearing of sounds, in speech for the proper reproduction of the sounds heard, in visual perception for associating each sound with its printed symbol, and in blending in order to join the sounds to form words.

To become skillful in the phonetic approach a pupil must know the sounds for which letters and letter combinations stand; he must be able to give one or more sounds for each letter or letter combination. If the reading teacher is to direct his efforts toward a pupil's specific needs, he must find out just which sounds are not known. The following list of sound elements is suggested for initial diagnosis:

> consonant sounds
> > single consonants
> > consonant blends as *cr* in crown and *str* in strap
> > consonant digraphs: *ch, sh, wh, th, ph*

> vowel sounds
> > single long and short vowels
> > two-vowel combinations as *oa* in boat
> > diphthongs as *oi* in boil

> common syllables
> > *ing* in going   *ed* in jumped and started
> > *er* in taller   *a* in among

Many pupils in the reading project needed some training in each of these three areas. In a few cases, however, phonics had been overstressed in the school program, and the pupils' major approach to word recognition was through letter sounds. As a result, attention was focused on the mechanics of reading rather than on the meaning of the passage. Such pupils needed guidance in the use of context and in visual techniques. Because of their varying needs, retarded readers had to be considered individually and provided with the kind of training that would enable them to acquire skill in the phonetic approach and to integrate phonetic, contextual, and visual clues in the efficient recognition of words.

Testing Consonants

First it is necessary for a teacher to discover the extent of a retarded reader's knowledge of consonant sounds and his methods of word attack. During reading activities, the teacher takes notes of individual weaknesses and progress. If the efforts of both the pupil and teacher are to be channeled toward specific weaknesses, however, a more direct approach is necessary. For example, a letter sound test for individuals may consist of a typewritten or printed list of the lower case letters arranged miscellaneously or of a page of reading material on which the teacher

a)   PUPIL'S PAGE

1.	dig	big	pig	wig
2.	cat	mat	fat	hat
3.	rip	dip	tip	lip
4.	weed	need	seed	feed
5.	not	got	hot	pot
6.	he	me	be	she
7.	trust	rust	just	must
8.	kill	mill	sill	will
9.	may	lay	say	play
10.	fine	mine	wine	shine
11.	bow	cow	now	how
12.	sick	tick	lick	pick
13.	back	quack	tack	pack
14.	rest	vest	nest	best
15.	bit	hit	lit	sit
16.	hen	men	ten	den
17.	can	ran	van	man
18.	win	pin	tin	bin
19.	pet	met	net	yet

Teacher's List: (words to be read aloud by the teacher)

Line	1. big	Line	11. now
	2. cat		12. pick
	3. dip		13. quack
	4. feed		14. rest
	5. got		15. sit
	6. he		16. ten
	7. just		17. van
	8. kill		18. win
	9. lay		19. yet
	10. mine		

At another sitting different words may be selected
for the teacher's list.

has underlined the letters to be tested. The pupil is told to give the sound of each letter as the teacher points to it. The teacher may demonstrate by pointing to the letter *s* and giving its sound. Standardized oral tests may be used for the same purpose, as well as teacher-made tests, for both groups and individuals. Samples of teacher-made tests follow.

a) *Single Consonants.* The pupils underline or encircle on their individual sheets the word on each line that is read by the teacher. The teacher gives whatever explanation is necessary to enable the pupils to understand the directions. This test was given to groups of pupils who were functioning at only a first or second grade reading level.

b) *Consonant Blends.* Pupils underline or encircle the word on each line that is read by the teacher. The teacher gives whatever explanation is necessary to enable pupils to understand the directions. This test was given to pupils who knew individual letter sounds and were reading at the primary level.

c) *Consonant digraphs.* Consonant digraph lists may be used with individual pupils who are reading at a primary level and in whose oral reading or speech there is evidence of difficulty with specific digraphs. As the pupil reads the list, the teacher notices whether or not the digraph is pronounced correctly and with confidence. Similar lists can be made for any other digraphs that are found difficult for some pupils.

---

c)   **ch**

Initial ch		Final ch	
chop	chart	inch	catch
child	cheese	ranch	pitch
chase	chin	lunch	punch
chick	chair	much	teach
chum	cheer	match	coach

---

sh

Initial sh		Final sh	
she	shade	fish	fresh
shoe	ship	flash	splash
shall	shave	rush	dish
share	sheep	crash	wish
should	shore	blush	brush

b)   PUPIL'S PAGE

1.	sell	well	swell
2.	clap	cap	lap
3.	mock	sock	smock
4.	sin	spin	pin
5.	drip	dip	rip
6.	bow	blow	low
7.	sap	nap	snap
8.	sip	slip	lip
9.	rake	bake	brake
10.	pay	play	lay
11.	trap	tap	rap
12.	tin	twin	win
13.	gay	ray	gray
14.	sold	cold	scold
15.	cramp	ramp	camp
16.	kill	sill	skill
17.	fight	fright	right
18.	tick	stick	sick
19.	peach	reach	preach
20.	stain	strain	train
21.	slit	spit	split
22.	scream	seam	cream

Teacher's List: (words to be read aloud by the teacher)

Line		Line	
1.	swell	12.	twin
2.	clap	13.	gray
3.	smock	14.	scold
4.	spin	15.	cramp
5.	drip	16.	skill
6.	blow	17.	fright
7.	snap	18.	stick
8.	slip	19.	preach
9.	brake	20.	strain
10.	play	21.	split
11.	trap	22.	scream

At another sitting different words may be selected for the teacher's list.

Teaching Consonant Sounds

In some cases, reading retardation is so extreme that pupils know only very few letter sounds. When an individual really knows a sound, he is able to hear it clearly, produce it distinctly, and associate the visual symbol with the spoken form. In reading a familiar word, he immediately recognizes the individual letter sounds in their functional settings and his response to the word as a whole is automatic. When he meets an unfamiliar word that is phonetic, he is able to produce the individual sounds and blend them together to form a word which he recognizes as one he has heard and perhaps even spoken.

In learning the consonant sounds then, the pupil must have opportunities to listen to words in which the particular sound appears in various positions—initial, medial, final; he must produce the sound in numerous words and associate each sound with its printed symbol. These words may be in the form of either original lists built by the individual or group, or assigned exercises like those given in phonics workbooks.

Some retarded readers know the sounds of the individual letters, but they have to be taught to blend them to form syllables or words. At first the pupil listens while the teacher demonstrates the process of prolonging one letter sound until the next is begun; then he and the teacher together blend the sounds to form words. Gradually the process is speeded up and the teacher allows the pupil to complete a word by himself. Pupils who attack unfamiliar words by a spelling method can be trained to substitute the letter sounds for the letter names in a blending approach. The blending technique can be applied also to the letters of an unfamiliar syllable and to the syllables of a polysyllabic word. For some retarded readers blending is an extremely difficult technique; therefore, it is desirable for them to have only a very brief practice period of this type followed by a satisfying reading experience. As they gain skill, they think the sounds instead of saying them and by degrees change from the slow oral blending procedure to the more efficient silent approach characteristic of mature readers.

Since the material suggested for testing consonants is designed mostly for diagnostic purposes rather than for measuring progress, it may be used also for teaching consonant sounds. For example, the test for single consonants on page 217 makes good practice material if the pupils are asked to read the words across a line or down a specific column; or a game may be played after the four columns have been lettered A, B, C, D. One pupil chooses a word silently and then gives its location by line number and column letter. For instance, he says "2-B" and another pupil answers, "mat." The test for consonant blends may be used in a similar way. Many other exercises appear in various workbooks and may be adapted to the needs of particular individuals. When exercises are used in teaching, it is important to remember that the retarded reader must have numerous opportunities to apply his knowledge of sounds to reading. As his new learnings function in meaningful context, they become "second nature" to him, and he is able to give his attention to the meaning rather than to the mechanics of reading.

Some consonant sounds are more difficult than others and are often mispronounced by seriously retarded readers. The reading teacher should endeavor to differentiate between pupils with careless speech habits and those who have real difficulty in pronouncing specific sounds. All pupils profit from speech training, but the latter require the guidance of a speech specialist.

A teacher of very seriously retarded readers will find it helpful to have on display or readily available for use a series of cards or a chart to be used as a pronunciation key for consonant sounds. A common word with a pertinent illustration is printed for each consonant:

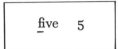

For such self-help aids needed by many pupils again and again, the teacher will find it worth while to use materials of good quality and to take the time needed for careful preparation.

The consonant blends and digraphs are taught to pupils who know the sounds of the individual letters. Again, as in the case of single consonants, hearing the blend or digraph clearly and reproducing it accurately are the first steps to be taken. Association of the sound with its printed symbol follows. A blend or digraph may be misread because the pupil does not really see the individual letters comprising it and as a result reads the word *string* as *sting*. In such instances, the teacher calls attention to the difference and prints both words on the blackboard or in the pupil's notebook so that he may compare them immediately. In this way the need for closer observation and finer discrimination becomes obvious to the pupil. Other suggestions for improving visual discrimination may be found in the section "Employing a Visual Approach." Another reason for the misreading of blends and digraphs is that the pupil has had no previous contact with the particular symbol. An oral check of his performance on an exercise like the following one not only will provide practice but also will help the teacher locate the difficulties that exist.

a) Discrimination of initial consonant blends.

The pupils are asked to put a line under the word which makes each sentence correct. Oral checking is a necessary follow-up of this exercise. To reinforce learning, the correct response may be placed on the black-

"C" That Sounds Like "S"

To the pupil:

In each of these words the letter "c" is sounded like "s." Read the words to yourself and then read them aloud.

Initial "c"	"c" in Other Positions
cent	ice
city	race
celebrate	peace
center	price
cigarette	force
cellar	mice
cider	produce
central	exercise
cereal	recess
certain	receive

To the pupil:

Draw a line under the "c" that is sounded like "s" in each of these words: (The written exercise must be followed by an oral check.)

circus	accept
bicycle	circle
practice	civics

Soft "G"

To the pupil:

In each of these words the letter "g" is sounded like "j." Read the words to yourself and then read them aloud.

Initial "g"	Final "g"
gem	age
gentle	badge
germ	bridge
giraffe	cage

To the pupil:

Draw a line under the soft "g" in each of these words:

geography	garbage
garage	gorgeous

board. The remaining words in parentheses may be used for supplementary oral practice.

We went to the park to (pay, pray, play) ball.
There is a (scrap, strap, slap) of paper on the floor.
The grass is green in the (spring, string, swing).
A bee's (string, sling, sting) hurts.
"America" was (swung, sung, stung) by the class.
What was your (store, score, snore) in that game?
A (stream, scream, steam) of water came down the mountain.
He will (swell, sell, smell) you a pencil for a dime.
Be careful not to (slash, smash, splash) your dress with water.
This ink will (stain, strain, slain) your clothes.

After a pupil has learned the basic consonant sounds, he may be taught the variations in pronunciation of some of the consonants such as the "s" sound of "c." Sample exercises appear on page 222.

Testing Vowels. Pupils' needs in the area of vowel sounds can be discovered in the various informal and formal ways described for diagnosing consonant errors. Long vowels usually do not present a special problem, and for most retarded readers it is not necessary to test them formally. Short vowels in the middle position in a word tend to cause the greatest difficulty. Sometimes pupils do not perceive the letter form clearly and confuse *a*, *e*, and *o*. At other times the cause of the difficulty is auditory or phonetic in nature; retarded readers often have difficulty in distinguishing between the short sounds of *a* and *e* and of *e* and *i*. They seem never to have heard a difference and, therefore, are unable to show it in their pronunciation.

A sample group test for discovering confusion among the short vowel sounds appears on the following page 224.

In this test, pupils associate the visual symbol with the sound as it is produced by the teacher. Pupils in the group who have difficulty with vowels are identified readily. For them, further diagnosis may be made by having the individual read aloud the various words in the test as the teacher records confusions such as "bat" for "bet" and "hot" for "hat." It may be necessary to isolate the vowel to find out whether or not the pupil actually hears the particular vowel sound and knows how to reproduce it. A need for training in auditory discrimination and in phonetics may be indicated.

Pupil's Page:

Draw a circle around the word that the teacher says. Read all four words across each row before you draw a circle around the correct one. (The teacher may use any directions that will be clear to the pupils.)

1.	bit	bat	but	bet
2.	big	bag	bug	beg
3.	hat	hit	hot	hut
4.	stick	stack	stuck	stock
5.	pit	put	pat	pot
6.	sang	sing	song	sung
7.	bad	bud	bed	bid
8.	peck	puck	pick	pack
9.	lock	luck	lick	lack
10.	pan	pen	pin	pun

Teacher's List: (The teacher selects one word from each line and reads it aloud.)

1. bat		6. sang
2. beg		7. bed
3. hit		8. pick
4. stock		9. lock
5. put		10. pun

At another sitting, different words may be selected for the teacher's list.

Vowel Combinations

Two-vowel combinations and diphthongs can be tested by means of oral reading of lists like the following:

eat	heap	oil	spoil
seat	clean	boil	noise
hear	year	coin	point
seal	feast	join	poison
beam	rear	avoid	moisture

Testing of other vowel combinations can be accomplished in the same way if the teacher feels that it is necessary. If the word lists used for informal testing purposes are printed on large charts or typewritten on individual papers, they can be re-used as practice material. Exercises in workbooks may be cut out and mounted and also used for diagnostic and teaching purposes. Gradually the reading teacher acquires an assortment of testing and teaching materials suitable for various pupils in a particular school.

Teaching Vowel Sounds

The teaching of vowel sounds is similar to the teaching of consonants. Attention should be given to the suggestions for the re-use of test material for instructional purposes, to the desirability of having a pronunciation key in the form of cards or charts, and to the need for giving the pupil a clear picture of the sound of the letter and for helping him reproduce it. Training in hearing and reproducing sounds accurately may have to be given greater emphasis in dealing with vowels. Because of the frequency and seriousness of short vowel difficulties on the part of retarded readers, most of the teacher's efforts will be concentrated on that particular area of vowel sounds.

a) *Short vowel exercises.* When a diagnostic test reveals a weakness in a particular vowel sound, oral work on lists of words containing that sound is needed. Practice in hearing the sound in context and in pronouncing words in which it appears helps the child become so familiar with the sound that he has no difficulty when he meets it in reading. The teacher may find it valuable to begin with a basic list of words for each short vowel sound. Some teachers prefer a list that includes words in which the short vowel appears in the initial position as well as words containing medial vowels. Here is a sample list for short ĕ:

ten	exit	left
desk	west	egg
end	effort	empty

A list for each vowel sound may be developed from individual contributions by the members of the group. Pupils may spontaneously give words containing a particular short vowel sound or find such words in their readers. In addition, sentences containing several words in which the particular sound occurs may be used for purposes of testing and practice.

After a pupil has learned the individual sounds with which he has had difficulty, discrimination exercises for vowel confusions may be given. Exercises like those on page 226 may be used first as tests and then for instructional purposes. The follow-up may take the form of oral correction accompanied by the writing of the answers on the blackboard. The latter precaution is taken to avoid any confusion in associating the particular sound with the printed letter.

b) *Short vowel games.* Drill on simple words should not be overdone as it may become very monotonous, especially for the older retarded reader. To avoid an unfavorable attitude toward language activities, a teacher may devise an original exercise based on words at the pupil's

Samples:

Medial Vowel Discrimination

Draw a line under the word that makes the sentence right.
1. He (sat, sit) down on the chair.
2. John took his (bat, bet) to the game.
3. He (hit, hot) a home run.
4. The red light says you must (step, stop).
5. He made a (shop, ship) in the school (shop, ship).
6. The two teams (ran, run) a race.
7. A dime is the same as (tin, ten) cents.
8. The boy will (fell, fill) the pail with water.
9. The dog likes to play and (ran, run).
10. The teacher (led, lad) the class to the door.

Discrimination Between ă and ĭ

Draw a line under the word that makes the sentence right.
(has or his)

1. Who (has–his) my coat?
2. Where is (his–has) hat?
3. The boy (has–his) a book.
4. He lost (has–his) pen.
5. Father put on (his–has) hat.
6. He found (has–his) books.
7. Who (has–his) a penny for me?
8. Here is (his–has) mother.
9. He (has–his) a big dog.
10. Where is (his–has) pet?

Discrimination Between ă and ŭ

Choose the word that makes the sentence right. (ran or run)

1. That boy can_____fast.
2. The dog_____after the fox.
3. Did you_____home?
4. I_____home.
5. Who_____for class president?
6. I like to_____.
7. Who_____to the corner?
8. Billy_____faster than Jimmy.
9. Can Mary_____fast?
10. Who will_____a race with me?

interest level which he uses in his recreational activities, hears on the radio, sees on television programs, or reads on the sports page. Vocabularies pertinent to hobbies, seasonal sports, and other areas of interest serve as material for enjoyable oral and written exercises. Ideas for games may be found in various workbooks. A sample exercise follows at the top of page 228.

c) *Long vowels.* The long vowel sounds do not present much difficulty. Usually a brief explanation enables the pupil to grasp the idea that a long vowel has the sound of its own name. Then he can apply this knowledge to the reading of words like *plane, old,* and *used.* Long vowel sounds are generally learned as they appear in the sight vocabulary.

d) *Exercises for discrimination between long and short vowels.* After the long and short vowel sounds have been studied separately, they may be presented together for further practice. Instant recognition of common words presupposes an ability to distinguish between the short and long sounds of vowels. Oral preparation and/or follow-up is a necessary part of exercises used for this purpose. In preparation for the interpretation of diacritical markings found in dictionaries, pupils may be directed to place either the long ($\bar{a}$) or short ($\breve{a}$) symbol over the particular vowel being studied. Sample exercises of various types are given here and at the bottom of page 228; many others may be found in workbooks.

Long $\bar{a}$ — Short $\breve{a}$

Draw a circle around each word that has a long $\bar{a}$ sound.

can	gave	grand	pat
cane	plant	blame	ran
made	brave	wave	shake
sad	lame	gate	plate

The underlying principle may be deduced and the pupils given the opportunity to apply it in similar exercises for the other vowel sounds.

e) *Two-vowel combinations.* The teaching of the most common two-vowel combinations (*gain, seat, coat*) has a place in the program of the retarded reader. Too much emphasis, however, should not be given to drill on the vowel combinations. As a pupil adds words to his sight vocabulary, he learns other sounds of this type, e.g., for the *ea* combination various sounds occur: *learn, great, head.* Vowel combinations like *ou* which has so many different sounds (*though, fought, rough, through*) need not be taught as such but rather in relation to new sight words. Some attention may be given to the most common sound of the various vowel combinations which the pupil meets most frequently in his reading materials. Exercises like those on page 229 may be used when they are needed specifically.

| Yankees | Red Sox | Phillies | Dodgers | Cubs |

Put the words listed below on the right vowel teams:

fence	cap	stretch	drop	up	miss
catch	bat	ran	mask	stands	inning
slid	left	send	belt	pen	under
run	bunt	box	club	sock	lot
fan	center	on	pop	cut	hit
win	bench	pitch	mit	stop	umpire

Samples:

catch	fence			
_____	_____	_____	_____	_____
_____	_____	_____	_____	_____
_____	_____	_____	_____	_____
_____	_____	_____	_____	_____
_____	_____	_____	_____	_____
_____	_____	_____	_____	_____
_____	_____	_____	_____	_____

Make the Vowel Say Its Name

Read the words that follow, then add an "e" to each word. Now read the new words.

can _____	hat _____	rat _____
mad _____	tap _____	fat _____
plan _____	pan _____	pal _____

Discrimination Between Long a and Short a

Draw a line under the right word.

1. Planes travel at a fast (rat, rate).
2. This morning there was frost on the window (pan, pane).
3. I went up in an air (plane, plan).
4. The policeman shot the (mad, made) dog.
5. The actor did a (tap, tape) dance.

Pronounce these words:

train	grain	brain	waiter	mail
maid	tail	faint	pail	sailor

Fill in these blanks with other ai words.

_____ _____ _____ _____ _____

_____ _____ _____ _____ _____

From the individual lists, a group list may be drawn up on the blackboard or chart and recorded in pupils' books. Words that might appear in such a list are:

paintings	raid	explain	refrain	obtain
complain	slain	trail	attain	contain

Teaching Syllabication

When a pupil reaches a third grade reading level, he encounters an increasing number of words of more than two syllables. Word recognition techniques which he has already acquired are not adequate for his new needs. Some knowledge of syllables is necessary not only for purposes of word recognition in reading but also for the spelling of words used in writing activities. After some progress in written expression has been made, a knowledge of syllabication will aid a pupil in dividing a word which must be broken at the end of a line. Motivation for the study of syllables springs from the learner's awareness of the need for and the function of syllabication in his reading and writing experiences. It is a skill that is very valuable for many of the more advanced pupils in the special reading programs. Some who read at a fifth or sixth grade level have acquired many word recognition techniques but have not had sufficient training in syllabication. With the acquisition of skill in this area, their achievement in comprehension and in speed often increases rapidly.

a) *Introducing syllabication.* Breaking a word into syllables is a skill that is difficult to acquire. It is developed gradually by the retarded reader as he meets words in context that lend themselves to syllabic analysis. In teaching syllabication, it is desirable to give attention first to compound words whose meanings are derived from their parts (A) and then to other compound words (B). Lists like the following can be drawn up by teachers and pupils and analyzed:

(A)	airplane	moonlight	seashore	outdoor
	fireman	shipwreck	bluebird	driftwood
(B)	handsome	hardship	quarterback	instep
	butterfly	understand	overboard	pocketbook

Next the pupils may be introduced to two-syllable words formed by the addition of a common ending. Words that may be used for teaching and practice are given here:

seeing	started	warmer	lightly
helping	needed	shorter	softly
going	waited	taller	slowly
flying	sounded	louder	swiftly
raining	hunted	faster	quickly

The syllable *a* at the beginning of a word is difficult for retarded readers and may be studied at this time if the teacher feels that the pupils need it. Practice on words like these is a valuable aid to word recognition:

ago	along	alike	alone	again
about	around	among	afraid	away

The syllabication of words with a double consonant is not difficult for pupils who have had experience in dividing compound words and two-syllable words with common endings.

The Same Consonant		Different Consonants	
dinner	apple	window	outline
puppy	sudden	after	breakfast
follow	battle	corner	welcome
better	offer	problem	almost
supper	summer	furnish	children

Pupils who are familiar with the preceding types of syllabication are probably ready for polysyllabic words. If, at first, words of the phonetic type are used, pupils may work out the pronunciation of any unfamiliar syllable by means of the sound-blending technique they have used for monosyllabic words.

potato	conductor
capitol	independent
patriotic	planetarium

In the next list, words are included that are not entirely phonetic. Some of them have common syllable combinations such as *ation* and *intro* which are recognized and pronounced as units rather than as two syllables.

automobile	introduction
graduation	paragraph
television	typewriting

Kottmeyer gives good suggestions for words that can be used with retarded readers in developing ability in syllabication. . . . The word lists that have been given in this section . . . can be adapted for use in developing many of the word recognition skills discussed in other sections.

As pupils participate in syllabication activities certain simple principles evolve. Attention may be drawn to them, but this does not imply the memorization of rules. Some of the learnings about syllables that will become evident are given here:

Every syllable contains a sounded vowel.

When a word has more than one vowel sound, it is broken into parts or syllables.

Sometimes a vowel forms a syllable by itself; e.g., a-mong; vi-o-lin.

Double consonants usually are separated; e.g., val/ley.

A consonant between two vowels usually is joined to the vowel that follows it; e.g., to/tal.

When the suffix *ed* is added to a word ending in *d* or *t*, it forms a separate syllable; e.g., fold/ed; plant/ed.

b) *Activities for developing skill in syllabication.* The following activities help pupils become aware of syllables:

(1) Listening to a word pronounced by the teacher in a natural manner in order to hear the parts or syllables. The pupil's syllabication of the word is checked with the dictionary or by the teacher who may wish to have the correct response shown on the blackboard. Variations in this exercise may be arranged.

> Words are presented to the group by pupils who have previously checked the syllabication. In accordance with the direction given, pupils' responses may take the form of: telling or writing the number of syllables heard; actually writing the word and dividing it into syllables; writing only the first syllable.

(2) Dividing compound words presented in printed form into their two parts—sunshine.

(3) Classifying words in columns according to number of syllables.

One Syllable	Two Syllables	Three Syllables
let	after	afternoon

(4) Dividing polysyllabic words by drawing lines between syllables— re / mem / ber

(5) Adding prefixes and suffixes to root words.

    *un*happy   walk*ing*   sleep*y*

(6) Using the dictionary to check one's own syllabication of a word.

5. Employing a Visual Approach

The visual approach is important in word recognition

This approach is helpful in discovering the identity of unfamiliar words. It is used in conjunction with context and phonetic clues and includes various degrees and kinds of observation. If efficient and effective guidance is to be given to retarded readers, it is necessary for the teacher to find out just what visual techniques each pupil has acquired and which of the essential ones he lacks. This calls for a consideration of both diagnosis and training in the area of the visual approach.

Diagnosing Weaknesses

As pupils read in their ordinary activities, many of their difficulties in using a visual approach are revealed. The two extremes of this approach to word recognition—superficial observation and concentration on details—are found in almost every group of seriously retarded readers. Superficial observation may take the form of guessing a word on the basis of either its general appearance or an outstanding characteristic. For instance, the general shape of the word *scissors* is long and rectangular whereas the word *run* may be enclosed in a comparatively short rectangle. A word like *telephone* with extensions above and below the base line is irregular in contour and is distinguishable by its uneven appearance. Guessing a word by means of an obvious feature is illustrated by the child who remembers the word *flies* because of its tall initial letters, or *look* by the two *o*'s that remind him of eyes, or the word *build* because of the letters that extend upward and connote the meaning of the word.

Such visual hints if used along with context suffice at the beginning of a child's reading experience. As he advances beyond the initial reading stage, however, he meets an ever-increasing number of words more or less similar in appearance or in an outstanding detail, *three* and *there*, *went* and *when*. Although the rapid observation of obvious clues no longer meets his needs, the retarded reader often clings to this infantile method instead of advancing to the level of visual analysis which demands closer observation and finer discrimination. Cursory observation, however, is adequate for most of the word recognition needs of adults because of their years of contact with printed words and their habitual reliance upon context clues. It is, therefore, a method which is not discarded as pupils learn to read but one that is quite limited in use until some maturity in reading has been achieved.

An analysis of the teacher's list of pupils' errors will often reveal weakness in visual discrimination as well as in left-to-right directional attack. For example, the words miscalled by one pupil in a week included the following:

> *through* for *thought*   *felt* for *left*
> *mouth* for *month*   *and* for *said*

The teacher notices that the pupil seems to guess words on the basis of their general appearance or of a specific detail and fails to observe distinctive parts. In addition, the pupil appears to require training in focusing on the initial parts of words and in observing words consistently from left to right. In the same way, a teacher will often discover a single error in discrimination which occurs over and over in one pupil's miscallings. Perhaps it is a confusion of the visual appearance of the letters *m* and *n*; correction of a mistake like this may clear up many word recognition errors.

In contrast to the rapid, inaccurate observation of words just discussed, there is another type which also causes difficulty. Some retarded readers become so engrossed in a detailed study of a word that they have difficulty in seeing the word as a whole and in remembering the part of the selection they have just read. This may be due to an overemphasis on phonics and a lack of training in utilization of the context. Pupils who make an exaggerated study of a word or who observe words superficially probably have had little or no experience with two other aspects of the visual approach, namely, locating the elements of a word that are most useful in discovering its identity and studying the structure.

One more weakness in the visual approach found frequently enough among retarded readers to be mentioned here is the inability to substitute one consonant or vowel for another. For instance, a pupil who knows the word *right* and is acquainted with the consonant sounds should be able to recognize *night, light,* and several other words. The technique of replacing one letter by another to form a new word is a key to an ever-growing reading vocabulary and a source of great satisfaction to older boys and girls functioning at a low reading level.

In addition to the informal appraisal of visual techniques based on everyday reading materials and observation, a teacher may check directly for specific weaknesses by formal means. Special word lists may be used for this purpose such as those given in the section on the phonetic approach. For the recognition of these isolated words, a pupil cannot rely on contextual clues but is forced to reveal the visual and phonetic aids at his command. Standardized oral reading tests also are used for diagnosing word recognition difficulties and often disclose patterns of error for an individual or for a group.

Guiding Pupils in Developing Skill in the Visual Approach

The weaknesses and strengths discovered in the diagnosis of the visual approach indicate the type of training required by each pupil. For retarded readers with so many gaps in learning, it is important that time and effort be directed toward their specific needs.

In guiding children in attacking unfamiliar words, emphasis is placed on the analytic method rather than on word synthesis. The word to be examined is introduced as a whole; next, one or more parts are extracted for study and then the whole word is presented again. This procedure has replaced the older method of synthesizing individual phonetic elements and discovering the word thus formed. For all word study exercises mentioned hereafter, teachers are urged to use the analytic method. The visual analysis of words embraces several skills:

> Noting general appearance
> Seeing an outstanding detail
> Detecting familiar parts
> Finding small words within larger ones
> Recognizing similarities and distinctive features

The first two require little discussion because many retarded readers have acquired these skills and rely on them almost exclusively. For the few who need guidance because of their extreme consciousness of word details, phonics is temporarily abandoned and emphasis is placed on building a sight vocabulary and on utilizing context clues. Each of the other skills will now be discussed.

a) *Detecting familiar parts.* An important skill in the analysis of word forms is seeing a familiar part of a larger word, such as the base word *break* in un*break*able. Pupils in the reading project were trained to detect known parts of words taken from context; these words were either printed on the blackboard or in the individual's notebook. Each word was then examined and the familiar element underlined or delineated in some other way. The pupil was asked to think of other words in which the same known part appeared or to find them in his reader. He made his own list on which he indicated the base word. Similar lists were built cooperatively by groups of retarded readers who needed this kind of training.

After pupils had learned how to locate familiar word parts, they gained further skill and also increased their reading vocabularies by means of word-building exercises. For example, the word *appear* was placed on the blackboard and pupils were asked to add the various common endings—*s, ing, ed.* The new words were then printed on the blackboard or on individual lists. A pupil or the teacher suggested that *ance* be added to form a new word and *dis* prefixed to the base word. Thus retarded readers learned to associate the printed forms of whole words and word parts with the spoken forms already familiar to them. Exercises that develop skill in seeing word parts are included in the discussions of discrimination and syllabication that follow. Helpful exercises are suggested also in the section entitled *Building A Meaning Vocabulary.*

b) *Finding small words.* Visual analysis of a word may reveal the presence of a small word within the longer one. This discovery is most valuable when the little word is useful in working out the pronunciation of the whole word and is related to its meaning; e.g., *airmail.* It is advisable generally to conduct oral rather than silent exercises in developing this skill. Locating the short word sometimes hinders the child in his attempts at word recognition, for example, focusing on *eat* or *at* in *great,* or *his* in *this* is confusing because of the differences in sound. Therefore, indiscriminate assignments that require the finding of small words within long words should never be given.

c) *Recognizing similarities and distinctive features.* Among retarded readers there was found a great lack of skill in recognizing the distinctive features of words. For most retarded readers, a few individual lessons on seeing the distinctive features of words they had confused yielded satisfactory results. When a pupil made so-called careless mistakes in word recognition, the time used in showing him the difference between the word as it appeared in the reading material and his miscalling of it was indeed worthwhile. For instance, a pupil read the word *present* as *president.* The teacher printed on the blackboard or on the pupil's paper the two words *present—president* and had the pupil look at each word and say it syllable by syllable or sound by sound if necessary. Attention was drawn to the differences between the two words, in length, in number of syllables, in the number of letters that extend above the line, in the presence or omission of the dot over a letter. Thus the details of the word *president* that differentiate it from the word present were highlighted. Similarly, pupils were taught to compare words frequently confused by retarded readers:

except–expect	what–that	quite–quiet	palace–place
want–wait	where–there	them–then	dog–boy

This kind of instruction was followed by word analysis assignments that called for the particular type of visual discrimination in which the individual needed practice. Observation was sharpened through exercises that required comparison of one word with another similar in some part. For example, in order to complete each sentence that follows, pupils were forced to give attention to the element that was different, that is, the middle part of each of the word choices.

The new boy has a stamp   collection
                                      collision

I like to swim in warm   winter
                                   water

Suggestions for Exercises in Visual Discrimination

Exercises found helpful for retarded readers in the development of various types of visual discrimination are given here. The teacher, of course, first calls attention to the difference between the words confused.

Many different exercises should be given for overcoming weaknesses in the following types of discrimination. If there is not clear perception of word beginnings, there is slight chance of proper identification of words. Similar exercises may be given to force attention to middle and final parts of words.

Reversal of Whole Word

Oral Directions

Copy the word saw from the sentence on the blackboard.
Draw a line under the first letler of the word saw.
Give the first letter sound in the word saw.
Write the first letter of the word saw.
On page _____ in your book find a sentence with the word saw.
Read it to me.

Draw a line under the words that mean "has seen."

saw   was   was   saw   was   saw

How many words can you say without a mistake?

| saw | won | no | pot | tap |
| was | now | on | top | pat |

Choose the correct word.

1. The boy (was, saw) a good moving picture.
2. We (now, won) the game.
3. Supper is (on, no) the table.
4. I like to spin my (top, pot).
5. She is a (pat, tap) dancer.

Partial Reversal

Fill in the right word in these sentences.

there   three

1. The _____ boys went fishing.
2. Put your library books over _____.
3. Can you name _____ big league baseball teams?
4. We knew _____ would be many pupils absent on the holy day.
5. The shop teacher sent _____ boys for the wood.

Configuration

Draw a line under the word that makes the sentence right.

The circus (house, horse) danced.
The president lives in the White (Horse, House).
The policeman rode a beautiful (horse, house).
Please come to my (horse, house) for dinner tonight.
Black Beauty is a story about a (horse, house).

Riddles	Put a box around the right word.	
1. It has a door.	horse	house
2. It can jump.	house	horse
3. It eats hay.	horse	house
4. We live in it.	house	horse
5. It has four legs.	house	horse

Draw a line under the word "horse"	Draw a line under the word "house"
horse	house
horse	horse
house	house
horse	house
house	horse

Medial Vowels

Draw a line under the word that makes the sentence right.

1. Tom $\frac{\text{want}}{\text{went}}$ to another junior high school.

2. What game do you $\frac{\text{want}}{\text{went}}$ to play?

3. We $\frac{\text{want}}{\text{went}}$ to play basketball tomorrow.

4. The girls $\frac{\text{want}}{\text{went}}$ to their sewing class.

Draw a line under the word that means "has gone."				Draw a line under the word that means "to wish."			
went	want	went	want	want	went	went	want
want	went	went	went	want	want	went	want

Initial Part of Word

Oral Directions

1. Draw a picture of a baseball bat.
2. Write the word <u>bat</u> under it.
3. Draw a picture of a hat.
4. Write the word <u>hat</u> under it.
5. Draw circles around the letters that are not the same in these words.
6. Draw a line under the word that tells something you wear on your head.

Confusion of Letters

Write the word that is missing in each sentence.

(but, put)   The boy_____his books away.
(month, mouth)   In what_____is your birthday?
(bug, dug)   The squirrel_____a hole for his nuts.
(gum, gun)   John gave me some chewing_____.
(kid, hid)   Mother_____our Christmas presents.

Omission and Insertion of Letters

Can you say these words?

Be careful of the tricky letters!

tap	tip	sick	say
trap	trip	stick	stay
bed	tick	food	pay
bled	trick	flood	play
pace	back	soon	gay
place	black	spoon	gray

---

21. WORD PERCEPTION AND ENRICHMENT

David H. Russell and Etta E. Karp

The accurate perception of words and phraes may be called the first step of the reading process. To his perception the child must add understanding and interpretation of the word symbols, but these cannot be useful if the first perception is inaccurate. Reading depends to a considerable extent, accordingly, upon the original impressions or perceptions of the printed page.

The day of reliance upon one method of teaching word perception and recognition is largely gone. Instead, the skillful primary teacher helps children to develop four or five ways of identifying or recognizing words for themselves. The child who is a good reader in the primary grades is able to use several or all of the following methods of "attacking" new or partly known words:

1. By configuration or general shape. The word "grandfather" has a shape different from the word "boy."

2. By some peculiarity in the word, such as the double *o* in "moon."

3. By use of a picture clue—matching the word and part of the illustration.

4. By use of a context clue—using the meaning of a sentence or paragraph to make an intelligent guess at a word.

5. By recognition of a familiar part in a longer word, where such a technique applies, as "mother" in "grandmother."

6. By phonetic analysis—using the initial consonant or common phonogram or other sound clues to discover the whole word.

Reprinted with the permission of the publishers from David H. Russell and Etta E. Karp, *Reading Aids through the Grades* (New York Teachers College Press), pp. 22–51. Copyright 1938, 1951, by Teachers College, Columbia University.

7. By structural analysis—knowing common prefixes and suffixes, recognizing syllables and other parts, especially useful in the intermediate and upper grades.

Since different children learn in different ways and have different abilities, they should have a chance to learn all of these seven ways of recognizing words and to grow in the ability to combine two or three or four of the most suitable methods in attacking any one word.

Many of the devices and activities below will help develop these word recognition and identification abilities as well as build up a sight vocabulary which children can recognize automatically. In addition, many of the activities are devised to help the child who is having difficulties or making consistent errors in perceiving words. A list of the most frequent of these errors is given below. The exercises have been classified in such terms as omissions, initial sounds, configuration, and reversals so that the teacher may select an activity which will help a child overcome a difficulty or provide a broad and varied approach to developmental problems of word perception.

EXAMPLES OF COMMON WORD PERCEPTION ERRORS

1. Omissions of letters, syllables, words

Child reads:
"place" for "palace"
"very" for "every"

2. Reversals

Complete:
"was" for "saw"
"on" for "no"
Partial:
"left" for "felt"
"tired" for "tried"

3. Letter confusion

b, d, p, q
"dig for big"
"pack" for "quack"

4. Substitutions

Letter:
"that" for "what"
"swed" for "sled"
Word:
"in" for "a"
"the" for "an"

5. Letter sounds and syllable sounds

Initial sounds:
"was" for "has"
"ran" for "can"
Wrong middle:
"get" for "got"
"big" for "beg"
Final sounds:
"has" for "had"
"big" for "bed"

6. Configuration	Similarity in physical appearance of words:
	"stick" for "stone"
	"hand" for "band"
7. Wrong endings	Addition, omission, confusion of endings:
	"wants" for "want"
	"walk" for "walked"
	"faster" for "fastest"

1. GENERAL WORD PERCEPTION

41. *Airplane.* Draw a spiral path on a sheet of paper, with a hangar at the end of the path. Divide the path into sections in which are printed drill words. Two players have an object representing an airplane and duplicate sets of 1″ x 2″ cards with the same words that are on the path The game begins with both airplanes in the lower left space and each player's cards face up. The first player reads the word on his top card. If the word is the same as the one in the first space of the path, his plane is moved to that space. If not, he may not move. His card is placed on the bottom of his deck and the other player takes his turn. The winner is the person whose airplane reaches the hangar first.

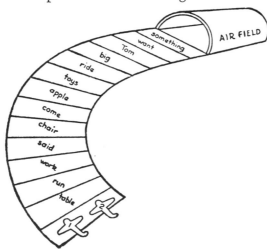

42. *Card drawing.* Print on cards words needing practice. Place the cards face down on the table. Children in the group take turns drawing cards and reading the words printed thereon. If it is misread, a card is returned face down to the bottom of the pack. The winner is the person with the largest number of cards when the stack is gone.

43. *Erase a word.* Children are asked to choose sides and stand in two lines at right angles to the blackboard. The teacher writes on the board two lines of words or sentences of equal difficulty, as many words or

sentences as there are children. At the signal the first child in each line says the first word in his column. If he is correct, he is allowed to erase the word. This game is in the form of a relay race.

44. *The picture dictionary.* The child or the teacher makes a scrapbook that is indexed. Both capital and lower-case letters are used. Illustrations are prepared or cut from old magazines, primers, papers, and advertisements. As soon as a word is learned, the child pastes on the proper page the picture which corresponds to the word. If the word is "automobile," a picture of an automobile is pasted on the "A" page. Later the teacher may drill on words in the dictionary by giving the child small cards on which are printed the words he has learned. The child has to find the picture that tells the same story as the word, and place the word under the picture. Good picture dictionaries have been published by the Garden City Publishing Co., Garden City, N.Y. (*A Picture Dictionary for Boys and Girls*), by Grossett and Dunlap (*A Child's First Picture Dictionary*), by Simon and Schuster (*The Golden Picture Dictionary*), and by other firms. There are, however, several advantages in the home-made dictionary: (*a*) it contains all the words that the child is using, and only those words; (*b*) it is individual; and (*c*) the child has the added interest of making it himself.

45. *Finders.* (played like "Bingo"). Each player has a card marked off into twenty-five square blocks. In each block a word is printed. On a small pack of cards, each the size of a block, words are printed. The teacher shows the cards one at a time. The child who has the displayed word on his card raises his hand, pronounces the word, points to it, and is given the small card, which he places over the appropriate word on his card. The child who has five words covered in any direction is the winner.

46. *Word race.* A chalk line is drawn on the floor to represent the starting line. A second line is drawn parallel to the first and as many spaces away from it as there are words in the game. (The spaces may also be marked off with chalk, or the floor boards may be used.) Each player has a cardboard figure to represent him. The figures may be numbered or named by the players. The players place their figures on the starting line. The teacher holds up a card. If the first child can read it correctly, he is permitted to advance his figure one space. The child whose figure first crosses the goal line is the winner.

47. *Self-learning with picture cards.* Cut oak tag into cards of handy size, such as $3\frac{1}{2}''$ x 5", and have the children paste on them pictures cut from old books, magazines, newspapers, etc. Under each picture print the word or phrase that tells about the picture and print the same word on the reverse side of the card. Give cards to the children, who learn to associate the printed symbol with the picture. After continued practice with picture and word, present the reverse sides of the cards showing only the printed words. New cards may be added as the child progresses.

48. *My word book.* All the words the child learns can be put into his

vocabulary book, *My Word Book*. This book may be illustrated by the child, or pictures may be cut from other sources and pasted under each word to illustrate it.

49. *Picture cards and tracing.* For the slow learner this device can be used with modifications as needed. Fewer pictures are given at one time. As the picture side of each card is presented, the teacher pronounces the word under it. The child pronounces the word, and then traces it with his finger. He does this as many times as is necessary to recognize the word shown without the picture.

50. *Matching card game.* A set of printed word cards is used. Each word occurs on four cards. The players are each dealt three or five cards. Five cards are placed face up on the table. If the first child to play has a card in his hand marked "horse" and there is a "horse" card on the table, he may expose his card, pronounce the word, and place the two "horse" cards face up in front of him. If he does not have a card which matches any of the exposed cards on the table, he must discard one of his own cards, and draw another from the pack. If he has a matching card, but cannot pronounce it, he places it on top of the card on the table which it matches, and draws a card from the pack. If a child can make more than one match at a time, he may do so. Drawing a card from the pack ends his play. The second player follows the procedure of the first, except that he may match with and pronounce any cards face up on the table and take them. For example, if the first player has taken "horse," and the second player has a "horse" card, he may take the two cards in front of the first player. Another player possessing the fourth "horse" card may in turn claim the three "horse" cards already collected. The same procedure is followed with respect to the pairs or triplets of cards that collect in the center of the table because of failure on the player's part to pronounce them. When the pack of cards is exhausted, the players continue as before, except that they do not draw. Thus the hands are soon played and the game is over. The player with the most cards before him has won.

Other games may be played by changing the rules and manner of play to conform to any simple, well-known children's card game.

51. *Fishing for words.* Word cards are folded and the open ends are pinned together with a large straight pin. (Care must be taken to use steel pins, or hairpins, as a magnet will not pick up ordinary pins.) They are then placed in a large fish bowl (or a box). The child throws into the bowl a piece of string with a small magnet attached and pulls out one of the "fish." If he can read the word on the card he may keep it; otherwise it must be thrown back into the bowl. He may keep a record of the number of words correctly read each day.

A similar device may be used in simple flash-card drill. The cards are placed in a row on the blackboard ledge. A pupil takes as many cards as he can read correctly.

52. *Treasure hunt.* The teacher places before the children a large box filled with small objects or pictures. Printed word cards corresponding to the objects or pictures are arranged along the blackboard ledge. Each child closes his eyes and draws an object or picture, for which he must then find the corresponding word.

53. *Wheel of chance.* A large cardboard clockface is numbered from 1 to 12 (or more) and fitted with a large movable hand. The hand can be held in place by means of a large fastener. Alongside the clockface the same number of words or phrases are printed either on the blackboard or on a large sheet of paper. A child is called on; he flicks the hand with his fingers, sees the number at which it stops, then reads the corresponding printed word or phrase.

1. had
2. come back
3. want
4. jump the fence
5. likes
6. barn
7. went
8. something
9. what
10. here
11. ran away
12. play

54. *Matching words with pictures.* Pictures may be used to illustrate useful words other than nouns. For verbs, a small card is used. At the left in a box is a sketch of a man performing some act, such as running, throwing, or sitting. To the right of the picture are three words, only one of which tells the same story as the picture. The child indicates the correct word by drawing a circle around it or by some other method of marking. (See drawing.) Other cards may illustrate "over," "under," "left," "right," etc.

SLEEP

RUN

EAT

55. *Color cards.* Cards are prepared with black and white drawings of objects which have a characteristic color. Under the objects are printed directions, such as: "This is a tree. Color it green." This teaches not only the words but also the colors.

56. *Word and picture hunt.* The children open their readers to an assigned page with a picture on it. On the blackboard, the teacher prints a list of words. The children read the words and associate them with the objects in the picture. For example, for a detailed home scene, such words as the following may be printed on the blackboard:

girl	ice cream
children	pink
table	blue
window	dog
chair	mother
cake	baby

This may be either a written or an oral reading exercise. Oral work may be done with a reader. For a written exercise, a picture from an old book, magazine, or newspaper may be used. The children print the word under the object or place a small card with the printed word on it under the appropriate picture.

57. *Labeling.* Labeling is a worth-while device only if it is made meaningful. When children bring in toys, these may be labeled. Shelves in the classroom closet should be labeled to indicate places for various supplies: for example, clay, paint, scissors, paper, chalk, pencils, etc. Children's hooks in the wardrobe may be labeled, and the children may be encouraged to learn the names of their classmates.

58. *The bulletin board.* Interesting pictures with a word or two about them in very simple language may be placed on the bulletin board. Colorful book jackets from children's books are also good bulletin board material.

59. *The news corner.* The News Corner may be used for announcements or any news pertaining to the children themselves, such as "We are going on a trip tomorrow"; "Betty has a pretty new red dress."

60. *Special vocabulary book.* If children are interested in special kinds of stories, such as animal or adventure, they are encouraged to collect words or print words that are essential in reading and enjoying their particular interests. These words are listed in a special book.

61. *Writing stories.* The child writes or dictates his own story, which the teacher types in primer type. The child may then read this story and exchange stories with the other children. Later these stories may be bound into books.

62. *Rapid presentation (Tachistoscope).* For quick recognition of words, the teacher may make a very simple tachistoscope. Cut a piece of oak tag or cardboard to convenient size, 5″ x 8″ or any other size. Fold back about ½″ along each of the long sides. This serves as a tray to hold the printed materials. Cut an opening in the center wide enough to allow the usual size of printed material, and fasten another piece of oak tag or cardboard to it to serve as a shutter. Printed words on separate slips of paper or cards are slipped into the fold on the underneath side. When

the screen is operating, the slips of paper or cards are placed behind the opening but are hidden by the shutter. Screen and slips of paper are held upright with the left hand. The thumb holds the paper or card against the screen. The right hand lifts the shutter and then lets it drop. The

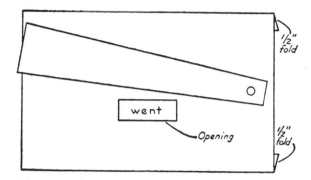

right hand is also used in changing cards to be flashed on the screen. The word is exposed for about one-quarter to one-half second. If the word is missed, the shutter is opened and the child is allowed to inspect the word carefully and try again.

63. *Surprise stories.* Use a difficult abstract word in a nonsense jingle or story, or paraphrase a song using the word to be learned. Print the story or song on the blackboard before the children come to class and call attention to it when all are assembled. Then encourage the children to take turns reading it, or singing the new song. Keep this surprise story on the blackboard until the children are familiar with the words. Change the stories frequently and encourage the children to look for them on the board. For example, to teach the word "of":

> Of all the pets,
> Of all the rabbits,
> Of all the squirrels,
> Of all the kittens,
> Jo-Jo was the best.

Or to teach the word "here," which frequently presents difficulty, the following jingle could be used.

> Here we go
> Here we play
> Here we run
> Here we stay
> Here we stay and play
> Here, here, here.
> Here we walk
> Here we talk
> Here, here, here.

64. *List of nouns to illustrate the alphabet.*

a — apple	n — nest
b — boat	o — orange
c — cat	p — pail
d — duck	q — queen
e — egg	r — rooster
f — fox	s — sack
g — goat	t — tail
h — house	u — umbrella
i — ice cream	v — vest
j — jacks	w — wagon
k — kite	x — xylophone
l — lamp	y — yard
m — mouse	z — zebra

Some attention should be given to individual letters only after the child has accumulated a good sight vocabulary of words and phrases he knows automatically. The letters are valuable as the child learns initial consonant sounds or vowel sounds and in developing readiness for later dictionary work.

65. *Omissions.* When a child omits one or more words in reading a sentence, the teacher writes on the blackboard the sentence *as the child read it.* Above this she writes the sentence as it appears in the book. She then asks the child to point out to her the differences between the two sentences. The child is thus made aware of the fact that each word has a definite meaning and is of importance in the sentence.

66. *Missing words.* For a group that has special tendencies toward omissions, the teacher may prepare cards, each card bearing one word of a sentence. Each child is given one of the cards, and takes his place in a line in such order that the sentence may be correctly read. Then individual children may be told to sit down, thus removing their words from the sentence. The children read it again with the words missing and make the discovery that the sentence has either changed in meaning or lacks meaning entirely when all the words are not there. Similarly, the sentence may be broken up in a variety of ways.

A similar technique may be used for building sentences. The cards are given to the children as above; then the child who has the first word of the sentence stands up and holds the word so all may see it. The child who thinks he has the second word stands next to the first and shows his word, and so on until the entire sentence is correctly built. Any errors in the sentence building will usually be corrected by the children.

67. *Phrase cards.* The use of phrase cards will be found of great assistance in correcting the error of omission. Short, easy phrases should be used at first, such as "all day," "they ran," and "into the house." When these have been thoroughly learned, longer and more difficult phrases

may be introduced. Phrases may be used which tell a story when put together.

68. *Answering with phrases.* Short phrases from a story read in class may be placed along the blackboard ledge. The child may be asked to find the answers to a question, as "Where did the little dog run?" The child would be expected to pick out a pharse, such as "into the house."

II. REVERSALS

69. *Reversals.* The child traces over a word with which he has been having difficulty. The word is written in fairly large letters. As he traces over each letter he vocalizes the sound of that letter, making the sound last as long as it takes him to write the letter, thus coming out even at the end of the word with both sound and tracing. Encourage him to blend the sound of one letter into the next.

70. The teacher holds up a card that is covered with a marker or sheet of paper. The marker is moved slowly to the right, so that letters are exposed in proper sequence.

71. *Stop and go.* Words frequently reversed, such as "was" and "no," are printed with the first letter in green and the rest in red. Children are told to observe lights, starting on the green and stopping at the red. The same words in regular pencil should then be placed beside the colored words and read after them.

72. The teacher holds up a printed word card. She then slides over it another card which has a small opening in it. The opening should be small enough to expose only one letter at a time. When all the letters have been exposed, the card is moved along to a larger opening which shows the whole word.

73. If the child knows some numbers, the teacher gives him a paper ruled off into blocks—as many blocks as there are letters in the word to be studied. The blocks are numbered from left to right, as 1, 2, 3 for a three-letter word. If the word to be learned is "was," the child writes *w* in the first block, *a* in the second, and s in the third. This gives training in the habit of reading from left to right.

Words Frequently Reversed

am	lap	no	pal	rat	star	ton
bad	ma	north	pat	raw	tap	top
dab	nap	now	peek	saw	tar	war
deer	net	on	pot	spot	team	was

Words Partially Reversed

even	from	felt	spilt	stop	tried	trial
never	form	left	split	spot	tired	trail

III. Confused Letters

74. Letters frequently confused are *b, d, p, q; t, f,* and *l; m* and *w; u* and *n;* and all the vowel sounds. As an aid in teaching the difference between *b* and *d,* between *t* and *f,* and between *p* and *q,* the teacher can point out that although these letters look somewhat alike in shape, they face in different directions. Occasionally a trick device may be thought out by teacher or pupil. For example, Peter, aged eight, who had trouble with *p* and *q,* finally remembered *p* because it stood for Peter and it turned to the right and he, Peter, wrote with his right hand.

75. Print the letter *b* on a card and the letter *d* in identical size on tracing paper. Place the paper on the card and have the child point out the differences. Remove the tracing paper and show the letter *b* again. The same technique may be used with sets of words beginning with the confused letters, such as "big," and "dog"; "pig" and "quack." One word is printed on a card, the other on tracing paper. Encourage the children to notice parts which are different. Remove the tracing paper, place it alongside the printed word, and ask for differences.

76. The teacher may have pictures illustrating words that begin with *b* and *d,* such as "boat," "duck," etc. The pictures should be pasted alongside the rounded part of the letter. That is, a picture of a boat should be pasted next to the lower part of the *b* and to the right of it. A picture of a duck should be pasted next to the lower part of the *d* and to the left of it. In each case the picture accents the direction of the rounded part of the letter.

77. In teaching letters show variation in length, number, and location of ascending and descending lines. Encourage the child to find individual differences within a word (in its physical appearance) which will aid him in distinguishing it from other words of similar appearance.

78. To help children differentiate letters frequently confused, the following little "stories" may be used with or without pictures to illustrate.

This is b	This is p
b is on the line	p is down below the line
b is tall like a building	p is long on the bottom
b looks to the right.	p looks to the right.
This is d	This is t
d is on the line	t is on the line
d looks to the left.	t has a little hat.
This is m	This is n
m is on the line	n is on the line
m has two little hills.	n has one little hill.

After these letters have been studied, the following riddles can be given:

Who am I	Who am I?
I am tall like a building	I am on the line
I look to the right	I have a little hat
Who am I?	Who am I?

79. To help identification of lower and upper case letters, use illustrations of the same object in various sizes.

I am little b	I am big B
I am little	I am big.
my name is b	My name is capital B
My sound is—.	My sound is —.

IV. SUBSTITUTIONS

80. After the child has learned the correct production of the sound, it may be practiced first with the addition of a vowel, as l, "*lo*"; then with the addition of a vowel and consonant, as "*lot*"; then at the beginning of a variety of words; then at the end of a variety of words, as "sea*l*," "fee*l*," "rai*l*"; then in the middle of a variety of words, as "co*l*or," "jo*ll*y." The child may also be asked to suggest words which begin with a particular sound.

81. Extensive drill on context clues will help eliminate many substitutions. The child should be taught to see that the word which he has substituted for the correct one cannot have much meaning in relation to the sense of the words which he has correctly recognized. Example:

Correct sentence:	The bear went to sleep in a hollow log.
As read:	The bear went to sleep in a hollow dog.

The child can be led to see that in this sentence "a hollow log" makes sense, whereas "a hollow dog" does not.

82. The child may be trained to look beyond a word which is troubling him to discover whether the following few words will give him any clue to the meaning of the difficult word. A distinction must be made here between blindly guessing at a word, and the intelligent use of known words and context clues.

Lem lived on the top of a h – – – mountain

Teacher: "What word can you think of that begins with *h* that might tell something about the mountain?"

Another method of teaching the intelligent use of context clues is the completion sentence. Example:

R – – – fell from the clouds
run   rain   rat   roll

V. Initial Sounds

83. Initial sounds should be taught before medial or final sounds. The best letters to start training are *f, g, b, c, h, l, m*. Ask the group to listen carefully to the pronunciation of words like "feet," "feel," "face," "funny," "fun," "from," "for." The children listen for the initial sound. They may be told that all these words begin with the letter *f*. Elicit the sound from the children and have them associate the sound with the name of the letter. Then encourage the children to give other words which begin with the same sound. Also have the children think about the way their lips and tongues feel as they say the word.

84. *Initial and final sounds.* The following initial sounds and blends are very common in the primary grades: *st, wh, br, ch, dr, tr, cl, gr, pl, sm, tw, fl, sw, sp*. Final blends used as word endings are: *sh, ch, al, on, ck, ly, nk, lk, nt, rk, se, ty*. Two-letter combinations given as a single sound are: *th, sh, ch*.

These letters or blends should never be taught in isolation. They should appear in words the child has learned in his basic sight vocabulary before they are studied as letter sounds or blends to be used in identifying new words.*

85. The teacher writes words on the blackboard and the children are called on to underline in a particular color or draw lines between sounds that are alike. A list such as the following is used:

sat, see, cow, big, pig, said, says, something, barn, ball, Jim, etc.

86. *Rotating wheel.* Two circles, one smaller than the other, are fastened together through their centers in order to rotate freely. The

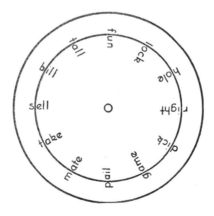

*Althea Beery, "Development of Reading Vocabulary and Word Recognition," Chapter VIII of *Reading in the Elementary School*. Forty-eighth Yearbook, Part II, of the National Society for the Study of Education. University of Chicago Press, 1949.

centers may be fastened by a large brass fastener. Initial consonants are printed on the large circle, and phonograms are placed around the edge of the smaller circle so that different words can be formed. By rotating the larger circle, initial consonants can be combined with the same phonogram. This device can be used to stress initial sounds, common phonograms, final sounds, etc.

87. The teacher places printed cards on the blackboard ledge. She then pronounces a word in her natural tone of voice, and a child is called to go to the board and pick the card containing a word that begins with the same sound as the one pronounced.

88. The teacher dictates a series of lists of three or four words, each series beginning with the same sound. The children write the letter representing the initial sound heard.

89. The teacher has a list of consonants on the blackboard like g, h, p, s, etc. She pronounces a word, and then a child points to the letter on the blackboard with which the pronounced word began.

90. The teacher draws five squares on the blackboard. In the left-hand corner of each is a consonant, and beside each a list of phonograms. The children are asked to give the initial sound and then form the words.

w all ay ell		b at all ell it
	s ail ell ay ame	
h at ay all ow		c all ame at ake

91. The teacher lists words on the blackboard and the children put a circle around all the words that begin with the same initial sound.

92. *Word building race.* A number of word families and three or four sets of consonants are placed in envelopes. The envelopes are passed out to the children, and the first child who correctly assembles all his words wins.

93. *Word hospital.* The teacher lists on a large card the letter combi-

nations representing the word families thus far studied, such as "ate," "ill," "ail." Each of these letter combinations appears in the list as many times as the teacher wishes, but the same combination should not appear twice in succession. At the bottom of the card is an envelope in which there are many small cards, each bearing a consonant sound. The child then tries to find how many good words he can make out of the "sick families" by placing the consonant sound (medicine) in front of the letters that represent the family.

Again, using this same device, the chart may present the consonant sounds, and the envelope contain the family endings. Or, at a more advanced stage, both the chart and envelope may have some consonant sounds and some family endings. The game may also be played by teams through the use of several identical charts and envelopes.

94. *School census.* The teacher cuts from stiff paper pictures of an apartment building (or a house). Each picture is prepared in such a way that a card bearing the name of a word family can be attached to it. Slits are cut, into which slips with initial sounds can be inserted; and another slit is cut, or an oak tag strip is pasted on like a pocket, to hold a "family" name card. (These houses may be built by the children as a part of some other activity.) Two, three, or more houses may be used.

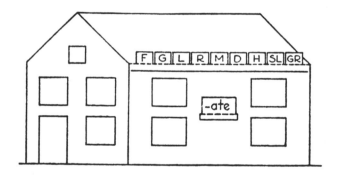

The children are then divided into as many teams as there are houses. Each house is then labeled with a "family" name, such as "ate" or "ill," and each team is given a number of slips containing consonant sounds and phonograms. The object of the game is to take a school census of the houses to find out how many "children" (known words made from the "family" on the house and the initial sounds on the slips) can be found in each house. When a "child" is discovered, the slip bearing the initial sound which made the "child" is inserted into one of the slits of the house.

95. *Riddles.* The teacher writes the name of one word family on the board, such as "ame." She says to the children, "I am thinking of a word that belongs to the 'ame' family. Can you guess what it is?" A child who responds goes to the board and either writes a consonant in front of the

family, or chooses a letter card from the blackboard ledge to indicate his guess. For example, the child selects an *l* and says, "Is it 'lame'?" The teacher may then write the word "lame" on the board, saying, "No, it is not 'lame'." Another child suggests another word in like manner, and it is written on the board under "lame," and so on until the right word is found.

96. *Finding partners.* The teacher passes out to half of the class cards bearing word families, and to the other half of the class cards bearing consonants or phonograms. The children with the consonant and phonogram cards pass around among the other children to see if they can make a word by combining their cards. When a word has been made, the child says, "We made_____with our cards," until the entire class is paired.

97. *Sound dictionary.* A scrapbook is used, the edges of the pages being so cut that they can be thumb-indexed. As the various consonant sounds are being studied, the child finds pictures in old magazines, and so forth, of objects or actions, the word for which begins with the sound being studied. These pictures are then pasted in the appropriate place in the book. Later, if the teacher wishes, the correct word may be cut out and pasted beside the picture illustrating it. Phonograms may also be taught by this device. The child thus makes his own picture dictionary, which can be used for future reference.

98. In teaching the sound of phonograms or digraphs, it may be found helpful to use such stories as these: "B lives in this house, and L lives in this one. B invites L to go for a ride in his automobile, so they ride along together as BL." "G was out rowing in his boat when he met R, whose boat was leaking, so G took R into his boat, and they rowed along together as GR." "S and H went horseback riding. H's horse got hurt, so they rode back home on one horse together as SH."

99. *Matching word parts.* Divide a sheet of oak tag into ten sections 2" x ½". Print one word on each section, using ten words containing the consonant blends and phonograms that have been taught, such as "grass," "bring," "crack," "string," "stand," "sheep," "chop," etc. Cut the words apart so that all cards will be the same size. Then cut each word in two, dividing it after the initial blend. Place all pieces in an ordinary envelope and have the child or children assemble the words.

100. *Initial blends.* After initial consonant sounds have been learned, initial blends may be introduced. Tell the children to listen to first sounds in words pronounced. In a natural tone of voice pronounce words like "chilly," "cheese," "chicken," "children," "cheat," "chop," "chimney," "chip," etc. Elicit from the children the sound of *ch.* Other words with the same sound are given by the children. As the list of blends learned increases, children may draw from a box cards on which are printed words beginning with the blends they know. The child who draws a card gives another word beginning with the same blend as the word he draws.

After two-letter blends are learned, three-letter initial blends can be given, such as those in "spring," "sprain," "thrash," "thrush," "street," etc.

VI. FINAL SOUNDS

101. The child is given ear training by being made aware of words that rhyme. The teacher gives a word like "day" and encourages the child to suggest words that end in the same sound. These words are listed on the blackboard, and parts that sound alike may be underlined.

102. The child writes his own jingle booklet to illustrate word families, such as:

> I play
> All day
> In the hay.
> All day
> I play.

103. The teacher puts a list of words on the board, such as "rose," "jump," "run." The teacher pronounces all the words on the board, pointing to them as she does so. She then says "nose," and the child points to the word on the board that sounds like it.

104. The teacher prints a list of seven or more words at the left of a large card. She then gives the child a large number of small cards, each bearing a word. The child hunts through the small cards for words that will rhyme with the words on the large card. When such a word is found it is placed at the right of the rhyming word on the large card. This method can be used for seatwork.

105. In a list of thirty or forty words the child indicates the words that rhyme with a given word by drawing a line under them.

106. The teacher has large charts illustrating vowel sounds or families. For example: a chart having the family "ail" printed in large letters at the top might have a picture of a "pail" in the lower portion of the chart; "ate" might be illustrated by "gate"; "ed" by "bed"; and so on.

107. *Finding families.* The children are divided into four or five teams. The captain of each team holds a large card with a family ending printed on it. Each team has a different family. Along the blackboard ledge there are word cards facing the board. There are as many word cards for each family as there are children in each team. At a given signal the children hunt through the word cards to find one that belongs to their family, the name of the family being held in full view by the captains. The team that wins is the first to have each member showing a card bearing a word belonging to the family indicated by his captain.

108. *Lost children.* The teacher appoints one of the children to act as "police captain." The other children are "policemen." The teacher an-

nounces to the police captain that she is "Mrs. Ill" and has lost her children while shopping. The police captain then tells the policemen to hunt for them. Some of the policemen might look through the "Bureau of Missing Persons" (a box containing a number of words, some of which belong to the "ill" family). Others might look in the parks (along the window ledges there are more word cards, face down), or in the streets (on the desks or along the blackboard ledge, where there are more word cards). The policeman who finds the most children may be rewarded by a "medal" or a "promotion."

VII. MEDIAL VOWEL SOUNDS

109. When the children have been introduced to differences in sounds of the short vowels, further practice should be given in context reading. Multiple-choice sentences can be given that will make the children focus attention on the medial sound. For example:

> The cat sat on the (rig, rag, rug).
> The pig was asleep in the pig (pan, pin, pen).

110. Still later practice in context reading should make the children focus on the total word. Multiple-choice sentences should be constructed that include initial and medial letter differences. For example:

> The bear was fast asleep in the (hut, log, leg).
> The farmer was in his (bag, hat, hut).
> Snow White was in the last (bed, led, bad).

111. The teacher writes the word "bell" on the blackboard after the children have learned the phonogram, "ell." The children are asked to give words that rhyme with it. The word "bell" is changed to "ball" and the teacher or children show that a change in one letter changes the sound and the word. The children then give words rhyming with ball and encircle parts that look alike in the words.

112. *Card calling game.* On small cards, say, $3'' \times 5''$, print words with different vowel sounds, such as "pig," "hat," "wig," "can," "ran," "sat," "bit," etc. Shuffle the cards and give four to each child. A small pack should be left face down on the table. The first player reads a word from any of his four cards. If another player holds a card that contains a rhyming word, he must give the card to the player calling for it. The next player receives a chance to call any of his words. When a player fails to get a card from any of the players, he may draw from the pack on the table. If he still fails to get a rhyming word, or if he cannot read the card he has chosen, he must discard the card he called. The player with the most cards at the end is the winner.

VIII. Sounds in General

113. In teaching letter sounds it may be found helpful to identify as many of these sounds as possible with familiar sounds.

For example:

wh　What sound do you make when you blow out a candle?
r　What sound does the lion make when he roars?
sh　What sound does Mother make when she doesn't want you to wake Daddy?
ch　What sound do you make when you sneeze?
ow　What sound do you make when you hurt yourself? (au)
o, ow　What sound do you make when you are surprised? (oh!)
oo　What sound does the wind make when it blows around the house?
s　What sound does the radiator make when steam is coming out?
gr　What sound does a dog make when he growls?
m　What sound do you make when you eat something very good?

114. *Picture book of sounds.* For children who have difficulty with certain sounds, the teacher keeps a book filled with pictures of objects that begin with the specific sounds. For words beginning with the letter *r*, pictures such as rat, rooster, rake, etc., can be used; for words with *sw*, sweater, swing; for *sl*, sled, slate, slide, etc. Children are shown the pictures and told to name them. This gives the child more practice with the sounds and helps in identifying initial or other sounds.

115. In words beginning with *wr* and *kn* the *w* and the *k* may be referred to as the "lazy w" and the "lazy k," because they are "too lazy to say their own names."

116. The teacher puts on the board an assorted list of words. The children are told to copy them in groups according to their families or according to the initial consonant sounds.

This procedure may also be used for an oral exercise, the teacher reading the words and the children sorting them into appropriate groupings. Example:

List

low	boy
mate	mend
bend	show
toy	gate
game	lame
shell	tell

Groupings by Families

low	mate	bend	toy	game	shell
show	gate	mend	boy	lame	tell

Groupings by Initial Sounds

| low | made | bend | toy | game | shell |
| lame | mend | boy | tell | gate | show |

117. The recognition of word elements may be expedited by giving the child a quantity of printed materials (magazines or old books) and having him draw a circle around the element being studied wherever it may occur in the printed material. For example, if the element is *sh*, the child would be expected to circle such words as "shut," "crush," "pushed."

When the element has been learned, give exercises in prefixing it to other real words, as "out shout," "elf—shelf," "in—shin."

118. The teacher reads a list of words, such as "bat," "Ted," "sit," "fat," "tell," which either end or begin with the same letter sound. The children indicate whether the sound being drilled upon (*t* in the above sample) is at the beginning or the end of the word. Care must be taken not to give words ending in *ed* which has the *t* sound, as in "jumped." When the child has become fairly familiar with the sound, words may be introduced which contain a sound somewhat like the sound being studied, just as *d* for *t*, or *p* for *b*.

119. The teacher lists words on the board to illustrate the effect of changing the vowel, or of inserting an additional vowel, in certain short words. Examples: "rug—rag," "bat—bit," "but—bet," "met—mat—meat."

120. The child is shown how final *e* changes the sound and meaning of words. Final *e* makes the preceding vowel "say its own name." Whenever possible this should be dramatized or illustrated by pictures. For example: The teacher shows how to change "cap" to "cape." She holds up a boy's cap with the word "cap" pinned to it. When she adds the *e* she removes from within the cap a doll's cape. Or she changes "can" to "cane." A small cane may be withdrawn from a can at the addition of the *e*.

121. The child is shown the difference in the meaning and the sound of words when a double vowel is substituted for a single vowel. Examples: "met—meet," "bet—beet."

IX. CONFIGURATION

122. The teacher discusses differences in words, noting differences in length and height and directing attention to striking characteristics in certain words. In words like "weather" and "winter," she notes the difference in length; in words like "tall" and "bell," the characteristic differences between *t* and *l*, *all* and *ell* are discussed.

123. A word which is causing trouble may be printed on transparent

paper. The child then finds the same word by placing the transparent paper over words in a known sentence until he comes to the word which exactly coincides with the one on the transparent paper. Example: If the child confuses "boy" and "big," the word "big" might be written on the transparent paper, and he might be asked to find it in several sentences, the first few of which would not contain the word "boy."

> The house is big.
> The dog is big.
> The big cat is black.
> The boy is big.
> The boy has a big cat.
> The big boy has a dog.

124. The teacher selects a word with which the child is having difficulty, writes it on a card in cursive or manuscript, and hands it to the child. The teacher pronounces the word, and the child repeats it. Then he traces over the word with his finger as he says it (either orally or silently). He then writes the word without copy, saying the syllables to himself. The word is now presented to the child in printed form, and subsequently used in context.

125. A short story containing many familiar words of similar appearance is written on the board or mimeographed. The children read the story, which is fully discussed in order that they may clearly understand it. The children then select from the story words which look alike, and these words of similar appearance are grouped together on the board. The children read the sentence in which each word occurs, discovering that although the words look alike, they have different meanings. Example:

> Don is a little boy.
> He has a big dog.
> The dog is brown.
> The big dog is Tip.
> Tip plays on a log.

126. A picture of an object may be presented at the left of the paper. To the right are three sentences using three words of similar appearance in the key position. The child is told to draw a line from the picture to the sentence that tells the same story. Example:

> This is a boy.
> This is a dog.
> This is a day.

127. Cards are prepared containing words which have the same general appearance. (The words may be selected from those with which the children are having configuration difficulties.) Each word appears on two cards. The children are given the cards and asked to find the pairs of words exactly alike. A score may be kept of the words correctly paired.

128. Groups of words are printed on the board and the children are directed to draw lines under the words which are the same as the key word above each column. For example:

stone	wall	winter	wanted	doll	shine
stick	ball	wanted	whistle	ball	shore
stitch	tall	winter	would	doll	shake
stone	wall	winter	wanted	dole	shin
stein	mall	warmer	while	doll	shine

129. Difficulty in distinguishing between certain similar words, such as "band" and "hand," may be overcome by constructing sentences, nonsense or otherwise, which contain the confused words.

A *band* leader's *hand* must be very quick.
The sun *shines* on the *shore*.
The little *children* took care of the baby *chickens*.
In *winter* the *weather* is cold.

After reading the sentences, there may be discussion of word differences. The same thing may be done with letters which are confused. Sentences may be written using the confused letters and practice may be given in noting letter differences.

The *b*oat was full of *d*ucks.
Put *P*addy down *q*uickly.

130. Different types of completion sentences can be given which employ words of similar appearance.

Boys and girls live in ———.
——— live in barns.
houses   heather   horses

A ——— is the home of a bird.
Clean children are ———.
near   nest   neat

The leader gave the ——— for them to ———.
sign   sing

A ——— cannot sleep in a ———.
horse   house

131. *Matching phrases in sentences.* At the left of a card or paper two or three phrases of two or three words of similar appearance are written.

Directly opposite each phrase is a sentence using the phrase. The child is told to underline in the sentence the phrase which appears opposite it. Example:

big boat   Peggy has a big boat.
big goat   Peter has a big goat.

A similar device is one in which a sentence using a phrase is not directly opposite the phrase which it contains. The child is told to draw a line from each phrase to the sentence in which that phrase occurs. Example:

big horse   The farmer has a big home.
pig house   The farmer rides a big horse.
big home   Pigs live in a pig house.

132. The class reading may be used as a basis for drill on configuration by use of the questions with multiple choice answers, thus:

When did Peggy go to school?
in water
in winter
in wanted

X. ENDINGS

133. Using a circular piece of oak tag, the teacher prints words (nouns, adjectives, or verbs) around its circumference. At the center she affixes five long strips of oak tag, each shaped like the large hand of a clock. Each of these hands bears an ending, *er, est, ed, s,* and *ing.* The teacher points to a word and asks the child to select one of the endings on the pointers (or hands) which can be added to the word and make a good word.

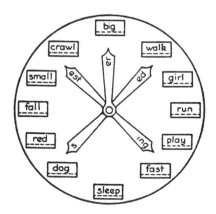

With this device, the teacher gives a sentence to the child, using one of the words on the chart, but not in its proper form. The child must select the ending for the word which will make it correct. Example:

> The teacher says, "The little boy ——— (pointing to the word "walk" on the chart) to the house." The child will then select either *s* or *ed* from the five pointers. Teacher: "This horse is ——— (pointing to the word "fast") then the other." The child should then choose *er*.

134. The rotating wheel may also be used for practice in word endings. On the outer circle, print words like "play," "jump," "slow," "run," "big," etc., and on the inner circle print endings *ed, er, ly, ing, s*, etc. Dictate a sentence, such as "Jane was ———," point to the word "play" on the outer circle, and have the child find the appropriate ending on the inner circle.

135. To furnish drill in recognizing differences in word endings, the teacher puts three columns of words on a chart; for example,

walk	walked	walk
jumps	jump	jump
water	water	wanted

The child underlines and pronounces the word in each row that is different.

136. Pictures on a chart are used to illustrate objects shown singly or in pairs; for example, two apples, one cup, two cups, one tree, etc. The child is given small printed word cards containing the singular and plural of each object on the chart. He chooses the word that goes with each picture.

137. A list of words is written or printed on the board, with considerable space between the words. The teacher will then ask the children which words in the list can be changed by adding *s*. This letter she will add to the words indicated (when indications are correct) with colored chalk. She will then ask which words can be changed by adding, for example, *er*. Should a word to which she has already added an ending become too involved (as it will in the case of "walk," "walks," "walked," "walking," for instance) she will write the entire word again under the original and add the ending to it.

138. The child is given a card containing several sentences from each of which a word has been omitted. He is also given an envelope containing an assortment of words. Each word is represented in several forms, singular and plural for nouns, comparative and superlative for adjectives and adverbs, and the various tense and number forms for the verbs. The child is supposed to find the correct word for each blank. Example:

> My doll is ——— than Peggy's.
> My doll can ———.
> The dog ——— with the ball.

Among the possible words will be: "big," "bigger," "biggest," "walk," "walking," "walks," "play," "playing," "played," "plays."

139. The child is given a card containing sentences, such as:

> Peggy is play ———— with her doll.
> Peter ride ———— the horse.
> This tree is big ———— than the house.

An envelope containing endings accompanies the card. The child is to select the proper endings for the unfinished words.

A variation of this device is to give in the sentence a variety of forms, only one of which is the correct form. Example:

> This tree is big, bigger, biggest than the house.

The child is to draw a circle around the correct form.

140. Oral drill on word endings may be conducted by having the teacher say, "I can runs, run, running." The child is to select from the sound the one which is correct.

141. Prepare a paragraph and ask children to supply the endings.

Dick and Tom were play————. They play———— near the barn. Tom saw two baby rabbit————. Tom call———— to Dick. The children ran after the rabbit————. The fast———— rabbit got away, but the other got stuck in the fence. Dick pull———— him out.

XI. IMMATURE HABITS

142. Slow-learning children are often lip readers in the beginning stages of reading. The teacher, however, encourages the child to read with his eyes only. Before the lesson begins the teacher asks the children, "With what are you going to read?" The children are taught to understand the reply, "With our eyes only." Teacher: "Yes, with our eyes because our eyes can go faster than our lips." Slogans to remind children may be used. "We read with our eyes wide open, our lips closed, and our finger still." "Let only our eyes be our guides." In extreme cases the child may put a finger to his lips to discourage movement while reading silently.

143. *Pointing.* A child who points with his finger should be encouraged to use a pencil or a marker instead, as a first step in getting rid of what may be a necessary habit at a certain stage. Then he may be gradually trained to read without pointing.

In the early stages of drill to eliminate the habit of pointing, the child should be given very short sentences. Examples:

> Peggy ran.   Dan ran.   Peter ran.   Sally ran.

When simple sentences such as these can be read without pointing the length of the sentences may be very gradually increased.

Peggy ran away.	Dan ran away.
Peter ran very fast.	Sally ran very fast.

A book marker may be used by children who have extreme difficulty in following their reading from one line to the next.

XII. Context Clues

144. When a child encounters a new word which he cannot read, the teacher may encourage first reading the rest of the sentence and then coming back to the unknown word. This teaches the child to anticipate meaning. The teacher may say: "Read the rest of the sentence and see whether it will help you know what the word is." The teacher may also ask guiding questions, and make comments or suggestions that will lead to the meaning. For example, if the new word is "toys": "Baby Ann saw many —— in the store window." The teacher asks, "What do you think Baby Ann saw when she looked in the store window?" If the child answers, "A doll," the teacher suggests other possibilities. "Yes, she may have seen a doll, but what are some of the other things she may have seen that begin with the letter *t*?"

145. New words should often be introduced in sentences that give their meaning or by questions that will lead to their meaning. For example, to teach the word "smashed," the teacher may ask: "What do you think happened to the cup when it fell?" To teach the word "yawn," the teacher may ask: "What do people sometimes do when they are sleepy?" When the correct words are elicited, the teacher prints the words on the blackboard for further study.

146. New words may be anticipated by a study of illustrations. The children look at pictures, name new objects, or suggest happenings or endings. The vocabulary used in the discussion may be recorded and studied.

147. McCullough[*] has suggested that context clues may be of at least seven different types. These should not be studied and classified as such by the children, but the teacher may have them in mind when directing children to the context to make a good attempt at a new word. The types of context clues are as follows:

1. *Definition.* Bill and Tom played together; they were good *friends.*
2. *Experience.* Father gave Rover a bone to *chew.*
3. *Comparison.* It is no longer cloudy; it is *sunny.*
4. *Synonym.* Mr. Brown and Mr. Clark, next-door *neighbors.*

[*]Constance McCullough, "The Recognition of Context Clues in Reading," Elementary English Review, 22:1–5, 38, January, 1945.

22. DEVELOPING A MEANING VOCABULARY
Board of Education of the City of New York

A large number of the pupils selected for special reading instruction in the junior high school project had inadequate vocabularies that limited their power to get meaning from what they read. Many of them had fair command of word attack skills and could apparently read most of the words they met in the books they selected. But a little questioning often revealed that their ability to sound out a word was no guarantee that any meaning was attached to it. A child who could pronounce "boon" or "pelt" correctly might have no idea what the words meant. When he did not have fairly accurate meanings for the words he seemed to recognize, he could not understand what he read. He was in the same position as a competent reader who can read aloud a sentence in an unfamiliar foreign language without having any idea what it says.

For the pupil in the earliest stages of reading, vocabulary difficulties were less obvious because most readers on the easiest levels use familiar subject matter, many illustrations, and a simple vocabulary. Since work with nonreaders on the lowest levels was highly individualized, the teacher could explain word meanings as needed. But the pupil who could read independently on a third year level or higher met many new words on his own. If he read a certain popular book on boats intended for a *third year level*, he met the following words: shallow, sturdy, midstream, lounges, dugout, merchant, warriors, sullen, route, clipper, paddlewheel, keelboat, fuel, harbor, packet, modern, launched, hull, compass, constant, prowl. Furthermore, in material about more unfamiliar subject matter—prehistoric times or adventure in the Far West—the vocabulary difficulties became even greater.

Since meager vocabularies were strikingly prevalent among retarded readers, it was important to help them expand their stock of word meanings and to give them techniques for coping with new words independently. They also needed better understanding of words assumed to be familiar to them since they often had only vague ideas of the meaning of relatively common ones. It was felt that extension of their vocabularies should not be left to chance, but should be an important part of a reading program. Both incidental and direct approaches were used.

The comparative merits of these two approaches have been the subject

Reprinted from *The Retarded Reader in The Junior High School: A Guide for Supervisors and Teachers*, prepared by the staff of the Reading Guidance Center, Division of Instructional Research, Publication No. 31 (September 1952), pp. 80–88. By permission of J. Wayne Wrightstone, Bureau of Educational Research of the New York City Board of Education.

of a good deal of controversy. Both types are effective and should be used to the fullest extent possible. The discussion of specific approaches [follows] . . .

1. EXTENDING CHILDREN'S EXPERIENCES AS A SOURCE OF NEW CONCEPTS AND VOCABULARY

Many of the retarded readers who were studied during the junior high school project had a meager store of experience. They had grown up in environments providing few cultural advantages and little opportunity to extend their vocabularies. Some of them had spent most of their lives within an area of half a square mile.

The relationship between a rich background of experiences and a good vocabulary is a positive one; it is desirable, therefore, to provide illuminating group experiences for such pupils as a means of vocabulary enrichment. Perhaps the surest way to vocabulary growth is in the informal discussion that takes place before, during, and after a group experience. Key words and unfamiliar ones should be explained and pupils should be encouraged to use them in discussions and reports. Children can express their ideas more clearly when their concepts are clear, and the new vocabulary growing out of shared experiences and ideas is sure to have more vivid and accurate meaning than that obtained in formal word drills. A class that has visited behind the scenes of a department store in order to observe its workings acquires a large number of accurate concepts and new word meanings in the course of planning and carrying out the trip and engaging in follow-up activities. Related reading is more easily comprehended because the vocabulary is already familiar.

Vocabulary can be enriched also through indirect experiences. Audio-visual aids—pictures, film strips, slides, sound and silent movies, radio, and television—have become abundant and furnish the basis for explanation and discussion of important or new words.

2. ENCOURAGING WIDE READING

The vicarious experiences provided by wide reading of interesting books are another important source of new word meanings. Unfortunately, reading for recreation is often shunned by poor readers who regard reading as a chore. They therefore miss the frequent casual contact with words that helps deepen and enrich meaning. In the junior high school project, especial care was expended on the choice of materials provided for independent reading. Publishers' lists were scrutinized for books that were high in interest for the age group and yet had a level of difficulty sufficiently low to allow fluent, pleasurable reading.

3. Making Children Word-Conscious

It was found that the pupils in the reading program could be stimulated to a lively curiosity about words and a desire to acquire a wider vocabulary. The enthusiasm of the teacher was an important factor. Pupils had fun in discussions in which they vied with each other in suggesting more precise substitutes for overworked words like *nice, awful,* and *interesting*. They learned to be curious about unfamiliar words and to bring to class new ones heard in radio or television programs.

They kept a record of new vocabulary acquired during the pursuit of hobbies, or in art experiences, or in the development of a unit of work. Colorful words, idioms, and striking expressions were also included. The words were listed on the bulletin board or on charts by the teacher; the pupils wrote them with illustrative sentences in individual notebooks or in card files like the following:

Theme—Television

Front of card	Front of card
dial	screen

Back of Card	Back of Card
Tom turned the dial to Channel 5.	Our new set has a seventeen-inch screen.

The retarded readers in the junior high school project were greatly interested in puzzles and word games. These often appealed to pupils who had a brief attention span where books were concerned. Puzzles were mimeographed for individual use or put on charts or blackboards for group use. Children with special interest or ability were encouraged to construct puzzles to be used by other children. Nonconsumable cross word puzzle material as well as the ordinary kind is available.

Fill in the missing letters.

an animal	b._____
something to sleep in	b._____
something to sweep with	b._____
a yellow fruit	b._____

---

4. ENCOURAGING THE USE OF THE DICTIONARY

Dictionaries and glossaries are valuable aids in arriving at a precise meaning, and their use should be encouraged. Pupils frequently avoid the use of dictionaries because the only ones available to them are too hard for them. Excellent ones on very easy levels were used in the junior high school project and the pupils were taught how to use them. These had easy vocabularies and large type. Picture dictionaries in color were used with the poorest readers. When possible, each child had a dictionary or easy access to one.

A glossary is included in many basic readers and is a useful introduction to dictionary study because it gives only the difficult words in the book in which it appears. Pupils who have good control of techniques for looking up words efficiently are more likely to make use of dictionary aids than those who flounder about. The development of such techniques is discussed in the section on special study skills, page 629.

5. TEACHING THE NEW WORDS OF A READING SELECTION

Frequently, direct teaching of word meanings was effective with pupils in the reading groups. Reading assignments that contained significantly new concepts or vocabulary were always better understood if the concepts and vocabulary were clarified carefully before silent reading took place. However, new words were never taught in isolation, but always in meaningful context, as during the introductory discussion of a story. It cannot be stressed too strongly that drilling on lists of isolated words to develop word meanings is useless for retarded readers.

In planning directed reading activities, the teachers were careful to choose a selection that did not present too many new words at a time. They then looked over the selection for words or expressions that were probably unfamiliar to the pupils and needed to be specially presented. Manuals and workbooks issued by publishers to accompany readers are helpful in giving ideas for presenting difficult words in stimulating ways.

Clarifying new concepts and vocabulary before reading takes place is significant also to the teacher of subjects other than English. It is essential in those subjects to anticipate difficulties in an introductory discussion in much the same way as the reading teacher does. Each content field has its own technical vocabulary. Especially in such fields as science, mathematics, and social studies, concepts must be thoroughly developed if the words representing them are to be clearly understood. Many children can perform the processes of multiplication and division without knowing what *multiplication* and *division* really mean. The subject vocabulary should be introduced gradually and reinforced by diagrams, pictures, and other visual aids that are available. For retarded readers with meager vocabularies, it is more advisable to teach thoroughly the meaning of a few technical words than to require verbatim recitations of a host of vaguely understood definitions.

6. Establishing Independence in Finding Meanings from Context

In the Bureau's work, it was found that retarded readers were likely to ignore words that were unfamiliar and to make little effort to determine their meaning in any of the numerous ways that efficient readers employ as a matter of course. As a result, these poor readers were often satisfied to gain from reading matter only a hazy and inaccurate notion of what the writer intended to say. These children were in need of techniques that would enable and encourage them to deal successfully with words that were completely unfamiliar or with known words that were used in unfamiliar ways. They often learned to become independent in their search for meaning.

The technique most useful to good readers is that of determining word meaning from the context; that is, from the setting in which the word is found. Poor readers profit from specific instruction in the use of contextual clues, since that is the quickest way and, for words with several meanings, like *count*, the only way in which meaning may be determined. On the earliest reading levels, the context is used chiefly for help in recognizing the form of a word and pronouncing it, because the pupil usually knows its meaning; but later on the pupil increasingly employs contextual clues to understand word meanings.

The importance of skill in using contextual clues becomes obvious when one considers that the words *scurry, horizon, wharf, gravel, desperate, descended, stallion, drifting,* and many others of equal difficulty occur in the third reader of a well-known basic series. In a directed reading activity the teacher helps with such words. When the pupil, however, reads this book independently, he can understand most of these hard words if he uses the aid of context. In a well-written reader, the meanings are usually clearly indicated in sentences similar to this:

The rat scurried to its hole when it heard the cat coming.

Some Types of Contextual Clue[1]

(1) A common and very helpful contextual clue that might well be used by more writers of books for children is the *definition* that occurs within the same sentence. The definition may take various forms similar to these:

The sabot or wooden shoe is worn by some French farmers.

Polaris—the North Star—is one of the best known stars.

The pup, which is the baby seal, can be seen on the rocks.

Condiments, such as cinnamon and pepper, were once very expensive.

(2) In the above examples, the meaning of the unfamiliar words was made clear by words or phrases that were more or less synonymous. Sometimes *an antonym* or a *contrast* may point out meaning as in the following:

Some parts of the lake were deep; others were shallow.

The mouse squeaked in a tiny voice, but the lion bellowed.

(3) The child's own *experience* serves to help him, as in the following:

In order to free the boat he severed the rope with his knife.

In the experience of the child, a knife is used for cutting. The phrase "free the boat" also helps give meaning to "severed."

(4) Similes are sometimes a guide. The meaning of *droned* is suggested in a sentence like this:

The speaker's voice droned on like the humming of a bee.

(5) The presence of *illustrations*—pictures, diagrams or maps—helps illuminate word meaning.

In order to convince pupils of their ability to use context clues, a paragraph or two may be written on the board. Blanks are substituted for certain rather obvious words like this:

[1] This is discussed more fully by Constance McCullough in "The Recognition of Context Clues in Reading," *Elementary English Review*, 22:1–5, January, 1945.

Sam used to take a good lunch with him on his hikes. He usually made some _____ of fresh bread and peanut butter or meat. Then he liked a tomato or two and some _____ like peaches or cherries. He knew that after a long _____ in the woods he would have a good appetite.

The pupils are then asked to suggest what words have been omitted and to give reasons for their choices. As was pointed out in the chapter on word recognition, this study of context is valuable in developing comprehension.

The same technique should then be applied to a paragraph that has a few difficult words. Words should be chosen for which very clear clues are present, so that wild guessing may not be encouraged. The paragraph is written on the blackboard with the difficult words underlined. Pupils read the paragraph and then try to give the meaning of each word by using its context. After discussion of "guesses" by the children, the dictionary is consulted to check the accuracy of the guesses. Such practice should lead pupils to use clues and combinations of clues habitually in their independent reading. It is important that they learn that meaning clues should be hunted out before the dictionary is used. Reading should be interrupted to consult the dictionary only in cases where clues to an important word are so vague that the meaning of a passage is not clear. Pupils with meager vocabularies who are faced with the problem of looking up words in the dictionary several times on each page are likely either to regard reading as laborious and unattractive chore or to skip over all unknown words and be satisfied with loose approximations of the meaning of what they read. In some circumstances, teachers find it advisable to give pupils the meanings of words as needed. Teacher judgment plays an important part in deciding when to do this, so that pupils become neither discouraged on the one hand, nor over-dependent on the other.

Simple words with multiple meanings like *net, arm, bear, can,* were an important source of confusion to the poor readers in the Bureau project. They had not learned to use the context as a guide to meaning and were not sharply aware that one word might have many meanings. The pupil who knew about a candy *box* or *boxing* gloves was likely to be bewildered by:

> The sentry stood in his box.
>
> The box stayed green all winter.
>
> The driver leaped up to the box.

Exercises like the following proved successful in calling pupils' attention to contextual clues to meaning:

Next to the phrase in the first column, put the number of the phrase in the second column that finishes the sentence correctly.

I went to the fair	3	1. when he put the player out.
The umpire was fair	___	2. we shall go on a picnic
If the weather is fair	___	3. and ate popcorn.

Double Talk

Some words look and sound alike but have more than one meaning.

1. I like to skate.
2. He looks like his father.

What is the meaning of like in the first sentence? In the second? Finish these sentences to show that you understand the meaning of the underlined word.

1. A bat flew _____.
   Tom bought a new bat and _____.

2. The child's face is _____.
   Face the class when _____.

3. Please hand me _____.
   My hand is _____.

4. What kind of candy _____?
   The kind man _____.

Read these pairs of sentences that use the same word. Find the underlined word in Column 1 that means the same as each word in Column 2 and write the number.

1. Fred saved ten dollars.   rescued (2)
2. The boy scout saved his friend's life.
3. The movie was over at nine o'clock.   across
4. Jump over the puddle.
5. The rest of the class is reading.   be still
6. Try to rest after lunch.

7. MAKING A DIRECT STUDY OF WORDS

Many of the retarded readers enjoyed uncomplicated exercises and games that dealt with uses of words. Exercises, however, were not used to the virtual exclusion of techniques previously described, but in moderation. Motivation was provided to make such study a pleasant and profitable experience rather than a boring routine to be gone through simply because it was assigned.

It was found that this kind of study was most effective when the approaches were varied. The exercises below are some of the many kinds that were used. Similar ones may be found in various reading workbooks. With a few exceptions which are indicated, those given here can be adapted to use for any reading level. They can be used as the basis for teaching and as practice material for independent work by the pupil. In the oral discussion preceding independent practice, some groups will need more explanation and samples of procedure than others. The blackboard is a useful aid for this presentation.

Oral and written exercises can be used to reinforce meanings through:

> Classifying words
> Using synonyms and antonyms
> Understanding question words
> Studying common prefixes and suffixes
> Studying the origin and development of word meanings

a) *Classifying words.* An effective way of helping the child to a broader vocabulary is to provide him with the opportunity to examine meaning by considering the relationships between words. In these exercises, word meanings are considered in order to determine in what categories they belong or to find the relationship of part of an object to its whole. Both simple and more advanced vocabulary are used in order to show that the exercises can be adapted to various levels of difficulty.

Word Puzzle

Cross out the word which does not belong in each list. In Group 1 you will cross out the word *made*.

1.	2.	3.	4.
climb	whisper	jacket	elephant
walk	sing	house	squirrel
jump	play	glove	sweater
made	talk	stocking	tiger

5.	6.	7.	8.
scissors	above	pitcher	quarter
needle	later	umpire	nickel
egg	around	catcher	dollar
thread	below	shortstop	money

9.	10.	11.	12.
airplane	candy	hunter	milkman
radio	bitter	fisherman	butcher
movies	sweet	shoemaker	cousin
television	sour	trapper	carpenter

Cross out the words that don't belong.

1. People: man, girl, book, boy, dog.
2. Food: ink, egg, milk, spoon, bread.
3. Money: dollar, table, quarter, dime, chair.

Match the "part" to the "whole." Write the correct number from Column 1 next to each word in Column 2.

1. branch	airplane 5 _____
2. page	eagle _____
3. cloud	tree _____
4. feather	book _____
5. propeller	building _____
6. finger	
7. room	

Add a word that belongs to each line.

1. sister   mother   uncle   _____
2. weeks   minutes   hours   _____
3. cherry   peach   apple   _____
4. window   wall   door   _____

Write these words under the correct headings below:

stadium, inning, infection, umpire, thermometer, champion, doctor, bicycle, medicine, nurse, hockey, goal, dribble, temperature, skates.

Hospital Words   Sport Words
_____   _____

_____   _____

_____   _____

b) *Using synonyms and antonyms.* A study of synonyms and antonyms leads not only to deepening of meaning but also to flexibility in oral and written expression. While it is undesirable to have pupils learn a word-for-word definition of *synonym* and *antonym*, frequent use of the terms will add them to the child's vocabulary. The exercises with synonyms can also be used for antonyms and vice versa. Exercises of this kind may be used either with or without the dictionary.

Words That Are Synonyms

Match the synonyms, which are words that mean the same. Choose the word from Column 2 that is the synonym of a word in Column 1 and write it in the correct space.

1.	2.
below_____	bring
brook_____	sure
certain_____	crawl
several_____	some
creep_____	show
	under
	stream

Which Word Means the Same?

Underline the word in the second column that means the same as all of those in each group in the first column.

I		II
speech talk words	may mean	people book language
merry happy gleeful	may mean	restless joyous loud

Comparing Words

Underline each pair of words that mean the same.

sad	happy
love	like
loud	soft
close	shut
allow	permit

Antonyms

In each line below find a word which means the opposite of the first word in the line. Draw a ring around it.

little:	part, big, house
short:	whole, hear, long
dirty:	clean, cold, grow
found:	let, lost, hard

How Else Can You Say It?

There are often many ways of expressing the same idea. From this list of words choose those which will complete the sentences without changing the thought of the first sentence in the group.

sprang	yelled	shouted
cried	hastened	needed
found	leaped	hurried
ran	touched	bounded

1. Robin Hood jumped across the stream.

   Robin Hood _____ across the stream.
   Robin Hood _____ across the stream.
   Robin Hood _____ across the stream.

2. "Strike one!" called the umpire.

   "Strike one!" _____ the umpire.
   "Strike one!" _____ the umpire.
   "Strike one!" _____ the umpire.

3. The fireman rushed into the burning house.

   The fireman _____ into the burning house.
   The fireman _____ into the burning house.
   The fireman _____ into the burning house.

---

c) *Understanding question words.* The retarded readers sometimes answered questions incorrectly because they did not understand what was being asked. Often they actually read the question word incorrectly, so that "how" became "who" and "were" became "where." These children needed practice in distinguishing between the words in print and had no trouble with the word meanings when the confusion was cleared up. Sometimes, however, pupils pronounced question words correctly but did not clearly understand their meaning. Exercises like these were useful for developing the meaning of such words:

Who? When? Where? How?

Here are some parts of sentences. Each part answers one of the questions above. Next to each one write the correct question word.

1. At home — where
2. The two girls —
3. Next year —
4. On foot —
5. Very slowly —
6. In the park —
7. To the baseball game —
8. With all his might —
9. During the storm —
10. On the sidewalk —

Underline the words that tell where.

outside	downstairs
tomorrow	here
policeman	quickly
cellar	center

Underline the words that tell when.

early	January
since	doctor
mountain	summer
sky	within

Underline the words that tell who.

uncle	woman
between	haystack
afternoon	princess
clown	captain

Put the numbers of the questions next to any sentence that contains an answer. Some sentences may have more than one number.

1. How many?   2. When?   3. Where?   4. To whom?

_____

__2, 4__   David gave his stamp collection to his sister when he was fifteen years old.

_____   They arrived at the station a minute too late to catch the train.

_____   All the children except Anna and Jerry want to go to the park.

d) Studying common prefixes and suffixes. A vocabulary can be extended through discussion of the most common prefixes and suffixes and the changes that they effect. This kind of word study is suitable only for pupils who are not very retarded in reading. For pupils on the lower reading levels, such study should be avoided except as it arises in the development of word attack skills. In any case, meanings of word parts should be developed in informal discussion and formal memorizing should not be required. According to a study made by Stauffer,[2] the most common prefixes are:

ab (from)	in (into)
ad (to)	in (not)
be (by)	pre (before)
com (with)	pro (in front of)
de (from)	re (back)
dis (apart)	sub (under)
en (in)	un (not)
ex (out)	

Some suffixes which merit special attention are *tion, er, y, al, ous, ment, ful, less*. The meanings of suffixes do not appear, in general, to be so constant as those of the prefixes.

The attention of pupils can be drawn to the changes in meaning of complete words, as in:

happy	unhappy
read	reread
farm	farmer
help	helpless
improve	improvement

[2] STAUFFER, R. G. "A Study of Prefixes in the Thorndike List to Establish a List of Prefixes That Should Be Taught on the Elementry School." *Journal of Educational Research,* 35:453–58, February, 1942.

Substituting a Phrase

Find another way of saying the underlined word without changing the rest of the sentence. You may use more than one word to explain.

Sample: I liked the story so much that I reread it.

       I liked the story so much that I read it again.

1. The people were unfriendly to the stranger.
   The people _____ to the stranger.

2. The dentist tried to make the drilling painless.
   The dentist tried to make the drilling _____.

We Can Build Words

Directions: In each column write the prefix before the words. Notice how the prefixes change the meaning of the words.

un	re	dis
happy	write	agree
lucky	read	courage
even	tell	appear
true	fill	like

Directions: Each sentence below has a word after it. From the prefixes listed above add one to the word which will make the sentence correct. Then write the word in the blank space.

1. Soap and water make dirt _____. (appear)
2. We do not want to play this game with _____ sides. (even)
3. Please _____ the book after you have finished it. (place)
4. I do not believe that story because it is _____. (true)

We Can Build Words

Directions: In each column write the suffix after the words. Notice how the suffixes change the meaning of the words.

ful	ly	ment	less
wonder	slow	improve	pain
help	quick	agree	help
care	kind	enjoy	sleep

Directions: Each sentence below has a word after it. Put the word in the blank space and if necessary, add one of the suffixes to the word to make the sentence correct.

1. The children had a_____time at the circus. (wonder)

2. You will have to move_____if you want to be on time. (quick).

3. The storm left many families_____. (home)

4. The_____in his work pleased him very much. (improve)

---

e) Studying the origin and development of word meanings. Children can be made sensitive to and curious about words by a lively presentation of English as a constantly changing language. Archaic expressions like *methinks or betide* were once in common use. New inventions, human experiences, the slang of teenagers contribute new words, some of which become a permanent part of the language. The origin and meaning of common idioms are also worth exploration. Very retarded readers also enjoy this kind of activity if it is largely oral.

In the following exercise, pupils are to distinguish between outdated and recently coined words.

Today's or Yesterday's?

Put these words in the column in which they belong:

jazz, rayon, surrey, betide, television, plastic, maiden, zipper, trundle-bed, helicopter, radar, lad.

	Today's	Yesterday's
Sample:	jazz	surrey

The Animal Kingdom

Some of our expressions have come to us from the animal kingdom. A few are given below. Can you fill in the missing words?

as strong as an _____

as wise as an _____

as stubborn as a _____

as quiet as a _____

as sly as a _____

as busy as a _____

Can you add other "animal expressions" to this list?

bear hug
monkey business
horse sense
lion hearted
fish story

Idioms

Idioms are expressions that don't mean exactly what they say. In fact, using their exact meaning gives humorous results!

See if you can underline the meaning that really shows what the idiom means.

1. Bob caught her eye across the room. Did he

   a) shut the window?
   b) throw it back?
   c) exchange glances with her?

2. During the lesson his attention wandered. Did he

   a) walk around?
   b) lose interest?
   c) take notes?

3. The famous movie actress dropped out of sight. Did she

   a) hurt her ankle?
   b) become forgotten?
   c) sink through the floor?

Match Mates

Each phrase underlined in Column 2 means the same as an idiom underlined in Column 1. Match each idiom with its meaning as in the first box.

Column 1	**Column 2**
1. No one liked Jim because he always went around with a <u>chip on his shoulder</u>. **[c]**	a. I went home by the <u>quickest</u> way.
2. Because he was in a hurry he took <u>a short cut</u> through the woods. **[ ]**	b. The mother <u>scolded</u> the child for playing with matches.
3. Mother was so angry at the delivery boy that she <u>gave him a piece of her mind</u>. **[ ]**	c. It was clear from the way the boy acted that he was <u>looking for a fight</u>.

The development of a meaning vocabulary should not be regarded as a separate phase of reading instruction. The enrichment of vocabulary is inseparably bound up with the other aspects of reading such as word recognition, general comprehension, and the pupil's own background of ideas.

The importance of oral practice in building meaning vocabularies cannot be stressed too much. This is especially true for the most retarded readers who have not yet acquired much of a reading vocabulary. The pupil should be encouraged to use his new vocabulary in daily speech and in creative writing.

D. Improving Comprehension Skills

23. HOW TO COPE WITH DEFICIENCIES IN BASIC READING SKILLS THAT BLOCK PROGRESS IN LEARNING ACTIVITIES

Gerald A. Yoakam

That there are in basic reading skills serious deficiencies that block learning, especially at the middle-grade and high-school levels, is widely recognized. How to cope with these deficiencies is, to a large extent, an unsolved problem. Many children could use reading in learning activities to greater advantage if it were not for their inability to use basic reading skills effectively. Even at the graduate-school level we find a considerable number of students who read less well than they could were they more effective in their use of basic reading skills.

THE PROBLEM FACED

At the root of the difficulty lies some uncertainty about what are basic reading skills and what are the special skills required to read materials of different kinds in an effort to master the facts, principles, and generalizations that constitute the content of reading matter which is intended to inform rather than to entertain. The practice of teaching children to read for general meaning, which has been so common in the past, made no provision for teaching them to read for study purposes and did not provide them with the basic reading skills required in many learning activities. While the situation is now improving through a recent return to systematic teaching of fundamental skills, there are still many persons who remain unconvinced that systematic, sequential development of basic reading skills is essential if the large majority of children are to learn to use reading as a tool for learning. Pupils are now found in the middle and upper grades who have reading difficulties resulting from a lack of systematic development of basic reading skills in the 1930's and early 1940's. This lack occurred because of a mistaken idea that children can learn to read without guidance, instruction, and practice.

In the opinion of the writer, we shall not learn to cope with deficiencies in basic skills that block progress in learning activities until all teachers learn to recognize the importance of basic reading skills and how they function in the reading process. Far too many teachers in the upper levels of our schools have had little or no training in teaching children to read and do not understand how reading ability develops with the maturation of the learner. Too many upper-grade and high-school teachers assume that the child *has learned to read* in the lower grades and that, if children cannot *read to learn* in the middle and upper grades, it is the fault of the teachers at the lower levels. They fail to realize that all teachers who use books in teaching must be teachers of reading if the children under their charge are to use reading as a tool for learning. They must learn to direct the reading of textbooks, reference books, encyclopedias, pamphlets, magazines, newspapers, and other informational materials if the child is to succeed in learning through reading. They must assume responsibility for teaching the new and strange concepts which appear in the content fields and must teach the child how to read for the purposes appropriate to the subject matter with which they are concerned.

NATURE AND TYPES OF BASIC READING SKILLS

In order to understand our problem better, it seems necessary that we consider the nature of basic reading skills. Some teachers of basic reading are clear in their minds as to the meaning of the term *basic reading skills*. According to the dictionary, the word *basic* means fundamental. Basic reading skills are fundamental reading skills. But fundamental to what? They are fundamental to all reading of whatever kind. They are the common foundational skills which are used in all types and kinds of reading and without which the reader cannot read. Without these basic skills the child not only will fail to read for enjoyment but will fail to read to learn, which is ordinarily a more difficult matter. All teachers should be able to recognize the presence or the absence of the fundamental skills in the reading of each child and should realize the necessity of dealing with deficiencies in these fundamental skills when they are recognized.

It follows that every teacher should be able to identify basic reading skills. He should learn to recognize the common deficiencies in these skills which are found among inefficient readers. Time does not permit a complete analysis of all the basic reading skills in detail. We shall mention some of the common deficiencies and then attempt to suggest ways of coping with them. Among those that interfere with reading as a tool for learning are the following:

1. Lack of a stock of sight words which the child can recognize auto-

matically without analysis. A reader cannot read fluently without an adequate stock of sight words.

2. Lack of independence in word recognition; inability to attack words that present difficulties, to identify them, to pronounce them, and to associate meaning with them.

3. Inability to use the context in acquiring new meanings and in identifying new words.

4. Lack of ability to recall and use past experience in making meaning out of material being read.

5. Lack of insight into the function of reading and inability to make sense out of printed material.

6. Lack of ability to conceive and accept purposes for reading and to enjoy the acquisition of ideas.

7. Inability to understand the differences between reading for information and reading for amusement and to understand the nature and purpose of historical narrative, expository, and descriptive materials, and the difference between fact and fiction.

8. Lack of ability to read for a variety of purposes and failure to adjust the reading rate and technique to different purposes.

9. Failure to acquire common study skills basic to all kinds of reading, such as ability to locate material; ability to get the main idea; ability to get the main idea; ability to read for details; ability to answer questions; ability to solve problems; ability to evaluate, select, and organize, to outline, summarize, remember, report, and use ideas.

This brief review of deficiencies in basic reading skills is, of course, inadequate and merely suggestive, but many of the items constitute the deficiencies which most often interfere with the success of children in reading for learning. Unless these abilities can be developed among the great majority of children, there is little prospect that the use of reading as a tool for learning can be very much improved in the near future.

METHODS OF IMPROVING BASIC READING SKILLS

Having attempted to identify the difficulty, let us now proceed to consider some suggestions on how to cope with it. I shall assume that many of my readers are teachers of the social studies, elementary science, health, and other subject matter, although certainly not by the traditional textbook procedure. Nevertheless, your pupils must read to learn, and you have problems due to their inability to do so. Recognizing that many children now in the middle grades and in junior and senior high schools cannot use basic reading skills effectively, what can you do about it? The suggestions which follow are, of necessity, stated briefly and somewhat dogmatically, but it is my hope that they may help teachers to cope better with the problem of improving the deficiencies in basic reading skills which block progress in learning:

1. Discover how well the children in your classes can or cannot read. Survey their reading abilities. Use analytical reading tests or informal objective tests of your own to locate areas of difficulty. Observe and note signs of difficulty with basic reading skills.

2. Determine the reading capacities of pupils. By the use of either group or individual intelligence tests, find the mental ages of the pupils. Determine whether their reading ages are below, equal to, or better than, their mental ages.

3. Locate those children who because of low capacity will always read at the lower levels.

4. Identify the children whose reading achievement is a year or more below their reading capacities. Note the areas in which they are weak. Give these pupils some remedial instruction aimed at their specific weaknesses.

5. Make a survey of your reading materials. Find the readability levels of your instructional materials. These will generally be above the average comprehension level of your pupils.

6. Search for materials relating to your units of work that have as wide a range of difficulty as the range of reading abilities in your group. Arrange these materials for the use of your pupils and guide them in their use. The use of one of the readability formulas will aid you in finding materials of suitable levels of difficulty. Such materials may be hard to find, but, if you can find them, you will be rewarded.

7. Assemble all the visual materials available that will aid in enriching the experiences of your pupils, teach them new meanings, and add to their understanding. Use such materials to enrich the children's listening vocabularies, develop new concepts, and arouse interest in reading for learning.

8. Use the materials of different levels of difficulty to adjust the reading task to the abilities of your pupils. Some children can read quite well at a fifth-grade level but falter and fail at a seventh-grade level. The intake of ideas must be adjusted to the child's rate of learning.

9. Develop a program of reading instruction based on the specific needs of the children. The purpose of the program should be developmental rather than remedial. Your object is to develop all the basic reading powers to the limits of the child's capacity to learn, not to bring all children to read at the same level of achievement; for the latter is an impossible task. It is possible to teach most children to read better, but it is not possible to teach them all to read at the same level.

10. When assigning reading to be done, direct and guide the children so that each child has a clear idea of what is to be done and how to do it. As a teacher of reading to learn, you are responsible for careful assignment of tasks and for instruction and guidance in how to perform each task. Most of the reading failures and much of the reading retardation that exists today could have been prevented if teachers had learned to take more care in directing the child's learning.

11. Develop new concepts basic to the understanding of new material in advance of their occurrence in material to be read by the child. Make sure that basic concepts are understood before leaving them. Utilize every possible aid to meaning to make the concepts known to the child, including verbal, aural, and visual aids as well as direct contact with processes, institutions, and events.

12. Attack specifically weaknesses in the basic skills of word recognition, or, if you are a teacher in a departmental set-up and do not have responsibility for developing the basic reading skills, confer with the basic reading teacher concerning the weaknesses you observe and arrange specific practice on those skills which are interfering with learning activities.

13. Try to develop insight into, and understanding of, the importance of reading to learn and seek to make such reading significant and satisfying to the learner. Failure on the part of the child to make sense out of material which should contribute to learning activities leads to the careless, heedless reading so often apparent in the curricular fields and to lack of effort on the part of the learner.

14. Abandon the idea of equal achievement by all and seek rather to develop in each child the ability to read as well as he is capable of reading. It is far better that a child read well on some level, even though it is below that of his group, than that he constantly experience frustration due to his inability to cope with material that is too difficult for him to read.

15. Realize that it is your responsibility to aid the child to learn to read for the purposes which are appropriate to the material in each curricular field. There are certain adjustments which children must learn to make to materials of different kinds; and, while as a teacher of basic reading skills, you should teach the child to read for the purposes common to the various fields, as a teacher of social studies you must aid him to read social-studies materials in ways appropriate to that area.

16. The fact, however, that you are a teacher of a special field not wholly responsible for basal reading skills, especially in the departmentalized work of the upper grades and high school, does not excuse you from responsibility of doing all you can to aid children who are deficient in the basic reading skills and do not have any other person to help them. The teacher in the subject areas should be familiar with the essential basic skills of reading and how they operate. At times, special individualized help and even small-group instruction should be given in basic skills, or in a skill that is interfering with a child's progress. As a teacher of social studies or science, you cannot simply shrug your shoulders and blame the teacher lower down in the grades for the shortcomings of the child. You must do what you can to help him when his learning is blocked because of the lack of some needed skill. By asking a child to read aloud the material of his field, you can often discover certain weaknesses in word recognition which can be overcome by appropriate sug-

gestions, guidance, and practice. Deficiencies in basic reading skills must not be allowed to interfere with the child's learning through reading if it is possible by effective teaching to overcome the difficulty.

17. Always adjust the reading task to the ability of the pupils. In light of our knowledge of individual differences, the common assumption of many teachers that all middle- and upper-grade pupils and all high-school students can read and profit from the same textbook must be abandoned. This does not mean, however, that children should not be challenged by attempting to read materials which make heavy demands upon their powers of interpretation, but the task should be one that is possible for the children to perform if they make the maximum effort. Attempting to have the children read with a maximum effort at all times, however, is unwise. Periods of maximum effort should be interspersed with periods of fluent reading, in which the ideas are achieved with comparative ease.

18. Do not expect that all children can make the same contribution to the unit of work. Let the more able children find, read, assimilate, organize, and report ideas that will enrich the experience of the less able and thus give them the satisfaction of sharing their ideas with others.

19. Observe and appraise the performance of children constantly. Discover weaknesses before they have had the effect of slowing down progress and killing interest. Remedy weaknesses as soon as they are discovered. Prevention of reading disabilities is far better than curing them after the child has experienced unhappiness and frustration caused by his inability to do what is expected of him.

24. IMPROVING COMPREHENSION

Board of Education of the City of New York

It has already been pointed out that when a pupil enters the junior high school he finds that he is expected to be able to use reading as a major tool for learning. Good readers can do so, but many poor readers now reach the seventh grade who formerly would have been held back in the elementary school. Hence, both teachers and poor readers feel disappointed and frustrated when the latter fail to get meaning in reading *Julius Caesar* or an explanation of what *energy* is.

Reprinted from *The Retarded Reader in the Junior High School: A Guide for Supervisors and Teachers,* prepared by the staff of the Reading Guidance Center, Division of Instructional Research, Publication No. 31 (September 1952), pp. 89–99. By permission of J. Wayne Wrightstone, Bureau of Educational Research of the New York City Board of Education.

1. SOME FACTORS THAT CAUSE POOR COMPREHENSION

Poor comprehension may be due to a variety of factors

Before a remedial program is begun, it is important for teachers to find out why a child does not understand what he reads. In the Bureau project, an attempt was made to determine what general factors were responsible for the poor comprehension of each pupil selected for instruction. In each case, one or more of these factors was found to be involved.

a) *An inadequate background of experiences.* When the child's understanding is limited by a narrow field of experience, it is advisable to:

Enrich his background of ideas by providing him with a variety of direct and indirect experiences.

Encourage him to read material of many kinds. A variety of easy materials should be on hand in the classroom.

Precede silent reading activities with explanations and discussions of difficult concepts that he is to meet.

b) *A narrow meaning vocabulary and a poor language background.* The poor readers who had little opportunity to hear good English language patterns at home sometimes had difficulty in understanding what they read unless it was written in the simplest style. This was true not only of bilingual homes, but also where English was the only language. There is a need for developing good oral language in both the elementary and junior high schools, especially in the primary grades where formal book reading can be deferred. Pupils who have an inadequate language background need many opportunities to speak and listen to good English.

c) *Lack of efficiency in using techniques for recognizing unfamiliar words.* Constant interruption of the flow of reading to puzzle over words interferes with thought getting. Many pupils, even those who achieve fourth or fifth year scores on achievement tests, need practice in word recognition skills.

d) *Verbalizing—the ability to read material aloud glibly without having much idea of what it means.* Verbalizing may be the result of previous overemphasis on mechanics or on oral reading with neglect of thought getting. Another effect of overemphasis on oral reading was voiced by an anxious seventh-grader who recognized her own symptom: "I can't understand what it means unless I hear myself say it out loud."

e) *Reading everything too fast or too slowly.* In the junior high school project it was noted that some pupils had developed the habit of reading all material quickly and superficially, no matter how difficult it was or what their purpose in reading was. Others always read slowly and painstakingly, even when they wanted only the gist of an easy selection. The child's deficiency was discussed with him to be sure that he understood the goal toward which he needed to work. When he habitually read too fast, the teacher gave him exercises which required accuracy in noting details and minor points. The over-careful child needed an abundance of easy interesting material to develop fluency and also profited from exercises which he read quickly to get the general significance.

f) *Failure to develop an attitude of demanding meaning from reading.* Many of the retarded readers read passively, satisfied with any meaning they got without any attempt to dig further. Others read with wandering attention and were easily distracted by random thoughts or slight classroom incidents. Lack of concentration is sometimes a symptom of emotional difficulty; in many children, however, it may be evidence that they have never developed interest in reading. For independent reading, these children especially need easy, satisfying material—about their interests and hobbies, or perhaps about adventure. In directed reading activities, children concentrate more easily when thought-provoking questions are assigned in advance of silent reading.

g) *Lack of training and practice in specific comprehension skills.* Often it was found that children had been given practice only in answering questions about specific details or in reproducing a simple story orally. It was obvious that such a limited approach to getting meaning was inadequate for many of the reading jobs the child needed to do. He sometimes had fair control of the mechanics of reading, but he was in need of practice in specific comprehension skills.

The teacher should be on guard against assuming that poor comprehension always calls for remedial teaching. A pupil may fail to comprehend because the books he is asked to read are too hard for him in general. This is, of course, very common. It cannot be stressed too strongly that children must be supplied with materials they are able to read. When materials are too difficult, pupils abandon the effort to get meaning. This is true not only in reading activities but also in content subjects. If Johnny can read only stories on a maximum fourth year level in the reading room, he surely cannot understand a textbook written on a seventh year level in the science or social studies room. In the junior high school project, improvement in reading frequently went unrecognized by teachers of other subjects. A pupil whose reading score had gone from 3.5 to 5.5 could still not read an eighth year textbook and, to the casual eye, might appear to be as retarded as ever.

2. IMPROVEMENT OF COMPREHENSION THROUGH TRAINING IN SPECIFIC SKILLS

The growing variety of educational experiences in which the child is expected to use reading as a tool has made teachers more than ever aware of the importance of developing comprehension skills. The child who must solve a mathematics problem, or prepare a concise report, or defend a point of view, must be able to do more than passively read the content of a selection. He must be able to do what McKee calls "the scratching and clawing that is often essential to arriving at an adequate understanding of the meaning intended by the writer." Many children have no idea of how to "scratch and claw" for meaning. Consequently, we find the pupil who, faced with reporting on the gist of an article, copies verbatim portions of it—or the pupil who plods through all reading matter in the same way, no matter what his purpose or the type of material.

Repeated urgings to the child to read more carefully have little effect, and will probably not develop in him that automatic mental self-checking device that good readers impose on themselves. He needs direct instruction and practice in specific techniques that will enable him to read thoughtfully. Even in his earliest reading, the child's attention should be directed to a vigorous search for meaning. On the lowest reading levels he can learn to interpret pictures, follow simple written directions, anticipate what comes next in a story, draw pictures to illustrate what he has read, make up titles for stories, tell the most important events, or find details of color and size. Systematic development of comprehension skills not only gives the retarded reader competence in those skills, but more important, brings about greater accuracy and deeper understanding in all his reading. The gradual development of these abilities is very important.

Comprehension skills may be analyzed in various ways

There is wide agreement that fluent oral reading is not an assurance that any depth of comprehension has been attained. On the other hand, there is a good deal of variance in the conclusions of authorities as to what comprehension really is. Specialists on the subject of reading have suggested lists of comprehension skills that are very different as to number and variety. This difference can be seen in the types of comprehension response which well-known standardized tests try to measure. The examples below show only a few of the many ways in which reading comprehension has been analyzed.

Iowa Every-Pupil Tests of Basic Skills[1]
Test A, Part I: Reading Comprehension

Skills Involved in Paragraph Comprehension:
1. To recognize the main idea or topic of a paragraph.
2. To select the main purpose of a paragraph.
3. To grasp an idea not explicitly stated in the paragraph.

Skills Involved in the Location and Understanding of Details:
1. To recognize and understand an explicitly stated fact.
2. To recognize and understand implied facts and relationships.

Skills Involved in Organization of Ideas:
1. To recognize common elements in incidents or paragraphs.
2. To select main co-ordinate ideas.
3. To select co-ordinate ideas which are subordinated to a given idea.
4. To recognize proper time sequence.
5. To recognize the common element in two subtopics and select a third subtopic co-ordinate with the first two.

Skills Involved in Grasping Total Meaning:
1. To draw conclusions from an article.
2. To select the best title from given titles.

The Shank Tests of Reading Comprehension[2]

1. Answering a direct question on content details.
2. Answering an implied question on content details.
3. Answering an implied question on content meaning as a whole.
4. Determining whether or not the contents stated a given idea.
5. Selecting words or thoughts to which given words refer.
6. Determining whether given statements are true or false.

Gates Basic Reading Tests
(See Appendix A, Section I, 13, p. 451)

1. Reading to get the general significance or main ideas in passages.
2. Reading to see or predict circumstances or evidence implied by but not given in the passage.
3. Reading for precise and exact understanding of what is given, as in the case of reading directions.
4. Reading to note details.

The plan used in the Bureau project is discussed in the following pages. It was developed for usefulness in teaching rather than testing. Many of the items overlap or might be listed in more than one category.

[1] Examiner's Manuals for Test A Elementary; Advanced. Boston: Houghton Mifflin Co., 1945, p. 12; p. 16.

[2] SHANK, SPENCER. *Student Responses in the Measurement of Reading Comprehension*. Cincinnati, Ohio: C. A. Gregory, 1929, p. 53.

It is certainly not intended that the list be followed in sequence for teaching purposes. Neither is it intended that the teacher feel that she is responsible for "covering" the entire list. The deficiencies of the pupils themselves and the opportunities and demands of curriculum and subject matter will suggest when and how much practice should be given.

While each component skill may be useful by itself in certain reading activities, the main purpose in giving training in the specific items is to bring about more alert reading and generally better comprehension. Pupils are to practice noting details or selecting a topic sentence partly because these abilities in themselves are useful in certain study activities, but chiefly because of the way in which they improve general reading ability. The suggestions and exercises for improving comprehension are arranged according to this plan:

The efficient reader gets the literal meaning and finds details.

Finds and recalls details directly stated
Gets sensory impressions
Follows directions

The efficient reader selects the main idea and gets the general significance.

The efficient reader sees relationships and makes inferences.

Uses verbal cues to establish relationships
Identifies antecedents
Predicts the outcome
Sees details indirectly stated
Follows a sequence of events
Sees the author's organization and recognizes the relationship of subordinate ideas to the main idea
Sees cause-and-effect relationships, draws a conclusion, makes judgments, etc.

The efficient reader reacts to what he has read.
Thinks critically
Appreciates

3. APPRAISING PERFORMANCE THROUGH STANDARDIZED AND INFORMAL TESTS

It is important to know the pupil's strengths and weaknesses in comprehension

In formulating a plan of instruction, the teacher will want to find out the pupil's specific needs. One way he can do this is by studying performance on standardized tests of reading. The achievement score (usually in the form of a grade score) gives only the pupil's general level of comprehension. The actual test papers give further information. It is useful to go over the papers of poor readers question by question to see what kind of errors they are making. An analysis of wrong answers reveals in which area weaknesses lie. In the case of certain skills a large number of children may need training; in others, perhaps only a few may need help. It is usually found that pupils do far better in literal interpretation like finding details than in other categories. There is a tendency in many classrooms to ask questions of a factual nature to the virtual exclusion of those involving reasoning, where the function of details is to support inferences and conclusions.

The teacher will learn much about the kind of reading his pupils are doing through his own informal tests and observations. Tests can be devised to provide information about a single type of skill or about more than one. They may be similar in form to the exercises given in this chapter or to standardized tests, and they should not be rigidly timed. Suggestions for planning informal tests of comprehension are given in Educational Research Bulletin No. 10—*The Informal Appraisal of Reading Abilities*, p. 19.

4. THE PLACE OF THE SKILLS APPROACH IN IMPROVING COMPREHENSION

The skills approach should form only a part of the total reading program

The teaching of specific comprehension skills is not to be regarded as the whole or even the major portion of a program for reading improvement. Perhaps the main goal in teaching reading is to lead children to an enduring pleasure in reading. Since true recreational reading involves a strong desire to find out what the page says, it is a valuable means for improvement.

Another important means to improvement is the related-activity approach. In that approach, the child's use of reading is related to his activities, as in reading done before excursions, or for units of work, or about hobbies, or sports. That avenue used alone has limitations in the case of seriously retarded readers who need more than incidental practice for mastery of specific reading techniques. It should, however, form part of a remedial reading program whenever possible. If remedial reading is given by a special reading teacher, close cooperation with class teachers is necessary, so that activities can be related.

The pages following present suggestions for practice in comprehension skills. Most of the skills listed in the outline on page 293 can be developed to a certain extent at any reading level, but both the materials used and the complexity of the questions asked should be adapted to the pupil's ability. This is very important in teaching retarded readers. Starting at the point where the child is, or even below, will yield satisfying dividends in the pupil's achievement and in a more favorable attitude to reading.

Overteaching a skill is to be avoided. A child who can do exercises in finding details so easily that he hardly has to think, should not continue with that kind of practice merely to finish a particular set of exercises. Workbook or other practice material which is used as "busywork" becomes meaningless and monotonous and the slow reader is quick to become bored and to work mechanically.

Each sample exercise in the section following was devised for practice in some specific skill. Practice, however, should not be limited to improvement in a single skill. Frequent opportunity should be given pupils to maintain the skills learned previously by answering a variety of questions on what they read.

In no case should the exercises be regarded as a substitute for teaching. They are presented here both to clarify the type of skill they exemplify and to serve as guides for teachers who want to write original materials. Exercises should not be assigned for independent practice *until after teaching has taken place.*

Many of the exercises suggested in these pages can be used with material taken from books actually in use in the reading room. Well-written readers are often a trustworthy and convenient source of adaptable selections. Care should be used to choose paragraphs or stories that are especially suited to the specific skill that is to be practiced.

5. Suggestions for Developing Comprehension Skills

The efficient reader gets the literal meaning and finds details

In the earliest stages of reading, much of the development of literal comprehension is carried on in conjunction with word recognition and vocabulary study. Therefore, many of the exercises in the two preceding chapters are useful for developing ability to read phrases and sentences.

A good deal of reading calls for attention to specific statements. A child making a model plane, for instance, must observe and follow directions precisely as they are given if he is to be successful. This preciseness is especially useful in study reading of a careful and thorough kind.

a) *Finds and recalls direct details.* The pupil who has developed the habit of reading too superficially often has difficulty in noting and remembering details. Ability to observe details in reading is useful in many activities; e.g., in ordering sports equipment from a catalogue or understanding a newspaper account of a fire.

Pupils who are deficient in getting literal meaning may for a time need practice in finding details directly stated rather than those that are to be inferred. If the comprehension level is very low, the questions will have to be worded like the answer that appears in the passage read as in Question A below. Later the wording of the question may be varied as in Question B.

Example:

The wood of the balsa tree is the lightest wood we have. It comes from Ecuador. It is so light that it is used in life preservers. Balsa wood is also strong. We use it in airplanes.

A. What is the lightest wood we have?
B. Which wood is the lightest there is?

The ability to find directly stated facts and details is basic to higher skills of an inferential type like making judgments. Some pupils seem to guess wildly when they need to reason from what they read. These children benefit from first finding the specific phrases or sentences that bear on the inferences that are to be made. Questions may take these forms:

Find the words that tell that_____
What sentence shows that_____
Read the sentence that proves that_____
Underline the words that mean _____

Questions in practice exercises may ask for such details as *who, what, where, when, how big, what color*, and so on. Short-answer exercises are especially useful in this type of practice: completion, multiple choice, matching, true-false. In order to discourage guessing in answering questions, pupils may be asked to defend their choice....

b) *Gets sensory impressions.* The poor reader is often helped by being encouraged to form mental pictures of what he reads. He may be asked to tell what he sees or to draw a picture for a passage describing a vivid scene, as of a "white-sailed boat rocking on a sunny sea beneath blue skies." For this purpose the teacher may select suitable passages containing colorful details.

The same technique may also be applied to realization of details appealing to other senses—sound, smell, taste, and touch. Pupils may select telling words and phrases such as *crackling* fire, *blaring* trumpet, *sour as a lemon, soft as a baby's skin, thundering* waves, *smell of roast beef cooking in the oven.* Such practice is effective in vocabulary development also. The ability to synthesize significant details into a mental picture is a useful skill in many areas and can be developed by teachers of various subjects. In literature classes, the visualization of descriptive passages as of a violent storm, a busy street, or a junk shop enhances understanding and appreciation of verse or prose. In arithmetic, the

---

Play in Central Park

Why not spend the day at Central Park in Manhattan? You can reach it by any of the subways that go to that borough. (If you live in Staten Island, you will have to take the ferry first.) Get off at any station from 59th Street to 110th Street, depending on which spot you plan to visit.

There are many kinds of sports going on in Central Park. You may roller skate, bicycle, play tennis or baseball. When the ponds freeze over in winter you can ice skate too. The Wollman Memorial Skating Rink near 63rd Street is an artificial ice rink that has skating from November to March. If you like rowing, you can hire a boat. There will usually be a sailor or two rowing on the lake, too.

You can visit the Zoo and watch the seals and bears outdoors or make funny faces at the monkeys indoors. You can eat at a good cafeteria near the Zoo. There are beautiful walks and gardens in the park also.

For more information on Central Park, telephone Manhattan Recreation, REgent 4-1000.

1. You will have to take the ferry if you live in
   (a) Manhattan   (b) Staten Island   (c) Central Park
2. Where is the Wollman Memorial Skating Rink?
3. What animals can you see at the Zoo?
4. Can you bicycle in Central Park? _____ (Answer yes or no.)
5. You can ice skate from November to _____.
6. What telephone number will you call when you want more information?
7. List all the sports mentioned in Paragraph 2.

---

visualization of problems, as in calculating areas or distances, aids in understanding a problem.

c) *Follows directions.* Poor readers often respond inadequately to written directions. Many teachers recognize this deficiency and frequently give written directions since following written instructions is an important use of reading.

Fundamental practice in this comprehension skill can take place in a variety of situations. Written directions can be given for independent study and practice, class procedures, constructing simple objects in crafts or art classes, using or storing materials, following recipes, and doing simple science experiments. With retarded readers, it is advisable to have a group discussion after the first silent reading of more complicated directions, such as, what to do in an emergency or how to reach a place to which the class is taking a trip.

The technique of reading and following directions should be explained and demonstrated to pupils. Reading should be precise and thorough. In the case of simple step-by-step directions, it is enough to read them quickly to get the idea of what is required and then read and follow out each step. In this type of directions the main skill required is "noting details."

Even the most retarded reader can learn to follow written directions. Material should be geared to his general reading ability and may be as simple as:

> Put the pencil on the table.
> Write your name on the blackboard.

Sometimes following directions involves not only noting details, but also visualization of what is to be done and an understanding of the sequence of steps.

Though practice in following directions is most effective in real situations, it can also be given with prepared exercises. These may involve such content as rules for tricks and games, procedures for constructing model airplanes and boats, rules of etiquette, routes to places and the like. Evidence of understanding can be shown in the carrying out of instructions or answering of questions on the content.

How to Make a Potato Stamp

Cut off about a third of a potato. Draw a simple design on the flat side of the larger piece. The first letter of your name, a star, a heart, or a tree would be easy to start with. Cut along the design with a knife. Then cut away the part of the potato outside the picture you drew. The design should stand about a quarter of an inch above the rest of the potato.

You can use the potato stamp on paper or cloth. Brush some paint on the design and press the stamp down firmly. Practice doing this until the picture is clear and neat.

Your stamp will be useful in many ways. Two good ways are printing gift wrapping paper and decorating paper napkins for parties.

1. Write a list of all the things you need for making and using the stamp.
2. Where should you draw the design?
3. Two good designs to start with are_____ and _____.
4. How far should the design stand out on the potato?
5. Here is a list of some things you have to do to make a stamp. Put them in the right order. Write the number in the space before each sentence.

_____ Draw a picture.

_____ Put some paint on the design.

_____ Get a potato.

_____ Cut away the potato outside the design.

_____ Use the stamp on cloth or paper.

The efficient reader selects the main idea and gets the general significance

Much of the time, we read to get the general meaning of a paragraph or selection. When we read a newspaper, a novel, or a magazine article, we usually find that all we want is the author's main ideas. This kind of reading should be more rapid than that needed for noting details.

Many retarded readers lack skill in reading for a general impression. Some of them tend to read all material too deliberately, and miss the main point because they get lost in detail. Others read sentences as separate units of thought. These pupils need specific training in reading for total meanings. In training pupils to read for general ideas, either narrative or informational material may be used. For retarded readers, particularly, it should be carefully selected with certain qualities in mind:

The main idea should be clearly apparent, even obvious, especially when this skill is in its early stages.

The passages should not contain an undue amount of obscuring detail.

The material should be suitable for quick reading and present no problems of new vocabulary or unusual sentence structure.

At first only brief paragraphs should be used. Longer paragraphs or a selection of several paragraphs can be used as skill is developed.

Pupil response can be oral or written—by underlining, matching, or writing a sentence. Practice should take a variety of forms as in the suggestions below:

a) *Finding the topic sentence* when it is clearly stated. The topic sentence is usually the first sentence of a paragraph. (The sample paragraph under Item b below would be suitable.) It is important that pupils know that a good paragraph is a group of sentences that tell about one thing.

b) *Reading a paragraph and selecting the central thought* from a list of sentences or phrases:

A good hiker knows how to take care of himself. He does not drink water from a spring or brook unless it is marked safe. He watches out for harmful plants like poison ivy and poison oak. When he goes on a long hike, he takes along a warm sweater and wears shoes that are strong and comfortable.

What is this paragraph about?

(1) What to wear on a hike.
(2) What a Boy Scout must do on a hike.
(3) How to keep safe on a hike.

c) *Giving the central thought or summarizing the gist* of a paragraph in an original sentence:

What does this paragraph tell about?
What is the main idea of this paragraph?
This paragraph is mainly about_____

d) *Selecting the central thoughts* from several paragraphs of a story:
Read these paragraphs about training pigeons. Then number the titles at the bottom of the page to match the paragraphs.

1. Training pigeons is an interesting hobby that many boys enjoy. It is not an easy hobby. To do a good job you must be gentle and willing to work hard. You can teach these birds to race and carry messages. You must also feed them, exercise them, and take care of them when they are sick.

2. The birds used for training are called homing pigeons because they can find their way home from far away. They are not the kind you see in the park. Homing pigeons are very strong and are able to fly great distances. Champions can fly over a thousand miles. They also fly very fast. Birds that are well-trained can fly a hundred miles in less than three hours.

3. The pigeons should be fed twice a day. They like corn, peas, and wheat. They have no teeth so they need to eat grit—bits of rock or shell—to help grind their food. Feed stores sell specially mixed pigeon foods.

4. Homing pigeons are kept in pigeon houses called lofts. The size of the loft depends on the number of birds. It can be made of old boxes and wire screening, but must have a good roof and a floor. It should be set in the open so that birds can find their way back.

_____How to Feed Pigeons

_____Why Pigeons Are Strong

_____Pigeon Houses

_____What Homing Pigeons Can Do

_____How to Buy Pigeons

_____A Hobby That Is Interesting but Not Easy

e) *Writing titles* for a paragraph or for a longer selection; choosing the most appropriate title from a group of titles; matching each title in a list of titles to its corresponding paragraph in a story or an article:

It was a wonderful pie! It made the whole kitchen smell good. The crust was crisp and melted in the mouth. The cherries were sweet and the dark red juice oozed out over the plate.

Make up a title for the paragraph you have just read.

or

Choose the best title:

(1) A Pretty Pie
(2) Pie for Lunch
(3) A Delicious Pie

f) *Composing headlines* for story paragraphs. The characteristics and functions of newspaper headlines should be discussed in preparation for this activity. Pupils can also be asked to select the best headline from several given to them. Short, simple human interest stories make good practice material:

Writing a Headline

The other day, some men working in Yankee Stadium got a big surprise. A fox dashed out on the baseball diamond. The workmen chased it from first base to home plate but it got away. Finally it ran under the bleachers and disappeared. People are wondering how a fox got into Yankee Stadium.

Write a headline for the story you have just read.

or

Choose the   (1) The Fox
best headline: (2) A Big Surprise
                    (3) Fox Hunt at Yankee Stadium

g) *Getting the general significance* of a passage concerning the feelings and emotions of a character:

Robert sprang to his feet when he heard the news. He threw his cap up in the air. A grin spread over his face and he yelled, "Yippee!"

1. What was the news he heard?

     (1) His brother was ill.
     (2) His team had won the football game.
     (3) His class was going to have a test in arithmetic.

or

2. How did Robert feel?   (1) frightened
                                (2) happy
                                (3) sad

h) *Using special cues to the main idea* supplied by the author; e.g., titles, subtitles, sideheads.

The efficient reader sees relationships and makes inferences

The ability to see relationships is essential to comprehension. Even in material of the simplest type, the relationship of idea to idea must be carefully observed if understanding is to take place. The retarded reader often shows marked deficiency in this area. He does poorly in answering questions that require him to "tell why," to draw conclusions, to "read between the lines"; he has difficulty in making an outline or recognizing which portions of material are pertinent to his purpose. He needs practice of various types, some of which are suggested below.

a) *Uses verbal cues and signals to establish relationships.* Pupils often miss relationships between ideas because they do not utilize important word signals that help in getting an author's meaning. For example:

To show sequence of ideas or paragraphs—*first, second, in the first place*

To indicate opposing or contrasting ideas—*however, but, still, yet, although*

To herald additional or reinforcing information—*besides, also, furthermore*

Observance of word signals often helps in an understanding of the organization of a selection as when paragraphs are introduced by *first, second, third.* Even more important, such signals help retarded readers who usually have trouble with complex sentences. Harris suggests that the poor reader's difficulty in reading complex sentences often results from unfamiliarity with the meanings of words that introduce subordinate clauses. He points out that many pupils are not accustomed to speech and conversation which employ these connectives. He recommends oral practice in constructing sentences, and in paraphrasing or rephrasing ideas with connectives like:

who, which, what, that, from whom, to which, how, like, so as, in order to, because, since, until, as soon as, before, while, as, after, following, if, unless, provided that, whether, should, as well as, all but, hardly, except, without, although, however, moreover, therefore, nevertheless.

An exercise like this may be used:

Easy: I am hungry (and, but) I shall wait till lunch time to eat.

Harder: It is raining. (Therefore, However) I shall take an umbrella.

b) *Identifies antecedents.* The retarded reader sometimes fails to understand a passage clearly because of confusion regarding the correct antecedent of a relative pronoun or other reference word. The confusion is especially likely to arise when the antecedent is in one sentence and the word that refers to it in another. A partial list of reference words is:

he, it, its, his, him, who, which, they, their, them, this, that, there, each, one, none, many, such, first, last, former, latter.

Pupils can be asked to find the antecedents of reference words as they occur in directed reading activities, or an exercise of this sort may be devised:

Some birds fly south in winter and north in summer. However, many stay in the same place all year.

Many means _____.

> Yesterday we built our clubhouse. We started at seven in the morning. We made it of old boxes and tin sheets.

It refers to_____.

c) *Predicts the outcome.* The competent reader develops the habit of anticipating content. He is often fully conscious of this process only when he reads stories of high suspense like adventure or detective fiction, but the habit persists with other materials too. The effect of thinking ahead is to intensify a critical and interpretational approach to the printed page, a continuous process of inferring and judging. Success in anticipating or predicting events or outcomes of what is read is dependent on other skills like noting important details, following a sequence of events, and understanding cause and effect relationships. Practice may be given in various ways:

> Pupils read to a designated point in a story and several of them tell how they think the story goes on. The class then evaluates the suggested endings, backing up their approval or disapproval by references to what they have already read.

> Before reading takes place, pupils are asked to guess from the title and illustrations or from the first paragraph what the story will be about.

> Exercises can be prepared in which short unfinished narratives are used.

> Pupils are asked to choose what happened next from a group of several suggestions. The choices given should be those which will lead to a conclusion based on clues given in the story.

d) *Sees details indirectly stated.* In the Bureau project, it was found that poor readers often failed to gain insight into what they read because they grasped only those details that were explicitly stated. Sometimes these pupils were unaware that any but literal meanings were available in the reading process; thus they failed to look for the implications that would lead them to more than a superficial understanding of what they read. Furthermore, they tended to read each sentence as a separate unit; they failed to establish relationships between ideas in different sentences.

Authors count on having these relationships established by the reader. Except in the easiest materials, they write in the expectation that the reader will infer certain additional information from what is on the printed page. A story or article in which every detail was explicitly stated would be a dull affair. Even a simple passage like the following shows how the author depends on the reader to fill in gaps:

> Tom walked around town looking for Skipper. He asked people if they had seen a big white dog with black spots. He looked in the park and down by the river. Over and over he whistled and called, "Here, Skipper!" But no Skipper came. Skipper had disappeared.

In the above paragraph, implied ideas rather than direct statements answer such questions as:

Who was Skipper?
How did Skipper look?
Was Skipper in the park?

e) *Follows a sequence of events.* Retarded readers rarely have trouble in following a sequence of events in very simple, short narratives. They can usually "tell the story" orally without too much trouble. But they fail to keep in mind a clear story line when presented with a more complex narrative. Inability to follow a sequence of events or ideas affects reading of nonfiction as well. Simple story material can be used at first and more complicated kinds later:

Have pupils retell stories and anecdotes orally to encourage them to note the order and relative importance of events. Other pupils listen critically for incidents omitted or out of place.

Help pupils use word cues to establish a time sequence where indicated by time-words (like *one o'clock, Monday, July*) or by such words as *first, next, then, later, finally.* Also, questions like these may be used:

What did the boys do first when they got to the clubhouse?
What did the soldier do after the war was over?
Where did the traveller go then?
How did she feel the next day?

Ask pupils to list events in chronological order or ideas in logical order following a reading of a selection. This kind of practice is more difficult than those above. An example of this type of exercise is given in Question 5 of the exercise on page 299.

f) *Sees organization and relationship of subordinate ideas to the main idea.* Poor readers rarely bother to notice an author's plan of organization. As has been noted above, they tend to read one sentence after the other without the habitual analysis and appraisal that a good reader employs.

It is always useful to observe the pattern of a piece of reading material. The reader is thereby able to follow a line of reasoning and understand conclusions reached by the author; he can select important ideas and pass over unimportant details; he recalls and retains the material better; he finds it easier to take useful notes and summarize.

Retarded readers are likely to be unaware that well-written material is constructed according to a pattern. While the form of simple selections can be discussed with pupils, the teacher will find it desirable to delay formal outlining of selections until certain skills have been thoroughly acquired. Perhaps the best starting point is to give practice in finding the main ideas, first of one paragraph and later of a longer selection.

The pupil also needs practice in finding the connection between a main idea and ideas subordinate to it. For this, it is important that he should know that a well-written paragraph is the development of a single main idea. All the other ideas explain the main idea. Paragraphs used in this kind of practice should be carefully selected for their clear development. Well-written textbooks often contain adaptable material.

Following are suggestions for planning lessons and exercises:

(1) A topic sentence followed by a list of related and unrelated ideas is presented. Pupils are asked to select the related ideas.

Study the Topic Sentence. Then read the sentences below it. Put a check next to the sentences that tell something about the topic sentence.

Topic sentence: Swimming is not hard if you learn to do certain things.

Keep your legs nearly straight while you kick.
Take a breath each time you turn your face out of the water.
Wear your best bathing suit.
Keep your fingers together when you practice the arm stroke.
Pack your lunch in a brown paper bag.
Kick your feet three times to each arm stroke.
Keep practicing the arm and leg stroke.
Keep your eye on the ball as you swing the bat.

(2) Same as (1). The pupils are asked to select unrelated ideas.

(3) A paragraph is presented. The main topic is selected in a discussion or indicated by the teacher. Pupils are told how many supporting ideas to find.

(4) Same as (3). The number of subordinate ideas is not indicated.

(5) Pupils are given a paragraph in which one or more unrelated ideas are included. Pupils are asked to find these.

(6) Pupils who read well enough can be given practice in outlining selections using formal outline forms. Though formal outlining is sometimes useful, it is not necessary to the understanding of simply constructed material. Outlining is discussed on page 318.

g) *Sees cause-and-effect relationships, draws a conclusion, makes judgments.* Since children do not tend to read more thoughtfully just because somebody thunders "Think!" it is valuable to provide them with guidance and specific opportunities for inferential reading. Some of these opportunities have already been described under the headings "Predicts the outcome" and "Sees details indirectly stated."

Teachers find that well-chosen thought questions lead to more reflective reading than those which simply call for factual details. Compare, for instance, "What did Mary decide to do?" with "Was Mary's decision a wise one? Why?" The second question necessitates finding the answer to the first and then viewing it in relation to other ideas in the selection. Pupils can demonstrate in discussion how they arrive at their answers, citing statements in the text.

If pupils have difficulty in drawing conclusions and making judgments, they may first need practice in answering cause-and-effect questions to which the answer is directly stated in the text. However, as soon as possible they should be asked to make inferences from the information given there.

Who Said It?

Here are some things people say. At the bottom of the page is a list of people. Match what is said with the person who says it.

1. May I have the next dance?
2. Kill the umpire!
3. Calling all cars! Calling all cars!
4. Please don't pinch the vegetables.
5. Please step to the rear.

_____policeman

_____fireman

_____boy

_____bus driver

_____baseball fans

_____grocer

Questions like the following stimulate pupils to reason:

If Bob had not seen the car speeding down the road he would not have _____.

What reason did the old man have for not speaking to his neighbors?

Ellen was unhappy because _____.

This story proves that:

1. It is better to give than to receive.
2. It is pleasant to get gifts.
3. Rich people should give big presents.

Why do we wear light colored clothes in summer?

The efficient reader reacts to what he has read

The comprehension skills described so far have dealt with ability to get an author's meaning, either directly expressed or implied. The reader does not, and should not, stop there. He reacts to and appraises the author's ideas. His evaluation may be purely objective or may have subjective elements as well.

a) *Thinks critically.* Objective evaluation, often called *critical reading*, is sometimes reserved for superior readers by teachers and authorities on reading. Critical reading, however, depends basically on critical thinking which involves both skills and attitudes that should be developed from the very beginning. Pupils who do not read well enough to practice evaluation techniques independently may take part in oral discussions of material even if it has to be read to them. Such discussion is particularly valuable in the social studies, though it should not be limited to that area.

Opportunities for learning often arise naturally, as when pupils ask why two newspaper stories disagree. The level of the problems selected for discussion should not be too difficult, but it should also be taken into account that junior high school pupils who read on a fourth year level are interested in more mature issues than eight-year-olds who read just as well. Some types of critical evaluation are:

(1) Discriminating between fact and fiction

Is this a true story? Pick out the sentences (or ideas, or facts) that tell you.

(2) Recognizing "slanting" of information

Is the author trying to convince us of his point of view by appealing to our emotions or by giving us facts?

Tell which of these ads is really factual:

Eat our purer, better-tasting ice cream.
Our ice cream contains 12% butterfat.

(3) Examining the truthfulness and validity of the author's statements

Who is the writer? Is he an authority on this particular question? Are his facts up to date?

(4) Recognizing and selecting ideas relevant to the pupil's purpose

Here is a list of sentences about New York City. Check every sentence that would help you find out how New York City takes care of the health of its people.

b) *Appreciates.* Subjective elements are prominent when our thinking about what we read is colored by our emotions and feelings. Opportunities for developing appreciation occur in:

Getting the general tone of what is read and sensing the purpose of the author—humorous, sarcastic, serious

Considering the author's language—color words, rhythm, style

Relating what is read to personal experience

Giving reasons for liking or disliking material

Reacting to humor—cartoons, jokes, stories, films

6. READING PURPOSE

The reading purpose determines the approach

In general, we read for either of two broad purposes: recreational and informational. Many times our goal is both, as in the case of the sports enthusiast who reads about baseball or hockey.

In addition to the general purpose of getting recreation or information, we usually read with some specific purpose in mind—to solve a problem, to reproduce the material later, to follow a story, to find out how to play a game or construct an object. The specific purpose not only affects the choice of reading matter but how it is read. For instance, the pupil whose hobby is stamp collecting may read a book about philately with as much enjoyment as he reads an exciting story of adventure, but his approach will be different in the two cases. For one thing, he will probably read the story faster. For another, he may use different comprehension skills. In reading the book on stamps, he may need such skills as noting details, following directions, determining the relevance of content, selecting main ideas, and drawing conclusions. The exciting story may require these too, but will probably chiefly call for following a sequence of events, anticipating action, making inferences, and getting the emotional tone.

Retarded readers need help in varying their approach to reading materials. Since they tend to read everything in the same way, they need to be taught that their approach to reading matter should be influenced by what they want to get out of it. They should learn that thinking about the purpose of their reading and looking over the material before they read will help them to save time and do a better job. The teacher should demonstrate this frequently in advance of silent reading. Some considerations are:

The suitability of certain reading speeds for specific jobs:

Skimming to locate specific details or relevant passages, to choose books, etc.

Rapid reading to get main ideas or the gist of a story.

Slow careful reading for following directions, for memorizing facts, for understanding explanations.

The usefulness of using first one speed and then another. For example, if the task to be done involves finding information on the Statue of Liberty for a unit on New York City, the pupil may need to skim a page or two to locate pertinent material and then read the part carefully.

On what occasions to reread and how much of a selection to reread. Some reasons for rereading are:

to understand difficult ideas
to find answers to questions
to understand difficult sentence structure, figures of speech
to memorize significant ideas or details
to enjoy a well-liked selection again
to react critically to material read

Rereading should always be purposeful. It is of little benefit when it is done in response to suggestions like, "When you finish the story, read it over again."

Application of appropriate comprehension skills. It is especially important to show pupils that the approach to story materials is usually different from the approach to study reading.

25. SPECIFIC METHODS OF TEACHING CERTAIN COMPREHENSION SKILLS

Board of Education of the City of New York

TEACHING THE UNDERSTANDING OF A SENTENCE

A proper understanding of an involved sentence depends upon the ability to separate the main idea, or core idea, from the many descriptive words, phrases, and clauses which surround it. This is really equivalent to a knowledge of the essential grammatical element of a sentence. It requires first, an awareness that a sentence may contain many elements which are subordinate to the main idea, and that they have been included as a kind of "dressing" for it. It demands, next, a recognition of the various *purposes* for which these subordinate elements have been

Reprinted from *Reading Grades 7–8–9: A Teacher's Guide to Curriculum Planning Bulletin, 1957–1958*, Series No. 11 (1959), pp. 85–104. By Permission of the New York City Board of Education.

included—to describe, to tell where, when, why or how. Finally, it requires the ability to apply this knowledge of sentence structure while in the very act of reading, in other words, to seek for the meaning through the core words *even if they are separated by various intervening expressions*.

A close correlation between grammar and reading is necessary if this ability is to be taught as a specific skill. A familiarity with the terms *verb, subject word, phrase* and *clause* will facilitate the lessons for both teacher and pupil.

TEACHING THAT CERTAIN PARTS OF THE SENTENCE ARE SUBORDINATE TO THE MAIN IDEA.

Teacher and class work together from a given "skeleton" of a sentence, adding words to give it "body". E.g., boy-ate-cake

1. Add words that will *describe* the boy and the cake. (adjectives, phrases)
   The dirty-faced little boy ate the chocolate cake.
   The dirty-faced little boy in the ragged sweater ate the chocolate cake.

2. Add words that will tell *how*. (clause)
   The dirty-faced little boy in the ragged sweater ate the chocolate cake as if he had never tasted cake before.

3. Add words that will tell *when*. (clause)
   As soon as the woman's back was turned, the dirty-faced little boy in the ragged sweater ate the chocolate cake as if he had never tasted cake before.

4. Remove all the added words to show that the main idea still remains. (Note: Many similar sentences may be described orally and at the blackboard, the difficulty of the topic depending upon the reading level and interest of the class.)

   e.g., Immigrants settled in America.
   Because they had been persecuted or had poor living conditions in their homelands, millions of *immigrants* from European countries *settled in America* during the last half of the 19th century.

PRACTICE IN THE RECOGNITION OF THE VARIOUS PURPOSES OF SUBORDINATE CLAUSES.

Teacher may select sentences at random from any grade level text and work with group.

1. Find all the descriptive words and phrases which have been used to give a clearer picture:

    In their letters, the pioneers wrote in glowing terms about the rich and wonderful land with its snow-capped mountains, its tumbling streams, and forests of oak, pine, and fir.

2. Find the parts of the sentence which have been included to give the element of time:

    The states in the southern part of the continent, after many years of wars with England and among themselves, formed the Union of South Africa.

3. Find the parts of the sentence which have been included to tell *where*:

    This part of Burma, near the mouth of the Irrawaddy River, is the greatest rice-producing region in the world.

4. Find the parts of the sentence which have been included to give a reason, to explain *why*:

    The hostile Indians, realizing that they were far outnumbered by the white settlers, wheeled their horses about and fled.

SELECTING THE MAIN IDEA BY APPLYING A KNOWLEDGE OF SENTENCE STRUCTURE.

Underline the words which express the main idea. Test your selection by reading the underlined parts to see whether the idea will "stand alone."

1. Where parts of the main idea are not widely separated:
    In some places, *the marble*, which is carved in fine delicate patterns, *looks like lace*.

2. Where the main idea is intact but at the end of the sentence:
    Hale and hearty at 69, now a rancher in California, but visiting here for the convention, *Mr. Roberts posed willingly* for the press.

3. Where the main idea is intact but in the middle of the sentence:
    One day, as he sat in the beautiful church of Pisa, his native city, *Galileo noticed the motion of the heavy ornate lamp* which hung over the altar.

4. Where parts of the main idea appear at the beginning and end of the sentence:
    The southern people, inasmuch as most of the slaves remained faithful and continued to work on the plantations, *were not entirely without food*.

5. Where the main idea is broken by several subordinate elements:
   The trail-blazing party which is penetrating deep into Byrd Land to locate another base for American scientists *was reported moving again* after being stalled for two days by a blinding snowstorm.

   In many of the Asiatic countries *the people*, who have been hindered for centuries by poverty, ignorance and superstition, *have made little progress*, as compared with the people of the western world.

6. Where the usual subject-verb pattern is reversed:
   In the frozen north of the Scandinavian countries, where few plants can survive the cold, *live the Lapps*, a strange wandering people.

STENOGRAPHIC REPORT OF A LESSON ON FINDING THE MAIN THOUGHT OF A PARAGRAPH

Motivation and Introduction

Of course you have noticed newspaper headlines. What purpose do headlines serve? Obviously, headlines give you main ideas. Many of the books and magazines you read do not have these useful headlines to help you find main ideas. What can you do when headlines are missing? Why, make your own headlines, of course! When is your headline a good one? When it states the main idea.

Today we are going to learn how to find the main idea of a paragraph by working first with main-idea expressions.

Would you consider the word *giraffe* a good newspaper headline? Why not? It doesn't tell you enough about giraffes. You ask yourself immediately, "What about giraffes?" A headline, like a main idea, must tell what the whole paragraph is about.

Development—The Steps

Now, how are you going to select the main idea to put into your headings? It must fit the paragraph exactly. Perhaps we can see this idea more clearly if we use a list of words:

cubs-colts-puppies-lambs-kittens

Although these are all different from each other, yet there is an idea that fits all of them. Which one of the following ideas would best fit the list above?

dogs-animals-wild animals-young animals-food

(Let the class go through the list and then elicit from pupils that both *animals* and *young animals* would be two possible terms, but that *young animals* is the better because it is more specific. Follow with other lists until pupils understand that a main-idea expression must be "just right," neither too large nor too small.)

Now we will see what we can do with a paragraph. True, all the sentences are different from each other, yet there is one sentence in the paragraph that gives the thought of all the others. We call this the key sentence. It is a key to the main thought of the whole paragraph.

Read the following paragraph silently:

Wars are very harmful. Thousands of soldiers are killed. Much property is destroyed. Many innocent women and children suffer unjustly. Wounded and discouraged fighting men return home to begin a new and uncertain life.

(Can the pupils see that each sentence, in its own way, is showing how harmful war is?) What is the thought of the key sentence? With which of the following topics would you match the main thought (expressed as a phrase) of the key sentence?

1. The killing of soldiers
2. The suffering of women and children
3. The harmfulness of war

Why is the third topic the best? (Let pupils explain that the third is all inclusive. Let pupils read the sentences that prove that wars are harmful.)

(Use more samples of paragraphs which are followed by this type of multiple-choice topics before proceeding to the next step.)

This exercise was not very difficult because we had a list of topics from which to choose. Now let us see what we can do with a paragraph where you have no list from which to choose.

Although the giraffe has a long throat, he cannot make a sound. Other animals may bleat or bark or bellow, but not the giraffe. He goes through his entire life voiceless. He is one of the few mute animals in the world. Even when he is in great pain, he cannot make a sound.

What is the key sentence? What is the main thought? Read a sentence that proves he cannot make a sound. What word in the sentence proves it? Read another sentence to prove the same point. Indicate the word. (Slow procedure is very important in order to make sure that every child gets the concept.)

What must every sentence in the paragraph do? (Tell something about the main thought—i.e., that the giraffe cannot make a sound.)

(Continue this procedure, using simple paragraphs containing key sentences at the beginning of the paragraph.)

Now that we have found main ideas all by ourselves, let's go on to the next step to see if we can make up paragraphs that will be able to "stand up" against all criticism. Have you ever made "stand-up" paragraphs? They're fun to do. Someone in the class says a key sentence. He stands up in front of the class. Other people in the class think of sentences that should go into the paragraph. As they add other sentences, they stand up behind the key sentence. The "paragraph" is a row of people standing at the front of the room. When all the "sentences" have taken their places, they repeat their sentences one after the other, just like a paragraph.

After you've heard all the sentences once, you may think they should be in different order or that some sentences do not belong to that key sentence. If so, some sentences may have to sit down and others "change places" in the line.

Let us see what we have done so far in our study of the paragraph. In what sentence did we find the main thought of the paragraph? Where in the paragraph was the key sentence? (At the beginning.)

Now let us go one step further today. Not all paragraphs are written with the key sentence at the beginning of the paragraph. Some paragraphs have their key sentence concealed in some other part of the paragraph.

For example, read the following paragraph silently:

Two high school students were seriously injured in football games last Saturday. The week before, three players were hospitalized. Football has become a dangerous sport. The piling up of players in a scrimmage often leads to serious injury. Perhaps some rule changes would lessen the danger.

What is the key sentence? In what part of the paragraph do you find it? What is the main thought? Read one sentence that proves the main thought. [Let the pupils see that each sentence proves that football is *dangerous.*]

[Follow the discussion with additional samples in which the key sentence is in some other part of the paragraph, not at the beginning.]

Application

[Let the class bring the social studies text to class on the following day. The pupils will look for paragraphs that illustrate the two concepts stressed in the lesson:

1. Paragraphs with key sentences at the beginning

2. Paragraphs with key sentences in some other part of the paragraph]

TEACHING RECOGNITION OF DETAILS THAT SUPPORT MAIN IDEA

Introductory Remarks to Pupil

Main ideas, although they are important, are not sufficient by themselves. Suppose the key sentence is "He was a new boy but very popular." This statement alone is not convincing enough. What can be said to convince you that the boy was so popular? The author can add these thoughts: "He had a friendly smile which everyone liked. He knew how to tell a joke. Girls found him interesting. Boys liked him because he would never show off. Everyone called him by his first name, even his teachers."

Notice that only the key sentence says that the boy was popular. The rest of the sentences contain related details, such as "could tell a joke," "was interesting to girls," "boys liked him," "teachers called him by his first name." Yet these details all help to prove his popularity.

You will find that most paragraphs are written this way. There is usually a key sentence that expresses the important idea which the rest of the paragraph has to support. One must not expect, however, that every paragraph *everywhere* will be like this. But it is very helpful to learn how to recognize details that support the main idea.

Sequential Exercises and Devices

A. With the Help of Cue Words (first, another, etc.)

Illustration: There are *four* seasons in the year. The *first* is spring, when all nature awakes from its winter sleep. *Another* is summer, when all plant and insect life live their fullest. The *third* is autumn or fall. At this time nature prepares for its winter sleep. The *last* season is winter, when the warming snow prepares the underground seed for the coming spring growth.

Let pupils explain how the clues help to point out the details that prove the main idea.

1. Teacher and pupils can now prepare directions for parents attending "Open School Week" or similar functions. In order that parents may be able to see as much of the school as possible, a step-by-step program will have to be developed. The writing of such a program will necessitate the use of many cue words.

2. Show how cue words help in all the subject areas.
   e.g., directions in shop work, rules for a game, instructions for cooking, agendas for class meetings or guidance discussions, etc.

B. With Cue Words Removed

1. Pupils may be asked to re-write a short paragraph, removing cue words. (This type of exercise should determine whether the pupil has a good understanding of "cue words".)

2. Teacher writes a topic sentence on board. Pupils develop topic without the use of cue words.

3. Pupils select paragraphs from a social studies or mathematics text-book with cue words absent, and compare with paragraphs that have cue words present. Discuss the "readability" or ease of getting the main idea from each.

C. Noting Relationship of Supporting Details to Central Thought

1. Introductory suggestions by teacher, statements that have to be *proved*—"More penmanship should be taught." "Senior hats are affecting the rest of the school." Pupils then add details of proof.

2. In preparing material for magazine or yearbook, teacher may ask, "Who is the most popular boy in the school?" Pupils list factors supporting their choice.

3. Teacher to ask question, "Did you have a good time over the week-end?" or "Was it a pleasant vacation?" Answers to be supported by list of experiences written on board. (Though methods 1, 2, and 3 are done orally, transfer can be made to reading. This inter-relationship among the language arts should be encouraged and emphasized.)

4. Have pupils select a vivid passage from a story or poem. What details make it vivid?

5. Have pupils select a character that they like or dislike. What details has the author written to give that impression?

6. Apply to social studies content where the author makes some significant statement that "causes," "results," "influences." Does the author support his central thought with supporting details? What are they?

D. Recognizing the Presence of Irrelevant Details

1. Teacher to prepare a list of categories (e.g., "shelter," "transportation," "communication") under which are listed some irrelevant items, as well as those that are appropriate. Pupils to locate these and explain why they are appropriate or irrelevant.

2. Teacher to prepare short paragraphs, each containing one irrelevant detail. Pupils to locate these and explain why they are inappropriate.

Welcomed by dozens of smaller ships, the superliner "United States" steamed gracefully up the harbor. She had just completed a record crossing of the Atlantic. Thousands of people lined the piers to see the new "Queen of the Seas." *Long before the ship docked, there was an automobile accident on the main pier.* America had regained her supremacy on the seas.

3. Pupils prepare their own paragraphs containing one irrelevant detail. Exchange papers, and have classmate locate the error. Cross out irrelevant detail, and replace the phrase or sentence that supports the central thought.

4. Prepare agenda for class meeting or guidance conference. Pupils' discussion to follow agenda. Person who comes up with irrelevant topic is "out of order." (Here, too, we see how the language arts can be combined.)

5. Apply to other subject areas and outside reading. Have pupils bring in items that show the presence of irrelevant details.

E. Additional Exercises for Recognizing Details

1. Show a picture to the class for 10 or 15 seconds. Ask pupils to describe what they saw. Then show the picture again. Compare the effect of omitting details from a picture with the effect of ignoring details in a reading assignment.

2. Place a series of unfamiliar pictures along front of room. Have pupils read, silently or orally, a number of given paragraphs, each describing one picture. By reading carefully for details, pupils will be able to decide on a title for each picture.

3. For slow readers—combining details with drawing. Present for reading a colorful, descriptive paragraph. Have pupils draw picture from details presented in paragraph. Show how attention to details can affect an entire picture.

4. Teacher to prepare a series of short paragraphs, each of which has one word that is obviously out of place, i.e., does not fit in with the meaning of the rest of the paragraph. Have pupils find this word, cross it out, and replace with a word that is in accord with the meaning of the paragraph.

TEACHING THE ABILITY TO ORGANIZE AND OUTLINE MATERIAL

A. Practice in Perceiving the Relationship of Words and Ideas

Step 1: Grouping objects according to common characteristics as an aid to recall.

(a) Skim over the following list of items, then see how many you can remember.

ruby	boat	lion
deer	elephant	diamond
plane	sapphire	car
pearl	tiger	sled

(b) Now group the same items under the headings *jewels, vehicles, animals.* You will see that by organizing them into groups according to common characteristics, you have made it easier to remember them.

Step 2: Organizing names with historical or special significance into related groups.

EXERCISE: List the following under the headings: *Explorers and Inventors*

Columbus, Marconi, Bell, Magellan, Fulton, Cabot

EXERCISE: Group the following under *Land, Air, Water*

submarine, dirigible, dogsled, dugout, helicopter, canoe

Step 3: Organizing ideas expressed as topics.

EXERCISE: List the following under the headings *History, Mathematics, English*

Writing a composition
Finding the square root
Discussing the Revolutionary War
Learning rules of grammar
Studying the Monroe Doctrine
Solving a problem in percentage

B. Practice in Changing Sentences to Topics

1. Organizing ideas to show how they are related to each other, or outlining, can be simplified by using topics instead of complete sentences. By keeping only the important words we can retain the main idea but express it in a shorter form:

SENTENCE: There are many uses of electricity.
TOPIC: Uses of electricity
SENTENCE: The automobile has had a strong influence on our American way of life.
TOPIC: Automobile a strong influence

EXERCISE: Condense the following sentences into topics by omitting unnecessary words.

(1) The Parthenon is an excellent example of Greek architecture.

(2) There were many evils in the feudal system.

(3) Paris is one of the great fashion centers of the world.

2. It is sometimes necessary to change the order of the words or make other minor changes in the order to express the meaning in a topic:

SENTENCE: The monasteries served many purposes.

TOPIC: Purposes of the monasteries

SENTENCE: There are definite steps in making a papier-mâché mask.

TOPIC: How to make a papier-mâché mask

EXERCISE: Change the following sentences to topics in the above way.

(1) Diving for pearls involves many dangers.

(2) There are a number of ways in which college students may earn money.

(3) The floods caused great and widespread damage to farm lands.

EXERCISE: In the following list decide which are topics and which are sentences.

(·1) The correct way to plant bulbs.

(2) Uses of the coconut palm.

(3) The success of the invention was amazing.

(4) Custer's last stand.

(5) The enemy suffered a crushing defeat.

(6) How glass is made.

C. Practice in Perceiving the Relationship Between the Main Topic and Sub-Topics

1. A main topic expresses the key thought in a paragraph. The details that prove or support the main idea are sub-topics. In the following illustration the main topic is shown in italics. Note how the other topics are related to it:

Good health habits
Brushing teeth regularly
Bathing frequently
Eating well-balanced meals

EXERCISE: In each of the following groups of topics underline the one you consider the main topic.

a. Daniel Defoe
Great English writers
William Shakespeare
Jonathan Swift

      b. Great mineral wealth
         Excellent fisheries
         Resources of Alaska
         Extensive coal fields

2. It is often necessary to invent a main topic for a group of ideas by seeing how they are related to each other.

    EXERCISE: For each of the following groups of sub-topics, compose a main topic that will show their relationship to each other.

      a. Loose rugs on slippery floors
         Poor lighting in dark places
         Objects left lying on steps

      b. Felling the trees
         Sawing the trunks into lengths
         Loading the logs on sleds

      c. Dense, dark growth of trees and vines
         Unfriendly savage natives
         Wild animals

    EXERCISE: From an unsorted list of topics select two which are main topics and under each one list the related sub-topics.

    Shearing the wool
    Developing a new vaccine
    Examples of scientific progress
    Protecting the herd from coyotes
    Breaking the sound barrier
    Sheep ranching in the West
    Building an atomic submarine
    Taking the flock to pasture

D. Practice in Finding Main and Sub-Topics Within a Paragraph

1. In some paragraphs the author gives you certain word clues which help as guides in outlining. Words like "first," "next," "another," point out a listing of sub-topics. In the illustration below note the *outline form* which is used:

    There are good reasons for Denmark's success. *First*, the government encourages adult education. *Second*, it has established a reputation for excellent dairy products. A *third* reason is found in the cooperative farm.

    Outline I. Reasons for Denmark's success (main topic)
           A. Adult education (sub-topic)
           B. Reputation of dairy products (sub-topic)
           C. Cooperative farm societies (sub-topic)

EXERCISE: Outline the following paragraph in the same way.

There are some interesting facts to recall about Brazil. One is that it is the largest country in South America. It also has the mightiest river in the world. Another fact is that it produces two-thirds of the world's coffee.

2. Another type of paragraph lists events in a sequence. The author may give you outline helps by using such words as "after this," "later," "then."

Georgia was the last of the thirteen colonies to be settled. James Oglethorpe first received a land grant from the king. Then in 1733 he planted a colony at Savannah. At the end of twenty years, Georgia became a royal colony.

Outline: I. Settlement of Georgia
   A. Oglethorpe received land grant
   B. Colony begun at Savannah
   C. Royal colony in 1753

EXERCISE: Outline the following paragraph, using the time sequence as a guide.

Athenian boys were trained to have beautiful bodies. First, their bodies were well oiled. Then they spent hours at the wrestling grounds practicing many sports. After the exercise was over, they scraped off the oil and bathed in fresh water.

3. A third type of paragraph may indicate a comparison. It may point out likenesses and differences, advantages or disadvantages, causes and effects. You will now have two main ideas and will have to extend your outline:

Paraguay and Uruguay have little in common except their size. Paraguay is poor and isolated. It is landlocked and has no mineral wealth. It has many boundary disputes with its neighbors. Uruguay, on the other hand, has fine grassland for cattle raising, an excellent seaport, and is prosperous and progressive.

Outline: I. Paraguay a poor country
   A. Landlocked
   B. No mineral wealth
   C. Boundary disputes

   II. Uruguay a prosperous country
   A. Fine grassland
   B. Excellent seaport
   C. Progressive

EXERCISE: Outline the following paragraph, using two main topics.

Think how much farther advanced were the Europeans who discovered America than the natives they first found here. The Europeans had built wonderful churches and castles, had made great sea voyages, and given the world stories and poems. The Indians lived in tents or huts, wore skins or simply woven garments, and used the most primitive of tools.

E. Practice in Outlining Longer Selections

1. The following topics are from a selection about the Pony Express. Note how the related ideas suggest the main topics by the relationship of their common element.

Stagecoach and wagon trains slow
Boat around Cape Horn took months
No railroad past Missouri River
Pony Express from St. Joseph, Missouri to Sacramento, California
Covered 1900 miles in 8 days
Relays of men and horses used
Man rode 75 miles before resting
Carried mail in leather pouches
Braved weather and Indian dangers

Outline: I. Why a fast mail was needed
      A. Stagecoach and wagon trains slow
      B. Boat around Cape Horn took months
      C. No railroad past Missouri River
   II. How Pony Express worked
      A. Ran from St. Joseph, Mo. to Sacramento, Calif.
      B. Covered 1900 miles in 8 days
      C. Relays of men and horses used
  III. The Pony Express rider's life
      A. Rode 75 miles without resting
      B. Carried mail in leather pouches
      C. Braved weather and Indian dangers

2. Group the following notes, taken from a selection on *Our Forests*, in outline form. Use three main topics of your own.

Trees cut for construction of ships, building, furniture
For wood pulp to make paper
For mine props and railroad ties
Destruction by forest fire
Blighting due to disease and insects

Damage by storm, winds and ice
Experimentation with tree diseases
A system of fire prevention

3. When we take notes on a subject from more than one source, it is necessary to decide the order in which to outline the topics. In the following list of topics, number them in the order in which they should be listed to show the proper sequence of events.

(a) Unwinding the silk from the cocoon
Weaving the silk into fabric
Raising the silkworm
Selecting the best cocoon
"Weighting" the silk threads
Twisting the fine threads into one heavy one

(b) The gas light era
Burning sticks used as torches
The electric light bulb
Fish and whale oil in lamps
Animal fats used for candles

4. From the following unsorted list of topics on the life of George Washington, form an outline. Three of the topics are main topics. Decide their proper order before beginning the outline. (Topics 9 and 11 are sub-topics under 6)

(1) Advice on foreign entanglements
(2) Service in French and Indian War
(3) Career as a soldier
(4) Victory over British forces at Yorktown
(5) People's choice as president
(6) Early life in Virginia
(7) The winter at Valley Forge
(8) Washington, the statesman
(9) Desire to become a sailor
(10) Commander of American forces
(11) Work as a surveyor
(12) Leadership of a young nation

5. In organizing several broad topics in one outline, it is necessary to be sure that they are all related to one chief topic. Note how the three broad topics in the illustration are related to the chief topic expressed by the title.

I. How seeds are scattered by wind
II. Help of animals in dispersing seeds
III. How water carries seeds

Title: Seed Dispersal

6. Decide on a general topic for the following related topics and express it as a title.

   (a)   I.   Ancient superstitions about disease
          II.   Early scientific ideas about germs
        III.   Modern medical theories

   (b)   I.   Distrust among European nations
          II.   Nations pledged by opposing alliances
        III.   Rivalries over territories and trade

F. Using an Outline to Obtain a Better Understanding of a Selection After Reading

In the following illustration note how the topic sentences have been regrouped under main ideas. These in turn lead to a general conclusion or summary for the entire selection.

   I.   Man exchanged goods even in cave days.
       Tribes exchanged deer meat for arrowheads.
  II.   Man progressed from tribes to nations.
       Leaders seized power and territory.
       Man began to think in wider terms.
 III.   Trade between tribes became trade between nations.
       Exchange has developed slowly and steadily.
       Trade in world is now complex.

   I. Need for exchange always existed.
      A. _____
      B. _____
  II. Trading ideas grew with civilization.
      A. _____
      B. _____
      C. _____
 III. Man's complex world demands complex trade.
      A. _____
      B. _____

Main ideas summarized into one general statement: As man has changed from a simple way of life to a complex one, trade has changed from simple barter to a big business.

TEACHING HOW TO GRASP AN ORGANIZED UNDERSTANDING OF A LONGER UNIT

Children tend to "summarize" by reading a selection and copying verbatim the sentences which they consider important. They usually show poor discrimination, quoting unimportant details, omitting essential facts or missing the author's ideas completely. The ability to summarize intelligently, either mentally or in writing, depends of course upon the numerous reading skills already outlined, such as recognizing key thoughts, signal words, relevant and irrelevant details, etc. However, applying these skills in composing an adequate summary, combined with the ability to translate the author's words into one's own, is a separate technique. The following procedures are presented as aids toward its development:

A. Practice in Expressing a Single Idea in Briefer Form

1. Use the italicized key words to compose a summary sentence:

   In his annual message to Congress that year, the *President, James Monroe, issued* the *warning* which has since come to be known as the *Monroe Doctrine*.

   Summary: The Monroe Doctrine was a warning issued by President Monroe.

2. Select the key words yourself and use them in a summary sentence:

   A compound fracture, often incorrectly described as one where the bone is broken in two or more places, is actually one in which both bone and skin are broken.

B. Practice in Summarizing a Single Idea in the Reader's Own Words Instead of the Author's

Write a summary sentence, but express the italicized parts in words which you yourself might have used:

   Both of these organizations have *certain elements of strength* and *certain elements of weakness*.

Summary: Both organizations have their good and bad points.

   We should all be *informed*, at least in a general way, as to *what constitutes a legal offense*.

Summary: We should all know something about recognizing violations of the law.

(NOTE: Some exercises may require the use of the dictionary, a practice too often by-passed in composing summaries.)

C. *Practice in Summarizing a Long Sentence Briefly and in the Reader's Own Words*

Find the key words which indicate the main idea, then write a brief sentence in your own words to express it:

> Dr. Walter Reed was among the army doctors who were called in during the fight against yellow fever to determine whether, as many thought, the terrible disease was spread by the sting of a mosquito common in the tropics.

Summary: Dr. Walter Reed's job was to find out whether a certain mosquito was the cause of yellow fever.

D. *Practice in Summarizing a Paragraph*

Most paragraphs follow an idea or thought arrangement or pattern. The summary of a paragraph should follow the same arrangement. Recognition of the type of pattern is a definite guide for anticipating and composing an *adequate* summary.

1. Summarizing the paragraph which *lists* or *enumerates*

This type of paragraph includes, in its topic sentence, signal or guide words which tell you what kinds of details will be included. They may be: "for these reasons", "the principal causes", "in many ways", "several kinds of", "the parts of", etc. Your summary should include these details, stated *briefly* and *in your own words*.

> In recent years the people of the South have learned that they cannot depend entirely on the cotton crop, so they have turned *to other activities*. Near Birmingham, Alabama, there are many iron and steel foundries. In other sections we find lumber mills, as well as paper and pulp mills. Most important is the manufacturing of cotton cloth and other textiles, such as nylon.

Summary: Besides growing cotton, the South now manufactures iron and steel, lumber and paper, cotton cloth and other textiles.

2. Summarizing a paragraph which emphasizes a *time sequence*

The ideas in this type of paragraph follow a time order. Signal or clue words may be: "and this time", "the next step", "the first event", "the following year", "soon after", "finally", etc. In writing your summary use similar guide words to help you follow the thought pattern:

Before World War I, Germany was doing a huge business in world trade. *Then* her defeat in that war gave her trade a setback. She recovered *after a while,* but a second defeat in World War II destroyed her high rank in world trade for several years. *Then* she was allowed to resume her trading operations. *Today,* her ships are again seen in busy ports and the "Made in Germany" label is appearing on products in the world's markets.

Summary: *Before* World War I, Germany did a great deal of world trading. *Then* she was defeated in two wars and her trade suffered, but *today* she is again exchanging goods with the rest of the world.

3. Summarizing a paragraph in which the arrangement shows a *comparison of ideas*

   In this type of paragraph, the author may wish to point out causes and effects, likes and differences, conditions before and after an event, advantages and disadvantages, reasons for or against, etc. Your guide here will probably be *two topic sentences.* Your summary should also contain *two main ideas to show the comparison.* Signal words which will help are: "before and after", "some-others", "then-now", "once-today", "on the other hand", etc.:

   At one time, all the land which now makes up the state of Oklahoma was one great plain which was used for grazing. Ranchers from Texas *used to* drive their big herds of cattle up to feed on the good grass. While this is *still* fine grazing land, Oklahoma *now* uses much of it for the growing of cotton.

   Summary: *At one time* Oklahoma's land was used only for grazing, but *now* it is used for cotton growing as well.

4. Summarizing a paragraph in which the author's aim is to give a *reason or explanation* of his main idea.

   In this type of paragraph you may be guided by signal words or phrases such as: "because", "for this reason", "due to this", "therefore", "on account of", "as a result", etc. These indicate that your summary should include the reason, *stated briefly* and *in your own words.* Using similar guide words in your summary will help you to follow the author's idea:

   When Hitler offered peace terms to Great Britain, the British people knew that they could not accept them. He promised to leave the British Empire intact, although Germany was to keep the land which she had already conquered. *Because* they had learned, through a sad experience at Munich, that Hitler's promises were worthless, the British rejected his offer now.

Summary: The British people turned down Hitler's peace terms *because* they knew from experience that he would not keep his promise.

E. Supplementary Exercises

1. Anticipate from these key sentences whether your summary would *list details, show a comparison, show sequence* of events, or *give a reason*:

   a. The embargo had some disastrous effects on the welfare of the city. (A list)

   b. Life in the city may have more difficulties than life on a farm. (A comparison)

   c. The farmer who grows wheat has his own special worries. (A list)

   d. Creating a beautiful statue is a slow, painstaking process. (A sequence)

   e. Their spokesman was ready to justify their rebellious acts. (Reasons)

   f. There are arguments for and against fluoridation of our water supply. (A comparison)

2. Read the selection, then choose the sentence which you think summarizes it best. Explain why the others are inadequate.

   There are definite reasons why anthracite coal costs more than bituminous. First, it is found chiefly in only one region of our country. Therefore, when it is carried to other places, there is the added cost of railway transportation. Second, there is not a large supply in any one section of the region where it is found, and mining operations must be set up in each place. Finally, it is difficult to mine because the seams are not near the surface of the earth. It could be mined more cheaply if it were easier to find and bring to the surface. Then it could be sold at a lower price.

   a. There are several reasons why anthracite costs more to mine than other coal.
   b. Anthracite is more expensive than bituminous because: *first*, it must be transported to many places; *second*, it is not abundant in any one place, and *third*, it is difficult to mine.
   c. Anthracite coal is expensive because it is very difficult to mine.

3. Skill in using the newspaper will be helpful in learning how to summarize. Newspaper men remember that "news rises to the top

like cream on the milk". Their summary appears in the lead paragraph, telling the why, who, what, and where of the news story. Practice writing a first paragraph for a news story.

4. Practice with selections from narrative and descriptive poems, by writing your own summary of the author's idea.
   Hiawatha, Paul Revere's Ride, Robin Hood, Evangeline

E. Appraising the Results of Remediation

26. AN APPRAISAL OF CORRECTIVE AND REMEDIAL PROCEDURES IN INTERPRETATION

Ruth Strang

The best corrective and remedial procedures in improving interpretation are developmental. That is, the most effective remediation (1) is based on diagnosis of the student's present performance in interpreting different kinds of passages, (2) begins where the student is, and (3) from that point follows, step by step, sound developmental sequences.

For example, Patricia, an attractive, socially poised girl of fourteen, was seriously retarded in reading. Her interpretation of words and paragraphs was fantastic. She seemed to think that any response, however wild, was better than none—it might cover up her lack of knowledge. She was embarrassed when called upon to read aloud in class and even tried to hide from the reading teacher her basic lack of word-recognition skills. One of her assets was a good oral vocabulary. Growing up in a cultured family, she had learned to hold up her end of a conversation.

Remedial work to improve her interpretation began with her basic attitude toward reading. It was necessary for her to learn that printed words had meaning, use, and purpose for her—a fact which she should have learned in Grade I. Her present teacher took advantage of every

Reprinted from *Promoting Growth Toward Maturity in Interpreting What Is Read,* W. S. Gray, Compiler and Editor, Supplementary Educational Monographs No. 74, pp. 201–205. By permission of the University of Chicago Press, copyright 1951 by the University of Chicago Press.

opportunity to give her experiences in which correct interpretation of printed matter made a real difference: looking up a friend's telephone number, reading a menu, reading directions for knitting a sweater, finding a funny story to tell to the group. Next Patricia went through the stage of learning basic word-recognition skills, following many of the methods so clearly described in Gray's *On Your Own in Reading.*[1] By beginning with words already included in her oral vocabulary, she made rapid progress in this difficult task of clarifying the confused associations she had formed in her frantic attempts to "give the right answer." Only after she had acquired the basic ability to comprehend the literal meaning of words was it possible to move into the more subtle aspects of interpretation. Once Patricia had accepted this developmental approach, she was willing to begin where her difficulties in interpretation originated and to move through the developmental stages which, for one reason or another, she had skipped or neglected.

Another generalization that might well be made at the beginning is that the most natural remedial procedures are the best. In support of this view, Richards emphasizes the fact that language is mastered most readily through its use and in the pursuit of meaning.[2] One might imagine a scale with the most natural procedures at one end and the most artificial at the other. Natural procedures would include stopping to interpret a word, a metaphor, or a sentence while reading, translating it into one's own words, making comparisons between meanings, and organizing or systematizing scattered perceptions of meaning. Artificial procedures might be typified by drill on a list of words.

Within the developmental sequence for different individuals, a variety of procedures will be helpful. Let us begin with those on the most natural end of the scale suggested above. From there we will proceed to the more formal methods used in improving interpretation.

BACKGROUND FOR INTERPRETATION

What experiences do the students have that will help them interpret the meaning of the passages they read? What new experiences can the teacher offer them? Each word in their vocabulary has acquired its meaning from a series of experiences. Remedial work in interpretation means providing the individual with relevant experiences.

In the primary grades, the teacher who inherits a group of children who think of reading as word-calling makes a special effort to see that experience precedes reading. Similarly in the upper grades, the ingenious

---

[1] William S. Gray, *On Your Own in Reading.* Chicago: Scott, Foresman & Co., 1948.

[2] I. A. Richards, *How to Read a Page,* pp. 53–54. New York: W. W. Norton & Co., 1942.

teacher will provide as many firsthand experiences as possible: field trips, handcraft, simple experiments in science, spontaneous dramatizations, or sociodrama. At all ages, the pooling of experiences is the next best prelude to reading.

In a junior high school class of retarded readers, filmstrips were skilfully used to aid interpretation. For example, in the Eye Gate House filmstrip "Rip Van Winkle," one slide showed Rip's wife going after him with a rolling pin. Underneath the picture was the statement that Rip's wife was a *termagant*. Apparently this situation was familiar to these boys; none of them had any difficulty in interpreting this word. The mimeographed questions which the pupils answered after viewing the filmstrip were directed toward the practical interpretation of the story. Among them were the following:

> What kind of person was Rip Van Winkle?
> Which of his characteristics annoyed his wife?
> What does the word *termagant* mean as used here?
> Why did he go with his dog into the mountains?
> What kind of story is this—a true story, a fanciful story, a tall tale, a fable?

In a high-school group, motion pictures were used to give background for the reading of Shakespeare, Dickens, and Scott. Whenever possible, retarded readers should see a worth-while film treatment of the book they are about to read. The motion picture gives them a visual acquaintance with the setting, the times, and the people, which is then enriched by the reading of the book. By this means pupils also become aware of the special contribution of motion pictures and of books.

WRITING, LISTENING, AND SPEAKING: AIDS TO INTERPRETATION

Since interpretation has its roots in experience, remedial measures that begin with "experience reading" are sound. It is common practice in the primary grades to use the children's own dictated "stories" as reading material. Elementary pupils make their own single-word picture-books and books recording discussions or accounts of experiences. Though less frequently used with older children and adolescents, this procedure remains effective.

Writing aids interpretation in another way. In order to interpret skilfully, the reader must be almost as creative as the writer; he must go through a similar process. He sees reading as discovery. He discovers the structure of thought which the author has created. In reading poetry, he sees the pictures, hears the sounds, experiences the feelings that the author wanted to convey. In the field of science, the reader follows the scientific method; to make his hypothesis or generalization, he gathers facts from the printed page in much the same way that the author gathered the facts from firsthand experience. Practice in constructing clear paragraphs, in writing reports of documentary plays, and reports of experiments, descriptions of how to make and do things, gives the reader experience on the sending end of the communication process. From this experience he derives a critical attitude toward the reading of newspapers, magazines, and books.

Listening improves interpretation in a similar fashion: the skilful listener has a clear purpose, raises questions, anticipates answers, relates and reviews main points, and is alert to implied meanings. As the pupil becomes more experienced in listening, he has less difficulty in interpreting printed material. Killgallon[3] suggested the use of recordings that give a progression of experiences: commercials of the patent medicine type; other commercials; radio oratory of many kinds, including addresses by a scientist, a politician, "a man with a cause"; a fine professional reading of parts of a play, poem, or story. Interpretation of the spoken word makes a pleasant introduction to the interpretation of printed material.

Speaking also underlies the interpretation of printed matter. In the primary grades, children interpret their first printed words and sentences in the light of the associations which they have formed with spoken words. Through practice in oral language, they learn to organize and express their thoughts. This ability is basic to reading. If an individual has not learned to express his own ideas, he is not ready to interpret an author's ideas. For such a person, remedial work should begin with the building of oral-language patterns. He should have interesting experiences to relate or discuss, should feel a need to explain his ideas to other persons, should have frequent opportunities for conversation, and should read selections related to his experiences.

INTERPRETATION WHILE READING

Practice in interpretation is most effective when given in context. When a class encounters an unfamiliar word, a pictorial phrase, a metaphor, it is often profitable to take time out for interpretation. Individuals may pool their impressions of the word, describe the images evoked by the pictorial phrase, and discuss the kinds of comparisons implied in the metaphor. Thus, they will bring out clearly the many potential meanings, associations, and feelings which are involved. They can track down the literal meaning of a word and try to see how other meanings have become attached to it.

[3] Pat Killgallon, "Recorded Sound Aids," *Elementary English*, *XXVII* (March, 1950), 174–75.

If they first study, the more obvious figures of speech such as are found in slang ("out like a light"), in advertisements ("Is coffee your Waterloo?"), and in newspaper headlines, they will begin to understand the kinds of jobs words do. They will recognize the feelings attached to certain words and will understand why writers, especially poets, select words for their power to produce emotional response.[4]

CHECKING INTERPRETATION

Interpretation can be checked in a number of ways: by means of drawings, freely written responses, discussion, answers to questions, introspective reports, and action. The drawings made by little children constitute one of the most effective and interesting ways of checking their interpretation of what they have read. Their drawings indicate the elements that have been most meaningful to them, and also reveal their misconceptions. One child in Sunday school expressed his concept of the flight into Egypt by drawing an airplane with four figures in it. Three of them—Mary, Joseph, and the Babe—were identified by their halos. When asked "Who is the fourth person?" he replied, "That is Pontius, the pilot." Such drawings indicate possible misinterpretations. In the upper grades, asking the pupils to draw diagrams or charts is a useful way to test the accuracy of their interpretation of technical material.

Freely written responses explaining more fully the meaning of a word, phrase, sentence, or longer passage reveal the adequacy of students' interpretation of printed material. It often requires a paragraph or more to explain a single word in context. The student starts with the primary, concrete meaning of the word, and describes the object or action to which it originally referred. He then traces the shifts which its meaning has undergone. Finally, he discusses the meaning which the word has for him in its present context. Phrases, sentences, and whole paragraphs can be similarly dealt with.

Discussion is a generally enjoyable way of checking students' interpretation. Alm[5] described a book discussion which used the small group or "buzz session" technique. The class had all read or listened to several stories about family life which they then discussed in small groups. This sharing of responses deepened individual students' interpretation of the books and resulted in keener insight concerning the lives of the characters discussed.

Questions may be used in connection with discussion or as an additional check on comprehension. The questions may be directed toward

[4] Edward F. Gordon, "Teaching Students To Read Verse," *English Journal*, XXXIX (March, 1950), 149–54.

[5] Richard S. Alm, "Buzz Sessions about Books," *English Journal*, XL (January, 1951), pp. 12–15.

any aspect of interpretation. For example, some questions may call for interpretation of the author's mood, intent, and purpose. Other questions may focus on the meaning of words and phrases—literal meaning, word origin, and connotations. Many questions will concern the actions of characters—why they behave as they do. Other questions may emphasize critical reading—the inferences or generalizations that may be made and the evidence supporting them.

Introspective reports are also enlightening; they often reveal misinterpretations. Smith[6] has given an excellent illustration of a fifth-grade boy's misinterpretation of Lincoln's "Gettysburg Address." His limited concepts made it impossible for him to get its deep significance.

Interpretation can sometimes be checked by action. Children in the elementary grades may fail to carry out their committee responsibilities or may fail to be in the right place at the right time, because they have not accurately read the notices on the blackboard or bulletin board. Failure to understand a recipe may result in a strange culinary product. Inability to interpret the specifications in shop or in a chemistry laboratory, or to follow directions for building a radio, becomes evident in the student's practical work.

INSTRUCTION AND DRILL IN INTERPRETATION

It is helpful for the student to have awareness of the process of interpretation. Practice is not enough. As he has experiences in interpretation, such as have been described, the student needs to develop methods of interpretation which he can apply in many other situations. Students may be given instruction in interpretation before being exposed to a new experience. After students have tried to interpret a passage, they can describe the methods that seemed to get the best results.

Although the natural, developmental methods are generally the most effective, occasionally there is place for drill on separate aspects of interpretation. Children in the primary grades may need drill in word recognition. In the army reading program, a filmstrip was used to teach basic words in geography.[7] One section illustrated words related to the land (*continent, mountain, plain, desert*); another pictured words referring to water (*ocean, river, lake*). An exercise interesting to high-school and college students is one in which the meaning of an unknown word can be learned from the context.

Drills on the more subtle aspects of interpretation have also been constructed on the multiple-choice pattern. The danger is that drill of

[6] Nila Banton Smith, "Reading: Concept Development," *Education*, LXX (May, 1950), pp. 549–50.

[7] Paul Witty, "Reading of Social Studies Materials," *Elementary English*, XXVII (January, 1950), p. 4.

this kind may attempt to express subtle relationships by means of stereo-typed replies. It would be better, as already suggested, to express these more complicated aspects of interpretation in freely written responses or discussions.

Concluding Statement

Methods for improving interpretation cover a wide range from the most natural to the most artificial, from the most analytical to the most superficial. Since interpretation is part of the total reading process, and reading is part of the total development of the individual, remedial procedures are necessarily developmental; as such, they are often subtle and complex.

27. INTERPRETATION OF THE RESULTS OF STANDARDIZED READING TESTS

Jeanne S. Chall

Essentially, tests are only samples of behavior and measure only what a person does at a particular time and place. Some people do their best reading on tests; others do their poorest.[1] In interpreting the test results of a *class* or *school*, the "best" and "worst" performances may balance out, and the average scores may represent the group's actual perform-ance. For the individual pupil, however, it is well to remember that his test performance is only a sample of his daily functioning, and the sample may be biased. Furthermore, tests are samples of the particular skill or ability tested. Reading is a complex of skills encompassing many general and specific abilities, understandings, and attitudes. Although standardized reading tests purport to measure the most important as-pects of reading, they lag behind our recognition of these factors at all levels.

The reading readiness tests correlate positively, but not perfectly, with success in beginning reading. It is therefore not surprising to find

Reprinted from *Evaluation of Reading*, Helen M. Robinson, Compiler and Editor, Supplementary Educational Monographs No. 88, pp. 133–138. By permission of the University of Chicago Press, copyright 1958 by the University of Chicago Press.

[1] Alex C. Sherriffs and Donald S. Boomer, "Who Is Penalized by the Penalty for Guessing?" *Journal of Educational Psychology*, XLV (February, 1954), pp. 81–90.

that Mary, who scored below average on the readiness test, is more advanced at the end of the first grade than John, who scored above average. The high school or college student who scores below the mean on a standardized reading test may in fact be a better reader, from the viewpoint of integrating and using what he has read, than the student who scores above the mean.

The assumptions that standardized test results may not always be unbiased samples of a student's reading ability and that the standardized reading tests do not measure all the important objectives of reading instruction, especially for a particular school,[2] often lead to rejection of standardized tests in favor of informal teacher observations. However, standardized reading tests, even with their limitations, can make an important contribution to reading instruction. The remainder of this paper will suggest how the results of standardized reading tests can be interpreted to evaluate, first, achievement and, second, instructional needs.

TEST RESULTS AS MEASURES OF ACHIEVEMENT

The most common use of standardized reading tests is to determine over-all reading achievement of individuals and groups in comparison to that of the general population. The grade levels or percentile ranks afford both a measure of achievement and a comparison with the population on which the test is standardized. The results reveal the level in reading achievement of a school system, a class, or an individual. But what we do not know is how "good" or "bad" the results are. For this, we must take into account the capacities of the students. Test scores alone tell us "how much" but not "how good."

For example, if one third-grade class in a school averages at grade 3.9 on a reading test, and another at only 2.8, we cannot, from this information alone, determine which can be more proud of its achievement. By merely scoring at the national norm, the first class may not be doing well enough, since the children may be superior in intelligence and should be achieving even higher. The class that scored below the national norms may be below normal in intelligence and may, in fact, be achieving even better than the first in terms of capacities of the children.

Since the capacities of poor readers are often underestimated, their low reading achievement may appear justified. According to expectancy formulas, pupils may appear to be achieving up to their capacities. Also, since children are selected for remedial and corrective programs on the basis of discrepancies between their intelligence quotients and reading,

[2] Walter W. Cook, "Tests, Achievement," in Walter S. Monroe (ed.), *Encyclopedia of Educational Research*, pp. 1461–78. New York: Macmillan Co., 1950.

the children who have "low" intelligence quotients because of poor reading will be penalized further. We often reason erroneously that children achieve below grade level in reading because their intelligence quotients are low. The truer picture is that in many instances their intelligence quotients, as revealed by group tests, are low because their reading is so poor.

LIMITED RANGE OF READING TESTS

Standardized reading tests designed for a few grades frequently give a distorted picture of reading achievement, particularly at the extremes among the poorest and the best readers. The selections and vocabulary are suitable for typical students in those grades. Hence, if students are significantly retarded or advanced for their grade, they will be unable to reveal their true achievement levels.

It may well be that the usual finding that bright children do not work up to potential is sometimes due to the restrictions at the upper levels of achievement tests. The best achievers cannot show how well they can really read because they can complete all items.

It would be well to select tests for those who achieve at the extremes on the basis of their estimated reading level rather than their grade placement. Two or three levels of standard tests may have to be given to one grade if the range of reading is wide. Where this cannot be done, the lowest achievers should be retested on lower level tests and the highest achievers on tests designed for higher grades.

THE INFLUENCE OF RATE

Slow readers, especially above the primary grades, often find it impossible to complete the test before time is called. For this reason, some tests now give longer time limits. Some even have separate sections that are designed to measure rate of reading. However, unless the time limits on vocabulary and comprehension are long, the scores of slow readers will be affected adversely.

To illustrate, the following were culled from test batteries of three children who were given additional time to complete their tests:

Reading Comprehension Tests with:	Level of Test	Standard Time Grade	Untimed Scores
1. Ample time limits	For Grades V–VI	5.0	6.2
2. Ample time limits	For Grades V–VI	4.9	6.2
3. Very short time limits	For Grades IV–VIII	7.3	11.2+

Which of the foregoing are the truer scores? If our purpose is to measure power of comprehension, then the higher ones are probably more accurate. When a school uses tests with short time limits, perhaps some adjustment can be made to permit those students to finish who think they can continue. A test may be scored both with and without time limits by drawing a line under the last item completed within the specified time. Such dual scoring gives additional information about instructional needs.

TEST RESULTS AS INDICATORS OF INSTRUCTIONAL NEEDS

The grade equivalents from standardized reading tests can give clues to selecting appropriate reading materials, to suggesting the level and type of reading instruction, and to grouping of students.

The grade scores from the reading comprehension subtests of survey and analytic tests indicate the general level of difficulty of material that can be read. In most instances a score of 4.5 indicates that a pupil can read with a reasonable degree of facility and understanding material on a fourth-grade level of difficulty. If a junior college freshman averages only ninth-grade reading level, it means that his textbooks should be easier than those published for average college freshmen. Therefore, the grade level scores from standardized tests can help the teacher set the level of basic reading instruction. If groups are formed, the grade scores can be used as the first approximation of the level of the basal reader most suitable for that group.

Some teachers assume that the standardized test scores indicate a pupil's frustration level or top level of performance and have therefore selected readers on a grade lower than the standardized test scores. This may not always be wise, since for many children, especially those who lack confidence or have an unusually slow rate of reading, the standardized scores may give a minimal estimate of performance. Such children can actually benefit more from a higher level of materials. Informal tests on the basal readers should supplement the standardized scores in order that children be given instruction neither too difficult nor too easy for them. This is especially important for retarded readers, who may be discouraged further by basal readers several grades below their maturity levels.

DIAGNOSTIC INTERPRETATION FOR GROUPS AND INDIVIDUALS

The most penetrating kind of interpretation of standardized test results is concerned with the pupil's strengths and weaknesses in reading. To answer questions about specific aspects of reading achievement, the analytic or diagnostic type tests, with separate subtests, are especially useful. However, even the survey tests (the usual reading tests on achievement batteries), if studied and interpreted carefully and supplemented with oral reading tests or just "listening" to the pupil read, can be used to diagnose specific needs.

Limitations of space prevent my going further into this particular aspect of interpretation. However, some basic issues which should be considered suggestive will be discussed.

DIAGNOSTIC INTERPRETATION AT THE ELEMENTARY SCHOOL LEVEL

Most reading readiness tests afford a separate evaluation of knowledge of concepts, understanding of directions, visual discrimination, auditory discrimination, and visual-motor co-ordination (copying). These subtests are usually too short to give a reliable index of each aspect of readiness, but they can give the teacher a clue to weaknesses that can be observed more thoroughly by informal tests. For example, if a child scores low on the visual discrimination subtest, his teacher can look for this deficiency in class activities in matching of pictures, forms, words, and letters.

Recent findings on the importance of visual[4] and auditory discrimination[5] for success in beginning reading suggest that the results from these particular subtests should be studied carefully to locate those children who may be weak in these areas.

In general, the readiness subtests can be divided into two areas— language background and specific auditory-visual skills. These two areas are not highly intercorrelated, and if a child is high on one and low on the other, the kind of instruction needed to get him "ready" would differ. If a child is high in language background and low on auditory and visual skills, he may not need the enriched experiential background usually considered a must for "low readiness" children. He may, instead, need more concentrated help in matching words and letters and in listening for rhymes and beginning sounds.

On the primary, intermediate, and upper elementary levels, most of the standardized silent reading tests contain only two subtests—word meaning and paragraph reading. Separate grade scores are derived for each subtest. Usually the two scores are fairly close to one another. However, it is not uncommon to find significant discrepancies between the subtests. Some children may score considerably lower on the word

---

[4] Jean Turner Goins, *Visual Perceptual Abilities and Early Reading Progress.* Supplementary Educational Monographs, No. 87. Chicago: University of Chicago Press, 1958.

[5] Donald D. Durrell *et al.,* "Success in First Grade Reading," *Journal of Education,* CXL (February, 1958), 1–48.

meaning subtest than on the paragraph reading part. What does this mean? If we consider only the names of the subtests, we may infer that the pupil needs help in word meanings and that general comprehension will also improve if the child's meaning vocabulary is expanded. However, in some instances his meaning vocabulary is quite extensive for his age, but he cannot recognize the words. Thus faulty word recognition may lie behind the low word meaning score. On the paragraph comprehension subtest, context may be used to arrive at general meaning. Thus paragraph comprehension scores may not be affected as much by poor word recognition, especially for brighter pupils. A standardized or informal oral reading test, together with a diagnostic test of word analysis skills, can determine whether the problem is primarily word recognition, word meaning, or comprehension. If the oral reading score is low and word analysis skills limited in a child with normal or above normal intelligence, we can usually infer that the major problem is not comprehension but probably still word recognition.[6]

On the other hand, higher scores on oral reading tests together with significantly lower scores on silent reading tests may indicate a need for help in comprehension and rate. However, here too, especially if the pupil has normal intelligence, the lower silent reading test scores may reflect a difficulty in working independently or in concentration—abilities needed for completing a standardized silent reading test.

As mentioned earlier, beginning with intermediate grade levels, rate becomes an important factor to consider. Power of comprehension may be considerably underestimated if the time limits are short. Since reading instruction would differ depending upon whether the major problem is rate or comprehension, it is well to analyze the scores and the test booklets to see whether rate is a problem.

What about the diagnostic and analytic tests that give separate grade scores for word meaning, different kinds of comprehension, rate, and study skills? The profiles of scores on such tests can help pinpoint strengths and weaknesses. Thus it may be found that a group of eighth-grade pupils score high on comprehension of details and low on comprehension of main ideas and critical reading. Appropriate steps can then be taken to remedy their weaknesses. However, for very poor readers, the discrepancies in scores may reflect not so much the specific weaknesses in different kinds of comprehension and study skills but a more fundamental deficit in reading skills. Each of the analytic tests requires a minimal reading ability to make the subtest scores meaningful. If the pupil still has difficulty in reading the words, the weaknesses indicated by the tests may not be too helpful for remedial purposes.

[6] Jeanne S. Chall, "The Roswell-Chall Diagnostic Reading Test of Word Analysis Skills: Evidence of Reliability and Validity," *Reading Teacher,* XI (February, 1958), pp. 179–83.

Diagnostic Interpretation at High School and College Levels

Most standardized reading tests at this level are of the analytic type with many subtests. The same points about analytic tests made above for the upper elementary tests are relevant here as well. At the high school and college levels the content of the tests and methods of testing rate and comprehension vary so much that careful interpretation is needed.

Some tests contain passages of a general nature; others contain only social science and natural science materials. It is therefore more essential than for the elementary levels to study carefully the test manuals and the critical reviews in order to interpret what the results mean for instructional goals.

Some of the tests for high school and college students have unusually short time limits on all subtests. For example, one student in Grade XII scored at the fourth-grade level on rate, fifth grade on comprehension, and sixth grade on word meaning.

To show how rate can influence comprehension scores on a test, I administered to him two subtests of a silent reading test widely used in high schools and junior colleges. This test has short time limits. He was given as much time as he needed, however. The subtests were then scored two ways—according to the standard time allotted and by the additional time he needed. The following were his percentile ranks on the word meaning and paragraph reading subtests:

	Percentile Rank— Twelfth-Grade Norms	
	Timed—standard testing procedures	Untimed—given time to complete the subtest
Word meaning	5	58
Paragraph comprehension	1	74

When given as much time as he needed, he was able to achieve average scores for his grade.

Since a deficiency in comprehension is usually associated with lack of intelligence, it is essential that we measure power of comprehension which is not influenced by rate.

Concluding Statement

There is more to interpreting the results of standardized tests than drawing profiles of grade scores or percentile ranks arrived at miraculously by modern scoring machines. As in medical diagnosis, the final decision about what the scores mean rests with human interpretation. The data secured from our more elaborate tests must ultimately gain their meaning and wise use from the teacher, the psychologist, and the administrator.

28. THE READING HABITS, ATTITUDES, AND ACHIEVEMENTS OF HIGH SCHOOL DROPOUTS

Harold Newman

Because poor readers, many of whom are high school dropouts, face a bleak unemployment future, school systems throughout the country have launched reading improvement programs. Although published evaluations of such programs are not infrequent, the author is not aware of any published follow-up study of vocational high school students who dropped out of school after having received remediation in reading.

This article will be limited to a consideration of the reading attitudes, habits, and achievements of students who became dropouts subsequent to remediation. To provide the reader with a more meaningful context, it will be necessary to give some important preliminary information.

Group Studied

Out of a total of 184 students who were enrolled in the author's remedial reading classes between September, 1958 and June, 1961, there were 51 who dropped out of school after receiving an average of thirteen months' instruction in reading. Thirty-four of these were accessible and available for participation in this study. Data obtained from these students' cumulative record cards, information secured from personal interviews, and standardized reading test scores comprised the materials used in this report. At the time they were interviewed, the median number of years that had elapsed since remediation was 3.0.

The subjects, all of whom lived in a lower socio-economic area of South Jamaica, ranged in age from twenty to twenty-three. Only five came from broken homes and, surprisingly, within the last four years, not a single family had moved out of the immediate neighborhood. The

Reprinted from *High Points*, Vol. 48 (March 1966), pp. 36–48. By permission of the New York City Board of Education.

formal education of their parents was limited in large part to the elementary school. Both parents of only three dropouts had completed high school. None had supplemented their education by taking evening courses. The principal wage earner in all but two cases was the father. Most of the mothers remained home to take care of their children. None of the fathers was engaged in highly skilled, proprietary, or professional jobs. With the exception of one who was unemployed, all worked at a trade requiring semi-skilled or unskilled labor.

Prior to entering high school, 24 dropouts had been placed in slow learners' classes. Six had been classified as mentally retarded. Once having entered high school, they experienced academic failure in many of their subjects during their entire school attendance. Only two dropouts achieved passing marks in all subjects, whereas 32 of them failed more than half. The one purely vocational subject, shop, was failed as frequently as were academic subjects.

Of the 34 dropouts, five had been reported by their teachers as being severe behavior problems. Among the infractions which their teachers had reported to the dean were using abusive language, disrupting classes, fighting, stealing, and cutting classes. Although the majority of these school leavers were not on the dean's blacklist, many were rated as unsatisfactory in citizenship by most of their teachers.

The median age of the subjects in this study who left school was 18—the peak period of withdrawal occurring between completion of the tenth grade and the first semester of the eleventh grade.

Adverse school experiences were mentioned as reasons for leaving school more frequently than all other reasons combined. Lack of interest in school work, dissatisfaction with the manner in which subjects were taught, poor marks, unsatisfactory relations with the school staff and classmates were among the reasons given for dissatisfaction and frustration in school. Financial reasons for withdrawing included the desire to obtain jobs in order to become self-sufficient or to contribute to the support of their parents. Other reasons mentioned less frequently were parent negativism to their remaining in school and the desire to have a good time with their friends.

This tabulation of factors associated with school dropoutism is obviously oversimplified since dropping out of school is seldom traceable to a single factor. This decision usually results from an accumulation of various experiences, attitudes, and pressures over a period of time.

Motives for Wanting to Improve Reading

In order to ascertain whether the dropouts had any special reasons for wanting to improve their reading, the author asked: "Do you want to improve your reading? If so, why?" Only one dropout answered in the negative. Most dropouts gave two or more reasons for wanting to improve their reading. From among the reasons given in Table I, those dealing with furthering one's vocational status received the widest response. Every dropout was keenly aware that his prospects for getting a job and advancing on his job depended on his ability to read well.

TABLE I

The Dropouts' Motives for Improving Their Reading

Motive	*Number of Responses
Improvement of vocational status	34
Satisfaction of basic personal needs	19
Meeting social demands	18
Others	15

*Total number of responses exceeds number of dropouts because of multiple responses.

The satisfaction of certain personal needs of daily living was another strong incentive to reading improvement. Being able to read signs and maps, passing a driver's test, reading contracts to avoid getting "stuck" when purchasing a car, building a hot rod car, etc. are included in this category.

Social satisfactions sought through improvement in reading skills were the desire to understand what other people were talking about, taking part in social conversation, and reading and writing letters.

Among the responses tabulated under "Others" were such desiderata as being able to understand books and articles on a variety of subjects, and the ability to read difficult words faster.

A certain amount of caution should be exercised in accepting the opinions and conclusions of dropouts as fact. There is always a chance that their perceptions may be affected by a desire to invest their statements with a halo of respectability. Taken at face value their statements seem plausible and realistic. Unfortunately, however, there is a wide gap between what one intends to do or what one knows he must do and what he actually does. During the interval of time which had elapsed between their leaving school and the date of the interview, only four dropouts had had additional schooling. One dropout whose reading was seventh grade was able to pass a correspondence course while serving in the United States Navy.

None were engaged in job training programs, either because the jobs in which they were engaged didn't have any or because they did not have the basic educational requirements to succeed in them. None of the dropouts were seeking or receiving special help designed to improve their reading ability. Since opportunities for advancement in jobs sought required a higher level of reading ability than the dropouts possessed, it is difficult to see how they could attain these positions.

The Extent and Nature of Their Reading

One of the aims of remedial reading instruction in the author's classes was to foster an interest in reading as a means of obtaining information and pleasure. In the curriculum research report, *Reading in The Secondary Schools*, the chief reason for stressing the improvement of reading is "to establish the place of reading as a factor in the student's life." What role does reading play in the lives of the girls and boys who left school? The author asked each dropout several questions designed to elicit information concerning the amount of time they spent reading and the extent and nature of their reading of books, newspapers, magazines, and comic books.

A glance at Table II shows the total amount of time which the dropouts said they spent in their daily reading. The average amount of time which the non-graduates spent "yesterday" was twenty-one minutes whereas the usual amount of time averaged twenty-five minutes. It is difficult to say which of the two, time spent reading "yesterday" or "usual" time spent reading, is the more reliable answer.

TABLE II

Approximate Time Which Dropouts Devoted
to Their Daily Reading

Number of Minutes	Number of cases Yesterday	Usually
0	3	5
5-10	3	10
15-20	8	3
21-30	6	8
More	4	8

The dropouts confine their newspaper reading to the *Daily News* and the *Long Island Press*—newspapers which contain an abundance of pictorial material and appeal to the dramatic and the sensational. The extent of their reading is indicated in Table III. Asked to indicate what part of the newspaper interested them most, they cited local news, world news, sports, and comics in that order. The respondents candidly admitted . that they were most interested in reading articles on gossip, accidents, rape, murder, robbery, and fires; in short, the lurid and the sensational. The second most popular part of the newspaper dealt with the international scene. Of the respondents who had cited this section as their first or second choice, only two were knowledgeable about the current scene. Those who read the sports section did so to obtain the latest information about a particular sport; for example, boxing, baseball, or basketball. They knew their subject well. The dropouts who read comics regularly were among the poorest readers.

Table III shows the extent of the dropouts' reading of magazines. Among the magazines read were these:

MAGAZINES ABOUT CARS		PICTORIAL MAGAZINES	
Hot Rod	6	Look	6
Custom Craft	1	Life	4
Car Craft	1	Ebony	4
Motor Trends	1	Jive	1
Speed Machines	1	Jet	1
Cars Illustrated	1		
MAGAZINES OF ROMANCE		SPORTS AND HOBBY MAGAZINES	
True Confessions	2	Field and Stream	1
Love	1	Outdoor Sports	1
Secret Romance	1	T.V. and Radio	1
Movie Glamour	1	Popular Mechanics	1

TABLE III

Distribution of Responses Concerning the Frequency of
Reading Printed Matter

Type of Material	Frequency		
	Regular	Occasionally	Never
Newspapers	15	15	4
Magazines	9	13	12
Comic books	5	9	20

Ebony and *Jive* are magazines featuring Negro news and personalities. *Hot Rod, Custom Craft, Cars Illustrated,* and *Speed Machines* feature new developments in car construction and design. *Secret Romance, True Confessions,* and *Love* contain intimate stories, usually of an autobiographical nature.

The one thing that virtually all of these magazines have in common is an abundance of pictures. The dropouts maintained that pictures made what they read come alive. They also made for easier reading. Magazines like *Hot Rod, Popular Mechanics,* and *Motor Trends,* are not easy reading. But the dropouts admitted that they did get something out of reading these magazines because of their ability to read and interpret diagrams. What knowledge did those who read *Life, Look, Ebony,* and

Jet derive from their reading? The author is of the opinion that the readers of these magazines browsed through them in a superficial manner, paying more attention to pictures than to print. When asked to tell what article they had read in the magazine of their choice, most of the dropouts answered with a blank stare. It would appear that although these magazines do contain articles of genuine merit, they are rarely read. In general, the dropouts' reading of magazines was spotty, unselective, and uncritical.

An inspection of Table III shows that comic book reading is least popular. Among the comic books regularly read were *Superman, Batman, Flash Detective, Bugs Bunny, Donald Duck,* and *Sad Sack.*

Only seven dropouts reported reading a book at the time they were interviewed. Three said they were "brushing up" on math, science, and shop in order to become more knowledgeable about these subjects. Another boy said he was reading *Blackbeard, the Pirate,* an "easy" book. One girl was reading a mystery story. When the author asked these dropouts to briefly describe what they enjoyed most about these books, only one seemed able to respond in a meaningful way. It seemed to the author upon further questioning that six of the dropouts may have merely thumbed through the books they claimed to have read. Among the twenty-four dropouts who were not reading a book at the time they were interviewed, eight said they hadn't read a book subsequent to leaving the reading class, and seven confessed that they had never completed a book in their lives.

It would appear then that reading plays an unimportant role in the lives of almost all of these former students. Much of their reading is superficial and unselective and it is doubtful that it could contribute very much to their cultural development.

Their Reading Achievement

In accordance with a requirement of the Vocational High School Division of the New York City Board of Education, all remedial reading teachers administer a standardized reading test to their pupils at the beginning and at the end of the period of instruction. The difference between the initial and final scores is used as a measure of reading growth. At the beginning of the term in which remedial reading instruction began, Form A of the *Nelson Silent Reading Test* was given to all pupils enrolled in the author's reading classes. Form C, an alternate form of the test, was administered at the end of the school year (late May or early June) to determine their reading progress. Table IV suggests that groups with higher initial mean scores tended to make greater progress in less time than those groups with lower initial mean scores. The group whose initial reading level was fifth grade and above made almost twice as much progress as the groups whose reading levels were below fifth grade.

Regardless of the severity of initial reading retardation, each group showed gains which exceeded normal expectancy. Table V indicates that although the group which was initially reading below third grade managed to raise its follow-up reading scores by 1.4 years, this improvement still placed most of the group below a fourth grade reading level. Table VI suggests that subsequent to remediation those groups whose mean scores were below fifth grade continued to make slight gains. The group whose final mean score was above fifth grade showed a mean loss of five months at time of follow-up.

It would seem that the greatest gains made by the dropouts occurred during remediation. Subsequent to remediation, about three years later, they seem to make very little progress, probably because they do so little reading.

Suggested Improvements

Since almost all the dropouts were dissatisfied with their present reading performance, the author asked them what improvements the school could make in its reading program in order to develop better readers. Their comments are listed *in toto* since they merit serious consideration:

Instruction and Application

Teach them to sound out words and look them up.

Have pupils who are better in reading help those who are not.

Help them become less embarrassed with their problem.

Do more reading out loud and have pupils get into the habit of listening to corrections made by teachers and pupils.

Let them read out loud for a few minutes, not for a few seconds.

Teachers in all classes should spend more time helping kids with their reading.

Tell them to practice reading out loud to their parents at home. They'll learn more.

Show them how reading improvement will cause them to be able to talk about different subjects.

Teach them how to listen.

Get them into the habit of reading books.

Teachers of all subjects should teach phonics so that the kids will be able to figure out the words.

They should go slower and ask more questions to determine if what they're teaching is understood.

They should not use big words when they explain things.

Curriculum and Materials

Interesting books should be given so kids don't get bored.

They should be easy enough to be understood so kids don't get disgusted.

Give us more reading periods.

Longer reading periods.

More library periods so we can read books that are enjoyable.

Give special help to the kids who leave the reading class.

Use SRA kits throughout the school.

Give us less homework so we can complete it.

Keep pupils who read at same level in one group.

Separate girls and boys. They make it difficult for us to concentrate.

Pupil and Teacher Attitudes

Pupils must want to learn if they're to profit from being in the reading class. Otherwise teachers are wasting their time.

Children must be given more help in the earlier grades so that when they come to high school they won't have such a problem.

Kids must learn not to give up so easily.

Teachers shouldn't jump down their throats when they miss a question. They should be patient.

The dropouts' suggestions indicated the need for more extensive reading instruction in all subject classes, more effective teaching techniques and procedures, more satisfying pupil-teacher relationships and an abundance of materials which are appropriate to their needs, interests, and abilities.

TABLE IV

Reading Achievement of Thirty-Four Dropouts Based on a Comparison
of Their Initial and Final Mean Scores

Reading Score	N	Initial Mean	Range	Final Mean	Range	Mean No. Terms of Instruction	Mean No. Months Gained Per Term
Below 3.0	13	1.9	0–2.9	3.5	2.0–3.7	2.9	6.3
3.0–4.9	17	3.7	3.0–4.9	5.1	3.6–8.3	2.3	6.8
5.0 and up	4	6.2	5.2–8.8	7.8	5.9–9.5	1.3	12.9

TABLE V

Reading Achievement of Thirty-Four Dropouts Based on a Comparison
of Their Initial and Follow-Up Mean Scores

Reading Score	N	Initial Mean	Range	Follow-Up Mean	Range	Mean Gain In Years
Below 3.0	13	1.9	0–2.9	3.3	2.0–6.7	1.4
3.0–4.9	17	3.7	3.0–4.9	5.7	2.8–9.3	2.0
5.0 and up	4	6.2	5.2–8.8	6.9	5.2–10.0	.7

TABLE VI

Reading Achievement of Thirty-Four Dropouts Based on a Comparison
of Their Mean Final and Follow-Up Scores

Reading Score	N	Final Mean	Range	Follow-Up Mean*	Range	Mean Gain Or Loss In Years
Below 3.0	7	2.6	2.0–2.9	3.3	2.0–6.7	+.7
3.0–4.9	13	4.1	3.1–4.8	4.4	2.8–9.3	+.3
5.0 and up	14	6.7	5.4–9.5	6.2	3.6–10.0	—.5

*Median years out of reading classes at time of interview = 3.0
Range = 1.2–4.0.

Reflections

The dropouts in this study probably were potential dropouts long before they had reached high school. Their reading retardation was in evidence in the early elementary grades and became rather conspicuous in junior high school. By the time they had reached high school, their mean reading retardation had increased to *six* years. The fact that all of them made better than average progress when special instruction in reading was given (Table IV) implies that they have unrealized potential for improvement *within the supportive atmosphere* of the *reading class* and that there is the possibility that even greater improvement could have taken place if remediation were provided on a school-wide basis. There is the suggestion that it may be unwise and wasteful to program seriously disabled readers to half a day of shop subjects (only two passed them) when they are unable to read blueprints, job sheets, and/or work manuals.

Comments made by the dropouts suggest that the school was not meeting their needs adequately. Reading materials used in other classes seldom reinforced or enhanced work done in the reading classes. Teachers often maintained standards of achievement which were both unrealistic and difficult for retarded readers to attain. Seldom were the students asked to suggest the kinds of practice and instruction that seemed of most value to them. Some teachers were difficult to understand because they did not satisfactorily clarify their explanations. Others proceeded at too quick a pace, failing to allow for repetition and review. Dropouts frequently mentioned that their reasons for leaving school were related to poor teaching techniques and methods.

Implications of Findings

The implications of these findings are that the teachers' methods, materials, objectives, and goals must be realistically adapted to their pupils' needs and abilities; that the pupils be helped both to identify their difficulties and to evaluate their progress toward eliminatiing them; and that ample provision be made by all teachers for systematic instruction and practice in developing reading skills.

It is unrealistic to expect a student whose reading level is fourth grade to read a daily five-page assignment from an eighth grade social studies text. Pupils must meet with some measure of success if they are to experience the satisfactions of learning. Every subject class teacher should use the results of survey and diagnostic testing in order to help him to plan together with his pupils a realistic program of rehabilitation. When achievement is based on the progress that pupils are capable of handling, then success should be possible within the limits of their abilities.

On the premise that more effective teaching techniques and practices result when teachers are helped either to solve or face more realistically their own instructional problems, it is recommended that a reading consultant be appointed to schools of the type studied. This person should be a master teacher in one or more subjects as well as a reading specialist who is intimately acquainted with the reading problem of vocational high school youth. In addition he should help teachers use appropriate materials, provide them with an opportunity to observe demonstration lessons, discuss concrete ways in which they may weave the teaching of reading skills into their lessons, show them how to diagnose reading difficulties, and conduct reading workshops.

Although the dropouts in this study appear to have some insight about the nature of their problems and what to do about them, they are not able to mobilize whatever positive attributes they possess in order to upgrade themselves. They desperately need some type of vocational guidance and counseling as well as a very thorough program of remediation in reading designed to enable them to acquire the essential skills requisite for occupational mobility.

It is unlikely that their reading interests, attitudes, and achievements, even their entire response to education, were positively conditioned or stimulated by their parents. Because of the important role that parents play in shaping the attitudes and habits of their children, it is essential to enlist their support in reinforcing the school's role. The apathy and indifference which many parents have toward school must be modified through a personalized educational program.

It is therefore suggested that the Board of Education appoint a Parent Consultant to schools of the type studied. This person could be a college graduate who majored in social work and human relations and who has both theoretical and practical knowledge of the problems and needs of disadvantaged children and their parents. His responsibilities would include discussing with parents ways in which they can help to provide the proper encouragement and stimulation of their children's education; helping them to see that the school offers many opportunities for their children's vocational, social, and cultural development (if this is true!); helping them to raise their own aspirations and those of their children with regard to educational, social, and vocational achievement; providing them with information about social agencies which may be helpful to them; and providing opportunities for them (most crucial if they lack the wherewithal to upgrade themselves) to improve their skills in the basic school subjects.

There are few more challenging problems in the educational world than that of improving the reading ability of our nation's youth, but particularly that of the potential and the actual dropout. It is hoped that these reflections will serve as a guide in helping schools effectively deal with this problem.

CHAPTER IV

APPROACHES TO
READING IMPROVEMENT

29. INDIVIDUAL INSTRUCTION

Harrison Bullock

The non-reading pupil in the secondary school is invariably a difficult problem to himself and to his school. Much can be done for him in the regular or remedial classroom, both to help him improve his reading and to achieve other important learnings. Certain aspects of his difficulty, however, may be such that they require individual attention. Often this can be achieved within a school; sometimes private tutoring may be required; occasionally expert psychological help must be found.

Individual help—tutoring—for pupils, whether offered by teachers or by a professional specialist, is always expensive either in money or in time sorely needed for other purposes. Schools are not usually able to focus on one pupil the amount of expert professional attention required in thorough and systematic individual instruction. Generally it cannot be made available except when most urgently needed.

Obviously, a non-reading pupil in a secondary school needs to learn to read. His failure in reading, however, is generally associated with lack of fulfillment of other, even more basic needs. Attention to these other needs is always important and frequently absolutely necessary if the pupil is to make progress in reading. Under special instruction better attention to a pupil's unfulfilled needs is possible than can be provided in the classroom.

Reprinted with the permission of the publisher from Harrison Bullock: *Helping the Non-Reading Pupil in Secondary Schools* (New York: Teachers College Press), pp. 131–170, Teachers College, Columbia University, copyright 1957.

A teacher should learn to recognize the need for deeper psychological study than he is himself equipped to make, and should be able to refer a pupil for such study when necessary. The fact is, however, that there simply are not enough psychologists and psychiatrists to work with any but the most seriously disturbed non-reading pupils, and in many communities expert psychological help is virtually unavailable for pupils. Fortunately, a teacher or counselor who is experienced and sensitive and who has real empathy with pupils can help the non-reading pupil. Such a teacher, knowing what sort of progress may be expected, having some idea of procedures helpful with non-reading pupils, and understanding the various factors which may operate to block progress, can work significantly for the benefit of these pupils. In doing so, the teacher at the same time deepens his own understanding of problems faced by pupils, and improves his ability to provide them with significant help.

It is neither necessary nor desirable for the teacher to take an entirely psychological approach in working with these pupils. Hidden motives, of course, are ever at work in everyone, but this is no reason for careful scrutiny of every chance action or remark for hidden significance. Psychotherapists have their valuable function; their training is long and rigorous, leaving little opportunity for other types of training and experience which make for successful teaching. A teacher, likewise, has no opportunity for the specialized training necessary to successful psychotherapy.

In performing his function as a tutor, however, a teacher can well borrow certain of the psychotherapist's techniques of interviewing and observation. The teacher should first attempt to become well acquainted with the pupil and to establish a relationship of mutual confidence, even of affection. He should be alert to feelings in the pupil and facts in the pupil's life which might have a bearing on the reading disability, so that he can formulate a hypothesis as to its causes and a tentative plan as to what might be done about them. The teacher should be alert for signs in the pupil's behavior which tend to support or to suggest modifications in the hypotheses and in the plan. Frequently there will appear evidence of factors which cannot be overcome, as, for example, defective intelligence. Such evidence may not necessarily be conclusive, and should not be so considered. Nevertheless, it should stimulate the teacher to find other means by which the pupil may progress without depending on that factor which appears hopeless. There may perhaps exist a combination of factors which will effectively prevent a pupil from ever learning to read, factors about which the teacher can do nothing, such as certain conditions in the home environment, persistent parental attitudes, unfavorable trends in the child's individual history, defective vision, hearing, or intelligence. These do not in themselves prevent the teacher from helping the pupil in other ways to understand himself, to come to terms with his disabilities, and to achieve those parts of his education which are not absolutely dependent on ability to read.

For effective individual work with a non-reading pupil, then, a teacher should be alert to indications of factors which may account for the pupil's disability, and how or whether they can be overcome. If the disability cannot itself be completely overcome, its crippling effect on the pupil may perhaps be minimized.

In the present chapter a case study will be used as an example of how work with an individual pupil can serve these purposes:

1. It can help the teacher to a sympathetic understanding of the specific pupil. In this chapter information disclosed during the work with Juan Garcia will be evaluated for its bearing on his reading disability and on the personal problems associated with it.

2. Through careful study of one non-reading pupil the teacher can learn much that is true of other non-reading pupils. While Juan Garcia was an individual with his own unique life situation and problems, nevertheless many of his feelings about his reading disability and his reactions to reading situations are not unique to him. Thoughtful consideration by the teacher would suggest some which would seem to stem from ordinary human nature or adolescent folkways. The more opportunities a teacher has to observe non-reading pupils closely, the better qualified will he be to determine what is peculiar to an individual and what is to be expected in other non-reading pupils.

3. Individual instruction can help the pupil achieve better understanding of himself and come to terms with his reading disability and the problems associated with it. As will be seen, Juan Garcia had far to go in this respect, and most of his achievements were in this area.

4. With individual help from his teacher or tutor, a non-reading pupil may gain in reading skills, provided he is motivated and emotionally ready to apply himself to such learnings. Juan Garcia was not really ready for this and his progress in reading skills was modest indeed. While he made some gain in sight vocabulary, he tended to resist instruction or practice in methods of word analysis. Despite occasional motivation to read for purposes important in his own estimation, his fear of or resistance to reading was greater than he could overcome, so he remained a non-reading pupil, so far as his school was concerned.

The account of the case study of Juan Garcia which follows is reported in such a manner as to suggest not only the specific problems of this particular boy, but also some teaching procedures that may be used with any non-reading pupil. As to whether the time spent during the course of an entire year, working individually with this boy, was really worth while—this is a question which must be considered in the light of the facilities available for service and the pupils who need it.

THE CASE OF JUAN GARCIA

At the time of his referral, Juan was a small, black-haired, olive-skinned, fourteen-year-old Puerto Rican boy with quick, jerky movements and unusual alertness. Through the course of the eight months during which he attended the Reading Center he grew rapidly, so that he ended the period on the verge of adolescence, although he began as a small boy. His health was poor, as attested to by his paleness and his frequent absences. He made and broke appointments for a tonsillectomy throughout the spring months.

He was born in Puerto Rico, and came to the United States at the age of six. Shortly after the family's arrival here, the parents were divorced, so that Juan had at least three difficult adjustments to make at the time he should have begun learning to read: He had to learn a new language and become accustomed to a strange country; he had to go through the period of family disharmony which culminated with the departure of his father from his home; and he had to begin school. His English was not marked with any noticeable Spanish accent, but was far from adequate to his needs for expressing himself. The impression he gave was not so much of a foreigner learning to speak the language as of a strongly non-verbal native.

Physically he was weak and puny, and there was something about his personality that led other boys to bully him. He came to hate school, absenting himself as much as possible on the slightest pretext.

First Interview with Juan. Juan's mother brought him to the Reading Center for the initial interview with the worker. She regaled the worker with the difficulty of keeping Juan in school. He was so small that boys picked on him, took his lunch money, and so on. He did not want to go to school for that reason and also because he could not read. She wanted to arrange for a medical examination to discover what could be done about his slow development, and wanted the Reading Center to give her a letter which would arrange for such an examination. Worker agreed to do this that day. She said she was very discouraged about his reading, and unless he improved she thought she might send him back to Puerto Rico. Worker then took Juan into the interview room, where he seemed dejected and apathetic, perhaps as a result of overhearing what his mother told the worker.

W: What school do you go to?
J: I dunno.
W: Don't you know the name of your school?
J: Hancock Junior High.
W: Do you know anybody else who comes to the Reading Center?
J: Yeah. One of my friends. He says he comes once a week.
W: How often do you want to come?
J: Every day. I like it here. It's better than the other school.
W: Tell me why.
J: In my school they always hit you and fight.
W: Do they hurt you sometimes?
J: Yeah. . . . The principal. . . . There was a boy, they were gambling and the

mother came and the assistant principal came and slapped them all around. He hit 'em. He was gonna take 'em to the home.

W: Did they call the cops?

J: Yeah. They took 'em away.

W: What kind of boys were they?

J: They were bad.

W: Were they friends of yours?

J: No, I didn't know 'em.

W: Are there other bad ones too?

J: Yeah.

W: Tell me about them.

J: They hitch on the busses. They want to go home fast.

W: Did you ever do that?

J: No.

W: Didn't you ever hitch on a truck in your life?

J: A truck on skates, yes. . . . Running after the truck.

W: Tell me more about how you get along with the boys.

J: Oh, I don't like them.

W: Don't you like any boys? Who's your best friend?

J: Nobody.

W: Don't you have any friends at all? *(Juan nods.)* Tell me about your friends.

J: My friends are bad.

W: What's bad about them?

J: They curse all the time.

W: Curse. . . . You curse too, when you're mad, don't you?

J: Yeah . . . but not much. If I see a nice girl, they come along and take her away.

W: They take her away? How?

J: They push me away.

W: Oh, I see.

J: They start showing off.

W: They start showing off. . . . Do they think they want her more than you do!

J: Yeah.

W: Do you have a girl friend of your own?

J: No.

W: Do you want one?

J: No. I don't like girls no more.

W: Why not?

J: I dunno. They're bad.

W: They're bad? What's bad about them?

J: You spend your money on 'em and in a couple of days they quit you.

W: Oh, I see. . . . You don't want your girl to quit you.

J: No.

W: Did you spend your money on a girl?

J: Yeah.

W: And she quit you?

J: *(Nods)* She lived in Kenny's block.

W: I see. . . .

J: There's some boys in our block, smoke cigars.

W: How old are they?

J: Sixteen, fourteen.

W: Are they bigger than you?

J: No, my size. . . . One of the boys is Fernando. He thinks he's big.

W: Is he the boss?

J: Yeah, he thinks he's something.

W: He's really tough is he?

J: He's the baddest boy in the block.

W: What does he do that is so bad?

J: He always starts with the kids.

W: What do you mean, he starts with them?

J: They're playing dice, so he goes and pushes the kids away.

W: Oh, I see . . . picks on them.

J: Yeah.

W: He's bigger, isn't he?

J: A little bigger than me.

W: He's gotta be, to do that. The kids wouldn't let him do that unless he was pretty big.

J: Yeah, sometimes they jump him, too. *(Story of how he tried to break up a game, and the kids all ganged up on him and beat him up.)*

W: Did he take that? Or did he take it out on somebody?

J: He takes it out on the little kids.

W: What does he do to them?

J: He beats 'em up.

W: Did he ever beat you up?

J: No. He tried it.

W: How did you keep him from it?

J: I got my friend.

W: Is he your best friend?

J: No. He's from my class, fifth period and fourth. So I called him and he said to leave me alone. Sometimes that kid speaks for me, so when I want to hit somebody bigger than me he goes and push the kids away. . . . I went to Central Park and caught a pigeon.

W: Was it alive?

J: Yeah. I've got him two weeks now.

W: Two weeks? When he grows up is he going to be a homing pigeon for you?

J: Yes, he's a clinker. *(Describes bird's appearance.)*

W: What do you feed him?

J: Pigeon food, flies, corn, and little pebbles.

W: Does he know you when you come?

J: Yeah. He ducks out of the cage and comes. Sometimes he gets to my shoulders, and he goes on my finger, and I feed him. He watches television.

W: Oh, does he? Does he like it?

J: Yeah, he likes it.

W: Did you make a cage for him? What kind of cage is it?

J: *(Describes the cage and how he made it.)* How long does this take *(the recorder)?*

W: Oh, that'll go for about an hour.

J: All of it?

W: Do you want to hear what you're saying?

J: Yeah.

W: All right, then we can turn this back and let you listen. *(They listen for about three or four minutes.)*

J: That doesn't sound like me.

W: It certainly does.

J: No . . .

W: *(Laughing)* It just doesn't sound like you sound to yourself, that's all. Do you like your voice?

J: Yeah . . . It sounds funny.

The preceding discussion of the sound of Juan's voice on the recording machine provided a natural and tactful opportunity for the worker to explore the boy's attitude toward his physical development. His feelings on the subject were well reflected in the subsequent conversation which explored three sources of discouragement to him: his size, his vulnerability to the aggression of other boys, and his lack of school success.

W: Say . . .your mother was talking about getting something to make you grow. How do you feel about that?

J: I never grow.

W: Don't you want to grow?

J: Yeah. I don't want to stay small.

W: Is it embarrassing to stay small?

J: Yeah. All the girls say they want big boys.

W: And you want the girls to like you.

J: Yeah.

W: What do they like in big boys?

J: . . . And the worst is, the big kids they bother you. And there's another boy named Fred, who thinks he can fight . . . *(Voice trails off, sadly.)*

W: And if you're big you can take care of yourself better.

J: Yeah.

W: They can't gang up on you. . . . Let's see your muscle.

J: I have none.

W: No muscle? *(Juan shakes head sadly.)* Well . . . tell me more about school.

J: I don't know nothing.

W: You don't know anything? Why not?

J: I just sit down in class and watch the kids . . .

W: You didn't pay any attention to the teacher?

J: No. . . . Sometimes I pay attention and know something. . . . But when she calls on me to read I tell her I don't know the page. She gives me zero.

W: She gives you a zero because she thinks you don't know the page, but really it's because you can't read.

J: My friends are like that. Some of them can't read nothing either.

W: Is it a special reading class?

J: No, it's the whole class, the official class.

W: The official class?

J: Yes. Some of them read, some don't. And some of them don't read. They're sixteen . . . and seventeen years old.

W: You're going to be sixteen some day, too. Do you want to be? *(Juan nods.)* Why?

J: I want to get big, ride a motorcycle. . . . I was on a motorcycle.

W: You were on a motorcycle once?

J: Yeah. In back of the motorcycle.

W: Who was driving?

J: Some man I know.

W: A friend of yours?

J: Yeah. He took me for a ride, and my friends.

W: Where did he take you?

J: He took us all around the block, fast. It's nice on the bumps. I'd like to be a cop on a motorcycle.

W: You'd like to be a cop on a motorcycle. *(Pause)*

Apparently Juan had had his say on this subject. The conversation turned to Juan's experiences in the summer Reading Center, and then to his eighteen-year-old brother.

W: What does he do?

J: He goes to vocational school. He's going to graduate this year.

W: Did he grow up pretty big?

J: About your size.

W: About my size? Is that why you want to grow up big yourself?

J: I'm gonna break his head. I'm small and he keeps on hitting me.

W: He picks on you because you're small? That's too bad.

J: Yeah.

W: I wonder why he does that. Do you make him mad sometimes?

J: Yeah, I call him a cow.

W: How would you like it if he called you a cow?

J: I wouldn't. I'd call him right back.

W: What would you do if some little kid called you a cow?

J: I'd break his head. Some kid, named David, he calls me a spick.

W: It's not a nice thing to call somebody, is it.

J: No. I threw him down in the cellar.

W: How old is he?

J: Seven.

W: I see. He won't call you a spick again, will he.

J: No, he kicked me on the knee yesterday.

W: And what did you do then?

J: I went after him, and then his father came down.

W: And told you to pick on someone your own size, did he?

J: Yeah, and some kids told him to shut up.

W: I see.

J: Nobody likes that kid, cause all the time he's gambling. Seven years old, he always wins.

W: Does he cheat?

J: No, he's just lucky.

Juan's resentment of his brother was certainly more than a matter of being "hit" by him. No small part of it, no doubt, was the unfavorable comparison between himself and his more successful older brother. One may well speculate about the possible effects on Juan's achievement throughout his years in school of being expected to live up to the standards set by this brother. Among his brother's points of superiority was his size. Juan had already expressed his discouragement at his own small stature; his brother's greater stature, added to the other resentments, must certainly have been hard for him to take. It is interesting to observe how Juan's conversation shifted from the ways in which he felt that his brother bullied him to the ways in which he himself attacked, not too successfully, the seven-year-old David.

Juan then picked up some of the reading material on the table, read it laboriously, needing help on nearly every word, although some of the material was at the first-grade level.

With the mood of this first interview set by Juan's mother's great discouragement and by her statement that she might possibly send him back to Puerto Rico, the interview may perhaps be considered largely exploratory of his feelings and attitudes. He brightened up only at the talk of pigeons and the motorcycle. It was also exploratory of his reading ability. He chose for himself a copy of *My Weekly Reader*, edition number one (first-grade level), and the delightful *Find Out Book*, out of the variety of reading materials displayed on the table for his own choice.

Juan's Attitude Toward School. Juan's mother had spoken of the boy's unhappiness at school, how the boys picked on him, and how he had occasionally taken to playing truant. The boy expressed his own attitude toward school in the following excerpt.

W: What does your mother want you to do?
J: Graduate next year, but I don't want to do nuttin.
W: You're not going to do anything.
J: No.
W: You're not going to graduate next year?
J: Maybe. I'm goin' to the ninth. I might quit school.
W: You might quit school. Then what will you do?
J: If my mother lets me.
W: You want to quit school.
J: I don't like school.
W: You don't like school, do you.
J: Everybody teases me.
W: Everybody teases you.
J: 'Cause I don't know how to read. They all bother me.
W: They tease you and bother you because you don't know how to read. You don't like that, do you.
J: No. They keep picking. . . . (*Voice trails off.*)

A month or two later he told of transferring to another school farther from home, but where he did not know any of the boys. Apparently the tormenting stopped from then on, for Juan always expressed preference for the new school. Its biggest attraction, of course, was the nearby swimming pool, where the physical education classes had weekly sessions.

Juan's Attitude Toward New York. His dislike of life in New York and his nostalgia for Puerto Rico were so intermingled in the following excerpt that it is sometimes difficult to know which he might be talking of at a given moment.

W: How old were you when you came to New York?
J: Six.
W: Were you happy to come to New York?
J: No.
W: Why?
J: Didn't have no fun.
W: Did you come in the airplane?
J: Yeah.
W: Was it fun riding on the airplane?
J: Yeah. I was playing ball. But me and my sister and my brother was sick. My brother was getting sick in the airplane. My sister was sick when we landed.
W: You were glad when you landed, weren't you?
J: No.
W: Why don't you like it in New York?
J: You don't have no fun. You can't play in no woods.
W: That's right, there aren't any woods here, are there?
J: And you go in the woods and get lost, and there are big hawks there, eat people. They're black ones. They pick up chickens.
W: They pick up chickens, live ones?
J: Yeah. Little pigeons, little birds. . . . You can go hunting. Right in the nest you see a little bird and you can shoot him down. You can eat those . . . those . . . those things.
W: Did you live in the country there?
J: Yes. And you go fishing. You catch eels like that . . . with your hands. The water . . . the rain comes down and its deep . . . then a couple of days and it dries up. And there's just that much water where the holes are and the fish go in there. And you catch tropical fish. All the tropical fish comes from there. And there's quicksand down there, too. We used to jump over it. *(Long description of a very narrow trail across the quicksand.)*

This nostalgia for the woods and countryside of Puerto Rico probably accounted for his fascination with wild life, woods, and country here. His interest in animals never flagged, whether wild creatures in the woods, pigeons in the streets of the city, or caged animals at home.

Juan's Bilingual Ability. The boy was genuinely proud of his ability to serve as interpreter at school. He found satisfaction in this recognized intellectual achievement. Nevertheless, one can but wonder what his Spanish must have been if, as he said, it was less adequate than his command of English!

W: Which is easier for you, to talk Spanish or to talk English?
J: English.
W: Do you have to stop and think to talk Spanish?
J: Yeah. Some people at school were trying to talk to me. I was the only Spanish kid in the class, so the teacher calls me to talk to the mothers of the Spanish kids in the other classes. They don't talk too much, the people, English.
W: Oh, they don't talk English at all.
J: No.
W: So you translate for the teacher.
J: Yes.
W: That's pretty good.
J: But sometimes I can't say the word in Spanish. I always forget.
W: You can say what they say in Spanish in English, though, can't you?
J: Yeah.
W: That's pretty good; that takes brains. It isn't easy, you know, to talk from one language to another. *(Juan laughs, absently counts small pictures of animals around the cover of a book.)*
J: Twenty-eight altogether.
W: Can you name them? *(Juan names them)* Can you name all those in Spanish just as fast?
J: No.
W: Try it. *(He does, most of them.)* Well, you're pretty good at that.

He then gave the worker a brief lesson on the names of animals in Spanish.

Juan Goes to the Doctor. When his mother first brought Juan to the Reading Center she expressed the desire to have the boy checked by a doctor to determine whether his development was normal and whether there might be any physical difficulties underlying his difficulties in learning. At her request the worker wrote a letter of referral which she could take to the clinic so that the examination might be arranged. During the second interview Juan told the worker that an appointment had been arranged. He seemed quite eager and hopeful about it, so the next week the worker asked Juan about it.

W: Well, did you go to see the doctor the other day?
J: Yes. *(A loud pounding noise commences in the hall.)*
W: There's a lot of noise out there. Would you mind shutting the door for me please?
J: Yes. Can I get a drink of water?
W: Go ahead and get your drink. *(Juan went out, reappeared a couple of minutes later.)*

J: Do you want me to shut the door?

W: Please. Thanks. You told me that you went to see the doctor the other day. Tell me about it.

J: Yes. I forgot the letter.

W: Oh, did he give you a letter for us here?

J: No, I forgot the letter in the car.

W: Oh, the one to give him.

J: Yes. My father's car. We went in my father's car. I forgot the letter in the car. I put it in the trunk.

W: The letter I wrote.

J: Yes. I forgot to give it to him. I forgot it and couldn't go down again.

W: Oh, you didn't go see him at all, and he didn't examine you.

J: No. We didn't have time. We got there at one o'clock.

W: What time were you supposed to be there?

J: At ten.

W: Oh, you had to go back and get the letter. Is that it?

J: No. And they don't take no letters from school.

W: Oh, I see. Who do they take letters from?

J: The doctors.

W: What are you going to do?

J: My mother's going to take me to some private doctor here.

W: To some private doctor? What do you want him to do?

J: Examine me.

W: You want to be examined; have you ever been examined?

J: Yes.

W: What does he do when he examines you?

J: They examine all my body. And they examine inside.

W: And what did he say when he examined you?

J: Said I was okay.

W: He said you were okay. Well, what do you want this doctor to tell you about?

J: That I'll be okay.

Parents and teachers will recognize in the sudden need for a drink of water a familiar juvenile evasive maneuver. The reason for it was momentarily obscured by the disturbance in the hall, but became abundantly clear in the contrition with which the boy explained his failure to see the doctor and to deliver the letter of referral. He had a hard time making this clear and was almost crying by the time the worker had grasped the idea. Here the boy's weakness in communication very noticeably got in his way.

The whole fiasco of the visit to the doctor, the forgotten letter, going at the wrong time, and so on, was typical of the lack of responsibility in Juan and perhaps in his family, manifesting itself in frequent absence and tardiness at school and at the Reading Center. In this particular instance Juan obviously felt terribly guilty.

During the next week Juan's mother finally took him to a doctor, with the worker's note of referral which had been left in the locker of the car. The doctor phoned the Reading Center and informed the worker that Juan's development, while slow, was within the normal range for boys of his age, that his short stature was characteristic of Puerto Ricans. To the doctor the boy seemed to be in good health.

The doctor said that he was "intrigued" with Juan, because he seemed so "bright and alert," and because he had had enough initiative to hold several jobs, as in a five-and-ten-cent store and a vegetable market; also that his conversation seemed so well-informed and alert that the reading disability appeared more associated with some emotional block than with lack of capacity.

The doctor referred Juan back to the Reading Center with negative findings as to glandular or developmental deficiency. He suggested that the boy might require the attention of a child psychiatrist.

The next week, while in the midst of a conversation about the pigeons outside the window, Juan ventured to announce in his own way that he had at last seen the doctor.

J: They call you, the clinic?
W: The doctor? Yes.
J: What he say?
W: What did he say to you?
J: Nuttin. He says that I got nuttin.
W: That you're fine.
J: Yeah. And what did he tell you?
W: He told me that you were fine, too. Was the doctor nice to you?
J: Yeah.
W: What did he do?
J: He 'zamined me and he asked me questions.... It's big, that place. The hospital.
W: Great big building.
J: Twenty floors.

Instructional Objectives with Juan. The worker observed several facts about Juan which suggested the following objectives in working with him:

(1) The boy found considerable difficulty in expressing himself verbally; therefore it seemed well to encourage expression in any medium possible, language, clay, drawing, painting, or acting.

(2) He had difficulty understanding, as well as using, language. His command of speaking and listening was so meager as to offer little promise of early success in reading. The worker, therefore, wished to provide motivated language experiences for him, both in listening and in talking.

(3) His frequent exhibitions of negativism no doubt had deep roots, beyond reach of exhortation or superficial suggestions. Nevertheless, it seemed well to attempt to encourage manifestations of maturity and assumption of responsibility in him, and to minimize so far as possible his tendencies toward childishness and dependence. For this reason, his

attempts to exercise independence and reject domination, even though they might seem negativistic, were not rejected.

(4) He had very definite and strong interests. It seemed well to exploit these, attempting to build word recognition in areas of interest to him. Here, if anywhere, would be motivation for reading.

(5) His reading ability was so low as to be virtually useless to him. He scored grade 2.4 on the vocabulary section of California Reading Test, Elementary, Form DD. This is below the score obtained by arbitrarily marking the test form, as reported in Chapter II above. On the comprehension section of the test, he found the task so discouraging that he did not attempt enough to achieve any score at all. The worker, therefore, should contrive situations where even this very slight reading ability might prove useful to him in obtaining information he desired.

Instructional Procedures with Juan

To carry out the instructional objectives, and to work successfully and harmoniously with a boy of Juan's disposition, it was necessary that the instructional procedures be kept very flexible. A variety of materials was always on display about the room, from which he was free to choose, although sometimes at his place at the table something the worker considered particularly appropriate would be awaiting Juan's arrival. The boy could and often did ignore this particular material.

Sometimes he felt like conversing. Other times he wanted to paint or model. Still other times he felt like working on a specific reading task. He well knew that his wishes and feelings in this regard would be respected, and it is doubtful that he ever undertook any particular task from a sense of duty to the worker.

The worker's intention was to guide and be ready with a suggestion for an activity, if Juan wanted a suggestion, but to enter into any activity which the boy would choose. For reasons mentioned later in this chapter, the worker felt that he should deemphasize the painting and modeling activities. This he did by storing the paints and clay out of sight, but when Juan requested them, they were brought forth.

It will be noted that teaching phonics has not been specifically listed as an instructional objective. Juan's skills of phonetic analysis of words were most rudimentary: initial consonants, occasional final letters, and sometimes familiar words within longer words. Still it seemed best not to press phonics with him for the following reasons:

(1) He had been exposed repeatedly to instruction in phonics during his eight years in school, always without successful learning. By now he associated phonics with failure in reading. It was better for him to work by methods which were not so unpleasantly associated.

(2) He corroborated this judgment by his reactions on those occasions

when the worker encouraged him to attempt to sound out a word. Juan would stiffen, become negative, or attempt to change the subject.

(3) Any attempt to insist on his application to drill in phonics would have negated the other instructional objectives, and might well have resulted in his withdrawal from all instruction.

(4) Juan's general level of intelligence was such as to promise relatively little success in any attempt at learning through the application of abstract general rules to specific situations.

Attempting, therefore, to keep the instructional techniques in harmony with the instructional objectives, the worker attempted as far as possible to make use of the boy's existing interests. Perhaps the high point of Juan's entire experience at the Reading Center, from his point of view, was the activity which will be described first.

An Excursion to the Country. Juan's interest in animals and the country suggested that he might greatly enjoy an outing and that many language experiences might be found in such an experience. The following account of the planning and follow-up of the excursion at the Reading Center tell a great deal about Juan. One day when Juan arrived at the Reading Center the worker asked him an unusual question.

W: What do you know about chinchillas, anything?
J: Chinchillies? Yeah.
W: Ever seen one?
J: No. They're black.
W: Gray.
J: Some of 'em are black.
W: I guess there's some black on them. You have seen chinchillas, have you?
J: Yeah. They make fur coats.
W: Yes, but very expensive though.
J: They bite.
W: Do they? Did they bite you?
J: No, but I know they bite.

Juan had a position to maintain as an authority on small animals. His first dogmatic assertion, that chinchillas are black, was coolly received, although the worker did not explicitly deny the existence of any black chinchillas. Juan's assertion that they bite was safer, even without first-hand evidence. His contradictory testimony as to whether he had seen chinchillas was probably due to lack of understanding of the questions asked him.

W: Well, how would you like to come out to Pennsylvania to see the chinchillas on a lady's farm?
J: Yeah.
W: Would your mother let you?
J: Yeah, and Kenny, too. Do you mean in the summer, Pennsylvania?
W: No, in a week or so. On election day. You don't have school then, do you? We can make it a holiday. You see, I know somebody in Pennsylvania

who raises chinchillas. Same person who—

J: She got a farm?

W: Yes, she has a farm.

J: Any horses?

W: No. Lots of chickens, lots of rabbits, and chinchillas and ducks. Would you like . . .

J: Yeah. I like to go to a farm.

W: Well, we'll see if we can do it. Ever been to Pennsylvania?

J: No.

W: Ever been on a farm?

J: No.

W: Never? Haven't you ever been on the farm at the zoo?

J: Yeah, the farm zoo at the Bronx zoo?

W: M-hm. They have farm animals up there.

J: They don't let me in.

W: Why, 'cause you're too big?

J: Yeah.

W: Have you ever seen a cow close to?

J: I never pet 'em.

W: You've never petted a cow. Didn't you ever see one in Puerto Rico?

J: No. Yeah, I've seen bulls. They ran after my brother.

Plans and arrangements were made. Juan was a bit offended that the worker wanted to start at eight o'clock instead of six in the morning, but otherwise he was very happy about the prospect of the excursion. Perhaps the trip itself is best described in Juan's words:

The Trip to Pennsylvania

Early in the morning we got ready to go to Pennsylvania. We started to go to Pennsylvania. We crossed the George Washington Bridge. Then we passed the George Washington Bridge. We passed a lot of farms. We saw many cows and pigs and goats.

We crossed another bridge. That bridge that we crossed was to get to Pennsylvania. And then we went a lot of miles to get to the farm. When we got there, we couldn't move. Then the lady came out of the house. She asked our name. We told her our names. She asked if we were hungry. I said yes. She said let's go feed the rabbits. Then she said we'll feed the rabbits after we eat.

Then she said to sit down on the chair. Then she brought the food. Then we started to eat. We finished eating. Then we went out to see the animals and chickens. We found chicken eggs. We left the eggs alone. Then we looked around. Then we found a goose sitting on six eggs. We left her alone. Then we went up the hill. There was a lot of corn. We started to pick the corn. Then we started to peel the corn. We came down the hill.

Then we went to the blacksmith. He made us a ring out of horseshoe nails. We went back to the house. We went back to the house. We were going home. We went in the car. Then we said goodbye to the lady.

We started off home. We got lost in the woods with the car. We came out of the woods. We found the teacher's friend. We went to his friend's house.

They said hello to us. They asked our names. We said our name is Juan and Kenny. They told us to come with them in the parlor. Then they gave us a lollypop. Then they took us down to see their animals. They showed us their steer. The steer's name was Stewpot. And the goat's name was Crosspatch. They showed us how to milk a goat. They gave us milk. They showed us rabbits and then they started wrestling. Kenny put the nuts in the barrel that they picked from the tree. They still were wrestling. Then we started to go. They started the car.

Then we went in the car. Then we went home. When we got to the tunnel we crossed the tunnel. Then we got home. My mother was worried. When she saw the car stop, then she knew I was in the car. Then the car stopped. I got out of the car. Then I went up to my house. I ate. I went to wash myself. I went right to bed.

JUAN GARCIA

It is interesting to note that no mention was made of the chinchillas, which were, after all, the original purpose of the whole trip. The omission of the chinchillas was characteristic of Juan in his resistance to suggestions of any sort. This dogged independence maintained by Juan remained through the entire series of interviews. It was strongly in evidence when Juan arrived at the Reading Center the week following the excursion.

He greeted the worker with a demand for another excursion to Pennsylvania the following day, which happened to be a school holiday. Worker explained that he would have no holiday and could not arrange a trip for that day. Juan did not accept this response, and kept returning to the demand periodically throughout the interview.

Juan went to the window to look at the pigeons on the roof outside. He walked to the table, picked up the microphone, held it close to his mouth and loudly said "hello" into it. Worker motioned to the chair where the clay and the books were laid out for Juan. Juan walked around the table and sat on the opposite side.

This was his declaration of independence of the worker, perhaps partly in return for the worker's refusal to take him on another excursion the next day. These small manifestations of independence can be healthy in a boy outwardly as submissive as Juan. It is possible that his failure to learn to read was likewise, in part, an unverbalized resistance to domination; if so, the only hope in overcoming the reading disability would seem to lie in helping him find means of maintaining his independence with less handicap to himself. The great value Juan placed on his independence emphasized the importance of the worker's not permitting himself to be trapped into a too directive teacher role.

He dictated the story while he manipulated a lump of clay in his hand, making various forms. While the worker was busy writing the story as dictated, Juan would sometimes remark about what he was doing with the clay. Other times he would lapse into silence as he manipulated the clay. He made in turn a couple of round "forts," manned by tiny figures shooting at each other, a face mask which he dubbed "Frankenstein," and a rowboat complete with fisherman and fishline. The fisherman was later taken from the rowboat and turned into a monkey, which was swung from a vine, fashioned from what had been the rowboat's oars and anchor. After a minute or two of each silence, worker would read the last half dozen or so lines of what had been dictated, and Juan would always continue with a few more sentences. No further pressure was placed on Juan to continue the story. He seemed to want to continue, although he would be blocked by difficulty in expressing himself. Hearing what he had written seemed to help him to go on. Occasionally he would misstate something, correcting himself when he heard how it sounded when read back. Worker always repeated each word as he wrote it down for Juan. Sometimes Juan would mock this by repeating the word after worker, or would dictate a word at a time. Other times the dictation would go quite fluently as Juan seemed to forget the part that worker was playing as amanuensis. On several occasions the worker suggested content to the story, as following from something Juan had just mentioned. Each time Juan ignored the suggestion, going on in his own way.

After finishing the story with rapid dictation as fast as the worker could write, Juan picked up the microphone and talked right into it, "No more!" then whistled and made various noises into the microphone. He looked at the story which filled both sides of the paper. "All that? Where's the end?" He took worker's pen, put an X after the last word of the story, then wrote his name below.

This was a remarkably creative session for Juan. He not only produced a variety of figures modeled from clay, but while doing this he authored a story of impressive length. His pride in his creation was demonstrated by the big X at the end and by his signing his full name to it. He even managed to read it surprisingly well, finding enough recognizable words to reinforce his memory of the content. His only failure for the session was in his attempt to persuade the worker to take the boys on another excursion the following day.

Art Materials Used in Interviews. Mention has been made of how Juan manipulated clay while he dictated his account of the excursion. The idea of using art materials in his reading sessions began one day when Juan, exploring some shelves in the interview room, came upon some jars of fingerpaint.

J: Who paints here?
W: Would you like to try that?
J: Yeah. I can make a picture.
W: All right. Have you ever done that kind of fingerpainting?
J: They teach that at school in our class. They teach it in art class.

The boy got out paints and paper, and began to work with the sure movements of experience, saying practically nothing. He started in black paint, adding other colors, experimenting with the effects of different kinds of strokes. He seemed entirely at home in this medium, although his results were not particularly attractive nor as satisfying to him as had been the actual process.

The next week, when Juan entered the interview room, he found a piece of modeling clay awaiting him on the table. The boy's interest in fingerpainting had led the worker to wonder whether he might also enjoy free use of clay as a medium of expression and for relief of tension during the interview. For a boy whose verbal capacity for expression is as limited as Juan's, a manual outlet of some sort can be very helpful and relaxing. The pleasure he found in manipulating the clay while talking and dictating his story was quite apparent. He expressed himself readily with the clay, but only haltingly in speech.

Since the boy seemed to have real esthetic appreciation, as well as pleasure in manipulating clay and fingerpaints, the worker decided to get him a set of watercolor paints, with the idea that the boy might turn out products which would be as satisfying to see as to make—more than could be said of the fingerpainting or the clay. As it happened Juan was absent the day the paints arrived, so the worker wrote him a letter telling him of them. The next time he entered the Reading Center Juan's first words were:

J: Painting set you got, you wrote in letter?
W: Yes, I have some painting things here today.
J: I got a nice picture to draw.
W: You have a nice picture.

Juan got materials ready, went out for water, returned and without a word commenced sketching a jar of flowers, then painted it in water colors.

W: What kind of flowers are they?
J: I donno.
W: Where did you get the idea of them?
J: Seen that picture in school.
W: Oh. You saw it in school.

Having nothing more to say on this subject, Juan painted on in silence for awhile. When he finished his picture worker complimented him on it and suggested that he sign it. He then took another sheet of drawing paper and started another painting. The boy sometimes painted in silence, sometimes talked of various matters on his mind. Presently he finished his second watercolor painting, a picture of a witch by a fire under a big tree. He signed this picture too, then he took the clay from the worker and began to manipulate it.

W: What are you going to make? (*Juan manipulates the clay.*)

J: I know what. Wait. (*Works it for some time.*)
W: Is that going to be an auto?
J: Guess that.
W: What is it going to be? Sled? Sleigh?
J: Sleigh. For Santy Claus.
W: Oh, Santa Claus. Are you going to draw a picture of him?
J: Yes. I'm going to draw Santa Claus. I got art class in school.
W: And you like the art class. (*Long pause.*)
J: (*Pounds clay.*) I not draw him.
W: You're not going to draw him.
J: I gonna make elephant.

For a fourteen-year-old boy to be talking thus of Santa Claus would seem a reflection on his emotional maturity. Probably Juan's decision not to make Santa Claus came of a conclusion that this was no suitable subject for so old a boy. The fact that Juan thought of him in the first place might be due to a longing for the security of early childhood which was shattered for him by the family's move from Puerto Rico to New York, followed shortly by the separation of his parents when he was six years old.

After he had completed the elephant, Juan made an "old-time bathtub" of a pre-1890 shape. After talking about this for awhile, Juan destroyed the tub, worked the clay; his next opus turned out to be a caterpillar with ears. Then he made a rattlesnake.

J: Now we paint it.
W: Paint won't stick on this clay.
J: Yeah, it will.
W: No, this is greasy.
J: Now it will. (*Prepares to paint.*)
W: This clay is not made to take paint. Paint a picture if you like, but please don't try to paint on the clay.
J: Will be nice if it gets hard.
W: Yes, but this kind of clay is made so it won't get hard.

Juan played around with the clay snake for a moment, then coiled it as though it were ready to strike.

W: Did you ever have a pet snake?
J: No.
W: Did you ever hold a snake?
J: Yes. Garter snake. And one day I killed it. I don't know what kind it was.
W: Why did you kill it?
J: This one was a bi-i-ig one, 'bout this big. I s'pose it was a water snake. We were in a rowboat. Nearly hit the boat. And I hit him with the oars. Was nice and big. We took him out of the water. . . .

The story continued as the tape recorder came to the end of the reel. While worker was reversing the tape Juan surreptitiously tried to paint the clay snake, with poor success as the paint gathered in drops on the oily surface.

W: (*Very softly.*) You painted it, didn't you, Juan.
J: Painted off.
W: It doesn't go on right. See, it goes on in little drops.
J: I paint with paints, but I don't know what kind of clay is this. I made speckles. I'll use water.

Juan got most of the paint off the snake. Then he started to clean up the table and to put things away. He rinsed the paint brush and put it away wet. Worker suggested that he wipe off the brush; Juan took a paper towel and started to wipe the tops of the cakes of paint. He couldn't or wouldn't understand what the worker wanted him to do, and the worker finally wiped off the wet paint brush.

Too often a teacher gets trapped in this sort of situation. Part of a teacher's responsibility, of course, is to see that things are done correctly and this can lead a teacher to help a child to avoid mistakes, thus preventing the child from learning from his own experiences. In this instance the worker correctly predicted the outcome of attempting to paint modeling clay, but by telling the boy not to do it he challenged him to disobey. Then, when Juan did try painting it with the inevitable results, instead of being a learning situation it was a case of disobedience, and Juan was led to feel guilty. Life in and out of school is full of prohibitions which, for the sake of safety or the good of society should be heeded. It is best that the teacher not unnecessarily add to the list of prohibitions. Here no harm was done by the attempt to paint the clay in itself. Before and after the incident, however, the worker put the matter in such a light that the boy was led to feel unnecessarily guilty. Feelings of guilt can nullify any constructive results of an interview or lesson.

Probably Juan's feelings of guilt contributed to his misunderstanding of how to wipe the paint brush. This was the third occasion in this one interview when he failed to understand instructions. It is perhaps legitimate to wonder whether this failure was entirely difficulty in communication or whether it included a more or less conscious resistance to being taught. It is quite possible that this was Juan's habitual response to teaching whenever, for one reason or another, his anxiety was aroused. It is not easy for a teacher to know when lack of understanding in pupils is truly that and when it is a form of evasion or escape. One can judge a child's motivation only as the total pattern of his behavior becomes apparent through growing acquaintance over a period of time. The safest assumption here is of a bona fide misunderstanding unless the evidence is overwhelmingly otherwise. A teacher must guard against irritation and resentment at being "played for a sucker" by this device, and try to understand why the pupil finds it necessary.

This interview was marked by several expressions of resistance and independence on Juan's part. He spent the entire time modeling in clay or painting in watercolor. He completely ignored the reading materials which were on display as usual. Perhaps this was due to the novelty of the paints; perhaps it was because of a current mood of resistance to reading generally.

Juan certainly could express himself far better with the clay and the paints than in talking. Between these materials and his limited speaking ability, he brought out far more feelings in this interview than he did in any of the interviews where speech was his sole medium of communication. As might be expected in any severely retarded reader, the feelings were heavily loaded with anxiety and hostility. While airing them may simply increase one's own consciousness of them, it may also help one to cope with them. It is probable that the worker here was too much the teacher, too anxious to show the pupil what to do and how to do it, and too little inclined to help the pupil face the feelings he was bringing out to make effective use of such activities in casework. For this reason, he did not bring out the paints or clay in subsequent interviews unless the pupil requested them.

Juan Portrays His Family. Several times after the worker decided to keep the art materials in an inconspicuous place, Juan asked for the watercolors. On one occasion he painted a girl whom he named Frances.

W: Is she your girl friend?
J: No, I ain't got no girl friend. I don't like girls. They're pains in the neck.
W: Is Lupe a pain in the neck?
J: No, she's my sister.
W: I see. Well, Frances looks nice. How many are in your family? You, your sister, your brother, and your mother?
J: Yes.
W: Well, that's four. Would you like to draw a picture of your whole family?
J: Okay. (*He did so, beginning with himself, tightly drawn in pencil.*) You know who that is?
W: That must be Juan. Is that right?
J: That's right. (*He drew his sister the right proportionate size. She also is rather tightly drawn. He makes very obvious spectacles about the eyes.*) You know what that is?
W: Glasses?
J: Yeah. (*His brother is the right proportionate size, and is drawn with his arms raised at the sides, with muscles flexed. There is one bump on the right arm, two on the left.*) Muscles.
W: Oh, he's proud of his muscles. Is he strong?
J: No.
W: Does he think he is?
J: Yeah. We fight sometimes. Sometimes he fights with my sister. Sometimes I fight with my sister. Sometimes I fight with my brother. (*He is now drawing his mother.*) . . . (*Apropos of nothing evident*) We went out. We went

to a Chinese restaurant yesterday. We went to eat with my friend. *(He drew his mother's feet. He was careful to make shapely ankles and high-heeled shoes. He cackled to himself as he drew these.)*

W: And that's your mother standing with her hands behind her back.

J: No. She has her hands on her hips. I forgot to draw the hands. *(He draws them.)*

W: Does she stand that way when she's happy or mad?

J: Happy.

W: How does she stand when she's mad? *(J. demonstrates, hands on hips and a scowl on his face.)* Oh, so that's how she looks when she's mad. *(Juan starts coloring the picture with crayons.)* Oh, so you're wearing your green sweater . . . and your blue jeans. . . .

J: And black shoes.

W: And black shoes . . . and your sister has on a yellow sweater . . . and a green skirt . . . and your brother has on a red sweater, and his muscles.

J: Forget the muscles. Now he's stretching himself . . . *(After giving his mother an orange blouse, black belt, and purple skirt, he colors everybody's shoes.)* Everybody has black shoes. *(Finally he takes the paint brush and puts "flesh color" on all the faces and on his hands in the picture. He had previously added a guinea pig on the picture of himself. In coloring the picture of his mother he covered over the hands so they were no longer visible and once more appeared to be held behind her.)*

W: Now you should write everybody's name under their picture. *(He writes his full name under his.)* You can just write one name under the others.

J: How do you spell Lupe? *(W. tells him, and J. writes it, beginning with a small letter.)* And how do you spell Bennie? *(W. tells him.)* I can't spell my mother's first name—

W: You don't need to. Just put down what you call her. What do you call her?

J: Mother or Ma. *(Worker spells it for him.)*

Worker was interested to see how Juan would hint at his relationship with members of his family in drawing his picture of the family. Whatever they might signify, the following clues emerged as he drew the "family portrait":

A. His brother was showing off his muscular arms.

B. When the worker seemed to be paying too much attention to the muscles, Juan admonished him to "forget the muscles."

C. He very meticulously depicted his mother's ankles and highheeled shoes.

D. He omitted his mother's hands at first, corrected the omission when it was brought to his attention, but omitted them again in the coloring, so that the pencilled ones were obliterated.

Juan's attitude toward his brother, showing his strength until the boy was sick and tired of it and wished to "forget the muscles," was quite obvious from the picture and borne out by various references to his brother in the course of the interview.

His attitude toward his mother was more obscure. It was surely no accident that he so carefully portrayed her feet and ankles; the first time he omitted the hands might have been accidental, but obliterating the ones he had added when the omission was called to his attention, so that she ended up handless, may have been more than accidental. Here again was an interesting avenue for a therapist to investigate. For a teacher to attempt such an investigation, however, could not accomplish anything particularly constructive for the boy, and could perhaps lead him to more anxieties than he already suffered.

Juan Dictates a Story. The following story demonstrates something of Juan's sense of humor. It was used in various ways after it was dictated by the boy.

J: Let's find a story.
W: All right, you find a story. Well, if you want to tell me one, we can go in the other room and type it. Do you want to tell me a story?
J: Yeah.
W: Okay. What's it going to be about?
J: A monkey.
W: All right. Is that the name of the story, "A Monkey"?
J: Yeah. *(He dictates the following story to worker.)*
W: Do you want me to read to you, what you wrote, so you'll know how it goes?
J: Yeah.
W: "I was walking in the park with a baby pigeon in my hand. I looked down. There I saw a baby monkey. The monkey had a sweater on. I picked him up. He went all around my head playing with my hair. I put him down and he started running. I ran after him. He went up a tree. I went up the tree. I pulled his tail. He started screaming. He came down off the tree. I brought him to the lake. He found a stick. The monkey started throwing the stick in the water. I told the monkey he wanted to go home. So I took him home, put him to bed, and he fell asleep." Do you know what you forgot in that?
J: What?
W: What did you have in your hand at the beginning of the story?
J: The pigeon?
W: What happened to the pigeon?
J: I brought him home.
W: Did you get it all squeezed when you were chasing the monkey up the tree?
J: I put the thing down.
W: Was this a true story?
J: No.
W: Maybe you made it up just now.
J: Yeah.
W: Well, okay. We'll go and copy that and that will be all for today. Okay, Juan.

They went to the typewriter, where Juan copied the story, completely disregarding capitalization and punctuation. Erroneous letters were corrected by typing the correct letter after the wrong one. When the time was up and worker suggested that work be stopped, Juan grinned and said, "One more line." He copied three before he would stop. He had no comprehension of the individual words he was copying.

The use of a typewriter with retarded readers can be very valuable. The motivation of the machine as a gadget is high; it can turn out printed materials, moreover, even for the most poorly coordinated pupil. Juan was greatly fascinated by the typewriter and would have used it often, if a suitable machine had always been available at the Reading Center.

Worker brought out the story again the next week. He held it so Juan could look on, and read it with modifications.

W: *(Reading)* "I was walking in the park with a baby pigeon in my hand. I looked down. There I saw a baby monkey. The monkey had a sweater on. I picked him up. He went all around my head playing with my hair. I put him down. He started running. I ran after him. He ran up a tree. I climbed up the tree. I pulled his tail. He started screaming. He came down off the tree. I threw him in the ocean."

J: The ocean?

W: Is that what you said?

J: No.

W: What did you say?

J: I said, uh, that I ran after him.

W: No. He came down off the tree. I threw him down the well.

J: Oh, yes. I brought him down the well.

W: "The monkey started throwing the stick at me. I told the monkey he wanted to go home. So I took him home, put him in his bed, and knocked him in the head until he fell asleep."

J: Haha! No.

W: Isn't that what you said? What did you say if not that?

J: I brought him to bed and he falled asleep. That's all.

The worker's misreading of Juan's story was intended to motivate him to check the text to find out exactly what it did say. Worker held the paper so he could do just that; Juan preferred, however, to depend on his memory rather than his reading ability. The story was, of course, far beyond his ability to read by himself; the worker's hope was that the boy could at least follow and recognize a word or two in the setting of his own story.

Worker decided here to use the Fernald method of letting the boy trace words until he knew them. He wrote the following words from Juan's story in two-inch letters on the three-by-ten-inch sheets that fitted the file box:

was	then	with	pulled	put	he	tree
walking	monkey	saw	my	him	ran	his
park	played	he	hair	down	up	tail

Worker had Juan find them in the story, telling him what the words were as Juan found them. Then he asked Juan to read the story.

J: "I was walking in the park. Then I seen a monkey. Then I played with him. The monkey pulled—the—wait; the monkey—"
W: No. "I played with the monkey."
J: "The monkey. He pulled my hair. I put him down. He—He—"
W: "Then."
J: "Then he ran up the tree. I pulled his tail."

Worker showed Juan how to study the words by tracing them with his finger and saying the words to himself as he did so. Then Juan wrote the words on a paper. When there were enough words to write a short sentence, he would write a sentence using them. This done, he would file the words alphabetically in the box. Eight of the words were studied in this way, before it was time to close the interview.

A kit is published to make use of the Fernald system of learning words through kinesthetic tracing. This is known as the *A to Z Speller.*

There is a booklet of words, each on its own three-by-ten-inch page, perforated to be torn out and fit into an alphabetical file box. On an earlier occasion, Juan had noticed the box on the table in the interview room. Juan took out the book, went through it and recognized the following twenty-one words:

and	do	in	little	see	to	us
at	good	is	man	so	too	we
baby	I	it	she	the	up	zoo

He missed the other seventy-four of the ninety-five word list.

J: *(Sadly)* No more.
W: No more. Do you want to learn these words?
J: *(Ignoring the words but looking at the tabs.)* What's these, the ABC?
W: See if they're right. *(Juan reads the letters.)* That's good. Can you sing them? *(Juan does so, out of tune.)* Good.

Presently he counted the letter separators in the file box.

J: There's twenty-six letters in the ABC.
W: That's right. There are twenty-six letters in the alphabet. Can you say it without looking? Try it.
J: A B C D E F G H I J K L O P Q R S T U V W X Y Z.
W: Pretty good. You made a couple of mistakes, otherwise all right.
J: M-hmm. A B C D E, no wait a minute. A B C D E F G H I J K L, H—
W: No, L, M *(They say them together as far as P, after which Juan says them alone.)* That's good.

Special Worksheets to Provide Vocabulary Drill. Juan's reading ability was so low that any practice material had to be very simple and repetitive. The following examples show how the worker attempted to meet Juan's ability and special interests in this sort of work.

Worker gave Juan a sheet prepared for him, consisting of a series of statements about the various small animals he enjoyed talking about.

Each statement had one word wrong, to be corrected by him. He needed help on nearly every word, but after receiving help the first time he met the word, he seemed to keep it in mind from then on until he had completed the lesson. (His corrections are indicated in the parentheses.)

Dear Juan:

There are some mistakes on this paper.
Can you find the mistakes?
When you find a mistake, cross it out.
Put the right words above the mistakes.

Feeding Animals

Guinea pigs like to eat hamsters. (Lettuce)
Chinchillas like to eat guinea pigs. (Carrots)
Pigeons like to eat Juan Garcia. (Corn)
Rabbits like to eat chinchillas. (Carrots)
Chinchillas are red. (Gray)
Parakeets are black. (Green)
Pigeons are green. (Black)
Juan Garcia likes to eat chinchillas. (Chickens)
Juan Garcia is green. (White)
Juan Garcia goes to Lincoln School—(Adams School)
Parakeets like to eat Adams School—(Parakeets' food)
Guinea pigs do not bite Juan Garcia. (Crossed out *not*)
Hamsters do not bite Juan Garcia. (Crossed out *not*)
Chinchillas like to bite Adams School.—(Lettuce)
Juan Garcia does not like hamsters. (Crossed out *not*)
Juan Garcia does not like guinea pigs. (Crossed out *not*)
Juan Garcia does not like chinchillas. (Crossed out *not*)
Juan Garcia does not like pigeons. (Crossed out *not*)
Juan Garcia does not like rabbits. (Crossed out *not*)
Juan Garcia does not like parakeets. (Crossed out *not*)
Juan Garcia likes to bite rabbits. (Yes)
Juan Garcia likes to bite guinea pigs. (No)
Juan Garcia likes to bite parakeets. (No)

Juan was instructed that the last words of the following sentences were mixed up, that he would find the right ending elsewhere on the page. He changed the last word in each instance to the word in the parentheses:

Dogs eat lettuce.	(bones)
Cats eat bones.	(fish)
Rabbits eat garbage.	(lettuce)
Guinea pigs eat anything.	(corn)
Calves eat corn.	(hay)
Ponies eat fish.	(hay)
Goats eat chicken feed.	(anything)
Pigs eat fish food.	(garbage)
Chickens eat milk.	(chicken feed)

Pigeons eat hay.	(corn)
Fish eat carrots.	(fish food)
Baby dogs are called calves.	(puppies)
Baby cats are called bunnies.	(kittens)
Baby rabbits are called kittens.	(bunnies)
Baby cows are called puppies.	(calves)
Baby goats are called chicks.	(kids)
Baby chickens are called kids.	(chicks)

On the following he wrote what the words were, drew the appropriate picture, and wrote a comment about each:

G - - - - - p - - -	Guinea pigs	I like them
P - - - - - -	Pigeons	I like them.
D - - -	Dogs	I like them.
C - - -	Cats	I like them.
R - - - - - -	Rabbits	I like them.
F - - -	Fish	I like them.
G - - - -	Goats	I don't like them.
P - - -	Pigs	I don't like them.
C - - - - - - -	Chickens	I like them.
C - - - - -	Calves	I like them.
P - - - - -	Ponies	I like them.

Finding Needed Information in a Book. Once Juan arrived at the Reading Center and announced that he was going to buy some guinea pigs next week. He asked if he could see the book which told what they eat and how to take care of them. Worker got the copy of *The Find Out Book*, and Juan found the page for guinea pigs by looking in the table of contents to find out what entry began with G. He copied the list of foods they eat, identifying them by their pictures in some instances. Where pictures were ambiguous, worker had to help him. He learned to recognize the words for the foods, so that he could recognize the words out of context and without reference to pictures.

Grass	Cabbage
Lettuce	Apples
Celery	Beets
Carrots	Rye
Oats	Wheat

The worker wrote sentences for Juan, using these words and other words which could easily be found in the book. (E.g., pigeons, chickens, cats, etc.) Juan read the sentences very laboriously. He also read the three pages concerning guinea pigs in the book with much help and encouragement from the worker, often forgetting words he had recognized on the previous line. In the midst of this reading, he remarked that he didn't like having to read it, because he could not remember what it said. Worker assured him that he would read the whole thing to him after he had finished reading it for himself. This was done. Then Juan asked permission to type the list of words telling what guinea pigs eat, so he could take it home. He did this also very laboriously.

This particular book, *The Find Out Book*, is an unusually fine book for a boy like Juan, who is extremely limited in reading but fond of animals. It contains interesting and important factual material concerning almost any domestic animals a child is likely to be caring for. Facts are presented about their way of life, their care of young, and the feeding and care of the animals. It is well illustrated with much material which helps to build up reading vocabulary, and which presents many picture clues to words in the accompanying text, which is written at second-grade difficulty.

Reading to Juan. One day when Juan arrived at the Reading Center he was attracted by a bright new book which had just been received. He leafed through it, looking at the pictures.

W: Do you want me to read you one of these?
J: Yeah.
W: Which one?
J: Let me find one. . . . This one.

In this way he selected "Pat and the Magic Shoes," "The Magic Rain-cloud," "Roise Jumps the Fence," and "The Stubborn Witch." After reading the last story, the worker asked,

W: Did you like that story?
J: Yeah. I like witches and story about witch.
W: You like stories about witches. Was this witch like the other witches you've heard about in stories?
J: No.
W: What's the difference?
J: The other witch stories tell about the witch kills the prince.
W: Yes? And this one didn't. You like fairy stories, don't you? Who reads them to you?
J: My sister. . . . The story after this one, the Golden Goose, I think, or the shoemaker. Read the shoemaker.
W: You read that one already, didn't you? Oh no, not this one. "The Elves and the Shoemaker." *(Reads)*
J: That was nice. I've read that story before. . . . The golden goose. You got the Golden Goose in there?
W: The man who killed the goose that laid the golden egg, you mean?
J: Yeah.
W: Let's see if we can find it.

The boy selected several more stories, generally from the pictures.

Although the book was written at the third- or easy fourth-grade level, it was far beyond Juan's ability. Hence the worker read to him such stories as he selected. There is a real place in work with a non-reading pupil for him to listen to stories read aloud by someone who can read fluently. The sharing of enjoyable experiences out of a book can help counteract the non-reading adolescent's many previous unpleasant associations with books. The worker had Juan look on while he read, following the pictures and sometimes helping to read key words in the text, drawing freely from picture and context clues. This made the reading a shared activity, even though the boy could not feel that he was actually reading himself.

Juan's rather juvenile level of interest and fantasy was revealed in his selections and in his attitude toward them. Very often this is the case with pupils of Juan's age and mentality. They may be ashamed to display it among their peers, but, like Juan, they may be quite willing to ask for stories they like.

Conclusions

Juan's inability to learn seems to have been part of a general linguistic inadequacy, as speaking and understanding of speech were inadequately mastered arts for him. His general intelligence seems not to have been seriously inadequate, being at least within the dull-normal range. There may have been, however, certain psychological advantages to him in not learning to read. He might, for example, find satisfaction in receiving individual sympathetic attention from adults. This would seem to indicate that significant gain in reading would have to await psychological developments in the boy or in his family environment. He seemed to need and to be able to profit from experience calculated to improve his ability to communicate and to receive communication in the form of language. Here seemed the best possibility of success in teaching him, more promising than in techniques of word recognition, which he seemed to resist.

A pupil like Juan can be very discouraging to a teacher who is too strongly bent on teaching him to read. The boy's responsiveness and interest in fields other than reading, however, suggest that much could be done to help him in many other ways. A teacher who was ready to recognize any significant growth in the boy's ability to meet situations, particularly linguistic situations, and not too much worried about reading as such, could find much satisfaction and accomplishment in working with a boy such as Juan—to say nothing of the liberal education the boy could provide the teacher in the ways of pigeons, guinea pigs, and the rest.

Perhaps Juan's greatest emotional need was to accept and to find acceptance from his own contemporaries. At the beginning of the series of interviews, he was repeatedly expressing hostility toward other boys and girls. The change in schools for him seemed to relieve some of the acuteness of this feeling in him. His helplessness and dependence on adults seemed to abate gradually during the course of the interviews;

this development found expression in his various ways of showing his independence of the worker. During his last few interviews he came to the Reading Center in company with two other boys, one of whom had been on the excursion to Pennsylvania with Juan. Juan displayed a growing ability to participate in normal give-and-take and banter with these boys. He lost, too, any dread of displaying his reading difficulties and was now quite willing to tackle reading tasks in the presence of others.

By the end of the year Juan showed many physical and behavioral signs of maturation. He was no longer evasive about attempts to read, nor did he continue to show signs of fear of reading. He continued to maintain his freedom of choice and independence of the worker, but no longer found it so necessary to proclaim this through negativism.

True, at the end of the year Juan was still essentially a non-reading pupil. But the year seemed to have been well spent. Through the combined influence of normal maturation, a change in schools, his experiences in the Reading Center, and perhaps other influences not known to the worker, he had developed a far more positive attitude toward reading than he had known at the beginning of the year. His prospects for success in many endeavors—including reading—seemed much brighter than at the outset.

30. NONDIRECTIVE THERAPY FOR

POOR READERS

Virginia Mae Axline

Many teachers have sighed despairingly over the poor reader and have asked with a note of weariness in their voices "Are the poor readers here to stay?" for they, like the other "poors" seem to be always with us. The reading problem is so universal that the research in that field is overwhelming. And yet, in spite of all the excellent work that has been done, we still have the group of persistent nonreaders who show every evidence of having the capacity to learn to read, but who, for some reason or another, do not engage in the active participation that is necessary to

Reprinted from *Journal of Consulting Psychology*, Vol. II (March–April, 1947), pp. 61–69. By permission of Virginia Mae Axline and the American Psychological Association Inc. Dr. Axline is the author of *Dibs: In Search of Self* (Houghton Mifflin, 1964) and *Play Therapy* (Houghton Mifflin, 1947.)

bring forth sound and meaning from printed symbols. No one can effect constructive change in another person without the active participation of that person and his desire to change. To create in the individual a desire to change, and to secure the active participation necessary to accomplish the change, is sometimes a very real problem. If a pupil has the capacity to learn to read but is not utilizing that capacity, what can the teacher do to release it?

There have been many attacks upon this problem. It has been recognized for a long time that children do not learn to read until they have built up "reading readiness." Just what do we mean by "reading readiness?"

Classroom experience, research, and the evaluation of both have stressed certain factors that are considered necessary for successful reading progress: the mental age of the child, his social and emotional maturity, experiences that give meaning to vocabulary, adequate skills to enable the child to translate the printed symbols into meaningful words. Certain physical conditions are also important. The child's vision, hearing, and speech are significant factors. Research studies have indicated many influences that seem to enter into the reading problem: handedness, sex, family background, health, nutrition, and others. The schools have earnestly attacked this problem and have contributed to a wealth of material that has increased our understanding. However, we still do not have an adequate solution.

To give the children experiences that can develop their vocabularies, and to give real meaning to reading by using many experience stories, are successful methods. But even these fail to teach some children to read. The use of many very easy books to give the child a feeling of success in his early attempts to read has been tried successfully. To wait until the child indicates that he is ready, that he wants to learn to read; and deliberately to avoid any pressure, so that the child remains relaxed and voluntarily seeks to acquire this skill when he feels a need for it, have also been used successfully. But these, too, have failed with some.

The kinesthetic approach, the phonetic approach, the nonsense-syllable approach, the whole-story approach, the silent approach—there are too many to enumerate them all—give the same results: successful in many cases, useless in others. These varied methods have one characteristic in common: the motivation of the teacher. These techniques are *direct* approaches. The objective is always clear enough in the mind of the teacher. She wants to teach reading, and every one of these devices is pointed directly down the road that says READING in big letters at the end.

Then, there are those exceptions at both extremes that throw a monkey-wrench into the best laid plans of the educators. For example, Mary is very bright, gets along well with the other children, seems quite mature emotionally (she is quiet and well-mannered), has excellent health, good care, a devoted family, excellent vision, hearing, speech, superior vocabulary, and multiple experiences that she can relate with vividness. But Mary cannot read; she blocks completely every time the small reading group assembles. And in the same class is Audrey, below normal mentally, undernourished, severe speech defect, fifty per cent vision, meagre experiences, poor health (she has a cold practically all winter), and yet Audrey can read anything she picks up and can relate it accurately to others. Exceptions, yes. But why?

This article is an attempt to describe briefly an experience with a group of thirty-seven second graders who were poor readers or nonreaders. It was a study that the teacher made in an attempt to determine what results could be obtained by a therapeutic approach, with the objective first of all a better adjustment of the children; happier children, relaxed, unhurried, natural children in the kind of situation that would free the capacities within each one, that would help the children gain a better understanding of themselves and so become better able to help themselves. The procedure is based upon the philosophy that is the foundation of nondirective psychotherapy. The application of this philosophy for the field of education presents a real challenge, and the attendant results seem worthy of more intensive study and research.

The basic philosophy is built upon one central value: a deep respect for the integrity of the individual and a belief in the capacity of an individual to help himself when that capacity is given optimum release. It is a respect that grants the individual the right-of-way to utilize the capacities within himself. It is a respect that implies that the individual has reasons for what he does, that he knows what he is doing, that he is best able to know how he feels and what he wants and why he feels the way he does. It is a respect for the inner self, rather than a "social respect." One might respect an individual for his ability to memorize facts better than anyone else, or to play a better ball game, or to play a musical instrument unusually well. That is respect for an accomplishment, for having obtained a commendable goal, for being able to do something better, and all of this rates high in a competitive frame of reference. In the nondirective philosophy the words "respect for the individual" are used to convey a recognition of the individuality of all men, and a belief that man is entitled to the right to develop to his fullest capacities. It implies that each man is different, that each one proceeds at his own pace, that each one operates within his limitations of one kind or another, but is never exploited for another's gain. This places the focus on the individual, measured against himself and not against others. We are concerned then with matching the inner capacities of the individual with the realization of those capacities in the world of reality. We accept the individual exactly as he is. The individual's behavior tells us a little about him, but there is a much greater part of the individual's inner life that only he knows; for try as we will we cannot penetrate the inner recesses of that self without the active and voluntary participation of the individual.

When we secure the confidence and trust of a little child and he shares his inner world with us, then we are impressed by the child's ability to cope with very serious problems. When the teacher is taken into the confidence of Billy and Mary and Dick, and hears snatches of the feelings and experiences that are a part of their lives, these children are no longer "problem children" to her. They are children who have reasons for being as they are. The teacher sometimes asks herself if she could do as well under similar circumstances. And so the teacher extends her complete acceptance to all the children, granting them all this under-standing. She tries to give them the opportunity and the permissiveness to be themselves in her classroom, to get their feelings and attitudes out in the open, to learn to know themselves, to release their tensions, and thus to clear the way for more positive and constructive growth.

In this class experiment it was the purpose of the teacher to provide the kind of experiences for these children that would be primarily thera-peutic, since she believed that this basic philosophy of respect for the child is a necessary prerequisite for any kind of functional learning. Therefore, the class program was designed to give the children ample ex-pression thru the mediums of art materials, play materials, free dramatics, puppet plays, music, creative writing (dictating their own stories), telling stories they made up themselves, planning for themselves, listening to stories, taking trips, sharing experiences, keeping the bulletin board up to date and alive, and living together in an atmosphere of complete accep-tance. In this framework their feelings and attitudes were not only accepted but clarified for them by an understanding teacher, and their ability to think for themselves and do for themselves was utilized as fully as possible. In the reading groups (there were four of them), they dictated their own stories, read them back, listened to stories, and read easy books. But the children were never compelled to join a reading group; they came to the group voluntarily. When they discovered, after testing the real permissiveness of the teacher's attitude in this regard, that she meant what she said and that the children only came into the group if they wanted to come, then they came. When they came, they were active participants, and willing to learn.

There were thirty-seven children in this group, eight girls and twenty-nine boys. Eight of the children were left-handed. Four of the children had serious eye difficulty. Eleven had speech defects. The intelligence quotients varied from 80 to 148 according to Stanford-Binet tests. The children came from average homes. There were five colored children in the selected group.

During the last two weeks of the first semester, the second grade teachers were asked to list the names of the pupils in their classes who, in their opinion, were seriously maladjusted in reading. Fifty children were so listed. (There were six classes of second graders in this school, the average class size being 38 per teacher.) The Gray Oral Reading Test was given to each of these children. Because each class had to contain a specified number of children, there were to be thirty-seven children selected for this "remedial reading" class.

The fifty children were then given the Gates Primary Reading Test and the thirty-seven who received the lowest scores were placed in this class. Unlike most remedial reading classes, these children were to have all their school work in one room with the same teacher, since these children's reading problems were considered to be a part of the whole child.

Observers visited the class once a week to record the behavior of the children. The teacher took brief notes of some of her talks with the children. Excerpts from the notes of the recorders threw an interesting light upon the emotional problems of the poor readers. These thumb-nail sketches indicated a need for something more important than reading skills for these children. They are random samples, not just the extreme cases.

Dick was a thin, hollow-eyed boy, almost nine and still in the second grade. He stayed on the outer edge of the group. He watched the others, said very little to anyone, and drifted around the room leaving behind him a trail of unfinished work. When, for a moment on rare occasions, he joined in the activities of the group there was soon a flare-up of trouble because Dick had moments of displaying a violent temper. He bit the other children, hit them, kicked them, shoved them. He was bigger than they. And just as quickly as it flared up, it died down, and he cried out his remorse, "I'm sorry! I'm sorry! I didn't mean to!" Dick played truant quite often. When he did his truancy was followed by reports from other children on the way to and from school, from neighbors, store-keepers, and the police. Dick stole, set fires, and committed acts of vandalism. Dick was not at all interested in reading, or in any other school work.

One day, during the children's "work period" Dick decided to paint. The teacher sat down beside him, smiled at him. Dick looked at her with a sad expression in his eyes. He was slopping black paint over his paper. Then suddenly he said to her, "Know what? I'm a bastard—just a dirty bastard and I ain't got no father and I never did have. My stepfather told me he wished I'd never been born. You know what a bastard is, don't you?"

"Yes," said the teacher. "I know. And it makes you unhappy when you think about it—and when your step-father talks to you like that." (Yes, the teacher did know he was illegitimate, but she didn't think Dick knew it yet.)

"I've got a sister," said Dick, and there was a note of pride in his voice. "She's pretty, like a doll. She's three. She's taking dancing lessons." He smiled briefly, then suddenly glowered, "I hate her," he said. "*I hate her.* She gets *everything.* They *love* her."

"She's a pretty little sister—and kind of nice, but sometimes you hate her because she gets things and you don't—and you think they love her better than they do you."

"Yeah!" Dick said. He smeared the paper vigorously. He stabbed it with his brush. Then he looked at the teacher again with a brief smile. "She's got yellow-curls all over her head," he said, "bright as the sun." He paused momentarily. "She's so sweet," he said. His smile changed again to a glower. "Someday, I'll get the scissors and cut them off!" he said. "I'll take the scissors and cut her *throat*. Then they'll feel bad."

"You think she's a sweet little girl—and pretty—but sometimes you feel like hurting *her* to get back at your mother and step-father because of the way they treat you, hm?"

"Yeah," Dick answered soberly. "I wouldn't just hurt her, I'd *kill* her and get rid of her so they wouldn't have her."

"Oh," said the teacher. "You mean you would kill her just to take her away from your parents."

"Yeah," Dick answered, glumly. He placed his other hand down on the wet black paint and smeared it around. "I wouldn't though," he said quietly. "I wouldn't hurt her. Not really. She's the only one at home who likes me. She runs out to meet me. I take good care of her. If anybody ever hurts her, why I fight them until they bleed."

"Then you really think a lot of your little sister and she thinks a lot of you— and you wouldn't hurt her or let any one else hurt her—"

"I'll say I wouldn't. It's my step-father I *really* hate."

There the teacher had a brief glimpse into Dick's inner thoughts. And there were many other times when the teacher sat down beside Dick and talked to him in this manner. Dick had a very real problem and he was not interested in reading, writing, or anything else. First of all he must find some release for these tensions and feelings of conflict. First of all he must feel accepted.

In this type of teacher-pupil relationship, where the children feel free to express their true feelings, where they feel that the teacher understands them, accepts them exactly as they are, and respects them, then they share with her their innermost world. The following very brief excerpts indicate the kinds of thoughts some of these children lived with. The teacher was never too busy to listen. The children came first. The reading, writing, and arithmetic came secondly.

Bill was busily hammering nails in a board. He was muttering to himself when the teacher stopped beside him. She stood there, watching him. He looked up and there were tears in his eyes.

"Something the matter, Bill?" she asked.

"No," he said, with a quivering lip. Then quickly he changed his answer. "Yes," he said. The teacher waited.

"Becky is having a birthday party and she says I can't come," he said woefully.

"Oh," said the teacher. "It made you feel unhappy when she told you you couldn't come." (When a fellow is seven a birthday party is an important event.)

"No," Bill protested vigorously. "I don't wanta go to her old party. I wouldn't ever go. I don't ever wanta go to anybody's party."

"I see," said the teacher. "Then it's not because you weren't invited to the party that you feel so sad."

"No," said Bill, wiping his nose on his sleeve. Then hammering vigorously on the nails, "She said it was because I was a nigger," he said, with a catch in his voice, but thrusting out his chin as he spoke. "But I'm *not* a nigger," he cried. "I'm *not* a nigger." The tears rolled down his cheeks. His eyes beseeched the teacher. "Am I?" he asked her. "Am I—a nigger?"

"It made you feel very unhappy when she called you that, didn't it, Bill?"

"I'm not a nigger," Bill said again, "Am I? Am I?"

"You're *not* a nigger. You're Bill," said the teacher. She looked at his blue eyes, his light brown skin, his brown curly hair. She thought of the little black clip that was attached to Bill's permanent record card. Here was Bill, meeting for the first time the race problem that would probably be like a shadow to him all the rest of his life.

"I don't care if she didn't ask me to her old party," he said.

"You really don't care about the party," the teacher said.

"Yes, I do," Bill said. "Yes, I do; I do care."

"You would like to go if you could, Bill," said the teacher. "I understand. You're unhappy when you're left out."

"Maybe someday I'll have a party and I won't ask *her*," he said.

"You would like to get even with her some day, maybe, hm?"

"Yes," said Bill. The tears stopped. He began to make an airplane—"Look," he said, "this is going to be a B-29." And Bill seemed to have weathered the storm.

Jenny had the habit of continually sucking her two middle fingers. She had driven her former teacher almost frantic with this habit. She was timic cried easily, stood around doing nothing but suck her fingers. One day she came in with her fingers bandaged. She chewed at the bandages nervously. When the teacher sat down beside her she thrust her bandaged finger out toward her.

"Something happen to your fingers?" asked the teacher.

Jenny nodded and returned them to her mouth. The teacher waited. If Jenny wanted to tell her she would.

"Daddy did it," she said.

"Oh?" said the teacher. "Your daddy?"

"With a butcher knife," she said, and her words came out with a rush. "He said if I sucked them again he'd cut them off and I did and I couldn't help it. I couldn't help it and he did. He got the butcher knife and he cut them almost off and they bled and I was afraid and I cried and he shut me down in the cellar and I'm so afraid of the cellar. There are rats down there." There was panic once more in Jenny's eyes.

"You really were scared, weren't you, to have your Daddy cut your fingers and then shut you down in the cellar because you cried?"

"Yes," Jenny said. "There are *rats* down there."

"The rats down in the cellar frighten you, too."

"Yes - yes - " Jenny said. And once more the bandaged fingers were in her mouth.

"Mama said the next time my fingers would probably be cut *clear* off," Jenny said.

"They really *are* scaring you, aren't they?" said the teacher. (What the teacher thought at this point must for the sake of propriety be censored.)

And Donald, one day, colored a picture taking infinite pains seemingly to achieve perfection. The teacher stopped beside Donald.

"Every tiny line just right," he said, peering at it through his glasses. "Oh! what'll I do?"

"You want it to be just perfect, hm?"

Donald looked up at the teacher.

"*My mother does,*" he said with considerable feeling in his voice. "I gotta take every paper I do home and let *her* see it. I gotta always be inside the lines. But I'd like to smear it all up!"

"Mother likes them perfect, hm? but you would like to smear this one all up," said the teacher.

Donald looked at the teacher and a mischievous smile flitted across his face.

"Do *you* care?" he asked.

"No," said the teacher. "I don't care. That is your picture. You do as you like about it."

"Ha!" said Donald—and he snatched up his black crayon and really messed it up. He laughed gaily.

"You enjoyed messing that one up, didn't you?" said the teacher.

"Yes," he said. He snatched up the picture, held it at arms length, gave a wonderful imitation of his mother.

"Now let me see! Oh Donald! Donald! Did *you* do this? Oh, I am *so* ashamed of you! Oh, what *will* I do?"

"Think mother will be upset, hm?"

"Oh yes," said Donald quite happily. "Yes," he sighed. "If she sees it. But there isn't any reason why she should see it." He got up and threw it in the waste basket. "Anyhow, it was fun," he said. And he got another piece of paper and prepared another picture that "mother would like."

"It felt good to mess up that one, but you think that you ought to do another good one to take home, hm?"

"Yeah," said Donald. "She *saves* all my papers."

(Yes, thought the teacher, I expect she would. She comes over every week and wants to know why we don't teach reading here like they did in the good old days when *she* went to school.)

Ronald B. and Barbara were allergy cases. They were nervous and easily upset at the beginning of the semester. They had been in a class where the teacher was very strict, and where there had been pressure applied to force reading. In this class, as a result of the absence of pressure, and an opportunity to relax and be themselves, the allergy symptoms disappeared, and in these two cases the progress in reading was quite high.

As the teacher checked the list of children who were members of this class she was impressed by the many serious problems that these children were facing:

Orville was the only child of a middle-aged mother and a seventy-year-old father. He talked about his room "where they locked him in" and how he "couldn't ever make any noise" and how he "wouldn't dare bring other kids home," and how his mother "rocked him to sleep at nights." Orville couldn't read. He couldn't do anything but stand around, it seemed. But Orville had an I.Q. of 148 and perfect health and perfect vision. His parents couldn't understand why he couldn't read. They really couldn't! It was not until his mother came over once a week after school to see the teacher for counseling that she began to understand things a little better. Orville gradually became an active member of the group, and began to explore his own potentialities.

The teacher noticed that all of these children had a serious problem of one kind or another. She checked the list on her roll book, and jotted down some of the things the children had talked about during the informal chats:

Nancy—"My mother and father are getting a divorce and I just cry about it. I don't want my daddy to never come home."

Bill—"Am I a nigger? Am I?"

Orville—"They lock me in my room at nights. I wouldn't dare bring other kids home. I can't ever make any noise. My mother rocks *me* to sleep at night."

Jim—"Anybody else ever says I steal and I'll bust 'em. Anybody else call me nigger—and they'll see!"

Edna—"Did you read in the papers how my father was murdered? Did you? Did you? I'm afraid to go upstairs at night. I'm afraid I'll—Oh, I don't know. My father was killed. They had a fight. And this man stabbed my father with a knife—I'm afraid."

Leonard—"I don't know anything. I'm dumb. My sisters say I'm dumb—I don't wanta do anything."

Arnold—"My mother got a new baby and they don't want me any more."

Malcolm—"I can't go out and play. Mamma said I might catch cold. Mamma said not to sit in a draught. Mamma said not to paint. It won't wash out—Mamma said—"

William—"I can't see it. What did you say? I don't know what you mean? I can't." (Vision less than 50 per cent. Hearing defective.)

Bruce—"Do you know where babies come from? I can tell you—Do you know what's the difference between boys and girls? It's *bad*—"

Mac—"I didn't have any breakfast. Well—we didn't get up in time. Yeah, this is my winter coat—I hope it don't get *too* cold—We don't have much heat at home."

Janey—"Mamma has gone away. Daddy says she ain't coming back. He won't let her. Yeah—they're going to get a divorce. I wish she would come back. She said she would—"

Donald—"I gotta always be *inside* the lines."

Jack—"Oh, I wouldn't dare. My father would beat me. I gotta take a book home. I gotta study."

Blair—"I don't care whether I *ever* learn to read. My mother says if I don't pass she'll have my dad lick me. Well, I *hate* reading. I *hate hate hate* it."

Ronald—"My cousin got all A's on his card. Mother hopes I can be as smart. My uncle is living with us now. He's crazy from the war. Whenever a car backfires he cries like a baby. Mother says we're going to have to get rid of him."

Allen—"Mamma makes me write my numbers to 100 every night. She wants

TABLE I

Reading Scores (in Grades) and Improvement (in Months) of the Therapeutic Group in Three and One-Half Months (Gates Reading Tests, Grades 1 and 2)

CHILD	WORDS			SENTENCES			PARAGRAPHS			I.Q.	REMARKS
	Feb.	May	Gain	Feb.	May	Gain	Feb.	May	Gain		
2B Group											
1. Nancy	1.35	2.43	10.8	1.57	2.1	5.3	1.5	1.95	4.5	100	
2. Bill	1.35	1.95	6.	1.52	1.62	1.	1.65	1.95	3.	116	
3. Orville	1.7	2.2	5.	1.35	1.8	4.5	1.5	2.05	5.5	146	
4. Jim	1.7	2.2	5.	1.35	1.8	4.5	1.5	2.05	5.5	80	Second Binet 112
5. Edna	1.2	2.2	12.	1.47	2.45	12.	1.7	3.22	17.	126	
6. Glen	1.2	1.3	1.	1.4	1.55	1.5	1.4	1.55	1.5	97	Speech Defect
7. Arnold	1.2	1.85	6.5	1.3	1.62	3.2	1.5	2.0	5.	99	
8. Mac	1.35	1.75	4.	1.2	1.58	3.8	1.3	2.5	14.	95	
9. William	1.6	1.85	2.5	1.4	2.1	7.	1.6	2.2	6.	90	Left-handed. Speech defect. Less than 50% vision.
10. Bruce	1.8	2.1	3.	1.6	2.2	6.	1.8	1.85	.5	92	Speech Defect
11 Balcolm	1.4	1.55	1.5	1.3	1.55	2.5	1.65	1.65	0	88	
12. Becky	1.65	2.37	7.2	1.48	1.65	1.7	1.5	2.4	9.	128	
13. Barbara	1.85	2.33	4.8	1.65	2.5	8.5	1.85	2.9	13.	90	
14. Benton	1.2	1.5	3.	1.4	1.48	.8	1.5	1.85	3.5	117	
15. Ronald	1.5	2.23	7.3	1.57	2.7	13.3	1.7	2.9	14.	113	
16. Leonard	1.27	1.6	4.3	1.42	1.53	1.1	1.7	1.75	.5	103	Left-handed Speech Defect
17. Tommy	1.2	1.9	7.	1.55	1.6	.5	1.7	2.0	3.	107	
18. Larry	1.6	1.9	3.	1.5	1.6	1.	1.9	1.9	0	109	

19. Jenny	1.8	1.9	1.	1.6	2.23	6.3	1.5	1.95	4.5	83	Second Binet 119
20 Dick	1.3	1.75	4.5	1.7	2.2	5.	1.8	2.0	2.	94	Speech Defect
21. Louis	1.5	1.75	2.5	1.5	1.75	2.5	1.5	1.6	1.	92	Second Binet 112
2A Group											
22. Donald	1.85	3.27	16.	1.58	1.8	2.2	2.0	3.2	14.	105	
23. Jack	1.35	1.9	5.5	1.6	2.15	4.5	1.75	2.75	12.	119	
24. Blair	2.5	3.1	6.	1.9	1.95	5.	1.9	2.1	2.	109	Left-handed
25. Ronald B.	2.4	2.5	1.	1.75	2.9	13.5	1.9	2.6	7.	111	Left-handed
26. Allen	2.2	1.75	-5.5	1.62	2.35	7.3	1.8	3.1	13.3	113	Left-handed
27. Ann	0	1.3	15.	0	15.	15.	0	1.5	17.	88	Second Binet 112
28. Arlene	2.15	2.15	0	1.58	2.20	6.2	2.00	2.75	7.5	98	Speech Defect
29. Jamey	1.95	2.27	3.2	2.1	2.6	.5	1.9	2.4	5.	100	Left-handed
30. Jerry	1.7	2.15	4.5	1.57	1.62	.5	1.9	2.1	2.	97	Poor Vision
31. Delores	1.7	2.43	7.3	1.58	2.35	7.7	1.8	2.3	5.	97	Speech Defect / Less than 50% Vision / Left-handed
32. Roger	1.6	2.23	6.3	1.8	2.5	7.	1.4	1.85	4.5	115	
33. Levin	1.9	2.1	3.	1.6	1.9	3.	2.0	2.11	1.	108	
34. Kenneth	1.5	1.5	0	0	0	0	0	0	0	89	
35. George	1.9	2.2	3.	1.9	2.2	3.	1.9	2.2	3.	100	
36. Burt	1.2	1.9	7.	1.3	1.8	5.	1.2	1.9	7.	115	
37. Rollo	1.2	1.3	1.	1.1	1.2	1.	0	0	0	97	

to know when we're going to have spelling lists. She wants to help me be a good speller."

Ann—"Daddy wants me to go back to the Catholic school. Mamma wants me to come here. Daddy wants me to be a Catholic, but Mamma doesn't. Daddy says—"

Arlene—"I don't feel good. I gotta stomach ache. My head hurts. Grandma is at our house now. She's sick in bed. Mamma thinks she's going to die. Do you suppose she will die? What is die?"

Jamey—"Mamma said if my brother started to school next year he would probably get ahead of me because he's smarter than I am. My brother is only five but he can read almost as good as me now. He's smart and I'm dumb."

Jerry—"My mother got a telegram from the War Department. My father's missing. Nobody knows where he is. The Japs probably got him. My mother just cries. He's probably in a Jap prison."

This gives a fair sampling. It seemed to indicate that in many instances the reading problem might have been caused by the child's emotional problem. Other things far more important to the child than reading loomed up on his horizon.

This class experience was built upon as many therapeutic procedures as it was possible to include. Every way of incorporating the basic therapeutic principles that was thought of and that could find a place in the scheme of things was put into practice. There was ample opportunity to find release of feelings and a means of self-expression in the art work, free play, music and rhythm, puppet shows, group and individual stories that the children dictated, and in free dramatics and group interaction. There was no pressure. Everything was on a voluntary basis. The children were respected. They were accepted completely. They were granted the permissiveness to be themselves, to express their real thoughts and feelings, to utilize the capacities within themselves. The children assumed the responsibility for themselves. It was thought that an experience which would help the children gain a better understanding of themselves and a feeling of success and self-confidence and personal worth was a necessary prerequisite for successful academic work.

At the end of the semester, reading and intelligence tests were given again. There were three and a half months between tests. The results of the first and second tests are given in Table I. The gains, given in months, can be compared to the normal expectation of 3.5.

The results of these tests are interesting in view of the fact that no remedial reading instruction was given, and that the reading class attendance was always on a volunteer basis, although most of the chlidren joined the reading groups regularly. There were over two hundred easy library books in the room which the children loved "to look at." There were many preprimers and primers available for their use.

Jim, Edna, Dick and Jenny were given a series of half-hour individual play therapy contacts once a week after school for a period of eight weeks.

In the cases of four of the children there was a noteworthy difference in the first and second Binet test. These tests were given by the same experienced psychometrician before and after the study.

This study indicates that a nondirective therapeutic approach might be helpful in solving certain "reading problems." It indicates that it would be worthwhile to set up research projects to test this hypothesis further: that nondirective therapeutic procedures applied to children with reading problems are effective not only on bringing about a better personal adjustment, but also in building up a readiness to read.

31. REMEDIAL READING FOR THE DISTURBED CHILD

Pearl Berkowitz and Esther Rothman

The disturbed child is one who handles his own life situations in a manner which is painful to him personally and through means which are frequently socially unacceptable. Whatever the outward manifestation of the maladjustment, the most obvious result is a history of social failure, even when intellectually the child is adequate and should have succeeded. Poor social adjustment and rejection by both family and community, of which the school is a part, add to the child's inadequate functioning. Emotional maladjustment can cause academic retardation, and academic retardation can contribute considerably to a child's emotional problems. When one considers that children spend the major portion of their waking day in school, the interrelationship between these two is apparent.

Regardless of the various types of children described as problems, the majority suffer from some degree of retardation in reading. The importance of a reading disability cannot be underestimated, for a reading disability is a disability in almost every area of learning. The child who has a reading disability is usually below grade level in spelling, writing, social studies, and so on. Thus, a reading disability can cause complete failure in school, and surely the child who is failing in all academic areas must suffer emotionally.

The overwhelming importance of reading failure and its relationship to other areas prompted a serious search for some types of new methodology in the teaching of remedial reading. What method could be devised to assure even a small measure of success in teaching a child to

Reprinted from *The Clearing House,* Vol. 30 (November 1955), pp. 165–168. By permission of Pearl Berkowitz and Esther Rothman and *The Clearing House.*

read who in spite of years of schooling has failed to learn to read? Frequently the child has become so discouraged with his lack of progress that to get him even to admit that he cannot read may be a major achievement. Once he has become willing to confide this fact to the teacher, then perhaps remedial reading can begin. The methods with which remediation was attempted, while they were tried with all children, were aimed particularly at the seriously disturbed child. The materials selected differed radically from those with which the child had consistently failed in the schools. The following description indicates, in general terms, the remedial techniques which were used with severely disturbed children who were reading retardates and who received reading instruction in a New York City public school located in the psychiatric hospital where they were patients for observation.

Disturbed children have great difficulty, when using ordinary textbooks, in centering their thought processes on realistic situations. They have developed a kind of phantasy world for themselves, and the implications of this phantasy are so pervasive that even when their thoughts seem to be based on reality, they become imbued with a bizarre quality. Frequently, their thought processes emphasize supernatural themes, and their art productions show gross distortions of realistic thinking.

Since these children apparently could not be approached through the use of commercial reading materials, it was felt that reading for them might be meaningful if they were permitted some distortion of reality as we know it and could imbue this reality with their own phantasies. Since phantasy is the basis for much of the child's experiential background, it is upon this background that his reading was based.

These reading materials, which have been called "phantasy booklets," permitted the child to express his phantasy in a socially acceptable way and utilized the art work in which he participated freely and with which he had previously achieved many satisfactions. The child was encouraged to articulate his phantasy in drawings, verbalize his accompanying ideation to the teacher, who typed or printed the story right on the drawings, and then attempt to read this material, which was actually of his own creation. Reading thus became a most satisfying activity, providing the child with the opportunity to express his own interests and to have these interests accepted by the teacher. For example, the following sentences were dictated by a ten-year-old child, one for each page of a four-page booklet in which he had drawn pictorial representations of the story he was planning to learn to read:

(1) This is superman who will scare away the wolves from the house.

(2) Superman is shooting electricity and lightning into the water.

(3) He saved the whales and the fish by killing the lions and the German submarine.

(4) Superman is a good guy and so is Dracula, Frankenstein, and bloodsuckers. They are all good to me. The end.

When the teacher accepts any and all such story material, regardless of its unreality, as if it were common experience, the child, perhaps for the first time in his life, can feel that he is an accepted part of a learning group, and is encouraged to pursue his studies further. When the program of phantasy reading is carried to its logical conclusion, the child soon develops a large enough reading sight-vocabulary to permit him to relinquish his own phantasy material as a source of learning in favor of available textbooks.

The adolescent who is somewhat inhibited artistically, and not so free in his art productions as the young child, is not able to utilize phantasy material in art expression. He was introduced to reading with a kind of unique word list. He was asked, "If you could learn only five or six words in your whole life, which words would you want to learn most of all?" The reading was then started with this word list. The words frequently were much more difficult than any the teacher would have chosen and sometimes seemed to have no reasonable order except in the mind of the child. The following are three such lists which were suggested by children aged nine, twelve, and fourteen who were complete nonreaders when the program began:

I	II	III
mother	girl	Wolfman
grandmother	stupid	Zombie
Jesus	institution	wife
Christ	electricity	weight-lifting
cat	interplanetary	Atlas
pig		

Amazingly the child who could not seem to remember "up up up" and "down down down" from one day to the next, when he tried to read from the usual primer, managed to learn and retain the words of his own choosing. Each day the list was increased and when enough words were learned, the adolescent was encouraged to attempt a phantasy book, using his word list, in which he dictated his own made-up story to the teacher, who typed it on a primer typewriter—a few sentences on each page. This story, with or without illustrations, depending upon the child's preference, was then used as a reader and the child learned to recognize his own thoughts in print.

Using the same personal reader type of format as the phantasy booklets, the tape recorder was added to the program as a further incentive toward learning to read. Following the pattern of the commercial R.C.A. Victor record readers, the child dictated his original story which was typed by the teacher, again only two or three sentences on each page. (A sound which means "turn the page" was invented by the child so that the few lines on each page could be made palatable as functional and fun rather than infantile.) The story was then read into the micro-phone and after that—for drill—the child listened to his own voice telling the story, while he followed it on the typed pages. The fascination of this activity seemed to be endless, and children appeared never to tire of hearing themselves; learning to read became really painless. The adolescents in particular responded to this method and even those who were able to read invented stories with very difficult words so that they too could be a part of this exciting activity.

Another attempt at using unusual material was made with songs. This method utilized a special type of song, written specifically for this pur-pose and designed to encourage movement and action. Action songs help children to express normal, natural needs in a socially acceptable man-ner. Children like to act with their bodies, to sway their hips, to reach up with their hands, to whirl their heads. These songs offered them opportu-nities for a variety of body movements, acting while they were singing. They had interesting and appealing themes. They were centered about children's phantasy, which is as real to them as reality is to adults: taking a trip to Mars, spending a day with a circus clown, or playing, in turn, every instrument in the orchestra. When the children learned the songs and enjoyed participating in this musical experience, the words of the songs were reintroduced in a new situation, namely, reading. The words were duplicated on separate sheets of paper and the child read from them, while he sang. In addition, to vary the procedure and to force attention to the words, the child was provided with a magnet and a metal bar. The child held the magnet under the paper, moving it from word to word; the little bar, resting on top of the paper, followed it, similar to the bouncing-ball type of singing in movie theaters.

This kind of word recognition drill is purposeful even when the pur-pose is obscured to the child. It is entertaining, done in a social situation, and focuses the child's attention upon words without his being aware that he is learning. The vocabulary used in the songs was simple, the tunes were easy to sing, and it was felt that many children transferred their enthusiasm for singing to an acceptance of learning how to read. Under these conditions the attention span of even the most distractible child was extended, and learning could take place without stress or pressure.

Another device which proved of interest to the disturbed child, helping him to maintain attention and participate with enthusiasm, was a battery-operated quiz-game type of reading drill. This consisted of a series of reading cards, superimposed upon the usual commercial quiz board with two leads and a red light, devised specifically to assist in sound discrim-ination and word identification. The cards were designed to teach phonics, word recognition, picture matching, vowel discriminations, initial consonant recognition, and so on. This game had real value because it held the interest of almost every child who attempted to work with it. They were intrigued by the mechanics of the game and delighted in the little red light which indicated a correct choice of response. The cards were structured in such a way that specific reading difficulties could be worked on either by a group or by an individual.

Of the five materials described in this paper, the most successful as new methodology were the phantasy booklets, the tape recorder, and the word lists. The other two seemed to be excellent supplementary devices for associated learning or specific drill activity. All of the methods had the quality of a uniquely structured learning situation, and those children who feared academic activity because of past failures were stimulated into learning with the presentation of different materials in an unusual manner. It is, of course, apparent from the activities described that many experimental methods were rejected as unsuccessful in favor of these before these five were utilized to any large extent. In addition, the very fact that this type of searching was necessary is an indication of our lack of complete success in the teaching of reading. No one method is the panacea for all children, and regardless of method there are those children who seem not to be able to learn. Even those who are learning seem at times to backslide and give little indication of the amount of effort which has been expended in order to help them. However, in spite of the failures and inadequacies in both our knowledge and our methodology, many children who seem to have had previously no ability to learn to read can actually be taught and can improve in their skill. With enough patience and a tremendous capacity for accepting uneven progress along with the fine successes, one can take a sanguine view of the studies made in the teaching of reading, and remedial reading teachers can look forward toward the evolution of better and more efficient methods in teaching reading to the academic retardate.

32. DEALING WITH EMOTIONAL READING PROBLEMS IN THE CLASSROOM

Lester R. Wheeler

Teachers know that feelings and emotions in some degree are present in all learning. They are aware of the emotional problems of poor readers, but are often confused as to the degree and remediation. This confusion may be somewhat elucidated by studying the symptoms of emotional problems and the remedial procedures. The general trend of

Reprinted from the May, 1954 issue of *Education,* by permission of the publisher, The Bobbs-Merrill Company, Inc., Indianapolis, Indiana.

research varies a great deal in the degree but all indicate a significant relationship between poor reading and emotional problems.

A review of recent research by Dahlberg[9] and others indicates a high incidence of emotional disturbance among poor readers. Weksell[25] found about 50% of poor readers in the freshman class in high school were also emotional problems. Robinson[21] reported a significant number of poor readers were emotional problems. Zalkas[31] maintains that since reading involves the whole child, any imbalance of the organism materially affects reading efficiency.

Bond[7] studied the factors adversely affecting the scholarship of high school pupils, and suggests that the teachers try to understand the psychological reactions of pupils who fail to do good school work. He also stressed the importance of better understanding of the development of fears about school work. Addy[1] emphasized that teachers working with retarded readers need to accept the children emotionally in order to remove or correct emotional problems in their reading.

Nila[16] maintains that the chief foundation of a successful reading program is trained personnel, differentiated reading instruction grouped according to levels of learning, and a well planned program which prevents frustrations in reading. Dolch[11] maintains one of the important factors in remedial reading is to restore the child's security and establish adequate emotional rapport. Harris[14] believes that motivation of the poor reader is of vital importance and teachers must convey to the learner the feeling that he is accepted, liked and understood. This indicates the importance of social factors affecting the child's feelings, emotions and progress in reading.

Delacato[10] made a study of the progress of a small remedial group to eliminate or reduce negative emotional reactions to reading. The experiment ran for six weeks and a wide variety of materials and methods were used. Gates Survey tests were given at the beginning and end of the experiment. A gain of about one grade was shown and the attitude of the group was materially improved according to teachers observations.

Smith[22] in discussing reading in 1953, maintains the teachers must realize that the first step in building reading success among children is establishing a sense of security and emotional stability. Robinson[20] maintains that emotional factors are significant causes of 10-20% of poor readers in the schools today. This indicates a general trend of the importance to the classroom teacher and others working with emotional reading problems.

The causes of emotional problems among poor readers probably conform to the multiple causation theory. This should be considered whenever we attempt to group or classify the emotional factors for discussion. Although the primary emotions, grouped under fear, love and rage, occur early in the child's life, they are influenced by heredity and conditioned into many different types of behavior patterns by training and various experiences. Osborn[17] divides the causes of emotional blocking among reading problems into: (1) primary factors such as sensory discrimination, illness, loss of school time, adverse home conditions, and speech defects; (2) secondary factors which center in disturbances of the home and has some, or all, of the primary factors as well as lack of understanding; (3) tertiary factors such as child's reaction to his situation, lack of confidence, shyness, social adjustment and other personality problems. In diagnosing emotional factors in reading it is difficult to determine whether the emotions are the cause or the result of poor reading. Our clinical experience indicates that the emotions may be both causal and resultant factors in reading retardation.

Emotional problems may be studied or grouped according to the following causes: (1) physical factors such as poor vision, hearing, brain injury, poor health, lack of physical energy, glandular disturbances, inadequate nutrition, lack of physical readiness, etc.; (2) mental factors such as slow learning ability, nervous instability, low in nervous energy, poor associative learning, and emotional immaturity, etc.; (3) social factors such as inferiority in social situations, lack of parental affections, poor social adjustment in the school and home, parental domination, etc.; (4) educational factors such as over-anxiety of teachers, unfair comparisons by teachers, fear of failure, dislike for reading, lack of readiness, delayed instruction, difficulty of materials, inadequate teaching, negative conditioning, lack of wholesome emotional outlets in the school, inadequate methods of evaluation, etc. Any such categorical grouping of emotional factors is inadequate due to various difficulties as to the amount or degree of overlapping, methods of discrimination, etc. Methods often used for discovering the emotional child are (1) standard tests (2) informal tests (3) interviews with children (4) interviews with parents (5) observations, etc.

A study of the symptoms of emotional disturbances may give some basic clues as to the causes for poor reading. Following is a check list of emotional symptoms that may be used by the classroom teacher. To discriminate between the degree of emotional behavior that may aid or retard progress in learning to read, the teacher needs a basic knowledge of the physiology and psychology of emotions, an understanding of child development, and experience in clinical and classroom teaching. As education progresses, the classroom teacher is called upon to assume a greater part in teaching and developing the WHOLE CHILD. A list of remedial suggestions is given to help formulate a program of prevention correction and remediation of the emotional factors that affect not only poor reading but other learning activities in the classroom.

SYMPTOMS OF EMOTIONS IN READING

Observe the child's reading and general classroom activities.
Check (√) any of the following symptoms.

____ 1. Child often bites his finger-nails.

____ 2. He seems to be ill at ease when he is reading.

____ 3. He has a tendency to stutter and stammer in oral reading.

____ 4. The child is often fatigued.

____ 5. He reads at a high pitched voice.

____ 6. He is generally restless in school.

____ 7. He is frequently emotionally disturbed.

____ 8. He is generally inattentive.

____ 9. The child is often over-sensitive about things in general.

____ 10. He is often over-anxious to learn to read.

____ 11. He is poor in all subjects involving reading.

____ 12. Child has poor study habits in reading and other subjects.

____ 13. He often has persistent fears.

____ 14. He shows wide variation on different tests.

____ 15. He may show symptoms of hyper-activity in and out of school.

____ 16. He seems to be insecure in social situations.

____ 17. He feels inferior in reading and general school work.

____ 18. He often wants to retire rather than work with the group.

____ 19. The child has a tendency to resent teacher or parental suggestions.

____ 20. He is often excited and later depressed.

____ 21. He often shows anti-social symptoms with the group.

____ 22. He has a tendency to withdraw from the group.

____ 23. The child feels he has few friends in school.

____ 24. He often craves affections in the school and home.

____ 25. He often shows symptoms of jealousy in social activities.

____ 26. In the same day he may vary one or two grade levels in his reading.

____ 27. He is often a behavior problem in school.

____ 28. He sometimes has temper tantrums.

____ 29. The child is unable to follow through a task in reading.

____ 30. He lacks general confidence, and depends too much on others.

____ 31. The child is afraid of failure and non-promotion in school work.

____ 32. He dislikes reading and most subjects involving reading.

____ 33. He often has emotional blocking in his reading.

____ 34. He often sets goals in reading impossible to achieve.

____ 35. He often does poorly on tests or examinations.

____ 36. He often shows a defeatist attitude toward reading.

____ 37. Emotional tensions increase the longer he reads.

____ 38. He often shows a great degree of inner resistance in reading.

____ 39. He is afraid to succeed.

____ 40. He is afraid to have fun.

____ 41. He often tries to cover up inferiority feelings by compensatory boasting.

REMEDIAL SUGGESTIONS FOR EMOTIONAL PROBLEMS IN READING

1. See that child gets wholesome food, adequate sleep, plenty of rest and recreation.
2. Correct all physical deficiencies which might hinder the child's progress in reading.
3. Change or shift the child's work when you notice fatigue, emotional tension and blocking in his reading.
4. If the child shows a lack of energy, a physical examination by the family physician is very desirable.
5. Encourage group approval to supplement teacher approval.
6. Use oral or audience reading only when the child volunteers or shows a definite desire to read to the group.
7. Use a social promotional plan, and evaluate child's progress in a variety of different ways.
8. Assist the child to adjust to the total classroom situation as well as to the children.
9. Allow the child to work in small groups on materials within his interest, social and independent levels of reading.
10. A careful analysis should be made of the child's learning by visual and auditory methods of teaching. Teaching emphasis should be on the child's best method of learning rather than on his poorest.
11. The teacher should deal with the whole child as far as possible.
12. Study the child's general emotional make-up and teach accordingly.
13. The teacher should meet the needs of the child rather than fit the child to the school and materials.
14. Carefully study emotional symptoms of child in his reading and general behavior and remove underlying causes.
15. The teacher should try to interpret the child's emotional behavior rather than evaluate his behavior.
16. Study the major and minor causal factors underlying symptoms.
17. Secure parental cooperation and work cooperatively with the child.
18. Establish a friendly relation with child and secure desirable emotional rapport.
19. The teacher should create and maintain a desirable emotional climate in the schoolroom.
20. Encourage the development of

a wholesome sense of humor in the child.

21. Have plenty of wholesome play activities in the child's school day.

22. Make full use of visual education techniques in your teaching.

23. Encourage child to read widely on his independent level of reading.

24. Teach the child on his instructional level in reading.

25. Keep the child out of his frustrated level in reading where materials are too difficult.

26. Discover child's hidden talents or the activities he can do well, and reward with adequate praise.

27. Use indirect methods of teaching reading as far as possible.

28. Use games, play therapy, and a variety of techniques in teaching the emotional child.

29. Maintain a folder and keep records of child's progress with accumulated materials for further diagnosis and study.

30. Teacher should proceed slowly in easy materials to build confidence, and gradually introduce material on the instructional level.

31. Encourage the child to read widely in easy material of high personal interest.

32. Maintain a clear and definite purpose for both teacher and child, and keep program well organized.

33. Assist the child after he has gone as far as he can by himself, and gradually build up confidence.

34. Provide opportunities to talk out fears and anxieties, and assist child in discovering harmless outlets for his emotions.

35. Keep calm yourself and remember that emotions are caught as well as taught.

36. Good methods of group teaching will often work with the emotional child as well as the normal child in reading.

37. Encourage child to face, and not run away from, his emotional difficulties.

38. Teach the child to learn self-control and emotional poise in reading.

39. Try to relax the emotional child, and teach him how to discount his emotional problems in reading.

40. Discourage day-dreaming and encourage the child to solve his problems as they arise.

41. Encourage the emotional child to select a task within his ability and finish or complete the task.

42. Praise work well done and inflate the emotional child in reading and general achievement.

43. A change of teachers may be advisable in a general program of remediation of the emotional child.

44. The evaluation of the emotional child should be indirect, informal and on the basis of the child's social, emotional and educational improvement.

45. Give the child an opportunity to release emotional tensions through outlets such as music, dancing, drawing, singing, rhymes, marching, skipping, etc.

46. One of the major roles of the

teacher is to develop emotional readiness, not only in the first grade, but through all grades.

47. Follow the law of relaxation and apply psychotherapy in the process of developing normal emotional growth along with reading.

48. Do not condemn or praise the child's emotional behavior but aid the child in general self appraisal.

49. Encourage the emotional child to interpret his emotional reac-tions and offer self solutions to his problem.

50. Try to give the child adequate security, improve his reading, and build up his emotional strength.

51. Remember that the teacher may be the emotional child's last resort. If she fails, there may be no one from whom the child may get assistance in removing his emotional problems which block or materially hinder him in reading.

REFERENCES

1. Addy, Martha L. "The Influence of Personality Traits on Reading Ability of Elementary School Children." *Journal of Educational Administration and Super-vision.* Vol. 32, (December 1946), pp. 555–58.

2. Anderson, Irving H. and others. *The Psychology of Teaching Reading.* The Ronald Press, New York, 1952, pp. 18–23.

3. Barbe, Walter B. "High Interest, Low Ability Level Reading Material." *Elementary English,* Vol. 30, (May 1953), pp. 281–84.

4. Betts, Emmett A. "Basis for Effective Reading Instruction." *Educational Administration and Supervision,* Vol. 26, No. 9 (December 1940), pp. 679–85.

5. "Factors in Reading Disabilities." *Education,* Vol. 72 (May 1952), pp. 624–37.

6. "Social and Emotional Readiness for Reading." *Educational Administration and Supervision.* Vol. 30, No. 3 (March 1944), pp. 139–64.

7. Bond, Jesse A. "Analysis of Factors Adversely Affecting Scholarship of High School Pupils." *Journal of Educational Research,* Vol. 46, (September 1952), pp. 1–15.

8. Carter, L. J. and others. *Learning to Read.* McGraw-Hill Co., New York: 1953, pp. 17, 20, 167.

9. Dohlberg, C. C. and others. "Psycho-therapeutic Principles as Applied to Remedial Reading." *The Elementary School Journal,* Vol. 53, (December 1952) pp. 211–17.

10. Delacato, Carl H. and others. "A Group Approach to Remedial Reading." *Elementary English,* Vol. 30, (January 1953), pp. 31–33.

11. Dolch, Edward E. "Success in Remedial Reading." *Elementary English,* Vol. 30, (March 1953), pp. 133–37.

12. Eddy, Claire Francis. "A Sixth Grade Teacher looks at Personality Development through Reading." *Reading Teacher,* Vol. 7, No. 1, (October 1953), pp. 29–35.

13. Ephron, Beulah Kanter. *Emotional Difficulties in Reading.* The Julian Press, Inc., New York: 1953.

14. Harris, Albert J. "Motivating the Poor Reader." *Education,* Vol. 73, (May 1953) pp. 566–74.

15. Knight, Elva E. "Personality Development Through Reading." *The Reading Teacher,* Vol. 7, No. 1, (October 1953), pp. 21–27.

16. Nila, Sister Mary. "Foundation of a Successful Reading Program." *Education,* Vol. 73, (May 1953), pp. 543–54.

17. Osburn, Worth J. "Emotional Blocks in Reading." *Elementary School Journal,* Vol. 52, (September 1951), pp. 23–30.

18. Page, James D. "Emotional Factors in Reading Disabilities." *Education,* Vol. 72, (May 1952), pp. 590–95.

19. Robinson, Helen M. "Causes of Reading Failures." *Education,* Vol. 67, (March 1947), pp. 422–26.

20. "Poor Reader, Why?" *Library Journal,* Vol. 78, (May 15, 1953) pp. 875–77.

21. "Some Poor Readers Have Emotional Problems." *Reading Teacher,* Vol. 6, (May 1953), pp. 25–33.

22. Smith, Nila Banton. "Reading in 1953." *Education,* Vol. 73, (May 1953), pp. 532-38.

23. Tinker, Miles A. *Teaching Elementary Reading.* Appleton Century Crofts, Inc., New York: 1952, pp. 35, 51, 58, 123, 237.

24. Wattenburg, William W. "Teachers Can Build Emotional Strength." *Education,* Vol. 74, No. 3, (November 1953), pp. 133–37.

25. Weksell, Wesley. "The Relationship Between Reading Difficulties and Psychological Adjustment." *Journal of Educational Research,* Vol. 41, (March 1948), pp. 557–8.

26. Wheeler, Lester R. "Dealing With Auditory Problems in the Classroom." *Education,* Vol. 67, (April 1947), pp. 511–15.

27. "Dealing With Vision Problems in the Classroom." *Elementary English Review,* Vol. 22, (October 1945), pp. 226–32.

28. Wheeler, Lester R. and others. "Indirect Methods of Teaching Reading." *Elementary English Review,* Vol. 22 (March 1945), pp. 106–8.

29. Wheeler, Lester R. "The Child Who Dislikes Reading: Causes and Remedial Suggestions." *Elementary English Review,* Vol. 23, (October 1946) pp. 267–71.

30. Young, Norman and others. "Implications in Emotionally Caused Reading Retardation." *Elementary English,* Vol. 28, (May 1951), pp. 271–75.

31. Zalkas, H. H. "What Research Says About Emotional Factors in Retardation in Reading." *Elementary School Journal,* Vol. 51, (May 1951), pp. 512–18.

33. SOME PRINCIPLES OF REMEDIAL INSTRUCTION FOR DYSLEXIA

N. Dale Bryant

Specific, severe disability in word recognition (dyslexia) is usually resistant to standard remedial procedures. Many children with dyslexia remain virtual nonreaders in spite of years of remedial work. Dyslexia cases can learn to read, but only if the teacher recognizes the nature and extent of the child's difficulties and uses procedures appropriate for dealing with those difficulties. Teachers need a frame of reference for planning remediation of these cases—some principles as well as techniques. The points outlined below represent an application of learning principles to the specific disabilities found in working with several hundred reading disability cases.* The principles are not inappropriate for teaching retarded readers other than those with dyslexia. Characteristics of dyslexic children have been discussed by many authors, notably Money (3) and Bryant (1). The relationship of dyslexia to other reading problems has been discussed by Rabinovitch (4) and Bryant (2). Bibliographies in these references provide a more comprehensive introduction to this extensive literature.

The following principles are not a method of remediation but are, instead, a partial framework on which effective remediation can be built. Several principles are common to all efficient learning. They are emphasized here because the learning difficulties of dyslexic children necessitate close adherence to general learning principles.

Principle 1. Remediation should initially focus on the simplest, most basic perceptual-associational elements in reading: perception of details within the Gestalt of words and association of sounds with the perceived word elements.

A child with dyslexia does not readily abstract and make generalizations like those that allow the normal child to improve basic skills of reading on his own. If a child is reading second grade material, merely practicing at this level can benefit some retarded readers, but a child with dyslexia is likely to continue to be confused. The teacher should focus remediation upon the child's difficulties and simplify the work so that

Reprinted from *The Reading Teacher*, Vol. 18 (April 1965), pp. 567–572. By permission of N. Dale Bryant and The International Reading Association.

* This paper results from an investigation supported in part by a project grant OM 225 from the National Institutes of Mental Health, Public Health Service, and a research grant from the Association for the Aid of Crippled Children.

confusion is avoided and the basic perceptions and associations are learned so well that they will not be forgotten.

One of the major problems exhibited by dyslexia cases is the difficulty in perceiving and retaining a detailed image of a word. This is seen clinically when a child recognizes a word on one line and is unable to recognize it, or incorrectly identifies it, on the very next line. The child is operating on rather minimal cues (often the initial letter, the length and general shape of the word) and the context of the selection being read. *Calling attention to the details within a word is an important aspect of remedial teaching.* Writing or even tracing the word is useful not only because of possible kinesthetic-tactile facilitation of memory but, perhaps more important, because the child's attention is called to each letter within the word. Another effective technique consists of presenting the word with one or more letters left out. As the child fills in blanks and finds that he is right, he is forced to become aware of the missing details. Flash cards or tachistoscopic practice can insure the rapid recognition of the details within words that is necessary in actual reading. Practice in rapid discrimination of words from other words that differ only slightly insures that the perception of details is well established.

A second major problem for dyslexia cases is the difficulty in associating sounds with letters and perceived word parts. This is a basic element of all reading by children who have usable hearing, and it functions in recognizing "sight words" as well as in its more obvious role in sounding out new words. Until basic symbol-sound associations are established, learning new words and increasing reading level are likely to provide only inconsistent gains. To get around the inability of the dyslexia case to abstract these associations from words he learns, the remedial teacher should focus on a single association or, at most, a few associations until practice has firmly established the relationship.

To be effective in reading, when the letter is presented as a part of a word, the associated sound must be quickly blended with other sounds to produce the word. The child should, therefore, practice with words rather than individual letters. The words should be chosen so that the particular sound association is the only process requiring effort for the child. Every word that is written, every letter filled in, or word briefly seen should be pronounced aloud so that practice of symbol perception and sound association takes place. *Always the pronunciation should be correct, aloud (so you know it is correct), and immediate.* If the child ever falters, the word should be pronounced for him.

Principle 2. Perceptual and associational responses should be overlearned until they are automatic.

An automatic response occurs when a response to a letter or word part becomes so well established that a person does not have to consciously try to select an appropriate response. For example, an immediate association of sound with a letter (or common combination of letters) is usually made by normal readers. All common associations should become automatic for good reading, including the modification of a sound because of another part of the word (as in the rule of silent *e*). In quickly recognizing a word, many component discriminations and associations are automatically made that otherwise would confuse or distract from other discriminations or associations.

To develop automatic responses for the basic discrimination of letters, and for the association of sounds, the child needs to overlearn these basic skills and to practice them in complex words. Flash cards, tachistoscopic practice to discriminate from similar words, or the rapid reading of sentences are useful in establishing automatic responses. *The teacher should not encourage laborious sounding out.* Simple enough tasks should be used in learning so that recognition is always quick. As learning progresses, the difficulty of the task can be increased until, even in difficult words, the association of sound responses to the word parts is relatively quick and automatic.

Typically, dyslexia cases cannot deal at any one time with many discriminations or associations that are not automatic, and this is probably a major reason for failure of remediation with these cases. Even three-letter words often cause confusion. Dyslexic children cannot single out the perceptual and associational elements basic to word recognition on their own, so the remedial teacher must present tasks which will cause the child to develop automatic responses in the basic elements of reading one at a time.

Principle 3. The remedial teacher should plan the learning experience and modify the presentation of the task and material on the basis of the child's performance so that the child is correct in nearly all of his responses, regardless of whether they are made aloud or to himself.

Incorrect responses can produce negative learning and confusion, as well as damage the confidence and motivation of the student. Every teacher has seen a child make an error and then have other errors snowball, even for tasks the child was previously able to do. This is particularly characteristic of dyslexia cases. They seem unusually vulnerable to confusion, perhaps because they have less depth and stability in their previous learning. Learning is based primarily on increments of correct response with immediate knowledge that the response is correct. *Any remedial session in which the child is allowed to make predominantly incorrect responses, particularly when he thinks even for a minute that they may be correct, is damaging to the child.* He may lose what he has gained, and may handicap future learning. Any time a child, who is trying, makes several errors in a row, it is likely that the teacher has made an incorrect judgment in selecting materials or tasks. Long delay in a response that should be automatic is in itself an error. Many concepts and techniques for keeping tasks within the capability of the child are the same as those described in articles on programmed learning.

Principle 4. When two discriminations or associations are mutually interfering, the following steps should be taken consecutively: (1) one of the discriminations or associations should be learned to an automatic level; (2) the second should then be learned to an automatic level; (3) the first should be briefly reviewed; (4) the two should be integrated, starting with tasks where only the difference between the two need to be perceived; and finally, (5) in graduated steps both should be made automatic when the task requires discriminations and associations in addition to the mutually interfering ones.

Mutually interfering discriminations or associations occur frequently and remain a source of confusion to the dyslexic learner. Probably the best example is the association of several sounds for a particular letter. Vowels look somewhat alike and are often used interchangeably by dyslexia cases. Complicating the situation is the fact that every vowel has more than one sound and that the sounds are very similar to those of other vowels. This is a major stumbling block for dyslexia cases because it is a basic perceptual-associational element of even simple reading (Principle 1). It is important to overlearn each symbol-sound association until it is automatic (Principle 2). Not only will this overlearning contribute to phonic skills in sounding out new words, but the association of the sound seems to give more definite structure to the visual image of a letter and facilitates its rapid recognition within a word. The problem facing the dyslexic child is that he has difficulty in abstracting the different letters and sounds in a normally complex situation, so *the remedial teacher must limit the discriminations and associations required* to the point that the child can successfully handle them (Principle 3). When presented visually with a particular vowel, the dyslexic child is likely to respond with any one of five short vowel sounds or with any other sound with which vowels are associated. These are mutually interfering discriminations and associations (Principle 4). Even his visual discrimination of vowels is often poor, perhaps because the vowels are not clearly differentiated in terms of sounds.

If the reading teacher can stabilize the discrimination of each letter and the correct association of a *short* vowel sound with the appropriate sound, most of the confusion can be eliminated. The child will then possess the stable skills which will allow him to go on and learn conditions under which specific vowels have long or other sounds. Following this principle, a teacher might work with simple words using a single vowel, such as short *a*, until the child correctly and automatically responds with a short *a* sound any time this vowel occurs in a word. Then a second vowel (e.g., *o*) would similarly be associated with its short sound until the perception and association became automatic. A review of the short *a* association would be made to insure that the later learning had not caused the forgetting of the earlier learning (retroactive inhibition). Then, since both of these associations would have been established, whenever the child knows that a word is going to contain a short *a* or that it is going to contain a short *o* sound, the remedial teacher would start with words which differ only in the medial vowel. All should be words that the child has previously perceived and sounded automatically.

The flash card presentation of pairs of words such as *cat* and *cot*, *hat* and *hot* would give the child practice in rapidly discriminating which vowel is present and also practice in giving the correct short sound associated with it. If the child has some trouble, the teacher should limit practice to a single pair of words (e.g., let the child know the word is going to be either *cat* or *cot*) so that little discrimination is required of him. If his recognition skills are somewhat more advanced, or after practice with simpler discrimination tasks, the child might know only that a card will be drawn from four specific pairs of words with which he has previously practiced.

Eventually, the task should be such that in flash card presentation or in the reading of sentences the child can rapidly and correctly discriminate the vowel and give the correct short sound association at the same time that he is discriminating any other combination of consonants. At that point he would be able to recognize and immediately pronounce any three-letter word having as its medial vowel either short *a* or short *o*. In fact, he should be able to perform correctly with nonsense syllables in which the medial vowel is either short *a* or short *o*.

Once he is stable in his discrimination of short *a* and short *o*, the entire cycle can be repeated with his learning a third vowel. After the sound association of a short sound with this third vowel is well established, the short *a* and short *o* words should be briefly reviewed. Discrimination of words containing this third vowel (e.g., *cut*) from similar words containing either the short *a* or the short *o* (e.g., *cat* and *cot*) could be practiced in increasingly more demanding tasks until any three- or four-letter word containing one of the three vowels can be identified in less than a second. The same procedure would be repeated with the fourth short vowel and the fifth short vowel with integration and practice each time.

Rate of progress will depend upon the child's impairment. Some children can establish automatic association of short vowel sounds with their respective letters in a few sessions. Other children may require months to become stabilized in even a few short vowel associations.

Of course, the foregoing example is only one illustration of the application of the principles. Such procedures would have to be incorporated in a comprehensive program. A full discussion of the application of the principles would be too long for this paper. Nevertheless, some examples of others areas might include the following: As nonphonic words are needed, they can be taught as sight words, reminding the child not to sound them out. Sight words should be overlearned with attention given to discrimination of details within the word. Once a child can recognize any brief short vowel word, his perceptual and associational skills are likely to be well established. Polysyllabic words can be introduced by combining known words. (The child is likely to introduce them himself and with reasonable skill.) Long vowel sounds can be taught by starting with words the child knows and showing him how they change when, for example, silent *e* is added, or when the vowel ends the word. Once basic skills are stabilized at an automatic level, routine remedial procedures using small steps and lots of reading will take a dyslexic child the rest of the way to adequate reading achievement.

Principle 5. There should be frequent reviews of basic perceptual, associational, and blending skills, and as rapidly as possible these reviews should involve actual reading.

Dyslexia cases are often thought to have poor memory, and, indeed, they do for reading material. This may be because their learning is not well established. It is essential that every skill that a child learns be frequently reviewed. This occurs normally in reading, but because of the low level of skill of most dyslexia cases and their avoidance of the reading situation, review must be planned within the remedial session itself. Review should always be slanted towards rapid perception, rapid discrimination, and rapid association—all need to be automatic skills. It is possible to obtain or to construct reading exercises which utilize only the skills the child has already learned, thus giving him practice in what he has learned and avoiding skills not yet established, thus avoiding confusion.

Remedial activities based upon the principles discussed above are not intended to be mechanically applied. Successful remedial instruction of dyslexia will be influenced by the extent to which the teacher can couple the richness of previous teaching experience with (1) skill in identifying the cause of the child's difficulty at any point in the lesson, and (2) ability to modify instruction so that only the most basic difficulty is worked on until it is solved and integrated. Within the scope of the principles outlined for work with dyslexic cases, many procedures can be used effectively—and finding new techniques should be a creative challenge to the teacher.

REFERENCES

1. Bryant, N. D. "Reading Disability: Part of a Syndrome of Neurological Dysfunctioning." In J. A. Figurel (Ed.), *Challenge and Experiment in Reading.* New York: Scholastic Magazine Press, 1962.
2. Bryant, N. D. "Learning Disabilities in Reading." In J. A. Figurel (Ed.), *Reading as an Intellectual Activity.* New York: Scholastic Magazine Press, 1963.
3. Money, J., Ed. *Reading Disability: Progress and Research Needs in Dyslexia.* Baltimore: Johns Hopkins Press, 1962.
4. Rabinovitch, R. D., Drew, A. L., DeJohn, R. N., Ingram, W., and Withey, L. "A Research Approach to Reading Retardation." In R. McIntosh and C. C. Hare (Eds.), *Neurology and Psychiatry in Childhood.* Baltimore: Williams & Wilkins, 1954.

34. CORRECTIVE READING IN THE CLASSROOM

Marianne Frostig

Three major approaches to the teaching of reading may be distinguished, principally on the basis of the materials commonly used. With the so-called basic approach the teacher uses the familiar basic readers, and the children are usually grouped according to reading achievement. During the reading lesson the children are told about the material they will read, and new words are introduced before they read. The individualized reading approach permits each child to make his own selection from a great variety of books, magazines, and pamphlets. The teacher gives assistance as needed. Each of these approaches has advantages and disadvantages for a total communication program. The language experience approach meets many of the disadvantages of the other two since in this approach the reading material is mainly composed by the children themselves. They tell their experiences in class and the teacher writes them down for later reading.

All of these approaches to the teaching of reading are valuable and each supplements the others. They are the three major lines of approach, and none can be neglected. Nevertheless, in teaching reading to children who have learning difficulties, whether the cause is emotional disturbance, brain damage or a developmental language disorder, it is necessary to modify and augment these approaches. This paper is devoted to an account of a variety of ancillary methods which should be used to supplement these approaches when teaching children with learning difficulties. But I should like to state most emphatically that these additional techniques can be used very effectively in the regular classroom as well as with exceptional children. They can speed up the process of learning to read for all children and help eliminate nagging difficulties that might impede even a relatively proficient learner.

Labeling

During World War I, Kurt Goldstein developed methods to rehabilitate soldiers who had suffered brain damage because of gunshot or shrapnel wounds. He found that some of those who had lost their reading ability were unable to regain the skill when taught by the regular methods

Reprinted from *The Reading Teacher*, Vol. 18 (April 1965), pp. 573–580. By permission of Marianne Frostig and The International Reading Association.

because the symbolic functions of their brains had been impaired. Reading involves a double symbolic process, for not only are the spoken words symbols, representing real things or events (the word *chair* stands for a real chair, *house* for a real house, *running* for a certain type of locomotion), but the printed words are symbols also, standing for the combination of sounds that make up the words.

To help soldiers whose ability to master symbols had been impaired by cerebral dysfunction, Goldstein introduced a method of matching words to pictures. Kindergarten teachers now often use a similar method by putting labels on objects or pictures in the room. When a child first sees the configuration of the word *chair*, it is meaningless to him, but when he sees it paired with either a real or pictured chair he can understand what it means. The child at this stage is only labeling, however; he cannot be said to be reading until he is able to recognize and understand the word alone, unsupported by the object or picture.

In teaching children with reading difficulties by this method, we usually start with just two words. The two words, cut out from an old workbook, and their matching pictures are put in an envelope fastened to the back of a page, ready to be matched with either the words or pictures pasted on the front of the page. When the child can match the words and pictures well, the identical two words are used again on the next page, but with a new word added, and this system is maintained. All three words are used on the third page, plus a fourth word. The matching can be repeated indefinitely, since the material to be matched is always available. The child should switch frequently between matching words with pictures and matching pictures with words. The words should be joined in as many ways as possible to form simple phrases or sentences. The words *run* and *Billy* can be written "Run, Billy," or "Billy, run," or "Billy, Billy, run!" for instance.

This method is, of course, limited by the fact that only words for concrete objects or depictable actions can be matched with pictures. Conjunctions and other parts of speech which exist for the purpose of organizing language cannot be illustrated. Such words as *the, to,* and *and* have to be added gradually to the illustrated words so as to make phrases and sentences. These words have to be learned by repetition, but only in the context of phrases or sentences in which their function is clear.

The labeling method has been found of particular value in teaching children suffering from specific dyslexia or more pervasive defects, such as mental retardation, who fail to learn by any other method. The process requires careful use and preparation by the teacher, but usually need not be maintained for an extended period. When the child has learned to match from nine to twelve words, he will very likely indicate that he has developed the ability to visualize words and will no longer need the help of pictures.

The Highly Controlled Vocabulary

All books designed for children just learning to read employ a vocabulary which is controlled to some degree, with new words being introduced slowly and with frequent repetition. But in teaching children who have learning difficulties, this process needs to be intensified. In preparing such children for reading a preprimer, for instance, it is advisable for the teacher to first compile original books for them, using the same vocabulary that is used in the preprimer. The teacher thus has control over the pace at which vocabulary is accumulated and can eventually provide each child with encouraging success when he tackles the printed book.

The teacher should write in the right upper corner of each page of each child's book the words that the child has learned in the order of their original presentation. In the middle of the page the same words are presented in story form. As soon as the child knows a few words, this presentation is made in as lengthy units as possible—phrases, sentences, and finally paragraphs—rather than in the individual words or two-word phrases which necessarily characterize learning by the matching method. Emphasizing larger word units avoids chopped and relatively meaningless learning, which lessens interest and fails to instill a feeling for the structure of language.

One or two new words should be introduced daily, and repeated daily for a sufficient period of time to insure overlearning. The list of words in the upper corner constitutes a record of the sequence. If a word is missed, the teacher can go back to the page on which this word was first introduced and review the succeeding pages. When necessary, a page is prepared without new vocabulary for the purpose of review. It is helpful to give the children familiarity with reading different kinds of print by composing the reading matter in the book from words cut from old textbooks, newspapers, and magazines, as well as from words written by hand in both articulated and cursive writing. Illustrations can be gathered similarly from a variety of sources or can be made by the children themselves.

Proper names which occur at this stage in most preprimers are best omitted, because they are not common vocabulary and because it is best to teach the children to think in a less specific way at first than by reading stories about a single family. The appropriate proper names can be introduced when the rest of the vocabulary has been learned and the child is about to read the book itself. When the child has learned to read one book in this way, he should learn to read others in a different series at a similar level before progressing to the vocabulary and stories of the next level.

Other commercially available books may be used in addition to primers and preprimers in such a way as to insure sufficient repetition of each word. For instance, the series called Easy Readers, published by Wonder Books, New York, has a highly controlled vocabulary and a great deal of repetition, but as with all commercial books, some words are repeated as many as thirty times and other words only a few times. Before giving these books to the children, therefore, all words which are likely to cause difficulty should be written on flash cards and learned beforehand. Words which are missed by the child in reading the book should also be written on flash cards or listed on a chart and taken home by the child for review.

The Easy Readers may also be used to develop other reading skills. A list of printed questions concerning the text can be prepared, glued to cardboard, and inserted in a pocket on the last page of the book. These questions help the child in developing certain areas of reading comprehension or reading skills, such as finding a certain bit of information on a particular page, finding the main idea of the story, finding a word which rhymes with a given word, and so on.

Teaching reading by the use of a highly controlled vocabulary can be adapted to work with both the usual basic readers and individualized reading programs. Insuring adequate mastery of the vocabulary beforehand greatly enhances the probability that the child will enjoy what he reads and will acquire increased motivation.

The Child's Own Book

A third auxiliary method consists of constructing a book based on each child's own experiences and using it according to the principles of the language experience approach, in which reading, writing, and oral language are integrated. The fact that the child's own experiences constitute the subject matter does much to assure his interest and cooperation.

The child is presented with a booklet made from newsprint stapled between sheets of construction paper, and he is told that the teacher is going to help him to make his own book. The teacher will necessarily have to steer the child closely to make sure that the vocabulary is appropriate to the child's level and is augmented sufficiently slowly. On the first page is pasted a photograph of the child, or a picture of any boy or girl, and the name of the child is written beneath it. Then one or two more words may be added so that a simple sentence can be written: for example, "I am Billy," or "See Billy." In writing the next page, the child can be asked what he saw recently that interested him, and the sentence constructed accordingly. It might read, "Billy, Billy, see the car," or "I see a dog." The incident to which this new word, *car* or *dog* refers is discussed, and the simple sentence may have all the qualities of a real adventure for the child.

I recall how successful this method was with Jim, a little boy from Alaska who had been sent to us because he had not been able to learn to read. He was at first very homesick for Alaska. His teacher talked with him about what he liked best there, and he told how he went out in a boat to fish with his father. For the first page of Jim's book, the teacher put a picture of a father standing by a boat, and the words were, "Jim, see the boat." Jim and his teacher talked about the construction of the boat, how it would be launched, and so on. For the second page, the teacher wrote under a picture of a father beckoning his son: "Jim, ride in the boat. See the boat, Jim. Jim, ride in the boat. See, Jim, see! See the boat." Jim told how the first time he went out in the boat he was so excited that he could not sit still and his father told him not to jump in the boat. So his third page read: "Jim, ride in the boat. See Jim ride. See Jim jump. Jim, Jim, jump not in the boat. Jump not in the boat, Jim." In the upper right corner of the first page the words used were written: *see, Jim, the, boat*. On the second page, the words used were written in the same order in the right hand corner: *see, Jim, the, boat, ride, in*. The words on the third page were: *see, Jim, the, boat, ride, in, jump, not*.

In this way the story was developed, and the entire preprimer vocabulary introduced with sufficient repetition. For the adult the story may seem somewhat inane, but for the child it represented a series of most pleasurable experiences.

Besides learning to read the words, the child should be taught to write them as soon as possible, and he should be encouraged to read his book to other children and discuss with them the contents of his book and theirs.

The Child's Own Book method need not be restricted to young children. It was found to be equally effective for teaching a group of nonreading adolescent girls between thirteen and seventeen years of age in a camp for juvenile delinquents near Los Angeles. These youngsters had not even mastered the preprimer vocabulary, and an attempt to teach them from a printed book would have evoked only a scornful refusal to work. The idea of making books of their own, however, caught their interest. Surprisingly, they did not choose as their subjects the lives of film stars or stories of crime or romance, as might be expected, but cooking, travel, and flowers.* When they had learned a basic vocabulary in the manner described above, they were told that they were now equipped to read a preprimer. They were at first reluctant to try, until it was suggested that they should imagine they were mothers wanting to read a story to their children, or older sisters reading to the younger members of the family. This imaginative touch stimulated them to read aloud in turn from a preprimer, and they were delighted with their accomplishment.

*A catalog is often a most helpful source for illustrations. In this instance a Sears-Roebuck catalog and a National Park brochure were used.

Phonics

The purpose of teaching phonics is to help the child to recognize the association between the phoneme and the grapheme—between the auditory stimulus, the sound, and the printed word or symbol. It is often possible to teach reading without the aid of phonics by using the whole-word method, but in our experience, the latter method is difficult, if not impossible, for children with certain disabilities in visual perception, nor does it give a child a tool with which to attack new words. It seems, therefore, that the whole-word method should be augmented by instruction based on phonics.

Teaching a child to associate the sounds of the language with the written symbols is especially difficult in English, because of the great disparity between many of the spelling and phonetic rules. Even the greatest admirers and promoters of the phonic methods, such as the author of *Why Johnny Can't Read*, cannot claim that more than 80 per cent of the words in the English language are phonetically written, and many maintain that the proportion is less. It is even difficult to teach rules of exception, since there are exceptions to the exceptions. For instance, when the letter *i* appears in short syllables, it is pronounced as in the word *bit*, *except* when it appears before the letters *nd*, when it is pronounced with a long sound (as in *kind*), *except* in the word *wind*, referring to air in motion.

For this reason, we place greater emphasis upon a functional approach to phonics than upon a systematic teaching of phonetic rules, but it must be acknowledged that opinion on this question is divided. Sabaroff (5), for instance, found that an experimental group of low achievers made progress with systematic instruction in the rules of phonics.

Color Cues

Our usual method is to associate phonemes with graphemes from the beginning, writing each distinct sound in a word in different color. The first words to be introduced are, of course, phonetically "pure," and it is best to introduce words containing short vowels first, then words with long vowels, and finally more complex sounds, such as diphthongs and digraphs. Where letter groups are pronounced uniformly, as, for example, the combination *ur* in the words *hurt, curtain, turn,* the letters in the group are written in the same color, to help the child learn the pronunciation of that particular combination. Sometimes it is necessary to teach a child to read only the initial letter in a word, at first, then the last letter, and finally the middle letter or letters. In these cases, the appropriate letter only is colored. Colors can also be used to teach syllabification, each syllable of a word being written in one color. Silent letters, such as the *e* in *those,* can be indicated by an appropriately insubstantial stippled effect so that the letter does not stand out from the background. We have not generally found it necessary to use the same color for one sound consistently, except in a few instances in which a child shows a particular difficulty which he can be helped to overcome by receiving a consistent cue, but we have found it useful to use consistently one color for *all* of the long vowels, and one other color for all of the short vowels.*

Kinesthetic Methods

The sense modality basic to the reading process is of course vision. Accurate space and form perception are essential. But when a child has disturbances in visual perception, the visual modality can be supported by the auditory even at the beginning of reading (as with the phonic instruction described above) and also by the kinesthetic modality. As kinesthetic activities are largely a matter of tracing, they not only provide training in reading but serve also to further writing and spelling skills.

Kinesthetic methods have other advantages as well. They form a bridge between the experience of an act extended in time, which occurs when we hear, and the experience of an act extended in space, which occurs when we see. Whenever we say a word or read it aloud, we experience an act which is extended in time. The *v* at the beginning of the word *visual,* for instance, is heard before the *l* at the end of the word. But when we read silently, we usually take the word in at a glance, and all of the letters seem to be perceived at the same time. The word is no longer perceived as extended in time, but as extended in space. It may be that it is just this translation from a spatial dimension to a temporal one, and vice versa, which makes it difficult for a child to associate words which he hears with the printed word. The kinesthetic method helps overcome the problem by forming a bridge between the auditory stimulus and the visual one. When we write or trace a word, it takes *time* to write it; we perceive that a time span elapses while we are writing. We also experience a spatial dimension as we see the word "grow" from left to right on the page. When a word is presented kinesthetically, therefore, it has both a temporal and a spatial dimension, which makes it easier for the child to connect the two experiences of seeing and hearing.

There are many modifications of the kinesthetic method. Pulliam (3) has suggested that children write in grooves, experiencing in this way the movement of the word and learning its kinesthetic pattern. For children

---

*We have not discussed the use of the Augmented Roman Alphabet in teaching reading because we have had no experience with it. It would seem to be a very worthwhile method, however.

with severe motor defects, it is helpful to write in clay or on some similarly resistant surface. Many clinics advocate the Fernald method (2) of first tracing words with the fingers and then writing them.

Blind Writing

The blind writing kinesthetic method deserves a detailed account because of its effectiveness with children whose visual perception is inadequate, as is often the case with children who have minimal brain damage.

Recent research (1, 4) has shown that even in small children the visual experience is stronger than the haptic one. ("Haptic" means the dual experience of touch and kinesthesia, which are combined, for instance, in taking an object in one's hand and feeling it totally while moving a finger over it to experience its shape.) When the children were first shown something which they experienced visually, and then felt the same object without looking at it, their final description of the object was in visual terms rather than in terms of touch. Because of this natural predominance of the visual modality, a child with a severely distorted visual perceptual sense is very seriously handicapped. It is necessary in these cases to train the child's less effective, but at least unimpaired, kinesthetic abilities so that he can perceive accurately by movement, as blind children can do. The kinesthetic modality can then be used to guide the visual one.

To teach the child to write and read by the blind writing method, the teacher first writes the letter or word on the chalkboard at a height which can easily be reached by the child. Then the teacher guides the child's hand while he traces the word with closed eyes. The elimination of visual stimuli enables him to concentrate entirely upon the kinesthetic experience. While the teacher guides the child's hand, she pronounces the word slowly, trying to use as much time for saying the word as the child takes in tracing it. With repetition, the teacher will feel the child's hand begin to follow the lines of the word independently. She can then remove her hand while he continues to trace, without opening his eyes and without her assistance. The next step is to have him make the connection between the kinesthetic and the visual modality by looking at the word as he traces it, and then as he writes it. The child is finally asked to find the word on a page in his book, to read the sentences in which it appears, and then to write it again. The use of cursive writing is a great advantage because of the uninterrupted flow of the kinesthetic pattern the child perceives, even though he has to make the association between the written and printed forms of the word.

Causes of reading difficulties. Difficulties in reading occur not only because of a specific difficulty with the reading process itself. They may be due to disabilities in comprehension or to a lag in any other area of development, such as in perception, motor skills (especially eye movements), language, and social and emotional development. The possible difficulties in any one of these areas are legion. But the corrective methods described above can be used with all children in the regular classroom during corrective reading.

REFERENCES

1. Birch, Herbert G., and Lefford, A. "Intersensory Development in Children," *Society for Research in Child Development Monographs,* Vol. 28 (1963).
2. Fernald, Grace M. *Remedial Techniques in Basic School Subjects.* New York: McGraw-Hill, 1943. p. 349.
3. Pulliam, Roy A. "Invented Word Cards as a Sensori-Motor Aid in Vocabulary Development," *Peabody Journal of Education,* 23 (July 1945), 38–42.
4. Rock, I., and Victor, J. "Vision and Touch: An Experimentally Created Conflict Between the Two Senses," *Science,* 43 (Feb. 1964), 3606.
5. Sabaroff, Rose. "A Comparative Investigation of Two Methods of Teaching Phonics in a Modern Reading Program: A Pilot Study," *Journal of Experimental Education,* 31 (Mar. 1963), 249–256.

35. CULTURAL ASPECTS OF BILINGUALISM

Miles V. Zintz

I. INTRODUCTION

If you had heard a great deal of Spanish before you started attending formal school, the sound pattern *"Cuantos años tiene Ud?"* would be very familiar. You would translate literally into English "How many years do you have?" and answer the question "How old are you?" A psychometrist administering an individual intelligence test asks a young Spanish-speaking child, "How many ears do you have?"; changing "ears" to "years," the child translates *"Cuantas orejas tiene Usted?"* as *"Cuantos años tiene Ud?"* and tells the examiner that he has *eight ears.* Since this answer is obviously absurd, the examiner recognizes the lack of understanding and clarifies the ear-year discrimination. Yet, how many similar word confusions in translation go undetected?

Reprinted from *Vistas in Reading,* J. Allen Figurel, Editor, Proceedings of the Eleventh Annual Convention, International Reading Association (Newark, Delaware, 1966), pp. 353–361. By permission of Miles V. Zintz and The International Reading Association.

Clara Gonzales, more than 40 years a teacher and principal at the Zuni Pueblo, tells about the fourth-grade boy who, when asked "Who was Magellan?" responded with "Magellan was the first man to drive his *sheeps* all the way around the world."

On the Navajo Reservation, a foreman came upon one of his Navajo workers loafing at his job. "You're getting away with murder," he said. To this remark the Navajo replied in a rather shocked manner, "Oh, no, I would never *kill* anybody." We may assume that *murder* has, for him, only its literal definition.

A second-grade teacher asked a reading group in the circle to recall what they'd seen in a picture after glancing at it and then closing their books. When an eight-year-old Navajo boy was asked to tell, he quickly responded, "I saw a *time*." He meant he had seen a *clock*. One can understand much about a culture by the language of its users.

While in English the clock "runs," the Spanish clock "walks." (In French it marches and in German it functions!) The English-speaking person must hurry to make use of time before it runs away, but the Spanish-speaking person may take a more leisurely attitude. The English-speaking person who arrives late for work tends to say, "I missed the bus," and thus makes himself the active agent and accepts responsibility for his tardiness. However, the Spanish-speaking person is more apt to say that the bus left him, and, consequently, does not make himself directly responsible! If dishes break because they fall out of your hands instead of because you drop them, language may be a good guide to the way a person perceives himself in his environment *(15)*.

Kaulfers illustrates clearly how language is an integral part of a people's culture. Language is the means by which thoughts and feelings are expressed; language guides our thinking about social problems and processes. Kaulfers says:

> How translation can defeat its own ends if words are merely transverbalized without regard for their pleasant or unpleasant associations is illustrated by the difficulties missionaries have sometimes had in trying to convert remote populations to Christianity. Most Eskimos, for example, eat no bread. Few like it, because it has no taste or smell. Consequently, early missionaries found it difficult to explain the phrase, "Give us this day our daily bread." To win the natives, they had to substitute "walrus, polar bear, and deer." This illustration is but one of many that could be cited to show how an expert command of a second language always requires a thorough understanding of the attitudes, likes, dislikes, customs, and standards of values of the people *(3)*.

When the late Professor Clyde Kluckhohn was consulting in Japan with people writing a "democratic" constitution after the end of the second world war, he asked a Japanese with a fair knowledge of English to translate back from the Japanese that phrase in the New Japanese Constitution that represents "life, liberty, and the pursuit of happiness." The Japanese rendered, "License to commit lustful pleasure" *(4)*.

Dora V. Smith, in her Kappa Delta Pi lecture *Communication: The Miracle of Shared Living*, tells the story of a little Japanese girl who was spending a year in an elementary school in this country *(9)*.

At Christmas time her American classmates sent a package to her school in Tokyo. They decided to write a letter to accompany it. When Reiko was asked whether she wished to add a line, this is what she wrote: "The boys and girls in America sound funny when they talk. We have to read in English, too. But they laugh and cry and play in Japanese."

Jade Snow was seventeen and had just arranged her first date without her mother's or father's permission. Her traditional Chinese father chastised her in this manner *(14)*:

Where and when did you learn to be so daring as to leave this house without permission of your parents? You did not learn it under my roof.

When Jade Snow tried to explain her behavior to her parents, her father angered and continued:

Do I have to justify my judgment to you? I do not want a daughter of mine to be known as one who walks the streets at night. Have you no thought for our reputations if not for your own? If you start going out with boys, no good man will want to ask you to be his wife. You just do not know as well as we do what is good for you.

II. CONFLICTING CULTURAL VALUES

In the Southwest, as well as in many other places in the United States, children come to school with a set of values and a background of experiences radically different from those of the typical middle-class Anglo teacher who teaches them. To teach these children successfully, the teacher must seek to understand them, to accept without rejection or insult their values, ideas, and everyday behaviors.

Since social scientists are agreed that cultural groups are not significantly different in levels of intelligence, schools must look to other areas of behavior to explain the poor academic achievement, the high drop-out rate, and the unemployability of these uneducated adults.

Some of the cultural values that teachers are apt to teach and reinforce are:

1. Competitive achievement and climbing the ladder of success;
2. Time orientation that is precise to the hour and minute and strongly oriented toward the future;
3. That there is a scientific explanation for all natural phenomena;
4. That change is to be accepted and anticipated;
5. That socially approved behavior is gregarious, out-going, competitive, and somewhat aggressive. (A Pueblo Indian child may have

been taught to be shy, quiet, reserved, conforming, and anonymous!)
6. That one can, to a considerable degree, by hard work on his part shape his own future destiny. Teachers emphasize that formal education is the instrument facilitating social mobility.

The following chart presents specific conflicts in the traditional values of the Indian child of the Southwest, the Spanish-speaking child, and the middle-class teacher in the American Public School (see pages 427–428).

Spang poses some questions for counselors of Indian students and predicts that many of the counseling techniques learned in formal university courses will not work very well unless the counselor understands:

How does one encourage an Indian student to become competitive when it is not in his value system to be so?

How does the counselor approach the problem of the Indian student who is failing because he does not compete but has the ability to do so?

What does the counselor do to instill in the minds of Indian students a desire to aspire to higher-level occupations?

How does the counselor encourage a student to seek medical help when he believes in "medicine men?" (11).

When Sad-Girl's grandmother decided that Sad-Girl must go away to the off-reservation boarding school to learn the white man's reading and writing, the grandmother arranged with the trader at the trading post to have her granddaughter registered for school, then arranged for her to ride to the trading post at the appointed time with the neighbors, the Yuccas. Enroute to the trading post, the Yucca children explained that the Navajo name was not sufficient in the white man's school and, after due deliberation, named her Rose Smith.

Later in the boarding school, she was awakened one night by the crying of her roommate in the lower bunk. She had been a bit frightened by the strange, muffled sound which the crying had made. Her first thought was that it might be the ghost of an earth person because she knew that ghosts appear only after dark and only on moonless nights. Rose must help her friend, Isobel.

If Isobel had contracted sickness or disease, it was because she had violated a taboo or had been attacked by a ghost or a witch. If the latter was the case and the spectral attack was very recent, it could be averted or lessened by certain precautions.

She fumbled her way through the darkness to the dresser. Her fingers slipped down, counting, until they arrived at her own drawer. Inside, carefully laid away with her change of underwear and her sweater, was a tiny sack of gall medicine. Grandmother had made it for her just before she left home, so it was fresh and potent. It was composed of dried and pulverized galls of many animals and was a sure cure for anyone who had unknowingly absorbed a witch's poison (5).

CONFLICTS IN CULTURAL VALUES IN THE MINORITY GROUPS IN THE SOUTHWEST

rican schoolteachers ...ure to place great ...e on:	Children from *traditional* Indian families may be said to have accepted:	Children from *traditional* Spanish-American families may be said to have accepted:
...ery over Nature. ...must harness and ...e the forces of ...e to work for him.	*Harmony with Nature.* Nature will provide for man if he will behave as he should and obey nature's laws.	*Subjugation to Nature.* An often observed reaction in the traditional Spanish American was, "If it's God's will."
...re-time orientation. ...ving in our society ...ure oriented.	*Present-time orientation.* Life is concerned with the here and now. Accepting nature in its seasons, we will get through the years, one at a time. "If the things I am doing now are good, to be doing these same things all my life will be good."	*Present-time orientation.* For the traditional Spanish-American family, the only important goal of life was going to heaven after death. One only passed through this temporal life to receive his "reward" in the next.
...l of aspiration. ...b the ladder of ...ss. Success is ...ured by a wide ...e of superlatives: *the most, the best,*	*Level of aspiration.* Follow in the ways of the old people. Young people keep quiet because they lack maturity and experience. This de-emphasizes experiment, innovations, and change.	*Level of aspiration.* "To work a little, rest a little." Follow in one's father's footsteps. Be satisfied with the present.
.... Success will be ...ved by hard work	*Work.* One should work to satisfy present needs. Accumulating more than one needs could be construed as being selfish, stingy, or bigoted.	*Work.* Work to satisfy present need. The Spanish American was particularistic in nature. He operated on emotional response rather than subordinating the individual to the societal institution. A businessman looks first at himself as a brother to the man who is asking for credit and second as a businessman who is dealing with a customer.
...g. Everybody ...d save for the ...e. "A penny saved ...enny earned." "Put ...thing away for a ...day." "Take ...of the pennies and ...ollars will take ...of themselves."	*Sharing.* One shares freely what he has. One of the traditional purposes of the Shalako was that a man could rather anonymously provide a ceremonial feast for the village if he were able to do so.	*Sharing.* Traditional pattern included sharing within the extended family group. In cultural transition, Spanish Americans suffered considerable economic poverty. Those established in the dominant culture accepted Anglo values in sharing.

American schoolteachers are sure to place great value on:	Children from *traditional* Indian families may be said to have accepted:	Children from *traditional* Spanish-American families be said to have accepted:
Adherence to time schedules. "Take care of the minutes and the hours will take care of themselves." In practice, we have become so enslaved to time schedules, we might be termed "clock watchers."	*Adherence to time schedule.* Time is always with us. The unhurried inexactness of the Indian with appointments has led to the expression, "He operates on Indian time."	*Adherence to time schedu.* The expression for "the runs" translated from tl Spanish is "the clock wa It has been said that th explains the "mañana atti which Anglos have obser\ in some Spanish Americar
Acceptance of change. Change, in and of itself, is accepted as modal behavior.	*Reaction to change.* We may follow in the old ways with confidence.	*Reaction to change.* We follow in the old ways wi confidence. The reason r not be at all the same as tl Indians, however. This li earth is endured only to \ eternal life in Heaven.
Scientific explanation for all behavior. Nothing happens contrary to natural law. There is a scientific explanation for everything.	*Non-scientific explanation for natural phenomena.* Mythology, fear of the supernatural, witches, and sorcery may be used to explain behavior.	*Non-scientific explanation natural phenomena.* Wit\ fears, and non-scientific medical practices were us\ to explain behavior.
Competition. Aggression. One competes to win. Winning first prize all the time is a coveted goal.	*Cooperation.* Remaining submerged within the group. Traditionally a man did not overtly seek offices of leadership or attempt to dominate his people. In sports if one won once, he was ready to let others win.	*Humility.* Acceptance of status quo.
Individuality. Each individual shapes his own destiny. Self-realization for each person is limited only by his capacities to achieve.	*Anonymity.* Accepting group sanctions, "sinking" the individual in the group, and keeping life rigidly routinized—all these place primary emphasis on conformity.	*Obedience.* Life was routinized, placed empha on obedience to the will of God.

III. THE INTERDEPENDENCE OF LANGUAGE AND CULTURE

The way in which the language is rooted in the culture is generally understood and accepted, but the implications for children's learning in school have not been explored. To master a second language and thus become a bilingual person included the possibility that such a person is still able to function in only one culture. Hence, he is a mono-cultural-bilingual person. If he lives in or internalizes the values of another culture and learns its language, he may, hopefully, become a bilingual-bicultural person. On the other hand, it is possible to live in a second culture and internalize the values and not learn the language and thus be a monolingual-bicultural person. This point is theoretical and not apt to happen, at least in any complete sense, since one cannot fully master a language without absorbing some of the thinking, feelings, and attitudes that are required for accurate interpretation of the language. Nor is one apt to acquire the thinking, feelings, and attitudes in a cultural setting without absorbing some of the language. It is the thesis of this paper that the basic *problems are those of biculturalism,* not bilingualism (10).

The scope of biculturalism may be illustrated if one thinks of the use of the word *father* in Anglo-America and in Zuni culture. For the Zuni Indian child, the word *father* represents his mother's husband, a man who enjoys his children as companions. He takes no part in disciplining his children, nor does he have any concern for their economic security. In his matrilineal society, the mother owns the property and her brothers assist in the rearing of and disciplining of the children. Further, it is said, that she may divorce this husband by leaving his shoes and ceremonial garb outside the door while he is away and that this act will be his cue to gather up these few belongings and return to his mother's house. Family organization is of an extended nature, and the marriage does not decree that a man-wife love relationship is more important than the consanguinal mother-son or brother-sister relationship. In short, in a matrilineal, consanguinal, extended family, *father* may mean a specific set of behavior patterns such as is described here.

Father, for the Anglo-American middle-class child, represents the legal head of a household who is held responsible for the rearing and disciplining of his children. His marriage to his wife is based on a conjugal, or love, relationship; and even if dissolved in a court of law, he may still be held accountable for her full support. For this child, *father* is a set of meanings derived from a patrilineal, conjugal, nuclear family relationship (16).

A Pueblo-Indian college student suggested that this understanding of the word *father* is also important to the Indian child's teacher:

It would sure help if the teacher knew who was directly responsible at home for the boy's behavior. I have heard the teacher say to a student, "If you don't do so and so, I'll tell your father." The Indian boy thought this was a big joke because he knew his real father would never lay a hand on him.

Four categories follow in which the language of one culture differs from the language of another:

1. Certain features of living are similarly manifested in both cultures and have similar significance. They overlap. Such areas include family relationships, school activities, food and shelter, tools, and recreation.
2. A second class of cultural features may have the same manifest in the countries being compared but have a different meaning; such as kinship terms, gestures, greetings, use of the eyes, manner of dress, etc.
3. A third class of features may have the same meaning in both countries but a different manifestation. For example, children get hungry before meals, but in Topeka they may eat crunchy corn crisps while in Thailand they eat dried squid or green guava.
4. In the fourth category are those cultural features that do not overlap in any way in the two cultural areas. In Burma, a student might hear that his aunt in the back country has just been eaten by a crocodile; yet, he cannot fathom the fact that trains run in tubes underground in many large cities (13).

IV. TEACHING ENGLISH AS A SECOND LANGUAGE

There's a story going around that involves a carpet layer who had worked all day installing wall-to-wall carpeting. When he noticed a lump under the carpet in the middle of the living-room, he felt in his shirt pocket for his cigarettes and they were gone. He was not about to take up the carpet, so he went outside for a two-by-four. Tapping down the cigarettes with it would be easy. Once the lump was smoother, the man gathered up his tools and carried them back to the truck. Then two things happened simultaneously. He saw his cigarettes on the seat of the truck, and over his shoulder he heard the voice of the woman to whom the carpet belonged. "Have you seen anything of my parakeet?" she asked plaintively (6).

Some of our behavior with boys and girls may be like this man's. Of necessity, we must often and all through each teaching day, make decisions based on our conception of what is happening at the moment. We are killing parakeets, figuratively, when we misjudge a child's ability, behavior, or only *his* reasons for his use of language that is not what we expect.

Dr. Allen suggests certain procedures in teaching language lessons to groups learning second languages:

1. Do *not* introduce a new *vocabulary* item at the same time that you are introducing a new *structure* pattern. Rather, teach new vocabulary in old sentence patterns; and teach new sentence patterns with old vocabulary items.

2. Do not teach two items that might be confusing during the same class period. For example, children need a few prepositions. Ruth Crymes suggests concentrating on these nine: *at, on, in, of, for, from, by, with,* and *to.* However, they must be taught one at a time, not all at once.

Also, Virginia Allen suggests *not* teaching word opposites as new concepts during the same class period. In the pairs, large-small, old-young, up-down, teach one of the words in one lesson and the other member of the pair after the first is understood. If the child tries to learn both at once, he may confuse the two completely.

3. Young children need words that are required for the use of fundamental grammatical patterns such as the names of the days of the week, months of the year, numbers to ten, and common adjectives.

Don't try to teach beginners all the words that pertain to clothing, shelter, food, or transportation: only the items in their environment that are important to the learners should be taught at this time.

At this point, the mastery of structure and sounds is most important; the size of vocabulary load must be subordinated to this mastery.

4. Do *not* spend drill-class time talking to the class about what they need to be learning. Do *not* present long lists of isolated vocabulary to work on, for example. Rather, strive for class participation as much of the time as possible. Work on patterns with zest and variations and keep the responses changing. Plan many substitution drills, expansion drills, and changing-sentence-order drills; and as soon as children are "comfortable" in group responses, move to smaller group and individual responses. For beginning groups many words can be taught through objects and pictures and through demonstration—pointing to objects, pointing to small models of furniture, or pointing to articles belonging to the students *(1).*

The six component parts of a school program of teaching English as a second language are:

1. *Experiences.* The teacher needs to capitalize on or to create experiences in which the need for speaking English is present. The child's acquaintance with the concept through first-hand and concrete experience should help to insure understanding of the idea and integration of the concept into his total background of experience.

Morris reminds us that learning cannot take place in a vacuum. Too often this accomplishment is what we are expecting when children are asked to deal with facts and concepts of an urban, industrialized society in terms of their own rural, nonindustrial cultural experiences.

Morris goes on to say:

A survey of commonly used social studies and science textbooks in the primary grades shows that they emphasize units dealing with cities, urban activities, and with the artifacts of a modern, industrial society—the large city fire department, factories, newspaper and telephone offices, machines and modern sources of power.

Morris attempted to meet this problem of vocabulary development by providing a series of fifteen field trips for first and second graders with language patterns planned for oral-aural practice both before and after the excursion (7).

2. *Vocabulary.* The teacher needs to develop systematically a vocabulary for expressing oneself. Acquiring a knowledge of words and practicing precise use of prepositions, idioms, synonyms, pronouns, and verb tenses are a never-ending task in language.

3. *Sentence Patterns.* The teacher needs systematically to develop *automatic control and fluency* in the use of natural and accurate English-language patterns. Children must habituate the commonest speech utterances and be able to use them with ease. Approximately 300 common English expressions constitute a large percentage of the language used in casual conversation in greetings, passing the time of day, and obtaining or giving information for satisfying one's needs. These are presented in detailed lesson plans for teachers in the *Language Guides of the Puerto Rican Study*; the "Teachers' Guides for Teaching English," prepared by the Philippine Center for Language Study; the *Fries American English Series*; and the *Teaching of Structural Words and Sentence Patterns.*

4. *Imitation of a good speech model in the vernacular.* The teacher needs to help the learner understand and produce precise sounds, rhythm, and intonation. This ability will be accomplished by imitation of a native speaker, or competent speaker, whose inflection, emphasis, stress, and pitch characterize a "normal form" of English speech. It will be helpful, at times, if the teacher knows the students' vernacular so that he will be aware of differences in the two languages in rising and falling inflections, words stressed in sentences, and whether the tone of voice affects meaning.

5. *Reading and writing.* The learner will not be expected to read and write language he has not heard and come to understand in oral usage. This fact means that reading and writing will be delayed until the learner has mastered a sizeable speaking vocabulary. When the learner demonstrates sufficient readiness, the teacher needs to teach all the developmental skills in reading. Continual emphasis must be given to understanding concepts and testing the child's ability to paraphrase meanings of concepts presented. Only when the child has reached this level of competency in the use of the language is he ready to develop writing as a useful skill.

6. *Contrasting English with the child's vernacular.* The teacher will

function with greater confidence if he knows something of the phonology, morphology, and sentence patterning in the child's language. This function will be discussed in the next section, contrasting English with the Spanish and Navajo languages.

Speakers of English as a second language need lots of help with minimal pairs. Minimal pairs are words that sound almost alike but have one phoneme that is not the same and that makes the two words entirely different in meaning. For example: live and leave; bit, bet, and beat; mit and meet; He's living here and He's leaving here; chop and shop; share and chair; chip and ship; chin and shin; shoes and chews; shock and chock.

They also need help with noun-plus-noun combinations—where to put the stress: Christmas tree; wrist watch; watch pocket and pocket watch; shoe box.

The *Miami Linguistic Readers* have been developed to give children these experiences with the English Language. The teacher's manuals contain much practice in sentence structure and in auditory discrimination of minimal pairs *(8)*.

What is important is that the student talks whether he makes mistakes. If he does make a mistake, the teacher should repeat the item as it should be but with no scolding or explanation. If the students are making too many mistakes, the teacher should look to his teaching. If the child does not talk, there is no language to try to improve.

As a result of an experiment carried out during the 1963–64 school year, Talley recommended a special, enriched language arts program, including the teaching of oral English as a second language; the study of idiomatic English expressions and the multiple meanings of words was to be implemented in the school system for all children who hear and/or speak a language in their home situations which is not the same in which they are required to function at school. After six months of working with experimental groups in fourth and sixth grades, the experimental groups made significantly greater gains on reading tests than did control groups; but what seems more significant, their mean-I.Q. scores on alternate forms of the California Test of Mental Maturity increased ten points while the control groups' increased only three points *(12)*.

V. Teaching Diagnostically

Many children are victimized by instructors who fail to realize that grade level is a statistical concept describing the midpoint in the achievement levels of a typical group of students. The term guarantees by definition that half of any normal group of pupils will achieve at grade level or above while the other half will achieve at grade level or below. To expect all or even most children to reach grade level or above is to expect an arithmetical impossibility. One might as well argue that 90 per cent of those who marry should be women (2).

Teachers' experiences in the slums strongly suggest an increase in remedial and diagnostic training in the view of prevailing needs. The most fruitful approach, in reading and arithmetic, appears to be an emphasis on remedial instruction and diagnostics: on determining not how poor a pupil is but what difficulties preclude his success. If we persist in emphasizing only a pupil's product—that is, his wrong answers and bad performance rather than the process he employs to derive answers—it is unlikely that the difficulties of learning will be determined or resolved. This experience reported for slum schools can be replicated over and over with the culturally different as well as the culturally deprived.

Skills in remediation techniques and diagnostic practices are perhaps two of the most obvious abilities of an outstanding teacher.

The ability to conduct a meaningful conference with parents is a powerful tool that too few teachers possess.

Too much formal school is so structured that success is impossible—for certain pupils. Competition can only occur within a range of uncertainty—that is, the range in which both success and failure are possible. It cannot occur where each participant does not have a chance: where the outcome of victory or defeat is predetermined. When the acceptable norm in a class has been based on the work of the typical middle-class Anglo, the culturally different, language-handicapped student has had defeat predetermined for him. In that reference, school "competition" becomes a daily punishment for those of low ability, for whatever reason. Under circumstances in which few participants have a chance to win, it is not strange that numerous students protect themselves by setting a low level of aspiration—that is, by not trying.

VI. SUMMARY

In New Mexico, the greatest problem in the primary grades is the teaching of oral English. Encompassing Hispano-American children, Indian children, and the newly identified culturally deprived children, this group constitutes a majority of New Mexico's school children. Teachers, principals, and supervisors of primary classrooms must become much more concerned with specific techniques for teaching English as a second language. This teaching cannot, of course, be successful unless it is predicated upon understanding the boys and girls—their life values, their living habits, and their levels of aspiration for the future. Any solution to the problem necessitates, on the part of the teacher, (1) an understanding of the significance of the cultural differences, (2) proficiency in the teaching of English as a second language, and (3) ability to use remedial-teaching methods appropriate to the level of functioning of the groups taught.

VII. SOME MATERIALS FOR TEACHERS OF ENGLISH AS A FOREIGN LANGUAGE

A. Books on Linguistics and Methodology

1) Cochran, Anne. *Modern Methods of Teaching English as a Foreign Language*. Washington: Educational Services, 1954.
2) Fries, Charles C. *Teaching and Learning English as a Foreign Language*. Ann Arbor: University of Michigan Press, 1947.
3) Stevick, Earl W. *Helping People Learn English*. Nashville, Tenn.: Abingdon Press, 1957.
4) Keesee, Elizabeth. *Modern Foreign Languages in the Elementary School: Teaching Techniques*. Washington: U.S. Office of Education, 1960.

B. Materials.for the Teaching of English as a Second Language

1) California State Department of Education, *Teaching English to Spanish-Speaking Children*, 1954.

   The Puerto Rican Study, Board of Education of the City of New York, Lists the following language Guides: *Teaching English to Puerto Rican Pupils in Grades One and Two*, 1957. *Teaching English to Puerto Rican Pupils in Grades Three and Four*, 1957.

   Teaching English to Puerto Rican Pupils in Grades Five and Six, 1957.

   These manuals contain an excellent discussion of the things a teacher needs to know about the Spanish language to effectively teach the Puerto Rican child to speak English. They also contain a long list of *speech patterns* on which teachers can effectively drill to make the child's oral English sentence structure conform to our "stream of speech." Address:

   > Board of Education of the City of New York
   > Bureau of Curriculum Research
   > 130 West 55th Street
   > New York 19, New York

2) English Language Services, *English This Way*, Twelve books for six years, New York: The Macmillan Company, 1963.
3) *English 900*, prepared by English Language Services, Inc., (New York: The Macmillan Co., 1964). Six books each, in order of difficulty, present and provide teaching practice on 150 sentence patterns.

4) Hornby, A. S. *The Teaching of Structural Words and Sentence Patterns*. Stage 1. London: Oxford University Press, 1959.

5) Philippine Center for Language Study, (Pasay, Philippines, 1961) *Guidebooks for Teaching English as a Second Language*. This study is being done in cooperation with the University of California at Los Angeles. Correspondence with Dr. Clifford Prator, Professor of English, University of California, Los Angeles, California, will obtain information about these materials.

6) *Fries American English Series for the Study of English as a Second Language*, (Boston: D. C. Heath, and Co., 1953–1957). Six textbooks have been prepared. Book I is designed for children, ages 10–14, beginning their study of English as a language. The Teachers' Guides are excellent. One guide book covers both Books I and II; but there are separate teachers' guides for Books III, IV, V, and VI. (Rojas, Pauline M., Editor.)

7) Wright, Audrey and James McGillivray. *Let's Learn English*, Parts 1 and 2. New York: American Book Co., 1955.

REFERENCES

1. Allen, Virginia French. "Teaching English as a Second Language," prepared for Western States Small Schools Project, Workshop; Flagstaff, Arizona, June 7–11, 1965.
2. Frymier, Jack M. "Ninety Percent Should Be Women," *Education*, 84, April 1964, 498–500.
3. Kaulfers, Walter V. "Gifts of Tongue or Tower of Babel?" *The Educational Forum*, November 1954, 82.
4. Kluckhohn, Clyde. *Mirror for Man*. New York: McGraw-Hill Book Co., Inc., 1949, 154.
5. Lampman, Evelyn. *Navajo Sister*. New York: Doubleday and Co., Inc., 1956, 93.
6. "Laughter, the Best Medicine," *Reader's Digest*, May 1964, 92.
7. Morris, Joyce. "Teaching English as a Second Language to Second-Grade Children at Santo Domingo School," *Research in Progress*, 1966, University of New Mexico, College of Education.
8. Rojas, Pauline M. *Miami Linguistic Readers*. Boston: D. C. Heath, 1965.
9. Smith, Dora V. *Communication, The Miracle of Shared Living*. New York: The Macmillan Company, 1955, 51.
10. Sofietti, James P. "Bilingualism and Biculturalism," *Journal of Educational Psychology*, 46:222–227, 1955.
11. Spang, Alonzo. "Counseling the Indian," *The Journal of American Indian Education*, 5:11–12, October 1965.
12. Talley, Kathryn S. "Effects of a Program of Special Language Instruction," unpublished doctoral dissertation, University of New Mexico, 1965, 114–121.
13. Van Syoc, W. Bryce. "The Scheduling of Cultural Materials in Language

Lessons," *On Teaching English to Speakers of Other Languages,* Virginia French Allen, Editor. Champaign, Ill.: National Council of Teachers of English 1965, 126.

14. Wong, Jade Snow. *Fifth Chinese Daughter.* New York: Scholastic Book Services, 1963, 163–165.
15. Woods, Sister Francis Jerome. *Cultural Values of American Ethnic Groups.* New York: Harper and Brothers, 1956, 35.
16. Zintz, Miles V. "Indian Children in Public School Classrooms in New Mexico—Next Steps in Research." *NMSSE Educational Research Bulletin,* March 1963, 14.

36. THE PRESCHOOL-
DISADVANTAGED CHILD

Queenie B. Mills

The truly disadvantaged-preschool child is on a collision course with reading failure in first grade unless something intervenes to prevent this academic disaster. Reading inability among all children is estimated as 15 to 20 percent. Among the disadvantaged children as a group the disability estimate is as high as 50 percent (8), and it is even higher in the case of children from severely impoverished backgrounds.

We are only now beginning to understand the full impact of severe deprivation on the preschool child. We still have much to learn about him and about ways of working with him to compensate for his learning handicaps. A number of well-designed experimental programs is in progress, but to date results from these are either incomplete or inconclusive. We still do not know enough to prescribe with confidence the type of program or programs that will ensure optimum learning opportunities for these young children. At this stage of our knowledge what kind of compensatory educational experiences should we provide for severely disadvantaged preschoolers to improve their chances for success in learning to read?

In this paper I shall attempt to identify the truly disadvantaged child and his specific disadvantages in relation to beginning reading, to describe some of his developmental and learning deficits, and to suggest some guidelines for teachers. Some of what I have to say is based on my

Reprinted from *Vistas In Reading,* J. Allen Figurel, Editor, Proceedings of The Eleventh Annual Convention, International Reading Association (Newark, Delaware, 1966), pp. 345–349. By permission of Queenie B. Mills and The International Reading Association.

experiences as an educational consultant with Project Headstart; some of my observations and suggestions are directly related to experiences I have gained from an exploratory project involving severely disadvantaged preschoolers at the University of Illinois.

THE SEVERELY DISADVANTAGED-PRESCHOOL CHILD

Who is the severely disadvantaged-preschool child? He is roughly between the ages of three and five, and he has not yet entered first grade. If he is enrolled in an educational unit other than a day-care center, it is either a nursery school, a pre-kindergarten, or a kindergarten. Chances are, however, that he does not yet attend a school of any kind. He is not merely a poor child; rather he is a child whose impoverished-family environment has had such an impact upon his early development that he is ill-prepared for either the behavior requirements of the classroom or the demands of the learning process.

There is a good deal of confusion about the descriptive label *disadvantaged* and quite some disagreement about its appropriateness. We seem to have run the gamut in short order from *underprivileged* through *culturally deprived* and *culturally disadvantaged* to just plain *disadvantaged*. This term, too, has its drawbacks; for it is easy to build a case for certain "disadvantaged" middle-class children as well as for those from lower-class families.

The fact is that there are many degrees of disadvantage. It should also be recognized that not all poor children are necessarily disadvantaged. A colleague of mine was born in an oil camp in Texas. His family moved constantly from one oil camp to another. He was fourteen before he and his five younger brothers and sisters first entered school. But he wasn't disadvantaged! According to him he was merely poor at that particular time.

The truly disadvantaged child in my frame of reference comes from a bottom-of-the-range, lower-class poor, multiple-problem family. His deprivations have been many and the impact has been severe. He has inherited poverty. And the enormous significance of his deprivation is that he is being socialized in a "culture of poverty" (7) which has already started to retard his cognitive development.

Research has demonstrated that such children have many developmental and learning deficits in common. They score well below their middle-class peers on standardized measures of intelligence; their language development is retarded and of poor quality; auditory and visual-discrimination skills are not well developed; and skills for coping with the expectancies of a teaching-learning situation are almost nonexistent (2, 6).

It would be incorrect, however, to say that there is a disadvantaged preschooler per se. A decided range of differences with respect to the degree of disadvantage exists even at the lower end of the deprivation scale. Moreover, these disadvantaged American children come from different ethnic backgrounds and live in different sections of the country. The Oriental child in California and the Hawaiian child in rural Oahu, the Mexican-American or the Indian child in the Southwest, the Puerto-Rican child in Spanish Harlem, the Negro child in a Chicago slum, and the Caucasian child in Appalachia have different needs and backgrounds. The great challenge is still the challenge of individual differences.

LEARNING DEFICITS RELATED TO PRE-READING SKILLS

There are a number of basic learnings related to reading which middle-class children acquire during the preschool period and which disadvantaged children fail to acquire. For example, Durkin (4) reported that books and "being-read-to" were experienced regularly and with pleasure by the early readers in her research project. Books and being-read-to are unknown quantities in the life of a young disadvantaged child. Because of this fact, he builds neither an understanding of what it means to read nor the desire to learn how.

It is pretty well agreed that we must have a child under attention if we are to teach him to read. Yet, one of the prime characteristics of the disadvantaged child at the preschool level is his notoriously short attention span. Related to this characteristic is the difficulty he has in following the teacher's directions. This child's predominantly physical approach to learning (3) may further complicate the problem of getting him involved in reading which, after all, is a fairly sedentary and abstract task.

I do not need to remind teachers that a high level of auditory discrimination is required of the child in the beginning stages of learning to read. Disadvantaged youngsters, however, appear to be surprisingly insensitive to subtle differences in sound. It may be that, living in unadulterated noise, they have learned how *not* to listen (3). The resultant learning deficit is a serious one. It is important that the child be able to distinguish "p" from "b". It is equally important that he be able to listen to and benefit from the language spoken by the teacher.

The young disadvantaged child is a language cripple. He is not, strictly speaking, a non-verbal child; but his verbal inadequacies are such that they present a grave threat to his success in learning to read. This child has not had many experiences with objects and ideas which are familiar to middle-class children. As a result he does not know what these things are or that they have names. Even the simplest pre-primer may present concepts and vocabulary that are altogether unfamiliar. Add to this the fact that his language is crude and limited, and the prognosis is not too bright.

Basil Bernstein (1), the British sociologist, has suggested that the language a child learns shapes and limits the *what* and *how* of his future learning. He describes two modes of verbal communication: *restricted* and *elaborated*. Restricted language is characteristic of the disadvantaged. Sentences are short, simple, often incomplete. It is used primarily for social interchange and is understood easily with a minimum of verbal cues. A kind of "disadvantaged pidgin," this type of communication affords little need for reflection. Elaborated language is more precise. The range of concepts, vocabulary, structural elements, and information is greater. It permits reflection and encourages the cognitive use of language as tools of thought.

Imagine a disadvantaged mother who wants to sweep the floor. Her young son is playing in the exact spot where she wishes to use the broom. She points toward the door and says, "Get out!" He obeys without responding verbally. This is restricted language. Now imagine a middle-class mother in the same situation. She might say, "Darling, Mother wants to sweep here. Would you please play in the other room for a few minutes until I have finished?" Something more must be done about this sentence than just listening to it. According to Hess and Shipman (5), the verbal categoric command, "Get out," cuts off thought; whereas the more elaborated message gives the child a reason for his mother's request. Given a rationale, it may encourage him to *ask* why in another situation. This type of verbal interchange may also encourage the child to learn to look for action sequences in his own behavior and in that of others. This more cognitive use of language is essential to interpretation in reading.

THE ILLINOIS NURSERY-SCHOOL PROJECT

Disadvantaged children have much to teach us about themselves. A two-group nursery-school project was initiated at the University of Illinois by Celia B. Stendler and myself on March 1, 1965, BHS—"Before Head Start"—that is, before the maiden summer voyage of the national effort in behalf of deprived four- and five-year-olds. The major purpose of the Illinois project was to gather descriptive data on severely disadvantaged preschoolers at two different age levels and under two different programs and to explore various approaches to parent education at this depressed level.

Both groups were housed in the Child Development Laboratory at the university and met for two and one-half hours five afternoons a week. Both were used as demonstration projects in the training of Head Start personnel.

The major criterion for selection was severe disadvantage. Public welfare officials and principals of schools in the most deprived areas of Champaign-Urbana were contacted for recommendations. It would be difficult to assemble a more bottom-of-the-barrel group of families than the ones we recruited. These were truly hard-core poverty cases. Moreover, the principals had nominated those families where there had been other children who had given the school real trouble over the years. To let the university take off some of the rough edges of behavior before this next child arrived on the kindergarten or first-grade doorstep was an obviously inviting temptation. Prayerfully principals made their recommendations, and we selected the most disadvantaged.

The children ranged in age from two and one-half to five years. They were divided into two age groups. Approximately one fourth of the sixteen children in each group was Caucasian, and the rest were Negroes. The older group was subjected to a highly structured situation using Piaget-inspired materials. The younger group was exposed to a more conventional and informal type of nursery-school program. Concrete experiences, concept development, and oral language were emphasized in both groups—individually and informally with the threes, and in small structured groups with the fours. The three-year-olds stayed at the laboratory for almost five months; but the four-year-olds were available to us for only three months.

The first thing we noticed about these children was that they were unable to manage space. Our playrooms are enormous. Unaccustomed to such freedom of movement indoors, they simply used the square footage as they would outdoor space—to exhibit open-field running. We learned shortly to break up this space, to limit the time for "free play" to twenty minutes at first, and to organize for "structured freedom." In this highly structured program for the four-year-olds, attention span was noticeably short and the activity level was very high. These two factors together necessitated a shifting program, versatile teachers, and small-group activities for short periods of time.

Next we learned that more teachers were needed in the four-year group than in the three-year group. A ratio of one teacher to four children appeared to be the most effective arrangement for small-group, direct-teaching activities. In contrast, the less structured, more traditional nursery school functioned well with only three teachers for sixteen children. Teacher personality undoubtedly had some effect on the situation, but it is a difficult variable to assess. Both head teachers were fine, intelligent, dedicated people. From observation, however, the younger children's teacher appeared to be somewhat warmer, more relaxed in her teaching style; and she was better trained to work with young children.

One of our most startling discoveries was the way these children used equipment. They threw everything they could pick up! A hole is to dig; a stick is to throw. A book isn't much different from a stick if you have never seen a book and you don't know what it is for or how to use it. Slowly, step by step we had to model how these concrete objects could be used. We were building concepts along the way. The old admonition not to make models for children to copy is still good advice, but it needs some modification. Children who have no built-in schemas for looking at picture books, listening to stories, or using paints and crayons need someone to model these activities for them.

One rather curious reaction was noted repeatedly in connection with the plastic toy animals. The children were afraid of them. They seemed unable to accept the fact that these toys were not real animals. When the gray rat-sized elephant was presented to one child, he ran away screaming, "He bi me! Bi me!"

These severely disadvantaged youngsters were capable of as much as ten to fifteen minutes of sustained play, but we learned early that it is important to guide or direct them before they reach some commitment to an undesirable activity. How to set limits and how to reinforce desirable behavior were perhaps our most challenging control problems. When we failed to use physical punishment, the children thought we weren't serious about the limits. On the other hand, praising a child for a task well done was no guarantee that it would be repeated.

The language deficits were severe in both groups, and much time was spent in the manipulation of concrete objects, naming, classifying, and helping the children to extend their spoken language. Even among these severely disadvantaged children, however, the range of language ability was surprising. For example, on the Templin fifty-item articulation scale, the scores ranged from 1 to 49 correct responses.

Both groups changed in language behavior. Test-retest gains on the Stanford-Binet over a three-month period were positive but not statistically significant. The average increase for the three-year-olds was 5 points; for the four-year-olds, 5.69 points. Shifts in scores on the Peabody Picture Vocabulary Test (PPVT) gave us better information. Initial testing on the PPVT was done after approximately two months in nursery school. The interval between testing was approximately two and one-half months. Average increase for the three-year-olds was 13.8 significant beyond the .025 level. Teacher ratings and structured parent interviews also indicated the improvement in language use.

GUIDELINES FOR TEACHERS

The following points are offered in summary as guidelines for teachers:

1. Not all young disadvantaged children are alike. They have different backgrounds, different needs, and may present different degrees of deprivation. Moreover, the range of individual differences within a group may be as great as it is among groups.
2. Learning deficits related to prereading skills are associated with auditory discrimination, concept formation, and language development. Compensatory educational programs should emphasize learning activities which will eliminate the existing handicaps.

3. Young disadvantaged children have to learn to be taught; therefore, at the preschool level, teachers should emphasize the "learning to learn" rather than the "learning to read" skills.
4. Teachers planning activities to help children "learn to learn" should give attention to helping children find pleasure in books and stories.
5. Always the teacher is the master key to the motivation problem with preschool-disadvantaged children. When there is mutual respect between teacher and child, the teacher can and must serve as a secondary reinforcer for the learning behavior she expects from him.
6. Since there is no one-best educational model for all disadvantaged preschoolers, compensatory educational experiences should be integrated with the best of traditional preschool practices (9, 10, 11).

REFERENCES

1. Bernstein, B. "Social Class and Linguistic Development: A Theory of Social Learning." In A. H. Halsey, Jean Floud, and C. A. Anderson, Eds., *Education, Economy, and Society*. Glencoe, Illinois: Free Press, 1961.
2. Bloom, Benjamin S.; Davis, A.; Hess, Robert. *Compensatory Education for Cultural Deprivation*. Working papers by participants in the Research Conference on Education and Cultural Deprivation. Chicago: Holt, Rinehart and Winston, Inc., 1965.
3. Deutsch, M. "The Disadvantaged Child and the Learning Process." In A. H. Passow, Ed., *Education in Depressed Areas*. New York: Columbia University Teachers' College, 1963, 163–180.
4. Durkin, Dolores. "Children Who Read Before Grade One," *The Reading Teacher*, January, 1961.
5. Hess, Robert D. and Shipman, Virginia C. "Early Experience and the Socialization of Cognitive Modes in Children," *Child Development*, 36 (December, 1965), 869–885.
6. Hunt, J. McV. *Intelligence and Experience*. New York: Ronald Press, 1961.
7. Lewis, Oscar. *The Children of Sanchez*. New York: Random House, Inc., 1961.
8. Riessman, Frank. *The Culturally Deprived Child*. New York: Harper and Brothers, 1962.
9. Sears, Pauline S. and Dowley, Edith M. "Research on Teaching in the Nursery School." In N. L. Gage, Ed., *Handbook of Research on Teaching*. Chicago: Rand McNally and Co., 1963.
10. Strodtbeck, Fred L. *Progress Report: The Reading Readiness Nursery: Short Term Social Intervention*. Chicago: University of Chicago, August 1963. Mimeographed.
11. Swift, Joan W. "Effects of Early Group Experience: The Nursery School and Day Nursery." In Martin L. Hoffman and Lois W. Hoffman, Eds., *Review of Child Development Research*. New York: Russell Sage Foundation, 1964.

CHAPTER V

MOTIVATING

RETARDED READERS

37. WHAT DOES RESEARCH TELL ABOUT THE READING INTERESTS OF JUNIOR HIGH PUPILS?

Arno Jewett

At the University of Texas a few years ago, I had a student teacher in an Austin junior high school who was a master in motivating student reading. This student teacher knew the personal reading interests of each pupil. Through observation and a reading questionnaire she had learned the favorite books, magazines, and authors of her students. From each student's cumulative reading record, which was passed on from grade to grade in the junior high schools, she knew the titles which these pupils had read and enjoyed. She knew their reading scores on a standardized reading test. And she knew the research findings concerning the reading interests of early adolescents. Also she had managed to read many of the new books for adolescents. Thus, she was able to guide the reading of her pupils, rather than turn them loose on a *free* reading program.

Before class started, this student teacher would bring two or three armfuls of books to the classroom. Soon after the beginning of the class, she would hold up a book, usually one with a jacket containing colorful pictures, and ask a question or two about the book, starting with its title

Reprinted from *Improving Reading in The Junior High School,* Bulletin No. 10 (Washington, 1957), pp. 26–33. Arno Jewett, Editor, United States Printing Office.

or book jacket. Then she would "sell" the book by telling about the conflict in it, by reading an exciting or humorous paragraph, by showing illustrations, and by getting a student who had read the book to tell how much he liked it. At this point, some boy and girl in the class would usually ask, "May I borrow that book?" Or the student teacher would say to one of her students, "John, you liked *Rocket to the Moon.* I'm sure you'd like this book, *The Lonely Sky.* Why don't you try it? Then, if you don't like it, return it in a day or two and I'll help you find one you do like."

Sometimes the student teacher spent one or two periods getting the right book in the hands of the right reader. After everyone had a book to read, students were given two or more free reading periods in class to get interested in the book. In brief, her purpose was to motivate extensive reading and to develop the habit of reading worthwhile books.

Perhaps, too, her utilization of reading interests helped the pupils to grow in reading ability, especially in vocabulary knowledge and reading comprehension. Two recent studies seem to support this idea.

In a recent controlled experiment involving 100 ninth-grade pupils in a large metropolitan high school, Margery R. Bernstein (2)[1] found that there was a definite relationship between a pupil's interest in fiction and his comprehension of it. Two narrative selections equal in readability (according to various formulas) but widely different in interest were given to the pupils. Comprehension scores made by the pupils on the more interesting selection were significantly higher statistically than the scores on the other selection. Miss Bernstein also reported that "The relationship between interest and comprehension existed for pupils of high and low reading ability and for retarded and non-retarded readers alike." In this study pupils also felt that the interesting material was easier to read.

In a study concerning the readability and interest of selected books for 113 retarded readers in grades 4–8, Robert W. Ridgway (7) also noted the importance of interest in reading. He found that "When interest in a book was high, the pupils ... tended to read above their measured reading levels. ... Books with high interest scores were frequently judged as about right in difficulty even though rated two or more grades above the measured reading level of the readers. Books with low interest scores were frequently rated as too hard even though actually on or below the reading level of the reader."

In a companion study dealing with the readability and interest of 20 simplified books for retarded readers in grades 7–12, Herbert I. Bruning (3) concluded that "There appears to be a rather definite relationship between a pupil's interest in a book and his rating of its difficulty." Books

---

[1] Bibliographical references are listed on page 451 at the end of this article.

written especially for retarded readers were ranked highest in interest by
Dr. Bruning found that when interest factors are comparatively weak,
the retarded readers. Adapted classics were ranked second. In addition,
pupils' judgments of a book's difficulty compare favorably with readability difficulty indicated by the Dale-Chall formula. However, when
the interest factor is strong, the formula does not seem to give all the
information needed.

In this situation, the interest factors inherent in the book and the
motivation which the pupil brings to the book are important. Perhaps we
need more research to determine how well present readability formulas
measure the interest which a book has for a youth or a youth brings to
a book.

What do we think we know about the reading interests which pupils
have in common between the ages of 12–15? We think we know a lot.
For more than 20 years there has been a continuous flow of studies about
reading interests of boys and girls.

In the main, these studies have agreed on the following:

1. Animal stories are enjoyed by both boys and girls in the junior high,
especially in the seventh grade. Favorites include a hero or heroine about
the same age as the reader or slightly older. Titles such as *Lassie Come-
Home* by Eric Knight, *My Friend Flicka* by Mary O'Hara, *Old Yeller* by
Fred Gipson, *The Black Stallion* by Walter Farley, and *Big Red* by Jim
Kjelgaard are seldom resting on library shelves.

2. Exciting adventure stories have always attracted teen-age readers.
According to a study by Evangeline C. Malchow *(5)*, adventure stories
appeal most when they contain suspense and serious danger. Boys like
bloody, violent adventure stories with dangerous situations. *White Falcon*
by Elliot Arnold, *Dark Frigate* by Charles Boardman Hawes, and *Call It
Courage* by Armstrong Sperry are typical examples. Girls prefer mild
adventure with a bit of romance about other girls fifteen or older. *Lasso
Your Heart* by Betty Cavanna is a typical favorite.

3. Mystery stories which are not too involved and which include young
people rate high. J. Harlan Shores *(9)* has reported that "As children
progress through the grades *(4–8)* they show increasing interest in
mystery stories and decreasing interest in cowboy stories and fairy tales."
Girls seem to enjoy mystery stories more than boys do *(4, 6)*. *Who Rides
in the Dark?* by Stephen Meader, *Mystery at Boulder Point* by Eleanore
M. Jewett, and *The Secret Cargo* by Howard Pease are the type of
mystery stories that intrigue junior high pupils.

4. Humor which is not subtle or ironical is often enjoyed by both boys
and girls, especially those who are above average in intelligence *(5)*.
Cartoons, jokes, puns, limericks, exaggerated situations and tall tales are
especially liked by most adolescents. Unfortunately, humorous books
appealing to early adolescents are in short supply. Among those widely

read are *Ben and Me* by Robert Lawson, *The Centerburg Tales* by Robert McCloskey, and *Cheaper by the Dozen,* by Frank B. Gilbreth and Ernestine G. Carey. Hank Ketcham's cartoon books featuring Dennis the Menace are scanned by tens-of-thousands of early teen-agers.

5. Patriotic stories are liked by many boys and girls, according to George Norvell's comprehensive study of the reading interests of over 50,000 pupils in grades 7–12 in New York State (6). Among today's favorites are *Thirty Seconds Over Tokyo* by Ted Lawson and Bob Considine, *The Story of the U.S. Marines* by George Hunt, *Of Courage Undaunted* by James Daugherty, and *Johnny Tremain* by Esther Forbes. Average and slow readers enjoy many of the titles in the American Heritage series, the American Adventure series, and the Landmark series. Teachers of social studies, core, and language arts have many excellent titles of historical fiction available to recommend to their pupils.

6. Biographies which describe the youth of famous men and women are interesting to average and bright pupils (6). Both boys and girls like biography; however, boys prefer biographies of men. Girls have a slight preference for biographies of women (6). In reading biography, many teen-agers are seeking clues concerning ways to become successful and to lead happy, useful lives. Biographies such as *Thomas Alva Edison* by H. Gordon Garbedian, *Narcissa Whitman* by Jeanette Eaton, *Abe Lincoln Grows Up* by Carl Sandburg, *We Came to America*, edited by Frances Cavanah, *River Boy* by Isabel Proudfit, *Albert Schweitzer* by Jo Manton, and *The Jim Thorpe Story* by Gene Schoor are in demand. Unfortunately, there are not as many biographies of women as there should be to satisfy girls' interest in this type of literature.

7. Science and aviation stories appeal to most boys. In his nation-wide study of reading interests of over 6,000 pupils in grades 4–8, Dr. Shores (9) found that boys are more interested than girls in reading about astronomy, geology, physical geography, science, space travel, Indians, airplanes and rockets. Dr. Norvell (6) also found that boys have a greater interest in reading about science than girls. Librarians report that current favorites include *The Spirit of St. Louis* by Charles Lindbergh, *Everyday Machines and How They Work* by Herman Schneider, *The Silent World* by J. Y. Cousteau, *This Fabulous World of Insects*, edited by Charles Naider, *The Exploration of Space* by Sir Arthur C. Clark, and *Great Adventures in Science*, edited by Helen Wright and Samuel Rapport. *Rocket Jockey* by Philip St. John, and *Space Cadet* by Robert Heinlein are among the science fiction titles that propel boys away from this confining earth. Two hundred outstanding science books are annotated in the pamphlet "Books of the Traveling High School Science Library," published by the American Association for the Advancement of Science and The National Science Foundation.

8. Boys like stories and books about outdoor life. Dr. Norvell found

that girls, too, enjoy stories of school games and poems about sports *(6)*. There is an abundance of sports stories for boys but not many for girls. Unfortunately, plots are often trite and characters stereotyped. Stories of outdoor life involving danger or animals and featuring a girl as a main character often have strong appeal to girls. Examples are *High Trail* by Vivian Breck, and *Going On Sixteen* by Betty Cavanna. *Wonder Boy* by William Heuman, *Backboard Magic* by Howard Brier, and the stories about famous American athletes by Gene Schoor and Henry Gilfondy circulate widely and rapidly among boys, provided the books are readily available. Sports stories often have a special appeal to boys who are reluctant readers or who are slow learners *(5)*.

9. Junior high girls, especially those who are thirteen or older, enjoy stories dealing with dating, romance, sentiment, and family relationships. Girls at this age, and some boys too, are concerned about problems of growing up and social relationships. Their interests may be partly satisfied through books like *Cress Delahanty* by Jessamyn West, *The Newcomer* by Clyde B. Davis, Paul Annixter's *Swiftwater*, and Nancy Barnes' *The Wonderful Year*. However, many teen-age books in this area are replete with saccharine situations, unrealistic solutions, and false values.

The importance of dating in the eyes of teen-agers is reflected in the sales of the most popular of the Teen-Age Book Club's paperbacks. Close to 300,000 copies of *Boy Dates Girl* have been sold. *Your Manners Are Showing* by Betty Betz is another favorite. Aubrey Shatter (8) found that girls like magazines dealing with fashions, romance, movies, and home-making. Studies by Robert L. Thorndike, George W. Norvell, and other persons have agreed that most boys in their early teens reject narratives in which girls or women play leading roles or in which there is a considerable amount of romance *(10, 6, 4)*. Occasionally, however, boys who are becoming interested in feminine behavior will ask a trusted school librarian for books by Betty Cavanna, Mary Stolz, and Rosamond Du Jardin.

There are many other research findings concerning reading interests of early adolescents. The amount of book reading done by young people, especially by boys, frequently begins to drop off sometime between the ages of 12 and 15. However, according to a study by Paul I. Lyness *(4)*, the amount of newspaper and magazine reading done by boys increases somewhat with age.

Miss Malchow, Dr. Norvell, and Dr. Thorndike have reported that except for mild adventure, biography, and humor, the sex of the reader is a significant factor in their choice of reading materials. At the onset of pubescence, and sometimes before, girls want stories with romantic interest. Television and other unknown factors may be causing these interests to come earlier for girls than they have in the past. Other researchers have concluded that literary selections offered in the classroom have had more appeal to girls than to boys and that more girls than boys like to read (9).

Superior, average, and slow pupils like "equally well the selections commonly studied in high school," concluded Dr. Norvell in his New York study. In an earlier study of the interests of 3,000 youths, however, Dr. Thorndike found that bright children read a wider range of titles and more science, biography, and informational material than other pupils, and that very bright youths read literary selections at an earlier age than average children. He concluded that bright children's interests are most like those of slow children who are two or three years older (10).

If a literary selection is well liked in a particular grade, Dr. Norvell found, it will usually be liked by pupils two or three grades above and below that grade. Also, there seems to be little difference in the reading interests of children living in metropolitan, urban, and rural areas (6).

What effect does television have on reading? There are varied views on this subject. William D. Boutwell, Director of the Teen-Age Book Club, has declared that "movies and television are books' best friends." He says that teen-agers look at films such as *Shane* and then read the book *Shane* by Jack Schaefer. In his latest report on television and its appeal to youth, Paul Witty (11) states that the average amount of reading done by pupils has not changed greatly during the past few years. In the May 12, 1956, issue of *School and Society,* he writes, "In 1955, 43 per cent of the pupils stated that they read less; 45 per cent, more; and 12 per cent, the same amount. . . . The group that reads less is regarded as a real problem by many parents."

There are, of course, possible weaknesses in some of the research concerning pupils' reading interests. In answering questionnaires about likes and dislikes, young people react the same as adults; they don't always say what they think. Furthermore, when youth are asked to name their favorite books, they are restricted in their response by what they have read or have had an opportunity to read. They may know *Two Years Before the Mast,* but not *Carry On, Mr. Bowditch*; or *An Old-Fashioned Girl* but not *Cress Delahanty.* Also, to a limited extent, reading interests change with the times. During and after wars, war stories are popular; during periods when dangerous mountains are scaled, books on mountain climbing have a vogue; and in scientific periods—like the present—youth are fascinated by books describing the wonders of the universe.

Briefly, no research can tell us all we need to know about our pupils' interests. We need to know the reading interests adolescents have in common, but we also need to be alert to what Henry and Jean are interested in reading on a certain day and what they would probably learn to like if we opened the gates to a wider, richer range of reading experiences. And that means that the junior high teachers need to know not only the best books of the past for teen-agers, but also the scores of thrilling books of excellent literary quality being published every year. Then the teacher can guide adolescents while they explore and enjoy the "wonderful world of books" together.

REFERENCES

1. Barbe, Walter. A Study of the Reading of Gifted High School Students, *Educational Administration and Supervision,* 38: 148–54, March 1952.
2. Bernstein, Margery R. Relationship Between Interest and Reading Comprehension, *Journal of Educational Research,* 49: 286, December 1955.
3. Bruning, Herbert I. A Study of the Readability, Interest, and Usefulness of Selected Materials for Retarded Readers in Grades Seven to Twelve, *University of Kansas Bulletin of Education,* 10: 22, November 1955.
4. Lyness, Paul I. The Place of the Mass Media in the Lives of Boys and Girls, *Journalism Quarterly,* 29: 43–54, Winter 1952.
5. Malchow, Evangeline C. Reading Interests of Junior High School Pupils, *School Review,* 45: 175–85, March 1937.
6. Norvell, George W. The Reading Interests of Young People, Boston, D. C. Heath and Co., 1950.
7. Ridgway, Robert W. A Study of the Readability, Interest, and Usefulness of Selected Materials for Retarded Readers in Grades Four to Eight, *University of Kansas Bulletin of Education,* 10: 13, November 1955.
8. Shatter, Aubrey. A Survey of Student Reading, *The English Journal,* 40: 271–73, May 1951.
9. Shores, J. Harlan. Reading Interests and Informational Needs of Children in Grades Four to Eight, *Elementary English,* 31: 493–500. December 1954.
10. Thorndike, Robert L. Reading Interests, New York, Columbia University, Teachers College, Bureau of Publications, 1951.
11. Witty, Paul. A Sixth Report of TV, *School and Society,* 83: 166–68, May 12, 1956.

38. ACHIEVING EARLY SUCCESS

Deborah Elkins

Teachers had very specific goals which helped them meet their major objectives of teaching children to read, to enjoy reading, and to gain the reading habit. One of these goals was to bring about early success, to give the feeling that now in a new school there was a new beginning.

Reprinted with the permission of the publisher from Deborah Elkins, *Reading Improvement in the Junior High School* (New York: Teachers College Press), © 1963, by Teachers College, Columbia University.

A Project with Juvenile Books

One way of ensuring early success was through the use of younger children's books. Many of these junior high school children could not read books of interest to them because in certain areas there are not sufficient numbers available with easy vocabularies. Therefore, it was necessary for the teacher to make easy books acceptable to these children, books of a more childish nature which they would ordinarily find insulting to their intelligence, to themselves as human beings growing into adulthood. Projects were organized around the use of little children's books. One class read such books to study the degree to which the author used the element of horror. Was there too much horror for little children? Was a book too "soupy" and lacking in "spice?" The teacher read them some psychologically oriented newspaper articles on the effect of fear on little children, and even some paragraphs from a psychology textbook. The children felt "grown-up" at thus being taken into the confidence of adults as equals. They read book after book. When at least six children had read a book, they gathered together to discuss and "officially" rate that book for the edification of parents. A one-sentence annotation was composed, a horror rating given, and the book was classified as recommended or not recommended. A bibliography for parents was prepared, mimeographed, and distributed to parents of younger children.

There were variations of this activity. One class studied "fantasy" in little children's books and tried to decide whether it was "a good kind"; another group became intrigued with endings of stories and tried to decide whether or not the endings they liked now as compared with those little children liked gave any indications that they had grown up.

The children were told why it was important for them to read "easier-than-they-wanted-to" books. In simple terms, the teacher explained how the eye works during the reading process, showed what happens to its performance when the reader meets too difficult or too many unfamiliar words. The children were aiming now at fluency, and fluency is gained when the eye is permitted freedom to move easily. The children loved these short technical explanations; they "made sense."

Since the books to be included in the bibliography had to be rated, and since the children who had read a particular book often could not agree on the evaluation, it was usually necessary for them to read their selections to younger children. To prepare for reading to younger siblings or neighborhood children, there was much preliminary reading and rereading and "practicing on each other." The book had to be read well in order to get a true reaction. The class discussed what kinds of reactions they would look for. At what point does the child ask a question? Where is his excitement greatest? Where does his interest lag? Does he seem amused, or is he really frightened? How do you know?

Here is an excerpt from a discussion with one of the teachers: "The children began the session without waiting for me to start the ball rolling. They couldn't wait to report on their success with reading to their younger siblings or neighbors. I used this opportunity to ask them to write about this experience. Later, as they talked, one child repeated that her brother had asked for it again and again, until she had to distract him to another activity. Another child read a book in which appeared the words 'strut' and 'waddle'. When I asked her how she managed to explain such hard words she said, 'I showed him'. And I complimented her on her ability as a teacher. I'm finding the use of easy books for reading to younger children an outstanding stimulus. Some of the children are even beginning to be amazingly relaxed with reading."

Though the children accepted the project wholeheartedly, much of this reading had to be done in school time, because many of the children, boys especially, would not "be caught dead" carrying a "baby book." Others had no fear about being seen with such an object. For the boys who "cared" we quickly found such books as *Squanto and the Pilgrims* (Harper & Rowe), and the Bobbs-Merrill *Childhood of Famous Americans Series*. These are more adult in content but at third- and fourth-grade reading levels.

Whether the class as a whole accepts and enjoys the sibling-book project depends to a large extent on the way the teacher handles it. That they do enjoy it is obvious from the following excerpts from a taped recording:*

MIKE: I compared the book to [with] two different little kids. I read it to one and then to another one, and I read one in the morning and one in the night, and I think it was good because they liked it because the one in the night didn't yawn. They were like this: "What's gonna happen next?" You know, they were lookin' like that.

※　※　※

MARILYN: The title of mine is *Play With Me*. When I first opened it, I made sure it has big letters so if they look on with me they can almost read it themselves. And they have big pictures in here.

※　※　※

CAROLINE: I read to a neighbor's little boy and little girl. The little boy was four, so I said to him . . . "Did you like the story" and he said, "Yeah because he won the prize," and all that.

TEACHER: What was the title of the book you read?

CAROLINE: *Bugs Bunny at the Country Fair*. The seven-year-old started reading it to me at first, and I told her that I gotta read it to her. She can read very good.

MIKE: Sunday I didn't have anything to do so I took out the book and I read it to my brothers, my two brothers and next-door neighbor's two children. It's

---

* From a recording of a discussion led by Mr. Eli Seifman.

by Dr. Seuss, *One Fish, Two Fish, Red Fish, Blue Fish*. Well, my brothers liked it because it rhymed and because there's two characters in it, Joe and Mike, that—y'know my brother's name is Joe, so they laughed and said it was *us*. They just enjoyed it, but the other boy and girl are in school—one is five and one in first grade. So the older one stood there reading it, and when I came to a part that this girl liked she almost memorized it.

Then I read another book, *The Cat in the Hat*. This was a story like, but it rhymed and they liked it more than *One Fish, Two Fish*.

TEACHER: How do you explain the fact that they liked one better if they are both by the same author?

MIKE: This book is just riddles and it doesn't have a very good ending, y'know, to the story. But in the other story the cat comes back and he cleans the house up and then they see the mother, and the mother asks how they kept the house so clean.

THOMAS: I'm surprised at that because usually when you go into a regular bookstore for children they always recommend Dr. Seuss books for children because they are so interesting and hold their interest.

TEACHER: That's right. Mike did say that the children liked both but they liked *Cat in the Hat* even better. Was that right, Mike?

MIKE: Yes, and George has *Cat in the Hat Comes Back;* it's the same thing, but continuous.

TEACHER: Maybe we can hear from George now. Did you read it to your young child yet, George?

GEORGE: I brought the child five books and let him pick, and he picked out *Cat in the Hat* and I read it to him. He started to read some too, and made a few mistakes. He liked the little cats; he had a whole bunch of baby cats under his hat and he liked that. It's like a trick, keeping a whole bunch of cats under the hat like that. . . .

TEACHER: Did he understand the ending?

GEORGE: Yes, he did, because he was the one that read it to me. I let him read that part. . . . He said "I like that last cat."

HILDA: I had the book, *Daddy's Picnic and other Stories,* and just read *Daddy's Picnic* to my next-door neighbor. She liked it because she said they had a good time. And she understood the ending because she laughed and clapped her hands.

TEACHER: Did anyone have any unusual experiences when you tried to read your book?

ROBERT: Yeah. You know, I have that book *Yogi Bear* that Brenda gave me, so my cousin came over and she's a pretty smart kid, so my sister let the bird out of the house and the kid followed the bird and paid no attention to the story.

*   *   *

SANDY: (About the book *Dumbo*) When I got to the middle of the book she ran away and started to fly around like the elephant, and I couldn't stop her.

TEACHER: What does that tell us about one of the answers we are looking for?

MARTY: She understood the story, because she goes flying around chairs and making believe her ears were wings.

*   *   *

TEACHER: Did anyone else have an unusual experience?

MARTY: I had a bird book, like Sandy's only a little bigger but not many words

in it. I read about all the birds in the winter go South and he starts crying, because he's so sorry they went South. He's really mixed up, and then I read on
and it says in the end Spring will be here and all the birds will be back, and
he yells, "hurrah hurrah."

ANTHONY: I was reading the story to my brother and stopped in the middle to
ask him questions and he said, "Shut up, Andy, and finish reading the story."
He wouldn't let me ask any more questions.

* * *

TEACHER: What sorts of endings seem to be the type that the children like?

CORINNE: I found they like happy endings like the ending of *Bugs Bunny* when
he won the biggest prize and all that. They like happy endings, not when
someone dies, and mysteries.

BONNIE: When the story is finished and they say the princess lives happily ever
after. They want to know what happened—is she going to have children after
that. They want the story to continue.

There are evidences here not only of the children's enjoyment, but of
what they are learning about human behavior as well as about reading.
For some, this was a new and real effort on their part to make a relationship with other human beings. It was new in the sense that to make
warm relationships was difficult for them. Now they were receiving fresh
satisfactions in this area of their lives. There is evidence, too, of their
seriousness about the project. The readers can see the aims of the teacher.
From this point on he could lead them to see the need for other classmates to read the same books to other small children and to discuss how
they themselves felt about the endings of those books. He could read
short stories to the whole class. He could use the books the children were
discussing to consider basic ideas such as: Should books for little children
be "true to life"? Did teen-agers want everything to end happily? Was it
"true to life" for family members never to quarrel? What *was* the
meaning of "true to life"? Or he could lead them into a consideration of
certain specific aspects of human behavior, using their observations of
the little children to do this.

SELECTING THE APPROPRIATE BOOK

Achieving the goal of early success at this crucial time in a new school
required other things of the teachers, too. When children were reading
on their own levels and, where feasible and desirable, were reading a
common story, teachers learned to read *to* children until they became
emotionally involved in their story, and then let them proceed on their
own wherever possible. In doing this, they hoped that the momentum
would carry them along. Their hopes were usually satisfied if the story
was properly selected. Teachers also learned to do the reverse of what
their inclination might be: to permit and even encourage children to
read books that could be finished at a few not-too-long sittings rather

than to expect them to read a book with many pages. "Skinny" books became acceptable.

Teachers realized that a book must never be permitted to drag on for a long time. They read with the child (or found a "partner" to read with him) to help him finish it in a reasonably short time; or they took it away and started him on, plunged him into, an easier, shorter one. This function seems a simple one to learn. Actually, it was one of the most difficult things for all teachers. In the first place, their acquaintance with children's books was so meager that they had no framework within which to make judgments quickly, almost on the spot, about what constituted a third-grade level book, or a fourth, or a fifth. Children came in with pocketbooks their big brothers were reading and tenaciously held on to them, refusing to surrender them for easier ones (except within the previously described project using younger children's books). At first there was almost complete unawareness on the part of a teacher that this book was quite impossible for that child. When he did realize it, such devices as the one cited above in which the teacher talked about eye-span helped some. Then, the teacher explained to children how to try a book on for "fit." If they missed more than two words in a large paragraph, and felt that they were not "getting" the story, this was not a good "fit." This rule of thumb helped in a limited number of cases. It was necessary to give daily demonstrations of books that were suitable. When teachers were sure that a particular book and child suited each other, the child read for the class and the performance was discussed.

USING THE "EXPERIENCE" STORY

Working with a common theme helped meet the goal of early success in another way, too, this time with the nonreader. There were three or four children in each group who could not read at all, or at least claimed they could not, and test results bore out their statements, sometimes because they simply marked the test "any old way," knowing they would not do well, or in other cases because they did not understand directions or because they really had no word recognition ability. With these children, it was necessary to work especially quickly to demonstrate that reading was a possibility for them also. For these, teachers used an adaptation of the "experience story" used by primary-grade teachers, but here it was on an individual basis. The teacher acted as the child's "secretary" during a period when others were writing and took down, verbatim, his story. This was given a title, the "author" was named, and the story was typed double or triple spaced in duplicate. Next day, the teacher gave one copy to the child and from the other she read to him as he watched his own. Usually there was a broad smile of real pleasure at seeing himself "in print" and listening to his own story being read. Almost invariably, the child was able to read his own story back to the teacher with a minimum of errors if too much time had not elapsed between creating it and reading it. The reason, of course, was that it was his own vocabulary, his own flow of words, and that he knew the content since it was his. Now he had just the mechanics to contend with, and he could handle the situation. Almost invariably there was a terrific boost to morale at this demonstration that he could learn to read. This process was continued under a variety of circumstances. A student teacher took over, or another child, a sociometric choice,* acted as his secretary for future stories, and later copied the teacher's technique of marking the words he had missed and of helping him to learn to recognize them. The child-secretary took his story down from dictation when the teacher was too busy with other things involving the whole class. An example of such a story follows.

Riding to School in the Rain
BY JOHN DOE

When I was coming from my house to school, I was in the rain. The rain was coming down in buckets and buckets. I was on my bike. I was riding to school. It was really coming down, the rain. My mother told me not to go to school because it was raining too hard. But I rode to school on my bike in the rain. The rain was coming down in buckets.

When I came to the school, I saw my friend. My friend's name is Tommy. Tommy came to school with his mother. Tommy's mother drove Tommy to school.

When I took off my raincoat, I went to the water fountain to get a drink of water because I could not get a drink of water from the rain. Then my teacher and I started to work with my reading. We worked on our words and we read the story I wrote last week. I got plenty of words wrong. I hope I don't get many wrong when I read this story.

Often children do not like to dictate personal stories. When the class is discussing a theme and the concepts around it have been built up in such a way that daily experiences of all children can be brought to it, getting an "experience" story is not difficult. If the class is discussing careers, and the children have held an interview with an adult engaged in the career the child thinks he would like, it is a simple matter to get a story out of him. The teacher need not worry about whether he is a "verbal" child or not, whether he will "give" or not. He now has something to say, and saying is no problem for him. Or if the class is talking and writing about ways in which families educate, and children are discussing younger siblings and observing them, and are observing what families do teach them informally by the way they talk with them and play with them and feed them, stories come readily. This focus has an added advantage: All the children are making a contribution to group ideas, and this child is not left out because he cannot read or write. It is still his story, even

*See Helen Hall Jennings, *Sociometry in Group Relations*, Revised Edition (Washington, D.C.: American Council on Education, 1959).

though someone else at the moment is doing the mechanical recording of it. If, on occasion, the contributions of all the children are mimeographed, for all to read, every class member feels he is receiving equal attention.

Teachers in the project also found that they need not wait for perfection before praising a child sincerely, but could note each little element of progress and could help the children be aware of this and of what it meant. Teachers had to learn not to let a day go by without making a hopeful and genuinely encouraging remark to the class as well as to individuals. Such a remark could be on paper or directly stated face to face, but it was necessary in some form to the morale of the children. However, mere encouragement and support without tangible achievement results were fruitless. Children had to see and feel that they were learning, were making progress.

39. GIVE HIM A BOOK THAT HITS HIM WHERE HE LIVES

Charles G. Spiegler

Culturally, he is bounded on the north by comic books, on the south by the pool parlor, on the east by the racing form, on the west by neighborhood small talk. Born into a home at cultural ebb tide, often raised midst turmoil and trauma, living in an intellectual ghetto, he sits in my classroom—annoyed to the point of hostility. I have asked him to read a book—any book—for a first report of the term.

The "he" I mean is no figment of my imagination. He is Barry Saltz, a 16-year-old future butcher of America (one of many such in my classroom); a present reluctant reader (one of many such in my classroom). Despite his 20/20 vision, it dismays him not an iota that he has never read a book cover to cover in all his 16 years, that he has never spent a rainy afternoon browsing in the library.

Scan the printed page? Not he!

I search my brain for a *book* that may appeal. "How about *Questions Boys Ask*,"[1] I recommend ever so naively, as I brandish a copy I own. "Naaah. . . . "

Reprinted from *Improving English Skills of Culturally Different Youth*, Doris V. Gunderson, Editor, Bulletin No. 5 (Washington, 1964), pp. 91–99. United States Government Printing Office.

[1] David W. Armstrong. *Questions Boys Ask*. New York: E. P. Dutton & Co., 1955.

I try sports, hobbies, deep-sea fishing—everything from prehistoric man of 5 million years ago to the stars millions of light years away. But I get a look that warns me—"Mister, you're wasting your time."

I am beginning to lose heart when one day it happens! I find the link I need to help move Barry Saltz from the desert island of ignorance about books he has for so long inhabited to the mainland of written words and ideas. It is a tiny link—no bigger than the cluster of warts on Barry's index finger.

Those warts really worry Barry, butcher-to-be, because as he put it, "They're gonna drive away my customers." So I ask him one day, "Why don't you get rid of them?" and learn, to my surprise, that he has an *idée fixé* about warts. They come from touching frogs, and maybe will vanish one day by magic, if you're lucky.

Sensing how deep his superstition about warts really is, I recommend a book, *Superstitious? Here's Why!*[2] urge him to read the section on warts, and agree to accept this as a report.

The result? *Mirabile dictu!* Barry Saltz practically memorizes that paragraph on warts and reads the book through cover to cover in one 4-hour sitting. Moreover, having finally gone to a library, he has now become aware of some very readable books about health and strength—a major interest. Before the semester is over, Barry Saltz can tell you all about *The Wonders Inside You*[3] by Cosgrove, *Magic Bullets*[4] by Sutherland, and *Boy's Book of Body Building*[5] by Pashko. True, he still refers to de Kruif's *Hunger Fighters* as "Hunger Pains"! Who cares! Barry Saltz is on his way!

Does it matter? Does it really matter that the Saltz nose now goes between the covers of a book? Is this a "summum bonum" commensurate with the effort expended? Yes, indeed! For, of all youth's divine rights during that precious period we call "The school years," I place very high the enjoyment of books. Learning how to earn a living is one thing; but in an age of steadily increasing leisure, learning how to live—joyously—is, to me, prime. And learning how to do it, among other ways, through books—is quintessential.

Perhaps no one has said it for me better than Paul Bueter, a 17-year-old senior who, after viewing *A Night to Remember*[6] on TV, was one of dozens who had remembered it vividly enough to ask for the Walter Lord original. Queried on why he wanted the book, having just seen the

---

[2] Julie Forsyth Batchelor and Claudia De Lys. *Superstitious? Here's Why!* New York: Harcourt, Brace & World, 1954.

[3] Margaret Cosgrove. *The Wonders Inside You*. New York: Dodd, Mead & Co., 1955.

[4] Louis Sutherland. *Magic Bullets*. Boston: Little, Brown & Co., 1956.

[5] Stanley Pashko. *Boy's Book of Body Building*. New York: Grosset & Dunlap.

[6] Walter Lord. *A Night to Remember*. New York: Holt, Rinehart & Winston, 1955. Bantam Paperback, 1962.

TV version, he gave what seems to me the classic answer to those who see TV as the substitute for reading—"Sure, it was good," he says of the TV performance, "but I don't know...I didn't really get the feeling of how it was on the *Titanic* on that black night.... How could you, with all those camera lights on the people?" In order for Paul to "really get the feeling" of that black night to remember, he needed more than brilliant camera lights. He needed the glow of his own imagination.

Yes, I'm glad I got Barry Saltz to read for other reasons. Just as we learn to write by writing, we learn to read by reading. It's not always that "Johnny doesn't read because he can't." It's often that "Johnny can't read because he doesn't."[7]

Yes, I'm glad I got Barry Saltz to read because I know that the meat upon which our Caesars feed is anti-intellectualism, "know nothingism." In the growing struggles between freedom and authoritarianism, it is better for us all that the Barry Saltzes be thinking, questioning, probing citizens—not vacuums or vegetables. Though there are many paths towards this end, I respect reading as one of them. I'm glad I got Barry Saltz to read.

As chairman of an academic subjects department in a New York City vocational school (from 1956 to 1961), I have had the chance to study hundreds upon hundreds of Barry Saltzes in their raw, untutored state. Coming from homes where the bedtime story at twilight had never been heard and where the television set had replaced the reading lamp, they sat in our classrooms with all the symptoms of cultural blight. Their median IQ score was 85, their reading scores were poor, and their practice of the language arts was unique. One boy who was asked at an assembly to read from Proverbs in the *Bible* prefaced his oral reading with the announcement that he would read some "proud verbs" in the *Bible.* Youngsters asked to write on the "Star-Spangled Banner" began with "Oh, say can you sing by the doors early light?" A lad, reporting on a TV show he liked insisted that the hero was "Quiet Earp." Once in a discussion, I used the term *bachelor of arts* and asked for a definition— "He's a guy who got away by staying single."

Family ties, as the ordinary middle-class youngster enjoys them, were *terra incognita* to many of my boys. Fully 20 percent lived at home with but one parent, the second having vanished, run off, or died. I had boys who had never been served a warm breakfast by mother since they could remember. I had boys who had never had a heart-to-heart talk with father. Yet let mother or father be called to school, on some matter disciplinary, and we were often invited to "Hit him! Whack him! I mean treat him like he was your own!"[8]

    [7] Estelle H. Witzling, "Johnny Can't Read Because He Doesn't," *High Points,* 38: 52–59, January 1956.

    [8] Charles G. Spiegler, "A Teacher's Report on a 'Tough School,' " *The New York Times Magazine,* Nov. 24, 1957.

Spawned in such homes, the Barry Saltzes never go much beyond talking of "Who's gonna win the fight next week?" watching crime shows on TV, going to the movies with their dates, ogling the girlie magazines. Of the 900 boys at my city vocational school, no more than 20 ever found it worthwhile to take in a Broadway play or a concert at Carnegie Hall even though both are little more than an hour from any boy's home. "That's for eggheads," Billy Brenner, 16, tells me when I offer him a ticket. "It's too far, anyhow. You come home too late." Yet two nights a week, religiously, instead of sitting down with his homework, he marches to the bowling alley where, until midnight, he enjoys a few short beers and the thrill of crashing a 16-pound bowling ball against the varnished pins.

Small wonder, then, that when we talk to them of *Silas Marner* they hear us not. Their ears are tuned to the change-of-period bell. We may appeal to them with a lovely print of an English landscape. They see it not; their eyes are on the clock. Desperate, we bring out the great, beloved classics which are on the world's permanent best-seller lists. With pomp and ceremony, with a laying-down of red carpets, with a lighting of candelabra, we introduce children to these classics. But we leave them unmoved. So, in quiet resignation, we affix to them the label "retarded readers"; and that great cultural divide between the middle-class teacher (reared on Shakespeare and Browning and Eliot) and the sons and daughters of "blue-collar" America (so often raised on comics, the movies, and television) becomes deeper and wider.

We've got to heal that breach, and we can! But this can be done only with understanding—the understanding that the Barry Saltzes are, as the late Elizabeth Rose of New York University put it "allergic to print"; that much of what we, his teachers, choose for him to read is not only *not* a cure for this allergy but also an *extension* of it; that only the book which "packs a wallop for him" may hope to effect a cure. The remedy? Begin with a book that hits him where he lives![9]

I learned this back in 1954 when, as a new departmental chairman, I walked into the middle of a cold war between most of the 900 students in the school and most of the English teachers. The issue at first was books, *required* books for classroom study. The battleground was the bookroom piled high with *Silas Marner* and *Giants in the Earth* (grand books for college-bound youth, but sleeping pills for vocation-bound youngsters). There was a curtain dividing pupil and teacher, which, though made only of paper and print, was no less formidable than today's Iron Curtain. You walked into classes where teachers were devoting a full term to *Silas Marner*, and you saw children with heads on desks and eyes shut. You walked into the library and rarely saw a

[9] Elizabeth Rose, "Literature in the Junior High School," *English Journal*, 44: 141–147.

youngster except with a prescribed booklist based on the predilections of his teacher. The long and short of it was that children were not reading, and teachers had thrown in the sponge with the excuse, "They can't!"

I believed they could, if we would but give a boy a title, a book jacket, a theme that rang true; if we could but talk to him colorfully about the world of books! Don't limit him to the confines of prescribed booklists or restrictive formulas for making book reports. Let the world and its infinite wonders be the subjects he may choose from, I begged. Let him begin with what he likes, appeal to his interests—and he will read.

When we inaugurated a 3-day book fair, displaying 2,000 books dressed in jolly jackets and written on hundreds of lively subjects I was sure youngsters liked, there was a shaking of heads among some members of the faculty. "I'll bet you won't sell a hundred books," one asserted smugly. "All these kids want is comics and girlie books. They won't buy anything decent!"

But they did. For 3 days, while English classes were cancelled, children browsed, read at random, bought or not as fancy struck them. And when the fair was over, we knew that these were the 3 days that had shaken our smug little world. The Johnnies who would buy "only comics and girlie books" had dug into their after-school-odd-job savings to take home 1,123 good books. Granted, Bill Stern's *My Favorite Sports Stories* and *The Real Story of Lucille Ball* were best sellers, but not far behind were the *Burl Ives Song Book, The Red Pony,*[10] and books of science fiction. And higher than anyone dared predict were *The Cruel Sea*[11] and *Mutiny on the Bounty.*[12]

Though no teachers were panting down the students' necks to "read this!" they did guide student choice. Some, like the big, broad-shouldered lad who was about to buy *The Scarlet Letter*[13] because he thought it was a football story, needed guidance. Some, like the nature lover who was about to buy *A Tree Grows in Brooklyn*[14] because he thought it was on target for a report he was making on trees, needed guidance. Others passed the proffered help, however, and bought many books with vocabulary loads somewhat beyond their level. It didn't matter. "Interest," George Norvell, former New York State Supervisor of English, has said, "leaps over all reading barriers, including vocabulary."[15]

Johnny wasn't sleeping through "Lit" class by now. We relegated *Silas Marner* to a basement storeroom and gave the youngsters livelier fare.

[10] John Steinbeck. *The Red Pony.* New York: Viking Press, Inc., 1959.

[11] Nicholas Monsarrat. *The Cruel Sea.* New York: Alfred A. Knopf, Inc., 1951.

[12] Charles Nordoff and James Norman Hall. *Mutiny on the Bounty.* Boston: Little, Brown & Co., 1932.

[13] Nathaniel Hawthorne. *The Scarlet Letter.*

[14] Betty Smith. *A Tree Grows in Brooklyn.* New York: Harper & Row, 1947.

[15] George W. Norvell. *The Reading Interests of Young People.* Boston: D. C. Heath & Co., 1950.

Booker T. Washington in his struggles for an education became a far more genuine superman to them than the comic book man with wings. It was *Kon-Tiki*[16] on the perilous Pacific that replaced Eliot's nineteenth-century England. You could now walk into a class studying *Kon-Tiki* and see Jimmy Kolofney at the blackboard writing a letter of congratulations to Thor Heyerdahl. While he is expressing his admiration for the Skipper and "that crazy, wonderful think you done," seven boys are rehearsing in two separate corners of the room: three of them in one corner play the crewmen of the *Kon-Tiki*; the other four make up a TV panel that will ask the intrepid voyagers all about the dangers, the thrills, the uncertainties of their venture.

Before long all eyes are focused on Jimmy's letter on the blackboard, to correct it—because "You can't send junk to a big shot like that." Later the class turns to the TV panel, which raises some incisive questions on the madness, the glory, and the thrill of adventure dear to any boy's heart. It also raises a question or two that better-bred boys might not ask: "Didja ever 'chicken out'?" "Hey, didja miss girls?" The end-of-period bell rings in the nick of time.

By the end of the year, the majority of our 900 students were reading at least a book a month. Many were doing far better. Library circulation had gone from 600 to 1,500.

Neither "climax" nor "denouement" cluttered up book reports now. As make-believe salesmen, kid critics, Hollywood producers, television panelists, they reported in terms they knew. "I like," "I love," "I hate," "I get mad," "It's great," "exciting," "heartwarming"—these terms indicated how books hit them. "I love that book because it suits my taste," wrote Johnny Gallardo about *Lives of a Bengal Lancer*.

Whatever the individual taste, we had given each of those 900 students a sporting chance to satisfy it. Now that the fair was over and the appetite whetted, I began to observe, ever so occasionally, especially after lunch, a paperback under the arm of a lad or two where earlier in the day there had been a lunch bag. Boys were beginning to walk off their hero sandwiches with short strolls to the neighborhood paperback gallery, sometimes bringing back a sample or two. Soon we discovered the Teen Age Book Club[17] whose titles caught the fancy of many. We were beginning to establish a rapport between children and books, helping many of our boys buy them cheaply, start their own libraries, and see for themselves how "even the smallest library is a veritable Treasure Island that takes no *Hispaniola* to reach—its buried riches no pirate's chart to locate."

This is not to boast that success was absolute and universal. We still had lots of lads like Lenny Kalter who equated the carrying of books with the role of the sissy. It wasn't until Miss Isenberg (public librarian

---

[16] Thor Heyerdahl. *Kon-Tiki.* Chicago: Rand McNally & Co., 1950.
[17] Teen Age Book Club, sponsored by *Scholastic* magazine.

assigned to visit our classes regularly to bestir the reluctant dragoon)
had introduced young Master Kalter to Henry Gregor Felsen's *Hot Rod*[18]
that Lenny could identify with a character in a book—in this instance
Bud Crayne, *Hot Rod's* hero, and lover of speed. Lenny borrowed the
book, devoured it, then became so avid a reader on the subject that *Street
Rod*[19] (also by Felsen), *Mexican Road Race*,[20] *Thunder Road*,[21] and
The Red Car[22] were finished within 2 weeks. Then he began searching
the stacks all over the city for "anything by Mr. Felsen." When he heard
that we were planning to invite an author to visit our assembly and set
the keynote for our next Book Fair, he volunteered to write the first
formal letter of invitation he had ever written in his life—you guessed
it—to Gregor Felsen.

Last, but hardly least, let me suggest how television far from proving
a menace to reading, as is so often alleged, proved a boon. My major
premise here is that culturally deprived youngsters limit their horizons to
the four walls of the home, the four corners of the neighborhood, and, as
with many of my boys, the six pockets of the pool table. Television is
their new window to the world. Through it they find the fullest, richest
array of new interests man has ever known. Where or when, for example,
in all recorded history could so many Americans in the year 1962 with a
flip of the dial take an hour-long journey through the White House, with
its gracious First Lady as hostess and guide?

My minor premise is that interest is the key to reading. My conclusion
follows naturally. Television, by creating interest, can become the road
to wider reading.

I saw it strikingly one morning in April of 1956. I was sitting in my
office composing my weekly bulletin when the door burst open and two
of my boys came dashing in.

"Got somp'n by Ogden Nash?" came the breathless query.

Slowly I raised my head.

"Who?"

"Ogden Nash—you know," they exclaimed, "the guy wid dose crazy
rhymes."

My pen dropped; my ears perked up. Surprised, indeed delighted, that
my boys were interested in reading one of America's most literate
creators of verse, I asked: "You boys doing a book report on Mr. Nash?"

"Nope!" they parried, "no book reports—we just wanna read sump'n by
him. We went to the library, but the other guys beat us to it. *You*
got sump'n?"

[18] Gregor Felsen. *Hot Rod.* New York: E. P. Dutton & Co.

[19] Gregor Felsen. *Street Rod.* New York: Random House, 1953.

[20] Patrick O'Connor. *Mexican Road Race.* New York: Ives Washburn, 1957.

[21] William Campbell Gault. *Thunder Road.* New York: E. P. Dutton & Co., 1952.

[22] Don Stanford. *The Red Car.* New York: Funk & Wagnalls Co., 1954.

Happily I had. And happily, Tommy Gorman, a 15-year-old butcher-to-be, and Peter de Stefano, a 16-year-old baker-to-be, walked off with every copy I owned of *I'm a Stranger Here Myself*.[23] When you realize that before this day the closest Tom and Peter had come to voluntarily exposing themselves to rhythms and rhymes was the "popular song sheet," you realize what a move forward they had made.

This did not erupt full grown from the head of Zeus. It happened at a time when their English teacher found the going rough as he started a unit on poetry. So he looked for help. Since television was not a dirty word in our school, he looked to see how that week's TV programing could help. And lo, that Sunday Ed Sullivan could! For Sullivan had invited Noel Coward to read from the works of Ogden Nash to the background music of Saint Saens, as played by Andre Kostelanetz. So the homework assignment for that Sunday said, "Watch Sullivan"—not just the song, not just the dance—but *all* of it! With the results we have seen.

Teach a little "dialmanship" and TV can become an Aladdin's lamp far more wondrous than the Arabian original. Our librarian, too, recognized that and arranged a bulletin board entitled *IF YOU WATCH: WHY NOT READ*. If you watch the weather spots, why not read *Weathercraft*[24] by Spilhaus, for example? If you watch Leonard Bernstein, why not read *Leonard Bernstein*[25] by David Ewen?

If, in fact, we really want to introduce the culturally deprived youngster to books he can read on subjects he wants to read about, we are living in an age of huge abundance. For, in truth, this is the Golden Age of Writing for Youth, with many magnificent series available to them; with real writers (Quentin Reynolds, Dorothy Canfield Fisher, John Gunther, to name but a few) writing for them.

I cannot begin to tell you of the many, many hundreds of "juveniles" I have read myself with admiration, and been privileged to review and annotate, with a very high respect for what they can mean to children, and, with genuine appreciation for what they have meant even to ancient old ME.[26]

The job of preparing the proper materials for the customer we are talking about is, however, far from complete. So formidable, indeed, is this task, with both the textbook and the trade book, I would take a leaf from the book of the Ford Foundation man who recently recommended a *Vice President-in-Charge-of-Heresy* for every school system—by proposing a *Vice President-in-Charge-of-Searching for-and-Finding-Materials-Written-So-That-the-Children-We-Are-Concerned-With-Will-Read-Them-*

[23] Ogden Nash. *I'm a Stranger Here Myself*. New York: Little, Brown, 1941.

[24] Athelstan Spilhaus. *Weathercraft*. New York: Viking Press, 1951.

[25] David Ewen. *Leonard Bernstein*. Philadelphia: Chilton Books, 1960.

[26] The reviews of the books under this category appear in the section called "Books You May Like," in Marion Monroe, Gwen Horsman, and William S. Gray. *Basic Reading Skills*, Chicago: Scott, Foresman & Co.

With-Interest. As my first piece of advice to said VPI, I would urge: "Listen to the children you are serving." Here are their answers:

1. The subject has to be worth it to us. We like books about animals, aviation, careers, hobbies, sports, the sea, westerns. We love lots of adventure, plenty of excitement, slews of interesting facts about science and things.

2. Don't treat us like babies. We may not be such "hot' readers, but that doesn't mean if you give us an easy book about ducks on a farm we'll cackle over it gleefully. We had that stuff in the third grade, remember?

3. Give us lots of good pictures, good drawings, and big print. As one of the fellows said, "I can't read when the print on the pages is so small. After a while I lose my eyesight."

4. You have to know how to write. Maybe the fellow who likes to read a lot will stand for some boring parts, but not us. If you want us to read don't beat around the bush but come to the point. Give us a story that pushes us to go on to the next page and the next page—and we'll stay with it.[27]

Let us search out the books which, as Robert Lawson has put it, will give these kids " ... the chuckles ... the gooseflesh ... the glimpses of glory" they love. The books are here, now, asking to be discovered and enjoyed.

Books and reading are a staple in such a program not only for the well-endowed, but also for *all* the children of *all* the people. Only in the faith that there are no "second-class" citizens in our schools, a faith conceived, nurtured, and cherished in pride for nearly two centuries, can we hope to rise to the urgent tasks ahead. I am supremely confident that we shall.

[27] Charles G. Spiegler, "Reading Materials for Retarded Readers," *Materials for Reading*, Supplementary Educational Monographs, No. 6. Chicago; University of Chicago Press, 1957.

CHAPTER VI

READING IMPROVEMENT

PROGRAMS

40. HELPING CHILDREN TO READ

Gertrude Hildreth

The remedial program was by no means restricted to direct work with books and other printed materials, although the children had been enrolled especially for help in reading. To integrate the summer's work, training in reading, combined with recreational activities and including a period for planning and discussion, was carried on daily. This program was organized as an integration of activities centering about the major group interests and embracing varied educational experiences. The program was entitled "Pleasant Adventures with Books." From the outset we wanted the children to feel that reading would be fun and as well worth doing as other activities in which they were more successful. The program provided a series of experiences not only closely related to the children s interests, but adjusted to their learning requirements. Although the six weeks' period was too short to do more than study each case and begin the retraining, it gave us an opportunity to initiate a comprehensive program. Suggestions for further training that grew out of the individual remedial program for each child were made at the end of the term. These suggestions were made in the form of recommendations sent to the parent and the school.

Although the program was considered "remedial" in a technical sense,

Reprinted with the permission of the publisher from Gertrude Hildreth and Josephine L. Wright, *Helping Children to Read* (New York: Teachers College Press), pp. 19–58. Copyright 1940 by Teachers College, Columbia University.

the term remedial was never used before the children. Actually, in most respects the procedures differed little from those used in modern teaching with normal children, except that they were more highly individualized. The major objectives were:

1. To restore the child's confidence in his ability to learn to read.
2. To restore interest in reading.
3. To help the child gain actual skill in deriving meaning from the printed page.
4. To help him use his reading in functional ways, such as following directions and the like, to relate reading to varied activities.
5. To enable the child to read with enjoyment even though the reading was on a simple level.
6. To help him gain skill and poise in oral expression, and to develop fluency in conversation.

Specific objectives for individual children developed as the project progressed.

The Classroom and Its Equipment

The classroom was furnished and arranged quite informally to suit the activities carried on. Conventional classroom seating was abandoned for tables and chairs, bookshelves, and work space. On entering the room the children found plants in the windows, bright pictures on the walls, colorful curtains, and books in new jackets. Almost daily the chairs and tables were rearranged for meetings of the reading club and other group or individual work projects. Several corners were separated from the rest of the room by bookshelves, and furnished with tables where children could work quietly alone. Folding screens were available for use in blocking off individual work places.

The general equipment included bulletin boards, two typewriters, three rubber stamping sets, anagrams, alphabet cards for writing practice, paints and crayons, toy animals, clay, drawing paper, paste, scissors, colored construction paper, and notebooks.

The instructional materials for reading work were of two kinds: First, a library of three hundred recreational and informational books, varying in subject, with a wide range in reading level, selected for their appropriateness to the project. There were also pamphlets and magazines, scrapbooks, series readers. Second, a supply of workbooks, work sheets, study-type exercises, and appropriate materials for making necessary devices for individual cases.

Chairs and tables of the right height were selected for the children, and each one was assigned a definite place in the room. Later, seating was rearranged in order to group the children who had similar difficulties. Several brightly colored and well illustrated books were spread out on two reading tables so that on entering the room the first day of school the children could go to the tables and handle the materials freely.

The Daily Schedule

The class met daily from 8:30 until 12:20. A schedule was worked out in cooperation with music and art teachers of the Summer Demonstration School so that in addition to the reading work and regular classroom activities the children could have music, art, and gymnasium periods. The program included, in addition to more direct work in reading, attendance at assembly, clay modeling, painting and drawing, swimming, music, rhythms, and shop work. The program of special activities was as follows:

	MONDAY	TUESDAY	WEDNESDAY	THURSDAY	FRIDAY
9:30–10:00					Assembly of the Demonstration School
10:30–11:00					Music
11:00–11:30			Music		
11:30–12:00		Clay work		Fine arts Shop	
12:00–12:20	Swimming		Swimming		

The first two weeks served as an orientation period in which the children became acquainted with their classroom environment, with the teacher, and with one another. They were encouraged to choose from the classroom library books of appropriate levels; they took a trip to the zoo which stimulated questions about animals and led to an interest in animal stories; they attempted to write stories; they engaged in classroom discussions about animals and their habits; they took various reading, spelling, intelligence, and diagnostic tests.

The class was kept together as a group for at least one hour daily. This seemed desirable to build up morale. During this period the teacher had opportunity to make announcements, plan future work, discuss various projects, encourage children to participate in class discussion, and make group assignments. This proved to be one of the most helpful periods of the day. At other periods the children worked individually with the interns. By treating the class as a social group at the beginning of the term and for daily periods thereafter, the social relations among the group early established were maintained.

No two daily programs were ever the same, but after the first week the daily succession of events and activities had much in common. The following is an illustration.

July 8th:	8:30– 9:00	Individual work
	9:00– 9:30	Reading test
	9:30–10:00	Assembly
	10:00–10:30	Class discussion
	10:30–11:00	Reading Club
	11:00–12:20	Special activities

Other illustrations are on page 493.

Art work done during the art period was posted about the room for the children to enjoy, and also in order that they might derive satisfaction from seeing a finished piece of their own work displayed. Stories about the pictures were written and these often provided material for future reading periods.

No one theme characterized the class work throughout the term; instead, several interests ran parallel from time to time.

The Trip to the Zoo

A trip to the zoo was taken early in the session to stimulate an interest in animals and a desire to obtain additional information about them such as reading would furnish. This trip also provided a common experience for teachers and pupils. Each child took a notebook and pencil on the excursion. Student teachers accompanied the children so that there were two or three children under the guidance of each student. When the children reached the zoo they were permitted to wander where they liked and were encouraged to sketch the animals or to copy the names from the placards on the cages. During the discussion period before the trip the children listed the animals they would like to see. This was done with the teachers help and with some use of the dictionary by the more advanced readers. When the children reached the zoo they attempted to find these animals by comparing their lists with the names on the cages. Many of them printed the names in the same capital letter forms used on the placards.

The day following the trip a class discussion resulted in plans to collect animal pictures for a scrapbook and to draw, paint, and model the various animals that had been seen. All the lists of animals compiled by the children during their trip were pooled and copied on the blackboard by the teacher. In order to make an index for their scrapbook, it was pointed out to the children that an alphabetical arrangement of the words would be desirable. This was undertaken by a group of children and resulted in discussion of alphabetical arrangement, reference to the dictionary, and finally in a list somewhat as follows:

bear, black	camel
bear, brown	crocodile
bear, polar	elephant
bear, snow	fox, red
bear, sun	fox, silver
bison	etc.

The list ended with yak and zebra. The trip to the zoo led to a discussion of animals and their habits, which in turn aroused an interest in animal stories. Letters and visits relating to the zoo were exchanged with another class in the Summer Demonstration School. Following the trip, our class drafted a note to the neighboring class, asking whether they would like to hear about the trip. A note was soon received inviting our group to visit them and describe what they had seen.

The children made books for mounting their drawings. The books were labeled "My Book of Drawing." Printing the title pages of these books led to a discussion of letter forms. The teacher put the alphabet of small and capital letters on the board to facilitate writing.

The trip to the zoo served as an "ice breaker" for social contacts among the group and furnished an opportunity for valuable natural language expression.

The Reading Club

Early in the term a reading club was organized, with each person in the class as a member. The children enjoyed nominating and voting for the officers of the club, who included a president, a secretary, and a "helper." The helper was selected because of his ability to read better than the others and because he therefore would be able to assist anyone who needed help when reading before the club. The purpose of the club was to motivate the children's oral reading and to provide for them an audience situation. Books read before the club varied in reading level from preprimers to fourth grade readers. Reading was accepted and praised by club members when it represented the best effort of the child reading. They soon learned to make constructive criticisms and to rejoice genuinely when those who chose primary material read it smoothly and with expression. After each child read, the president asked for suggestions and remarks from the audience. If a child came to a club meeting unprepared, he was stopped at once by the president and advised to study before appearing again. The secretary was responsible for the program. He tacked on the bulletin board a large piece of paper on which children wrote their names and the date on which they would be prepared to read.

If a story was long, the child who selected it would tell part of it and read only the "most exciting," "the funniest," or the "best" part. Often a child presented a long story by reading and telling a certain part each day. This was looked forward to with great pleasure by the others. The primer and preprimer readers were always tolerated, but those who read primers were often urged to "work hard so you can read a more interesting story." Books other than textbooks were often chosen. Children were urged to select "easy books" for reading club. As the school term advanced, they read at sight and were not required to put so much time upon their preparation. The teacher often put her name on the club program and read to the children when her turn came. The secretary always announced the program and called upon the various members in turn. The president opened and closed the meetings. This provided an invaluable audience situation for the children, most of whom needed more practice in oral reading before a group. Meetings of the reading club were held during the group work period. The teacher at first placed on the board notices about the reading club. For example, "When would you like to read? Please put your name here. Be sure to write the date." Later this was done by the secretary of the club.

	Stories		Poems
Date	Name	Date	Name
August 1	Phil	August 1	Elizabeth
	Bernard		
	Alex		

For a typical meeting, each child got out the book on which he had been practicing. The children were divided into groups which were numbered 1, 2, 3, 4. Each group came up to the front of the class as guests. The chairs were placed in a circular arrangement. The groups were called to read in turn. During the club meeting, each child was instructed to put a marker with his own name in his book and listen quietly to the others. Typical selections made early in the term were from the Elson-Gray preprimer, the Gates-Huber, *Round the Year*, and *Peter and Peggy*, a story about "Charlie and His Dog," a fire engine story from *The Fireman* (Kuh), *Mr. Brown's Grocery Store* (Read), *Along the Busy River* (Keelor), *The Bear Twins* (Hogan), and *Trains* (Coffin). Other selections were "Big Black Rooster," and "Kit Carson and the Bears." On one occasion the teacher made the following notation: "When F read to the group in reading club today several children commented on his improvement. One child said, 'He goes on a smooth road' (meaning he phrased well), and another said, 'He deserves to improve, he worked so hard.' On another occasion the class clapped after one of the members had read a poem.

Almost daily, at first, the teacher read to the group in order to give them a better background for understanding the terminology and ideas they would encounter in books and thus broaden their experience with language. This reading also aided in maintaining interest, introducing variety, and giving an opportunity to hear oral reading correctly done. The reading included both poetry and stories. The children enjoyed most hearing stories and poems on a very simple level, appropriate for children about two years younger than themselves.

The reading club was continued through the term with increasing selection by children of reading material, stories, poems, and books, as well as discussion of the books read. After being read to, the children were sometimes required to answer comprehensive questions on their reading, to discuss the story, to write out what they liked best about the story, to write their ideas about the story, to write answers to comprehension questions, or to write original material. This was not required to the point of spoiling the enjoyment of the stories. The following account illustrates a typical meeting.

The teacher showed the children some books selected from the room library. She gave the titles and told something about the contents of each book. The children were asked to select the one they wished to hear read aloud. They chose *Blaze and the Gypsies* (Anderson). The teacher read part of the story and then placed it on the book table. She also read part of *Firefighters* by Floherty. One child selected Stryker's *Little Dog Ready*. The teacher continued with reading from Orton's *The Secret of the Rosewood Box*. All these special books were placed on the table in the front of the room or were given to children who wished to finish the stories. This activity was carried on in an attempt to help the children form the habit of picking up books in free time instead of turning to other activities. One day, after reading more of *Little Dog Ready*, the teacher wrote on the board sentences about the story. The children helped compose the sentences: "Ready is the name of a nice little dog. He wanted some fresh air. He met a big yellow dog. The dog turned his head. Ready was a very polite dog. He never gave up hope." One child then read the story to the group. The teacher inquired, "If you were going to write still more of the story what would be some of the hard words you might want to use?"

The children volunteered "tired," "home," "Master Dick," "happy," "again," "flowers," "window." They were directed to copy the first part of the story from the board and then to finish it, using some of the ideas suggested by the additional words. When this work was completed, the children took turns reading their stories about "Ready." The group decided which one should go in the next edition of the class newspaper.

On the day the story of *Little Dog Ready* was completed, the teacher suggested to the group that perhaps Miss Fiske's children (the ungraded class) would like to read it too. The class then wrote the following letter:

Lincoln School
New York, N. Y.
July 29, 1938

Dear Miss Fiske,

We have a very good book. We think your class would like to read it.

The children were asked to add anything else they wished to complete the letter. After the letters were completed and the teacher had looked them over, they were sent in with a copy of *Little Dog Ready* to Miss Fiske's class.

Shortly after the term began, a newspaper project was initiated by two of the older children. They came to the teacher one morning with the comment, "We have been working with the printing press (a rubber stamp marking set). We thought we'd have a newspaper and print news of the class to be put on the bulletin board." The teacher asked, "When will it be ready?" They answered, "Friday. We'll call it the Summer Newspaper."

The teacher capitalized this interest at once because she appreciated the numerous ways in which such a unit could become integrated with many-sided reading activities and interests. In fact, the teacher had intended to suggest a newspaper unit, had the children themselves not proposed it, since she was convinced that a newspaper project would unify experiences and provide opportunities for social contacts and work for the group as a whole. It would also involve functional practice reading and integration of the various activities under way.

The word "newspaper" was placed on the blackboard, and in the process of writing it the teacher pointed out that it was made of two small words. At the same time the group practiced finding the "er" sound in their own names and other familiar words.

The children discussed features of a newspaper, "weather," "the date," etc. The class decided on the duties of officers needed for making and running their paper. An editor and reporters were suggested, as were sports editor and society editor. Then they decided on the number of reporters and the best people for the jobs. A staff was duly elected to run the paper. Finally the following list was written on the blackboard:

Editor	Society reporter
Assistant editor	Art reporter
Weather reporter	General news reporter
Sports reporter	Printers

It was planned to have the reporters collect news items to put in each edition from week to week, and to mount pictures cut from daily papers. Others in the class helped prepare the items; they wrote original stories, typed materials, printed the newspaper headlines, and cut out pictures to be put in the paper. These articles and pictures were filed by the children in large manilla envelopes which were labeled and tacked up on the bulletin board. When it was time to assemble the paper, some of the articles contributed were read by the teacher to the class. The teacher helped because it was difficult for the editors to read all the material written in the various children's handwriting. Two stories on the same topic were found and the children learned that the editors must read them and select the better one. They took the material out of the envelope on one occasion to see whether it was appropriate. One boy decided that comics should be included in the paper. A sign "Editor" was printed and placed on the editor's desk. The teacher occasionally read various articles that had been submitted and asked for appraisal by the class. On one occasion the weather report was so badly smeared that it could not be used. This brought forth a discussion on the need for and advantages of neat, careful, and accurate work.

Copies of "My Weekly Reader"[1] were distributed after plans for the class paper were formulated. The children examined copies with interest and found in the printed sheets many suggestions to follow for their own news sheet. One day, when the children had completed their respective tasks on the newspaper, the teacher inquired what other suggestions might be made for improving the paper. On the blackboard was placed the following outline:

The Summer School Newspaper

Weather
Pictures
Scoop
Articles written or copied by the children
Picture section
    Pictures clipped from newspapers and pasted
    on the sheets.

The teacher then told of a mysterious scoop. The term "scoop" was explained by one of the children. The teacher held up the paper on which the "scoop" was written in large blue letters. The children tried to read the "scoop," which said

Swimming
Extra swimming period
Today at twelve o'clock
This is a surprise

On July 15 a folded copy of the first newspaper was exhibited. It was in

[1] Published by the American Education Press, Columbus, Ohio.

two sheets of newsprint, measuring when folded 15 x 22 inches. The name of the paper and the date were printed with the rubber stamping set. Children's contributions, in their own handwriting or typing, were merely pasted on this sheet. The story editor told the group about his work on the newspaper. He gave suggestions about some of the stories and told why he could not use them. The children passed the paper around the class and scanned it eagerly for their contributions.

After the edition was completed, the stories, news items, and other written material were mimeographed and distributed so that each child could have his own copy of the paper, see his own name in print, read the material as often as he liked, and take it home to enjoy. Pictures which could not be reproduced were given a notice in the mimeographed edition, telling the name of the child who drew the picture and the subject of the picture. At the reading club meeting, the teacher read at random several articles from the mimeographed edition of the paper, stating the child's name and glancing at him before the reading. The children then took turns reading their contributions. There was general group discussion of the material. Miss Fiske's class was invited to share in enjoying the paper. Two editions were completed during the six weeks' term.

Provisions in the Program for Individual Work

Individual work in reading was carried on throughout the term coordinately with the reading club, the newspaper, and other group activities. Individual instruction was provided for chiefly in the following ways:

1. Through materials—having on hand an adequate supply, varied in character and appropriate for all achievement levels, and selecting each child's materials to harmonize with his requirements.
2. By providing individual drill periods for each child every day, apart from the group, under the supervision of a student-teacher.
3. Through activities within the class on an individual basis, e.g., individual contributions to the newspaper projects, individual preparation of stories for the reading club.
4. Through contributions made by pupils on an individual basis during group reading activities.

This individual work was done under supervision by the advanced student-teachers or interns who were enrolled in the class for this experience and who were given regular college graduate credit for their work.

At practically no time during the first three weeks were any two children reading from the same book. Later, as several proved able to read together, sometimes as many as three children enjoyed the same material.

Larger groups were then formed. In connection with their individual work, children read aloud from various books, worked with flash cards, used reading workbooks, prepared progress charts, made scrapbooks, prepared word lists, and practiced spelling and writing. The specific techniques used in individualized instruction are described in the next chapter. When the children could not be worked with individually, they were given seat work assignments, such as using workbooks, cutting out material for a scrapbook, printing for the newspaper with a rubber stamp outfit, reading a book in preparation for reading club. Some of the children assembled the paper by pasting the contributions on large sheets of newsprint, others cut out pictures after having read directions, and one child copied a paper he had previously written which had been refused by the editor of the newspaper.

Work of the Student-Interns

The student-interns were primarily responsible for the individual work carried on with the most seriously retarded cases. During the first week the interns gave individual diagnostic tests and closely observed each child, both in the classroom and in the individual workroom.

The interns encouraged the children in the selection of workbooks, hypotheses as to the causes of the children's disabilities and outlined readers, and storybooks adapted to their abilities. They formulated programs for conducting individualized remedial work. They kept daily systematic records of the children's responses and development, prepared individual work materials, selected appropriate books and workbooks, and developed remedial techniques suitable to each case. In addition, each intern visited the home of at least one child, interviewed parents concerning the problem, did individual teaching daily with one or more children, did some group teaching, and observed the regular room teacher work with the class for one hour or more daily.

The interns sent letters to the children's former schools requesting information concerning their previous work. They studied the materials in our classroom library in order to evaluate it for teaching purposes. They established rapport with the special teachers in the Summer School and with physicians who examined the children.

A daily discussion group was attended by the interns, during which meeting the nature of the program was explained, children's problems were studied, remedial techniques were discussed, and teaching plans were made. This group discussion often related to problems of individual children. A student-intern reported that G read with his eyes very close to the page, suggesting the need for a more thorough vision examination. Should he have glasses? Another student raised the question of the level of reading material a child should have. The suggestion was made that now possibly second grade should be tried. A suitable reader and coordinated workbook were recommended. A similar question of reading difficulty arose in connection with another child who was rapidly reaching a point where he could profitably handle more difficult material.

The reasons for P's continued difficulties were sought by the intern who had been working with her. At first poor vision had been suspected, but a visit to the home and adequate tests confirmed the fact that the child's vision was normal. The various reasons for the types of difficulties the child showed and their persistence in spite of intensive training were discussed in detail. The intern inquired, "Is her difficulty due chiefly to innate dullness?"

The individual workers conferred with the classroom teacher daily at the conference period in order to coordinate the work done individually with the program as a whole.

Those student-interns were most successful who quickly established sympathetic rapport with the child, who appreciated the total problem most comprehensively and understood it most thoroughly, who gained the best understanding of the child in all his learning activities. An important phase of this work was to help the child adjust himself emotionally to his reading problem.

We found it very helpful for one worker to stay with a given child and work with him daily at the same place and time, for a period, in order to systematize the child's work and study habits and promote efficiency in practice. Interns found it a most profitable practice to talk over the child's mistakes with him, to let the child explain his difficulties, and to explain in turn to the child how he could work to overcome them. The value in individual work with the intern resided in the secure feeling the child gained when he felt someone was interested in his progress and was there to help him out of his difficulties. When this contact was re-established daily, the child and teacher gained a rapprochement that was invaluable in rehabilitating these slow learners. However, there is danger in overdoing this close personal relationship, especially if the teacher grows so fond of the child that she becomes too lenient with him, allows him to dawdle, excuses his errors too readily, and becomes blind to his faults or too sentimental and emotional over his desirable or undesirable qualities. The child must not become over-dependent on one teacher, otherwise he never reaches the point where he can help himself. The teacher in her intimate individual relations with the child must maintain a mature, well-poised attitude—sympathetic, yet objective and impersonal in character. Only thus can she evaluate the child's responses fairly and help him to get on his own feet.

Several student-interns who worked with the most seriously retarded cases individually, almost to the exclusion of any group work, maintained this sympathetic personal relationship admirably, yet at the same time required the child to face his limitations, gain independence, recognize his errors, comply with requests, stick to schedule, give maximum attention, gain self-control, and help himself out of difficulties. These student-interns grew in appreciation of the intimate relationship between reading trouble and behavior problems.

Grouping

Individual reading work was necessary at first until children gained confidence. After the second week it was apparent that there were some pupils who were quite similar in achievement level and retraining needs. At the same time they were not too different in personality or too antagonistic socially to work well together, and were mature enough to work with others. In other cases several boys at about the same reading level and having similar difficulties could not be grouped together because they could not tolerate each other socially. Several individuals required individual attention as clinical cases throughout the term and never reached the point where they could work profitably or successfully in the presence of other children. On several occasions D adjusted successfully to others, but worked without much profit. Gradually the more mature and stable children were grouped in twos or threes. Later the groups were increased to three or even four children. It was apparent, however, that the larger the group beyond five, the less marked were the individual gains, and the greater the waste of time. Sometimes group work took place in the individual workrooms; at other times in corners of the classroom. In the latter case, the class teacher called groups in turn, while others continued working at their seats on assignments previously made.

These remedial groups were not organized solely on the basis of test scores. Had we used such test data as the sole criterion for grouping, we would have made many serious errors. We had to consider the child's personal likes and dislikes for other children in the class. Some children with identical test scores did not work well together, or had distinctive needs that could not be met when they worked with certain other children in the group of the same reading difficulty level. Difference in chronological age was often a factor in this grouping. We found from experience that any grouping could not be considered final, but must be shifted from time to time. Some children progressed more rapidly than others, even though originally they were equivalent in ability and achievement. As far as possible we arranged the classroom seating so that children who were to be handled as a group at any time during the day would already be seated at the same table or near enough to be grouped without loss of time.

The Use of Reading Materials

In our program we stressed the use and examination of books which provided a sufficient range and variety to meet all our needs, including some books that were stimulating to look at, even though they were too difficult for any of the children to read. During the first week, we discovered that we had tended to grade the reading work for most of the children on too high a level. As the individual diagnostic studies began to indicate each child's needs more precisely, this error was corrected.

Careful supervision was exercised over book selection. Only a few things were called to the children's attention at a time. The teacher arranged two tables, one with the label "Poems," the other "Stories." Appropriate books were placed on each table. A list labeled "Good Books" was placed on a chart. (This list was compiled by the children, not by the teacher.)

By the end of the term we concluded that series readers had been our main dependence in the actual business of reteaching reading. This was primarily because of the sequential, overlapping, controlled vocabulary. In many cases, too, we had been able, in sets of readers, to find appropriate content, or at least material that the children did not resist. The use of series readers is highly recommended for individual work, particularly the newer series that offer several books and supplementary booklets at each grade level. The advantage in using commercially prepared primary books over such mimeographed pamphlets as the instructor might prepare lies in the large quantity of such material obtainable, its excellent format, its carefully controlled vocabulary, its good clear type face. Few teachers have the time or the skill to prepare the quantity of content material that these retarded children require as they gain skill in reading. For practice they need a number of very simple books rather than excessive drill on a pamphlet or two. One child, for example, read eight primers before going on to a first reader.

In many cases the workbooks we tried were too difficult for our groups. The children could not often be trusted to carry through a workbook assignment without considerable help from a teacher. This might have been caused by poor work habits previously established.

We had the usual difficulties with materials that experienced teachers invariably report when discussing remedial work. In spite of the variety of materials at our command, our stock was still inadequate. It lacked sufficient easy material suitable for older children that was scientifically scaled in vocabulary and calibrated to the learning rate of slow children. The pictures were too immature for the older children in the group. Some of the more colorful books and those most interesting in content could not be used because of their erratic and uncontrolled vocabulary. This material, however, could be safely read to the class.

We realized as time went on that it was confusing to have many books on display at one time. With too much material about, the children were likely to handle books aimlessly and not become genuinely interested in any. It tended to put the children on their own responsibility for selection too soon.

Books Enjoyed

The books the children listed on their "Good Books" chart as ones most enjoyed, or books they asked the teacher to read to them during reading club meetings included the following: *Book of Indians* (Holling); *Fire, Fire* (from the Picture Scripts Series); "Sounds of the Traffic," a poem; *Toby Tyler* (Otis); *Billy and Blaze* (Anderson); *Make and Make Believe* (Gates-Huber); *Little Dog Ready* (Stryker); *Adventures of Peter Whiffen* (Meadowcroft); *Little Elephant Caught Cold* (Washburne and McConnell); and *The Singing Farmer* (Tippett).

A similar program was conducted the following summer during which session it was found profitable to shorten the time of the children's attendance. They came to school at 8:30 A.M. and were dismissed at 10:30 A.M. The student-interns thereby had a free hour following their work with the children in which they could plan the work of the next day. They were not, however, required to do their planning at that time, but could attend college classes at that hour if they wished to do so. The students met with the instructors for a required conference hour from 11:30 to 12:30 daily. Thus this program shortened the required attendance period for the children and gave the student-interns more time for planning.

SPECIFIC INSTRUCTIONAL TECHNIQUES

In working with each child's individual reading problem, we adhered to several basic principles:

1. We studied the child's emotional attitude toward his reading difficulty and adapted our method of teaching to this attitude.
2. The work with the children was individualized as much as possible.
3. The materials selected and assigned were appropriate to the child's actual reading achievement level as determined by diagnostic test scores and practical tests of reading.
4. In arranging each child's program we used materials in carefully graded sequences, with a carefully controlled vocabulary affording maximum repetition.
5. Work in word analysis and word study was kept intrinsic in the

daily assignments. Isolated word study, when this was given, was based on meaningful reading content.

6. At every point in the program, maximum stress was placed on meaning, comprehension, and understanding. Whenever we had a choice between the familiar and meaningful and the unfamiliar item which lacked meaningful associations, we chose the former as more suitable for reading exercises.

7. Specific limitations were not worked on with intensive drill in isolation, but the child's total social adjustment problem was considered in planning the remedial program.

Drill an Integral Part of Program

Since preliminary evidence had indicated that these children were slow learners and had little tendency to "transfer" abilities or techniques acquired from one situation to another, we concentrated on teaching the children as directly as possible by methods closely allied to normal reading processes. A wide diversity of techniques and devices was employed to maintain or arouse interest in reading, and specific practice was given the children in order to overcome deficiencies revealed in the diagnostic tests. The specific techniques used to give the children more skill at their weakest points are described in the following pages. The exercises used for drill were made an integral part of the total reading program.

We wanted the children not only to improve in reading techniques but to get to the point where they would pick up books voluntarily and examine them with interest, or express a desire to read them. To do this, we had to overcome their tendency to avoid reading and to fiddle with the typewriter, scribble on the blackboard, get out paints and paper, annoy other children, get into mischief, or sit with an apathetic air until the teacher came to the rescue. The children had all developed undesirable behavior patterns because of their inability to fit into their regular school classes, and getting them to settle down and gaining their individual attention was a major problem which the teacher worked on assiduously.

We found that the children were most attentive and relaxed when they were being read to. Even the most restless child would sit quietly and listen intently. This activity was therefore good practice. To relieve strain the teacher also had the children rest in their chairs for a few minutes after particularly strenuous work or play.

Courtesy and manners were emphasized, as were "rules of the road," the need to be quiet and orderly while working, the need to share materials with others, to await one's turn, and to refrain from criticizing another child destructively or ridiculing another's efforts.

Each child required a somewhat different emphasis in his remedial program. Several children needed far more training in attacking new words and in speech training than others. Child A showed that he could profit from "writing-out" practice. This would have been dull and unnecessary for other children.

In K's case an attempt was made to create a desire for reading by selecting easy material and telling or reading enough of the story to interest her, so that she would want to read it; by making reading seem to her a less serious business, a more joyous experience; by showing friendliness toward her; by attempting to build up a feeling of security, self-confidence, and satisfaction.

In F's case we tried to correct poor reading habits, such as finger pointing, word-by-word reading, inability to hold books properly, and careless habits of word attack; to develop an interest in reading and accurate comprehension; to develop ability to concentrate on material for a longer period; to overcome restlessness; and to instill a desire to read well.

For N we first built up a basic sight vocabulary by having him read several primers, *Peter and Peggy, Nick and Dick, Dick and Jane.* We reviewed names of letters and sounds of initial consonants, especially those less well known, introduced the short and long vowel sounds, and read a first reader and workbook, *Round the Year* (Gates-Huber), taking phonograms as they came up in workbook and reader. We reviewed each day the unfamiliar words, vowel sounds, and phonograms studied thus far; we trained him in careful observation of words, directing attention to the beginning parts of words, teaching him to look through the whole word from beginning to end and to discriminate between words that look familiar. He kept a daily chart of the number of repetitions and word errors, trying to make fewer each day. After his confidence was restored, we worked on phrasing, increasing the eye-voice span, and for better expression, encouraging his attempts to sound new words and to think about the content. The child gained through group activities also, but worked best when apart from the other children.

In H's case we began with easy word comparisons, e.g., "ran" with "run." We used the *Peter and Peggy* workbook; tested rate of reading with the Elson Preprimer; practiced reviewing in order to gain speed; taught needed phonic elements, such as "ew," worked on phonic sounds— k i f e bl sh; flashed a list of words which he had encountered in reading and which he had typed on flash cards. (The boy typed the words as he learned them.) All the work was oral, in order to prevent guessing and picture reading. Occasionally he worked with one other child.

Techniques for Changing Unfavorable Attitudes

Several features of the program contributed automatically to an improved attitude toward reading, the removal of antagonistic moods, and the achievement of better emotional satisfactions. Some of these features were:

1. Individual work (which prevented embarrassment).
2. Grouping of pupils having similar difficulties so that no child felt himself below others in skill.
3. A program of activities in which success was inherent.
4. The use of easy material which gave each child a feeling of success. (In M's case we found that reading simple stories orally gave him a feeling of satisfaction in performance.)

We stressed "Reading is fun," "Learning is like a game," "See how far you can go," "Can you win?" We tried to develop certain attitudes toward reading, such as reading has surprises and excitement in it, reading helps you out, reading is useful, you can all do it if you practice. All work was dramatized by the teacher as much as possible in order to keep it from becoming drudgery. We always capitalized upon the children's assets, such as their maturity, the first faint signs of interest in reading, or their interest in activities that would motivate reading. Such reading skills as the child possessed were put to use. We attempted to create an atmosphere of ease and enjoyment during individual instruction. We allowed the children to follow their inclinations as far as we possibly could, so that they would develop confidence in their own ability and would begin to read easy books of their own accord, thus helping themselves.

Everything had to be extremely easy for the child who habitually asked, "Do I have to do that?" In J's case, to restore confidence, we began with a first grade book. This book was quickly finished and J began a second grade book. After this, all reading was done in books of third grade level. F was encouraged by keeping "My Reading Alone" chart, on which he was to record the number of pages read alone, an idea that pleased him greatly.

The important thing was to get the children over the plateau on which their learning had stopped and from which they had difficulty in taking off because of a heavy load of discouragement. Fear that they would fail again in undertaking something in which they had previously failed presented a problem requiring patience and skill to handle. Talking with the children about their mistakes helped both teacher and child.

Previously G had tended to fail in school, but this time he was elected class president. On one occasion, when during a drill period he gave letter sounds correctly, one child commented, "He knows them because he is class president." This worked wonders in re-establishing the boy's morale.

The teacher made lavish use of praise in motivating improvement. One morning she praised the group for good work habits during an independent work period. Another day the group talked about the improvement that members of the reading club had shown. P commented of N, "He was not so bad. He has a nice way of sticking to a job."

Increasing Word-Recognition Skills

One of our major problems was increasing the children's skill in word recognition. The pupils had not only very limited recognition vocabularies, but little idea of how to work out or study a new word when they came to it, and seemed confused or helpless on meeting new words. Yet there could be little fluent oral reading, little accurate silent reading, until word-recognition skills were improved. The children needed more practice in examining words, in associating visual perception of word forms with sounds and meaning, in learning how to study words efficiently. Especially did they need a great deal of easy reading material in which the load of new words was not too heavy.

Several children had such meager sight vocabularies and such limited skill in word analysis that it was thought unwise to begin with an elaborate phonics program. The children would have been discouraged and would have refused to cooperate. The first step in improving these children's stock of sight words was to use very easy material which contained new words only at rare intervals. These new words were first experienced in context and consequently were easy to learn. Children were encouraged to try to guess new words from context. C at first could not get the unfamiliar words from contextual associations, consequently he was urged to skip over the unfamiliar word, to guess at it, and, when through, to reread the sentence, putting in the new word to see if it would make sense. At first he did not have enough self-confidence to try this alone. He was still blocked by unfamiliar words, but he gained in skill as the teacher encouraged his slightest effort. C used the *Peter and Peggy* primer at first as his textbook. The teacher often typed different stories for him to read, using the same vocabulary.

Other types of exercises used to build up a sight vocabulary through context reading follow.

The teacher discussed the details of a story beforehand, and developed new words during this discussion. These she presented on the blackboard or on paper for the child's inspection. Difficult words were reviewed in completion exercises. The following is an illustration.

Bob gave the squirrel some . . . .

The man lived in a little . . . . in the woods.

He had a big . . . . Would you . . . . if you saw him?

gun hut nuts run

A check was sometimes made of all the words missed in a child's first reading, and rereading was done after these words had been discussed and studied. In some cases the teacher listed errors on the board, had the child review the words, and reread the selection in which errors were made.

Words that constituted errors in daily reading were, in some cases, typed on flash cards and frequently reviewed. Often these cards were typed by the children. This was not necessary for all children. Workbook materials with exercises containing questions to be answered were helpful because they required precision and close attention to individual words. This was done largely under the teacher's supervision.

Often difficult words were isolated by having a card placed over a page; a slit in the card revealed troublesome words. By means of this device the child could examine their structure better and develop skill in analyzing them. This was the next step needed to build independence in word recognition. "Families" of words were sometimes typed in a group, one word of the "family" being familiar to the child, the others being easily guessed by comparison, as *hair, fair, pair*.

The simpler drill methods which were effective with duller, more stolid children did not work with L. It was better not to tell him hard words, but to let him read on and make mistakes until he lost the drift of the story and became bewildered; then he was forced to go back and reread in order to correct himself. This was only possible with a child who had a strong urge to understand the story—one who would go to the work of figuring out the hard words for the purpose of enjoying the story.

Word Analysis and Phonics Techniques

After the most immature children gained a feeling of confidence by being able to recognize a larger number of words at sight, it was possible to increase their flexibility in attack on new words through exercises in word analysis and phonics techniques. Obviously, if a word cannot be sensed or understood from a cursory glance in conjunction with meaning clues, then the child needs to be able to identify the word through analysis, trying to guess the word from a partial analysis if that will suffice. The chief problem here was to show children how to isolate the key sound elements and then to build associations between these sounds and their vision symbols, a translation process which must function automatically while the child reads.

These activities were not carried on in any conventional, formal way. On the contrary, drill in word analysis was as varied as each case required, and was kept closely integrated with content reading. This work was kept to the minimum, so as to avoid any artificiality in the program. We did not first start with phonetic elements, teach these in any logical system, and then expect the child to apply them in his content reading and word-recognition practice. Instead, when, in the child's experience, it was apparent that practice in word analysis or sounding out the elements would help, the child was given instruction.

The danger in any emphasis on separate phonic elements lies in the tendency to spoil eye-movements within words. The child, having learned "ing," looks for "ing" in "spring" instead of sounding the word from the beginning. With overemphasis on sounding isolated word elements children not only form wrong eye-movements, but have difficulty in applying what they have learned to the actual reading process, and in addition become bored or disinterested. Again and again, in our cases, it was obvious that some children had previously learned to recognize the elements and sound them properly, but this ability had not improved their skill in reading.

In the program we had no separate drill periods for uniform practice in phonics, but there were occasional reviews for short periods of time with individual children or small groups who needed practice. Diagnostic exercises were used to discover the children's weaknesses in word recognition or in phonic ability, and only those needing it were given this kind of help.

Among the various techniques used in increasing word-analysis skills both visually and aurally were the following:

Attention was first centered on the beginning sounds of the words with which the child had difficulty, or the specific differences in the words he often confused. These were compared with words familiar to him, such as another child's name or his own name, the name of his city, or any word he knew by sight.

Children were taught to see familiar small words within the larger words, to sense syllables, and to get a better impression of general word form and structure. Alert children who were reading in context seldom had to go to the extreme of painfully sounding the entire word and blending the sounds. Children were given practice in listening for words in poems that rhymed. Lear's *Book of Nonsense Rhymes* was used. Practice was given in analyzing difficult words met in reading; the teacher pointed out familiar parts of a word and urged the child to guess what it was from context clues. Often only the initial blend or consonant was familiar. When this type of practice was going on, children were never told words until they had made some attempt to work them out. Several children did not know the actual names of the respective letters in the alphabet. They needed this knowledge so that they could talk about the separate letters within words. They were taught these letter names and encouraged to use them when discussing words. Naturally they were taught that the separate letters had both names and sounds, and they learned to distinguish the two. Occasionally they were given practice in listing all the words they could think of that begin with "s" or with some other sound. This was an informal exercise carried out in the spirit of a game, more often related to spelling exercises than to reading.

Phonetic elements were recognized by relating them to words encountered in the child's experience. After the class had taken the trip to the zoo and were engaged in making a scrapbook of animal pictures, there were exercises of the following sort:

Teacher: "Do you remember the yak which we saw at the zoo? With what letter does it begin?" (Child guesses "u.") "Listen to these words we use every day: *yes, yellow*. Who can spell *yes*?" Teacher wrote it on the blackboard. "Who can spell *yellow*?" A child spelled it and the teacher wrote it on the blackboard under *yes*. Teacher: "*Yak* goes under *yellow*. With what letter shall I begin *yak*?" Child: "Begin it with *y* like *yes* and *yellow*." The word was then spelled correctly by the child.

Looking for familiar elements and listening for familiar sounds in words was much practiced. The child whose name was "Barbara" discovered that it was similar to "car," "ajar," "far," and "garden." We helped her to see the identical elements in words by placing the words on the board and indicating the similarities. The "ar" part was found and identified in several old and new words. Other exercises included: building up words such as: remark—remarkable, help—helpful; studying endings: ness, ly, ful, tion, ing. In studying the effect of final "e" on the vowel in a one-syllable word, we gave several exercises to drill on this rule, making *cane* out of *can*, *rode* out of *rod*, etc.

We tried to build up word associations by noting distinctive characteristics, such as: "thought" has "t" on the end; "through" hasn't, but we must hear the "r" in it.

The dictionary was introduced. Words were divided into syllables by older children and checked with the dictionary. Words were sounded in syllables, and then blended as a whole. Children were pleased to learn that they could analyze and pronounce new words in this way. A chart was kept for one child, showing the new words he could sound for himself. This, however, did not interest all the other children.

The teacher frequently gave ear training to develop greater sensitivity to sounds, using words as they came up in connection with stories and poems read in class. As an aid children were required to listen to each other while they were reading, to criticize and evaluate each other's enunciation and phrasing.

In view of our experience with these cases, we suggest that, as a safeguard and preventive measure, all children should be checked for their knowledge of phonics: all consonants, all short vowels, all vowels with final "e," phonograms related to words met in their first grade reading vocabulary. All of the preceding should be taught in connection with the words the children find in their reading and in their actual experiences, such as trips and other activities.

Correcting the Tendency to "Spell Out"

"Spelling-out" tendencies had to be eliminated as speedily as possible. The children needed to break the habit of giving equal attention to every letter in a word. Emphasis on the word study techniques cited in the preceding section and practice in easy content reading served indirectly to correct "spelling out." From the beginning the teacher discouraged this habit in all cases and encouraged the child to use phonetic and context clues, to pronounce the words for himself whenever possible.

Comparatively little use was made of writing or tracing as aids to reading. But in H's case and several others, such practice was given incidentally when it seemed appropriate. Tracing over words was never used as a sole corrective, but served to supplement and reinforce visual and auditory perception of words. It was found useful chiefly in centering attention on word structure, and was restricted to the slowest, least mature children.

Words habitually miscalled, such as *there, their, those* and *these*, were written on the blackboard with colored chalk for the middle letters. Manuscript style writing was used habitually by the teacher in her blackboard writing. We believe it is essential that every primary teacher be an expert in manuscript writing so that she can compose bulletin material quickly and with maximum legibility.

PRACTICE FOR SMOOTHER, MORE EXPRESSIVE READING

Various methods were used to help the children read more expressively, to overcome the tendency to read monotonously "word-by-word," to neglect phrasing and punctuation marks. These difficulties were overcome naturally as the children increased in ability to read meaningfully, as they began to understand the reading process, and to enjoy reading. Increased skill in oral reading was accompanied by new insight into the thought back of the words. All children who required it had daily practice in oral reading.

To overcome the word-by-word reading method, the teacher often read the sentences to the child and had him read them back in a "smooth, easy way." She gestured with a long sweep under words and had the child follow her pencil as fast as it moved.

In order to give the children a better sense of rhythm in phrasing, the teacher demonstrated with gestures, or illustrated what she meant by smoother rhythm through the analogy to "horse and buggy" versus the automobile. "The horse and buggy go bumpety-bump over the road; the automobile runs along smoothly." She placed a simple sentence on the board, and then read it aloud several times with proper phrasing. She asked, "Am I riding smoothly in an automobile, or in a wagon over a bumpy road?" The two methods of reading were demonstrated; then she asked, "Can you make your voice go nicely like this?" The separate phrases were underlined on the board. Then the children took turns trying to "get more smooth places." The emphasis was on reading groups of words, reading in "sweeps." All the work was done with easy and interesting material that the children really liked to read, material in which they could readily pronounce all the words.

To develop longer eye-sweep, the child was instructed to follow the words with his eyes as fast as the teacher read aloud to him. There was a better attempt at phrasing when this was done. The teacher sometimes read a paragraph and then asked the child to read the next paragraph in order to demonstrate smoothness in reading. Or a page was read for the child and he was asked to read it back more in the style and rhythm the teacher had illustrated in her own reading. Reading with a natural voice —reading as we speak—was stressed and illustrated.

Some children were encouraged to look for phrases marked off by vertical pencil lines in his or the teacher's book. The teacher wrote on the board phrases chosen from the story to illustrate the natural breaks in the sentences. The children then attempted to locate phrases and these were put on the board. Various games and contests were used to improve phrasing. For example, the student-teacher and M read in dialogue. M appeared to enjoy this especially. As an added help to the slowest children, a line card was sometimes placed under the line being read. This tended to discourage pointing to the words.

During the term, a student-teacher suggested that choral speaking might be effective with these slow learners, to improve enunciation, rhythm, and phrasing, as well as to give more opportunity for group work. Choral speaking was tried experimentally with a group of three children who participated eagerly in this activity. They prepared to recite in unison "A birdie with a yellow bill" and "Poor old Jonathan Bing." M enjoyed this thoroughly and was responsible for much of the success of the venture. He showed particular talent in enunciation and rhyming. The practice gave valuable ear-training. The children learned the lines, rehearsed apart from the class, and then accompanied the recitation with appropriate gestures. On a previously announced day they entertained the group with their choral speaking recitation with such success that the actors were asked to give an immediate repeat performance. Reading the parts of a play and giving imitation broadcasts proved to be valuable experiences for some of the children.

No use was made of the mechanical apparatus or of specially spaced material and the like for phrase work. In the first place we scarcely had time to experiment with it, and in the second place we thought we could accomplish our aims in perfectly normal ways.

Too often oral reading is considered more mechanical, less meaningful than silent reading. We hear it said, "He should be doing more silent reading so that he can give more attention to comprehension." We believe that oral reading can be just as meaningful and contribute as much to comprehension as silent reading, provided checks on comprehension are constantly employed. In our experiment more use was made of oral than of silent reading, partly because the children were generally on low reading levels, and also in order that the teacher-interns could check daily on the errors made. Oral reading was also used for the greater interest it gave the children. It helped them to concentrate attention, and gave concomitant practice in language and speech. These children needed to hear themselves read, to reinforce the connection between speech and reading.

Speed of Reading

We consider it unnecessary and artificial to isolate speed of reading and drill on it as a separate skill. We find that speed takes care of itself when the child is properly motivated, when he has materials simple enough for him to read, has word-recognition skills well in hand and a substantial stock of sight words, and when he reads meaningfully and enjoys it. All our cases improved in amount read in a given time as the specialized skills required for successful reading became automatized.

However, when we found that children who could read more rapidly tended to dawdle, we talked about the need for reading faster and actually paced the work for the child.

Sentences were placed on the blackboard, then they were erased quickly, and the children were asked to tell what they had read. They were cautioned to keep lips closed while reading. Practice in reading easy material silently under observation helped this.

The reading work was conducted in various ways to promote different ends. Sometimes there was "rapid" reading, unknown words being supplied when the child hesitated. The teacher, armed with a cardboard slip, kept the child moving along at top speed.

The teacher read aloud while several children, holding copies of the same book, grouped about her and tried to keep up by moving a card along under the lines. Attempts were made to have the child read ahead silently, "seeing more than one word at a time" to avoid regressive movements.

As children demonstrated their ability to read in larger thought units we reduced the amount of oral reading. Children who read material suitable for the third grade or higher should spend their time chiefly in silent reading. At this point our chief concern is not that a child be able to pronounce all the words correctly, e.g., "grackel," "troubled," "reason," but rather that he sense their meaning from the content, and fully understand the entire sentence or paragraph.

Functional, Meaningful Reading

We have shown in earlier sections how functional, meaningful reading was featured throughout the program, how the total program contributed to understanding and gave meaning to reading. The opportunity to read something that had real significance for them had been lacking in these children's early experiences with reading. All needed more practice in reading with understanding.

The teacher utilized every opportunity to give genuine purpose to reading. Notices and announcements were placed on the blackboard and instructions were given in print style writing. In addition the daily program was often placed on the blackboard, and other material was placed on charts posted about the room. The following are illustrations.

The teacher wrote on the board as the children dictated:

Things We'd Like to Do

draw	claywork
type	woodwork
swim	read better
paint	

The teacher placed these sentences on the board:

Miss Fiske and her boys and girls live in room 213. They invited us to visit them after our trip to the zoo and tell them what we saw.

This message was read aloud by the children as they came into the classroom. Some words gave difficulty, e.g., "invited," and "Fiske."

The teacher selected the best letter of those which the children had written to tell Miss Fiske's class about books our class had read. The letter was then copied on the blackboard. This was eagerly read by the children. Assignments for the use of the printing sets were put on the board. Earlier in the week the teacher placed on the board in manuscript style writing the following notice:

Reading Club

When would you like to read?
Be sure to write the date. Please put your name here.

F was given written rather than oral instructions for work during quiet period. He checked each item finished. For example, he was directed:

1. Read "Bunny plays a trick" in Book One.

2. Count the number of pages you read. Draw a line on your chart to show how many you read.
3. Do the seat work.

The daily program was placed on the blackboard, together with simple instructions the children were to follow. Samples of such programs and directions are the following:

August 2nd

Our Program

1. Poems
2. Reading Club
3. Miss Wright will read
4. Clay modeling

August 3rd

Our Program

8:30	Work with your teacher
9:30	Go to the play in assembly
10:30	Story hour
11:00	Music in Room 10
11:30	Poetry and reading
12:00	Go swimming

August 4th

Our Program

8:30	Work quietly at your desk
9:30	Work with your teacher
10:30	Poetry reading club
11:00	Miss Wright will read *Peter Whiffen*
11:30	Painting in Room 406

August 5th

Our Program

8:45	Assembly. When you return from assembly, work with your teacher
10:30	Work at your desk—Newspaper
11:30	Reading club
12:00	Swim! This is a scoop!

These people will go for their vision tests at 10:30. Someone will call for them.
Bill   May   Arthur   Charles

August 9th

Our Program

8:30	Work at your desk
9:30	Work with your teacher
10:30	We'll write
11:00	Music in Room 10
11:30	Reading Club. Miss Wright will read
12:00	Swimming

Improved comprehension was insured indirectly through care exercised in selecting content materials. Books were selected for the children on the basis of each child's expressed interest, content, and difficulty. We judged difficulty almost solely in terms of the vocabulary repetition the child required. Our first trial with a book sometimes proved it to be difficult for the child, even though it was labeled a primer or first reader. In that case we found a book with fewer new or difficult words or one better adapted generally to the child's requirements. We took special pains to give materials in close sequence, each book following in terms of vocabulary and content the one the child had completed. We naturally selected books with the greatest amount of overlapping. The books that best met our requirements as to sequence were the carefully graded series readers. We also found in these materials the greatest overlapping in ideas, in situations, and in characters. We chose materials that in themselves would tend to insure comprehension. When the text was kept very simple, children were sometimes found not to be so dependent on picture clues.

Skill in anticipating meanings. The duller children had considerable difficulty in anticipating what would happen next in a story, yet skill in anticipation was necessary to speed up reading and to gain more experience in employing context clues. For P it was a real feat to try to imagine what the next word would be if she could not identify it at once. To improve this skill it was necessary to use material appropriate to the child's knowledge, mental level, and conversational powers.

As part of general training in anticipating while reading we helped the child anticipate the next page more quickly. The child needed to be thinking ahead of the point where he was actually reading. This involved having his hand ready to turn the page before he had completed enunciating all the words in the last line, if he was reading orally.

Comprehension was insured through reading of stories, asking questions on stories, discussing meaning, talking about the ideas in the pictures, and writing out ideas on stories read or told. Other aids to comprehension included discussing the story before and after reading, reading and discussing certain obscure ideas in the story, explaining confusing or unusual words, raising questions on the story, giving questions to be answered when the story was completed, etc. The child was asked a question when he failed to read intelligently. Children were stimulated to guess, to think ahead, imagine, and enjoy, to think over and relate what was satisfying in their reading.

The teacher discussed the meaning of the content with the child after a passage had been read. After reading his story of Lapland, Q was unable to infer the answer to the question the teacher asked him—why the nights in Lapland were so long. The teacher required him to reread phrases telling that the sun rose later and later and finally failed to shine all day. The child had not gotten the idea on the first reading, though he had read the selection as though he understood it. The best and most permanent gains appeared to come through this careful check on comprehension. Written assignments, made out by the teacher the day before, were kept very simple. Usually only a few questions or exercises were given at a time, but the teacher insisted on the assignment being carried out. Care was taken to be sure that the assignment was something the child could handle alone if he was to do it unsupervised.

Older children profited from instruction in the interpretation of punctuation marks as an aid to getting the sense of the material. There was insistence on careful attention to articles and tenses to help overcome careless habits.

Checks on Comprehension

The following are some of the devices used in checking comprehension in oral and silent reading.

Varieties of completion-type exercises—completing sentences—were used. M's favorite game was filling in the missing word in a sentence with a blank space for the missing word. He would pick out the missing word from a selection of slips and insert it in slits in the right place. Some children were checked daily on the comprehension of one of the stories read silently, covering the main facts in various types of exercises: multiple choice questions, "why" questions, "how" questions, "what" questions, yes-no or true-false questions. We could check the comprehension of most children by asking a few simple questions.

The story or part of the story was told in the child's own language and coming events were anticipated by the child from trends in meaning in the story.

To force attention to sentence meaning and important details, riddles were used which the child enjoyed reading orally.

Certain children were requested daily, "Tell me what you read." Even a sketchy report was accepted if the teacher felt satisfied that the child had read with comprehension.

Written directions were given for drawing, e.g.: "Draw a bear. Put a bee on his nose."

The comprehension questions and exercises contained in workbooks were found to be useful.

The Gates-Peardon Practice Exercise[1] books were used to help more advanced pupils in grasping the general significance of the story. Records were kept of exercises completed correctly.

In the reading club the teacher often used the technique of reading part of a story, stopping at the most exciting point, pausing at such a phrase as: "And there he saw a ——." Then she asked if any child would like to take the book and find out what happened next and then bring the book to reading club and let the whole class know what happened.

The "reading aloud" period contributed to comprehension in other ways. On one day the teacher read from *Little Dog Ready*. The children then wrote the story and read their stories to the class, or they dictated sentences about the story to put on the blackboard and then copied the sentences in their notebooks. Next they did clay modeling from the story of "Ready."

[1] The Gates-Peardon Practice Exercises. Bureau of Publications, Teachers College, Columbia University, New York City.

Reading for Enjoyment

Reading for fun was encouraged in many ways so that children would cover more ground and at the same time enjoy their work. One day, late in the term, the teacher came in with an armful of simple books. "Just to read for fun," she said. Everyone was instructed to choose any book he preferred to read to the class. They read at random from many books. Much improvement was shown. The teacher commented to the group that the children could read much faster than when they came. She observed that one child could not read the same material at all successfully when he first joined the class. This technique was tried several days in succession, until the term closed.

We did everything possible to encourage the children to select and choose books from among those we indicated as appropriate for them. We recommended, when the proper time was reached, that certain children select books to take home. The children were encouraged to keep one book in their desks to read just for fun.

These children at first had seemed unimaginative, limited in ability to visualize. Imagery was stimulated in several ways. After reading a colorful poem, the teacher would ask them to try to picture in their minds what they had seen while the poem was being read. "I want you to tell me what you see when I'm through. Perhaps you can paint a picture of one of the poems. Try to see pictures in what I read." The teacher read several poems and asked, "What does this make you think of?" The children showed much interest in the poems and several inquired where books with poems could be found.

Writing and Spelling

Practice in spelling and writing tend to reinforce and extend the child's consciousness and knowledge of words. Consequently we provided as many opportunities as possible for writing and spelling in functional situations.

Early in the term when the children were electing a class president, the teacher posted on the bulletin board the best statements the children wrote regarding the election. The newly elected president appointed a committee to judge the handwriting of these papers. As stated previously there was a letter writing project in connection with the reading of *Little Dog Ready*. The last day of school children wrote letters to their teachers thanking them for "all the nice things they had done."

Typical informal exercises were as follows:

The teacher would say, "I'll write 'summer school' on the blackboard. With what letter does 'summer' begin? 'school'?"

The children composed, "We voted for class president. We elected Bob." They copied these sentences. A committee was chosen to select the best sample of handwriting and to put this paper in the hands of the newspaper editor in order that he might include it in the next edition of the paper.

As much spelling and sounding as possible was brought in informally *whenever it was appropriate.* The children showed great interest in this. Spelling also motivated learning the alphabet letter names. In connection with attempts to spell the animal names, A remarked, "If you didn't know your alphabet you would be sunk."

Two typewriters provided for the class were much enjoyed by the children, who considered it a privilege to use them. We made no attempt to teach typing scientifically, but used the machines as incentives to better accomplishment. We obtained the best results when typing work was well motivated. The teacher would say, "Now let's see who can write or copy this letter well enough for Miss Fiske's class to read it." Or, "I'll post the best letters and reports." The typewriter served to introduce variety and hold interest. About half the class used the typewriters at some time during the term, typing stories and definitions, letters, bulletins and programs, and materials for the newspaper. Children who refused to write by hand or hated the task often typed instead and made good progress in spelling through the use of the typewriter.

Problems Presented by Left-Handed Children

No special methods were followed with the one left-handed child in the group because this sinistral child proved to have difficulties very similar in character to the other children. We did, however, encourage him to adopt comfortable positions, free from strain, for writing activities. We never called the child's attention directly to left-handedness, and made no effort to shift handedness. Parents were instructed not to mention handedness to the child, not to show concern over the matter in the child's presence, and to relieve the child's tension as much as possible through a hygienic daily schedule.

41. INTEGRATION OF THE LANGUAGE ARTS

Deborah Elkins

Many other sound procedures for helping children improve their ability to read were facilitated by the use of the common content theme as the basic procedure. For example, one important aspect of organizing the work to help children's progress in reading was integration of the language arts. The things talked about in class, the films shown as topics of conversation and written work, were around the same subject as that chosen for reading so that word meanings and whole ideas could be gained and concepts deepened.

WRITING

There was much, much writing. Not a day went by without some writing. This meant finding reasons for this activity which were real to the children. Those words which they were seeing in print were now being used by them, a process which fortified their reading skills. But more than that, the ideas gained in reading were being emphasized, and new ideas and concepts which would bring richness to their reading were being developed.

Reasons for writing were both "natural" and contrived. Children wrote, and did not mind correcting even a number of times, "stories" to be mimeographed so the whole class could read them. For example, "The Most Frightening Time of My Life" was the subject of one. This came within the context of the books they were reading in connection with their study of "horror in little children's books." The papers they wrote were corrected and mimeographed—everybody's, unless a child requested that his be kept confidential. There was a maximum of intense interest when the copies of the "booklet" were distributed, and this became the reading lesson for the day. Children talked to each other about what each frightening experience meant, there were many questions asked of each other, and the teacher led the discussion into channels which would enrich their understanding.

Even the children with grade-two reading levels wrote when the motivation was there—and did this without "secretaries." Here is an illustration of a "true story" written by a girl whose reading level was 2.3. As the children wrote, the teacher moved around the room giving whatever assistance was necessary with spelling or other mechanical stumbling blocks the children were encountering.

What I Don't Understand About Grownups

What can we do to make our mothers and fathers understand about love? When I want to go out, my mother and father says, "Stay in." My mother says, "I'll give you a boy on the head." I say that I love the boy. My father starts to yell. I walk out and when I come in my father tells me to do my homework.

Last night my brother told me to stay in with my father. I brought my friends inside. I said, "This is the boy I love." I'll not mention any names because he goes to this school. He is in class 7-S. His room number is 489.

At other times they talked and wrote of their observations of young children's reactions to the books they read to them. This was done in connection with the children's bibliography project, when the pupils found they needed tangible evidence for the record to help in making the final evaluation of each book. These written pieces of evidence were kept until five or six children had read the book and then these same children formed a committee which used the written evidence in rating the book as being appropriate or inappropriate for little children. All writing activities had a purpose real to the children.

Sometimes teachers used an idea to stimulate creative writing simply because it was an idea which they felt would appeal to the children. They did this even though at first the work was not correlated with the reading and discussions in which children were engaged at the moment. However, the teacher's ingenuity and planning led to a strengthening of the ties between the writing and the reading. For example, one teacher began a method which so intrigued the children that they continued it for a far longer span of time than she had ever intended. One day, she wrote four phrases on the board:

> pack of cigarettes
> discarded can of sardines
> dim street lamp
> kerchief

and proceeded to read a story woven around these phrases, a story which she had created but which the children thought was written by an "author." Then she led a discussion on what the children thought about the story, and was surprised at the depth of understanding about what makes a good story, for they were extremely critical and could generally be led to give reasons for each criticism. When she told them it was *her* creation, there was crestfallen silence and a feeling that this was not quite cricket. But when she explained that she feared they would not have been frank with her otherwise and that she, in turn, would be frank with them when they wrote, everything was "all right" again.

Next she put new phrases on the board:

> a broken pair of scissors
> a torn flag
> a crumpled letter
> a cast-off newspaper
> a shriveled old lady

One child pointed to his broken arm which was in a cast, as if to help her with her list. The children were all eager to write, even the nonwriters. Enough excitement had been generated for that. For the first few minutes they were completely engrossed in their task. Then began the need to share their creations. One boy nudged another and said, "See what I wrote." But the second boy was still busy and could not be bothered. The teacher at this point said, "I'll call time in a few minutes. Meantime don't disturb the others if you are finished. Everyone will have a chance to share his story with others."

The teacher called "time" before all the class had completed their stories and there was a roar of protest. But she promised time to finish later. One or two children read their stories; they were discussed and enjoyed (not evaluated to the extent that hers was), and then the children divided into groups to enjoy those written by others and to have theirs enjoyed. A few were chosen to share with the whole class, chosen by the children in groups according to criteria established with the children beforehand. Such criteria could be the "tallness" of the tall tale, or interesting beginnings, or surprise endings. Criteria had to be limited in number. Every child's composition was read but the whole class did not have to listen to all thirty of them, so there was no waste of time; there was wise use of class time. There was seriousness of purpose. The papers were so good that they were later used for intensive individual correction and mimeographed for a future reading lesson. (There was nothing personal here, so it was safe to use this procedure.)

The children enjoyed this activity so much that the teacher suggested they keep a little slip of paper as a bookmark in the books they were reading and, when they came across an expression or phrase which particularly intrigued them, jot it down to share with the class for writing purposes. Lists became so long that the next time a preliminary committee had to be chosen to limit the items to fifteen from which the children could choose.

A variation was suggested by the children when they read biographies. Two children read one biography. Each partner drew up his own secret list of phrases. On the day set for writing each gave his list to the other as a guide for writing the life of their great man.

Other writing experiences followed, each with emphasis on enjoyment, so children would want to continue to write. Children were assigned the task of finding incidents in their books which posed problems for people.

This meant some previous intensive work with them by the teacher before they were able to carry out such an assignment. The teacher read several short stories and several excerpts from novels, before they were able to grasp the idea. When each child had selected his problematic situation from his own book they met in groups to select one. The incidents chosen were presented in a read-and-tell method to the whole class who selected one for which they would like to act out creative solutions.

Several role-playing situations were acted out and discussed. Then, each child chose the one he liked best and wrote on why he felt it presented the best solution to the problem. If he felt none of them was feasible, he could write one that was.

In a book called *Teen-Age Companion*,[7] there is a story, "Top of the Mountain." When the teacher read this to the climax, it was one of such appeal to children of this age that they wrote easily about its possible ending, and really enjoyed doing it. Then the teacher read the ending and they discussed it together, after which two or three of the children's endings were read and discussed according to certain limited criteria. One such criterion was logical consequence: Does the ending follow as an outgrowth of what went before? Another teacher used the criterion, Is it true to life?

There were situations, however, where this method of selecting a child's story to be read to the whole class simply did not work. Such occasions occurred when the children were still so insecure that they could not "afford" to choose someone else's, when there were children who had never yet appeared "in print." This happened in the room of one teacher who made a practice of mimeographing only a select few of the children's stories, so that most children were never given an opportunity to be the chosen ones. Neither did this practice work when children were thrown together at random rather than by choice. But in classes where some self-confidence was already built, where the relation with the teacher was warm, children could tolerate this amount of competition. Otherwise, it proved far better to use groups to *help* each other, to put together several heads to assist each writer in meeting the criteria better than he had.

Other writing situations occurred in connection with predictions of what would happen in a story. This differed from the previously described procedure in which the teacher read to the climax and then had children write the ending. Here the teacher read with them up to an interesting point to help them plunge into the story. Then they discussed "whether you think Squanto will get away." Following this they wrote their own opinions and kept them until they read to see how correct were their guesses. If a common story was being read, children could keep a running record of their success in predicting. Later, they did it on their

[7] Frank Owen, *Teen-Age Companion* (New York: Lantern Press, Inc., 1946).

own with their individual books. It worked especially well where two children were reading the same book and sharing their written predictions. This whole procedure was also good motivation for reading more frequently and for longer periods on their own than might otherwise be the case.

All writing topics need to be close to the children's experience or concrete enough so that they are real to them. Usually, an imaginary assignment like "Write what you think Benjamin Franklin would say to his friend about Lincoln" is completely beyond them. But a preliminary discussion of the things the children like and dislike about their neighborhoods, followed by writing on the topic, which in turn is followed by a closer study of certain cooperatively determined phases of their neighborhood, can be realistic. This study can again be the subject of wide and enthusiastic writing and can be followed by a search, in the novels they are reading, for reactions (implied or expressed) of the characters in their books. Do people in books react to their neighborhoods as we have done? Such a sequence of activities is especially good with such books as Seredy's *A Tree for Peter* and Angelo's *Bells of Bleeker Street.*[8]

When the idea of children writing and even learning to *like* writing was first presented, one teacher remained silent for a long time and then exclaimed, "This is incredible! If I can get my children to write a sentence by the end of the year, I'll be happy." It took only a little time to "convince" her (and not verbally) that when children were assigned the writing of a sentence on a given unprepared, previously unconsidered topic, the stage was set for struggle. But children *will* write when there is something they can and want to say. This was an amazing young teacher, willing to try anything she saw the need for, anything that made sense to her and that she felt she could handle. The children began to write pages within a space of two weeks after this outburst, with the result that the teacher was walking on air, unable to believe her own success, trying to achieve the same results over and over again—and succeeding when the motivation was real—in order to prove to herself that this was not one of those miracles that happen only once.

One teacher used folklore as a focus for integrating all the language arts with reading. The children interviewed parents and neighbors for best-loved stories which had been handed down, and noted the place of origin. These stories were written up and discussed for similarities around the world. Then they took proverbs they knew and tallied these for content and "origin" (as far as they could trace) and tried to discover if any of the stories illustrated proverbs. Following this they wrote incidents of "real life" which illustrated some of the proverbs ("Haste makes waste," "Too many cooks spoil the broth." "A stitch in time saves nine" were favorites). Then they read folklore, or tales with folklore

[8] Kate Seredy, *A Tree for Peter* (New York: Viking Press, 1941), and Valenti Angelo, *The Bells of Bleecker Street* (New York, Viking Press, 1949).

flavor such as *The Cat Who Went to Heaven* and *Secret of the Andes* and *The White Stag*[9] to see which proverbs seem to be the most popular among folk tales.

Something must be said at this point about the treatment of written papers when the teacher corrects them. If too much correction on all compositions is standard procedure, children soon learn that the less they write the fewer the possible mistakes, and a one-sentence paper becomes the order of the day. But this does not mean that no corrections should be made. It is true that some papers are not returned to the individual for correction—especially those that are written in confidence. There must be an invitation to write in confidence, and children must know that those confidences will never be divulged. There is more than one reason why such papers should not be returned for correction: There are guilt feelings next day when confronted with what seemed appropriate the day before; when a child writes at length, "forgetting himself," it is a shock to see the number of red marks across that paper which meant so much to him emotionally. Such papers can be "corrected" in another way: the teacher makes note of the most glaring, most typical errors, and uses this list as a basis for teaching mechanics of writing. Otherwise, the whole basic purpose of the assignment is lost. And much is also lost in relation to the child's future willingness to write. Writing should be an exciting venture. There are many ways to encourage it, and other ways to kill it.

The process of having children read each other's papers in small sociometric groups has much soundness pedagogically and psychologically. If it is agreed that the children should write each day, ways must be devised by the teacher to save himself from being overwhelmed by papers to correct. It is impossible, physically, for him to do this each day when he meets several large classes. There are not enough after-school hours in which to do this when he must also plan ahead and make some attempt at becoming acquainted with children's books. What has happened in the schools today is that teachers, feeling they must correct each paper, have cut to a bare minimum, and even less, the time devoted to writing. Children must write, and teachers must read much of what they write since we assume all writing assignments have a very real purpose, real to the teacher as well as to the children. But that does not mean laborious correcting which does the children no good—and even hurts the educational process—and certainly does not help the teacher to do a better job.

In sociometric groups, children can find each other's errors. In cases where the group is made up of children whose knowledge is so meager that they cannot distinguish between correct and incorrect construction, or cannot agree on what is correct, the teacher serves as umpire. Children can often help each other far more readily than can the teacher. When

9 Elizabeth Coatsworth, *The Cat Who Went to Heaven* (New York: Macmillan Company, 1931); Ann Nolan Clark, *Secret of the Andes* (New York: Viking Press, Inc., 1935); and Kate Seredy, *The White Stag* (New York: Viking Press, Inc., 1938).

five children are reading each other's papers for content as well as for mechanical errors, five potential teachers are scrutinizing the same paper for ways in which they can help. A certain pride develops when a group can bring a paper close to "perfection" before the teacher sees it, and it is only the errors the teacher finds that "count." This prevents carping, a child's feelings being hurt because a peer criticized him, and develops a spirit of community helpfulness.

A child who writes deserves an audience. Sometimes that audience is the teacher only, especially when papers are written confidentially. Too often, the other children are the audience for thirty-five young people as they stand up and read their individual papers, one after the other—a deadening process. Children are interested in the first few that are read, but soon no one is listening and the procedure becomes mechanical. The small-group procedure eliminates this drawback and puts the responsibility for correction, for perfection, exactly where it belongs—on the children. When teachers correct constantly with too fine detail, the children become dependent on them to judge. Children should learn to take increasing responsibility for those judgments. Besides, this process is fruitful because the children are reading. Each child reads four or five papers by his classmates and scrutinizes them for two purposes.

It is surprising how quickly children learn to work in groups when they begin with short periods and are given definite tangible tasks to do which are truly group tasks and which cannot be done either individually or by the whole class. Too often the young teacher plunges into long-term committee work without giving himself and the children any previous training, without thinking through the *why* of the particular group task, without knowing the basic difference between tasks which are essentially individual and those which are truly group, and without planning the procedure step by step.

In the school situation portrayed here, where teachers or children seemed not yet ready to handle this type of set-up, sociometric twosomes, or partners, served essentially the same purpose for a time, and had the added advantage of training children to work together with one person before asking them to function in small-group activities. Here again it was the individual teacher working with his class who explored ways appropriate for him and for them and determined the goals toward which they were striving. Some teachers rarely went beyond the partner arrangement with a particular class; others gradually increased the group size for some children while they permitted certain other children to continue to work as partners; still others managed relatively early to set the "work tone" of the class in such a way that small-group work was comfortable and profitable for all; some soon learned to use both small groups and partners, whichever was most appropriate for the learning purpose.

Most teachers needed encouragement. Some were fearful of permitting thirty children to work together in fifteen teams. They were afraid of discipline problems, of a few teams "cutting up" and "spoiling it for others." These teachers had to educate themselves and the children. One did it by running a series of role-playing situations, one a day, in which two children showed how each would handle the written work of his partner. These role-playing situations were discussed by the teacher and class until the seriousness of purpose was established and both teacher and children were confident that they knew what to do. Another teacher preferred to work with one row of "double desks" (about one-third of the group) while the rest of the class occupied themselves silently reading their individually chosen books. When the teacher felt that these children knew how to proceed, he moved on to another row another day. One teacher preferred to use partner arrangements as a prestige activity, and children who could handle themselves were given the opportunity. Others had to work individually and wait for the teacher to come around so they could read to him. When such children thought they could work with another child, they informed the teacher and were promptly given an opportunity to demonstrate that ability. The responsibility was on each individual child to decide when he was ready.

The point here is that teachers, too, have individual differences. If a technique or method is psychologically and pedagogically sound, it will "work," but only when the teacher is given an opportunity to explore ways suitable and comfortable for him to make it work.

Reading Skills: Vocabulary Building and Word Recognition

Organizing reading around the common theme approach provides a "natural" for extending vocabulary without which progress in reading cannot be made but which, in turn, reading helps to expand. When children are learning to read, the vocabulary in the book must be familiar —words they know through listening, words which are meaningful experientially. Later, reading is used to increase vocabulary, to gain new experiences, to learn new words.

By and large, the children in this project worked at both levels. They were interested in materials which would bring them new experiences, but their reading levels dictated that the words, on the whole, must be known to them, except for those that were to be used for learning word-analysis skills. And these had to be few enough so that the meaning of the selection was not lost by the necessity for laboriously figuring out too many words, and so that discouragement did not set in.

Vocabulary is increased through experience. How do children learn the meaning and use of *unruly*, or *deceive*, or *floundering*, or *emphasize*, or *falter*? Teachers should use the new vocabulary in meaningful natural context, so that children become familiar with the words and what they mean before they are asked to struggle with them in a reading selection. Teachers should continue to use them at frequent intervals so that the words, and the concepts and experiences attached to them, become useful tools to the learner. This is how very young children learn language—they hear a word over and over again until they are able to attach meaning to it, until they are able to use it. It solves no problem, nor is it teaching, when a teacher uses a word once, writes it on the board, and expects children, to whom the written word is still a bewildering phenomenon, to recognize it without difficulty in the reading text. Often a story is read to children for the sole purpose of introducing words whose concepts are otherwise difficult to teach. The story provides the basic experience with the word or words, the teacher uses them meaningfully and repeatedly, and the children are encouraged to use the words as they write and speak. Taking time to build ideas creates opportunity for building vocabulary.

For example, a tape recording of a forty-minute lesson in which the teacher was introducing the project of reading to younger children reveals that he used the word "reaction" several times and that before the end of that period the children were using it as part of their own vocabularies. Here are a few excerpts from that lesson:

TEACHER: In order to get this list of little children's books as a guide for parents, we'll have to study little children's reactions to the books you read to them. For example . . .

* * *

TEACHER: How will you be able to tell what the little child's reaction is? If he doesn't like the book, how may he act?

* * *

TEACHER: In our report we'll put down the reaction of the little child. We'll say, Now there are some people who liked this book even though it didn't have a happy ending.

* * *

THOMAS: I agree with Mike. Probably you won't find one person that has the same reaction with [as] the child.
SANDY: If I read the same book to two children and they don't have the same reaction, what will I do?

No one method of word recognition was relied on exclusively. Children had to learn how to anticipate meaning as they read, and to use this skill as an aid in recognizing a new word. They needed, also, to be able to identify the basic word in a derivative. Basically, teachers in the project used two simple processes for reteaching skills of using context clues: One was the leading question which directed the child's thinking toward the word not recognized in order to help him find clues. Does the story take place at night or in the daytime? What does Susie want for a birthday present? Another way was to have the child skip the bothersome word and continue to read to the end of the sentence, returning to the word to see if context helped. Teachers helped the whole class to discover how to do this for themselves and for others. If one child asked another for help, the second child asked a question connecting the unknown with a clue to guide him, or he urged him to read to the end of the sentence, skipping the word temporarily and returning to it when he had the complete thought. It was necessary for some children to have these processes emphasized daily, for only when all the children knew what was being done, and why, could assistance be given. Being able to verbalize, to intellectualize the processes and the reasons, not only helped the child who asked for aid, but the child who was giving it, for there were many times when he too needed help with the same skill. Most important of all, children began to feel that they were *learning how to learn*, that they could attack the problem intelligently.

Another process which was taught was in one sense a part of the process of using context clues. In another sense, it served as motivation to go on in spite of difficulty and also as a check on the children's comprehension. It served to emphasize comprehension as a basic feature of vocabulary building. It was the process of predicting events. What do you think is going to happen? To answer this intelligently, one must have understood what went before, and this would provide a focus for more intelligent reading of what was to follow. This was emphasized in almost every reading session in which common skills were taught to all, and in which common reading materials were used.

Once the child had learned the vocabulary, he needed opportunities to hear the words, to see them, to use them in a variety of different situations. The teacher continued to use the words in a natural way at intervals which were first short, then longer. These words appeared frequently—perhaps in the written directions teachers gave to children. The day after the children read their stories to siblings, the teacher wrote on the board, "Describe the reaction of your child to the book you read." This whole process of providing sufficient experiences necessary for vocabulary building, of using new words in a variety of situations, of using the context to help figure them out, was facilitated by the theme approach of teaching reading. Who plays the *role* of *arbiter* in your family? Do different people play different roles? There are *arbiters* in books too, in books about families and about teen-agers, and children can watch for situations in which people *arbitrate* at home or in school or among peers. The point is that the children must be enabled to build a substantial vocabulary around areas that are allowed sufficient time for study, and which include consideration of ideas requiring a particular vocabulary for their expression.

Phonics, as a method of teaching word-analysis skills, has made the headlines for the past few years—to such an extent that it is difficult for teachers to view phonetic analysis objectively. When it is viewed objectively it is seen as one of several procedures used to help a child with word recognition and analysis. To teach through this method, using isolated words, bears little fruit for several reasons: (1) The children's chief difficulty is reading for meaning, reading to find out what someone else is saying to them. Learning phonetic analysis through isolated words only increases the lack of meaning reading holds for the child. (2) The children have not yet learned that reading can be a pleasurable experience. Learning in this way only strengthens the frustration of their earlier sad experiences with the reading process. (3) Teachers often find that many of the children who are still having difficulty with reading have already "had" this method. It did little for them then, and emphasis on it is not likely to improve the situation now.

Other aids to word recognition must come first: context clues, for example. Then phonetic analysis can be used in meaningful context as the child is grappling with a word. Teachers in this project taught phonetic analysis only after they knew that the child was reading fluently and with meaning. Unfortunately, the children who seemed to need phonetic analysis most could not profit from it, even at junior high school age, when more children can use this method than could previously. It took a certain degree of mental maturity to *see* the similarity of *sound* on the printed page. Teachers did not find necessary a highly complicated and intricate method of teaching phonetic analysis. They simply used it as needed to help a child who was "stuck" as he read, and made sure that the whole word was kept intact, that letters were not sounded in isolation. For example, if a child failed to recognize the word *smudge* and did not even attempt to attack the initial sound, the teacher helped him arrive at the meaning from the context. Once the meaning was clearly established they read together to a point in the story at which it was reasonable to stop, and then went back to the troublesome word. The teacher isolated the whole word from its sentence, writing it on a piece of paper (or on a 3 x 5 card so the child could file it for future reference). He mentioned several known words beginning with *sm:* smell, small, smoke, smile. When the *sm* sound—as it is seen in print— was clearly established, the child was helped to get the next part of the word: *smudge* is like *smell* in the way it begins, but in the latter part it is like *fudge* or *judge.*

None of this drill or teaching of a "new" skill was undertaken while the child was reading in an audience situation. It was when he was reading to the teacher alone, or to his partner, or when he asked for help during silent reading periods, that most of such instruction was given.

As a child gained in his ability to figure out words for himself, and as the teacher gained in resourcefulness in finding materials suited to each child's ability, there was much less need for teaching new words before reading a common selection. The reading activity began to be used for learning new words.

Teachers used very few different types of written drills and exercises; it was not necessary to burden them with the task of learning about a great variety of drills or with devising ways to implement them. Nor did they feel such drills were particularly useful for the children. They did use a very few, only on occasion, only for a very specific purpose, and only for a few selected children. One was for the purpose of helping children distinguish between words that were giving them difficulty, words such as *then* and *than*, *where* and *when*, *whom* and *what*. For this the teachers prepared a list of phrases using the vocabulary the children had already learned, and asked them to circle, for each phrase, the correct word that followed.

working in the laboratory	Where	When
after the busy season	Where	When
during the recess period	Where	When

The teachers spent some time on syllabication, stressing the division of words according to sound rather than following the dictionary. They realized that there is difference of opinion among lexicographers as to exactly how some words should be divided. Previously, they had followed the practice of having the children look up every word in the dictionary—a time-consuming procedure. Teachers realized that there is a hierarchy of values when the school day is limited. Some words were checked; the dictionary was not a forgotten tool. But first things must come first. In all cases, the words used were those encountered in current reading material.

Teachers found value in the use of "cut-up stories" to be reassembled. They worked with the children, helping them discover the transitions from paragraph to paragraph. These stories were mounted on cards, paragraph by paragraph (sometimes two or three paragraphs on one card to make it easier for the children to succeed in this task), and the children put them together into a sequential story.

In all cases, stories were in the context of the theme under consideration and used the vocabulary necessary for that consideration. Stories were obtained from discarded books and from *Practical English* (a weekly published by Scholastic Magazines, Inc.); some of the stories used had been written by classes of children who were more verbal. Interest in this activity was as high as if it had been a picture puzzle.

Nor were teachers averse to using *Classic Comics*. Some of these were quite appropriate to discussions at hand, had high interest value, and repeated words often enough for children to learn to recognize them. When a small group of children in one class obtained the *Classic Comic*, "The Magic Fountain," interest reached a peak. Some of the children played the parts of the characters while others read the explanations and setting. The teacher reported that "they followed the text eagerly; when one hesitated, the other one helped him. They attacked words as a team." Here, figuring out words and written ideas became a group project about which children could actually become excited.

Spelling

Even spelling was taught in such a way as to aid with word recognition in reading and with vocabulary extension. The city-wide spelling list was used more to satisfy the teachers than for any other reason, because the list was largely in isolation and had little connection with the content teachers and children were considering. There were spelling lists from other sources which were given even greater attention: an individual list drawn from the words the child really tried to use in his writing, and a composite list made up of words that were commonly misspelled in the children's written work.

The children were told, even encouraged, to indicate their need for help whenever they felt they could not spell a word properly. It was explained to them that seeing the word written incorrectly made it more difficult to "unlearn" than if it were set down correctly to begin with. Also, they were led to believe that recognition of the fact that they could not spell a word was a step forward. When a child raised his hand for help, the teacher went to him immediately with a 3 x 5 slip of paper or card and wrote the word on it in large letters. The child copied it and continued to write. When his piece of writing was completed he wrote the word three times from memory, each time covering what he had written.

The teacher had previously taught the children how to learn to spell. Visual memory was stressed. They must not look at a copy of the word while they wrote. They could look carefully, all they wanted to, at the word before they wrote, but when they wrote, the word must not be in sight. Most of these children had a history of having copied words twenty-five times, without learning to spell them. They did not need to. There was the word above to look at each time they wrote it. Most of the children had a common difficulty in reading. They failed to note details. They could note them as they copied them but that is where the noting ended. Now they had a copy of the word enlarged so that details stood out. Now they studied the word before writing and noted the details carefully enough to carry them in their "mind's eye." Spelling "out loud" was discouraged; visual memory, necessary in spelling correctly, was encouraged.

Since the words were those that children used frequently, and since the content of what they were writing was correlated with what they were discussing and reading, this method fortified word recognition in reading. After a very few weeks, it became evident that children were making a start at noting details, noting differences between *where* and *were*, *thimble* and *thistle*.

GRAMMAR AND USAGE

Grammar and usage were also taught with indirect focus on strengthening word recognition. Teachers used the method of building up sentences instead of the usual tearing down. For example, the teacher (or children) named an action word, let us say "crawls," and the children thought of as many things that crawl as they could. Then the order was reversed, and a noun was named—"automobile." The children listed as many verbs as they could, describing what an automobile does. Thus, they not only gained the basic feeling for how a sentence is created, but the verb or the noun—*crawl* and later *automobile*—which was to remain constant while they created the other part of sentence, was a word which needed reinforcement for reading, either because of word-attack skills or word recognition.

The process was continued as time went on, never reverting to sentence analysis, but always using the creating process of building sentences, always keeping one element or one part of speech constant. It was this constancy which gave the opportunity for teaching reading skills and vocabulary and usage. If children confused *lie* and *lay*, these became the constants. The children were called upon to change the rest of the sentence; they now had an opportunity to truly learn the difference.

Later, the adverb and adjective were introduced by keeping the noun and verb constant and changing first one modifier and then the other. Even clauses were taught this way, and difficulties with sentence structure remedied. For example, if children wrote *Because I went home* and called this a sentence, it was difficult to explain by rules why it is not. But if *Because I went home* was kept as the constant clause and the teacher called for another clause which finished its meaning, which told exactly what happened when you went home, it was much less difficult to teach independent and dependent clauses. The children were in the meantime creating new ideas, learning to recognize whatever words were consciously used by the teacher over and over again.

Teachers were. not concerned with whether these particular children could name each part of speech; they were concerned with their writing creatively and meaningfully and accurately. They were concerned with having all procedures used fortify the children's reading skills. Yet it is interesting to note that children learned more about the names of the parts of speech than teachers had hoped they would. This occurred only in cases where teachers gave them an opportunity to show what they knew through the building process. When the test consisted of a sentence already created by someone else, and required the children to name the parts of speech of the various words, they were at a loss. But then, so were the others who had been taught by the method of parsing.

ORAL READING

The basic procedure of using a constant theme approach to individualizing the work gave opportunities for still other practices, too, practices of extreme importance in strengthening the children's reading ability. For example, it offered opportunities for teachers to find occasions for oral reading. They realized that oral reading should continue to be an important part of the program, even though silent reading predominated.

Because most children read well by the time they reach junior high school, teachers often tend to forget the role played by oral reading in the process of learning to read. It is through oral reading that a teacher can diagnose a child's difficulties; it is through this process that children are motivated to read better, to practice their reading beforehand. This does not mean that each child should be asked or even permitted to stumble through a passage with thirty-five peers as audience. Audience situations can be provided in other ways. There are, again, the small sociometric groupings which can serve the purpose. There are times when children can share something with only one other classmate. This became evident in one routine procedure which teachers found very fruitful—the use of the first five minutes of every core session for oral reading in "duets." Each child had an outside reading book on his own level, whether it was on the Westward Movement or fantasies for young children or an adventure story. In the adventure-story sequence children were trying to come to some conclusion about what constituted adventure. Did you have to risk your life? Was there adventure in every-day life? Was the same experience adventure for everyone? A standard homework assignment was reading from that book every night. Each child had a mimeographed chart on which he made certain entries.

Then he prepared the paragraph he liked best for reading to his classmate. After reading to his classmate he entered two or three words in the proper column, words he would like to be able to recognize more readily. This work was begun as soon as the children entered the classroom, even while the teacher was on hall duty. Any questions were referred to the teacher. As soon as the teacher returned he circulated around the room, listening, advising, noting progress, making comments of encouragement on the charts wherever this was warranted. In other words, at the start of each day, every child had a chance to read aloud and be heard, and the time consumed was only five minutes.

Teachers frequently used plays for oral reading. For example, there

READING PROGRESS SHEET

NAME _____   CORE TEACHER _____   CLASS _____

Date	Title of book	Time begun / Page begun	Time ended / Page ended	Minutes per page	Words for practice	Most exciting part or part I liked	Teacher's comments

was *Seeing the Elephant*[11] by Dan Totheroh when they were studying the Westward Movement, or scenes from *I Remember Mama*[12] when they were considering what children learn from families. There were several short plays in earlier issues of *Practical English* which teachers saved for this kind of use. Since these were common readings, they were not given to children to struggle with alone. Always the teacher worked with them, even to the extent of first reading it to them while children watched their books. Soon they lost their self-consciousness about reading aloud and everyone wanted to read at sight. In all cases, teachers had to hold out for silent preparation beforehand, for it was in the motivated practice of these materials that children developed their skills.

Much work was also done with choral reading of poetry. It was necessary to use simple uncomplicated poems, for the sentence structure in poetry is not easy for children who are poor readers. But "Casey at the Bat," done in chorus, was always a "big seller" as were ballads and many other pieces of poetry. This method of choral reading provided motivation for rereading many times until words were recognized in the natural course of events. The teacher did a good deal of reading aloud so that the children could see and hear him express an emotion which was aroused by words on a cold printed page. In addition it was through his oral reading that a teacher could introduce the children to many new books, open up new vistas and new ideas. The children still needed models for good reading, and most of them had no source other than their own teacher. As the children watched the teacher enjoy reading, they began to sense that people derive pleasure from this thing which caused them so much difficulty. Also, there was a community of feeling when the teacher read to them. It was good for children to feel this closeness—connected with books—with other human beings. Some children had experienced it in their early years when their parents read to them; others had probably never experienced it until they entered school. Now there was anticipation of pleasant relationships with teacher and classmates whenever the teacher picked up a book to read to them. This atmosphere was important in changing the children's attitudes toward books.

The tape recorder has numerous ramifications and unending possibilities for oral reading. Its motivational powers are unquestioned. Children will practice and practice untiringly, without a murmur, in order to perfect a passage for the recorder. It is an excellent device for showing children how much they have improved in ten weeks, let us say, and thus it can provide further motivation at a time when interest lags or the tasks involved in learning to read become difficult. It is also a way of taking

[11] Dan Totheroh, *Seeing the Elephant* (New York: Dramatic Play Service, 1939). This play was one of the America in Action Series of one-act plays for young people.

[12] John Van Druten, *I Remember Mama*, in *Three Comedies of American Family Life*, edited by Joseph Mersand (New York: Washington Square Press, Inc., 1961).

care of individual and small-group problems: The teacher (or some more advanced member of the group) reads a story onto the tape for children who are still on a considerably lower level. These children work alone later, listening to the tape and at the same time watching the book (one with which they would be unable to cope without such assistance). Then they try reading it without the tape, noting the words at which they are blocked. They may play the tape as many times as they feel necessary. The words they do not know furnish material for work with word-attack skills.

When the children themselves feel that they have improved, they ask the teacher for a special hearing or for an extra chance to use the tape for recording their progress. It is their responsibility to know when they are improving, to know when they've gotten "that certain feeling." The teacher also encourages each member of the class to observe the progress made by the partner with whom he does his daily five-minute reading and to encourage him to demonstrate that progress.

Plans must also be made within the context of work organized around a common theme and around certain concepts related to it to create opportunities for rereading many selections. Each rereading should be done for a different purpose. This does not affect work with the individual books the children are reading, but applies to the common stories and plays. The use of plays and choral reading of poems, and the high motivation they offer for reading, have already been discussed. Motivation for rereading stories has to be planned, too. Children need to understand the reason for rereading both in terms of their own skill building and in terms of the function the reading activity will serve. A function already considered is reading to younger children. There are many devices that are fruitful, each according to the story itself and the needs of the class. For example, with the "Tell-Tale Heart"[13] by Poe, which may have to be read in good measure by the teacher, only simple questions are needed as motivation for rereading because the story is a gripping one—such questions as: When do you first become aware that this man is insane? What are the other places where Poe makes you more and more sure that this is a madman?

There are usually differences of opinion which become evident as they are aired in the ensuing discussion, and this provides the motivation for a partial third reading. Who is right? How do you know? Prove your point with evidence from the story.

Other stories require different types of motivation for rereading. For example, "Ski-High,"[14] by B. J. Chute, is fun to read as if it were a play. So the children reread to decide how many scenes there will be, and

[13] In Rewey B. Inglis, *Adventures in American Literature* (New York: Harcourt, Brace and World, Inc., 1952).

[14] In Frances T. Humphreville and Frances S. Fitzgerald, *Top Flight* (Chicago: Scott, Foresman and Company, 1961).

exactly where each will begin and end. When everyone has made his own individual judgment, a discussion follows to resolve the differences, and a partial third reading is achieved when children are asked to present "proof."

Another group of stories lends itself best to reading up to the climax, after which the children write the endings. Then the "real" ending is read, followed by the reading of a few created by the children. A discussion follows along these lines: "Some of you have happy endings; others sad. Why did you choose that kind?" Children are asked to give particulars from the story itself—a rereading process. "The author did not mean that the ending could be anything at all—either happy or sad. He gave you cues all along. Can you find them?" Stories suitable for such analysis are Leonard Ross's "Cemetery Path"[15] and Guy De Maupassant's "The Necklace."[16]

42. SPECIAL READING CLASSES

Harrison Bullock

The previous chapter, considering the non-reading pupil in the regular class, mentioned the desirability of special remedial instruction in reading for such pupils. Suggestions were made of ways in which the regular classroom teacher could give him help in reading when special classes are not available. A trained reading specialist, however, can more systematically appraise and meet the non-reading pupil's potentialities and needs in reading.

Remedial teaching is far more than a special technique of instruction. It is instruction based on diagnosis. The diagnosis is a continuing process, inseparable from the instruction. For this double process to be effective, remedial groups must be small enough for it to be carried out with individual attention to the needs and progress of each pupil. The regular classroom teacher cannot always be expected to do an adequate job of diagnosis plus instruction in the corner of the room while the rest of the class is studying history. That an occasional exceptional teacher seems

Reprinted with the permission of the publisher from Harrison Bullock: *Helping The Non-reading Pupil in Secondary Schools* (New York: Teachers College Press), pp. 106–130, Teachers College, Columbia University, copyright 1957.

[15] In Matilda Bailey and Ullin W. Leavell, *Worlds To Explore* (New York: American Book Company, 1951).

[16] In M. E. Speare, *The Pocket Book of Short Stories* (New York: Pocket Books, Inc., 1941).

to succeed at it is greatly to the teacher's credit, but scarcely to be expected generally.

The present chapter will consider this process of remedial teaching as it may be carried out in a special class of pupils organized for the purpose. It will begin with glimpses of teachers in action, followed by consideration of principles of operation applicable to this work.

The first visit to a remedial reading class will be reported as a minute-to-minute diary of happenings in the class over a period of three hours. The other classes are reported in less detail.

Mrs. Silver's Junior High School Reading Club

The attractive new junior high school building was so crowded already that the only room available for the "Reading Club" was a dreary basement storeroom. The inadequate windows in one corner could only be opened a few inches, because of their accessibility to vandals. This meant that the room was poorly ventilated and that the hall door had to be kept open. The room was made cheerful and attractive, however, with pictures and many books on display. This touch of color and interest saved the room from the gloom and dreariness inherent in its situation.

Mrs. Silver was able to plan an effective remedial program because she had been allowed to schedule very small groups and to select pupils for each according to similarity of needs or abilities. This provision for small classes and for permitting the teacher to schedule the pupils in her own way made it possible for her to deal with difficult pupils a few at a time. Her own planning, attitude, and management, however, created and preserved the relaxed, friendly, constructive atmosphere in the classes.

The minute-by-minute account of the morning's activities follows:

9:00 Girl 1 comes to desk, reads to teacher.
9:02 Three boys and two girls enter room, are greeted individually by name. Boy 1 asks permission to go to a club instead of reading class. A friend is with him to support his request. Teacher asks friend where he belongs, sends him to the class where he belongs. Teacher discusses request with B1, finally putting decision over to next day. B1 takes his work, goes to his seat. Other boy and the two girls who entered with him are already at seats with work they have taken from shelf at front of room. Teacher resumes work with G1 holding her to exactness in reading, but finding much to praise in the girl's performance.
9:10 Teacher dismisses G1, invites G2 for individual work. G2 comes to desk, sits down, waits while G1 finishes chatting with teacher.
9:12 G1 finally takes seat. Chats a moment with G3. G2 reads a story she has written to the teacher.
9:15 Teacher for the first time addresses class as a whole: "Who knows what a syllable is?" G3 volunteers answer, has difficulty expressing

it, is assisted by teacher. Class back to individual work; teacher back to work with G2.

9:20 Teacher leaves G2 working at her desk, while she goes about room checking work by various individuals. She sits down and spends some time with B1. Is warmly appreciative of progress he is showing.

9:25 Teacher is back at her own desk with G2. G1 comes up, sits down on chair at other side of teacher.

9:30 G4 enters, explaining that she forgot to come to reading club today. Teacher has G1 and G2 sit together to work cooperatively. G3 comes to desk, receives considerable phonic instruction (e.g., inserting the various vowels between P and T).

9:35 Fire drill. Pupils wait expectantly until teacher has given instructions on what to do before they leave. Teacher and pupils very calm and matter of fact about the procedure.

9:45 Back in room. Activities resume where they left off. There is apparently no residue of excitement from the fire drill.

9:52 Teacher dismisses G3 to her seat, calls B1 to desk for individual instruction.

9:56 G2 comes to desk with question, is sent back to her seat. "You had your turn; this is Henry's turn."

10:00 Bell. Teacher tells B2 to come to her desk at beginning of period next time, because she didn't get to him today. Dismisses children, who leave quietly, after replacing their work envelopes.

10:02 Three boys and two girls enter, are greeted by name. They take their work envelopes off shelf at front of room and go to seats.

10:03 Teacher works with G4. Has her attempt reading with one eye at a time. Apparently this girl is new to the class. Teacher gives her a notebook. "I want you to write me a story before you do anything else. The name of the story is 'Myself.'" Girl takes seat in back of room, starts working on the story.

10:08 Teacher circulates about the room watching children at work. They are working on stories they have selected for themselves in McCall-Crabbs *Test Lessons in Reading*. She helps them with words and encourages them generally.

10:12 B6 comes in late. Teacher greets him by name, says nothing else to him until he has picked up his work envelope from the shelf at front of room. She then asks him to account for his tardiness, tells him what to do under similar circumstances next time. This is done in a positive, but friendly manner; no threat expressed or implied. The teacher continues the individual help at various places about the classroom as pupils direct individual questions at her. B6 goes right to work like the others, without specific assignment. Apparently he knows just what is expected of him.

10:21 Somebody says he is ready. Everybody closes book and listens as B4 reads. After he finishes reading his selection, he reads the questions, while other pupils put answers in their notebooks. After all have finished with answers, teacher reads correct answers and pupils check their own work, reporting how well they did. After B4 comes B5, then, very tensely, B6, next G5, finally B3. After all have finished, teacher briefly evaluates the work of the entire group, viewing it against her educational objectives in the lesson, which she explains to the class. Pupils evaluate their own performances and their "improvement."

10:50 Teacher goes back to desk, working individually with B4. Meanwhile rest of class is working independently with their story books from the library table. B6 takes out of his pocket a copy of "Ciba Clinical Symposium," containing colored photographs of oral surgical conditions and technics. Occasionally he will show one of the pictures which particularly interests him to a pupil or pupils sitting near him. This is not done covertly; apparently he feels safe in this.

10:55 Teacher works at seat with B3.

10:58 Teacher calls B6 to desk to work individually.

11:00 Bell. Pupils put work away and leave quietly.

11:02 B7 enters, is complimented on how nice he looks today. He takes his work to his seat as other pupils enter and do likewise. Each is greeted by name as he enters. G6 goes to teacher's desk for individual work. Others work at their seats.

11:09 Teacher dismisses G6 to seat, calls G7 to desk for individual instruction.

11:11 Teacher dismisses G7 to seat, calls B9 to desk. B9 is a very big and rather mature boy, but an extremely weak reader. She gives him much gentle, tactful help.

11:16 B9 is dismissed to seat. Teacher circulates, supervising pupils' work at seats. They are working with Sangren and Wilson, *Instructional Tests in Reading*, Grade I, Form A.

11:20 She has the entire group work together on this material, reading aloud from it. G6 is working with something else. "Aren't you working with us?" G6 shakes her head. "Don't you want to work with us?" G6 shows what she is doing. Teacher accepts this, makes no more issue about it.

11:24 Much noise in the hall. Door must necessarily be open to permit ventilation of the room. Teacher and pupils are obviously annoyed by the noise, but apparently little can be done about it. Lesson continues.

11:40 Noise in hall gets much worse. Teacher grimaces, leaves room for a moment, then returns. Presently a man's voice in the hall seems to be taking command of the confusion there. Noise subsides slightly. Lesson continues.

11:45 Group work is finished. Pupils resume individual workbook work. Teacher calls G7 to desk for individual instruction. She finds that G7 seems worried about her progress, reassures her not to worry.

12:00 Bell. Pupils replace their work envelopes, leave room quietly, some of them with individual brief words with teacher.

After the class left, the teacher explained that she would accept any pupil needing special work in reading, and would work with him as he was capable. She said that she recognized the existence of emotional and environmental factors as contributing to reading disability; where nothing could be done about such factors directly by the school, she attempted to build up confidence and success as far as practicable within the framework of her own classes. She said she helped to foster this by grouping pupils in such a manner that they could help each other, but would not be working with too many classmates far above or below their own ability.

In her conduct of the classes she seemed careful to keep her attitude casual and pleasant, so that pupils might feel free to relax in her room. She was strict in her standards of work and conduct, obviously tolerating no "nonsense;" infractions of her standards, nevertheless, seemed to be taken in stride. She gave the general impression of realizing that pupils were trying, that they needed and would welcome help, so that they would eventually meet her standards.

Much of her success may be attributed to a positive, forceful personality, as well as a sympathetic understanding, but this force was kept well under control. There was no feeling of threat, but there was an impression of undefined resources available to the teacher when needed. In an atmosphere of understanding, patience, and confidence, even the most difficult and disturbed pupils seemed able to relax and to learn.

An interesting postscript on this visitation came after a copy of the minute-by-minute account of the three hours in the class had been sent to the teacher. She responded with the following letter, which in many ways expressed the philosophy of her work:

I appreciated your thoughtfulness in sending a copy of your observation more than I can say. "To see ourselves as others see us" is always a thought-provoking experience.

I was pleased that you liked what you had seen and the detailed account of your observation made it possible for me to view the morning objectively, myself.

From the point of view of the observer, I think I might have been more critical, delighted as I was that you hadn't been. But, for the sake of your broader study, you may be interested in what I see in the report.

The teacher, from my point of view, may be overzealous. There should be more pause for good fellowship and less "drive." These are high-strung, troubled children, and I felt that, in her zeal, the teacher seemed to lose sight of that.

Retardation in reading has been the source of their most acute scholastic defeat. The seriousness of their failure has been impressed upon them at home and in school. The job of the teacher of retarded children is to provide lightness as well as enlightenment. The teacher, from your observation, or rather from mine, took herself too seriously. This, I think, is a valid criticism.

I used to start each hour with cookies—bribes, the children called it. After reading your report I decided to go back to bribing again.

Thank you for affording me the opportunity of taking notice of my professional self. It was revealing and therefore significant.

An observer might be inclined to consider Mrs. Silver's criticism of the class procedure rather more severe than would seem justified. Probably one of the most important factors in her success as a remedial teacher, however, was the fact that she saw fit to make such a criticism. Her use of "bribes," it might be observed, differed greatly in spirit from the use of prizes and rewards, for they were to be given the pupils at the beginning of the period; they were to demonstrate good will and affection to the pupils regardless of performance. They could help establish a bond between teacher and pupils, a bond which might facilitate cooperative endeavor.

Miss Grace's Party Atmosphere. Miss Grace gave the impression of being a gracious hostess at a young people's party, one who knew what interests children and how they feel about things. The pupils apparently had this impression of her, for they came into the classroom with an attitude of expectancy of interesting things to happen, and greeted her personally in a manner neither deferential nor familiar, but rather as someone who had shown them a good time in the past and could be counted upon to repeat in the future.

Her classroom was basically not attractive, having been designed as a teachers' lunchroom with prominent sink and gas range. But its large south window and the display of colorful books and the neatly lettered illustrated charts made it bright and cheerful, reflecting Miss Grace's manner.

One period of her class began inauspiciously, because three of the five boys who entered at the beginning announced that they were required to take a science test at this particular time. In Miss Grace's school the issue of what to do about tests on days when pupils were supposed to go to remedial reading was a problem, for she had to release the boys during the test, even though it spoiled her plans for the period. For the two boys remaining, she got out copies of a beautifully printed English illustrated edition of "The House That Jack Built," with colorful old-fashioned pictures. They were evidently her own books. She introduced the book with the old-fashioned nursery rhyme in an enthusiastic but natural manner. Her attitude toward the book and toward the big adolescent boys was such that there was no feeling that the book was in any way juvenile. She taught the archaisms and unfamiliar concepts (e.g., malt, maiden all forlorn, shaven and shorn, etc.) as curiosities to intrigue the pupils. Her enthusiasm and conviction on this occasion was able to "sell" this rather surprising bit of literature to a pair of unlikely pupils.

When the other boys were finished with their science test and returned to the room in the middle of the period, she had finished "The House That Jack Built" and had begun a "word wheel" game. The returning boys noticed the attractive new books and wanted to read them, so she told them they might take them home with them. Then she went on explaining the word wheels. One of the boys disregarded her instruction to put the book aside and watch what she was doing. He read "The House That Jack Built" to himself, forming the words with his lips, occasionally voicing them. The teacher disregarded this, finally acknowledging it verbally by excepting him in a general instruction given the rest of the class. With that he closed the book and joined in the activity.

He had been keeping track of what the others were doing all the time he was reading.

At the end of the period, after working on phonics by the "word wheel" method, the teacher introduced that curious word, *antidisestablishmentarianism*, with the usual fascinated response. She apparently knew what interested eighth graders and how to gauge and sense their interest. She also seemed to sense the limits of their attention span.

The next class came in and spent the entire period with no outside interruptions or distractions. She began this period with *antidisestablishmentarianism* with much the same results as in the previous class. The bulk of this period was spent with a homemade reading game of bingo, based on word endings. The pupils played enthusiastically and Miss Grace's "hostess" manner was much in evidence. The pupils seemed to like the game. When one of them suggested trying a new game which had been prominently displayed on the teacher's desk, the others quickly outvoted him, preferring to continue bingo. The pupils played to win, but were good sports on losing. On one occasion a boy obviously passed up an opportunity to capitalize on a girl's accident in exposing a card; the teacher praised his sportsmanship, pointing out that, according to the rules, he could quite properly have taken advantage of this "break." They finished this game and had just set up the materials for the other new game when the bell rang. The pupils all groaned with frustration at having to discontinue their game before it had fairly begun. They helped pick up the equipment of the game and left the room with goodbyes for Miss Grace.

Miss Grace was young and attractive, enthusiastic and optimistic. The bond of real mutual affection between her and the children was evident in the way they greeted each other, her manner toward the pupils, and by their response toward her.

She explained her philosophy of remedial teaching as involving recognition of pupils' need for affection, experience of success, confidence, and work at their own level. As she said, "The more disturbed they are, the more enthusiastic they are about any success they have." She made no reference to pupils' case histories or individual problems.

Miss Grace was apparently new to her work. Her great assets were her attractive appearance and personality, her enthusiasm, and her liking for and understanding of pupils. With experience would come increasing attention to the diagnostic aspects of remedial work, and to individual needs of pupils. Meanwhile in the atmosphere of her classroom, teachers can find a standard worthy of emulation.

Miss King's Carefully Planned Classes. Miss King was a much more experienced teacher than was Miss Grace. Her manner was more calm, more matter-of-fact, less affectionate. Obviously the pupils enjoyed her class, but their enthusiasm was less warm, for the atmosphere was more work than party. She, too, used games in her teaching. She had a large assortment of the commercially prepared reading games on hand. She would participate in the games enough to teach the pupils how to use them, but when the pupils knew how to play them, she would leave them on their own with the games, while she worked individually with pupils. The games were used as learning exercises which the pupils might use with a minimum of supervision, so that she could give them more individual attention than would otherwise be possible.

Each pupil had an individual envelope with work in it which was assigned by Miss King, and which was performed under her supervision at the beginning of the hour. The second part of the hour would usually be devoted to some group activity involving reading, perhaps enjoying a filmstrip together and reading the captions or making up their own captions, perhaps listening to one of the pupils read a selection he had prepared, perhaps learning to play some new reading game under Miss King's supervision. The final few minutes would be spent by most of the pupils playing some game together, while Miss King worked intensively with individual pupils, perhaps on work in their envelopes, perhaps simply in conversation with them.

Miss King felt it of great importance to keep careful case histories of each pupil, filling in with information gleaned from the pupils themselves, from other teachers, from counselors, from school records, and from parents. With many of the pupils she felt she had a fairly good idea of the nature of the difficulty which underlay their reading disability; with these pupils she felt she could plan work which would meet their needs quite accurately. With other pupils she was less certain of the true nature of their difficulty; their work she planned more tentatively. With all pupils she tried to observe carefully their response to their work and their apparent progress through it.

Perhaps Miss King was rather more obviously "scientific" in her approach to the pupils than they themselves would quite like. Perhaps they felt a bit more "pushed" by her knowledge of what they needed than they did by Mrs. Silver's more sensitive approach. If they felt this way at all, it would probably be due more to Miss King's attitude toward them than to her actual methods. A teacher who felt free to respond with a warm, natural friendliness to pupils would have no difficulty with such methods, although the pupils would probably appreciate more opportunity to participate actively in planning than either Miss King or Miss Grace gave them.

Mr. Witt's Emphasis on Evidence of Progress. Mr. Witt's remedial reading program was on a different basis from the others. It was programmed in place of the regular English class for each of the pupils in his senior high school, meeting daily. He described his philosophy of remedial work in the following terms:

The first requisite is the recognition by the pupil of his problem. Then he should have a reading test. The teacher should discuss with him on the basis of this test, in terms he will accept, his ability to learn. He should be conditioned by the successful experiences of many other children assigned to the class. The class should be kept small, not in excess of twenty to twenty-five, ideally fifteen, enough for the pupil to be with other students of similar handicap. The class should:

1. Provide successful reading experiences.

2. Set up mechanical scoring, graphs, etc., procedures that he can use constantly to evaluate his improvement in speed and comprehension.

3. Provide suitable materials for free reading as well as materials for "techniques of reading."

4. Receive standardized tests at beginning and end of term.

Once the student is motivated, there is no substitute for reading in the "improvement of reading."

Obviously much of Mr. Witt's procedures were aimed more at the retarded readers who already had some reading ability on which to improve than at the non-reading pupil. Graphs of improvement in speed and comprehension are meaningful to pupils who already can read and comprehend, if only haltingly. Nevertheless, bringing a non-reading pupil into such a program can help to motivate him to bring his reading to the point where his own graph will commence to rise; he will be working on standards set by people of comparable ability. The confidence and hope inspired by a teacher like Mr. Witt can lead a pupil perhaps for the first time to put forth efforts, motivated by a growing appreciation of the contribution reading ability can make toward the fulfillment of his own needs.

The limitation of Mr. Witt's approach is with the pupils who are most resistant to pressure. Some pupils seem able to accomplish things only in their own time and in their own way. While Mr. Witt would himself recognize this fact and adjust assignments to each pupil's own pace, nevertheless the visible evidences of progress and the perhaps unspoken but implied urge to excel one's classmates, a strong motivation for many pupils, can arouse resistance in others, particularly those who may lack confidence in their own competitive ability in this regard. If competition is to be a constructive motivation, there should be reasonably equal opportunity for each pupil to win. The resistance to use of visible progress records can be minimized if each pupil's individual record can be kept private so that he and the teacher are the only ones who need know of setbacks and learning plateaus.

The next few observations, more brief than the foregoing, illustrate how a remedial teacher may help non-reading pupils find occasion and material for reading in their daily life and interests.

Road Signs. There were seven boys in Miss Smith's junior high school special class for non-reading pupils. When they arrived in the room they found a list of messages on the blackboard:

No Parking Allowed	Detour
Men at Work	Danger
School, Go Slow	Dead End
One Way	Keep to Right

Miss Smith: These are signs I saw on the way to school. How many of you saw them? (*All of the group had seen at least some of these signs.*) Jim, you are learning to drive. What would you do if you saw this first sign? (*She points to "No Parking Allowed."*)

Jim: "No Parking." I'd find another place to stop.

Miss Smith: That's exactly the thing to do. But do you know the last word of the sign?

Phil: "No Parking Allowed," isn't it?

Miss Smith: That's right. Sometimes it does just say plain "No Parking" as Jim said it. What else does it say sometimes?

Nick: "No parking permitted?"

Peter: "No parking here?"

Miss Smith: Yes, I've seen all those in different places. Now, suppose you were driving and saw this word on a sign. (*She points to "Detour."*) What would you do then?

Paul: It looks something like "Danger," but it isn't that.

Miss Smith: No, it isn't. (*Pause*)

Jim: Does it mean road closed?

Miss Smith: Not exactly that, either. It is a French word which means to turn aside. What does that suggest to you?

Bill: Like you don't go straight ahead. You take a road that goes around, you know, and then comes back to the same road.

Miss Smith: How many would do that if you were driving and came to this sign, "Detour?" (*There is general agreement.*)

Similarly, the other signs were read and the meanings made clear. The pupils were asked to be ready the next period to report on signs and other reading that was necessary in their everyday lives.

Reporting on Shows. Most pupils are greatly interested in television and motion picture shows. This interest may be used in improving the oral expression of pupils, and in preparing beginning reading materials for them.

One overage junior high pupil, a discipline problem, and a non-reader with marked speech difficulty, surprised his teacher by his enthusiastic and lengthy account of a movie he had seen. He had been particularly impressed by the way one of the characters had spoken a particular phrase, "Make up your mind." He pronounced this with accuracy and precision. The teacher wrote his account of this picture, had it typed, and used it as reading material the next period.

Popular Songs. Many adolescents are enthusiastically addicted to the current song hits. Mr. Palmer made effective use of this interest in popular songs as displayed by a group of non-reading pupils. Their reading ability was practically zero; they were new in the special reading group, and needed success in reading.

Mr. Palmer had them dictate the words of a song, as he wrote it on the blackboard. They knew the song well enough so that they could "read" the verse on the board with ease. When a skeptic objected that he already knew the song, Mr. Palmer let the pupils prove for themselves that they could recognize individual words from the song when written alone or in sentences, where they could refer back to the original verse if necessary. Several of the boys were so intrigued with this that they copied it down to take with them. Also, boys in the group whose knowledge of the words of the song was a bit uncertain, found that they could go through the entire verse with the written version there in front of them. They could read enough to fill the blanks in their memory and remember enough to fill the blanks in their reading.

In this particular class session, the song happened to be "The Tennessee Waltz," and the words "darling," "lover," "sweetheart," and so on provided occasion for a bit of good-natured banter back and forth. Not every group of pupils could maintain sufficient self-control under this type of stimulus; the teacher who wishes to use the words of popular songs in class may well consider which songs are appropriate for study with the particular class in question.

Advertising Slogans. Many advertising slogans become extremely familiar to non-reading pupils through the radio, television, and hearing people repeat them. Cutting these out of magazines and newspapers so they are associated with the familiar trade mark, and also presenting them written or printed in a style different from the advertisement can help to add these words, as words, to their reading sight vocabulary.

OPERATION OF SPECIAL READING CLASSES

Almost all the procedures described so far can be adapted to the use of the small special reading class. In the present section, which is concerned with principles of operation of special reading classes, teachers may see ways in which the teaching procedures can be applied in special reading classes.

First we shall consider use of the time of the remedial teacher to best advantage. The important problem of selection of pupils for remedial instruction will come next, followed by a discussion of the inseparable problems of diagnosis and remedial instruction. Specific problems of method, not discussed elsewhere in the study, will receive consideration here, as will reading materials. Finally will come the all-important problem of emotional considerations affecting success in remedial classes.

Utilizing the Time of the Remedial Teacher. When a school is fortunate enough to have a trained remedial teacher available, how can this teacher's time be used to the best advantage?

If every pupil with reading ability more than one year behind mental age were considered a candidate for remedial instruction, a very large number of remedial classes would be needed to accommodate them all. A well-qualified reading specialist can very helpfully spend part of his time as consultant for other teachers who have retarded readers in their classes. In this way he may be of better service in helping more pupils meet their reading needs than he would be spending all his time teaching remedial classes in reading. He cannot hope to find a place for all pupils needing remedial reading instruction in his classes, but he can help teachers to find ways of helping them in their regular classes. And he can concentrate his direct attention on pupils most in need of it.

Obviously, remedial classes small enough to permit individual attention are expensive in terms of teacher time. Groups with non-reading pupils or emotionally disturbed, severely retarded readers should be kept at minimum size. Pupils with less severe retardation and without serious emotional difficulties can often work well in somewhat larger groups. There is no advantage in very small groups, however, unless the teacher is prepared to give highly individualized instruction. Fortunate are the non-reading pupils who have an opportunity to be in a very small remedial group with a teacher who is able and willing to utilize the particular advantages of such a teaching situation.

Very important among the duties of the remedial teacher or the reading specialist is the determination, in cooperation with counselors and subject teachers, of just which pupils, non-reading or retarded in reading, will best be able to profit by experience in the remedial groups, and in which specific group each will best fit.

Selection of Pupils. Since remedial classes in reading are so expensive in teacher time, proper selection of pupils for these classes is an important consideration, so that the opportunity of remedial instruction can be offered those most in need and best able to benefit from it. Selection should be made by the remedial teacher in cooperation with counselors and subject teachers so that no teacher gets the impression that the remedial program is not meeting the reading needs of many pupils who most need it. Without proper selection, the remedial class is likely to be filled with pupils whose reading is considered inadequate, but whose potentiality for improvement is not appraised. Such a class can well become a "dumping ground" whose primary function appears to be to relieve regular classes of the burden of non-reading pupils and other problem cases. Under such conditions an effective diagnostic and remedial program is usually not possible.

The concept of reading potential has been described as a pupil's potential reading ability, as contrasted with his actual achievement. Generally speaking, pupils should be selected for remedial classes on the basis of reading potential rather than merely poor reading ability. The pupil whose reading potential is farthest above his reading ability would be the one most in need of remedial help. The pupil who is reading very poorly but who is close to his potential is not as much in need of the remedial instruction as the one whose actual reading may be better, but whose potential is very much higher.

Emotionally disturbed pupils or pupils highly resistant to reading or to all instruction frequently are badly in need of remedial instruction; however, significant improvement may be for them less probable than for other pupils. With such pupils in the class, its total capacity for improvement of reading is not as great as when more promising pupils fill the class. Experience of success in a class with a skilled remedial teacher can be highly beneficial to such pupils, however, in emotional adjustment as well as in improvement of reading. The objectives of remedial classes in a given school, whether emphasis is to be given to emotional help for disturbed pupils or to improvement of reading ability generally, will determine the policy toward selection of such pupils.

Size of class and the remedial teacher's preference for methods will determine the heterogeneity or homogeneity of such a class. Somewhat larger groups may be handled if the teacher can group pupils according to similarity of needs and abilities. Mr. Witt's suggestion that a pupil should be with others of a similar degree of handicap is sound, although complete homogeneity is probably about as far from possibility in a remedial as in any other class.

Classes having been scheduled and pupils selected, the next consideration is what goes on in them.

Diagnosis and Instruction Inseparable. Before the remedy can be devised or applied, the nature of the difficulties must be known. Thus the first function of the remedial teacher is diagnosis.

As a diagnostician, the remedial teacher is responsible for determining the specific difficulties in reading, and if possible something of their underlying causes. It is futile to attempt to catalog every specific difficulty a non-reading pupil may have, for many of them are of relatively little importance until the pupil has developed some basic reading skill. Thus such matters as eye-movements, fixations, and other mechanical skills, important though they may be in the development of efficient reading habits, will concern the remedial teacher working with non-reading pupils less than the amount of reading ability the pupil actually has, compared with his reading potential. The teacher is also concerned with the extent of the pupil's sight vocabulary.

Determination of underlying causes may be impossible, or it may prove relatively simple. The teacher who is familiar with the various factors which tend to block development of reading ability can frequently find these factors in the life of a child through observation, conversation with the child or his parents, school records, or reports from other sources. Very often these factors are beyond the power of the school to correct. Often teachers must accept the existence of such factors and help the child to function as well as possible in spite of them. Sometimes awareness of their existence will itself suggest means of circumventing them. At other times it may appear best for the teacher to concentrate on the matter of helping the pupil to find a variety of satisfactions, some experience of success, personal acceptance, and a happy place for himself in at least one part of his school life, regardless of how much may be accomplished in reading. Miss Grace and Mrs. Silver were very careful to see that all their pupils found at least this much satisfaction in their remedial classes.

It is doubtful that a remedial teacher of reading often is able to arrive at much more than a tentative diagnosis of the reasons for a pupil's reading disability; this diagnosis must always be subject to revision as additional facts become apparent. The diagnosis of the nature of the reading difficulty is not as difficult as determining its cause, of course, although it too must be subject to revision as development occurs and as new facts come to light. It is, nevertheless, important that the diagnostic process continue, for it has great bearing on the concurrent instructional process.

Instruction does not await the outcome of diagnosis; it is actually inseparable from it, often commencing even before the teacher has had opportunity to make diagnostic observations. A large part of the activity in a remedial class in reading is in the nature of a planned routine, based on the characteristics and interests of the group of pupils, but designed to permit the teacher to observe and provide for individual needs among the pupils. As with all good teaching, of course, these classes utilize many different avenues of learning, such as those discussed in Chapter VI. Pupils learn from each other, from the teacher, from the printed page, from audio-visual media, and through various types of activity. Some of these activities deserve special consideration as related to the needs of non-reading pupils.

Kinesthetic Approach to Remedial Reading. Fernald for many years carried on a program of remedial instruction using kinesthetic activities to increase word recognition, as well as for other learnings. By repeatedly tracing words written in blackboard-sized script, while they said the words quietly to themselves, pupils would gradually build up a sight vocabulary of words. These words, on large cards, the pupils would file alphabetically for reference as needed. Fernald reports consistent success with the method, which was indeed used for many years in her highly successful reading clinic. While its use with pupils whose cases are reported in this book was not as consistently successful as Fernald reports, it can be very useful, particularly as one of a variety of approaches.

Fernald's theoretical advocacy of the kinesthetic approach for remedial work is based on the assumption that some pupils learn best through visual or auditory channels, while others learn through kinesthetic channels. These latter pupils are the ones who fail to make satisfactory progress in schools where the predominantly visual or auditory approach

is used; given the opportunity of learning kinesthetically they soon overcome their disabilities. Gates and others have questioned the adequacy
of this reasoning in explaining reading disability. Nevertheless it does
point up the value of a variety of sensory approaches.

A combination of visual and auditory channels of learning is involved
in reading aloud. This familiar school practice has long been subject to
discussion and not a little misunderstanding.

Reading Aloud. Traditionally, in the popular mind, learning to read
means reading aloud. Pupils and their parents take it for granted that in
a reading class pupils are expected to read aloud. Many teachers take it
equally for granted. Other teachers, familiar with research findings on
the futility and even harm of the common practice of expecting pupils to
follow in their books while one pupil haltingly gropes his way aloud
through a text he does not know, may feel that all reading aloud is
undesirable. And yet, puzzled about ways and means of teaching non-
reading pupils without some reading aloud, they may defy either the
research findings as they understand them, or else their conscience, and
ask pupils to read aloud.

Oral reading, of course, is a job in itself. The effort to read aloud can
prevent a child from gaining full meaning from what is read, unless he
reads it silently before or after his oral performance.

Overemphasis on oral reading can lead a child to bad reading habits—
vocalization, lip-movement, word-calling. It leads to emphasis on sound
rather than thought. But oral reading is not all bad; it serves valid
purposes of its own.

There is a real place for reading aloud in a special reading class. It is
an excellent diagnostic procedure, by which the teacher is able to gauge
a pupil's difficulties in reading and appraise his sight vocabulary. With
non-reading pupils who are sensitive about failure, such reading aloud
should be done, of course, privately by the pupil in individual conference
with the teacher, while the rest of the class is otherwise engaged. Similarly, pupils may help each other in pairs or in very small subgroups. No
pupil with reading difficulty should be expected to display his disability
before his class, of course, although much may be gained from having
him demonstrate his ability to read something he has prepared. Mrs.
Silver had an effective use of this procedure, requiring the other pupils
to close their books and listen carefully so that they could answer questions posed by the one who had read aloud. Another approach is to have
a pupil read to entertain his classmates with something he has himself
enjoyed.

Pupils with disability in reading need opportunity for reading aloud
material which they already know, to prove to themselves and to their
classmates that they can indeed read something; the teacher needs an
opportunity, through hearing a pupil read aloud at sight, to appraise
needs and progress. The remedial teacher can safely include reading
aloud among the learning activities of the special reading class, provided

it never becomes a public demonstration of failure and that it never is an unnecessary and monotonous duplication of what the other pupils can see printed right in the pages of their books before them.

The question now arises: What books should pupils in remedial classes have before them?

Reading Materials in Remedial Classes. If pupils are to improve their reading ability, they must have much practice in reading. The classroom for remedial reading needs, therefore, a wide variety and a vast quantity of reading materials, suitable to the ability of the pupils. For pupils who can read as well as fourth-grade level a wide variety of materials is available; for non-reading pupils provision of varied and easy reading materials is a difficult problem. This problem was discussed in the previous chapter, as it applies to work in the regular classroom; it remains a problem in the remedial classroom. Primary-grade reading materials, suitable for non-reading pupils in level of difficulty, are too often quite inappropriate in subject matter and interest level.

Periodicals like *My Weekly Reader* should be available at the various levels of difficulty and should be collected in folders for browsing. Such materials are carefully graded and they are timely. Even secondary school pupils can often find interest in the primary grade *Weekly Readers.*

Books of interesting information, well illustrated, can often be of value to non-reading pupils, even though the text may be slightly more difficult than they can be expected to read. They will go to such sources for information they may wish, and with the aid of the pictures may make good use of them. Books written for elementary school pupils on such subjects as animals, automobiles, sports, how-to-do-it, magic, nature, industries, airplanes, and so on can both motivate natural practice in reading and provide experience in it. Pupils should not necessarily be expected to be able to read such materials aloud word by word; they should, however, be expected to get their information from them accurately. Often they may need generous assistance from the teacher with some of this sort of reading. A good children's encyclopedia, profusely illustrated, can be invaluable to non-reading pupils. *The Golden Dictionary* and *The Golden Encyclopedia* are often much used by the non-reading pupils for accumulation of facts.

For non-reading pupils, commercial materials being as scarce as they are, homemade materials of various sorts are often needed. Stories composed by the pupils or teacher may be typewritten and illustrated either by pupil-made drawings or by illustrations cut from back numbers of magazines. Such magazine illustrations may also be used in vocabulary-building posters, illustrating meanings of various words.

A typewriter can be indispensable in a remedial classroom, both as a motivating device and for its practical use in preparing homemade reading material for pupils. Many pupils love to copy stories they have themselves written on the typewriter; this can be a privilege much prized, particularly by pupils of junior high school age.

A tape recorder in a remedial classroom would have value largely as motivation for reading aloud (what pupil can resist a chance to hear his own voice), as a record of a discussion, or to record interview material for a teacher to review subsequently as a part of a diagnostic study of a pupil. Like the typewriter, the tape recorder can be either a highly useful instrument or it can be a frivolous gadget, depending on how the teacher plans its use.

Reading games are many and varied, and they can be used as serious instructional devices. Pupils prefer to use them strictly for the game element involved, but under the teacher's guidance they can be made to serve both purposes well. Commercially prepared games are often available in book, toy, or school supply stores; a resourceful teacher and class can invent endless variations of these games and even construct original ones. Miss Grace's "word wheels" were made in this way.

The array of teaching materials on display in a remedial classroom can do much to set the stage for constructive work by the pupils. It can lend an aura of both interest and industry to the atmosphere of the room. This fact, plus the necessity for instant availability of a wide variety of materials, makes it almost essential that the remedial classroom have a permanent place in the school building. A teacher can hardly be expected to carry such an array of materials in a suitcase and set it up at the beginning of each period when he arrives in somebody else's room to teach remedial reading.

Attention thus far in this section has centered on what might be considered "supplemental" materials in the remedial reading classroom. From the pupils' point of view these may well be the most worthy of attention. They provide the real motive for reading. They provide the all-important practice without which improvement is sharply limited. They do not, however, always provide the necessary drill or planned practice work. There is a useful place for workbooks and practice materials, if not a dominant place. Pupils themselves often feel the need for practice, drill, and direct instruction. Such material should be selected for its suitability in terms of grade level and problems treated. Here, if anywhere, it may be possible to adapt use of primary grade practice material. Pupils can usually see the need for such practice, and in the privacy of the remedial classroom may engage in it. There is serious doubt as to the effectiveness of any practice material in which pupils engage unless they themselves feel the need for it. Probably the best policy is for the teacher to assign formal drill and practice only when pupils can see how it will help them meet some specific problem which blocks improvement in reading for them at a given time.

It may be well at this time to consider the place of drill in the remedial work of non-reading pupils.

Value of Drill. A non-reading pupil who has become convinced of both the need and the possibility of improving his reading skills will inevitably find that various deficiencies tend to block his progress. Very frequently it is lack of sufficient sight vocabulary which most bothers him. This may lead him to feel the need for drill in word recognition, and perhaps word analysis.

Word recognition may be practiced through the use of cards, games, fill-in workbook-type material, kinesthetic practice at tracing words, and so on. Phonetic analysis of words is of doubtful value for slow-learning non-reading pupils, although it may be of some help to pupils with a better grasp of abstractions, particularly if they have never tried it before.

Drill assignments given the entire remedial group at one time are not likely to be of much value to pupils, unless the teacher is able to contrive a situation in which all the pupils happen to feel the need for just this sort of practice at just this time, perhaps by making the need the focus of a game. Then the teacher has the responsibility for seeing that the learning is carried over into actual use by the pupils in situations other than the game or drill situation. However, it is far better to have pupils working individually on reading tasks meaningful for them, or working on overcoming deficiencies which have been blocking their improvement.

All talk of reading skills, drill, practice, materials, and so on is bound to be futile unless the pupil is emotionally ready to read. What contribution can the remedial class make to this emotional readiness in pupils? This is by no means the only function of a remedial class, but it is so basic that other functions are badly crippled unless it is successful.

Emotional Considerations. Reading disability often results from emotional disturbance of one sort or another; emotional disturbance almost certainly results from reading disability which continues well into adolescence. Remedial classes, therefore, have more than their share of emotionally unstable pupils. Mrs. Silver and Miss Grace subordinated nearly all other instructional considerations to this fact.

The great hope of success in remedial classes is that motivation for reading plus effective guidance for learning, in an atmosphere of optimism, assured success, and personal acceptance, can help to break the vicious circle. Frequently, by the time a pupil is well along in adolescence, the need for reading is so keenly felt, the motivation so powerful, that this atmosphere, with instruction and suitable materials available, almost seems sufficient in itself to start noticeable progress. At other times great patience is required. Motivation may be insufficient; emotional blocking factors may yet be too strong; instructional methods and material may be resisted. Still, little can be accomplished except in such an atmosphere of optimism, success, and acceptance; it may for a time be the only constructive influence the pupil can permit himself to accept from the school.

Factors which tend to spoil such an atmosphere should be carefully avoided in the remedial class. The teacher must remain optimistic and confident that the pupils will find success; opportunity for assured success must be provided repeatedly; possibility of failures must be avoided at all costs; pupils must be accepted and liked as persons by teacher and classmates. Successes and progress can be expected under such conditions, not equal or universal success, but enough to give hope for more successes in the future.

A great value to be found in the organization of remedial classes is the opportunity they afford pupils to witness and find encouragement in each other's successes and progress. Here there is no question of comparison with abler students. Here little bits of progress can be rejoiced in by all. This value can be found only in remedial groups, not in special work with a pupil carried on in a regular class, not in individual case work, valuable though this latter may be.

CONCLUSION

This chapter has not attempted complete consideration of problems connected with the remedial class. Its purpose has been twofold: To give the teacher interested in helping the non-reading pupil some general idea of the special contribution the special reading class can make toward helping him to achieve a usable reading skill; and to point out to the remedial teacher the particular needs of the non-reading pupil in the remedial class.

The remedial class can provide the non-reading pupil with trained attention and a satisfactory setting for the development of reading skills. In such a setting he requires more guidance and attention than do pupils who already have some reading ability on which to build.

43. WAYS TO DEVELOP READING SKILLS AND INTERESTS OF CULTURALLY DIFFERENT YOUTH IN LARGE CITIES

Kay Ware

When assigned the subject of developing reading skills among culturally different youth in large cities, one wishes he could invent a miraculous new formula to make the teaching of these skills a pleasant and profitable activity in the schools. Unfortunately, the mastering of

Reprinted from *Improving English Skills of Culturally Different Youth*, Doris V. Gunderson, Editor, Bulletin No. 5 (Washington: 1964), pp. 142–150. United States Government Printing Office.

the complex and elusive skills of absorbing meanings from textbook pages by children whose social milieu in large cities does not encourage this art becomes for them a tedious chore. We can therefore profitably review certain standard devices for the improvement of reading programs which will always be useful when prosecuted vigorously and constantly.

THE READINESS PROBLEM

There is evident a certain impatience in some quarters with traditional applications of the developed principles of reading readiness. There is some opinion that pupils will learn to read more readily if a formal and almost exclusively phonetic reading program is begun earlier, perhaps in the kindergarten, and that much readiness activity is only an aimless waste of time. Although it is doubtless true that some traditional readiness programs included occasional nonsense, there is no question but that reading, writing, and spelling are, essentially, artificial and derived aspects of oral language. Pupils can be inducted into these more artificial forms of communication only after they have mastered a useful oral vocabulary. The structural linguists tell us that the basic elements of intonation—stress, pitch, and juncture—and syntax are well mastered, if subconsciously, before children come to school. However, among typical preschool youngsters in underprivileged areas in the large cities, this observation simply does not hold. Notoriously, oral language of these children is probably the greatest single handicapping factor in the critically important business of a successful initial reading experience. To throw overboard the brutal facts of life which we have painfully learned about the readiness factors in reading over the past few decades would indeed be folly.

Experience in the large city schools shows conclusively that the great majority of these children have extremely limited conventional vocabularies, that they do not speak readily in the sentence patterns of children from more favorable environments, and that a typical basal reading readiness program sometimes requires three to four times as much time as is expected for the mythically "average" child. Obviously, these oral language limitations are reflections of the meagre and limited experiences of the children.

Anyone who considers the problem naturally assumes that it would be helpful to establish nursery schools for slum children at early ages, and that the major burden of such schools should be the development of backgrounds of experience which would in turn foster the growth of oral communication skills, essential prerequisites to the meaningful use of books. A sound kindergarten program, with essentially similar objectives, in smaller than normal group numbers, would strengthen and buttress such instruction. Now all this has been said before and said often, but it is equally true that the persistent application of these principles on a broad scale for those children who need it most has not been a distinguishing feature of our school reading programs.

UNGRADED PRIMARY PROGRAMS

When children with thin oral language preparation are introduced to formal primary reading programs in large groups, the chances for successful, sequential growth in reading skills are not promising for a large segment of the culturally different children. The very structure of the traditional graded school system presents a discouraging and unyielding facade. The philosophy of the graded school rests on the premise that one can identify a sequential cluster of reading skills which almost all children can master within a specified period of time. Now, it is quite realistic and practicable to identify the total sequence of basic reading skills from the most rudimentary and bumbling stage to that which requires the ultimate in facile perception and appreciation. But one must be most optimistic to expect that masses of pupils can be guided through this maze of complex skills at approximately the same rate by teachers who vary as widely in their range of teaching skill as the pupils vary in learning capacity.

Theoretically, the basic reading skills have to be achieved by pupils before they enter grade four in American schools. During the primary grades most attention is directed to a mastery of word perception skills through the use of narrative which recounts more or less typical incidents in the lives of middle-class suburban children. In grade four the reading material in the textbooks becomes predominantly expository, the vocabulary expands in the various curricular areas, and the child who has been struggling through the primary grade materials on the strength of some partially memorized sight vocabulary sees little purpose in laboriously trying to extract information from textbooks which he does not relate to any of his needs or interests. The streets and alleys, the poolrooms and taverns have a more alluring curriculum for him.

The arbitrary division of the sequence of basic primary reading skills into three annual graded segments is obviously incongruent with respect to the rates at which human beings learn any set of skills. Those who make our reading materials do, of course, with varying degrees of skill and wisdom, begin with the identification of the skills which must be mastered. They then create reading material calculated to develop those skills. That there are clearly discernible stages or clusters of skill in a typical first-grade program is quite apparent if from nothing else than the physical facts of bookmaking: there is, typically, a separate readiness book—or two; separate preprimers—one, two, or usually three; a primer;

and a first reader. Indeed, it would be most miraculous if one cluster of skills could be mastered by almost all pupils within a period of 180 to 200 school days.

Teachers who are poorly prepared to teach reading—and there is compelling evidence that many are—easily confuse the teaching of reading skills with the exposing of children to reading material. Thus, using a basal reading series, it is not uncommon practice for teachers to cover the pages of the readiness book in from 3 to 6 weeks, to hasten coveys of bluebirds, robins, and crows through the preprimers, primers, and first readers so that the "first year" reading program will be completed by the time the summer vacation begins.

Individual differences in learning rates are commonly bowed to by exposing the faster learners to more preprimers, primers, and first readers and by a token adjustment of reading materials to the child, e.g., the slow third-grade child reads from a preprimer.

The deceptive element in this kind of program is the fact that almost all children, when exposed to printed materials often enough, can pick up varying amounts of sight vocabulary without developing real word perception skills. Exposure to prefabricated reading materials designed for "average" conforming suburban children does not guarantee transmission of that basic tool of adjustment to traditional classrooms—the knack of deriving meanings and information from textbooks. As the slum child moves through the graded segments of growth which were never designed for him, his interest, if any, oozes away; and when the compulsory attendance laws no longer restrict his freedom, he escapes from his "concentration camp" and helps form the social dynamite in the jungles of our big cities, as Dr. Conant has pointed out to an all too indifferent American public.

There has been much superficial prattling about the ungraded primary school, the pedagogical machinery designed to remedy some of the factors in this situation, but there is no time now to discuss at any length its philosophy, its virtues, and its common misapplications. The rudimentary facts are these: If we have learned anything at all during these many years of teaching, we can certainly identify the stages or clusters of reading skills which will enable a child to learn from books. We also know that children differ widely—not only in the application of these skills, but also in the *rate* at which they can acquire them. Does it not then stand to reason that we should clearly set forth these stages in terms of skills, the mastery of which must be the true objectives of our teaching, and not in terms of the materials to which children are to be exposed? Must we not also have available all the objective means we can develop to measure the presence or absence of these skills in children, rather than the measures of a sight vocabulary which has accidentally stuck with children and which can be used most disarmingly in suburban school systems to inform the PTA that "we are four months above the national norm"? Must we not, then, move children from one stage of growth to another only after we have real evidence that the skills of the earlier level have been acquired? Must we not move thus in the progression of our teaching and learning without regard for the time which is necessary to do the job, whether it coincides with the semester units or the calendar or not? And must we not exert every effort and exhaust every administrative device to achieve these basic reading skills before we move the children into the first year of secondary education in the American school system? No administrative device, certainly, will automatically improve the efficiency of reading instruction; the ungraded primary school does, however, make improvement more readily possible and appears to be a particularly promising measure for the primary school populations of the large cities.

OTHER ADMINISTRATIVE DEVICES TO IMPROVE READING INSTRUCTION

Rooms of Twenty

No matter how meticulously we plan and execute an ungraded primary program designed to move children carefully from one stage of growth in skills to another, we shall have failures for a variety of reasons. In St. Louis another device has been employed in our effort to send into the fourth grade as few pupils as possible who are unable to work independently with textbooks. As a result, over the years thousands of pupils have been prevented from becoming reading clinic cases. For many years the pupil-teacher ratio has been 35. When pupils have spent 2½ or 3 years in the ungraded primary and have shown that they are still far from reaching the top level, they have been organized into groups of 20 and assigned to a clinic-trained teacher. The teacher is freed from the regular time-allotment schedule and is given the job of bringing her group through the top primary level in reading, language, spelling, handwriting, and arithmetic in one semester, or, at the most, two semesters.

Pupils of these teachers have consistently made twice the normal progress, as measured by standardized tests in these curricular areas. Teachers usually move 10 pupils out in one semester, but need a second semester for the other 10. Normally, from 20 to 60 such units are in operation each school year. With the right teacher and the right materials, this program has proved most useful in the slum areas of the city.

Reading Clinics

When a city school system has a strong classroom reading program and makes other provisions for mentally retarded pupils, a clinic staff with the services of a doctor, a nurse, clerical help, and 4 full-time teachers can service elementary schools with a population of about 15,000 pupils.

The St. Louis Public Schools maintain five such reading clinics, each of which provides diagnosis and remedial teaching for the schools of the district. Principals receive diagnostic service for their pupils upon request and are furnished remedial teaching for their more severe cases. Pupils continue to attend their home schools, and report for 2, 3, or 5 days of individualized instruction for 45-minute periods. Except in unusual cases primary school pupils are not given clinic service, but principals try to identify pupils who will need clinic help as soon as possible after they enter the fourth grade. Each year of delay in providing attention to severe reading problems which cannot be effectively dealt with in the classroom makes the problem more difficult to solve and alienates the child further from the school program.

In St. Louis we have used the reading clinics as teacher training centers which feed back into the schools dozens of teachers with realistic clinic experience. One teacher is permanently in charge in each of the five clinics, but each year three regular classroom teachers are assigned to each clinic for a year of training in diagnostic and remedial procedures. After the year of training, these teachers are reassigned to the schools, some as remedial reading teachers, some as teachers of "Rooms of Twenty," some as regular classroom teachers. Although such a system impairs the efficiency of the clinic operation to some extent, it does, in a large city system, return to the classrooms people who have the skill and experience to deal effectively with the problems which are typical of the culturally different children. At any rate, it seems quite clear that the big city school systems will always have enough deviate cases which cannot be dealt with effectively in a classroom situation to justify the kind of service which is offered by reading clinics.

READING MATERIALS

Basal Readers

There has recently been much criticism of the basal reading series which we commonly use in American schools to teach reading skills. Some of these criticisms have validity, but others show quite clearly a naive unfamiliarity with some of the problems of reading instruction and a tendency to oversimplify the problems. First of all, the use of a single set of basic reading materials in a large city system has much to commend it. The mobility of the pupils in the underprivileged areas of the big cities is extremely high. Some schools have practically a complete turnover of pupil population within 1 school year, and thousands of pupils attend four, five, or more different schools during the primary school years.

Unless these schools use common reading materials, and unless there is a transmission of pupil records—a strong feature of an ungraded primary program, pupils and teachers face a frustrating situation in trying to continue the sequential development of reading skills. Secondly, a strong program of reading instruction in the large cities with a high teacher turnover rate makes continuing inservice programs mandatory; and inservice work can be much more specific, direct, and realistic when a common body of materials is in use. Third, the teacher guides of the basal series, although they have grown extremely voluminous, have probably saved many a beginning teacher from hopeless confusion and discouragement and many a beginning pupil from failure.

The popularly used basal reading series, contrary to the cursory observations of critics who have not taught beginning reading do have more or less systematic programs of word perception skills. They are not evident in the pupils' books and this gives partly informed critics the impression that the basic word perception device is still "look-pray-and-say." However, the word perception program is cautiously and gingerly paced throughout the 3-year program. This caution results from the revolt against the highly mechanistic phonics programs which were jammed into the first-year programs of reading series several decades ago, which, incidentally, most nonteaching critics now offer as a newly discovered solution to all of our reading problems. This cautious pacing—for example, the excessive delay in teaching vowel sounds—distributes the word perception program over so long a period that pupils often fail to perceive the relationships of the parts. It also places the program into the hands of so many different teachers that sequential skill growth on the part of the pupils becomes very difficult to achieve. A return to an isolated, mechanistic phonetic program consisting essentially of tedious and repetitious drill, divorced from interesting and stimulating reading material, gives little promise of solving our problems. We do need different reading material for the culturally different child in the big city. One of its characteristics should be a simplified, closely paced word perception program which will make pupils independent in the word perception skills more quickly than at present.

The content of the basal readers is another matter. Naturally enough, the current story characters, their pets, and the family helpers constitute efforts to base reading material on the experience of "typical" 6-, 7-, and 8-year-olds on the thesis that such material will be more meaningful than the fanciful or moralistic content of the earlier readers. That a child in the slum districts finds the basal reading story characters difficult to identify himself with goes without saying. Some publishers are usually reluctant to bring out reading material for which there is no national market, and the current investment necessary to issue a basal reading series with its attendant paraphernalia may continue to give them cause for concern. Some of the minority group educators may also resist any attempts to produce reading material designed specifically for culturally different children.

This problem of educating culturally different pupils in the large cities, has, however, become so serious that some effort should be made to produce reading content which is more closely geared to the experiences of such children. The word perception programs should be more compact and aggressive, and there should be more simple expository content, in contrast to the present narrative. The teachers' guides should be simplified and curtailed, and much of the pedagogical jargon replaced with incisive, explicit English.

Remedial Reading Materials

Because many culturally different pupils are retarded in grade placement, there is great value in some of the reading material which has been developed for remedial programs. The essential characteristic of such material is that its interest level is more than customarily mature with respect to the reading difficulty. Thus, older pupils who have primary level reading skills can be motivated to read without laboring excessively over material in which they can find no interest.

Library

In the Banneker school district, where administrators and teachers have been carrying on an aggressive campaign to raise the achievement levels of culturally different pupils, successful efforts have been made to extend the reading experiences of children beyond the classroom. Pupils have the usual required outside reading lists at each grade level and are provided with classroom libraries, largely because of a lack of building space for central libraries and insufficient funds under the current budget to employ elementary school librarians.

The school principals have conducted an active campaign of education so that parents understand the importance of recreational reading and the school reading requirements. The public library has arranged a schedule for each of the schools to use the neighborhood branches and the bookmobiles. The librarians and teachers have a system of communication so that the children can get books at the proper reading level. Practically all the pupils in the district have library cards, and the library circulation figures are far higher than they ever have been before. When the city schools establish a sound and effective instructional program, it can profitably be supplemented by an equally vigorous supplementary or recreational reading program. Cooperation with the public librarians is usually not difficult to arrange, and the large cities probably have the best public library facilities available anywhere.

Central libraries in the elementary schools can do much to support and strengthen the classroom programs if enough money is spent to get a really adequate supply of books and to provide librarians. If this is not done, the already overburdened classroom teachers usually have to take on the additional chores. Judicious book selection to fit the needs of the pupils of the community can make the school libraries highly useful in promoting a love for books and for reading.

MOTIVATION: THE VITAL INGREDIENT

The educational situation we face in many areas of the large city school systems requires no elaboration. Our schools are textbook schools which attempt to transmit the cultural knowledge, attitudes, and skills of our civilization largely through the curiously artificial skill of drawing meanings from printed symbols. As mechanization of industry accelerates and as ever-increasing thousands of children huddle in the big city slums and housing projects, the need for the kind of school education our social and industrial civilization rewards can only grow greater. Before we conclude that a great segment of youth is unable to conform to the school regimen and curriculum, and that we must devise a totally new program of education to occupy these youth or to keep them off the streets, we had better make an all-out effort to make our current program succeed. There is some evidence to indicate that we can do much better than we have done in the past.

First, all of us who are engaged in this task need to face reality more fearlessly and honestly than we sometimes do. We are all now deeply concerned about this problem, largely because of fear—fear of the threat to our own security and comfort. It was not very many years ago that relatively few educators really cared whether the minority and culturally different children in the schools succeeded in getting the kind of education necessary to survive in our society, and all too many who were directly concerned with the problem considered the environmental influences too formidable to overcome in the classroom.

But changes are taking place. Dr. Samuel Shepard, director of the Banneker project in St. Louis, has tried, first of all, to induce the principals and teachers in his district to face up to the cruel fact that the academic achievement of the pupils was disgracefully low. He used objective measures of skill, with all of their admitted imperfections. He made graphic pictures of the results and made no secret of them. He takes the position that group intelligence test results are inaccurate because of their environmental loading and that a child's limitations in academic learning are determined only by his drive and determination. His principals and teachers have succeeded, semester by semester, in improving their pupils' achievement scores until they are currently respectable according to national norms. The principals and teachers are proud of their results, and they take pride in their work.

Secondly, he directed his efforts to getting parents to understand the relationship between formal education and the number of dollars one brings home in his pay envelope. He and his staff prepared a series of simple informative charts showing the facts of economic life. The principals urged parents to come to the schools. Dr. Shepard and his staff went, night after night, to every school in his district to tell the parents their story. The staff members explained how school achievement is measured, and they showed the parents just where their children ranked. They explained the importance of reading and how it affects performance in the other curricular areas. They talked about the importance of school attendance and homework; how parents can help the schools—to get the children off the streets, to provide a place to read and study, to turn off the television and the radio during study periods. They prepared a homework notebook, explained its use, and requested the parents to sign it each week. They distributed a parents' pledge of cooperation, a checklist for parents to follow. They have gone back again and again to report progress and to keep the parents working at their job.

Finally, they have told the same story to their students. They have arranged field trips to see people at work, to learn the educational requirements for the better jobs. They have tried to get them to places of cultural interest in the city, to expand their outlook and environment. Each semester they have visited each school to honor the children who have achieved well and those who have made the best gains. There is considerable evidence that these children see opportunities for themselves in the years ahead, and that they are beginning to understand the relationship of what they do in school to the kinds of lives they may lead.

Now these are not new educational inventions. This is not a new educational plan. These are determined and aggressive efforts to get a community and a people to change their attitudes and habits to conform to a completely new set of standards, to convince them that they are going to get a "fair shake" and that they had better be ready to make use of it. We have the answers to many of our problems. To overcome them we need only to apply what we do know—through the medium of dedicated, consecrated teachers with a great cause: To inspire children to make the very best of themselves as they face their world of the future.

44. A REMEDIAL READING PROGRAM

Harold Newman

The special reading classes at Woodrow Wilson Vocational High School were organized to cope with a school wide problem of reading retardation. Scores on the *Nelson Silent Reading Test Form A,* administered in September, 1958, indicated that sixty per cent of the students in the tenth year were reading more than four years below their grade level.

It was felt that special reading classes would be of value to these and other pupils who because of their reading handicap were unable to profit from their work in a regular English class. In addition, it was hoped that such a reading program, by ministering to the needs of retarded readers, could reduce grade failure, disciplinary problems, and possibly the number of school dropouts.

Aims of the Program

The remedial reading classes were organized primarily to serve the needs of pupils whose reading disability interfered with their school adjustment. The objectives of these reading classes were:

1. To help each pupil improve his reading skill so that he could experience greater satisfaction in his school work.
2. To help each pupil acquire those basic reading skills essential for the satisfaction of his personal, socio-civic, and vocational needs.
3. To help each pupil enjoy reading.

Selection of Pupils

Selection of pupils for the classes in remedial reading were based on these methods:

1. *The administration of a standardized reading test.* In March of each year Form A of the *Nelson Silent Reading Test* was administered to all tenth year pupils. Pupils whose reading level was sixth grade or below were selected as possible candidates for the remedial reading classes. New entrants from elementary and some junior high schools were not given special reading tests. Their previous reading scores were the basis for tentative selection.

Reprinted from *High Points,* Vol. 47 (January 1965), pp. 31–40. By permission of the New York City Board of Education.

2. *Recommendations by subject class teachers.* Two months before the end of each semester, all English teachers were requested to submit the names of pupils unable to benefit from instruction in a regular English class because of poor reading habits. These recommendations, based on observation of the pupils' everyday work habits, were a valuable means of identifying pupils who needed special help in reading.

3. *Referrals made by the guidance department.* In their investigation of reasons accounting for behavior problems, guidance counselors frequently found that poor academic performance was associated with inability to read class assignments. Because of this reading disability, many pupils would become annoyed at their inadequacy and become boisterous, apathetic, or withdrawn. The guidance counselors frequently sent referrals to the reading teachers asking that such pupils be considered for remedial instruction.

4. *Requests made by parents and pupils.* Occasionally a parent, becoming concerned about his child's inability to do his homework, would write a note to the reading teacher or visit the school to request special help in reading for his child. Also, pupils having difficulty in a regular English class might make a personal request to enter the reading class.

5. *Personal interview with the pupil.* Prior to placing pupils in the reading classes, eligible pupils were interviewed, because despite recommendations of teachers, guidance counselors, and parents, some pupils are reluctant to enter a reading class. They fear being labeled or stigmatized as a slow reader. Others are convinced that they can succeed in their regular classes if they apply themselves. The students' wishes are respected. Frequently pupils who originally refuse such help will voluntarily request it at a future date. On the basis of the interview, students are selected or rejected for special help. Preference is given to those pupils whose reading level is below 6.0, and who seem most likely to benefit from special instruction. Students are most often selected for remedial help when they are in their freshman and sophomore years.

Organization of the Classes

There were five remedial reading classes, each containing from twenty to twenty-five pupils who attended class five days a week for forty minute periods. Those who successfully completed the remedial reading course received academic credit in English.

The organization of the reading classes was flexible, pupils being permitted to transfer into and out of classes during the first six weeks and also at the end of the term. Ordinarily, they remained in the reading classes for one year unless they or their reading teacher believed a change was necessary. Pupils who transferred out of the reading classes went to Remedial English which simplified the work of the regular English class. Replacements for those pupils were selected from a waiting list.

INSTRUCTIONAL PROCEDURES

An informal diagnosis of the word analysis skills of the students revealed widespread inability to apply principles of phonetic, structural, and contextual analysis. In order to help them achieve more adequate word analysis skills, a three-pronged attack was necessary.

Phonetic Analysis

Instruction in phonics was designed to help students recognize, identify, and pronounce consonant and vowel elements in varied positions in words and syllables and understand simple generalizations such as those governing short and long vowels and the soft and hard sounds of letters like "C" and "G."

As an aid to understanding phonetic principles, with pupil help I devised an approach using pictures to illustrate the relationship between letters and sounds. These pictures served as mnemonic aids in helping to associate letter sounds with their visual equivalents. Among the exercises used to develop proficiency in the use of phonics were underlining rhyming words, making new words by changing the initial, medial, or final sound, spelling words containing short and long vowels, discriminating between sounds likely to cause misreading, and changing words by substituting double vowels for single vowels.

Structural Analysis

The fact that many students were unable to recognize inflected or derived forms of words highlighted the need for work in structural analysis. Help was needed in recognizing and identifying words formed by changes in tense, number, and degree; understanding the function of prefixes and suffixes; understanding basic principles governing contractions, use of the possessive case, changing "y" to "i," and syllabication.

Some of the exercises used to reinforce the learning of basic principles or generalizations were making new words by adding "ing," "er," and "ed"; writing out contractions; drawing lines between prefixes and suffixes; identifying root words; writing and recognizing compound words; changing "y" to "i" before "ed," "er," and "est"; dividing words into syllables.

Contextual Analysis

To encourage students to make intelligent guesses about the meanings of words encountered in their reading, I stressed the importance of rereading the sentence for clues to the meaning of the unknown word. Students were encouraged to make use of italics or bold face type; definition or direct explanation (e.g., A *spelunker*, a person who loves to explore caves, often has to carry a rope and a box of matches); comparison or contrast (e.g., Some parts of the story were interesting; other parts were *boring*); personal experience (e.g., After the person was tied up, he tried to *unfasten* the ropes.).

Frequently the students found that words could be "figured out" through a combination of contextual analysis and phonic and structural clues. Exercises like the following were used to encourage this approach: Because of the sl—— (*sleepy, slippery, sleet*) road, the man's car sk—— (*skipped, skidded, skated*) into another car.

Vocabulary Building

All of the students had meager vocabularies which impaired their power to understand what they read and heard. Vocabulary improvement consequently became an important part of the reading program. Several methods were used to build vocabulary.

Each student kept a notebook of words encountered in his in-school and out-of-school reading. These words tended to be related to social studies, trade subjects, and hobbies. The student entered the difficult word, its meaning, and a sentence illustrating its meaning. Once every two weeks each student was encouraged to talk about one or two words of particular interest to him. On occasion these talks were enlivened by blackboard illustrations.

Dictionary Work and Other Activities

Because most students failed to use dictionaries properly, I provided practice in these skills: alphabetizing groups of words containing the same initial letters, using guide words to determine which words will be found on a certain page, selecting the appropriate definition of a word which fits the context, using the dictionary as an aid to spelling and pronunciation.

Other word building activities included:

1. Listing on the blackboard pertinent words and idioms in the introductory discussion of a topic

2. Forming and diciphering words made up of prefixes, suffixes, and roots
3. Classifying words on the basis of their relationship to other words
4. Changing the meaning of sentences by using synonyms and antonyms
5. Discussing interesting word origins.

Oral Reading

Oral reading activities provided the pupils with an opportunity to apply their word recognition skills. Omissions, substitutions, reversals, and mispronunciations were diagnosed and provided material for future instruction. In general, students recognized the need to improve their vocabulary and speech. Instruction in oral reading for less seriously retarded readers stressed the importance of punctuation as an aid to proper enunciation, phrasing, and emphasis. This aspect of reading instruction was closely linked to that of increasing eye-voice span.

During literature lessons oral reading was frequently used to clarify an idea and to prove a point.

Silent Reading Activities

Low scores on the *Nelson Silent Reading Tests* and poor textbook comprehension pointed up the need for intensive work in deriving the main idea from a passage, relating the supporting details to the main idea, distinguishing between essential and non-essential information, and drawing conclusions and making inferences. *Basic Reading Skills For High School Use,*[1] *Practice Reader Series,*[2] *Reader's Digest Reading Skill Builder,*[3] *Reading For Meaning,*[4] and *The Reading Improvement Skill Test Series*[5] were helpful. When students had finished reading silently from *Teen Age Tales,*[6] *News Time*[7] or *Junior Scholastic,*[8] they

[1] William S. Gray, Marion Monroe, and Sterl A. Artley, *Basic Reading Skills For Junior High School Use,* Scott, Foresman and Company, Chicago, 1957.

[2] Clarence R. Stone and others, *Practice Readers Series* (Books I–IV) Webster Publishing Company, St. Louis, 1941–1944.

[3] *Reader's Digest Skill Builders,* Reader's Digest Educational Service, Pleasantville, New York, 1953.

[4] W. S. Guiler and J. H. Coleman, *Reading For Meaning,* Books 4–8, J. B. Lippincott Company, Philadelphia, 1955.

[5] Eleanor M. Johns and others, *Reading Improvement Skill Text Series,* Charles E. Merrill Company, New York, 1947.

[6] Ruth M. Strang, Ralph Roberts and others, *Teen Age Tales,* Books A,B, 1–6, D. C. Heath and Company, New York, 1953.

[7] *News Time,* Published by Scholastic Corporation, New York.

[8] *Junior Scholastic,* Published by Scholastic Corporation, New York.

were often asked to write answers to questions designed to test their ability to apply these comprehension skills.

The SRA Reading Laboratory,[9] which was used once a week, also contained interesting questions testing mastery of basic reading skills.

Free Reading

To encourage pupils to read for enjoyment the author set up a classroom library containing many easy to read books and magazines of interest to adolescent boys and girls. Students who were unable to find what they wanted were permitted to use the school library. During the free reading period, I guided pupils in selecting materials in keeping with their reading needs and ability levels, conferred with them about books they were presently reading, and gave some skills instruction.

EVALUATION OF RESULTS

The Vocational Division of the New York City Board of Education requires a standardized test to measure the reading growth of all pupils in remedial reading classes. At the beginning of the term in which remediation began, *Form A* of the *Nelson Silent Reading Test* was administered. A comparable form of the test, *Form C*, was administered at the end of the year to determine reading progress.

Table I

Table I on the following page indicates that groups with higher mean initial reading scores made more progress in a shorter period of time than groups with lower mean initial reading scores. The group whose initial reading level was fifth grade and above made almost three times as much progress as the groups whose reading levels were below fifth grade. Of interest is the fact that regardless of the severity of initial reading retardation, each group showed gains which exceeded normal expectancy. (Normal expectancy for normal students is a five month gain within a period of five months, or one term.)

The data in Table I actually understate the reading achievement of these students. Their reading gains are seen in truer perspective if one realizes that a large number of students made almost as much progress during the relatively short period of remediation as they had made during their entire elementary school years.

[9]Don Parker, *S.R.A. Reading Laboratory,* Elementary and High School Editions, Science Research Associates, 1960.

Teachers Evaluated Students

In order to measure student's academic adjustment after leaving the reading classes, social studies and English teachers were asked to evaluate their reading competency.

TABLE I

Reading Achievement of Seventy-Seven Students[*] Based on a Comparison of Their Initial and Final Mean Scores

Reading Score	N	Initial Mean	Range	Range	Final Mean	Mean No. Terms of Instruc-tion	Mean No. Months Gained Per Term
Below 3.0	25	2.2	0–2.9	2.1–4.0	3.4	2.7	5.3
3.0–4.9	30	4.0	3.0–4.9	3.8–9.0	5.9	2.2	6.7
5.0 and up	22	5.5	5.0–7.9	5.8–9.6	7.5	1.4	16.2

These students were still in school subsequent to receiving remediation during the period from September, 1958 to June, 1961.

Table II shows that more than 60 per cent of the students were deemed inadequate readers in both subjects. Less than 20 per cent were rated as possessing adequate reading comprehension in both subjects. No student whose reading score was below 6.0 was rated as having satisfactory understanding of both his social studies and English reading assignments. Almost all students whose reading score was on an eighth grade level or above were rated as adequate readers in both subjects.

A School-Wide Reading Program

Some would argue that those pupils deemed inadequate readers in social studies and English probably should never have been placed in reading classes because what small gains they made would be subverted by their inability to adjust to the more rigid requirements of "regular" classes. In view of the increasingly larger numbers of poor readers who are entering our schools, it would be wiser for subject teachers to modify their standards, procedures, and methods in order to help the academic adjustment of poor readers.

TABLE II

Distribution of Students According to Teachers' Estimates of Their Reading Competency in English and Social Studies

Reading Score at End of Remediation	N	COMPETENCY IN READING COMPREHENSION		
		Adequate in Both Soc. St. and English	Adequate in Either Social St. or English	Inadequate in Both Soc. St. and English
Below 3.0	14			14
3.0–4.9	28		3	25
5.0–5.9	10		2	8
6.0–6.9	10	2	4	4
7.0–7.9	6	4	1	1
8.0 and up	9	8	1	
Total	77	14	11	52

The isolated period of reading instruction should be abandoned in favor of a school-wide reading program. The remedial reading program must be broadened in scope to provide parallel reading-centered core sections in science, math, social studies, and human relations. The core provides a more personalized and functional approach to reading instruction and allows for greater teacher-learner continuity.

Improving a student's ability to read in specific content material will improve his general ability as well. The present isolated period of remedial reading would be replaced by a Communications Skills core in which reading would be the core around which a related language arts program could be developed. Several units in this core might be centered around the world of work. They would be designed to help pupils obtain occupational information and possibly some vocational guidance which could enhance their chances of obtaining jobs, holding them, and advancing in them. Reading material might include such topics as: applying for a job, behavior during the interview, proper work habits and attitudes, safety on the job, and union membership. Specific instruction in word analysis abilities, including phonics, structural analysis, and spelling, would be woven into the units. The work-oriented nature of the material would provide a functional approach to vocabulary, paragraph comprehension, and oral and writing activities.

45. BEGINNING READING PROGRAMS FOR
THE CULTURALLY DISADVANTAGED
Millard H. Black

How many of you ever have lived in a mining town, where the companies dominated the total economic and social structure? The tragedy of Appalachia is not alone in the physical need of the people. The depression years of the thirties showed me that there is more than one kind of poverty and that the most tragic, the most enduring, is that of the mind and spirit, a poverty unrecognized by those whose need is greatest.

Almost forty years ago I was a high school pupil in an Oklahoma mining town, where the population of 20,000 had no public park, no swimming pool, no boys' club, no library, no concerts. To our high school came an Australian, an ex-professional soccer player—not as football coach, but as music teacher. To the 150 of us who were in his band and orchestra and glee clubs, he brought glimpses of a life we had never imagined. He led us to see that there were symphonies and oratorios, as well as the nasal hillbilly songs and the rhythmic, emotional church music we had known all of our lives. It was he, rather than the English teacher, who revealed to us the music that lies concealed in the poetry of 17th and 18th century England.

Here was a teacher who came to a town which, while not poor economically, would have—by almost any other criterion—contended successfully for the doubtful title of "The Most Disadvantaged American City."

I am concerned, as I see vast sums of money being channeled into special school programs, that we school people will view deprivation either as an impersonal blight affecting such and such an area, or will consider only the economic and physical attributes of poverty. I would urge that we look into the needs of the spirit of the boys and girls who live in disadvantaged communities. As we are helping these young people to develop skills which can raise their economic potential, let us at the same time raise their cultural horizon.

What to *include* and what to *exclude* are sobering questions when a speaker is initially planning a discussion regarding beginning reading programs for the culturally disadvantaged. The nearer to the deadline, the greater the concern and frustration one experiences. Several alternatives present themselves: to report only those programs one personally has observed; whether to include those which have been described in

Reprinted from *First Grade Reading Programs, Perspectives in Reading,* James Kerfoot, Compiler and Editor, No. 5 (Newark, Delaware, 1965), pp. 150–172. By permission of Millard H. Black and The International Reading Association.

detail in school district or departmental publications but insufficiently reported in professional journals; or, as a third possibility, to include as well programs which already have been reported, in order to present a balanced picture of the kinds of experimentation which are being conducted. Whether to discuss only innovations or to include reports of the successful use of traditional methods and materials also must be resolved.

This report will concern itself with programs observed in Southern California; with the City Schools Reading Program, developed in Detroit; and with the experimental use of the Fries linguistic materials in the Philadelphia public schools.

Retardation in total language development among culturally disadvantaged children is an assumption common to many of the programs designed to facilitate growth in reading skill in pupils within this group.

A goal common to all the programs is the improvement of other facets of language, as well as reading.

Factors to be considered in reporting programs for a particular category include:

1. The specific application of methods also useful in many other kinds of classrooms.
2. The difficulties inherent in distinguishing among the needs presented by bilingual children—children who are culturally *different* but who may not possess other characteristics of cultural disadvantage —and by those who appropriately are termed "disadvantaged."

This discussion, with one exception, will focus upon the use of instructional materials or techniques initially designed for use with pupils of many differing backgrounds. The emphasis upon particular problems of the disadvantaged will be reported under the heading "rationale" as each program is described.

Six types of beginning reading programs will be discussed. The title of this particular report—and perhaps its greatest emphasis—is at variance with the subject of this fifth Perspectives in Reading volume: First Grade Reading Programs. I obtained permission to deal with the somewhat broader problem of "Initial Reading Instruction for the Culturally Disadvantaged." The reason for this point of view will be discussed in the last two categories. The types of experimental programs with which this report is concerned are:

1. Specially Designed Basal Instructional Materials
2. Adaptations of Commercial Materials
3. Programmed Basal Instructional Material
4. Phonic Emphasis Used to Supplement Instructional Materials
5. The Language-Experience Approach
6. Pre-School Communication Skills Development Programs

A brief discussion of administrative action designed to enhance the teaching of reading to the culturally disadvantaged also will be included.

SPECIALLY DESIGNED BASAL INSTRUCTIONAL MATERIALS

City Schools Reading Improvement Program.[1] Presses are busily turning out materials designated by authors and publishers as being "especially for the culturally disadvantaged." All too frequently, such materials have been written by persons who have no expertise; or are adaptations or rewrites of an earlier project which might or might not have been successful, either educationally or commercially. In some instances, these so-called specialized materials are little more than "color-me-brown" workbooks. These comments are not applicable to the City Schools Reading Program,[2] which will include all the readers and instruction.

Rationale. The materials were designed to introduce in beginning reading books non-Caucasian figures in other-than-affluent families. They also attempted to provide models of appropriate language structure through which the pupil might develop good usage.

Description of the Program. Whipple summarizes the unique characteristics of the program in this way:

1. The story characters represent races other than Caucasian, permitting pupils from multi-cultural neighborhoods to more readily identify themselves with the story content.
2. The development of correct speech patterns is promoted in "extraordinary ways." The "natural, familiar speech patterns of the culturally disadvantaged children" were introduced gradually and in accord with good usage. Thus it was hoped that the pupil could be helped toward correct modes of expression.
3. Unusually high interest value was provided, upon the assumption that because culturally disadvantaged children came from homes where reading is not a common recreational pattern, they have had "no pleasurable experiences in reading and lack the desire to learn to read."
4. Shorter, more numerous books (at the preprimer level) were provided in the city schools Series than is customary, so that the pupil may experience "the pleasure of accomplishment at the earliest possible moment, since he comes from a home in which long-term goals are seldom sought."
5. Social objectives, as well as skill objectives, are emphasized.[3]

---

[1] Gertrude Whipple. Appraisal of the City Schools Reading Program (Detroit Public Schools, Division for Improvement of Instruction, Language Education Department, Nov., 1963).

[2] Cooperatively developed by the Detroit Public Schools and the Follett Publishing Company.

[3] Whipple, *ibid.,* pp. 1–2.

The first three preprimers have the familiar family orientation, with this notable difference: the family unit which serves as the story-vehicle is Negro while Caucasians are represented by one little boy.

Whipple reports that "words for the basic vocabulary were chosen with great care. They were selected from a reservoir of words which are widely but incorrectly used. Active verbs were employed in relatively great number, for the child can act them out in the process of learning their meaning. . . . They gave preference to words helpful in developing a strong phonetic program."[4] Extraordinary repetition also was provided.

Belief in the basic educational value of the basal reader approach to initial reading instruction with culturally disadvantaged children was emphasized in the appraisal of the program:

> Progress in preparing reading materials for young children results, not from taking an entirely new point of departure, but from utilizing and improving procedures which have been found valuable in classrooms.[5]

Current Status. Detailed results of the use of the first three preprimers have been reported. Six first grade classes started with the city schools preprimers and six classes with the preprimers from a widely used basal reader series, designated in this report (as in the Detroit evaluation) as the "Standard Series." After a certain period, each class switched books. Immediately after completing a series, pupils were tested on that series to ascertain their progress. After both series had been taught, their relative interest appeal was determined, as were pupil attitudes toward characters in the two series.

The social ratings of the schools participating in the study were described by the investigator in this way:

> In summary it may be said that the Caucasian classes participating in this study were above average or superior in social and economic conditions. The Mixed classes ranked lower and included one class in which many pupils faced serious personal problems. As for the Negro classes, one Negro class was somewhat better than average in socio-economic conditions, while the other three Negro classes included the largest proportions of culturally disadvantaged pupils in any of the groups.[6]

The chief findings and conclusions of the experimental use of these materials were reported by Whipple to be:

1. *Racially mixed setting.* It was reported by the teachers that "the children made no mention of the fact that the group of playmates appearing in the city schools books is racially mixed. In all classes, Caucasian, Mixed, and Negro, the children manifested a marked preference for the City Schools Series. When asked to indicate the child character they preferred as a schoolmate and playmate, the children gave highest rank to the Negro

[4] *Ibid.,* p. 1.
[5] *Ibid.,* p. 2.
[6] *Ibid.,* p. 2.

characters. . . . Nevertheless, every evidence indicated that the choices were not made on the basis of race. . . ."[7]

2. *Verbal competence*. With the total group of pupils, the City Schools Series was significantly more effective than the Standard Series in promoting word recognition. In oral reading, the differences between the averages of the total population for the two series were slight, but with an apparent trend in favor of the City Schools Series.

With boys, the experimental materials were much more successful than the Standard Series in promoting oral reading skill. The average score attained by the boys on the City Schools materials was exactly the same as that attained by the girls on the Standard Series.

The most striking increase in oral reading skill through using the experimental material was for the Negro group; its number of perfect scores in the word recognition test was more than twice that on the Standard Series, a difference which was statistically highly significant. A correspondingly lower average number of errors was observed with the use of the City Schools materials.

3. *Desire to read*. High interest in the experimental material was evidenced, both statistically and in observed reactions of all pupils.

The City Schools Series also was especially popular with boys, and with the culturally disadvantaged group, most of whom were Negroes.

4. *Length of books*. It was reported by teachers that the smaller number of stories in each of the preprimers (as compared with the Standard Series) was an incentive toward growth in reading, in that pupils appeared to equate success with the early completion of a book.

5. *Social relationships*. While objective comparisons were not possible, the investigators believe that greater social growth occurred with the City Schools materials than with the Standard Series.[8]

This conclusion was reached by Whipple:

. . . data presented in this report have shown clearly that this city-oriented series is used successfully by culturally-varied urban children including those living in high as well as low socio-economic areas. It meets the needs of urban children in general, and is recommended for unsegregated use because the series as a whole is truly representative of city life.[9]

Research in Progress. Research necessary to the development of the readers is an on-going activity. However, an extensive experiment similar to that which validated the assumptions and content of the first three (of five) preprimers necessarily must be delayed until additional readers have been completed.

Miami Linguistic Series.[10] The Miami Linguistic Series is being used experimentally in a number of elementary schools, both in the Los

[7] *Ibid.*, p. 30.

[8] *Ibid.*, pp. 30–32.

[9] *Ibid.*, p. 32.

[10] Ralph F. Robinett. Production Director, *Miami Linguistic Readers, Level Four*, Miami, Florida: Board of Public Instruction, 1964, pp. i–ii.

Angeles City School District and in other districts in Southern California, as a part of a nationwide Ford Foundation Project directed by Pauline M. Rojas. These schools are situated in areas predominantly populated by persons of Mexican-American background. Since Ralph Robinett, Production Director of the Series and Assistant Director of the project, has reported in Chapter Nine on this particular project, it will not be described in this report.

Fries Linguistic Materials. Individuals interested in research on the teaching of beginning reading to culturally disadvantaged pupils through linguistically oriented materials are referred to Chapter Four by Charles C. Fries. In an address to the National Council of Teachers of English, Rosemary Green Wilson of the School District of Philadelphia described the initiation of an experiment in the use of linguistic materials.

Current Status. Gains of children involved in this program were described in this way:

1. Great gains in achievement for groups of our least mature, most under-privileged children in mastery of the alphabet, security in reading, enjoyment of reading, retention over the summer. (No nonreaders by end of year.)
2. Great gains from the rapid learners in permitting them at the end of one year to advance into the stage of "productive reading."
3. Concomitant gains in spelling and creative sentence and story writing.
4. Noticeable increase in interest in reading on the part of the boys in our classes.
5. Very favorable reaction on the part of teachers in the experimental program, even those who had taught thirty or more years.
6. Much more meaningful "independent learning activities" could be planned from the earliest stages.

Research in Progress. Continued research in the use of the Fries' materials for beginning reading instruction has been assured through a grant from the U.S. Office of Education.

ADAPTATIONS OF COMMERCIAL MATERIALS

An experiment cooperatively conducted by the Los Angeles City Schools and Occidental College involves the use of commercially produced non-basal reading materials[11] among classes representing different socio-economic groups.

Rationale. The assumptions upon which this research was initiated in the school year 1962–63 included these:

1. Boys would learn to read more quickly if they were instructed in sex-segregated groups.

[11] Selma Wasserman and Jack Wasserman. *Sailor Jack and Homer Potts,* 1961; *Sailor Jack and Eddy,* 1961; and *Sailor Jack,* 1960. Chicago: Benefit Press.

2. Boys would learn to read more quickly from high-interest material than from traditional primary level materials.

Description of the Program. Approximately 600 children in the first grade in various elementary schools in Los Angeles were taught reading in sex-segregated groups. Other variables, such as the sex of the teacher, the time of day of instruction, and the socio-economic level of the learner, were investigated.

During the year 1963–64, the second year of the research, experimentation was focused upon materials of instruction which were built around the male-interest-oriented books. In 1964–65, a variety of teacher-made supplementary materials, designed to intensify and reinforce the stimulus of the printed symbol, was added to the design. Included were:

1. An introductory sound film, produced by students of Jo M. Stanchfield, Associate Professor of Education, Occidental College, and principal investigator in this project.
2. Phoneme boxes, which consisted of teacher-prepared boxes for each child containing pictures which were representative of the letter or group of letters appearing on the card.
3. Individual flannel boards, with appropriate materials and individual blackboards and pocket charts.
4. Paper-bag puppets.

All of the above items were used in the structured readiness program, which emphasizes discovery and recognition of letter-sound relationships, rather than the spending of weeks upon weeks in a readiness activity book.

A wide range of supplementary materials to be used once the readers themselves were introduced also was developed. This included:

1. Printed practice or follow-up activities providing practice in the skill developed in each lesson in the reader.
2. Transcriptions (tapes) to be used at listening centers, providing each child an opportunity to re-read the textbook as he completed follow-up exercises in listening and following directions.
3. Colored slides of the pictures in the texts were used to develop new stories with repetition of the words learned in stories in the readers.
4. Study prints, based on characters and incidents in the books, enabled the teacher to develop the vocabulary of the readers in an auditory situation and provided incentives for pupils to write their own stories.
5. Short stories using the basic vocabulary in new situations were duplicated, providing opportunity for pupils to illustrate these newly learned words.

Current Status. At the end of the year 1962–63 test data revealed that separating the boys from the girls did not help the boys to learn to read better; the girls achieved significantly more in both the experimental and control groups.

Data for 1963–64 again showed no statistically significant differences between the scores of the experimental and control groups, although a trend toward greater growth by the experimental group was observed.

Test data were supplemented by two-hour interviews of each teacher in the experiment.

Stanchfield reached these conclusions concerning the culturally disadvantaged portion of the population of the study:

1. The *activity level* of boys, and particularly those who might be termed "disadvantaged," was much greater than girls.
2. When evaluating *verbal facility*, the teachers reported the frequent use of incomplete and fragmentary sentences, especially among the culturally disadvantaged. Stanchfield observed that when mixed classes were taught, some of the teachers erroneously believed that the boys and girls were participating equally.
3. *Auditory discrimination* was developed with greater difficulty among boys than girls, and that still greater difficulty and differences were observed among those pupils in low socio-economic schools. It was reported that it many times would take boys ten lessons to learn and recognize sounds that the girls could identify in three lessons.
4. *Listening skills* were less easily developed among boys than girls, and among culturally disadvantaged pupils than among those in higher socio-economic levels. It was observed that boys listened more effectively when more than one sense was employed; i.e., they were engaged in parallel use of vision, touch, etc.
5. The maximum *attention span* of first grade, culturally disadvantaged boys tended to be about 12 minutes, while that of girls was almost double that period. However, this observation was qualified by a number of teachers who observed: "It depends upon the activity. Boys can pay attention for a long time if they're doing something active and dynamic, either mental or physical."
6. In the area of *goals and motivations*, teachers reported that culturally disadvantaged boys were less anxious to please the teacher, less self-motivated in learning to read, evidenced less adequate work habits, and were less desirous of assuming responsibility than were boys of average or above-average economic level. Boys as a group also tended to be more deficient in these areas than did the girls.
7. In analyzing the *interests* of children in the experiment, Stanchfield concluded that culturally disadvantaged pupils did not adequately respond to the situations depicted in currently available primary reading material.

Research in Progress. Data from the most recent testing of pupils using for the first time all of the reinforcers developed during the summer of 1964 and included in the description of the program (above) now are being processed. Analysis of these data will not be completed for some time.

Stanchfield recently received a Rosenburg Foundation grant to pursue this experimentation in teaching beginning reading from high-interest materials. Tentative data will be available in 1965–66, but this phase of her work will not be completed until the end of the school year 1967–68.

Prognosis. If one may generalize from the experiments conducted by Whipple and Stanchfield which were alike in some respects, it may be tentatively concluded that beginning reading instruction with culturally disadvantaged pupils may be more effectively accomplished with materials which:

1. Provide opportunity, through illustrations and text, for pupils to identify themselves with the characters in the stories.
2. Employ speech patterns with which pupils are familiar.
3. Are high in interest value, an item of particular importance when teaching boys to read.
4. Provide *many* meaningful repetitions of vocabulary in an interesting manner.
5. Make provision for the shorter attention span evidenced by culturally disadvantaged children.
6. Facilitate early and continued success in reading.

PROGRAMMED BASAL INSTRUCTIONAL MATERIAL

Sullivan Associates Programmed Reading. The results of instruction with programmed reading material are being investigated in a cooperative project between UCLA and the Santa Monica and the Monrovia Unified School Districts. A Ford Foundation grant has been received by Arthur Lundaine, Professor of Education; and John McNeill, Associate Professor of Education, and Harriett Foster, Associate Research Psychologist, are responsible for the details of the project.

Rationale of the Program. The investigators believe that the Sullivan materials may possess two chief values:

1. Because the pupils may proceed at their own pace, unlimited opportunity to react to each learning task is provided.
2. Because verification of success is inherent in the completion of the learning tasks, continuing gratification or reassurance is provided.

Description of the Program. The Sullivan materials consist of fourteen basic books, seven of which the average first-grade pupil would be expected to complete during the first year of instruction. These are in the familiar workbook-type format and usable only by one pupil; a crayon whose marks disappear after about twenty minutes may serve to reduce the per-pupil cost of the program.

Two kinds of supplementary materials are available: a series of exercises designed to reinforce the skills developed in each book, and storybooks to be read independently in connection with each of the basic instruction books.

Current Status. The project was designed to investigate:

1. The influence of four variables as first-grade pupils were taught to read from the Sullivan *Programmed Reading* materials: (a) intelligence, as evaluated by the Binet or WISC; (2) sex; (3) bi-lingualism; and (4) socio-economic background.
2. Possible interaction effects with program and non-program subjects.
3. The manner in which the program is used by different teachers in the experiment.
4. The effects of using the publishers supplementary materials.

The investigators plan to compare pupils in relation to data obtained on each pupil in September (1964) before instruction was initiated; additional tests are scheduled to be administered in February, May, and October (1965).

In at least two schools, comparisons will be made of pupils of the experimental teachers under program (this year's first grade) and non-program (last year's first grade, now enrolled in the second grade) instruction.

Records of the number and titles of library-type books read by pupils also will be maintained.

No statistically significant differences in the achievement of the control and experimental groups were reflected in the data obtained from the tests administered in February. McNeill and Foster believe that while no conclusions can be drawn at this state of the experiment, that differences in average performance or in variability of individual performance may be found as additional data become available.

Prognosis. At this time, the investigators believe that more rigid controls need to be exercised in the way the programmed materials, as well as other materials of instruction, are used in the classrooms. It is their belief that variables are operative for which controls have not been provided, and that to the extent to which these variables are present the results of the experiment may not be definitive.

Therefore, it is planned that the present project will be completed as scheduled (October, 1965) and that a second phase will be initiated, in which the use of all instructional materials will be subject to less variation.

PHONIC EMPHASIS USED TO SUPPLEMENT INSTRUCTIONAL MATERIALS

Eclectic Phonetic Emphasis. This title may be a misnomer, for certainly the program observed at Ninety-third Street Elementary School in Los Angeles consists of much more than supplementary phonics drill.

Rationale. The very great concern of the principal of this school, located in a low socio-economic area and comprised almost wholly of Negro pupils, for the development of reading skills was expressed by him in this way: "If a child can read he can do anything; if he *can't* he can do nothing." Consistent with this philosophy, the school program centers around reading, emphasizing to a marked degree this phase of the communication skills.

Description of the Program Materials. In addition to using one of the two state-adopted basal series, workbook-type follow-up materials are used at all reader levels. Teachers also prepare, in addition to the exercises directly extending the skills taught in a particular lesson, oral reading exercises which provide both (1) opportunity to use new vocabulary and (2) exercises in following written instructions. Extensive use is made of cards with which pupils may match upper and lower case letters with a picture which represents the sound of that letter.

While this large school (1500 population) is organized in the customary grade-level pattern, each grade-level is further sub-divided according to reading ability; teacher judgment and the level of the material from which the pupil is receiving instruction are the criteria for this grouping.

At the beginning of the year, all children new to the school, excluding kindergarten and beginning first-grade pupils, are assigned to one of three orientation rooms. Here reading ability is evaluated and permanent assignment is made, usually a period of about one week.

Children who enter the school at other times are similarly tested and assigned by one of two special reading teachers. This is an on-going activity for the school will experience about 100 per cent turnover, with 40 to 50 per cent remaining for three to five years.

A final organizational factor is the use of the "divided day" schedule, approximately one-half the class arriving one hour after their classmates and similarly remaining in school one hour later. The teacher thus has a total group of only 15 or 16, dividing these into the familiar two groups for instruction. In most classrooms, the slow-readers are the ones who arrive at the earlier hour.

When all pupils have arrived in the classroom, the supplementary phonics lesson is held. All children participate, regardless of the reading group to which they belong. This supplementary phonics instruction is initiated at the beginning of the first grade at, according to principal Newell Bowman, "a rate comfortable for the pupils."

At the beginning of grade two, instruction is begun anew with the simplest phonics drills. The purpose of this complete re-teaching is to provide (1) review and (2) initial teaching for pupils who had not attended that school in the first grade.

Reading instruction is initiated in the second semester of the kindergarten as the pupils show readiness. In a kindergarten where there are few high achievers and the formation of reading groups is impractical, those few will be sent to a B1 room for reading instruction. A similar procedure is followed with the occasional child who enters kindergarten and already can read. The principal reports that "from 50 to 70 per cent of the more able kindergarten pupils will be reading by the end of the year, some completing the primer." At least a ten minute daily "story-time" is observed in all classrooms.

Current Status. As would be expected in a school where homogeneous grouping was employed, some classes are reading well above grade level; similarly, some are well below. However, when the scores of all B2 classes were grouped, the achievement appeared to be much higher than would be expected in a school located in a low socio-economic area.

Further evaluation will be made through comparing the achievement of pupils in this school with pupils enrolled in neighboring schools. These comparisons will be made on the data obtained in the regular city-wide testing program.

THE LANGUAGE-EXPERIENCE APPROACH

Yet to be discussed are programs which appear to me to offer maximum opportunity for developing the ability of the culturally disadvantaged child to communicate with others through reading. A significant body of research into the abilities of culturally disadvantaged children to communicate establishes this: these children do not listen as well as do more advantaged children; they do not speak as well; they do not read as well; nor do they write as well.

We accept the premise that pupils who have adequate command of oral language learn to read more efficiently and more economically than do pupils who are deficient in listening and speaking skills. This appears to me to point us to two major conclusions as we plan reading instruction for culturally disadvantaged children: (1) the values which accrue from using the language-experience approach; and (2) the importance—the *necessity*—of planned language instruction long before these children are ready to enroll in kindergarten or in the first grade.

The Language-Experience Program at Malabar Street Elementary School. In an address at the Washington Conference on Culturally Disadvantaged Youth, sponsored by the U.S. Office of Education, in May–June, 1962, Rosemary Green Wilson made the following statement:

The sooner we discard the term "reading program" and begin to think of a "language program," the closer we will be getting to the realities of the situation and a possible solution.

The sooner, also, that we accept the idea that speaking, reading, and writing *cannot* be taught effectively in the same way to children of highly literate parents and to children of completely illiterate or semi-literate parents, the sooner we will reach the public schools' goal of literacy for this and succeeding generations. Thus, will the myth of the same basic reading materials for all children be exploded. . . .

In the Malabar Street Elementary School in Los Angeles a broad experimental program in the total language arts program is being undertaken. Three areas of growth are being evaluated:

1. The language development of pre-school children in a rich, permissive school environment.
2. The language growth of kindergarten children in a similar environment.
3. The growth in reading through the language-experience approach.

Rationale. Among the assumptions upon which this program is based are these:

1. Language growth of children occurs to a greater degree in an environment which stimulates them to think, to explore, and to want to express themselves.
2. Children learn more from a curriculum which is based on their own culture and their own experiences.
3. The skills of listening, speaking, reading, and writing are inextricably interwoven and are most effectively developed through their inter-related use.
4. Among bilingual pupils, the school must capitalize upon the total language ability the child brings with him. The function of the program is expression, regardless of the language used by the pupil. Refinement of expression and skill in the use of English are later goals.

Description of Program. Understanding the child, appreciating his cultural background, and knowing about his home conditions are believed by Mrs. Jacqueline Ayers Hartwick, principal of the school, to be basic to successful working relationships among teachers, pupil, and parents. Teachers are encouraged to visit the homes of pupils; similarly, parents are encouraged in many ways to visit the school, to identify themselves with it, and to understand that the school and home have a common goal for the pupil—his growth in every aspect of his life.

The pre-school program is a cooperative one between the school and California State College at Los Angeles. Pupils in the experimental classroom are free to choose the activities in which they will participate, little control being exercised. However, pupils are stimulated to explore the many interest centers provided in the room. These science, music, art and other activity areas are frequently changed, providing the pupil with many new and, hopefully, interesting things to talk about. The usual large toys, sandbox, etc., are available for their use. Growth in vocabulary and language patterns are being observed closely. The language output of each pupil is recorded at intervals; ways in which new words appear to be learned or to be assimilated into the vocabulary of these three- and four-year-olds are studied. Recently, one boy was present at the storage box when the teacher discovered that a shovel he wished to use in the sand box had been stolen over the weekend. The child said nothing at the time, but some thirty minutes later he began repeating almost interminably "stolen, stolen, stolen. . . ." He then began to practice using the word in sentences, as "My shovel is stolen," "My dog is stolen," using the word in many, many different ways.

In the kindergarten, language activities are encouraged throughout the class period. Much discussion about activities which occurred outside school is encouraged. Stories are read and dramatized. Songs are sung. Art activities are related to things which have been discussed. Purposeful activity from which conclusions or generalizations may be drawn typify the program.

The first-grade reading program in this school, situated in an area populated almost exclusively by Mexican-Americans, emphasizes the use and development of all of the language skills. The program also is characterized by freedom for teachers to use approaches and techniques with which they are familiar and in which they are comfortable. All reading instruction centers around the oral language of the pupils; these children read materials which are meaningful because they have talked about an experience and, after talking about it, have either dictated a story to the teacher—as individual or group experience stories—or have actually done the writing. This kind of instruction is not unique; it occurs in thousands of classrooms each day all over the United States; but I believe that its importance in this discussion of beginning reading programs for the culturally disadvantaged lies in the attempt by the administrator of the school and the classroom teachers to understand the culture of the pupils —both the Mexican heritage which they possess and the events, big and little, which comprise the lives of the pupils and their parents. It is an attempt to develop a meaningful reading curriculum from the daily experiences of the pupils themselves, providing them with an opportunity to develop their listening, speaking, reading, and writing vocabularies out of things and activities with which they have immediate contact.

Efforts are made to employ experiences and activities out of the lives of the pupils themselves as topics of the experience stories. Unusual attention is paid to the use of definitive language by the pupil, help being given him in the selection of an appropriate word and in correct usage.

Through this joint pupil-teacher effort in oral vocabulary and usage, I believe that language control will be more readily developed than through our traditional approaches.

Using the divided-day program, reading is taught at a given time only to one-half the total number of pupils enrolled in the class.

The two major problems in using the experience approach in teaching disadvantaged pupils appear to be essentially administrative in nature:

1. How can the sequential development of word recognition skills be assured without the internal structure provided through the basal reader?

2. How can teachers be helped to become both comfortable and efficient in the use of a non-basal reader approach to instruction? This problem probably is of greater concern with older teachers and with teachers who are below average in performance.

Current Status. The research which supports this program is necessarily divided into two parts: (1) that of the language growth of the pre-school child, which will be reported through a dissertation; and (2) the growth in total language power of pupils in the regular K–6 program of this school. The values which derive from the instructional procedures being employed will become apparent as these pupils move into higher grades and become involved in the regular testing program of the school system, making possible comparisons with the achievement of other schools in the same community and with achievement of earlier pupils within the same school.

Compton Community Demonstration Area. Among the educational programs being sponsored in Los Angeles County by the Economic and Youth Opportunity Agency is one involving selected classrooms in the Compton City, Enterprise City, and Willowbrook Elementary School Districts. The teachers of these experimental classes continue basically to be responsible to the principal of the school in which they work and subject to policies adopted by their respective Boards of Education. They cooperate with the Project Director[12] and Educational Consultant,[13] who are responsible for program planning, supervision and in-service training, and administration of the experimental project. An important administrative aspect of this program is the payment of a salary differential of $80.00 per month; the teacher is thus reimbursed, at least in part, for the extra time and effort involved in the preparation of demonstration lessons, the keeping of research records, continuing attendance at in-service training classes, and in holding parent conferences.

The Enterprise District Project. Experimental programs in this almost

[12] Don Hodes, Project Director, Economic and Youth Opportunities Agency, Enterprise City School District, Compton.

[13] Thelma Henney, Educational Consultant, Economic and Youth Opportunity Board, Los Angeles.

totally Negro community include: (1) teaching reading to pupils in grade one and (2) the stimulation and further development of communication skills among pupils now in grade three. This latter program, emphatically *not* a remedial reading program, later may be extended to grades two and four.

Rationale. The first grade program, recognizing the language and experiential deficit found among disadvantaged children, attempts to:

1. Identify pupils at the end of the kindergarten program who are potential failures in reading.
2. Provide first-hand experiences which will stimulate pupils toward increased self-expression.
3. Provide, where possible, concrete materials for developing abstractions in all phases of the curriculum.
4. Assures success in initial reading experiences.
5. Stimulate general language growth.

Description of Program. Because of the essential similarity in goals and procedures among the various first grade classrooms in the total Demonstration Area project, the reading program at the McKinley school has been selected as being representative of the entire group.

The 25 pupils in the room were cooperatively selected by the kindergarten and first grade teachers, with the assistance of the principal and school psychologist, during the last weeks of the school year. The major criterion was the language immaturity displayed by these kindergarten pupils in comparison with their peers. A deliberate effort was made, according to Mr. Hodes, to select the pupils least likely to learn to read during their ensuing first grade experience. Five reading groups were formed very early in the fall, the teacher working with each group from 10 to 20 minutes. The basic reading lesson generally consists of a group dictated experience story. Reading and continued use of this story follow the familiar pattern. After the discussion and dictation have been completed, pupils individually illustrate some phase of the story; the teacher moves from child to child, writing for each a story to accompany his own drawing. These personal stories are bound in individual books, and repeatedly re-read.

Most instructions to the class as well as to individuals are printed and given orally only when needed; pupils read the instructions aloud before complying. Such statements as these are used:

Come to this chair.

Get ready to go out to play.

The language-experience approach is supplemented by twice-weekly use of preprimers, a related activity book, and a multitude of tradebooks.

Concerted and continued effort is made to have the pupils speak in complete sentences, a task requiring much questioning and repeating by both teacher and pupils.

Many school and neighborhood walks are taken. The class has been on "Listening Walks," "Leaf Walks," and "Smell Walks," among others. The group returned to check on things which had been observed and reported.

A unit in the social studies program, an adjunct in this classroom to language arts development, concerned—at this early age—professional and vocational choice. Under the topic "I Want To Be," pupils had described their ambitions and recorded the kinds of training required.

Parent cooperation is consistently developed. They were invited to the school to discuss the program in its inception, both by the principal and the president of the PTA. Of the 25 sets of parents, 16 came.

Current Status. The chief problems are reported to be parent pressures engendered by the informal nature of the program and local district policies making retention mandatory when certain norms are not achieved.

Research in Progress. While comparison with control groups is not anticipated, growth will be evaluated with the California Test of Mental Maturity and with the Lee-Clark reading readiness test. It is expected that individual anecdotal records will provide the greatest help both in assessing the growth of pupils and in recommending curricular or administrative change.

Youth and Economic Opportunity Board—Los Angeles City Schools Pre-School Education Program. The final project to be discussed is one directed toward early intervention in the pattern of language development of the culturally disadvantaged child. Pre-school classes were established in November, 1964, in two neighboring schools in a low-income community populated almost entirely by Negroes.

Rationale. The basic assumptions of the program are that children who live in culturally or economically disadvantaged areas:

1. Are deficient in experiences which prepare them for success in school.
2. Lack motivation toward achievement in our contemporary school programs.
3. Are deficient both in language background and in the total spectrum of communication skills.
4. May, through educational intervention, be re-oriented in their attitudes toward school and may be helped to develop skills necessary to this success.

Description of Program. The project was designed for pupils who were, upon enrollment, between 3.9 and 4.4 years of age. Two experimental classrooms were established; one of the programs was designed to provide maximum teacher-pupil guided interaction, with the pupils being directed in their movement to and from and in their participation in, activities relevant to the rationale described above. The second program envisioned equally detailed planning by the teacher, but much greater pupil-choice or selection of activities in which he would participate. In this report, the first program will be referred to as Program One; the second, as Program Two.

Goals of the programs are basically similar. They have been defined as the development of:

Physical Growth

Intellectual Growth

Social-Emotional Growth[14] [15]

The curriculum of the two projects also is basically similar. It has been defined for Program Two as developing:

I. Sensory Perception

II. Oral Language Understanding and Usage
   A. Listening for Directions; to answer questions; to enjoy stories and poems; to learn the names of things; to comment on a topic; etc.
   B. Speaking his name; telling his age; discussing and conversing; helping to plan activities
   C. Learning finger plays; nursery rhymes, stories, and poems

III. Music and Rhythms

IV. Social Studies Awareness and Understandings
   A. Becoming aware of the geography of the home, school, and community
   B. Learning about time, as it related to work, play, and rest
   C. Developing a feeling of civic responsibility, through caring for pets; helping to care for the room and equipment; and learning about the flag and about various holidays

V. Pre-Reading Understandings
   A. Auditory Discrimination
   B. Visual Perception
   C. Language Usage

VI. Arithmetical Understandings

VII. Science Awareness

VIII. Art Experiences

IX. Enrichment Activities, including trips to the: zoo; park; market; pet store; library; department store; shopping center; the beach; through the neighborhood; to the park on picnics

X. Outdoor Activities and Equipment, including: wheel toys; jungle gym; balls; sandbox; playhouse; water table; paint easels

XI. Health and Personal Cleanliness
   A. Developing an understanding of function of parts of the body
   B. Developing habits of personal hygiene
   C. Developing habits of good grooming

XII. Parent Program
   A. Home activities

[14] Bernice Christenson, "Pre-School Project 1964–65: 102nd Street School," Los Angeles City Schools, Division of Instructional Services, Curriculum Branch (Experimental Publication), January 1965.

[15] Los Angeles City Schools, Division of Elementary Education, "Experimental Pre-School Projects, 1964–65."

      B. Community activities
XIII. Body and Self
      A. Awareness of body and its parts
      B. Eye-hand coordination[16]

As was stated earlier, elements of the two instructional programs appear to be similar. Marked differences in the implementation of the programs were observed, in accordance with the design of the experiment. In Program One, the children are divided into three clusters, with an adult guiding and working with the children. While pupils generally are expected to rotate among their activities with the cluster of which they were members, individual selection of activities is possible within the cluster; greatest freedom of choice obtains in outdoor activities. The membership of the clusters varies from time to time, permitting the most able to progress at optimum rate. In Program Two a number of different interest centers have been established, with pupils generally being free to choose the center or activity in which they wish to participate. Providing an opportunity for the pupil to communicate with both adults and peers on an individual basis is one of the goals of the program.

The programs differ in terms of personnel, both salaried and volunteer. Program One employs a full-time teacher, 1-1/5 paid assistants, and the daily help of the mothers of two children in the class; these parents serve on a rotating basis. Parents are reported to have been very responsible in their attendance, and enthusiastic and cooperative in the assistance they have given. This opportunity for direct training of the parents is one of the strengths of the program.

An additional strength of Program One is a one-hour weekly group conference among parents and teacher. Here the teacher attempts to extending the understanding of the parents of the developmental patterns of the four-year-old child in addition to interpreting to them the curriculum. This has provided a base for continuing understanding between the school and home, and the larger community.

Program Two employs one teacher, one paid helper, and one volunteer assistant from a women's organization.

All personnel involved in the programs, as well as the principals of both schools, have commented on the regularity of attendance of the pupils, the unusually low transiency, and the growth in language experienced by these pre-school children.

Current Status and Research. Newton Metfessel and J. T. Foster[17] have developed "A Comprehensive Curricular and Evaluative Model for Pre-school Programs Designed for Educationally (Culturally) Disadvantaged

---

[16] Bernice Christenson, "Proposed Outline for Pre-School Education for Low Socio-Economic Level," Los Angeles City Schools, Division of Instructional Services, Curriculum Branch, November 1964.

[17] Center for the Study of Educationally (Culturally) Disadvantaged Youth, University of Southern California.

Preschool Children." Metfessel and Foster will compare the growth of children in this program in terms of these criteria:

1. Concept Formation
2. Creativity
3. Instructional Objectives
4. Parental Attitudes
5. Socio-Economic Status
6. Teacher and Teacher Aide Attitudes
7. The Achievement Motive
8. Curriculum Methods
9. Intellectual Abilities

No data are at this time available.

This paper began with a statement of concern that we may focus our consideration on programs *per se* rather than on their effect on the lives of children. In closing I would urge, through these lines from James Baldwin, that we continuingly ask ourselves whether our activities improve the status of a child, whether they enable some disadvantaged pupil to see new horizons of achievement and of hope. Baldwin writes that at the age of fourteen he:

> . . . began to feel in the boys a curious, wary, bewildered despair, as though they were now setting in for the long, hard winter of life . . . it was clear (that they) would rise no higher than their fathers. School began to reveal itself, therefore, as a child's game that one could not win, and boys dropped out of school and went to work.[18]

The concern of every person who has responsibility for education of the disadvantaged is to make of school a place where boys and girls are helped to realize that there is a life other than that they have now, and to help them develop the attitudes and the skills which will enable them to rise "higher than their fathers."

---

[18] James Baldwin. *The Fire Next Time.* New York: The Dial Press (1963), p. 32.

CHAPTER VII

A LOOK TO THE
FUTURE

46. WHAT'S AHEAD IN READING FOR
THE DISADVANTAGED?

Helene M. Lloyd

Today all aspects of reading instruction are in a state of ferment, and we who are caught up in this ferment find it difficult to separate trends from fads or to know exactly what is ahead in reading. Being part of the school system of a great city, however, I do see one major area of obvious need concerning which action *will* be taken because it *must* be taken. This imperative need is to improve the level of reading achievement of socially disadvantaged children. What can be done?*

There are, I believe, at least eight avenues of attack in meeting the reading needs of the socially disadvantaged child. We cannot rank the eight in order of priority; we cannot guarantee that each will function independently or will function in every circumstance. But in our all-out assault on the problem in New York City, the greatest promise of progress seems to be offered by these eight avenues.

Avenue 1. New types of tests will be developed to give a more valid picture of the disadvantaged child's capacity to learn to read. We must rapidly replace our present group intelligence and reading readiness

Reprinted from *The Reading Teacher,* Vol. 18 (March 1965), pp. 471–476. By permission of Helene M. Lloyd and The International Reading Association.

* This paper reports (with minor changes) remarks delivered by the author at a meeting of the American Association of School Administrators.

tests with measuring rods that do not militate against the disadvantaged and that, at the same time, give a true picture about the abilities and needs of all the other children in our schools.

A start in this direction has been made by New York City schools. We are developing in cooperation with the Educational Testing Service a new type of test for use with our first grade children next year in lieu of the group intelligence test. If the new test proves successful in grade one, similar tests will then be developed for upper grade levels. The New York City reading readiness test is also undergoing revision to take into account the affirmative assets of the socially disadvantaged.

Other examples of similar efforts to break free of the testing vise that binds us and militates against one group of children could, I am sure, be reported by others. Now that resolute action has been initiated, it is inevitable that we shall see in the years ahead a tremendous effort by school systems, publishers, and researchers for the development of new means and materials of appraisal.

Avenue 2. All-out efforts will be made in the years ahead to *encourage earlier language development* and to build necessary concepts. We know that language patterns are firmly implanted by the time a child is six years old. Therefore, the socially disadvantaged child must have our help with language and concept development in the preschool years.

This means that school systems in urban areas will have increasing numbers of nursery schools, summer playschools for preschool children, workshops for their parents. James B. Conant said that the more disadvantaged the neighborhood, the more important it is to have kindergarten and prekindergarten schools.

A pilot study using selected four-year-old children, now underway in six New York City elementary schools, is highlighting some of the values of a special preschool program for disadvantaged children. This study is being made in cooperation with the Institute for Developmental Studies, Department of Psychiatry, New York Medical College. The basic curriculum includes a regular nursery program with special emphasis in certain areas of cognitive development. Auditory and visual discrimination, concept formation, and language development are being stressed. The effect of this preschool program on later school achievement is being studied with mounting interest.

A special facet of the preschool enrichment program is the attempt to stimulate interest among the parents and to enlist their cooperation. Efforts are being made successfully to help the parents to understand the school experiences of their children, to develop a positive orientation to school, and to increase the reading skills and storytelling abilities of the parents themselves.

Teaching procedures in kindergarten are also being evaluated and analyzed in a companion program undertaken by the New York City Board of Education and the Institute for Developmental Studies. Additional studies of similar types are under way in other parts of our country. The results of studies to date emphasize that the kindergarten day should be lengthened, to five hours from the present two, two-and-a-half, or three hours. In addition, kindergarten should no longer be considered optional in urban areas but must be considered mandatory because of its contribution to language-concept development. Mandating kindergarten attendance will overcome the ironic circumstance that those children most in need of kindergarten experiences are frequently not even registered in our urban cities.

Avenue 3. The development of *urban-oriented materials* will be accelerated. This reading material must not be today's material with a few new stories, a few new words, or a few new photographs added. This material must be largely new, growing out of the interests, vocabulary, and experiences of *every* type of city child, including the socially disadvantaged. The material will include more than a series of basal readers; it will include a full and powerful gamut of skill kits, tapes, recordings, filmstrips, packaged materials, programmed materials. New materials will be prepared in all areas of the curriculum—social studies, health education, science, and others. Special emphasis will be placed on audio-visual materials and on materials the child can use independently, thus freeing the teacher for teaching other children to read. The need for new materials is great; all of us know we shall have to run in the years ahead to catch up with today's and tomorrow's needs in this area.

Avenue 4. The pre-service and in-service *education of teachers* in the area of reading will be improved. Today's drive for improvement in the quality of reading instruction, the need for which was underscored by the results reported in Mary Austin's book, *The First "R,"* will continue with increased momentum in the years ahead.

We know the classroom teacher is the key factor in any reading improvement program. In teaching reading to the socially disadvantaged, this teacher must not only be a skilled reading technician but also must have a sound background in mental hygiene and child guidance and an understanding of and respect for varying cultural and ethnic groups.

In urban centers, televised courses in the teaching of reading, with emphasis on mental hygiene and human relations, will be expanded and become a standard part of both in-service and pre-service training; for example, eight thousand New York City teachers enrolled in such a course on the teaching of reading at the primary level; six thousand, in a course at the intermediate grade level. These television courses, however, cannot be the main answer. Teachers and teacher trainees must get guided experience in teaching reading under the direction of highly-qualified reading specialists.

At the pre-service level, I believe this need will be met in the future by the expansion of the type of program Dr. Donald Durrell is using at Boston University, i.e., taking busloads of students to public schools on a regular schedule for work with children on a one-to-one basis in reading, or by an expansion of a program which we have initiated in New York City and which I shall describe later, the Campus School Program.

On the in-service level, the teacher will obtain highly qualified guidance in three ways:

First, and foremost, from his supervisor who, because of certification requirements or because of professional interest and need, will increase his skill as a reading technician. This increased skill in the teaching of reading will be necessary because of the ever-increasing leadership role of the supervisor in developing a quality reading program. The increased ability in reading will also be necessary because the supervisor will be and must be held directly accountable to the Board of Education and to parents for each child's progress in reading *regardless* of the number of reading specialists in the school.

Second, the teacher will receive help from a special teacher of reading assigned to his school to assist in the improvement of reading instruction. We have 539 such specialists in our New York City elementary schools and look forward to their working for some type of certification in order to ensure adequate backgrounds in reading.

Third, the teacher will receive help from college specialists working in and with the public schools.

The planned involvement of college personnel will result, I forecast, in the initiation of language arts resource centers located within clusters of schools in disadvantaged areas. It is to such a center that a teacher will come alone, or with colleagues, or with a few children. He may come for professional consultation, for demonstrations of new procedures, for assistance with special reading problems.

Two years ago in New York City, we facilitated pre-service and in-service growth through college involvement by the initiation of the Campus School Program, in which nineteen colleges now work closely with thirty-one of our elementary schools. We look forward to having this program expanded at all levels as a basic phase of our long-range program for the education of teachers of reading.

Avenue 5. There will be an *increase in* the quality and the quantity of the *special personnel* provided for upgrading reading in schools in disadvantaged areas. Just a few of these special personnel will be considered.

Speech specialists. We shall see within the next few years a new utilization of speech specialists in all schools in disadvantaged areas. We know that there is a close relation between speech problems and reading problems. The relation is such that one cannot readily solve the reading problem without first solving the speech problem.

In New York City, we are participating in a most promising study: instead of reserving the services of speech therapists to the elimination of stuttering and other deep-rooted problems of individual children, we are also using these specialists in a pilot project to upgrade the general speech levels of whole classes. The professional reaction to this project has been so affirmative that additional positions have been requested so the project may be expanded—another breakthrough toward reading progress.

Teachers of library. We foresee the day when the library will serve as the coordinating hub of every elementary school's reading program. The teacher of library will not only perform all the usual librarian services but will also maintain a rotating flow of books from the library to each classroom.

New York City, with other cities, is conducting a long-range drive to have school libraries with at least ten books for every child and a teacher of library assigned to each school. We now have 237 such positions in our 590 elementary schools and have requested 287 additional positions for next year.

Reading clinics. To meet the needs of the retarded reader who is emotionally disturbed, we will need more reading clinics in disadvantaged areas. From these areas particularly come children with grave, deep-seated problems that can be resolved only by the clinic team. Included on this team are the following: a reading counselor, speech therapist, social worker, psychologist, and when needed, the psychiatrist. These team members work with the individual child and/or his parents. We have eleven such reading clinics in New York City and are so gratified by their success that we are striving to increase this number to twenty-five.

Avenue 6. The reading program will be stabilized, particularly in disadvantaged areas, by the use of *adequate reading records.* A basic characteristic of children in socially disadvantaged areas is the excessive mobility of their families. Some children move seven, eight, ten times in one school year.

The shifting of children from neighborhood to neighborhood and from school to school, disrupting their own schooling as well as that of their less mobile classmates, has a disastrous effect on reading progress. In Manhattan, for example, the mean yearly mobility rate is 51 per cent. In several disadvantaged schools, the turnover is over 100 per cent a year.

To combat the ill effects of this mobility and to ensure systematic progress, New York City is using, on an experimental basis, a Reading Record Card, which is sent with the child's other records to his next teacher or his next school. This card provides a ladder of the reading skills and the child's progress up that ladder, as well as a record of the materials he has used. It provides orientation for his next teacher and eliminates his using reading materials he has already read satisfactorily in his former class or school.

Avenue 7. We will focus on more and improved *research studies in beginning reading* for all children, with special emphasis on the disadvantaged. I refer to the studies in first grade reading being encouraged by the United States Office of Education. Several studies have been approved, and researchers and reading specialists are working with some of New York City's first grade children, especially those disadvantaged children who are having difficulty understanding the meanings of words and who lack adequate skill in listening and speaking.

I urge that before any one of us makes drastic changes in our first grade reading program because of pressures from those who believe in more phonics, we wait until the fall of 1965, when the results from this nation-wide focus on first grade reading can be carefully analyzed in light of implications for our own school systems. After taking a hard look at these research results, then I urge that we take action if needed.

Avenue 8. We will find means to *stretch the school day and school year* to provide the required reading instruction time for socially disadvantaged children.

New York City has already taken giant steps in this direction by establishing After-School Study Centers in 163 elementary schools, 52 junior high schools, 40 high schools (13 academic, 27 vocational). These centers reinforce the reading programs in all schools with a percentage of 75 or more of Negro and/or Puerto Rican children. The centers are open from Tuesday through Friday from 3 to 5 P. M., and on Saturday from 9:30 to 11:30 A.M. Teaching is done by members of the day school staff who are familiar with the children's needs. Emphasis at the elementary level is placed on remediation in reading and mathematics, on homework help, and library activities. Requests are arriving daily for the establishment of these centers in other schools in New York City where the need is great. Correspondence received indicates that the pattern will probably spread in the near future to other cities faced with similar problems.

In the years directly ahead, other changes will be effected to improve reading. Boards of education in urban centers will, of necessity, also initiate plans for a twelve-month attack on reading improvement in school areas where the need is great. Yes, we are realists. We know that the cost will be great, too. The alternative, however, is to continue today's practice of having to use the fall months to retrieve the learning lost as a result of a two-or-three month vacation period and, thereby, reduce instruction time by approximately one third. Stretching the school year will be another way of helping the disadvantaged child make progress in reading.

What's ahead in reading? I have enumerated eight avenues so promising that they seem certain to develop into tomorrow's throughways. The important thing in this discussion, however, is not any one of these avenues, or even all of them together, but rather the assurance they offer that the situation can be corrected by people who are determined to correct it. What lies ahead in reading? *Action by people who are determined.*

APPENDIX

Specific Techniques in Aiding the Poor Reader

47. BASIC TEACHING SUGGESTIONS

Board of Education of the City of New York

The effectiveness of a reading program in a school is dependent to a large extent on the teaching procedures that are used. Experienced teachers know that some procedures are of much greater value than others in helping pupils to move to higher levels of reading achievement.

On the following pages are enumerated some of the time-tested reading-instruction procedures used successfully by experienced teachers. The suggested procedures are focused primarily on the early stages of reading, for two reasons:

1. Reading specialists and experienced teachers consider the readiness and beginning-to-read stages as crucial periods in reading instruction. It is during these periods that the child establishes the foundations for reading; more important, it is during these periods, also, that the child builds within himself an understanding of what reading is, of what it is for, and of the enjoyment that comes from reading. If instruction is ineffective at this foundational stage, negative attitudes toward reading are formed, poor habits are developed, and the child's reading progress in future years is seriously retarded.

2. Instruction at all levels of reading growth have not only unique characteristics but also strong common denominators. *Basic* procedures related to the teaching of reading at the foundational levels can be used again and again, in slightly modified form, in instruction at higher levels of growth.

Reprinted from *Sequential Levels of Reading Growth in the Elementary Schools* (1963), pp. 32–39. By permission of the New York City Board of Education.

The suggestions that follow, therefore, concern specifically what a teacher does at Level A in developing readiness for reading and at Level B in initiating formal reading from books, since these two levels together comprise the foundational stages on which all subsequent levels are constructed.

THE TEACHER BUILDS READINESS

Establishing readiness for learning is a basic consideration in the teaching of reading at every level of growth; but it is especially important when children enter the first grade, for this is where a firm foundation for a lifetime of successful reading must be started.

The boys and girls entering the first-year classroom bring with them varying expectations. Some are eager, some are fearful, but *all believe that they will learn how to read.* With skillful teaching and a sound reading program, all but a few children with special problems *will* learn to read. Readiness procedures are the key element in the sound reading program at this level; when children have had successful and effective readiness development, the teacher can lead them almost imperceptibly into beginning reading activities.

What kind of experiences comprise the readiness program? At least the following:

Experiences to Build a Background of Understanding

Children need opportunities to engage in many kinds of experiences that will give them understanding of words and will extend their speaking and listening vocabularies.[1]

Activities that will accomplish these purposes are block building, easel painting, finger painting, music, rhythmic activities, dramatic play, water play, working with clay, trying out and exploring other materials, bringing interesting things to school, collecting things, going on school trips and neighborhood trips, helping to compose experience charts.

Experiences to Build a Background of Skills

Children need opportunities, too, for experiences that will sharpen their sensory perceptions and develop the auditory and visual distinctions essential in reading. These experiences are necessarily varied and numerous.

[1] *Early Childhood Education,* Curriculum Bulletin No. 5 (New York: Board of Education of the City of New York, 1959), pages 13 and 52–57.

1. Provide listening experiences. To strengthen auditory discrimination and memory, utilize games, stories, songs, nursery rhymes, recordings, and radio programs.

2. Provide seeing experiences. To develop visual discrimination and memory; utilize pictures; filmstrips; motion pictures; televison programs; and games with objects, forms, letters, and words.

Experiences to Establish Pre-Reading Skills

1. Associate spoken words with meaningful concepts. There are legions of experiences in this category:

• Identifying and naming familiar objects, such as a ball, a crayon, a table. "Find the *ball*. Find the *crayon*. Walk to Jane's *table*."

• Following directions, like "Go to the door. Count the paper napkins for your table."

• Retelling familiar stories. Example: telling the *Three Billy Goats Gruff* in correct sequence.

• Dramatizing familiar stories. Example: the *Three Billy Goats Gruff* story.

• Developing experience charts, such as recording what the children wish to remember, creative stories, accounts of trips, weather charts, recipes.

2. Develop auditory perception. Experiences of this kind include:

• Identifying *gross* sounds: tearing paper, ringing bells, clapping hands.

• Identifying *less gross* sounds: cutting paper with scissors, breaking a piece of chalk, rattling keys.

• Identifying rhyming words in familiar context, such as "Little Jack Horner/Sat in the *corner*" and similar combinations in *Mother Goose* and other rhymes.

• Identifying rhyming words in *unfamiliar* context, such as teacher-composed rhymes like "Mary, *dear*/come *here*."

• Supplying rhyming words for riddles, like "I rhyme with *moon*. You eat with me. What am I?" (Spoon).

• Identifying rhyming words in oral series. In a controlled series, the child identifies a word that rhymes with the first word given, such as:

boat   boy   *coat*   book

In an uncontrolled series, the child must find any two words that rhyme without being cued by the beginning word:

father   *small*   cake   *ball*

• Supplying rhyming word in quick response to a word heard, such as

"Who can think of a word that rhymes with *shoe?*" (blue) "With *key?*" (see) "With *and?*" (hand)

• Supplying words starting with the same initial sound as a word spoken by the teacher, such as "Who can think of a word that starts with the same sound as the word *doll?*" (desk, door, David) "As the word *baby?*" (boy, book, ball); and other listening games.[2]

• Strengthening auditory memory by imitating sounds: clock, train, animal sounds.

• Strengthening auditory memory by reproducing sounds in varying rhythmic patterns, such as clapping hands or striking a triangle four times in even rhythm, or four times with two pairs and a pause between them.

• Strengthening auditory memory by reproducing context heard, such as from poems like *The Rain* ("The rain is raining all around . . ."), from songs like *Old MacDonald Had a Farm*, and in games such as *I Packed My Trunk*. In this last, one child says "I packed my trunk. In it I put a handkerchief." The next child says, "I packed my trunk. In it I put a handkerchief *and a coat*." Each child in turn repeats the whole story and adds one item. The last child tries to repeat the entire story with all items given, and in sequence.

• Strengthening auditory memory by following oral directions. These include a developmental series like this:

1 direction:	"Shake hands with me."
2 directions:	"Go to the front of the room.
	Tell the children your name."
3 directions:	"Come to the board.
	Draw a ball.
	Then erase it."
4 directions:	"Walk to the window.
	Look out.
	Tell us one thing you see.
	Hop to your seat."

• Strengthening auditory memory by reproducing stories read or told: retelling the story in sequence, telling principal events in sequence.

• Strengthening auditory memory by supplying the missing word that fits the context. The teacher gives a sentence orally, like "I saw a cat . . . the milk" (accept any suitable word) or "I saw a . . . hopping on the ground" (missing word must begin with the same sound as *red;* i.e. *robin).*

3. Develop visual likenesses and differences. Here, too, experiences should be varied and numerous:

• Observing real objects, to discriminate—

[2] David H. Russell and Elizabeth Fatherson Russell, *Listening Aids Through the Grades* (New York: Bureau of Publications, Teachers College, Columbia University, 1959).

Gross differences: 4 balls, 1 eraser
Less gross differences: 3 blue balls, 1 red one
Fine differences: 4 red balls, one has band
- Observing pictures of objects or people, discriminating—
Gross differences: 3 dogs, 1 child
Less gross differences (differences may be in color, size, shape): 3
apples, 1 pear
Fine differences: 3 bowls of different sizes
- Observing and arranging geometric forms—
Matching circles to circles, squares to squares, etc.
Arranging forms (can be felt shapes, to be placed on a flannel board)
in teacher-directed sequence
- Observing and discriminating the forms of letters—
Gross differences: O O O L O (or) e e t e e
Fine differences: H H N H H (or) h h h u h
- Observing and discriminating the forms of words—
Gross differences: father father boy father
Less gross differences: boy toy boy boy
Fine differences: was was saw was

4. *Associate ideas with meaningful pictures, labels,* and objects through
such experiences as these:

- Getting ideas from pictures of objects, people, actions—
First level (enumeration): identifying separate objects in picture
Next level (description): seeing a story idea in picture
Higher level (interpretation): inferring conversation; predicting
what might happen next in the story
- Connecting ideas with printed symbols is encouraged by printing and
posting placard labels to designate functional areas of the classroom,
like these:

- Connecting ideas with printed symbols is also encouraged by a work
chart that shows a picture and printed title of the room-duty assignment,
with an assigned child's name printed on a card beside the assignment
identification, like this:

* Strengthening visual memory by retention of the visual image of *real* objects: A series of objects may be displayed, then covered. One object is removed or added. The objects are uncovered again. Children try to identify the object that was removed or added.
* Strengthening visual memory by retention of the visual image of *pictured* objects: A series of pictures are shown. The children observe the pictures, then close their eyes so the pictures may be rearranged. On signal, children open their eyes and observe the new order. They try to reproduce the original sequence. To vary this activity, pictures can be taken away or added instead of, or in addition to, shuffling them.

Suggestions for a Typical Day's Plan

Almost all class readiness activities encourage, at least indirectly, the development of finer and finer auditory and visual discrimination skills. But a typical day's classwork should include 20 to 30 minutes of activity specifically devoted to the development of these discriminatory skills. The activities should be used at different times during the day as:

1. *Visual-discrimination* (5 to 10 minutes) experiences in which the aim is to distinguish, for example, gross differences in objects.
2. *Auditory-discrimination* (5 to 10 minutes) experiences in which the aim is to distinguish gross differences in sounds.
3. *Visual-memory* (about 5 minutes) exercises that aim to help children recall what they have seen. This activity is sometimes used as a game between major activities.
4. *Auditory-memory* (about 5 minutes) exercises that aim to help children recall what they have heard. This activity commonly involves the use of games or recordings.

On successive days and weeks, of course, other gradations ("less gross differences," "fine differences," and so on) of auditory and visual skills development are stressed to enable children to make finer distinctions and to master the essential pre-reading skills. Worth noting is the fact that some children need continuous reinforcement of pre-reading skills throughout the elementary-school grades.

THE TEACHER INITIATES READING

The line between reading readiness and actual reading is very fine, indeed, for the first grows into the second almost indiscernibly when the teaching is skillful. Moreover, readiness activities continue for a long while after children have started to read, the two activities overlapping and intermeshing so constantly and deeply that, after the start of reading, the two are scarcely separable. Readiness for new reading instruction is developed at every level of reading growth.

Children vary in the time when they are ready to begin reading. A few children are early readers who come to school already able to read with some degree of meaning and fluency.[3] Most children begin to read *from books* sometime in the first grade; but some boys and girls do not reach the book-readiness stage until second grade, and a few must postpone their use of books until even later. (For these late readers, readiness activities, specifically planned and taught, are needed throughout the early grades if these children are to have genuine success in their beginning-to-read activities.)

Developing the Sight Vocabulary

To develop the sight vocabulary essential at the start of reading, the teacher should focus on functional words that are *(a)* an outgrowth of daily experiences and activities and are *(b)* words needed for beginning to read from books. Successful procedures for developing recognition and understanding of sight words include the following:

1. *Provide real experiences.* Utilize the curriculum areas, centers of interest, special events, and all other class happenings that create interest in the important sight words.

2. *Guide discussion* to develop, to clarify, and to enrich the children's language expression.

3. *Use audio-visual aids* including pictures, films, filmstrips, stories,

---

[3] Reasons for not recommending premature reading are given by Dr. Mary Moffitt in "Reading and the Younger Child," published in *Teaching 600,000 "Johnnys" to Read* (New York: Board of Education of the City of New York, 1962), pages 8–13.

records, tapes, and so on, to bring the sight words into prominence in different contexts.

4. *Record experiences* on both chalkboard and charts to associate written symbols with meanings. Suggestions for effective use of experience charts:[4]

• Have meaningful reading (teacher, pupil) of the chart.

• Guide reading of selected parts of chart to establish meaning. This, of course, involves skillful questioning.

• Reinforce sight words by use of a variety of activities. For example, an experience chart may be prepared in duplicate; then one chart may be cut apart to provide sentences, phrases, and/or words for matching activities. Another example: dramatize the *action* words on the chart.

• Illustrate the experience chart.

• Direct choral reading of the chart for meaning, for phrasing, for fluency.

• Duplicate copies of the chart for the children.

• Accumulate different duplicated charts in individual booklets. The child reads the booklet by himself, reads it to his teacher, reads it to other children in his class or in another class, reads it at home to members of his family.

• Place copies of such booklets in the class library.

5. *Record* the child's individual dictated stories.

6. *Introduce pre-primers* or simple printed materials when the children have been taught the words that they will encounter. Waiting until the children know the words will insure a successful and gratifying initial reading experience for every child.

Developing Competence in Word Recognition

Word-recognition skills should be taught in meaningful context, proceeding from the known to the unknown, with the *children* as the discoverers of the generalizations. Among word-recognition skills to be taught are the following:

1. *Configuration clues,* which is the recognition of a word from its outline and shape, its length, height, its up strokes, its down strokes, and so on.[5] Examples:

---

[4] Adapted from *Experience Charts—A Guide to Their Use in Grades 1–3,* Educational Research Bulletin No. 13 (New York: Board of Education of the City of New York, 1952).

[5] Adapted from *Reading and Literature in the Language Arts: Grades 1–6,* Curriculum Bulletin No. 7 (New York: Board of Education of the City of New York, 1957), page 14.

Distinctive outline of the word *elephant:*

The up and down strokes of the word *dog:*

2. *Contextual clues,* which is the recognition of a word through the meaning of an adjacent picture or the other words in the sentence.

• Pictures on charts and in books, for example, serve as contextual clues:

My mother made a *birthday* cake.

• The meaning of a sentence may also serve as a contextual clue, if this skill is developed orally before it is used with symbols. Consider, for example, this sentence:

Blue and red are *colors* I like.

If the child does not know the word *colors* but does know all the other words, he infers the word *colors* from the meaning of the other words in the sentence.

3. *Phonetic analysis,* which is the association of sounds with letter symbols. Readiness for phonetic analysis includes auditory and visual discrimination skills that prepare the child for association of a particular sound with its letter symbol. Suggested teaching procedures:

• Draw upon *sight* words selected from among familiar reading material, such as experience charts and booklets.
• Children are ready for instruction in this skill when they know from three to five words containing the same phonetic element.
• Any phonetic element may be taught through procedures involving these four steps:

STEP 1. Auditory and visual discrimination
STEP 2. Generalization
STEP 3. Meaningful practice (reinforcement)
STEP 4. Application in reading materials

For example, to teach the initial consonant *F*:

STEP 1. The teacher uses such sight words as *fun, family, farm, funny, father*. The teacher guides the children to *hear* that all the words start with the same *sound*. She guides the children to *see* that all the words begin with the same *letter*. Then the teacher may ask, "What is the name of this letter?" The name *F* is supplied by a child or, if necessary, by the teacher.

STEP 2. Now the children make the generalization that the letter has a name and an associated sound.

STEP 3. Next the teacher provides meaningful practice. The children are led to suggest additional words beginning with *F*. Names of children in the class may bring in the use of the capital letter in a functional way. The children are led to locate pictures of objects whose names begin with *F*. The children supply missing words involving *F* in riddles, sentences, multiple-choice exercises, and so on.

The teacher may develop a picture chart as a self-help reference in connection with any phonetic sound. Example:

<table>
<tr>
<td>Children's pictures beginning with letter F are contributed to the chart.</td>
<td></td>
<td>The teacher writes the F word that describes each picture on the chart.</td>
</tr>
</table>

The chart accrues more and more pictures that begin with *F*, and words are written next to the pictures. The teacher and children say the words aloud frequently, stressing but not exaggerating the initial sound; the sound is not used in isolation.

For further practice, the teacher starts a "Key Word Chart" (after the children have learned several consonants) composed of a list of the known consonants, with a box next to each letter; in the box children see a picture to illustrate a word that begins with the indicated consonant. Like this:

STEP 4. Finally, after instruction in auditory and visual discrimination (Step 1), after drawing the generalization (Step 2), and after meaningful practice (Step 3), the girls and boys are encouraged to use phonetic analysis in their reading, not only alone but also in combination with configuration, contextual, and other word-recognition skills.

4. Structural Analysis, which means the recognition of a word by identification of the meaningful parts of words. Suggested teaching procedures include the following, which parallel the same four steps previously mentioned:

STEP 1. To develop the auditory and visual discrimination required, the teacher selects about five sight words that the children have used in many meaningful situations; for example: *jump, eat, talk, play,* and *help.* She writes the first word, *jump,* on the chalkboard and then asks, "John, jump!" As John is jumping, the teacher asks the class, "What is John doing?"

A child answers, "John is jumping."

The teacher calls attention to the fact that the action is a continuing one, then writes the word *jumping* beside the word *jump.* She proceeds similarly with the other words:

jump	jumping	play	playing
eat	eating	help	helping
talk	talking	*Etc.*	

Next the teacher asks the children to identify each root word in the second form; they frame it:

STEP 2. The children are guided to make the generalization that an ending has been added to each root word and that the ending is *ing.*

STEP 3. The third step is, of course, to provide meaningful practice. There are many possible exercises:

• The teacher may write sentences on the chalkboard, with one word omitted; she asks the children to supply the missing word. New words are utilized, too; for example:

Go to _____
                    sleep   sleeping

Mary is _____
                    laugh   laughing

• The teacher may provide opportunities in varied types of reading material to practice adding *ing* to known root words.
• The teacher gives direct practice in adding the ending to other known root words, pausing at times to review again the effect that adding the ending exerts upon the word meaning. This practice may include exercises with other previously introduced word endings, too, with a list developing like this:

toy	add *s*	toys	talk	add *ing*	talking
play	add *ed*	played	long	add *er*	longer
want	add *ed*	wanted	John	add *'s*	John's

• The specific point of structural analysis being taught naturally influences the nature of the practice exercises. In a lesson to recognize compounds, for example, the practice will include the words like *grand-mother, sailboat, something.*
• Other lists may show how *let us* becomes *let's, cannot* becomes *can't, do not* becomes *don't*, to develop readiness for contractions.

STEP 4. Finally—having established discrimination, made generalizations, and practiced the newly-learned skill—the children are encouraged to use the structural-analysis skill, both alone and in combination with all the other word-recognition skills, to unlock the meanings of unfamiliar words in reading context.

Gaining Independence in Word-Recognition Skills

Since the purpose of learning word-recognition skills is to use them independently, teachers establish procedures to encourage their independent use:

1. *Provide opportunities* for children to demonstrate their ability to use the acquired skills to unlock new words that they meet in their reading materials.
2. *Give encouragement and allow time* for children to try different

clues and word-analysis techniques. Guide the children's thinking with questions.

3. *Work with children in small groups* or on a one-to-one basis to help them apply the skills they have learned.

4. *Listen to the children's reading* and observe what they say when they respond orally, to diagnose their difficulties.

5. *Reteach needed skills* on a group basis or individual basis when the need for reteaching is demonstrated.

Providing Practice with Picture Dictionaries

When used skillfully, picture dictionaries make a major contribution to reading skill. Suggested procedures:

1. *Use the dictionaries to clarify and extend meanings* of words through such activities as these:

• First let the children look at the picture dictionary; let them study the pictures in general and see that meanings are associated with the pictures.

• Then have the children look at a particular picture and seek to associate it with a particular word.

• Later on, use the picture dictionaries for informal activities in the classroom. Children will enjoy using the picture dictionaries at home.

2. *Use picture dictionaries for directed activities for the whole class.* If the teacher wishes to stimulate discussion centered around a particular topic (animals, for example), an interesting presentation can be developed with the use of picture dictionaries, for children can find desired pictures and use them in discussion.

During the discussion the teacher may refer to the "Key Word Charts," if the beginning consonant has been taught, by asking the children whether they know the letter name of a new word. For example: bear.

"Who knows the name of the first letter of this word?"

"Who can find the key word that will help us with the beginning sound of the new word?"

A child finds the key word on the B chart and says it aloud.

In this manner children use many word-perception skills: picture clues, context clues, and initial-consonant clues.

3. *Use picture dictionaries for a group activity.* The teacher asks a group of children, each of whom has a picture dictionary, to find pictures centered about a particular topic. Children in this group find, show, and talk about the pictures.

The children develop the ability to associate a picture with the meaning of one particular word found in the sentence that accompanies the picture. For example:

bear

The bear is a big animal.

First the child reads the picture and the one word associated with the picture. Knowing the picturized word helps the child to unlock the meaning of other words in the sentence. He knows the word *bear* from the picture clue. The word *big* is already in his sight vocabulary. Now *animal* is unlocked with a context clue. The thought is directed in the child's mind to the word to complete the sentence, *The bear is a big* ————. The teacher has asked the children to find pictures of *animals*. The group has been talking about *animals*. The child almost automatically completes the sentence and has gained a new word.

This discussion might well be followed the next day with an experience chart on which the words *animal* and *animals* appear many times. In using the experience chart with the children, the teacher reinforces the vocabulary to which the children have been exposed through the use of the picture dictionaries. The teacher is also testing the children's visual and auditory memory of the selected words and providing opportunities for the children to use structural analysis (addition of *s* to *animal*), configuration clues (*animal* is a long word), and contextual clues (words in sentences on the experience chart). Thus, practice in all aspects of word-analysis can be provided.

Developing Comprehension Skills

Comprehension skills should be taught first on the oral level. First-hand experiences, centers of interest, daily living, storytelling, story reading, picture study and interpretation—all these provide opportunities for developing thinking skills that involve judgment, inference, and so on. The teacher capitalizes on situations that arise throughout the day. When the child sees the printed symbols, he is prepared to apply thinking skills he has already learned.

"The teacher's problem is to help the child translate the thinking he does in speaking and hearing situations to the printed matter before him."[6]

1. *Getting the main thought* is aided by such activities as the following:

ORAL STAGE: making up titles for experience charts, pictures, stories told or read by the teacher.

READING STAGE: choosing the best of several titles. The titles suggested by the children are written on the chalkboard and discussed. Selectivity and judgment enter into the choice of the most appropriate title. The thinking is most important. Another procedure is to list several sentences that tell what a story is mainly about, then similarly discuss them and select the most appropriate one.

2. *Finding Details.* Start with finding details that support the main idea, since finding the main idea and finding the supporting details usually go together.

ORAL STAGE: Start with a large picture showing action involving one or two characters (children, animals, etc.) with a simple, clearly-defined background. The children discuss the picture, suggest titles, and select the best.

The teacher asks, "What makes this the best title?"

The children study the picture anew and now find many details to support their choice. The teacher may wish to list these details on the board as the development proceeds.

• The teacher may read or tell a short, simple, familiar story. The children then express the main idea in the form of a title and contribute two or three supporting details.

• Before showing a filmstrip, the teacher may ask the children to try to remember two specified things; later, then, the details may be recorded on the chalkboard.

• Before the children listen to a recording, the teacher may ask them to remember certain things. These items may then be recorded after the listening experience. The ability to recall information is an important skill.

READING STAGE: Go back to a familiar experience chart, such as a work chart with a title and sentences with clearly-defined details. The children read to find supporting details for the main idea expressed in the title.

• Develop a new experience chart. The children suggest a title for it and find details to support their choice.

[6] *A Practical Guide to Individualized Reading,* Bureau of Educational Research Publication No. 40 (New York: Board of Education of the City of New York, October, 1960), page 69.

3. Determining sequence, another essential element of reading comprehension, is aided by such procedures as these:

ORAL STAGE: Read or tell a simple story to the children and then ask questions like these:

"What happened first?"
"What happened next?"
"What happened last?"

• Or, follow up the story by showing a series of pictures that cover the sequence of events. The teacher arranges the pictures in *incorrect* sequence along the chalkboard. The children retell the story, correcting the picture sequence.

• Show a filmstrip. Then the teacher guides the children in retelling the filmstrip story in sequence. The filmstrip may be shown again for verification.

READING STAGE: Use experience charts previously developed. First, the children reread the charts as a whole to recall sequence and review vocabulary. Then cut one copy of the chart into individual sentence strips. Shuffle the strips and give one strip to each of enough children to use all the strips. The children stand in front of the room and arrange themselves into the story sequence. The rest of the class participates by evaluating the sequence.

• Another sequence-determination activity is to have the children read a story and then to retell the events of the story in correct sequence. Guide the development by questions.

4. Following directions is a skill developed by activities such as the following:

ORAL STAGE: Make certain that the children have mastered the readiness steps in following directions. Develop skill in following directions through functional situations that involve classroom experiences in daily living—directions to monitors, for example, for the use of the centers of interest. Develop children's ability to follow directions in handling materials and in carrying out activities in the various curriculum areas.

READING STAGE: Utilize written directions that are needed in functional classroom situations, such as charts for various activities: "Before We Paint," "After We Paint," "Things to Do," "More to Do." Planning for a classroom party leads to somewhat similar charts, "What We Need," and so on.

• Utilize workbook directions for teaching purposes.

5. Drawing inferences is a phase of reading comprehension that is helped by such procedures as these:

ORAL STAGE: Use questions to elicit understanding of the actions of characters in a story and to get a reaction to an emotional tone. Develop sensory imagery. Lead the children from the literal level to the interpretative level.

• Show a picture with a story-telling quality; for example, a picture of a neatly-dressed little boy who is crying as he sits alone on the curbstone of a roadway. The children study the picture and then the teacher asks:

> "What is the little boy doing?"
> "How is he dressed?"
> "Why is he crying?"
> "What do you think happened?"

• Use daily experience in other curriculum areas, too:

> "What season is it?"
> "What is the weather like today?"

• Read or tell a story, and stop before the ending:

> "What would the ending be?"

• Show a filmstrip, and stop before it is finished:

> "What will happen next?"
> "Who can make up a new ending?"

READING STAGE: Lead very gradually from easy levels of interpretation to more difficult levels. Encourage the children, through questioning, to interpret both pictures and the text of pre-primers and other simple, pictured materials with brief textual content. Develop the children's ability to explain actions, to identify with story characters, to develop imagery, and to obtain increased satisfaction and pleasure from reading.

• Continue these skills with stories that the child can interpret on the basis of printed text with little help from illustrations.

Applying Comprehension Skills

1. Dramatizing Stories. Children apply organizational skills when they plan dramatizations:

> "What is the main idea?"
> "What details will be included?"
> "What characters will appear?"
> "What parts should we dramatize?"

Children carry out dramatization as another form of oral retelling of a story in their own words.

2. *Reading and Using Skills.* Encourage children to use comprehension skills in giving their reactions to varied materials they use—magazines, basal readers, trade books, workbooks, picture dictionaries.

"Therefore, in 'harnessing' thinking to reading, the teacher will help the child by developing these abilities at different times, through many different kinds of materials, and through many varied experiences."[7]

Introducing Work-Study Skills

In the beginning-to-read level of reading growth, learning the alphabetic sequences is the primary work-study skill involved, a skill developed through procedures like these:

1. *Using a picture dictionary* often sets the stage for developing a portion of the alphabetic sequences. For example, the teacher asks the children to find pictures of birds in the picture dictionary. One child finds and shows a robin.

"What is the name of the first letter?" asks the teacher.

"It starts with R," the child responds.

The teacher may then direct the children's attention to the alphabet charts in the room and asks, "Who can find that same letter for us?"

A child finds and indicates the letter R.

"What letter comes before R?" asks the teacher.

A child responds and indicates Q on the alphabet chart.

The teacher says, "Now let us look at our picture dictionaries to see whether the *same* letter comes before the R."

The children discover that the same letter, Q, does come before R. The same type of question and follow-up are repeated for the letter that follows R. The concepts of *before* and *after* are reinforced. The teacher says, "Let us say our letters, Q, R, and S." They say them and repeat them, and they have learned three letters in sequence.

If the children are relatively mature, the teacher repeats the procedure with another bird picture, and then more. The final step, eventually, might be to arrange pictures of birds in alphabetical order. Each child shows his bird-picture in the dictionary; children stand in proper sequence in the front of the room to represent correct alphabetic sequence.

• Some children make individual picture dictionaries from materials developed in the classroom.

2. *Using reference materials* reinforces alphabetic sequence mastery, not only because children enjoy such books as the alphabetic picture books in the library center which they use for reference and recreation but also because using all kinds of reference materials encourages the

[7]Loc. cit.

children to refer frequently to alphabet charts to check alphabetic sequences.

Introducing Library Activities

Both the materials in the classroom library and the concept of library organization have a place in the beginning-to-read level of reading growth.

1. *Handling library books* is an important phase of rousing interest in reading. The children learn how to hold a book, how to turn pages, how to read left-hand pages before right-hand pages, and many other book-management details. Later they learn how to use a table of contents and to refer to the page numbers in a book.

2. *The library-organization concept* begins, even at this early reading stage, by children practicing the classification of pictures. The teacher and children supply magazines, newspapers, coloring books, calendars, and greeting cards as a source of illustration. The teacher provides separate boxes or large envelopes bearing labels and/or indicative pictures; then the children sort the picture material into the appropriate containers—house pictures in one, pet pictures in another, and so on. Then when the class is learning about a topic for which the room has a picture-file resource, the teacher brings out the file and the children have a working set of materials for use in their classwork.

Later these same pictures can be used for bulletin-board displays, for dictated stories, for scrapbooks, or for starting new classifications for permanent class picture files.

Having had this experience, some children will want to start personal picture files as an independent activity.

48. THE TEACHING OF REMEDIAL READING

Board of Education of the City of New York

LESSON 8—READING FOR MAIN IDEA

Aims: To locate the main idea in a paragraph.
         To discover how the main idea is explained.

Reprinted from "The Teaching of Remedial Reading: Fifteen Remedial Lessons," *Teaching English for Higher Horizons* (1965), pp. 388–399. By permission of the New York City Board of Education.

Motivation: Anecdote about a student who could remember many facts in a story: dates, what people did, etc. Unfortunately, he could never tell the class what the author was trying to prove. If you were the reading teacher, how would you help him find the main idea?

List on
board

(*Anticipated responses:* Read the chapter heading, the small titles, the dark print used to introduce opening sentences, little notes in the margin, the opening and closing sentences of each paragraph.)

1. How would each of these suggestions help you find the main idea?
2. Which of these suggestions would help you find the main idea in a short story, in a newspaper article, in a science text?
3. How can we be sure that the sentence selected tells the main idea? (Needs explanation, examples. Most of the facts will explain it.)
4. Elicit Aim: What should we try to do in looking for the main ideas in the following paragraphs?
   a) Find the sentence which presents the main idea.
   b) Prove that it is the main idea.

Material:

Finding the Main Idea

1. There are four important reasons why foreigners come to this country. Some of them come here for the freedom of worship that our nation provides. Others come because they cannot endure the political persecution in their own land. Most of them, however, wish to escape from poverty in their own country and to enjoy the many opportunities that America offers to them.
2. Some immigrants come to this country for the freedom of worship that is encouraged here. Others come because they cannot endure the political persecution in their own land. Most of them, however, wish to escape from poverty in their own country and enjoy the many opportunities that America offers them. These are the four important reasons why foreigners come to this country.

Procedures:

1. *Let's warm up with these sentences.* Let's pretend each one is a main idea in its own paragraph. What facts or examples will you have to offer to prove each is a main idea?
   a. The automobile has many uses. (What are the uses?)

on
board

   b. Girls are better students than boys. (How? Why?)
   c. The traffic problem in New York City grows worse each year. (What is the problem?
   Why does it grow worse?)

2. *Distribute Material:*

    a. Have student read the opening sentence of Paragraph 1.

    b. If this is the main idea what will the author explain? Let's read the rest of the paragraph silently to see if reasons are given. Elicit responses.

    c. How can we organize our information to prove we are right? (outline)

    d. What shall we list as the main idea?

    —Foreigners come to this country for several important reasons.

    e. Development:

on
board

        (1) To *worship* freely
        (2) To escape *political persecution*
        (3) To escape *poverty*
        (4) To take *advantage* of opportunities America offers

    e. How many facts explain the main idea?
       What ties them together?

    f. Here is the same paragraph, (Paragraph 2), with the key sentence at the end instead of at the beginning. Does the paragraph seem different with the main idea at the end? Why?

    g. Which words does the author repeat to tie the sentences together?

    h. What does the last sentence do for the paragraph?

3. *Medical Summary:* (Return to students' responses to motivation.)

    a. Which of these suggestions have you found helpful in handling these exercises?

    b. What new approaches can you add?

4. *Drill material:*

Horses have almost completely disappeared from view on our streets and roads. Everyone uses an automobile instead of a carriage. Heavy carting that used to be done by wagon is now done by trucks of various sizes. The farmer's plow that used to be drawn by a horse is now pulled by a tractor. Heavy "combines" run by automotive power cut and thresh the grain and pour it into bags, and bind the straw into bales. Even the old-fashioned milk wagon vanished when the modern milk truck took its place.

    a. Read paragraph and underline the most important sentence (main idea).

    b. Place #1 in front of the first sentence that explains it, #2 in front of the next, and so forth.

    c. Have students read supporting sentences.
        (1) How is your sentence related to the main idea?
        (2) Is the word "horses" used in the sentence?
            How does the author use *suggestion?*
        (3) Which words are repeated or introduced in each sentence to suggest the disappearance of the horses?

Summary: How can our lesson today be of help to you in doing work in other subjects?

Lesson 9—Reading for Details

Aim: To increase comprehension by selecting details which develop the main idea.

Motivation: A newspaper reporter had been told to write an article about a flood. After observing the destruction and obtaining the facts, he divided his article into *paragraphs* about the following:

     I. Time and place of the flood
    II. Danger and suffering of the people
   III. Damage to property and crops
   IV. Rescue work

Procedure:

1. Write I, II, III, IV before each sentence below to show the *paragraph* in which it belongs. If a sentence contains a fact that does not relate to any one of the paragraphs, put X before the sentence.

    a. —————The flood occurred in sections of Illinois, Missouri, and Arkansas.

    b. —————By midnight, at least twenty persons had been reported dead.

    c. —————Damage to homes and buildings ran into uncounted millions of dollars.

    d. —————An examination showed that sixty percent of the crops have been ruined.

    e. —————Mr. Proctor, an artist, set up his canvas and painted pictures of the flood.

    f. —————Raging flood waters tore out levees that had cost thousands of dollars to build.

    g. —————The loss of life would have been even greater had the flood ocurred at night.

    h. —————Food and medical supplies were rushed to the flood victims by the Red Cross.

    i. —————Many people were ill and injured, and some had lost all trace of their families.

    j. —————All railroads and bridges in the area were washed out.

    k. —————Young crops were smothered by a blanket of muddy water.

    l. —————During this season, the area often suffers from vast melting snow and rising rivers.

m. ———A cold wave from the northeast increased the suffering of the people.

n. ———The Red Cross is asking for gifts of food, bedding and money.

o. ———It is anticipated that by the afternoon of the second day the flood waters will begin to recede.

p. ———Airplanes flew over the flooded areas searching for victims.

q. ———Hundreds of citizens aided soldiers and Red Cross workers.

r. ———The people rushed to the hills, hoping to obtain safety there from the flood.

s. ———A ferryboat capsized, and several people were drowned in the swirling deluge of water.

t. ———Soldiers were called out to assist the Red Cross in rescuing marooned people.

u. ———Adlai Stevenson was Governor of Illinois.

2. Now organize each *paragraph* in outline form by noting the appropriate letters under I, II, III, and IV.

Example: I.
   a.
   1.
   o.

3. Read *aloud* the text of each *paragraph* stating, in this order:

a. the Roman numeral and its heading (Example: I. Time and place of the flood).

b. the appropriate letter followed by the sentence (Example: Ia. The flood occurred in sections of Illinois, Missouri, and Arkansas).

c. (If time permits): the logical sequence in which you would arrange the sentences within each paragraph.

Assignment: Select a brief newspaper article. State the main idea and quote the lines answering any two of the questions: Who, Where, When, Why, What.

Lesson 10—Reading for Details

Aim: To develop skill in locating detailed information.

Motivation: Discuss the different types of information which can be obtained from the telephone book. Elicit situations in which efficient use would prove valuable.

Procedure:

1. Reading Practice Exercise Based on the Yellow Pages of the Manhattan Phone Book.*

* Practice booklets available from New York Telephone Company.

    a. What is the New York City Area Code Number?

    b. What are the phone and address of the F.B.I.?

    c. What is found on Page 5 of this booklet?

    d. What does the symbol O mean in the Subway Map?

    e. List the places and phone numbers where you can buy *Fiberglass Noise Control Products.*
      (Look under *Acoustical Contractors.*)

    f. List the places and phone numbers where you can get service and supplies for *Allen-Wales Adding Machines.*
      (Look under *Adding and Calculating Machines.*)

    g. What services are performed by *Custom Letter Service?* Where is it located and what is its phone number?
      (Look under *Addressing and Letter Service.*)

    h. What advertising agency specializes in Spanish language markets? Where is it located and what is its phone number?

    i. List the dealers and phone numbers of those who sell *Emerson Quiet-Kool Room and Home Air Conditioners.*
      (Look under *Air Conditioners—Room.*)

2. Reading Practice Exercise Based on the Manhattan Telephone Directory:

    a. List the numbers you would call for:
      (1) telephone repairs
      (2) business transactions
      (3) time of day
      (4) weather forecast

    b. How would you telephone Northern New Jersey?

    c. List the steps in correct dialing.

    d. How much would a station-to-station call after 9:00 o'clock and on Sundays cost you to:
      (1) Charlotte, N.C.
      (2) Seattle, Wash.
      (3) Cheyenne, Wyo. *Note:* These apply to the first 3 minutes.

    e. How much would a person-to-person call during the day cost you to:
      (1) Los Angeles, Calif.
      (2) Philadelphia, Pa.
      (3) Milwaukee, Wis. *Note:* These apply to the first 3 minutes.

    f. What does a 'beep' tone indicate if heard on your telephone line?

    g. What number would you call if you wished to place an order with Abraham and Straus Department Store?

    h. What number would you call if you wished to place a reservation at Las Brisas Hilton of Mexico?

    i. What are the addresses and phone numbers of all the Robert Hall Clothes Stores, Inc?

    j. What is the phone number of Stuyvesant High School? Its cafeteria? (Look under *New York City—Education Board of—School*)

Summary: Hand out folded slips of paper containing questions or situations requiring use of the telephone book. Have student stand in front of the room, stating aloud the steps followed and information secured. Seated youngsters should serve as checkers.

Examples:

a. You must telephone the Hotel Astor for a room reservation for a visitor.

b. You wish to learn the location of the library nearest your home.

LESSON 11—MULTIPLE READING SKILLS

Aim: To introduce students to the existence of different reading skills.
Motivation:

1. What is your feeling about the American who once said: "May she always be in the right, but my country, right or wrong."
2. You are going to read a selection which discusses this issue.

Material:

"Today, with the *emergence* of many new nations and the *consequent emphasis* upon *nationalism,* it is important to ask ourselves some thoughtful questions. Is it not possible to love one's own country without hating the natives of other countries? May one not be a patriot, ready to defend courageously the *traditions* and laws of his land without judging all the rest of the world fools or cowards? In all *conscience,* I must believe this possible; if it were not, I should be forced to make an unhappy *decision.* Rather than *delimiting* myself a Frenchman, or Englishman, or Nigerian, or American, I should voluntarily become a citizen of the world."
Anticipated vocabulary difficulties:

emergence	emphasis	traditions	decision	voluntarily
consequent	nationalism	conscience	delimiting	

Procedure:—Silent Reading of Paragraph

1. *Questions:*
   a. *Test for main idea*—Compare the point of view expressed in this passage with that of the "my country right or wrong" quotation.
   b. *Test for details*—With what kind of citizenship is "citizen of the world" compared?
   c. *Test for drawing conclusions*—It is possible, in the author's judgment to
      (1) admire another country and still love one's own
      (2) accept the existence of other people's courage

(3) value internationalism above nationalism
d. *Test for implications*—Faced with a foreign aid bill, the author of this paragraph would probably say—
    (1) I'm for it. My country is less important than world peace.
    (2) I'm for it. By helping the world, I see no reason why I am hurting my country.
    (3) I'm against it. The rest of the world is no concern of mine.
    (4) I'm against it. Helping the rest of the world will hurt my country.
    (5) I'll not vote at all. I don't care either way.

2. *Other skills that can be taught:*
  a. *Skimming:* How many questions does the author ask?
  b. *Finding key words:* How is "without" used each time it appears?
  c. *Relating ideas to one another:* Of what is the author certain?
  d. *Definition of abstract terms:* What is a "citizen of the world?"
  e. *Word attack skills:* What kind of effect do you imagine the word "coward" would have on someone if you called him that?

These procedures can be profitable with materials from class textbooks.

NOTE: You need not teach all these skills or even several of them. The kind and number of skills emphasized in any lesson will depend upon the level of the class.

Lesson 12—Remedial Reading in Mathematics

Aim: To distinguish between relevant and irrelevant facts in reading a *mathematical problem.*

Motivation: Discuss the costs of large household appliances and have students consider differences between outright and installment buying.

Procedure:

1. *Problem:* An insurance company *figures* that *depreciation* the first year is 30 percent of the cost, the second year 20 percent of the cost, and each *succeeding* year 10 percent of the cost. What would be the second-hand value of a car that is a year old and cost $2,000 when new?

2. Define the following words which have been written on the board before reading of the passage is begun.

    figures   depreciation   succeeding

3. Read the problem aloud instructing the students to follow with their rexographed copies. Divide the sentences into thought phrases and emphasize key words.

    An insurance company—*figures*—that *depreciation* the *first* year is

30 percent of the cost, — the *second* year (it is) 20 percent of the cost — and each *succeeding year* (it is) 10 percent of the cost. – – – What would be the *second* hand *value* of a car that is a *year old—* and cost $2,000 when new?

4. Discuss the passage with the following question-answer technique:
   a. *Teacher:* What is the meaning of the word *figures* as it is used in the first sentence?
      Elicit: It means calculates or sizes up or estimates.
   b. *Teacher:* What is meant by *depreciation?*
      Elicit: A loss in value.
   c. *Teacher:* What is meant by *each succeeding year?*
      Elicit: The next year, and the year after that, etc.
   d. *Teacher:* What is meant by *second-hand value?*
      Elicit: The car is a used car instead of a new car, so it isn't worth as much as when it was new.

5. Have students now read the passage silently to ascertain the fundamental problem:
   a. What is to be determined?
   b. What is given to help find it?

6. Conduct the discussion posing the following sample questions:
   a. *Teacher:* How can you restate the problem in your own words, as simply as possible?
      Elicit: A car cost $2,000 when it was new. We want to find its value when it is a year old.
   b. *Teacher:* What specific information is necessary in order to do this?
      Elicit: The cost when new and the depreciation the first year.
   c. *Teacher:* Are any facts stated which we will not need to use in solving the problem?
      Elicit: Yes. We do not need to know that the depreciation the second year is 20 percent of the cost, and we do not need to know that the depreciation each succeeding year is 10 percent of the cost.
   d. *Teacher:* Why do you think these facts are stated in the problem?
      Elicit: So that we will understand better how the value of a car continues to depreciate.

7. Have students refer to the passage, reading aloud the answers to these questions:
   a. What is your plan for solving the problem?
   b. How is the amount of depreciation expressed: in dollars or percent?
   c. Will your final answer be expressed in dollars or percent?
   d. Will the answer be larger or smaller than $2,000?

8. Now do the work necessary to solve the problem. (Write the following on board):

$2,000   (cost when new) $2,000
  x .30   (rate of depreciation)   −600   (second hand value of
  ———   ———   the car when it is a
 $600.00   (amount of depreciation) $1,400   year old)

Assignment: Direct the students to state a similar problem relating to a
large household appliance mentioned at the beginning of
the lesson.

LESSON 13—REMEDIAL READING IN SOCIAL STUDIES

Aim: To distinguish between fact and opinion reinforcing *social studies*
reading skills.

Motivation: Have you, or a member of your family, had the experience of
purchasing a commodity, highly recommended by its seller,
only to find it inferior in quality? (Examples: household
wares, clothing, insurance, correspondence course, etc.).
What checks could you have made to insure a wiser purchase? (Elicit: reliability of the vendor, comparative shopping, advice of an expert.)
We are also 'sold' information by newspapers and books.
How can we determine *the real thing*? How can we distinguish between a statement of fact and a statement of opinion?

Material: *Paragraph A*
Most Americans believe that the U.N. has lost its usefulness.
They are dismayed by the predominance of member nations
which they consider hostile to our national interests. Furthermore, they predict that the money we spend to maintain the
organization's world-wide activities would be sufficient to
wipe out poverty in this country within five years. It is likely
that a major movement will develop demanding withdrawal
of the United States from the U.N.

Paragraph B
Brazil is a country of great potential. It is the largest in South
America; it also has the mightiest river in the world. Moreover, its output in tin, copper, pulp, and coffee during 1963–
64 exceeded all previous records. The national per capita
income is now among the highest of South American countries.

Procedure:

1. Read *Paragraph A* and determine whether it is a statement of fact
or opinion. Be prepared to defend your answer by specific refer-
erences to its contents.

2. *Test for statement of fact or opinion:*
   a. Enumerate the nations which are hostile to the United States.
   b. What acts have they committed against the national interest of the United States?
   c. What two predictions are made? Can these be proved now?
   d. Which word clues indicate the nature of this paragraph?
   e. What does this statement express?
3. *Read Paragraph B.* Use the same critical thinking in determining whether it is a statement of fact or opinion.
4. *Test for statement of fact or opinion:*
   a. What information does this paragraph contain?
   b. How can the reader judge its accuracy?
   c. What other differences exist between assertions in *Paragraphs A and B?*
   d. What does this paragraph express?
5. How would you now define a statement of opinion?
   Elicit: a. something which expresses a feeling or belief
            b. something which cannot be proved in a reliable source
6. How would you define a statement of fact?
   Elicit: a. something we know has happened or has been done
            b. something that can be proved by a reliable source

Summary: Refer to aim. Why is it important to be alert to the above differences when reading a social studies textbook?

Homework: Decide whether the following statements express an opinion or a fact. State your reason for each decision.
1. I feel that Mary is happier in school than at home.
2. President Johnson was elected in 1964 by an overwhelming majority.
3. Red China will be admitted to the U.N. by a unanimous vote.
4. It looks as if it will rain tomorrow.

LESSON 14—READING FOR ORGANIZATION

Aim: To show the advantages of and need for organizing words and facts.
Motivation:

1. Show the class a number of pictures. Have them arrange pictures in proper groups (animals, birds, fruit, etc.).
2. Tonight, your mother will send you shopping to buy several things. These will require going to the grocery, to the drugstore and the bakery. How can you complete the shopping in the least amount of time without forgetting any item?
   Elicit: by first making a list classifying the commodities desired and grouping them according to the stores in which they can be found.

Procedure:

1. Show students a list of furniture in a moving van preparatory to being carried up to an apartment consisting of a kitchen, living room, bedroom, and bathroom. Using the board, direct students to assign the furniture to each appropriate room.
2. Discuss the value of organizing facts in this method.
   Elicit: such grouping helps one to visualize more clearly, remember more accurately, and work more efficiently.
3. How would this technique apply in studying school subjects: science, social studies, etc.?
   List on board unclassified words pertaining to other subjects; have students group these under proper headings.

Example:	multiply	test tube
	paint	brush
	microscope	compass
	easel	subtract

4. Check results. Drill by having one-half of class dictate a similar practice list to other half. Rotate until students have learned simple organization of words/facts and the advantages of this technique.

Assignment: Have youngsters bring in advertisements representing as many different products as possible. Use these for grouping exercises.

Lesson 15—Learning Parts of Books

Aim: To learn the parts of a book and their purposes.

Motivation: Let us suppose that a favorite aunt has taken you into a bookstore to treat you to a book. You are interested in making airplanes and enjoy leafing through books about military craft, famous flyers, different types of planes, etc. Since it is late, the owner of the store will allow you only a short time in which to examine his supply of books in this subject field. What is the fastest method you can use to learn the general contents of each book in order to determine which one to buy.

Material: A common student textbook in another subject; for example, social studies.

Procedure:

1. State that you plan to ask the class questions concerning the social studies textbook which will enable you to determine its contents in brief order. Direct the students to answer your questions orally; write the terms used and the responses to them on the board.

2. What information about the book is given on its cover?
   Elicit: *title, author, publisher.*
3. Where else is this information supplied? Elicit: *title page.*
   What other information is provided on the back of the title page?
   Elicit: *copyright date.* Discuss its importance.
4. What does the word *preface* mean? Direct the students to skim
   through the page. Elicit: the preface is a statement of the author's
   aim in writing the book. Direct one youngster to read the dictionary
   definition.
5. Turn to the next page. What is the purpose of the *table of contents?*
   Elicit: it tells the reader what the *body* of the book is, its arrangement, and the order of its appearance. It provides a rapid means of
   acquaintanceship with both the contents of the book and its pagina-
   tion. (Repeat the term *body* and elicit its definition.)
6. Turn to the back of the book. What does the word *glossary* mean?
   Elicit: it provides the meanings of the terms used in the book. How
   are the words arranged in this section? Elicit: in alphabetical order
   as in a dictionary.
7. What is the last part of the book? Elicit: *index.* What information
   does it give the reader? Elicit: the contents of the book in detail, in
   alphabetical order, with the page numbers listed. If there is enough
   time and interest, have the class examine the differences between
   the *table of contents* and the *index.*

Summary:

1. Demonstrate, by reviewing the terms and responses on the board,
   the extent of the information learned about the social studies
   textbook.
2. Direct the students to copy the terms and definitions in their notebooks: cover, title page, copyright date, preface, table of contents,
   body, glossary, and index.

Follow-up: Repeat the questions, using the same terms and definitions, in
   examining a second classroom textbook.

.49. READING LESSONS IN LANGUAGE ARTS
FOR THE FUNCTIONAL NON-READER

Board of Education of the City of New York

USING PHONETIC ANALYSIS TO RECOGNIZE WORDS

The ability to use phonetic analysis to recognize words known orally, or to pronounce new words, is most important to efficient reading. This ability includes recognition of initial consonant sounds, final consonant sounds, double consonant sounds, consonant blends, and vowel sounds. Lessons I and II that follow suggest methods of procedure and specific examples which the language arts teacher may use to develop specific phonetic analysis skills. These lessons are intended for the beginning reader in the junior high schools, and may be adapted for instructing the non-English speaking student. This adaptation involves a simplification of the questioning in column II and an increase in the oral repetition of new vocabulary contained in the lesson. The teacher may "upgrade" or "downgrade" the specific examples depending upon the needs, interests, and maturity level of the students.

In preparation for these lessons, it is essential that the teacher review the names of the letters of the alphabet, identify the vowels and consonants by letter names, and give practice in checking the vowel and consonants found in many one syllable words.

LESSON I

Phonetic Analysis Skill: Developing recognition of a specific consonant blend to aid in recognition of words known orally, or in the pronunciation of new words. (In developing this skill, please note that students are required to recognize sounds only as they appear in words. Students are never required to sound any letter or letters in isloation.)

Approach

PROCEDURE

1a. Relate an experience, the same as or similar to that below (see 1a).

Reprinted from *Reading in the Subject Areas, Grades 7-8-9,* Curriculum Bulletin Series No. 6 (1963–1964), pp. 90–109. By permission of the New York City Board of Education.

b. Through questioning, elicit from students the possible relationship that exists between the familiar experience and reading.

2. Question to elicit the purpose of the lesson and write it on the board.

DEVELOPMENT

1a. Say: Listen to this experience John had.

John made a telephone call to a friend. The friend called him by name as soon as John had said 'hello'. John didn't have to tell him his name at all in order to be recognized.

b. Q: How do you think the friend was able to recognize John before he could tell his name?

A: The friend recognized John because he was familiar with the sound of John's voice. It sounded "high", "low", etc.

Q: Can you think of any relation that exists between recognizing John because of the familiar sound of his voice and recognizing new words because we are familiar with the sounds contained in the new words?

A: Yes. If we are familiar with the sounds that are contained in new words, then we may easily recognize the words as we read.

2. Q: What do you think we shall learn in reading today?

A: We shall learn how a familiar sound can help us to recognize words known orally or to pronounce new words. (Write aim on the board.)

Direct Teaching

PROCEDURE

1. Present to class three familiar objects, the same as or similar to those below (see 1). Through questioning, elicit the names of the objects and write the names on the board.

2. Have a student read the three words on the board aloud and direct the class to listen carefully for the part of each word that sounds exactly the same. Put a box around the part of each word that sounds the same.

3a. Through questioning, have students note that the boxed off sound is made up of three consonants, and tell students the name given to a sound made up of three consonants blended together as one. (consonant blend)

b. If necessary, use a familiar experience to clarify concept of consonant blend.

4. Draw students' attention to the position of the consonant blend in each word and tell students the name given to a consonant blend in this position. (initial consonant blend)

5. Read to class a group of words, the same as or similar to the ones below (see 5) and tell students to listen carefully for the words that begin with the same consonant blend. (Auditory Discrimination) Check students' answers and write on the board the words that begin with this consonant blend. Have a student underline the initial consonant blend in each word. (Visual Discrimination)

6. Drill on recognition of this consonant blend by having students solve riddles, the answers to which have to begin with the same consonant blend. Write the correct answers on the board. Have the answers read aloud and have a student underline the initial consonant blend heard in each answer. (Auditory and Visual Discrimination)

7. Continue to drill on recognition of this consonant blend by reading sentences to class and having students count the number of words they hear beginning with the same blend. Check students' answers by writing the correct words on the board and underlining the same consonant blend in each word.

8. Using examples the same as or similar to those below (see 8), have students build words by substituting the consonant blend for underlined letter or letters in words. Have students check their answers by writing new words on the board.

DEVELOPMENT

1. Show the following familiar objects—
   piece of string
   book strap
   drinking straw

   Q: What are these objects?
   A: Piece of string
        Book strap
        Drinking straw

   List on the board: string
                        strap
                        straw

2. Say: While Lily is reading the words on the board, the rest of the class listen very carefully to hear the part of each word that sounds exactly the same.

   Q: Were you able to hear the part in each word that sounds exactly the same?
   A: Yes.
   Say: Draw a box around the part of each word that sounds the same. (Call on a student.)
        $\boxed{\text{s t r}}$i n g
        $\boxed{\text{s t r}}$a p
        $\boxed{\text{s t r}}$a w

3a. Say: Examine the boxed off sound in each word.
   Q: How many consonants make up this one sound?
   A: The sound is made up of three consonants.
   Say: We call a sound made up of three consonants blended together as one, a consonant blend.
   b. Blending ingredients in cake baking, voices blended in song, etc.
4. Say: Note that the consonant blend in each word is found at the beginning of the word. We call this an initial consonant blend.
5. Say: Listen carefully to this group of words. Note the words you hear that begin with the same blend as the word s<u>tr</u>aw.

> still
> strong
> stripe
> spin
> street

   Q: Which words did you hear beginning with the same blend as in the word straw?
   A: <u>str</u>ong
      <u>str</u>ipe
      <u>str</u>eet
   Write the words on the board as students give them to you, and have a student underline the initial consonant blend in each word.
6. Say: I know you like to solve riddles. See if you can solve these riddles. Remember that each answer must begin with the same sound as in s<u>tr</u>aw.
   Riddles: I'm thinking of a word that has the same meaning as brook. (<u>str</u>eam)
   What is the opposite of crooked? (<u>str</u>aight)
   What is used to carry someone hurt in an accident? (<u>str</u>etcher)
   Write the answers to the riddles on the blackboard. Have a student underline the same initial consonant blend ·in each word.
7. Say: As I read these sentences to you, listen for the words that begin with the same blend as in s<u>tr</u>aw.
   The <u>str</u>ong swimmer crossed the <u>str</u>eam with swift <u>str</u>okes. (Three words begin with the same blend as in straw: <u>str</u>ong, <u>str</u>eam, <u>str</u>okes.)
   The <u>str</u>ay dog was found on Fifth <u>Str</u>eet. (Two words begin with the same blend as in s<u>tr</u>aw: <u>str</u>ay and <u>str</u>eet.)
8. Write on board: <u>s</u>ing
      <u>l</u>aw
      <u>sp</u>eak

team
<u>b</u>ike

Say: Build other words by substituting the consonant blend as in
<u>str</u>aw for the underlined letter or letters in each word.

A: <u>s</u>ing   = <u>str</u>ing
            <u>l</u>aw   = <u>str</u>aw
            <u>sp</u>eak   = <u>str</u>eak
            team   = <u>str</u>eam
            <u>b</u>ike   = <u>str</u>ike

Summary

PROCEDURE

1. Refer to the purpose of the lesson written on the board, and through questioning, have students decide whether or not the purpose was achieved.
2. Have students read aloud the words recognized because they are now familiar with the consonant blend as in the word <u>straw</u>. Have students copy these words in their notebooks, underlining the initial consonant blend in each word.

DEVELOPMENT

1. Q: What did we say we were going to do today? Did we accomplish our purpose? How?
   A.   We were going to learn how recognizing a familiar sound can help us to recognize words. We did accomplish our purpose. Since we are now familiar with the consonant blend in <u>str</u>aw, we can recognize many words as we read.
2. Say: Read aloud the words you recognize because you are familiar with the initial consonant blend as in <u>str</u>aw.
   Examples: straw, strap, string, strong, stripe, street, strain, streak, stream, straight, strokes, stray, etc.
   Say: Copy the words above into your notebooks. Underline the familiar consonant blend in each word.

Follow-up Activities

Reinforce the learnings of this lesson by having pupils practice word-building activities, the same as or similar to the following.

PRACTICE EXERCISES

Substitute the initial consonant blend as in <u>str</u>aw for the underlined letter or letters in the following sentences:

The plane had no <u>w</u>ing. (<u>str</u>ing)
He was a <u>w</u>rong choice as a leader. (<u>str</u>ong)
Do you know how <u>l</u>aws are made? (<u>str</u>aws)
Look down at your <u>f</u>eet. (<u>str</u>eet)

Complete the following sentences by selecting the correct word from the words listed below:

straw—string—strike—streak

Tom had a long _____ on his kite.
The men were not working because they were on _____.
Horses sleep on beds of _____ .

A Final Note

The sequential steps described in the direct teaching of the preceding lesson, steps 1–8, may be used to develop recognition of initial consonant sounds, final consonant sounds, and consonant blends.
Examples:

Consonants	Consonant Blends
b, g	bl, fr, sc, spr, spl
c, h	gl, tr, tw, scr, squ
d, l	cl, dr, st, shr, etc.
f , etc.	sl, cr, etc.

The dictionary is the source for finding specific examples to clarify each step in the procedures of the lesson.

LESSON II

Phonetic Analysis Skill: Developing recognition of visual clues to the short vowel sound in words of one syllable.

Approach

PROCEDURE

1. Make a statement, the same as or similar to the one below (see 1), with regard to the contents of every word in the English language.

Question students about the meaning of the statement. Prove the validity of the statement.

a. List on board one syllable words to prove the validity of the statement.
b. Underline the vowel in each word.
c. Say the words orally, directing students to listen to the vowel sound in each word.
d. Draw students' attention to the difference or similarity in the vowel sounds.

2. State that vowels have many different sounds and that there are visual clues that help to determine the vowel sound in words of one syllable. Through questioning elicit the purpose of the lesson from the students and write it on the board.

DEVELOPMENT

1. Say: Listen to this true statement:
         "Every word in the English language contains at least one sounded vowel."
    Q: What does this statement mean?
    A: It means that every word in our language contains the sound of at least one vowel.
    Q: Do you think that even very short words, words of one syllable, contain at least one sounded vowel?
    A: Yes.
a. Say: We'll try to prove the validity of the statement. Here are some one syllable words you know.
    A: (Write on board)
         a—as in a book
         an—as in an apple
         the—as in the desk
b. Q: Is there a vowel in each of the words?
    A: Yes.
         Underline the vowel:
                a   an   the
c. Say: Note the same vowel in a and an. Listen as I say these words. (Say the words a and an.)
    Q: Did you hear the sound of the vowel in each word?
    A: Yes.
d. Q: Did the vowel sound the same or different in each word?
    A: The vowel sounded different in each word.
    Say: Now listen to the sound of the vowel in this word. (the) Tell students that the vowel in the word the sounds the same as the vowel in the word a.

Say: Even the above one syllable words contained a sounded vowel. Therefore, the statement about every word in our language containing a sounded vowel is a true one.

2. Say: You noticed that the one vowel had different sounds. There are clues you can see to help you recognize the vowel sound in many one syllable words. (Visual Clues)

   Q: What shall we learn in reading today?

   A: We shall learn to recognize some clues to vowel sounds in words of one syllable. (Write aim on board.)

Direct Teaching

PROCEDURE

1. Have students examine a list of one syllable words, each beginning with the same vowel. (Use the list below [see 1] or a similar one.) Have a student underline the vowel in each word. Read the words aloud. Direct students to listen to the sound of the vowel in each word. Through questioning, have students identify the vowel sound as the same in each word. Tell them what this vowel sound is called. (Short vowel sound.) Through questioning lead students to recognize the clue to the short vowel sound in these one syllable words. (Visual Clue I)

2. Have students examine another list of one syllable words where the vowel is in the middle of each word. (Use the list below [see 2] or a similar one.) Follow the techniques described in step 1, above, and through questioning, lead students to recognize the visual clue to the short vowel sound in one syllable words where the vowel is in the middle of each word. (Visual Clue II)

3a. Review the two visual clues to the short vowel sound in words of one syllable.
   Visual Clue I—Step 1
   Visual Clue II—Step 2

  b. Apply the clues to additional words containing the same vowel sound.

4. Use the techniques described in steps 1 and 2 of the Direct Teaching Procedures to check on recognition of the visual clues to the short sound of other vowels in one syllable words. Use the list of words below (see 4), or a similar list. (It is suggested that steps 1, 2, and 3 be developed in one lesson and step 4 be developed in several subsequent lessons, depending upon the needs and ability levels of pupils. Have pupils apply the learnings of each lesson to the recognition and pronunciation of words containing similar vowel sounds.)

DEVELOPMENT

1. Say: Look at this list of one syllable words:

    <u>a</u>d
    <u>A</u>l
    <u>a</u>m
    <u>a</u>s
    <u>a</u>t, etc.

    Charles, please underline the vowel in each word.

    Say: As I read these words aloud to you, listen to the sound of the underlined vowel in each word.

    Q: Did you hear the sound of the vowel in each word? What did you notice about the vowel sound you heard in each word?

    A: The vowel sound was the same in each word.

    Say: The vowel sound you heard in each word is called a short vowel sound. (ă)

    Q: Do you see any clue to the short vowel sound in the words on the board?

    A: Yes, the single vowel at the beginning of a one syllable word is usually a clue to the short sound of the vowel. (Visual Clue I)

2. List of one syllable words with the vowel in the middle of each word:

had	bad	gal
cad	lad	Sal
dad	mad	ham

    a.   Underline the vowel in each word.
    b.   Read words aloud and have students listen for the sound of the vowel in each word.
    c.   Identify the vowel sound as the same in each word.
    d.   Tell students each word contains a short vowel sound. (ă)
    e.   Look for a clue to the short sound of the vowel in each word. Visual Clue II: A single vowel in the middle of a one syllable word is usually a clue to the short sound of the vowel.

3a. Q: What two clues will help you to recognize the short vowel sound in one syllable words?

    A: Visual Clue I: The single vowel at the beginning of a one syllable word is <u>usually</u> a clue to the short sound of the vowel. Visual Clue II: <u>A</u> single vowel in the middle of a one syllable word is usually a clue to the short sound of the vowel.

    b.   Use the dictionary to locate additional words.

4. List of one syllable words:

<u>E</u>d	<u>Ne</u>d	k<u>e</u>g
<u>e</u>gg	b<u>e</u>d	l<u>e</u>g, etc.
	l<u>e</u>d	

if	is	sit
in	Bill	his
it	tin	bit, etc.

odd	don	rod
on	cod	Tod, etc.
	pod	

up	cup	bus
us	pup	Gus, etc.
	sup	

Summary

PROCEDURES

Through questioning, highlight the visual clues to the short vowel sound in words of one syllable.

DEVELOPMENT

Q: What clues may we look for to help us recognize the short vowel sound of the letter a in one syllable words?

A: a. A single vowel at the beginning of a one syllable word.

　　b. A single vowel in the middle of a one syllable word.

A Final Note

Separate lessons are indicated to develop recognition of the following visual clues to vowel sounds in one syllable words:

　　a. A single vowel at the end of a one syllable word is a clue to a long vowel.

　　　Examples: why – cry

　　b. Two vowels together in a one syllable word indicate a long vowel sound.

　　　Examples: meat – boat

　　c. Two vowels in a one syllable word, one of which is a final e, indicate a long vowel sound.

　　　Examples: face – lone

　　d. A vowel followed by the letters, r, l, or w, is neither long nor short, but is controlled by these letters.

　　　Examples: all, art, saw

The procedures used to develop recognition of the visual clues to the short sound of vowels in Lesson II may be used to develop any of the visual clues to vowel sounds listed in a – d above. The teacher simply substitutes examples to develop recognition of the specific visual clue.

USING STRUCTURAL ANALYSIS TO IDENTIFY LONGER WORDS

The ability to analyze the structure of words, using familiar portions to pronounce the words and to estimate their meanings, is a definite aid to word recognition and understanding. This ability includes the following sequence of skills:

1. Identifying the root of longer words: impossibility, racing, comical.
2. Identifying and understanding the importance of common prefixes and suffixes: re, ad, un, in, dis, ex, er, or, less, ful.
3. Estimating the meaning of new words through familiar portions: in compound words, playground; handshake—in longer words, unconstitutional; irregularity.
4. Recognizing differences in meaning or in shades of meaning in accordance with the accent: ob' - ject and ob - ject', des' - ert and de - sert'.

Before receiving instruction in the first skill listed above, students should be able to identify root words in longer words: as date, dating; hire, hiring, etc. This involves an understanding of the following phonetic analysis skill: In one syllable words that contain two vowels, one of which is a final silent e, a long vowel sound is usually given the first vowel letter. Examples: hire, date, etc.

Lessons I and II that follow suggest methods of procedure and offer specific examples which the language arts teacher may use to develop and implement specific structural analysis skills. In preparation for these lessons, it is essential that students are able to identify the syllables in two syllable words.

In Lesson I, separate lessons may be indicated if students are very severely disabled readers. The lesson may be broken down into two separate parts, first, to use familiar portions of compound words as an aid to pronouncing the words, and second, to use the familiar portions of compound words as an aid in estimating the meanings of the words. The teacher should keep in mind the ability and interest level of the students so that the examples can be "upgraded" or "downgraded" according to the needs of the students.

LESSON I

Structural Analysis Skill: Using familiar portions of compound words as an aid in pronouncing the words and a possible aid in estimating their meanings.

Approach

1. Describe an incident in which a problem arose that needed immediate solution. (Use the incident below [see 1] or similar one.) Through questioning elicit from students their suggestions on the solution of the problem.
2. Repeat the solution to the foregoing problem, and show students the relationship that exists between the solution of this problem and the problem of encountering long words in reading. Through questioning, elicit from students the purpose of the lesson and write it on the board.

1. Say: A scientist, a rock specialist, discovered a very unusual rock in his travels about the country. He wanted to examine the formation of the rock in his laboratory, but it was much too heavy for him to lift.

   Q: What do you think the scientist could do to solve his problem?
   A: The scientist could use a pickax to break the rock into parts so that he could carry a portion of the rock to his laboratory for examination.

2. Say: The scientist was able to break up the rock into smaller parts so that he could examine it. When we meet a long word in our reading, we can't take a pickax to break it up as the scientist did to the rock. We can only try to break the long word into familiar portions to help us pronounce the word and sometimes, to figure out its meaning.

   Q: What is the purpose of our reading lesson today?
   A: To use familiar portions of long words to help us pronounce the words and to try to estimate their meanings.
   (Write aim on board.)

Direct Teaching

1. Write sentences on the board. Include in the sentences, compound words, each composed of two words written together as one. (Use the sentences below [see 1] or similar ones.)
2. Direct students as follows, step by step, and through questioning develop the lesson:

    a. Read sentence one silently and examine the form or structure of the underlined words in the sentence.

    b. Separate each underlined word into its familiar parts, and pronounce each whole word.

    c. Consider the meaning of each familiar part.

    d. Try to estimate the meaning of the whole word, as it is used in the sentence.

    e. Use the dictionary to find the exact meaning of the word if it cannot be estimated from the meaning of its familiar parts.

3. Tell students the name given to words composed of two whole words pronounced as one.

4. Using the procedures described in step 2, have students analyze the form or structure of the compound word in the second sentence. Through questioning, have pupils discover that they cannot estimate the meaning of this word from its familiar parts but must use the dictionary to determine its exact meaning as it is used in the sentence.

5. Direct a student to find the meaning of the word in a dictionary on the junior high school level.

6. Have students analyze the compound words in sentences that remain on the board. Check students' work by having them pronounce the words and attempt to give their meanings. Have students explain whether they are able to figure out the word meanings from their familiar parts or whether they had to use the dictionary to determine their exact meanings.

DEVELOPMENT

1. Sentences on board:
    a. The boy was <u>shortchanged</u> by the <u>storekeeper.</u>
    b. The driver <u>sideswiped</u> the new car.
    c. The <u>cutout</u> on the sports car made a very loud noise.
    d. The record of the voyage was kept in a <u>logbook.</u>

2. Say: Follow my directions.
    a.   Read the first sentence silently and examine the form of the underlined words in the sentence.

    b. Q: Do you notice anything about the form or structure of the underlined words?

       A: The words are each composed of two familiar words:

<u>short</u> <u>changed</u>
<u>store</u> <u>keeper</u>

      Say: Because you recognize the two familiar words in each underlined word, you are able to pronounce the underlined words.

    c. Say: Think of the meaning of the familiar words in <u>short</u> <u>changed</u> and <u>store</u> <u>keeper.</u>

d. Q: Do the meanings of the familiar words give you a hint to the meaning of each whole word?—Can you estimate the meaning of each whole word?—

   A: Yes, the word shortchanged in this sentence means that less than the correct amount of change was given (Informal-U.S.) and the word storekeeper means the man who runs the store.

e. Say: By using the familiar parts of each word, we were able to pronounce the words and estimate their meanings.

   Say: Sometimes we are not able to estimate the meaning of a long word even though we are familiar with its parts. Then we must use the dictionary to find the exact meaning of the word as it is used in the sentence.

3. Say: We call words composed of two whole words pronounced as one, compound words.

4.   Sentence two on board:

   The driver <u>sideswiped</u> the new car.

   Q: Do you recognize the two familiar words in sideswiped?

   A: Yes—side and swiped.

   (Pronounce the word.)

   Q: What does the word swiped mean?

   Possible Student Answer:

   Swiped to me means snatched or stolen.

   Say: Then, in this sentence, the word sideswiped would mean that the driver snatched the side of the new car. Obviously, this is not correct.

5. The dictionary meaning of swipe is to strike a glancing blow.

   Q: Would the dictionary meaning be appropriate in this sentence?

   A: Yes, it would mean that the driver hit the side of the new car.

6. Compound words included in remaining sentences:

   cutout: meaning cannot be estimated from its familiar parts. Dictionary meaning: a valve in the exhaust pipe of an engine through which gases pass directly into the air.

   logbook: meaning cannot be estimated from its familiar parts. Dictionary meaning: book in which a daily record of a ship's voyage is kept.

Summary

PROCEDURE

1. Review the purpose and use of analyzing the structure of compound words. Stress the fact that familiar parts of some compound words offer broader hints to their meaning than others.

1. Q: Of what use to you is the ability to analyze the structure of
        compound words.
    A:
        a. It helps us to pronounce the words.
        b. It sometimes helps us to estimate the meanings of the words.
    Say: Keep in mind that you must use the dictionary to find the exact
        meaning of a compound word if you can't estimate the meaning
        from its familiar parts.

A Final Note

The following list may be used to give students practice in analyzing
the structure of compound words as an aid to pronouncing the words
and in estimating their meanings:

roadside	tailwind	headlong	larkspur
overcoat	breakdown	boxwood	nightclub
nightfall	patchwork	cattail	instep
pancake	watchdog	footloose	buttercup
lookout	raindrops	chairman	woodwind

Lesson II

Structural Analysis Skill: Recognizing the pronunciation of two syllable
                            words which look exactly alike but have
                            different meanings.

Approach

1. Write two related sentences on the board, the same as or similar to
    those below (see 1). Read sentences aloud, directing students to listen
    carefully to the pronunciation of the underlined words in the sen-
    tences. Through questioning, elicit the following facts from students:
    a. The underlined words look exactly alike but each is pronounced
       differently.
    b. Each of the underlined words has a different meaning.
    c. There are two syllables in each underlined word.
    d. Students do not know how the pronunciation of each underlined

word was determined.

2a. State that there is a guide that may often be used to determine the pronunciation of two-syllable words which look exactly alike but which have different meanings.

b. Elicit the purpose of the lesson from the students and write it on the board.

DEVELOPMENT

1. Sentences on board:

Today is my son's birthday.

I bought him a <u>present</u> and will <u>present</u> it to him tonight.

Say: As I read the sentences on the board to you, listen carefully to the pronunciation of each underlined word.

a. Q: What did you notice about the underlined words?

A: Both underlined words look exactly alike but each has a different pronunciation.

b. Q: What do each of the underlined words mean?

A: The first underlined word, <u>present</u>, refers to a gift and the second underlined word, <u>present</u>, denotes an act of giving.

c. Q: How many syllables do you hear in each word as I say the words <u>present</u> and <u>present</u>?

A: There are two syllables in each word.

d. Q: How was I able to determine how to pronounce these two syllable words that look exactly alike but have two different meanings?

A: We don't know.

2a. Say: There is a guide that can help you determine the pronunciation of two syllable words such as these.

b. Q: What shall we do today?

A: We'll learn a guide to the pronunciation of two syllable words that look exactly alike but have different meanings.

Direct Teaching

PROCEDURE

1a. Review the meaning of the first underlined word on the board. By questioning similar to that at the right, elicit from students the fact that the first underlined word refers to an object or a thing. Write the word "Object" on board.

b. Direct students to listen to the pronunciation of this word again to see if they can determine the part of the word that receives greater stress.

c. Write the word under the word "Object" on the board and underline the stressed portion of the word. (First syllable)

2a. Review the meaning of the second underlined word on the board, and by questioning similar to that at the right, elicit from students the fact that the meaning of this word denotes action. Write the classification "Action Word" on the board.

b. Direct students to listen to the pronunciation of this word to determine whether or not they can hear the part of the word that receives greater stress.

c. Write this word under the heading "Action Word" on the board and underline the stressed portion of the word. (Second syllable)

3. Using the procedures in steps 1 and 2, have students determine the pronunciation of additional two syllable words which look alike but have different meanings. Use examples, the same as or similar to those below (see 3). List each underlined word under its proper heading "Object" or "Action Word" on the board and underline the stressed (accented) syllable in each word.

4a. Have all words listed under the classification, "Object," read aloud and direct students to listen to the stressed portion of every word in the list. By questioning, draw from students the conclusion that greater stress (accent) is given the first syllable in each word that refers to an object.

b. Using the procedures described in step 4a, draw from students the conclusion that greater stress (accent) is given the second syllable in each word that denotes action.

5. Give students practice in determining the pronunciation of words similar to those at the right. Question students about their reason for the pronunciation given each word.

DEVELOPMENT

1a. Say: You said that the word <u>pres</u>ent in the first sentence means a gift.
   Q: Can you actually hold a gift in your hands? Can you touch it? What can we say this meaning of the word represents?
   A: We can see a gift, touch it, hold it in our hands. A gift is an object or thing. The word <u>pres</u>ent in the first sentence represents an object. (Write the word "Object" on the board.)

b. Say: Listen to the pronunciation of the word <u>pres</u>ent that refers to an object or thing. (noun)
   Q: Were you able to determine the part of the word, <u>pres</u>ent, that received greater stress?
   A: The first syllable of this word, <u>pres</u>ent, received greater stress.

c.   Write the word, <u>pres</u>ent, under the classification "Object" on the board and underline the first syllable of the word.

2a. Say: You said that the word pres<u>ent</u> in the second sentence means the same as the word, give.

Q: Was the gift <u>given</u> to anyone in the second sentence?

A: Yes.

Say: The word give denotes an action of some kind. Therefore the word pres<u>ent</u> is an action word. (verb) Write "Action Word" on the board.

b. Say: Listen to the pronunciation of the word that means to give: Present. Determine the part of the word that receives greater stress. (Say the word present)

Q: Were you able to determine the part of the word that received greater stress?

A: Yes, the second syllable received greater stress.

c. Write the word pres<u>ent</u> under the heading "Action Word" and underline the second syllable.

3. Sentences on the board:

The sanitation department collects <u>re</u>fuse three times a week in my neighborhood. (object)

I had to re<u>fuse</u> the invitation to the dance. (action word)

His school <u>re</u>cord is excellent. (object)

The teacher began to re<u>cord</u> the test marks. (action word)

A <u>per</u>mit is needed to drive a car. (object)

The boy's father did not per<u>mit</u> him to drive.

4a.

Object	Action Word
<u>pre</u>sent	pres<u>ent</u>
<u>re</u>fuse	re<u>fuse</u>
<u>re</u>cord	re<u>cord</u>
<u>per</u>mit	per<u>mit</u>

Say: As the words listed under each heading are pronounced, the rest of the class listen to the stress given to the underlined part of each word.

Q: Which syllable is given greater stress in all the words that refer to objects?

A: Greater stress is given the first syllable in words that refer to objects.

b. Q: Which syllable is given greater stress in words that denote action?

A: Greater stress is given the second syllable in words that denote action.

5. Say: Pronounce the following words. Give a reason for your pronunciation.

<u>per</u>fume	(object)
de<u>sert</u>	(action)
ob<u>ject</u>	(action)
<u>com</u>press	(object)

Summary

PROCEDURE

1. Refer to the purpose of the lesson written on the board, and through questioning, have students determine whether or not the purpose of the lesson was achieved.
2. Through questioning, highlight the guide that may aid in pronouncing two syllable words that look alike but have different meanings.
  a. In such words that refer to objects.
  b. In such words that denote action.

DEVELOPMENT

1. Say: We said we were going to learn how to pronounce two syllable words that look exactly alike but have different meanings.

   Q: Did we achieve our purpose?

   A: Yes, we did learn how to pronounce such words.

2. Q: Is there any guide which may help you pronounce two syllable words that look alike but have different meanings? Explain this guide.

   A: Yes, there is such a guide that often aids in determining the pronunciation of such two syllable words.
   a. Give greater stress to the first syllable when pronouncing words that refer to objects.
   b. Give greater stress to the second syllable when pronouncing words that denote action.

A Final Note

There are additional word-recognition lessons which the language arts teacher may use if students have already acquired an understanding of the skills described in the preceding lessons. In the social studies chapter of this manual, Lessons I, II, III suggest the procedures that may be used to develop the following word-recognition skills:

  I. To develop the ability to find the meaning of new words when they are clearly explained in the context.
 II. To find the exact meaning of words when no clues to their meaning appear in the context.
III. To understand that familiar words often have different meanings according to the context in which they are used.

The teacher may "downgrade" or "upgrade" the examples used to clarify the procedures by substituting simpler examples or more advanced examples, depending upon the needs, interests, and maturity level of the students.

USING THE DICTIONARY

For severely disabled readers, teachers may develop as an initial lesson procedures one through five in the lesson that follows, which deals with word placement in the alphabet. In a subsequent lesson, teachers may develop procedures six through nine, dealing with word placement in the dictionary. Teachers may adapt this dictionary lesson to meet the needs, interests, and maturity level of the students by substituting simpler or more advanced examples for those listed in Column II. In preparation for this lesson, it is necessary that the teacher provide a set of dictionaries for distribution to the class.

LESSON I

Work-Study Skill: Developing the efficient use of the dictionary in locating a specific word.

Approach

PROCEDURE

1. Have students participate in the following "timed" activity in order to have them recognize that they need help in locating words in a dictionary:
   a. Write a specific word on the board.
   b. Direct students to locate this word in the dictionary within a specified time limit.
   c. Observe the methods used by students to locate the word in the dictionary.
   d. Through questioning similar to that below (see 1d) determine the number of students who succeeded in locating the word and elicit from students possible reasons for some students failing to locate the word within the time limit.
   e. Tell students teacher's observations while they were locating the word, and explain to them that there is a quicker, more efficient way to locate words in the dictionary.
2. State the purpose of the lesson, the same as or similar to that on the right, and write the aim on the board.

1. Timed activity to determine methods students use to locate a word in the dictionary:
   a.   Write the word, pillage, on the board.
   b. Say: Locate the word, pillage, in your dictionary. I will allow you half a minute to find the word. (Pronounce the word pillage, as you point to it.)
   c.   Observe students approach to locating the word during the time allotted to them.
   d. Q: How many of you located the word? (Students raise hands in answer to question and teacher observes the approximate number of students who did not succeed in finding the word.)
     Say: Some of you were unable to locate the word, pillage, in the time allowed you.
      Q: Do you have any idea why you were not able to locate the word in the time allowed?
      A: We didn't have enough time to find the word.
   e. Say: As I watched you locating the word in your dictionary, I noticed that some students began to look for the word, pillage, in the beginning of the dictionary, and then proceeded to turn page after page trying to find the word. This takes too much time. That is why some of you did not find the word quickly. There is a quicker, more efficient way to locate words in the dictionary.
2.   Say: We shall learn a quicker, more efficient way to locate words in the dictionary. (Write aim on board.)

Direct Teaching

PROCEDURE

1. Through questioning, elicit from students specific information about the contents of the dictionary, the same as or similar to that below (see 1).
2. Briefly review the letters of the alphabet, and write them across the top of the board.
3. Through questioning similar to that below (see 3), have students divide the letters of the alphabet into four equal parts. Draw lines on the board to show these four sections. Direct students to examine the letters of the alphabet contained in each of the four sections, in order to determine the names of the letters contained in each section. (Note that the alphabet may be divided into three parts instead of four, if the teacher so desires.)
4a. Present a word card to each student, the same as or similar to those

below (see 4) and direct individual students to scotch tape the word card in its proper column on the blackboard, one under the other.
   b. Through questioning, have pupils explain why they placed each word card in a specific column.
5a. Have students examine the words in each column of the alphabet on the board, and through questioning, elicit the fact that the words are not in alphabetical order according to the initial letter of each word.
   b. Have students arrange the words in alphabetical order.
6. Question students about the similarity that might exist between the contents of the four columns of the alphabet on the board and the contents of four such sections of their dictionaries.
7. Direct students to divide the contents of their dictionaries into four sections. Have students note the initial letter of the words included in each section. (Note that the dictionary may be divided into three parts instead of four, if the teacher so desires.)
8. Review the initial letters of the words contained in each of the four sections of the dictionary. Write these letters on the blackboard in column formation. (Note that dictionaries vary according to grade level, number of entry words, etc.)
9a. Give students practice in turning to the specific division of the dictionary that contains words, the same as or similar to those below (see 9a). Observe students' activity in locating the correct section of the dictionary.
   b. Through questioning, elicit from students the value of the ability to locate words in a dictionary quickly.

DEVELOPMENT

1. Q: What does the dictionary contain?
   A: The dictionary contains a long list of words and their meanings.
   Q: How are the words in the dictionary arranged?
   A: The words in the dictionary are arranged in alphabetical order.
2. Say: I know that you are familar with the letters of the alphabet. Tony, say the letters of the alphabet as I write them across the top of the board, abcdefghijklmnopqrstuvwxyz.
3. Q: How many letters are in the alphabet?—(26)
       What is half of 26?—(13)
   Say: The thirteenth letter of the alphabet is m. (Draw a long line down the board after the letter, m, dividing the letters of the alphabet into two equal parts.)
   Example:
       abcdefghijklm | nopqrstuvwxyz
   Say: This line divides the letters of the alphabet in half. Letters a through m are in the first half and letters n through z are in the second half.

Say: The middle letter between a and m is g. The middle letter between n and z is t. (Draw a long line after the letter g and after the letter t on the board.)

Example:

abcdefg | hijklm | nopqrst | uvwxyz

Say: We have now divided the letters of the alphabet into approximately four equal divisions. Study the letters that are contained in each division for the next few seconds.

Example:

a to g | h to m | n to t | u to z

4a. Say: Place each of these word cards in its proper column on the blackboard:

abcdefg|hijklm|nopqrst|uvwxyz

fur	kite	robin	zest
bird	money	oven	x-ray
apple	jelly	time	unite
copy	ice	summer	victor
guard	lace	nothing	yellow
dinner	heart	pear	war
elf		queen	

b. Q: Is each word card in its proper column?
(Yes) How do you know?

A: The words in the first column begin with letters a through g. The words in the second column begin with letters h through m, etc., etc.

5a. Say: Look at the words placed in each division on the board.

Q: Do you think you would find these words listed like this in the dictionary?—No. Why not?

A: The words in the dictionary are arranged in alphabetical order. The words in each column are not in alphabetical order.

b.   abcdefg | hijklm | nopqrst | uvwxyz

apple	heart	nothing	unite
bird	ice	oven	victor
copy	jelly	pear	war
dinner	kite	queen	x-ray
elf	lace	robin	yellow
fur	money	summer	zest
guard		time	

6. Q: Do you think we can divide our dictionaries into four parts similar to the columns on the board?—Yes. How can we do this?

   A: We can divide our dictionaries in half, and then divide each half again so that we have divided our dictionaries into four similar sections.

7. Say: Divide your dictionary into approximately two equal parts.

   Q: What is the initial letter of the words found in the middle of the dictionary?—(the letter, l)

   Say: Then in this dictionary words beginning with letters a to l would be found in the first half, and words beginning with letters m to z would be found in the second half.

   Say: Now divide the first half of your dictionary into two parts.

   Q: What is the initial letter of the words found in the middle of the first half?—the letter, d.

   Say: Then words beginning with letters a to d are found in this section of the dictionary, and words beginning with letters e to l are found in the second section of the dictionary.

   Say: Divide the second half of your dictionary into two parts.

   Q: What is the initial letter of the words on these pages?—the letter, r.

   Say: Then words beginning with letters m to r are found in this section of the dictionary and words beginning with letters s to z are found in the last section.

8. Q: What are the initial letters of the words contained in the first division or section of your dictionary? The second division? The third division? The fourth division? Write on the board:

Sec. I	Sec. II	Sec. III	Sec. IV
a to ?	? to l	m to ?	? to z

9a. Say: Turn to the section or division of the dictionary where the following words may be located.

broom	- Section I
value	- Section IV
race	- Section III
pat	- Section III
girl	- Section I
winning	- Section IV

   b. Q: Why is it useful for you to know the letters contained in each of the four divisions or sections of your dictionary?

   A: If we have to locate a word in our dictionary, all we have to do is to note the initial letter of the word we must locate, and then turn immediately to the division of the dictionary that contains words beginning with that letter.

   Refer to the aim on the board:

   Q: Did we learn a way to locate words in the dictionary quickly?—Yes.

Q: What did we learn?
A: We learned to open the dictionary to the part in which the specific word is located.
Q: How can this skill help you?
A: This skill is a time-saver when locating words in the dictionary.

Summary

Review the purpose of the lesson and through questioning have students decide in what way this skill can help them.

A Final Note

When students have mastered the above dictionary skill, the teacher may refer to the following lessons which develop more advanced skills:
  1. Understanding the function and use of guide words.
  2. Understanding the use of diacritical marks as an aid to pronunciation. Before developing number two above, teachers must instruct students in the skill of selecting the correct definition of a word according to the context in which the word is used.

Conclusion

In order to further aid the retarded reader in the junior high school, the language arts teacher may develop more advanced reading skills when the students are ready. To do this, the teacher may use content material taken from any and all subject areas. Therefore, many of the lessons in the body of this manual may be adapted by the teacher for instructional purposes. These include lessons developing the ability to use contextual clues to word meaning, and finding the main idea of paragraphs. Several of the work-study skills lessons may also be adapted by the language arts teacher. Among these are the lessons which develop skimming and surveying, reading and interpreting graphic materials, and reading and following printed directions.

The exact procedures in each of the lessons should be followed as listed. However, the suggested subject area content, which develops the procedures, may be too difficult for retarded readers. The teacher should substitute appropriate material suitable to the reading level of the students.

50. SOCIAL STUDIES SKILLS LESSON PLANS

Board of Education of the City of New York

UNDERSTANDING PARAGRAPHS

The ability to recognize the main idea of a paragraph requires a number of important understandings. It requires the understanding that the separate thoughts or details of a paragraph relate to each other and that this relationship can be expressed as a topic or main idea sentence. It requires the understanding that the main idea sentence may be easy or difficult to find, according to the logical, or lack of logical, arrangement of the paragraph. The less obvious the arrangement, the more difficult it is to find the main idea. For example, some paragraphs directly express the main idea in the first sentence. Others express it in the last sentence or within the body of the paragraph itself. There are other paragraphs wherein the main idea is not directly expressed but must be inferred from the related details within each paragraph. Therefore it is important that pupils receive instruction in understanding paragraphs through a program of sequential development similar to that described in Lessons I, II, and III that follow.

The teachers involved in evaluating these lessons suggested that, as a time-saver, teachers rexograph the materials instead of copying them on the board.

Lesson I

Problem: In reporting on news articles, students show a need for understanding the main idea of paragraphs.
Required Skill: Finding the main idea of a paragraph when it is directly expressed in the first sentence.

PROCEDURE

1. Write the headline or title of a news article on the blackboard and read the first paragraph of the article to the students orally, directing them to listen carefully to note the sentence that suggests the headline. Use example below (see 1) or a similar one. (Step I).

Reprinted from *Reading in the Subject Areas, Grades 7-8-9*, Curriculum Bulletin Series No. 6 (1963–1964), pp. 11–27. By permission of the New York City Board of Education.

2. Question students about the sentence that suggests the headline and tell students what this sentence is called. (Main Idea) Write the sentence on board. (Step II)

3. Read the remaining sentences of the paragraph, one at a time, and prove that each sentence relates to the main idea sentence. (Step III)

4. Review the three steps listed above to find the main idea sentence of the first paragraph of a news article and write the steps on the blackboard or chart.

5. Have pupils use the three steps above to find the main idea sentence in the first paragraph of a news article similar to that at the right. (Check results.)

DEVELOPMENT

1.   Headline: Educational T.V. by "Phone"
        First Paragraph: Instruction is advancing on all fronts with the advent of educational T.V. by phone. A single teacher can personally instruct thousands of students in dozens of schools over special T.V. telephone lines. General Telephone and Electronics is bringing this modern form of education to the nation's schools through its own Operating Companies in areas of thirty-two states. This advanced educational system includes inexpensive T.V. cameras and receivers developed by a subsidiary company, Sylvania.

2. Q: Which sentence suggests the headline? Why?
    A: The first sentence, "Instruction is advancing on all fronts with the advent of educational T.V. by phone," suggests the headline because the headline is a condensed version of this sentence.
    Say: The first sentence in this paragraph is called the main idea sentence. The remaining sentences in the paragraph must relate to the main idea sentence.

3.   The sentence, "A single teacher ... over special T.V. telephone lines," gives information about educational T.V. by phone.
        The sentence, "General Telephone ... in areas of thirty-two states," gives more details about educational T.V. by phone.
        The sentence, "This advanced educational system ... by a subsidiary company, Sylvania," gives additional information about educational T.V. by phone.

4.   Read the headline or title of the article. (Step I)
        Read the first paragraph to find the sentence that suggests the headline. (Main Idea Sentence-Step II)
        Prove that each of the remaining sentences relates to the main idea sentence. (Step III)

5.   Headline: Weatherproofed Cars
        The modern car is weatherproofed to stay newer longer and to

protect the buyer's investment. Galvanized steel is used for the underbody parts that are most subject to rust. Stainless steel screws are used on all points exposed to the elements. A more durable four coat finish, with two outer coats of baked enamel, is put on every car.

LESSON II

Problem: The text students are using contains paragraphs in which the main idea is not expressed in the first sentence.

Required Skill: Finding the main idea of a paragraph when it is expressed in part of the paragraph rather than the first sentence.

PROCEDURE

1. Copy on the blackboard or chart, a paragraph, the same as, or similar to, that shown in the example below (see 1).
2. Clarify the meanings of difficult words included in the above paragraph.
3. State that there is a simple method for finding the main idea when it is expressed in any part of the paragraph.
4. Direct pupils to read the paragraph silently to get a general impression of the paragraph as a whole and question them about possible titles for the paragraph.
5a. Write the suggested titles on the blackboard.
5b. Have students read the paragraph again to select the best possible title.
  c. Then have students find the sentence that suggests this title. Tell students that this is the main idea sentence.
6. Underline the title and the main idea sentence and have pupils note is expressed in any part of the paragraph.
7a. Prove that each detail sentence relates to the main idea sentence.
  b. Draw pupils' attention to the clue words that indicate the sequential order of the details of the paragraph.
8. Review the steps used to find the main idea of a paragraph, as indicated below (see 8) and write them on the board or chart.
9. Have pupils follow the steps listed in 8 above to find the main idea expressed in additional paragraphs, similar to that below (see 9).

DEVELOPMENT

1. One reason the United Nations was created was to save succeeding generations from the scourge of war. Another reason was to reaffirm faith in fundamental human rights. Still a third

reason was to establish conditions under which justice and respect for obligations arising from treaties and other sources of international law could be maintained. Last of all, the United Nations was created to promote social progress and a better standard of life. The reasons for creating the United Nations were set down in its original charter. (From *Collier's Encyclopedia,* Vol. 19, 62c, 1956 Ed.)

2.   "Succeeding generations" means the generations that follow. "Scourge of war" means the punishment that war brings with it.

"Reaffirm faith" means to declare faith again.

3. Say: We will learn an easy way to find the main idea of a paragraph when it is expressed in any part of the paragraph.

4. Say: Read this paragraph silently. (Number 1 above) Decide the title you would suggest for it. Give reason for your choice.

5a.   Suggested Titles:
The United Nations
Reasons for Creating the U.N.
The Creation of the U.N.

b.   Best Possible Title:
Reasons for Creating the U.N.

c.   The sentence that suggests the best title: The reasons for creating the United Nations were set down in its original charter. (Main Idea Sentence)

6.   The main idea sentence is expressed in the last sentence of the paragraph. (Underline title and main idea sentence.)

7a.   Each detail sentence gives a reason for creating the U.N.

b.   Clue words:
One reason
Another reason
Still a third reason
Last of all

8.   1. Read the paragraph to form a general impression of its contents.
2. Decide on a suitable title for the paragraph.
3. Locate the sentence that suggests the title.
4. Prove that the remaining sentences relate to the sentence that suggests the title.*

9.   The Food and Agricultural Organization of the United Nations conducts programs to increase food production in many countries. The International Refugee Organization of the United Nations aids hundreds of thousands of displaced persons and refugees who are victims of political oppression. The Inter-

---

* Draw pupils' attention to the fact that the four steps just listed may also be used to locate the main idea of a paragraph when it is expressed in any part of the paragraph. (First sentence, last sentence, or within the body of the paragraph.)

national Labor Organization of the United Nations works for improvements in labor conditions throughout the world. An International Office of Education of the United Nations promotes educational and cultural cooperation among the nations of the world. There are many organizations in the United Nations concerned with bettering the living conditions of people throughout the world.

Lesson III

Problem: A section of the text includes paragraphs in which the main idea is not directly expressed.

Required Skill: Finding the main idea of a paragraph when it is not directly expressed but must be inferred from the paragraph as a whole.

PROCEDURE

1. Write a paragraph on the blackboard, the same as or similar to that below (see 1) and have students read it silently to get a general impression of the paragraph as a whole.
2. Question students about their general impression of the paragraph. Have them attempt to suggest a suitable title for it and elicit reasons for their inability to do so.
3. Underline on the board the different item that is mentioned in each sentence of the paragraph.
4. Have students re-read what is said about each different item to note the related thought common to all. Write the related thought on the blackboard.
5. Have students express the related thought in a sentence and explain that though there was no main idea sentence expressed in the paragraph, the main idea could be inferred from the related details within the paragraph.
6. Review the steps needed to infer the main idea of a paragraph. Write the steps on board or chart.
7. Use the steps reviewed in 6 above to infer the main idea in carefully selected paragraphs in which the main idea is not directly expressed, but must be inferred from the related details in all sentences in the paragraph. (See example in Number 7 below.)

DEVELOPMENT

1. In the early twenties, the Washington Conference and the World Court helped to bring about a more friendly feeling among nations. Before that, the League of Nations, established after

World War I, helped to avert some wars. In the late twenties, the
Paris Peace Pact did much to gain peace in the world. In 1945,
the United Nations was established to bring about world peace.

2. Q: Can you suggest a <u>suitable</u> tile for the paragraph? Why not?
   A: Each sentence seems to say something about a totally different
      thing.

3. Sentence 1 says something about the Washington Conference and
   World Court; sentence 2—the <u>League of Nations</u>; sentence 3—the
   <u>Paris Peace Pact</u>; sentence 4—the <u>United Nations</u>.

4. Washington Conference and World Court—<u>helped to bring about
   a more friendly feeling among nations.</u>
   League of Nations—<u>helped to avert some wars.</u>
   Paris Peace Pact—<u>did much to gain peace in the world.</u>
   United Nations—<u>was established to bring about world peace.</u>
   The related thought common to all—establishing peace in the
   world.

5. <u>Suggested Main Idea Sentences:</u>
   (1.) There have been many attempts to establish world peace.
   (2.) Many steps have been taken to establish peace in the world.

6. (1.) Read the paragraph and think of a suitable title for it.
        (Note that you are unable to suggest a title because each
        sentence seems to say something about a totally different
        thing.)
   (2.) Re-read the paragraph to find a common relationship existing
        among all the sentences.
   (3.) Express this common relationship in a complete thought.
        (Main Idea Sentence)

7. When Japan invaded Manchuria in 1931, the League of Nations
   was powerless to do more than censure her for this aggression.
   Subsequently, Germany, encouraged by the League's lack of power
   to act against Japan, rearmed and reoccupied the Rhineland. Then,
   in 1935, Italy followed suit by invading Ethiopia in defiance of the
   League. Finally, when the Soviet Union invaded Finland in 1939,
   the League was totally powerless to act because the world was at
   war. (Main Idea Sentence: The League of Nations was not an
   effective means of preventing war.)

A Final Note

There are additional, more complex main idea skills in which students
need direct instruction. The procedures listed in Step 8, Lesson II, may
be used to develop the following skills:

1. Where the main idea is expressed in only part of a sentence.
   Example: The atom bomb is recognized everywhere as a source

of destruction, <u>and yet atomic energy offers unbeliev-</u> <u>able peacetime possibilities.</u> It is already being used in industry. Atomic powered ships, planes, and cars, are predicted in the near future for use in everyday life. A small amount of atomic energy is sufficient to propel a ship to Europe. Atomic energy is being used effectively at the present time for detecting certain illnesses.

2. Where the main idea of a paragraph is expressed in two sentences.
    Example: <u>Carefully drawn plans are essential in the building</u> <u>industry in New York. So is the careful execution</u> <u>of these plans.</u> Architects make the original plans. Building contractors and workers erect the buildings according to the exact specifications of the plans. Architects supervise the construction to make certain the plans are executed properly. Inspectors from the building department also check to see that the plans are executed carefully.

UNDERSTANDING SKIMMING AND SURVEYING

Skimming is an art that has a definite place in the field of social studies. It is a kind of rapid reading, the simplest form of which is to locate a specific name, date, or single word, in lists or paragraphs. Comprehension of the entire selection is not involved here, for the "reader" remains oblivious to everything but his goal. Students who require corrective reading should receive instruction in this simple type of skimming. Students who are reading on grade level should be instructed in the more advanced types of skimming and surveying indicated by the problems described in Lessons I and II that follow.

Lesson I

Problem: Students need instruction in locating the answers to specific questions without reading an entire selection.
Required Skill: Developing the ability to skim content material in order to locate answers to specific questions.

PROCEDURE

1. Write a specific question on the board and review the type of rapid reading which aids in locating the answers to who, what, where, and when questions.

2a. Have students read the question carefully. State the "key" word that indicates the information required for the answer. Underline the "key" word.

  b. Through questioning, have students identify other words in the question that act as guides to the information needed in the answer. Underline these words on the board.

3. Direct students to turn to a specific page in the text to find the information indicated by the underlined words in the question.

4. Tell students to stop and check their answers by reading very carefully to determine whether or not they have located the correct answer to the specific question.

5. Have students examine other types of "key" words used in specific questions. List these "key" words on the board and indicate the type of information each one designates.

6. Review the procedures used in skimming to find the answer to a specific question. Write the steps on the board, or list them on a chart so that they may be used for recall.

7. Using the steps listed in step 6 above, have students skim to find the answers to other specific questions.

8. Review the importance of skimming to find the answers to specific questions.

DEVELOPMENT

1. Write on the board:
    Who was the first explorer to reach the new world?
    Q: How would you locate the answer to this question quickly?
    A: I would skim the material to locate a proper name which answers the question, who.
    Q: How would you locate the answers to questions that indicate where and when?
    A: I'd look for capital letters to answer where and numbers to answer when questions.

2a. Say: Then the word who in this question is a key word because it indicates that the name of a person is required to answer it, and proper names begin with capitals.

  b. Q: Are there any other words in this question that point to additional information needed to answer it?
    A: Yes. The words, first explorer, and new world, are guide words to the information needed.

3. Say: Turn to page . . . . Skim the page quickly to find the name of the explorer. Remember that a name is the only detail for which you are looking.

4. Say: Read the answer you have located very carefully to see if it answers the specific question.

A: The first explorer to reach the new world was _____.

Q: Is the specific question answered? Why?

A: The question is answered because we have located the <u>name</u> of the <u>first explorer</u> to reach the <u>new world</u>.

5. Write on the board:

   1. How did the crew react to the long arduous voyage? (<u>How</u> designates manner.)
   2. Why were the explorers looking for new trade routes to the east? (<u>Why</u> designates reason or cause.)

6. Chart:

   1. Read the question carefully.
   2. Select the key words in the question that pinpoint the information needed to answer the question. Underline them.
   3. Skim the material looking only for the information designated by the key words.
   4. Stop and read the information located to see if it answers the specific question.

7. Q: 1. Why was Spain so interested in financing many of the explorers' voyages?

   2. How did the explorers man their ships?

8. This type of skimming is an aid in locating specific information. It is a time saver.

LESSON II

Problem: Instruction is needed in determining quickly whether or not specific content material is relevant to a specific social studies problem.

Required Skill: Developing the ability to skim content material in order to determine its relevancy to a specific problem.

PROCEDURE

1. Write a social studies problem on the board, one for which pertinent content material is needed.
2. Have students examine the problem to locate the words that pinpoint the information this problem requires. Underline these words on the board.
3. Direct students to turn to the table of contents in their texts in order to locate the chapters listed under the unit to which the specific problem relates. Write the chapter headings and page numbers on the board.
4. Indicate another device used by authors to assist students in using a text.

5. Have the students turn to the summary of the first chapter and direct them to read it rapidly to get a general impression of its contents. Through questioning, elicit from students the answer to whether or not the contents of this chapter will help them solve the problem.

6. Use the same procedures described in step 5 to determine whether or not the summaries of the other chapters indicate that they are pertinent to the specific problem.

7. Refer to the chapters listed on the board and underline those which contain material pertinent to the problem. Draw students' attention to the fact that only some chapters contain pertinent material.

8. Reinforce the purpose and use of the type of skimming developed in this lesson.

DEVELOPMENT

1. *Problem:* Why did Spain, France, and England each lay claim to the New World?

2. Q: What clue does the word, <u>why</u>, give you in this question?
    A: The word, <u>why</u>, tells us that we should look for an answer that indicates a cause or a reason.
    Q: What clues do the words Spain, France, England, claim, each, and New World, give you?
    A: These words pinpoint the content required to solve the problem.

3. *Unit:* Europeans Discovered, Explored and Settled the Americas.
   Chapter I:
          Hunters from Asia Settled the Americas While Europeans Built Great Civilizations—pp. 2-27.
   Chapter II:
          Columbus' Discovery Opened a New World for Exploration—pp. 28-44.
   Chapter III:
          The French, Dutch, and English Explored North America and Founded Colonies—pp. 45-65.
     Say: The table of contents is one organizational device authors use to aid you in locating specific information.

4.   Say: There are other devices authors employ to assist you in using a text. For example, in this text, the author has placed a summary at the end of each chapter to highlight the important facts included in the contents of the chapter.

5.   Say: Read the summary on p. 26 <u>very</u> <u>quickly</u>.
     Q: What is your impression of the contents of this chapter? Do you think it contains information on why Spain, France, and England each claimed the new world?—No—Why not?

A: The summary indicates that this chapter contains information on America before the advent of the Spanish, French, and English.

6. Q: Skim the summaries on pp. 43 and 58. Do these chapters contain the information needed?

A: Yes, because these summaries indicate that chapters II and III contain information about the Spanish, French, and English in the New World.

7. Say: Look at the chapter headings. Notice that although chapters I, II, and III are listed under the one unit title, skimming the summaries of the chapters enabled us to determine quickly that only chapters II and III include relevant material.

8. Q: Of what value is this type of skimming?

A: This type of skimming is an aid in:
   a. Locating materials pertinent to the solution of specific problems.
   b. Judging the relevancy of such materials quickly.
   c. Saving time in selecting suitable materials.

A Final Note

The preceding lessons help to develop the understanding that the rate of reading is flexible according to the purpose of the reading. We "race" over material while engaged in the location of "key" words, and we slow down to a "walk" when understanding of the content is required. For example, we "race" over material when making rapid and skilled use of book divisions, chapter headings, etc. and we slow down to a walk when finding answers to questions that include the language of the context. For locating answers to questions that do not include the language of the context, the rate is even slower.

READING CRITICALLY

The ability to read critically is of utmost importance to every student. This ability cannot be left to chance development. It must be taught systematically in order that students develop the ability to judge the validity of statements found in printed materials. Students must be shown how to recognize slanted writings and biased opinions as they read, in order to be able to distinguish them from facts which can be proven. The lesson that follows describes the procedures that may be used in the early development of this reading skill.

LESSON

Problem: Guidance is needed in judging the validity of statements that appear in students' daily readings.

Required Skill: Developing the ability to distinguish between fact and opinion.

PROCEDURE

1a. Read a statement, the same or similar to the one below (see 1a).
 b. Question students to determine whether this is a statement of fact or opinion. Have students defend their answers.
 c. Record student response on board.
2a. Read another statement to the class.
 b. Question students to determine whether this is a statement of fact or opinion. Have students defend their answers.
 c. Record student response on the board.
3. Question students about statements of fact and opinion they encounter in their daily readings. List answers on the board.
4. Explain to students that reports use clue words to indicate that they are expressing opinions. Elicit from students a list of such clue words and write them on the board.
5. Elicit from students the items listed in step 3 which might express opinions without clue words.
6. Review the definitions of a statement of fact and a statement of opinion.
7a. Present several statements to students, directing them to decide whether each statement expresses a fact or an opinion. Elicit reasons for their choice.
 b. Check students' answers.
8. Review the importance of the ability to distinguish fact from opinion in daily readings.

DEVELOPMENT

1a.   "By 1970, the American population will probably pass the two hundred million mark. With this increase, we can anticipate problems related to housing, education, and conservation of natural resources." (From "News of the Week in Review," *The New York Times.*

 b. Q: Do you believe this is a statement of fact?
    A: No, this is not a statement of fact.
    Q: Why not?
    A: This statement predicts future happenings that cannot be

proven now. The word, probably, indicates a possibility for the future. This statement may be factual in 1970, but as of the moment, it is not a fact.

    Q: What would you say this statement expresses?

    A: This statement expresses an <u>opinion</u> of what someone believes may be true in 1970.

  c.   Write the word "opinion" on the board.

2a.   "The Federal Government spends about two billion dollars a year helping states with their aid to needy persons, needy through unemployment, disability, or family troubles." (From News of the Week in Review, "The New York Times.")

  b: Q: Do you believe this statement to be true? Why?

    A: Yes, this statement is true because it can be proven by using reliable sources that list the expenditures of the Federal Government.

    Q: What does this statement express?

    A: It expresses a fact that can be proven true.

  c.   Write the word "fact" on the board.

3. Q: Where in your daily readings do you find statements of fact and/or opinion?

    A: In newspapers, periodicals, etc. which has such features as:
        News Reports
        Market Results
        Editorials
        Letters to the Editor
        Political Speeches
        Advertisements

4. Say: Responsible reporters on reputable newspapers and magazines use clue words in their stories to indicate that they are expressing an opinion rather than a fact.

    Q: Think of some newspaper articles you have read. What words can you recall that indicated an opinion was being expressed?

    A: Claims, believes, thinks, considers, said to be, probable, etc.

5. Q: Which of the newspaper features listed in step 3 might possibly express opinions without the use of clue words?

    A: Advertisements, Newspaper Editorials, Political Speeches, etc. might omit clue words because these features generally do express opinions.

6. Q: How would you define a statement of fact?

    A: A statement of fact is one which can be proven true by using a reliable source, such as an encyclopedia, world almanac, etc.

    Q: How would you define a statement of opinion?

    A: A statement of opinion is one that expresses the feelings, thoughts, or beliefs of a person or persons, and one which cannot be proven true in any reliable source.

7a.   1. Scott Carpenter was the second American to orbit the earth.
            2. I consider your article, "How the West Was Won," the best that has ever been written.
            3. Scientists believe that a man may reach the moon in ten years.

b.   Statements:
            1. Fact—Can be proven in any reliable source.
            2. Opinion—A person's belief cannot be proven in any reliable source. Clue word is consider.
            3. Opinion—The belief of a group of people about future happenings cannot be proven at this time. Clue word is believe.

8. Q. Why is it important to be able to distinguish between a fact and an opinion?

     A: The ability to distinguish between fact and opinion helps us to recognize slanted writings designed to influence our thinking.

UNDERSTANDING WORK-STUDY SKILLS

As students advance in their schooling, more and more research reading is required of them. To do this reading, a working knowledge of basic study skills is essential. Students need to know how to organize the content of material they read, and how to make use of the organizational devices offered by authors to aid them in this task. Students need to know where to locate specific information in a reliable source, and how to use this source efficiently. Students need to know how to read and interpret graphic materials, such as maps, graphs, charts and diagrams that are included in the reading materials. These specific work-study skills should be firmly established during the junior high school years, and it is the responsibility of the social studies teacher to instruct students in these skills, if it is evident that instruction is needed. Lesson I suggests procedures the teacher may use to develop specific work-study skills basic to research reading.

LESSON I

Problem: In organizing a long unit of content, there is a definite need for instruction in understanding the purpose and use of an author's organizational devices.

Required Skill: Recognizing the author's devices (printing clues) as an aid in organizing a long unit of content.

PROCEDURE

1a. Have students quickly survey an entire unit in their texts to locate the different kinds of headings in the selection.

  b. Through questioning, elicit from students the reason they were able to locate the headings so quickly.

2a. Direct students to examine the unit heading carefully, and through questioning, establish how its style and size of type, and its position on the page indicate the importance of the content it introduces.

  b. Follow the procedures in step 2a. to establish the importance of the section headings and the paragraph headings.

  c. Through questioning, have students note the relationship that exists between the following headings:

1. Section Headings to the Unit Heading
2. Paragraph Headings to the Section Headings
3. Follow the procedures used in step 2 to show the relationship between other paragraph headings and the section headings that introduce them.
4. Have students re-examine the different kinds of headings contained in this unit, and show them how these headings offer an outline of the contents of the entire unit. Explain the following similarities:

    The Unit Heading to a title

    The Section Headings to topics that relate to the title

    The Paragraph Headings to sub-topics that relate to the section headings

5. Review the purpose of using an author's "printing clues" when organizing a long unit of content.

DEVELOPMENT

1a.   (The sample unit used here is adapted from: Hartman, Gertrude, *America, Land of Freedom,* D. C. Heath and Company, Boston, 1957, pp. 381–427.)

A NEW BIRTH OF FREEDOM

A NATION DIVIDED

The Manufacturing North and the Agricultural South
Slave States or Free States
States Rights
Immediate Abolition

ONE NATION OR TWO

Bitter Feeling Between the North and South
Honest Abe
A New Political Leader
The Rail Splitter Becomes President

ONE NATION INDIVISIBLE

Saving the Union
Freeing the Slaves
The Close of the War
Binding Up the Nation's Wounds

1b. Q: What made each of the headings stand out so that you noticed it quickly?

   A: Different kinds of type.

   Say: The author had a definite purpose in using the different kinds of type. Let's examine each heading very carefully to find out his purpose.

2a. Say: Look at the unit heading, **A NEW BIRTH OF FREEDOM.**

   Q: What kind of type is used?

   A: The unit heading is printed in black, bold-faced type.

   Q: Which letters are capitalized?

   A: Every letter is capitalized.

   Q: On what part of the page is it located?

   A: It is located at the top center of the introductory page of the unit.

   Q: What clue does this unit heading give you as to the content of the material it introduces?

   A: It offers a broad summary of the content of the entire unit.

  b.   Repeat the questions asked in 2a. to arrive at the following information:

     1.   The section headings are located off to the side and at the top of the page in black, bold-faced type, with every letter capitalized. Each section heading introduces one part of the content of the whole unit.

     2.   The paragraph headings are printed in black, bold-faced type, with the first letter of each word capitalized. Each paragraph heading introduces the content of the paragraphs that follow it. Each paragraph heading relates to the section heading that introduces it.

  c. Say: The entire contents of the unit, **A NEW BIRTH OF FREE-DOM,** are divided into three sections. Each section is headed as follows:

        A NATION DIVIDED
        ONE NATION OR TWO
        ONE NATION INDIVISIBLE

1. Say: Examine the section headings included under the unit heading.

   Q: Is there any relationship between the above section headings and the unit heading?

   A: Yes. The three section headings relate to the unit heading because each one suggests information about a new birth of freedom.

2. Say: Examine the paragraph headings included under this specific section heading:

        A NATION DIVIDED
        The Manufacturing North and the Agricultural South
        Slave States or Free States

        States Rights
        Immediate Abolition

Q: Do you see any relation between the paragraph headings and the section heading?

A. Yes. The four paragraph headings relate to the section heading because each one suggests one part of the content introduced by the section heading, **A NATION DIVIDED.**

3. See section headings and paragraph headings listed in step 1a.

4.

Unit heading (Title)

I. Section heading (Topic)
    A. Paragraph heading (Sub-Topic)
    B. Paragraph heading (Sub-Topic)
    C. Paragraph heading (Sub-Topic)

II. Section heading (Topic)
    A. Paragraph heading (Sub-Topic)
    B. Paragraph heading (Sub-Topic)
    C. Paragraph heading (Sub-Topic)

III. Section heading (Topic)
    A. Paragraph heading (Sub-Topic)
    B. Paragraph heading (Sub-Topic)
    C. Paragraph heading (Sub-Topic)

5. Q: How can understanding the author's "printing clues" help you organize a long unit of content?

    A: a. The "printing clues" offer a broad view of the contents of the entire unit.

       b. The "printing clues" aid in outlining the material for quick recall of its content.

A *Final Note*

In different texts, students will find other types of "printing clues" used by authors. For example, in the text *Exploring New York*, third edition, published by Harcourt, Brace, and Co., the authors, B. M. Wainger, D. W. Furman, and E. B. Oagley, used the following type of organizational device "printing clues" to the contents of the text:

THE IROQUOIS: People of the Long House	(Chapter Heading)
THE IROQUOIS	(Section Heading)
Reasons for Iroquois Success	(Paragraph Heading)
Iroquois Victories	(Paragraph Heading)
The Five Nations Confederacy	(Paragraph Heading)
INDIAN TRAVEL	(Section Heading)

Indian Trails Parallel Waterways	(Paragraph Heading)
The Great Iroquois Trail	(Paragraph Heading)
INDIAN INDUSTRY AND	
AGRICULTURE	(Section Heading)
Resources of the Land	(Paragraph Heading)
Indian Industry	(Paragraph Heading)
Men and Women Share the Work	(Paragraph Heading)
Indian Wampum	(Paragraph Heading)
The Uses of Wampum	(Paragraph Heading)

By examining the "printing clues" in the various headings above, it is evident that both by the size and style of type, and by the position of the heading on the page, the Chapter Heading gives a clue to the content of the whole chapter, the Section Headings give clues to the contents of the three parts or sections into which the chapter is divided, and the Paragraph Headings give clues to the contents of the paragraphs that relate to the Section Headings. Thus a broad view of the contents of the whole chapter is provided by an understanding of the organizational devices used by these authors. (Printing clues.)